# *Your Affectionate Husband*

For Jim —
With admiration and
warm personal regards

John Colmer
U.S.S. Iowa.

# "Your Affectionate Husband, J. F. Culver"

## Letters Written During the Civil War

*Edited by* LESLIE W. DUNLAP

*Dean of Library Administration, The University of Iowa*

*Notes by* EDWIN C. BEARSS

*Supervisory Historian, National Park Service*

1978

FRIENDS OF THE UNIVERSITY OF IOWA LIBRARIES

IOWA CITY, IOWA

**Library of Congress Cataloging in Publication Data**

Culver, Joseph Franklin, 1834-1899.
    "Your affectionate husband, J. F. Culver."

    Includes index.
    1.  Culver, Joseph Franklin, 1834-1899.
2.  Illinois Infantry.    129th Regiment, 1862-1865—
Biography.   3.   United States—History—Civil War, 1861
1865—Personal narratives.   4.   Culver, Mary, 1842-1920.
5.   United States—History—Civil War, 1861-1865—Regi-
mental histories—Illinois Infantry.   129th Regiment.
I.   Culver, Mary, 1842-1920.   II.   Dunlap, Leslie
Whittaker, 1911-              III.   Bearss, Edwin C.   IV.   Title.
E505.5 129th.C84          973.7'81'0924              78-25754
ISBN 0-87414-010-2

# CONTENTS

# ILLUSTRATIONS

# INTRODUCTION

The justification for publishing another lengthy account of the Illinois 129th Infantry Regiment during the Civil War [1] lies in the new views and additional insights provided in the letters of a volunteer who served from August, 1862, until June, 1865, in the Western and Southern theaters. The young man, Joseph F. Culver, of Pontiac, Illinois, which lies about seventy-five miles south and west of Chicago, had left Mary, his wife of less than a year, "to walk in the path of duty" (August 19, 1862), and he felt moved to write her a newsworthy letter several times each week. As the young husband repeatedly explained, he wrote, often under difficult physical conditions, because he simply wanted to talk with his wife. Lieutenant ("Captain" after June 28, 1864) Culver's letters were written as if he were engaged in conversation with a person seated across from his desk or writing table, and he took the time and trouble required to furnish a plenitude of detail because he wanted to share his life in uniform with his young wife at home. Because most of the men in his regiment resided in Pontiac or elsewhere in Livingston County, many of them were known to Mary, and Culver reported on their activities as well as his own. Similar circumstances led Mary Culver to write from Pontiac about occurrences there which possessed interest for her husband and others in his unit. The extent to which families of soldiers in a unit composed largely of residents of the same locality could become involved with each other is illustrated by Captain Culver's letter of July 4, 1864, written from the field near Marietta, Georgia:

> Thos. Moran [a young farmer] of my Company was killed. It will devolve upon you to convey the painful intelligence to his family; they live near you. He was a noble man & excellent soldier. . . . Tell his wife that if my life is spared I will write to her as soon as we get quieted down.

Many of Joseph Culver's observations about men in the 129th Illinois Regiment will interest few who are not concerned with the history of Livingston County in Illinois, but the richness of detail about the experiences of soldiers in his unit gives to the entire series of letters an importance which might not appear in reading selected documents in their entirety or many excerpts. For example, the number of individuals from Pontiac who visited the troops in the 129th Illinois Regiment and the number of men from the unit who traveled to Livingston County for one reason or another could not be realized unless one learned of the comings and goings of civilians and soldiers from letters in which Joseph Culver tried to keep his wife informed about the movements of mutual acquaintances. Young Culver's desire to share with his wife his experiences and reactions provides valuable glimpses into the mind of a Union soldier. Thus, the first report of the assassination of President Lincoln to reach Captain Culver was officially communicated on April 17, 1865, to the Union Army at Raleigh, North Carolina, yet not until April 23 when he had read the story in a New York paper did the writer conclude, "The death of the President is now established beyond doubt." Joseph F. Culver's 233 letters to his wife written during the Civil War constitute a rich source of information about the lives of soldiers who marched under Generals Rosecrans and Sherman across Tennessee, Georgia, the Carolinas, and Virginia, because their author was keenly aware of most of the events experienced by troops in his regiment and he found the time and took the trouble to write, and write, and write.

\* \* \*

The ancestry and family relations of Joseph F. Culver are easy to delineate because the history of his family and that of his wife's (Murphy) have been detailed in carefully prepared genealogies compiled by a daughter-in-law, Etta I'Dell Clarke Culver. According to her work, published in the 1920's and 1930's in typescripts, the first in this line of Culvers to come from England, James, settled about 1765 in Pennsylvania, where his wife (surname of Peterson) bore him three children, including a son, Joseph, who was born in 1791 in Cumberland County, Pennsylvania. Joseph Culver married Elizabeth Carey in 1812, and between 1813 and 1828 (?) the couple had eight children. Joseph's second wife (nee Martha Dunmire, born in 1809 in Franklin County, Pennsylvania) bore him six children, the second being Joseph Franklin Culver, who was born on November 3, 1834, near Carlisle, Pennsylvania.

Joseph Franklin Culver, the author of the Civil War letters in this volume, married Mary Murphy (born on March 17, 1842, in New Hartford, New York) on December 12, 1861. He left his wife before the birth of their first son (Franklin Allen Culver, born on September 21, 1862), and he was with his regiment in Tennessee when the boy died on October 30, 1863. Mary visited her husband in Nashville at the end of 1863, and their second son was born on August 25, 1864, while his father was with his regiment near Atlanta, Georgia. Six more children came of this union, including Chester Murphy Culver (born on October 5, 1870) who married Etta I'Dell Clarke, and their last, Essae Martha Culver (born November 15, 1882), who was to achieve national prominence as a librarian before her death in January of 1973. The Chester Murphy Culvers had two children, one of whom was William Clarke Culver, born on July 21, 1903, in Detroit and removed to Cedar Rapids, Iowa, where he opened in 1936 "Culver Motors," an automobile dealership. His son, John C. Culver, born on August 8, 1932, in Rochester, Minnesota, followed in his father's and grandfather's footsteps to Harvard University, and entered into the practice of law in Cedar Rapids before he was elected in 1964 to the Eighty-ninth Congress from Iowa's Second Congressional District. He was reelected four times, and in 1974 he was elected to the United States Senate. Senator Culver is the present owner of the Culver Collection, which includes the letters written during the Civil War to one of his great-grandmothers (Mary Murphy Culver, 1842-1920) by her young soldier-husband, Joseph Franklin Culver (1834-1899).

According to genealogist Etta I'Dell Clarke Culver, her father-in-law, Joseph Franklin Culver, who ordinarily will be referred to in this volume by his initials, attended common schools and an academy in Carlisle, Pennsylvania, before he entered Dickinson College. J.F.C. subsequently was graduated from the Iron City Commercial College in Pittsburgh, and he read law with attorneys in Carlisle, Pennsylvania, Wooster, Ohio, and Pontiac, Illinois. He taught in and served for two terms as the principal of a normal school at Burbank, Ohio. According to one account, J.F.C. moved to Pontiac, Illinois, because of the opportunities there described by a young friend, Samuel S. Saul, a native of Pennsylvania who had settled in the community. Another indicates that J.F.C. was induced to move to Livingston County to accept the position of deputy clerk which he held from 1859 to 1863. Like many other professional men in the nineteenth century who had located in small American towns, J.F.C. was engaged throughout most of his career in commercial activities, including banking and insurance, closely related to his practice of law. According to his military record, J.F.C. was five feet and ten inches tall, his complexion was dark, and his hair was "hazel black." Photographs of J.F.C. and of his wife taken while he was in the Army reveal them as alert and independent individuals who probably possessed considerable physical vigor.

The biographical sketch of Mary Murphy in Etta I. C. Culver's genealogical compilation entitled "Robert Murphy and Some of His Descendants" (1931) says little about her as a young woman other than that she was a Presbyterian who had a clear contralto voice. Her education, according to this source, was acquired through the efforts of two brothers and at a private school in Cleveland. She taught school for a brief period in Ohio and seriously considered returning to a classroom in Pontiac while her husband was away during the War. Mary Murphy had married on December 12, 1861, when she was nineteen and her husband was twenty-seven, but before the birth of their first child on September 21, 1862, the prospective father had enlisted on August 2, 1862, in the 129th Regiment of Illinois Volunteers.

J.F.C. became the first lieutenant of Company "A" in September of 1862, and he was promoted to captain on June 28, 1864. He was mustered out on June 8, 1865, at Washington, D.C. Particulars about the record of the 129th Regiment are given in the *Compendium of the War of the Rebellion* (Vol. III, p. 1100), but the activities may be grouped for convenience in several chronological periods. The regiment traveled from Pontiac by train to Louisville, Kentucky, where the men received basic training. During the remainder of 1862 and all of 1863, the regiment was assigned to guard railroads and other communication lines, chiefly in Tennessee, and in February of 1864 the regiment moved south to Atlanta and in November to Savannah. J.F.C. was detached from his regiment during General Sherman's celebrated "March to the Sea" to serve as a witness in a trial in Chicago, but he rejoined his unit in North Carolina and marched with his company northward across Virginia and down Pennsylvania Avenue in Washington, D.C., in the grand review held on May 24, 1865.

After the War, J.F.C. served for two years as mayor of Pontiac and was elected to a four-year term as county judge in Livingston County. He was active in local Republican politics and had a part in the establishment of the State Reform School at Pontiac. In 1879 J.F.C. removed to Emporia, Kansas, where he continued in the careers of banking and law begun in Illinois and was active in community affairs until a few months before his death on January 20, 1899. J.F.C. had received in 1896 a pension to compensate in part for certain physical disabilities believed to have resulted from his military service, and his widow received amounts varying from eight to thirty dollars per month until her death on November 27, 1920.

Before he enlisted in the army at age twenty-eight, J.F.C. had developed certain character traits which are manifested in his letters written during the War and which stayed with him during his post-war years in Illinois and in Kansas. Prominent among these was the unquestioning Christianity which pervaded his daily life. Before he entered service he had been licensed as an "exhorter" in the Methodist Church, and he was superintendent of a Sunday school in Pontiac. While in uniform J.F.C. attended religious services whenever possible, and he frequently delivered sermons and organized revival meetings for troops. Almost at the end of his military service, he wrote on April 18, 1865:

> Our meetings continue, & God is doing a great work for us. There were 10 forward Sunday night & 9 last night & numerous conversions. Over 160 have joined the church. . . . I preached last night from Mark, 16 Chap. & 16 V., and God was pleased to bless me.

In the 1870's he served without salary as the pastor of the Methodist Episcopal Church in Pontiac to assist the congregation to free itself from debt, and later in Emporia he was active again in Sunday schools and he helped to found the Grace Methodist Church.

J.F.C.'s relationship with his God was simple and direct; his letters are sprinkled with gentle Christian phrases relating to prayer and immortality, and he possessed unswerving faith in the wisdom of the Divine Will as it appears in human events. A telegram from Mary brought J.F.C. word of the death of his first son, and he responded that evening (October 31, 1863), "Let us cheerfully submit to the will of him who doeth all things well." J.F.C.'s complete confidence in the way events work toward ultimate good and his strong sense of duty left him free of fear and devoid of concern for personal safety. He volunteered for military service, because, as he wrote shortly after he left home (August 19, 1862), "I thought God & my country was calling me." His priorities were clear and clearly ordered. "Next to my God and my Country, I love my wife," he wrote on April 13, 1864, to Mary who was pregnant back in Illinois.

Other persistent characteristics of J.F.C.'s to be found in his letters are his preoccupation with his own health and that of others, his affection for his comrades in Company "A," his enjoyment of popular music, and his affiliation with Masonic orders. In almost every letter to his young wife, J.F.C. reported his physical condition which usually was superb: "I have almost reached my old weight, 186; I weighed 182 about two weeks ago. I believe I never enjoyed better health in my life" (August 28, 1863); and he described with precision the ailments and disabilities which beset others in his regiment. Moreover, he worried continuously about the health of his wife at home or on a trip to and from her and his early homes in New York and Pennsylvania.

J.F.C. served for a few months in the regimental headquarters and could have continued there, but he preferred to lead the men of his beloved Company "A." He wrote that his expenses had increased while he worked as a staff officer for his regiment and division, but he missed his relationships with the soldiers from Livingston County and desired to return to them. Before the fall of Atlanta, J.F.C.'s company experienced hours of "murderous" enemy fire, and in a letter to his wife he exulted, "I have a noble Company & my earnest wish so long cherished has been granted. I have been permitted to lead them in all their battles.'' And, when he rejoined his regiment after five months of detached service, he wrote to Mary, ''I am at home again. I found all the boys present in good health & most of them glad to see me.'' During the days which immediately followed his return to his company, the men teased J.F.C. about his lack of intimate knowledge of their memorable marches through Georgia and South Carolina (March 30, 1865).

J.F.C. had been a member of a cornet band in Pontiac, and it fell to him to try to raise money for the purchase of musical instruments for his regiment's band. He wrote to Mary about the airs played by bands in various camps, and he found enjoyment in singing with fellow soldiers and with others he met in the South. He requested his wife to send him the lyrics of a popular ballad, ''Mother Dear, Oh! Pray for Me,'' which she dutifully did. While garrisoned in Tennessee, the colonel of the regiment, Benjamin Harrison, later to become a president of the United States, on March 27, 1864, invited J.F.C. and several clerks ''into his house to sing.'' Colonel Harrison selected from the *Golden Shower* ''those pieces with which he was familiar, & we all sang with him. . . . We have been thus employed for over three hours. It was a very pleasant time for me, and I hope also profitable.''

The only mention made of Masonic connections in J.F.C.'s Civil War letters are passing references to emblematic pins exchanged between him and his wife, but the affiliation maintained for more than forty years must have been important to him for J.F.C. listed his achievements in Masonic orders in the letterhead of the stationery used in his Emporia law office the year before he died.

J.F.C.'s death evoked memorials from the Logan County (Kansas) Bar Association and from his Emporia Sunday school, and his funeral attracted a crowd of mourners. One Kansan noted, ''I presume there were few present who had not been befriended by him in some way. All the standing room was occupied inside and for about twenty feet outside each door.'' The lawyers in Emporia observed, ''He [J.F.C.] had accumulated very little wealth. In one sense his life was a failure, in another and better sense it was a grand success.'' J.F.C.'s body was taken to Pontiac for burial in a plot marked by a vertical stone which lists on its four sides the names of the Culvers and Murphys (including Mary Murphy Culver) who are buried there.

\* \* \*

As was mentioned above, J.F.C. as a soldier wrote letters to his wife because he wanted to talk with her, and most of his letters are in a relaxed, conversational mode. He introduces a topic of interest, moves to another, and returns to the first when and if additional thoughts come to mind. Events are described as he perceives them, and he realizes that a participant in a military campaign has next to no notion of the roles played by units other than his own. Rumors of unconfirmed events which circulated among J.F.C.'s troops are branded as such until the stories are supported or dispelled, and in most of his letters J.F.C. carefully notes his location and the date (and occasionally the hour!) of his writing.

J.F.C.'s letters to his wife were written amidst the difficulties encountered by the men in his regiment, and it is remarkable that he was able to surmount almost all of them. At times the extreme cold stiffened his writing hand, and he hastened to bring a letter (April 20, 1865) to a close when wind threatened to blow out his candle and leave him in darkness. A surface for writing frequently had to be improvised, and J.F.C. was resourceful enough to employ a cracker box for the purpose and he once carved a seat out of the side of a trench and used the level ground for a writing table. "It is very comfortable and has all the advantages of a cushioned arm chair." (August 5, 1864). Writing paper understandably was in short supply (May 3, 1864), but J.F.C. managed to secure enough sheets to continue sending letters to his wife. In one written on July 19, 1864, J.F.C. directed Mary, "Tell Lt. Smith [then at home on leave] we have used all his letter paper & envelopes and to bring a large supply with him." J.F.C. used the same pen throughout most of the War (June 10, 1864), and most of his letters were written in black ink and are easily read today. A half dozen letters were written in pencil, and these and letters written during the Atlanta campaign in light blue ink are barely legible. "This is blue but is better than none." (July 23, 1864). Five of J.F.C.'s letters written in August of 1864 defy accurate transcription and are not included in this compilation.

Recipients of mail from soldiers in American armies in Europe and in Asia will be surprised at the shortages of stamps experienced by men in Union armies in Tennessee and Georgia; J.F.C.'s need for postage was so acute that he asked his wife to send him "a dollar's worth" which she did more than once. Letters were sent home by the mails or by a soldier or civilian who was to travel from the regiment to Pontiac or to a town nearby. At times Confederate depredations of railroad lines interrupted the mails, and exchanges of letters between J.F.C. and his wife were delayed for weeks and, in at least one instance, for months. J.F.C. fretted when others in his regiment received mail and he did not, yet most of the letters written by Mary were delivered within a period of time which would seem reasonably short except to a young man who anxiously awaited news from a loved one at home.

Probably through his training in a commercial school in Pittsburgh, J.F.C. early developed an even and legible hand, but certain peculiarities which repeatedly appear have posed problems for the editor which had to be resolved. The size of particular letters, such as J.F.C.'s initial *C's,* leave his intentions regarding capitalization in doubt, and his final *s,* be it an old style *s* with a descender in a word such as "loss" or an *s* formed as a curlicue which flows into the formation of the first letter of the next word, did not confuse the recipient of his letters, but they present puzzles for the transcriber. J.F.C.'s informal prose was written without benefit of paragraph structure and regular punctuation, and these omissions have been filled by the introduction of indentations to mark new paragraphs and of commas, semicolons, and periods whenever the use of a convention will assist the reader to understand the meaning of the writer. J.F.C.'s misspellings are curious in that at times he will spell the first name of a close friend "C-H-R-I-S" [Yetter] and at other times "C-R-I-S", and he invariably left the *t* out of the name of General Joseph E. Johnston who commanded the Confederate army throughout General Sherman's campaign in North Carolina. J.F.C. was consistent also in his misspellings of certain frequently used words, notably "oportunity" and "immagine," and these have been corrected without ado. J.F.C. was not an illiterate; he wrote many letters under extremely trying circumstances, and he did not have at hand a dictionary. No attempt has been made to correct J.F.C.'s ungrammatical constructions, such as his frequent use of singular verbs with plural subjects and vice versa, because these do not hinder the reader's comprehension of the intended meaning. J.F.C.'s word order and his use of perfect tenses are susceptible of improvement, but these characteristics were of little or no consequence to him or to his wife and are reproduced without change in the transcripts which follow.

* * *

In addition to the 238 letters written by J.F.C. in wartime to his wife (the number includes five which are illegible), there are more than a hundred letters in the Culver Collection written by his wife, brothers and sisters, business associates, and fellow soldiers, plus a handful written by J.F.C. to his wife before and after the War and to others during the War. Mary Culver must have taken pains to preserve the letters from her husband, because she did travel to New York and Pennsylvania while he was away from home. The letters which she wrote and which are to be found today in the Culver Collection presumably were retained by J.F.C. until she visited him in Tennessee, and then she carried them back to Illinois. Late in the War J.F.C. reread letters from Mary still in his possession and then destroyed the documents to keep them from being read by others in the event of his capture or death (March 20, 1864, and April 9, 1865). J.F.C. received letters from members of his and his wife's family, which after answering he usually sent on to Mary for her information and enjoyment.

Many of the additional letters in the Culver Collection possess sufficient interest to warrant publication, but a halt had to be called somewhere, and this editor decided to limit the documents to be printed in this volume to those written during the Civil War by J.F.C. to his wife. Edwin C. Bearss, a professional historian, drew on the other letters in the Culver Collection in the explanatory notes prepared for the printed edition of J.F.C.'s 233 wartime letters to his wife. The existence of additional documents in the Culver Collection is mentioned here because some of them illuminate J.F.C.'s letters, and their retention for more than a hundred years reflects the value placed on these records by Mary Culver and by others in her family.

* * *

This edition of J.F.C.'s letters to his wife written during the American Civil War is a publication of the Friends of the University of Iowa Libraries, an organization formed in 1964 to encourage the development of collections of rare books and manuscripts in Iowa and at the University in Iowa City. The Friends publishes twice a year a periodical, *Books at Iowa,* devoted to scholarly articles describing books and manuscripts in the University Libraries and a *Newsletter* which contains information about recent developments in collections and services. The Friends has published important bibliographical compilations such as Frank Paluka's *Iowa Authors* (1967) and Frank Hanlin and John Martin's *Heirs of Hippocrates* (1974), and has distributed copies of these books and of others published by the University Libraries, such as *The Publication of American Historical Manuscripts* (1976), as bonus publications to members. These and related activities caused the Friends to welcome an opportunity to publish the Civil War letters written by Senator John C. Culver's great-grandfather.

The possibility of publishing this sizable group of letters had been considered about a decade ago by Senator Culver, and rough transcripts of most of the documents were typed and helpful explanatory notes were prepared from published sources and from unpublished documents in the Culver Collection and in the National Archives in Washington, D.C., by Edwin C. Bearss, historian in the National Park Service, who undertook the work as a labor of love. Comparison of the earlier typescripts of J.F.C.'s letters with the originals made plain that new transcriptions were needed, and the corrected typescripts and transcripts of letters which had not been copied at all were typed by my secretary, Doris Stuck. The index was prepared by John Schacht, and proofs were read by reference librarians in the University Libraries. Substantial encouragement for this very considerable undertaking has come from President Willard L. Boyd of the University of Iowa and from the University of Iowa Foundation.

On behalf of the Friends of tne University of Iowa Libraries, I wish to thank Senator John C. Culver for the opportunity to publish his great-grandfather's Civil War letters and for his support of the project through loan of the original letters and related materials and through his keen interest in seeing the project brought to a successful conclusion.

Leslie W. Dunlap
*Dean of Library Administration*

*Iowa City, Iowa*
*July 19, 1978*

---

[1] *A History of the One Hundred and Twenty-Ninth Regiment Illinois Volunteer Infantry,* a volume of 283 pages by William Grunert, was printed in 1866 at Winchester, Ill., and a compilation of letters written by two brothers who served in the regiment, A. A. and Charles Dunham, was edited by Arthur H. DeRosier, Jr., and published in 1969 under the title *Through the South with a Union Soldier.*

Mary  Murphy  Culver

Joseph Franklin Culver

# THE LETTERS

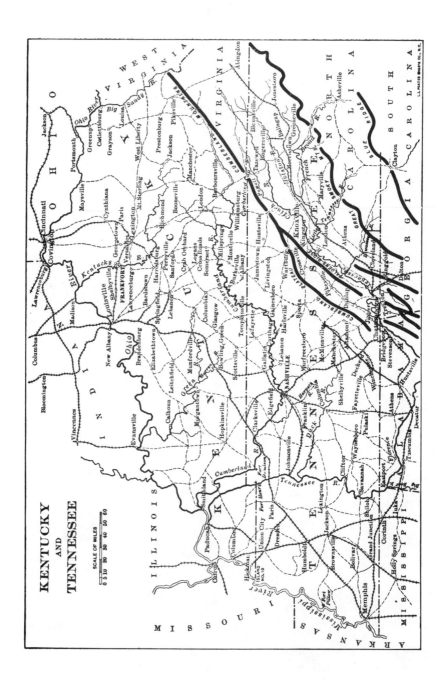

KENTUCKY
AND
TENNESSEE

SCALE OF MILES
0 5 10 20 30 40 50 60

Camp Worcester Kankakee, Ills. Aug 14th/ 62

Dear Wife

I arrived here all Safe on yesterday evening & have had several opportunities of sending letters home to-day but could not take time to write. Lieut. Smith went home this morning, & I have been trying to finish up the business of our organization, but it will occupy all of to-morrow. The health of the Camp is quite good; some few are ailing with diarrhea caused by eating too much green fruit but none seriously.

It is now eight o'clock. There is singing in almost every part of the camp, some sacred songs but many of different characters. I cannot say that I do not like Camp-life on this short trial though it affords but very few of the comforts of home. I have been interrupted for the last half hour by the return of a guard which I sent down to the city for some of the men who went away without a pass while I was thus engaged. A Stand was erected near our quarters, & now Speeches are being made by different soldiers, a great deal of cheering & noise accompanies. I am all alone, a privilege I do not often enjoy.

I hope you are well & happy; do not allow anything to give you trouble. I believe [God] requires this trial at our hands. Let us hope that we may have many years of peaceful Enjoyment in the future. "God ruleth all things well."

We go to Chicago on Monday next; if you wish, you and Mother can come up and spend some time. I hope you will be governed in the matter by Mother's judgment. She knows what is best. Our Camp will be one mile south of Camp Douglass & about three miles from Holmes's. The Street cars, I think, will run within a short distance. Write to me, directing your letter to Chicago.

I have not yet had time to think whether I have left any of my matters at loose ends. I shall try soon & take time to think them over. Do not always wait for my letters. You will feel happier, I believe, if you write often. Tell me all your troubles & let me share them with you. I have forgotten what you told me about Sammy; in fact, I was so much engrossed in business that I scarcely took time to think of anything that was not forced upon my mind, but I hope in a few days to be more at leisure. If anything demands my attention, please inform me.

I fear sometimes Sis & you must be lonely; gather all the Company around you possible. I would write to Sammy if I thought I could prevail on him to go & stay with you. Write me what you wish in the matter. Give my love to all. Write soon, & I pray that the Blessing of Heaven may rest upon you. Do not forget to pray for me, & may God preserve us both for the Enjoyment of many years [of] prosperity.

Your affect. Husband

J. F. Culver

 2

Head Quarters, Miller's Battery
Camp Douglas    Aug. 19th 1862

Dear Wife

I have delayed answering your letter from day to day expecting to answer it in person, but, as there is very little probability of our being Ordered to Pontiac, I shall occupy a few moments, after telling you how we are getting along, in answering your letter.

I came to Chicago this morning to see General Fuller,[1] but he is not here. I am now in Bro. John's [Murphy] Quarters where I found him looking well & Enjoying good health & Spirits. I left nearly all at Camp well: Byron Hopwood & Joseph Allen are quite ill & some few others ailing but none seriously. The men are very uneasy & anxious to go home, but we cannot get marching orders. It costs the government but 14 cents per day to keep us at Camp Worcester per man, while the cost at Pontiac is 40 cents. I fear the chances of our marching there are rather few. I am sorry that the Committee appointed to attend to that matter did not make an effort to get marching orders as soon as they concluded to organize a regiment at Pontiac. I know they would have succeeded.

Hand N. C. Cannon's letter to ? L Fleming & request him to answer & receipt for the note. I think I answered but am not sure. Preserve the letter of the Home Ins. Co. Put in the small drawer containing my receipts. If Charlotte Postlethwaite sends a receipt, put it in there also. If she should not write for 10 days, notify me, & I will write to her. I want her receipt for the money I paid her for Saul. I have forgotten the Amount, but there is an Express receipt in my Express Book which will show the Amount.

Dear Mary, I feel grieved that thoughts such as you have expressed in your letter should trouble you. I hope I shall be able to dispel them by uttering the true sentiments of my heart, sentiments that should have been long ago expressed but I feared you would think me guilty of flattery. You have been to me more, much more, than I ever anticipated in a wife: Good, loving, kind, affectionate, dutiful. O, May God bless you for the great good you have done me. When the world was almost a blank, your loving kindness opened up new Springs in my heart. You have made home the happiest place on Earth; you have created new desires for Heaven. I did not leave you from choice. God knew my heart, but I thought God & my Country was calling upon me, & I tried, as I ever shall by God's grace, to walk in the path of duty.

I should like very much to get home once more before we leave, but it is quite improbable. If not, do not think that I am unkind & that there are no home ties to draw me there. O, I never felt prouder of you in my life than when I saw you stem the great tide of Sorrow at my going & occasionally smile when I felt in my heart that the sacrifice was as great as could possibly be required at your hands. May God bless you for all your efforts & preserve you in peace & prosperity until in the dispensation of his providence I may be permitted to return.

Tell Maggie I shall endeavor to carry out her suggestion. I borrowed $50 - of Bro. John to-day to purchase a Sword. We have drawn no money yet. Write soon & often; tell me all the news. I have been so busy since I left home that I have had but little time to think how my business was disposed of. Give my love to all. Tell Leander [Utley] to write. I will write to him at the earliest opportunity. Be cheerful, & may God bless us with a babe which will in a great measure fill the void in your heart.

Your affect. Husband

J. F. Culver

---

1   Allen C. Fuller served from 1861 until 1864 as adjutant general for the state of Illinois.

 3

Jeffersonville, Sept. 24th 1862

Dear Mary

We arrived here all safe at 8 a.m. & are now making arrangements to cross the river to Louisville.[1] The Lieut. Colonel [Henry Case] went over this morning but has not returned yet. There has been considerable excitement on account of an expected attack by General Bragg, but it is currently reported this morning that he is retreating.[2] The Louisville papers this morning are urging the citizens to arm themselves.[3] No accidents happened save that a few of the men were left at various places along the road, having wandered off for water &c.

I hope you & the baby are both well. Kiss it for me. Give my love to all. Write soon as you can.

In haste, your affect. Husband

J. F. Culver

---

1   The regiment left Camp Pontiac on September 22 aboard a troop train. The soldiers breakfasted the next morning at Michigan City and had supper in the evening of the 23d at Indianapolis. *Through the South with a Union Soldier*, edited by Arthur H. DeRosier, Jr. (Johnson City, 1969), p. 23.

2   Gen. Braxton Bragg's hard-marching Army of Mississippi had reached Munfordville, where it captured the Union garrison on September 17, ahead of Maj. Gen. Don C. Buell's army. Bragg, having placed his army between Buell and his Louisville base, took position covering the crossing of Green River. To goad Buell into a rash attack on his chosen position, Bragg advanced one of his divisions. Buell refused the bait, and after four days Bragg, learning that his troops were down to three days' rations, in a "hostile country, utterly destitute of supplies," determined to abandon his position astride Buell's line of communications. Orders were issued for a supply train from the Confederate depot at Lexington to meet the army at Bardstown. On September 20 Bragg yielded the advantage gained and turned northeast. Buell, with the Confederate army out of the way, marched for Louisville, where he arrived on the 25th. *The War of the Rebellion: A Compilation of the Official Records of the Union and Confederate Armies* (73 vols., 128 parts; Washington, 1880-1901), Ser. I, Vol. XVI, pt. I, pp. 48, 1090-1091; pt. II, p. 542.

3   Although the crisis had passed, there was great excitement in Louisville on the 24th. "Every able-bodied man" was being impressed to take up arms for defense of the city or to work on fortifications. An attack was momentarily expected. *O.R.*, Ser. I, Vol. XVI, pt. II, p. 542.

 4

Head Quarters Company A, 129th Regt. Ills. Vol.
Camp near Louisville, Ky. Sept. 25th 1862

Dear Mary

We arrived here at about 6 P.M. yesterday & encamped just south of the city. I am informed there are about 100,000 men here.[1] Genrl. Buell will be here at 10 o'clock this morning with 40,000 more.[2] General Bragg, who was advancing on Louisville, has retreated & is reported in the neighborhood of Lexington.[3]

We had a trial of Camp life in earnest last night. We carried our supper across the river in our haversacks, without coffee, we eat our bite & lay us down to sleep. I had a rail for a pillow & the ground for a bed. I slept very well. At 3 o'clock this morning we were called & formed in line of battle & stood there until sunrise this morning. It was rather hard work after our long trip, but we must learn to stand it. All are well.

Louisville is a very fine place, but all was still as death yesterday. For the last 3 or 4 days, all places of business were closed; this morning they are opened again. Our rules are so strict that no one will get into the city for a while. We will be called out to drill shortly, & I must close.

Write to me soon. I wrote yesterday. We shall probably remain here for the present. Give my love to all. Kiss baby for me.

Your affect. Husband

J. F. Culver

---

1   On September 24, Maj. Gen. Thomas L. Crittenden had crossed Salt River with the advance of Buell's army and entered Louisville. Maj. Gen. Alexander McD. McCook's division followed Crittenden. By the 27th all of Buell's army had reached Louisville. The Federals had won the race.
Lieutenant Culver exaggerated the number of Union troops available for defense of Louisville. On the 24th Maj. Gen. William Nelson, the officer responsible for the city's defense, reported he had 35,000 men; that they were entrenched; and that he believed he could hold the city. With Crittenden came 12,000 men and six batteries, increasing the force camped in and around Louisville to 47,000. *O.R.*, Ser. I, Vol. XVI, pt. II, pp. 540-541; Robert E. McDowell, *City of Conflict: Louisville in the Civil War, 1861-1865* (Louisville, 1962), p. 89.

2  Culver was correct. Buell reached Louisville from Green River on the 25th with several brigades of his Army of the Ohio. It was the 27th before the last of Buell's troops entered the Louisville perimeter. Buell's field army numbered about 47,500. *O.R.*, Ser. I, Vol. XVI, pt. I, pp. 14, 111, 616; *O.R.*, Ser. I, Vol. XVI, pt. II, pp. 542-543.

3  General Bragg's Army of Tennessee had occupied Bardstown, 35 miles southeast of Louisville, on the 22d. The Confederate force at Lexington was the army led by Maj. Gen. Edmund Kirby Smith, which had advanced into Kentucky from East Tennessee. Bypassing Cumberland Gap, Smith's columns had routed the Federals at Richmond, Ky., on August 30 and had swept into the Bluegrass Region, occupying Lexington and Frankfort, and threatening Cincinnati. *O.R.*, Ser. I, Vol. XVI, pt. II, pp. 864-865.

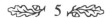 5

Head Quarters Company A, 129th Regt. Ills. Vols.
Near Louisville, Ky., Sept. 27th 1862

Dear Mary

We were marched at a late hour to this place, being about 4 miles from where we first encamped, through clouds of dust. There are about 12,000 in this division command[ed] by General Gilbert.[1] General Buell's army are concentrating at this place making in all encamped at this place about 200,000.[2]

There is but little prospect at present of our getting into a fight—Bragg, the only enemy near, has but 40,000 & will not attempt to do anything.[3] We are all in good health & spirits. We have 3 days rations in our haversack consisting of hard pilot bread & raw side meat which we cook by putting it on a stick & holding in the fire.[4] We have had nothing else since we left Pontiac. This morning we succeeded in buying [a] little coffee & are now making it. Co. A was fortunate last night in securing a shed used to husk Corn in, & I confiscated the overseer's room. I am at his desk, using his paper & ink. We have a very nice bed, wash stand, looking glass & desk. I hope we may remain here for a few days.

The sun is just beginning to rise. We have been drilling since 3 o'clock. We commence each day as early. No noise is allowed, & you would be surprised to waken up at daylight & find one or two hundred thousand men drawn up in line of battle.

I feel very thankful that our situation is no worse. The army of Buell's have been on the march for 32 day[s] on half rations all the time & often for three days without anything to eat. They look half starved.[5]

I hope to hear from you soon & know how you are getting along. I told [Charles] Custer to repair the fence around the lot I got of [Marcellus] Collins. You will please see that it is done & pay him for it. Give my love to all. Write as soon as you can. I have no postage stamps & shall have to send without stamp unless I can borrow.

Your affect. Husband

J. F. Culver

---

1   Charles C. Gilbert, a graduate of the U.S. Military Academy and Mexican War veteran, had been severely wounded at Wilson's Creek on Aug. 10, 1861. Recovering, he had been appointed acting major general on September 9, 1862, and placed in command of the Army of Kentucky, the unit to which the 129th Illinois was assigned. When Buell's Army of the Ohio absorbed the Army of Kentucky on September 29, Gilbert assumed command of the III Provisional Corps. *O.R.*, Ser. I, Vol. XVI, pt. II, pp. 530, 558; Ezra Warner, *Generals in Blue: Lives of the Union Commanders* (Baton Rouge, 1964), pp. 173-174.

2   There were on September 27 about 93,000 Union soldiers camped in and around Louisville. Like many people, J.F.C. was unable to estimate crowds. *O.R.*, Ser. I, Vol. XVI, pt. I, p. 19.

3   Between them, Generals Bragg and Kirby Smith had about 40,000 effectives. *Ibid.*, p. 1094.

4   "Hard pilot bread" is better known as hardtack.

5   Some of Buell's divisions had been marching and maneuvering since August 20, when Buell put General McCook's division in motion up the Sequatchie Valley. Confederate raids on the Louisville & Nashville Railroad compelled Union officers to put their men on half rations as early as mid-July. *O.R.*, Ser. I, Vol. XVI, pt. I, p. 279.

 6

1st Brigade, 4th Division, Western Department
Head Quarters, Company A, 129th Regt. Ills. Vols.
Louisville, Ky., Sept. 27th 1862

Dear Mary

I wrote to you this morning since which time I am informed that I cannot take my trunk with me. I have therefore put all my things in my trunk. I purchased a small valise being all I can carry.

It has been raining all day & is rather muddy; the troops have taken possession of all the buildings within the lines; & are doing very well. We are in Chapin's brigade & in General Gilbert's division.[1] The boys in Company A seem to be quite happy tonight & are busily singing in the Quarters.

Louisville is a very pleasantly situated place. I have not been much about the city, but what I have seen is rather fine. We are stationed on the outskirts of the city.

I have not heard from Bro. John [Murphy] since I arrived here. I have kept the brushes & c. as mother [Murphy] directed, & will send them to him on the first opportunity.

Write soon. Give my love to all. Tell Bro. Utley to write.[2] I can only get a few moments at a time & always feel like writing home first. We may be on the march soon, & I shall have no opportunity to write. You must not neglect in that event to write often. I have not yet written home [to Carlisle]. Send all my letters after you have read them if you think them interesting; but all business letters preserve carefully. I sent some money to Kankakee & expected a receipt. Please preserve it & tell me the bal. due as I requested him to inform me. Tell everybody to write. I should like to hear from some of [the] Remicks.[3] I shall try & write home soon.

Your affect. Husband

J. F. Culver

---

1  Three other regiments (the 23d Michigan, and the 102d and 111th Ohio) had been brigaded with the 129th Illinois to constitute a brigade commanded by Col. Marshall W. Chapin.

2  Leander Utley, a 37-year-old Pontiac Township farmer, was born in Providence, R.I., and had moved to Illinois in 1853. In 1860 Utley, a bachelor, was living in the same Pontiac hotel as J.F.C. On Jan. 7, 1861, he married Margaret Murphy, Mrs. Culver's eldest sister. Eighth Census, Livingston County, State of Illinois, NA; *The History of Livingston County, Illinois . . .* (Chicago, 1878), p. 652.

3  James W. Remick was a 39-year-old Pontiac Township farmer. Born in Franklin County, Pa., he had arrived in Livingston County in 1850. In 1856 he was elected sheriff and in 1860 clerk of the circuit court for Livingston County. Remick had married Sarah DeNormandie in 1844, and to the couple were born three children—Abbie, Lida, and Noah. *History of Livingston County*, pp. 648-649.

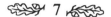 7

Head Quarters, Company A, 129th Regt. Ills. Vols.
Louisville, Ky., Sept. 29th 1862

Dear Mary

We returned about noon to-day from Picket duty. We had a very pleasant time being Quartered in a very beautiful grove. We brought one prisoner, a deserter from General Bragg's Army. He reported Bragg retreating.[1] Miller's Battery arrived here this evening. Bro. John [Murphy] was left sick in Chicago with fever but was getting better fast & will be here in a few days.[2] General Nelson was killed this morning by General Davis.[3] I have heard no one express any regret. He was disliked by the whole Army for being tyrannical, drunken & very unpleasant.

It is reported, & we all hope it is true that Buell has been removed & that General Hooker will take this command.[4] Thousands of Buell's men on every side of us proclaim him to be a traitor; that he withheld them when at one stroke he could have destroyed Bragg's entire army.[5]

We are all doing very well, but few sick & all generally cheerful. I expect to hear from you in a few days. My health is very good. Give my love to all. Yesterday was Sunday, yet I am sorry to say I did not think of it until nearly night. We were out early in the morning & marched out into the country. I was so busy that I forgot all about the day of the week. Bro. Cotton informs me that he did not find it out until he went down town.[6] Adjt. Plattenburg sends his respects.[7] He says you need not be uneasy as he will take care of me. He has brought his desk into our office & does business here which makes this the head quarters of the Regiment. Gagan arrived here day before yesterday.[8] He brought news for a great many of the company, & I was rather disappointed, but I know you were unable to go out, & I presume the rest did not think of it or know he was coming.

I hope you are doing well & by this time able to get around & I earnestly hope the babe is well & flourishing; that you may not have much trouble; that your health may not be impaired. May the blessings of Heaven rest upon you all for which I shall ever pray; As it is time to go to bed, I must say

Fairwell

Your affect. Husband

J. F. Culver

P.S. Our position has been changed today by an order from Head Quarters.[9]

---

1 Pvt. A. A. Dunham of Company C reported that some of the men believed the prisoner to be a spy, and he was put in the lockup. The prisoner, in stating that Bragg was retreating, had given misleading information. On September 29 Bragg's army was at Bardstown, where it had been for the past week, while Kirby Smith's divisions were camped in and around Lexington. Bragg's army on the 30th was increased by 8,000, when Maj. Gen. Carter L. Stevenson reached Danville from Cumberland Gap with his "fine" division. *O.R.*, Ser. I, Vol. XVI, pt. II, pp. 889-891; *Through the South with a Union Soldier*, p. 22.

2 Miller's battery (Company M, 1st Illinois Light Artillery Regiment) had departed from Camp Douglas on September 27. *Report of the Adjutant General of the State of Illinois, Containing Reports for the Years 1861-66* (Springfield, 1886); Vol. VIII, p. 665.

3 On the morning of the 29th, Maj. Gen. William "Bull" Nelson had breakfasted at the Galt House and was standing at the desk, when Governor Oliver P. Morton of Indiana, accompanied by Brig. Gen. Jefferson C. Davis and two other men, entered the lobby. Davis, "a small, sallow, blue-eyed, dyspeptic-looking man, less than five feet nine inches high, and weighing only about one hundred and twenty-five pounds," accused the powerfully-built, ex-naval officer Nelson of having insulted him at their last meeting. "Go away", the six-foot-four, 300-pound Nelson snapped, his manner expressive of his contempt for Davis. Other words followed, and Nelson slapped Davis with the back of his hand. He then turned his back on Davis and walked to the stairway. As he did, Davis secured a pistol from one of his companions and shot Nelson to death. McDowell, *City of Conflict*, pp. 99-101.

4 In Washington, officials at the War Department had become disenchanted with Buell's conduct of the Kentucky Campaign. On September 24 the decision was made to relieve General Buell and replace him with General Thomas, provided that: (a) the army was not in the presence of the enemy; (b) Buell had not gained a victory; or (c) Thomas was too far separated by geography to enter upon command of the army. The staff officer entrusted with this confidential dispatch, signed by General in Chief Henry Halleck, reached Louisville on the 29th. General Thomas, taking the position that Buell had completed preparations to move against the foe, telegraphed Halleck, asking that Buell be retained in command.
President Lincoln and his advisors, in view of Thomas' unwillingness to assume the responsibility, reconsidered their decision to sack Buell. Before the day was over, Halleck had drafted and forwarded a telegram, directing that the order changing commanders be suspended. *O.R.*, Ser. I, Vol. XVI, pt. II, pp. 538-539, 554-555.
The story reaching J.F.C. that Buell was to be replaced by Maj. Gen. Joseph Hooker, the popular commander of the Army of the Potomac's I Corps, was a garbled version of what was transpiring at army headquarters.

5 Col. J. C. McKibbin, the staff officer entrusted with the order relieving Buell, reported, there is "much dissatisfaction with General Buell" and "no probability of a fight within a week." *Ibid.*, p. 554.

6   Thomas Cotton, a 36-year-old minister, had enlisted as a corporal in Company K, 129th Illinois, at Pontiac on Aug. 2, 1862. When the regiment was mustered into federal service for three years, on Sept. 8, he was appointed chaplain. Cotton resigned on Aug. 6, 1864, because he was suffering from "bilious derangement," which had been aggravated by the terrible Georgia climate. This disability had induced a certain amount of nervous depression, which made it impossible for him "to move through the regiment with that glow of mental and social energy" that enabled him to succeed in his work. Compiled Service Records of Union Soldiers, NA.

7   Philip D. Plattenburg, of Pontiac, Illinois was 31 years old when he enlisted on Aug. 15, 1862, as a private in Company K, 129th Illinois. He was mustered in for three years' service, and appointed regimental adjutant on Sept. 8, 1862. Adjutant Plattenburg served with the regiment throughout the war and was mustered out at Washington, D.C., on June 8, 1865. *Ibid.*

8   William Gagan, a 29-year-old Irish newspaperman, had been appointed regimental sutler on Sept. 9, 1862, by Col. G. P. Smith. Eighth Census, Livingston County, State of Illinois, N A ; Regimental Papers, 129th Illinois, NA, RG 94.

9   The death of Nelson and the need to improve the organization of the army resulted in a sweeping reorganization on September 29. The divisions camped in and around Louisville were organized into three corps to be commanded respectively by Maj. Gens. Alexander McD. McCook, Thomas L. Crittenden, and Charles C. Gilbert. Chapin's brigade was redesignated the 38th and assigned to Brig. Gen. Ebenezer Dumont's Twelfth Division. Dumont's division was not given a corps assignment and would report to headquarters, Army of the Ohio. *O.R.*, Ser. I, Vol. XVI, pt. II, pp. 558-559, 595; Regimental Papers, 129th Illinois, NA, RG 94.

 8

Head Quarters, Company A, 129th, Ills. Vols.
Louisville, Ky. Octr. 1st 1862

Dear Mary

I thought I should get my trunk started to-morrow in which I have a note of this date but shall not succeed. I am happy to say my health is quite good. I read a letter from Lou to Allen, recd to-day in which she said you were doing well. It gave me much comfort.[1]

I hope I shall hear from you through some one soon & shall be happy when your health will permit you to write. Please take good care of yourself. [I] want to hear of your enjoying good health, & being blooming & happy. Kiss baby for me. Give my love to all & may the

Blessings of Heaven forever rest upon you. Strive to be cheerful & happy & trust in God.

Your affect. Husband

J. F. Culver

P.S. I sent my trunk key with Maples. Please get it.[2]

1 There were two Allens, both farmers, in Company A, Bartlett and Joseph. Twenty-four-year-old Joseph was mustered in as a private in Company A, 129th Illinois, on Sept. 8, 1862, at Pontiac. On Dec. 5, 1863, Joseph was detailed as a clerk in Maj. Gen. Lovell H. Rousseau's Nashville headquarters. He served in the Nashville headquarters throughout the remainder of the war and was discharged there on June 5, 1865. Lou Allen was Joseph Allen's wife. Compiled Service Records of Union Soldiers, NA.

2 Edwin R. Maples, the 29-year-old sheriff of Livingston County from 1860 through 1862, had been visiting the regiment, as an employee of Sutler Gagan. He left for Pontiac by railroad on the evening of October 1. *Through the South with a Union Soldier*, p. 25; Eighth Census, Livingston County, State of Illinois, NA.

9

Head Quarters, Company A, 129th Ills.<br/>Camp near Shelbyville, Ky. Octr. 5th 1862

Dear Mary

I received your letter just before leaving Louisville & did not have time to answer it. We are about 35 miles from Louisville; left there at 4 o'clock on Friday & marched until 10 o'clock next morning. We camped at Bull Skin run on the field on which the battle was fought last Wednesday morning. We arrived here about 10 o'clock last night & scarcely had lain down until we were ordered out as pickets about 1½ miles. One of us had to remain to take care of those coming in. As Smith & myself could not decide which should remain, both wishing to go with the Company, we cast lots & the lot fell upon me so I am in Camp this Sunday morning while nearly all the Company are on duty. We are all tired & sore, but I am one of the fortunate ones & feel very well. My health is quite good. I have found quite a number of old acquaintances in the Army here from Ohio, Pennsylvania & Illinois.

I was very happy to learn that you and baby were getting along so well. I scarcely expected you would be able to set up so soon. I felt like as if I should like to take you & baby both in my arms and carry [you] wherever you might wish to go. With regard to baby's name, I do not wish to add any. If I should be fortunate enough to return home, I may suggest; but for the present, I wish you to satisfy yourself, & I shall be very happy to submit. With regard to naming children, I always felt that the name is something of an index to the character. I know it is only a notion.

I do not know how many men are with us, but there must be several thousand. The Board of Trade battery is very near us; Miller's Battery is in the rear. I have not heard yet which will be attached to our Brigade.

I was sorry to hear that Bro. John was so sick & hope he will be able to join us soon. I sent my trunk by Express & hope it will arrive safe; I sent the Key by mail. I felt sorry to return so many things, but I could not take them with me.

I paid a visit to a house yesterday morning & also one this morning Sacked by our Army, & it made me heartsick; thousands of dollars worth of property destroyed that can be of no earthly use to the men. I surely do not blame any family for detesting the Army that will commit such depradations: Bureaus full of things sacred to a family broken to pieces & the contents scattered for rods around the house. I set down this morning to a splendid rosewood piano, as fine a toned one as I ever heard. It was covered with dirt; the ceiling had [been] broken by the bayonets of the men, & bruises & scratches from their guns, toilet & work boxes overlaid with shell & ornaments broken to pieces, & everything almost destroyed. The families, fearing for their lives, flying all over the Country. I could not depict all the horrors of war.

I shall have to see to our provisions. I may possibly have an opportunity to write again before we leave here. Give my love to all. I thought what a vast difference between these acres of men gambling & swearing & quiet Pontiac this beautiful Sunday morning. May God be with you & bless you all for which I shall ever pray. I shall be very happy to hear from you soon. I received all the letters you enclosed. I have been unable to answer the contents of your letter fully. I have written home twice since baby was born, both very hasty letters. I shall not forget, Dear Mary, to pray for you both. Give my love to Maggie & Mother. I intended to write to Bro. Utley but have not had time. Tell Johnie the Battery looks splendid. I left his things which Mother gave me with the Junior 1st Lieut. of his Battery. Write soon. Direct as before until we get into a more permanent Camp. Hoping God will bless & preserve you all until I return, I subscribe myself as ever

Your affect. Husband

Joseph F. Culver

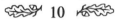 10

Shelbyville, Ky., Octr. 6th 1862

Dear Mary

I wrote yesterday but having no opportunity to send my letter I came to town this evening to mail it.[1] I am very well. The rebels are leaving the state from every quarter.[2] I see but little prospect of our getting into a fight for some time. The health of the company is generally good. Write soon.

Your affect. Husband

J. F. Culver

---

1 The 129th Illinois, along with other units of Dumont's division, marched from Louisville on the 3d. A diarist recorded, "The sun was tremendously hot, and as the water in our canteens gave out, no springs or creeks on our way, the knapsacks overloaded and heavy, it may be imagined that this our first day's tramp was anything but pleasant." Two days were required to march from Louisville to Shelbyville, a distance of 32 miles. William Grunert, *History of the One Hundred and Twenty-Ninth Regiment Illinois Volunteer Infantry . . .* (Winchester, Ill., 1866) pp. 5-6.

2 J.F.C. misinterpreted Confederate troop movements. On October 1 General Bragg, leaving Maj. Gen. Leonidas Polk in command of his army at Bardstown, had started for Lexington. Polk was under instructions to slowly retire to Bryantsville. At Lexington, Bragg ordered Kirby Smith with all his forces to Frankfort to assist in the October 4 inauguration of Richard Hawes as Confederate governor of Kentucky. At Lexington on the 2d, Bragg, learning that Buell's columns were advancing from the Louisville perimeter, ordered Polk to march at once toward Frankfort to strike the Federal army in the flank and rear.

Octr. 7th 1862
Camp Near Shelbyville, Ky., Head Quarters, Company A, 129th Ills.
Vols.

Dear Wife

We have had no opportunities for receiving mail from Louisville as yet, so that if any letters were sent I could not yet have received them. I wrote on Sunday & a short note yesterday & mailed them at Shelbyville. Since then we have moved our camp; for two days we were in an open field, very dusty. There has been no rain except a short fall shower last week since the first of July, & the weather is very hot.[1]

We are now in a very pleasant grove a short distance from our old camp, & I judge from appearances that we will remain here some time, how long I do not know. The general health of the Camp is good. Adjt. Plattenburg has been sick to-day but not seriously. N. W. Hill of our company has also been quite sick to-day but is much better to-day.[2] All the rest of our Company are well.

I have tried several times to compose myself & think over business at home but find it impossible. If anything arises, you will please inform me. I wish I could make suggestions, but my time is wholly taken up. I hope to hear from you by the first mail that arrives & hope to hear that you are quite well & baby flourishing. I have not received letters from any source yet except the one from you.[3] A letter would be very acceptable.

Mary dear, do not allow yourself to be lonely. You have the babe for Company, & as soon as you are able to go around, you must take plenty of exercise. Our time when together has been very happily spent, & I shall earnestly desire a return of such pleasant hours though I shall cheerfully respond to the call of my country & discharge my whole duty.

Bro. Cotton is holding a prayer meeting to-night near the hospital for the benefit of the sick. He is making himself very useful. Lieut. Smith is very well.[4] He received a letter from his wife on Monday & feels very uneasy. She seems to fret as much as ever. I do hope she will be more contented. It gives him a great deal of pain.

I have not yet written to anyone else in Pontiac, except to Remick on business, but hope I shall soon have time to write to many. May the Blessings of Heaven rest upon you for which I shall ever pray. May health & happiness attend you, & may we both be spared to enjoy many days & years of pleasure together. I feel that God will be with us.

Write soon. Give my love to all & believe me ever.

Your Affect. Husband

Jos. F. Culver

---

1   All accounts of the Kentucky Campaign refer to the drought and suffering caused by lack of drinking water. The battle of Perryville, fought on October 8, was precipitated on the previous evening when troops of Gilbert's corps lashed out to secure pools of water standing in the bed of Doctors Creek. Stanley Horn, *The Army of Tennessee: A Military History* (Indianapolis, 1941), p. 180.

2   A 24-year-old farmer, Nathan W. Hill was mustered into federal service as a private in Company A, 129th Illinois, on Sept. 8, 1862. He was promoted to corporal on Jan. 20, 1863, and to sergeant on May 9, 1863. Sergeant Hill was mustered out at Washington, D.C., June 8, 1865. Compiled Service Records of Union Troops, NA.

3   Until May 1, 1864, J.F.C. carefully preserved most of the letters received from his wife and relatives. The letter referred to, however, is missing from the Culver Collection.

4   John W. Smith of Pontiac enlisted as a 2d lieutenant in Company A, 129th Illinois, on Aug. 2, 1862. The 30-year-old lieutenant was mustered into federal service on Sept. 8 for three years. At Resaca, Ga., on May 15, 1864, he was wounded in the abdomen and shoulder. On Aug. 11, 1864, Smith was promoted to 1st lieutenant, and on Sept. 14 he resigned his commission, citing his wife's "delicate health." Compiled Service Records of Union Troops, NA.

 12

Direct to Louisville
Octr. 8th, 7 o'clock A.M.

Dear Mary

We leave [Shelbyville] this morning for Frankfort. I never felt better in health. May God bless you.
Farewell.

Your Husband

J. F. Culver

Head Quarters, Company A, 129th Ills. Vols.
Camp near Frankfort, Ky., Octr. 9th 1862

My dear Wife

We arrived here this morning about sunrise after a day & night's march, very tired, yet enjoying good health.[1] The mail arrived last night from Louisville but brought nothing for me. It is very easy for letters to miscarry.

I earnestly hope that you are all well. Will only stop here long enough to cook rations, & we will start in a few minutes on a two-days march. I think our destination will be Lexington but am not sure. There was a short skirmish here last night before we arrived, but the rebels left suddenly, a few wounded on each side.[2]

I shall expect to hear from you by next mail; I believe I have not missed a day writing to you since we arrived in Louisville.

May God bless you all, Farewell

Your affect. Husband

J. F. Culver

---

1 The 129th Illinois marched from Shelbyville on the 8th. General Dumont, having learned that Sill's division had evacuated Frankfort, pushed his soldiers hard. Word passed up and down the column that the Confederates had reoccupied the city. Dumont called on his people to make a night march. One of the men recalled, "No march has ever been so tiring to me as this one, being hardly able to remain in the column. Many of the men left the column and laid down by the road to sleep and rest." Grunert, *History of the 129th Illinois*, pp. 6-7.

2 Dumont's vanguard, as it approached Frankfort, skirmished with troopers of Col. John Hunt Morgan's Kentucky cavalry, who retired down the Versailles road. *O.R.*, Ser. I, Vol. XVI, pt. II, pp. 601, 925-926.

## 14

Head Quarters, Company A, 129th Ills. Vols.
Frankfort, Ky. Octr. 10th 1862

My Dear Wife

I wrote to you yesterday evening & supposed that before this we would be on our way to Lexington. The order was countermanded & we were sent to the heights west of the city to support a Battery. We are camped on a hill about 250 feet above the city giving us a fine view of all the surrounding Country.[1] I do not know how many troops are here but judge about 60 to 75,000.[2] The rebels are reported to be some ten miles south east of us, but, as we are only following up to support the Army in advance of us, we may not get a sight of them for some time to come.[3]

My health is quite good, though I am troubled with a slight cold. We get no news here & are not able to get any information about the plans here. We never know where we are going nor when until the order comes & seldom have more than five minutes to get ready. As our movements are so uncertain, you may direct all my mail to Louisville until we get into some permanent Camp. We get all our provision from that place & have better & surer opportunities for sending & receiving the mail.

We left some of our boys in Louisville sick; Luther Vandoren, Reason Syphers & A. A. Rockwell.[4] We left N. W. Hill in Shelbyville sick. We have not heard from any of them since. All here are well except some very sore feet. Frankfort is 60 miles from Louisville & has a very shabby appearance. It is the poorest looking Capital I ever saw.[5]

I have taken it for granted that all of our friends learn of me through you. I cannot find time to write much & that time I prefer to spend in conversation with you. I wish I could send you some of the fine cedar & pine trees that stand all around us. [Jonathan] Duff promised to let me have two of those pines in his garden for our yard. It might be well to have them planted this fall. I think the price is 50 cents apiece. Bro. Utley promised to have them planted.

Tell Bro. John [Murphy] I have not heard of Miller's Battery since we left Louisville.⁶ I hope he is well & able to be around before this. Do not let him come until he is perfectly well, or he will soon be sick again.

We suffer most for water. All the wells are dried up, & there has been no rain since 1st July. I hope soon to hear from you. I must go out to drill & shall probably be busy all day. Kiss baby for me. Do you call him Frank or Franklin? Give my love to all our friends. Tell them to write. May the Grace of God abound in all your hearts & the richest of Heaven's blessings rest upon my Dear wife & child. Farewell.

Your affect. Husband

J. F. Culver

P.S. Please send me one dollar's worth of postage stamps. I am out & cannot get any here.

---

1   On the 10th Colonel Smith sent two companies of the 129th to patrol the adjacent hills. No Confederates were seen, but from a black the Federals learned that the citizens had made off with a large number of tents left by General Sill's division when it passed through the area. Smith, on checking into this matter, recovered nine tents from one of the citizens. These tents were issued to the soldiers of the 129th, and provided a number with shelter from the cold rain which drenched the area on the 10th. G. P. Smith to Chapin, Oct. 11, 1862, Regimental Letter Books, 129th Illinois, NA.

2   J.F.C. has again overestimated the number of soldiers. On the 10th the only Union command in and around Frankfort was Dumont's division, numbering about 10,300 effectives. *O.R.*, Ser. I, Vol. XVI, pt. II, p. 658.

3   On Oct. 10 Kirby Smith's Army of Kentucky rendezvoused with Bragg's Army of Mississippi at Harrodsburg, 27 miles south of Frankfort. *Ibid.*, pp. 927, 931.

4   Luther Vandoren, a 19-year-old Nebraska, Ill., farmer, was mustered into federal service on Sept. 8, 1862, as a private in Company A., 129th Illinois Infantry. Private Vandoren was drowned in the Cumberland River, near Gallatin, Tenn., June 10, 1863. Reason Syphers, a 26-year-old Livingston County farmer, was mustered into federal service on Sept. 8, 1862, as a private in Company A, 129th Illinois Infantry. Private Syphers was given a medical discharge at Louisville on Nov. 1, 1862. Almon A. Rockwell, a 36-year-old Pontiac shoemaker, was mustered into federal service on Sept. 8, 1862, as a private in Company A, 129th Illinois Infantry. Private Rockwell was given a medical discharge at Louisville on Nov. 21, 1862. Compiled Service Records of Union Troops, NA.

5   Private Dunham echoed J.F.C.'s opinion of Frankfort. Writing his family on Oct. 17, he observed, "F is the poorest and smallest place for the capital of a state I ever saw. I had rather live in P. than to live here by all odds." *Through the South with a Union Soldier*, p. 28.

6   Miller's battery had remained in Louisville when Buell's army took the field. *Report of the Adjutant General of Illinois*, Vol. VIII, p. 665.

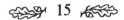 

Lawrenceburg, Ky.
Octr. 12th/ 62

Dear Mary

Recd. yours of 2nd day before yesterday & thank God that you are all well. Have been on hard marches for two days & leave here in haste this morning; do not know where we are going. My health is very good. Were out all day yesterday. Have not heard a sermon since the Sunday before I left Pontiac. Sunday is our busiest day.
Farewell. May God bless you all.

Your affect. Husband

J. F. Culver

Thank you for the P. stamps.

Provost Marshall's Office, Salvisa, Ky., Octr. 15th 1862
Head Quarters, Co. A. 129th Ills.

My Dear Wife

I wrote a line hastily yesterday morning not knowing when I should have an opportunity to write again. I have been aroused this morning at 2 o'clock A.M. by the arrival of Allen Fellows, Dr. Johnson & others from Louisville, left behind to attend the sick nearly two weeks ago.[1]

In another hour the Company must be called out to prepare for the march at Six. I think our destination is Herodsburg, some 12 miles south. Our Company is acting as Provost Guard to-night & have comfortable quarters in the Odd Fellows Hall. We had a very moderate march of 9 miles yesterday, & I feel quite well this morning.[2]

I was made very happy by the reception of your letter of Octr. 2nd, being only the second since I left home. You cannot imagine how anxious I am to hear each day from you & how happy to know that you enjoy such good health. How often since the receipt of your last letter I have tried to imagine how my wife looked (with baby at his breakfast) writing to me, & only this morning awakened suddenly to clasp you both in my arms when, lo! it was a dream, or how many times I have dreamed I was home in bed with you in my arms when I awoke & found the dews of Heaven falling upon me. Yet I shall content myself with endeavoring faithfully to follow in the path of duty & thank our God for the many favors & blessings conferred upon me in giving us all health.

We received a dispatch last night from Perryville stating that Genrl. Bragg was captured with 30,000 of his men. We can scarcely credit it as it is almost too good to be true.[3] We have six prisoners with us to-night & sent 100 to Frankfort yesterday morning. We will get near enough the battle field to-day to know all the particulars.[4] We suffer most for water, it being very scarce. We have had only two or three cold nights, rest of the time it was quite pleasant.

I am glad to hear that you have got Coal, but am sorry I am as yet unable to send you any money. I have felt considerable uneasiness lest you should not have sufficient. I do not know when pay-day will come around. I would like to know whether Jo Wolverton is urging the payment of my note now past due signed by Dehner & Russell as security; please enquire through Russell & let me know.

Miller's Battery is still in Louisville. The Board of Trade Battery is attached to our Brigade.[5] I saw Jas. Rollings in Louisville; he was then quite well. I shall be very happy to get a likeness of Mary & your boy. Kiss both for me.

I wish I had time to write to more of our Friends in Pontiac, but we are on the march nearly all the time & what little time we are in camp have no conveniences for writing. I should like much to get hold of a Chicago paper occasionally to hear how the war is progressing; we get no news here. I think we will succeed in clearing Kentucky soon, & we may get much farther south before the winter sets in.

Give my love to all our friends. I hope Bro. John [Murphy] may soon recover. I expected to hear from Utley before this but presume he is busy.

How are my business matters going on? C. I. Beattie was to pay Collins about $30 to be applied on the Dart Estate. Please ask Mr. Utley if it is settled; I do hope it is. I am sorry to hear of Mrs. Strevell's illness & hope she will soon recover.

I am happy to hear that you will so soon be able to attend S. School again. Please remember me to those dear children. How does the school prosper? I thought I should have had an opportunity to write to them before this & shall try to do so soon.

Remember me kindly to all, & now, Dear Mary, it has been my constant prayer that God would bless you & keep you. I may be spared to return to you & God may see fit to do otherwise, but thanks for his promises we shall all meet in Heaven. Do not forget to pray for me & may God's blessings ever rest upon you. Farewell.

Your affect. Husband J. F. Culver

P.S. A man in one of the Scott County companies was mortally wounded yesterday evening by the careless discharge of a pistol in the hands of one of his comrades. I have forgotten his name. It happened on the way from Frankfort. Both were left at Louisville & were on their way to the Regiment.[6]

---

1   John A. Fellows, a 30-year-old merchant, was mustered into federal service on Sept. 8, 1862, as a corporal in Company G, 129th Illinois. He was detailed as a male nurse, and on April 12, 1863, was appointed hospital steward. Fellows was mustered out on June 8, 1865, at Washington, D.C. Darius Johnson was mustered into federal service on Sept. 20, 1862, at Springfield, Ill., as 1st assistant surgeon, 129th Illinois Infantry. He was promoted to surgeon on March 6, 1864. Surgeon Johnson resigned because of disability from dysentery at Goldsboro, N.C., April 9, 1865. Compiled Service Records of Union Troops, NA.

2   The 129th Illinois, along with other units of the 38th Brigade, had marched from Frankfort on Oct. 11, taking the road to Lawrenceburg. On the 13th the regiment reached Salvisa. Regimental Letter Books, 129th Illinois, NA.

3   There was no truth to this rumor. At Perryville, on Oct. 8, Buell's army had battled Bragg's Army of the Mississippi. The Confederates, although they severely punished McCook's corps, had been compelled to abandon the field on the night of the 8th and retire to Harrodsburg, where on the 10th Bragg's and Kirby Smith's armies had rendezvoused. Union casualties at Perryville were 845 killed, 2,851 wounded, and 515 missing. Confederate losses in the fight were 510 killed, 2,635 wounded, and 251 missing. O.R., Ser. I, Vol. XVI, pt. I, pp. 1036, 1112.

4   General Buell had waited at Perryville until Sill's division joined him on the 11th. He then resumed his advance, expecting to battle Bragg at Harrodsburg, as his patrols reported the foe in force three miles south of that place. During the day, however, Bragg abandoned Harrodsburg, and, covered by a strong rear guard, retired across Dick's River and took position at Bryantsville. At Harrodsburg, the Federals on the 11th had captured some Confederate stores and about 1,500 prisoners, 1,200 of whom were confined to field hospitals.
The armies marked time on the 12th, while Bragg studied his next move. He had lost the initiative, and with the season of "autumnal rains" at hand it would be impossible to

subsist his armies over a supply line leading back across the rugged mountains of southeast Kentucky through Cumberland Gap. He therefore abandoned his position covering the crossings of Dick's River on the 13th and started his troops in two columns for Cumberland Gap. *Ibid.*, 1093; *O.R.*, Ser. I, Vol. XVI, pt. II, p. 611; Cist, *Army of the Cumberland*, pp. 70-71.

The prisoners referred to by J.F.C. had been captured by the cavalry screening the march of Dumont's division, as it thrust south from Frankfort. *Through the South with a Union Soldier*, p. 28.

5  There were three six-gun batteries (the Chicago Board of Trade, and the 13th and 18th Indiana) attached to Dumont's division. *O.R.*, Ser. I, Vol. XVI, pt. II, p. 662.

6  Private Dunham also mentions this incident, observing in his letter of Oct. 17, "Camped at Salvisa, Mercer Co., 10 m from Lawrenceburg. Scott Co. man shot by another by a pistol." A review of the "Regimental Returns" has provided no information as to the identity of the men involved in the shooting.

 17

Head Quarters, Company A [Octr. 16, 1862]
129th Ills. Vols., Camp near Crab Orchard, Ky.

My Dear Wife

I understand we will have an opportunity to send letters back to-morrow & am happy to be able to write. I have been quite sick for the last two days but am now much better. I have a slight Bilious attack, I think. We arrived here about noon to-day & are a little in advance of the main part of Buell's army, surrounded on every side by thousands of troops.[1] I met John Manker this evening, an old acquaintance of yours. He is Lieut. of an Ohio Company.[2] I presume there are many here I know when I come to find them.

We are now at the foot of that numerous ranges of mountains surrounding Cumberland Gap for which we are now bound. Through the supposed treachery of General Buell, the Rebel Army under Bragg has escaped into the mountains.[3] With the thousands of troops, he could have easily been taken, & when at Perryville without Buell's consent General Jackson attacked Bragg, there were troops enough within a few miles to have surrounded and outnumbered him 3 to 1, they were not allowed to come up.[4] Now we have 90 miles over mountains to the **Gap**, & I am informed we will be detained here some ten days giving the rebels sufficient time to fortify themselves.

It is boldly asserted that Buell & Bragg have been together every few days since they left Louisville, & I feel sure that if ever the troops ever get sight of Buell he will share the fate of General Nelson instantly.[5]

I have but little hope for the success of our cause while these things last. We will now march to Cumberland Gap at a cost of hundreds of lives; but these things cannot be too publicly talked of, do not commit me in them.

I wrote you quite a long letter a few days ago & hope ere this you have recd. it. If we remain here, I shall endeavor to write often. We have left a large number of men behind, sick & lost, a good many who gave out on the road. We were short 400 men in the Regt. when we arrived in Camp to-day, but many have arrived & they are still coming in. I hope by the mail from Frankfort I shall hear from you. Give my love to all. May the blessings of Heaven rest upon you. Farewell.

Your affect. Husband

J. F. Culver

---

1  Buell, learning on the 13th that Bragg had evacuated his position commanding the crossings of Dick's River and was in retreat, ordered his columns to pursue. Next morning at Stanford, one of Buell's divisions clashed with Confederate cavalry screening the retreat. About noon on the 15th, Crittenden's corps, which was spearheading the pursuit, entered Crab Orchard. Covered by a strong rear guard, the Confederates retired to Mount Vernon.

From reports submitted by his scouts, Buell knew that the roads by which the Confederates were retiring passed "through defiles, where a small force can resist with great effect a large one; where in fact the use of a large force is impracticable." In addition, he knew that the Rebels would use or destroy the small amount of forage in this sterile region. Buell accordingly decided to halt Gilbert's and McCook's corps at Crab Orchard. Crittenden's troops were given the mission of harrassing the retreating Rebel columns. *O. R.,* Ser. I, Vol. XVI, pt. I, p. 1029.

The 129th Illinois had marched from Salvisa to Danville on the 14th, to Stanford on the 15th, and to Crab Orchard on the 16th. At Crab Orchard on the 17th, the 38th Brigade was detached from Dumont's Twelfth Division and assigned to Brig. Gen. Robert S. Granger's Tenth Division. Regimental Papers, 129th Illinois, NA, RG 94.

2  John J. Manker had entered service as a private in Company B, 34th Ohio Infantry, and on Aug. 15, 1862, he had received his discharge to accept a commission as 2d lieutenant in Company E, Ohio Volunteers, 50th Ohio Infantry Regiment. Compiled Service Records of Union Soldiers, NA.

3  The story of Buell and Bragg being in collusion was common gossip in the 129th Illinois. Private Dunham wrote his family on Sept. 29 & 30, it was said that "if B. had been a mind to he could have taken Br. and his whole force at Green River, but Buell stopped them and let Bragg pass out." *Through the South with a Union Soldier,* p. 23.

There was no truth to these rumors. After his relief as commander of the Army of the Ohio, Buell's conduct was subject of an exhaustive investigation by a military commission. The commission, which focused its attention on accusations that Buell's tactics were dilatory, adjourned without making any recommendations. After more than a year awaiting orders, Buell was mustered out of the volunteer service in May 1864, and on June 1 he resigned his regular commission. Warner, *Generals in Blue*, p. 52.

4 Brig. Gen. James S. Jackson had commanded the Tenth Division, one of the three divisions constituting McCook's corps. At Perryville, on Oct. 8, Jackson's division on the Union left was assailed by elements of three Confederate divisions. Jackson was killed in the savage fighting which ensued and one of his brigades routed. The Confederate thrust was blunted by a fresh brigade, and the fighting shifted to McCook's right.

Because of the configuration of the terrain, the limited use of artillery, and the vagaries of the wind, no sounds of battle were heard at Buell's headquarters until about 3:30 p.m. It was for this reason, not a desire to subvert the Union, that Buell was slow in ordering Gilbert's corps to support McCook's hard-pressed divisions. Charles F. Gilbert, "On the Field of Perryville," *Battles and Leaders of the Civil War,* Robert V. Johnson and Clarence C. Buel, editors (New York, 1884-1887), Vol. III, pp. 52-57.

5 See J.F. C's letter of September 29, 1862.

~~~~ 18 ~~~~

Frankfort, Ky., Octr. 20th 1862

Dear Wife

I arrived here about noon to-day in charge of our Brigade train. I am Acting Brigade Quarter Master for a few days & came here after what was left, not having sufficient wagons to transport.[1] I shall start for Camp at Crab Orchard sometime to-morrow.

I have been quite sick for several days with a Bilious attack but am now much better. I left Camp night before last & rode through some 66 miles. I recd. yours of the 14th on my arrival here & yours of prior dates, 2 in number. Yesterday on the route, I met Maples about halfway out yesterday morning.[2] I am happy to hear that you & baby are so well & that Bro. Johnie [Murphy] is a little better. I earnestly hope he may get well soon.

I was fortunate enough to get a bed both nights out, & I think it accounts for my feeling so much better. It is the first time I have been in bed since I left home. Whoever "Livingston" is, he must have weak legs. I was tired but got along well enough. Allen Fellows is with the Regiment. I do not know how such reports get home unless some one was frightened. I have been ordered to do nothing as yet I was not able to do, & I anticipated hardships before I left home.[3]

I wrote to Bro. Utley at Crab Orchard & am glad to hear of Maggie's condition.[4] With regard to renting the house, I want you to suit yourself. I shall be satisfied with your selection of a renter. The all important point is to get the rent, for from present prospects there will be no pay forthcoming for months.[5]

I hope Bro. Thomas may receive the richest of Heaven's blessings.[6] My words cannot express what I feel. I have not heard from home [Carlisle], yet I requested that the letters be first sent to you. I cannot account for it. Have you written to Mother [Culver] yet, if not, will you not do so? We have been so much of the time on the march lately that I could not write as often as I wished.[7] I found another lot of stamps in one of your letters, again for which you have my thanks.

The Army when I left Camp were about to march; no one knew their destination. I may get a dispatch from them to-morrow. If so, I will let you know.[8]

I shall be very happy to see "Papa's Boy" & would like to see the boy's mother, too.[9] I sent my Bible home & took a testament; I had no way to carry it.

Consult Bro. Utley about renting: I think he will assist you. Should you rent it furnished, be careful of my papers, though I believe it will rent for more & be cheaper in the end to move the furniture out or keep one room. You will need some of it wherever you go. Be careful & reserve the privilege of taking possession at the end of each month.

It is getting quite late, & I have some business to attend yet to-night. I will answer yours at length when I get into Camp. Give my love to Johnie. I do hope he will soon recover, also to mother, Maggie, Mary, Leander, Thomas, Sammy &c. Kiss baby for me & tell Johnie to kiss my wife for me. Farewell. Write soon & often. You do not know how much good it does me; it is better than medicine. Send me a paper occasionally; I just got the news to-day of the last fight in the East some three weeks ago.[10]

Again Farewell.

Your Affect. Husband

J. F. Culver

P.S. Smith must have made a mistake.

26

1   When the 38th Brigade marched from Frankfort to Crab Orchard, the wagon train had been left behind. Lieutenant Culver, as acting brigade quartermaster, had the responsibility of forwarding the train and supplies stockpiled at Frankfort to the command.

2   See J. F. C.'s letter of October 1, 1862.

3   Much of the Civil War correspondence of Captain and Mrs. Culver has been preserved, but among the missing letters is Mrs. Culver's of Oct. 14. In this, she apparently referred to a letter from a soldier signed "Livingston," which had circulated in Pontiac, describing in exaggerated terms hardships encountered by the 129th Illinois on the march from Louisville to Frankfort.

4   Maggie was Mrs. Culver's eldest sister (24-year-old Margaret, the wife of Leander Utley).

5   Mary Culver, in the missing letter, had broached renting their house and moving in with her mother.

6   Bro. Thomas Murphy was Mary Culver's eldest brother. He was born in Ireland in 1835 and brought as a child by his parents to the United States. He learned the machinist trade and settled in Cleveland, where he found work with a steamship company. Etta I'Dell Clarke Culver, "Robert Murphy and Some of His Descendants," unpublished manuscript, p. 93.

7   Mary Culver, in her letter of Oct. 8, had mentioned receipt of a letter from Thomas, which she had forwarded to her husband. Mary Culver to J.F.C., Oct. 8, 1862, Culver Collection.

8   Buell on the 17th had notified General in Chief Halleck that if the foe's trains had passed beyond London, it would be useless to continue the pursuit. Whenever this occurred, Buell would "direct his main force by the most direct route upon Nashville, where its presence will certainly be required, whether for offensive or defensive objects." *O.R.*, Ser. 1, Vol. XVI, pt. II, pp. 621-622.

9   Mary Culver had promised to forward photographs of their month-old son, whom she referred to as "Papa's Boy." Mary Culver to J.F.C., undated, Culver Collection.

10  On September 17, 1862, the Army of the Potomac under Maj. Gen. George B. McClellan had defeated Gen. Robert E. Lee's Army of Northern Virginia at the battle of Antietam.

 19

Frankfort, Ky., Octr. 21st 1862

Dear Wife

I wrote to you last night & told you I should return to Camp to-day. I sent the train given in my charge, & not being able to get teams enough,

I am ordered to load the bal. on the Cars, & going by way of Louisville, take them to Lebanon where wagons will be furnished.[1] So I shall be in Louisville to-morrow if nothing happens. I have only one objection & that is getting so near home I feel an earnest desire to go there, but, before you get this, I shall be in the Southern part of Kentucky again.

I feel in better health to-night than I have for two weeks. I have had a very hard day's work & feel tired, but rejoice that the fever has left me & I am like myself again.

I shall not hear from you probably for a week as it will take me that time to get into Camp again, but there I am to have the picture. I did not think he [the baby] was large enough to make a shadow yet, much less a picture.[2]

I wrote in a hurry last night with regard to renting the house. I thought before I left that unless Bro. Sammy returned, it would scarcely be policy for you to remain there alone & especially as Sis would soon get tired. I spoke to Mr. Utley about it, & we concluded that as soon as you got right well again, you could spend your time at Mother's & Maggie's. He will attend to renting it if you tell him. I think Mr. McClary will make a very good tenant.[3] If you rent to him, get him to plant those other lots with something. I cannot say what is best to do with the furniture. I dislike to cumber Mother [Murphy] with it & dare not sell it at a sacrifice, as we may never be able to get more. So I leave you to exercise your judgment & if necessary sell it.

I shall try & send you my Gold watch from Louisville by express if I get time. I hope you will keep it running, as it will be better thus. It is not safe here & is too valuable to lose.

Did Utley ever get anything out of Dr. Hulsey for my other watch?[4] I hope to hear by your next that Bro. Johnie is much better.

Capt. Perry & I. G. Mott are with me to-night & going to Louisville.[5] Perry is much better.

Give my love to all. I should try to send you a photograph but have had no opportunity & less money. I may be able some day & shall be very happy to do so. May God Bless you all. I often think of you & pray for you. I should like to write to the S. School but cannot find time. Give my love to the dear children.

Hoping soon to hear from you, I remain, as ever

Your affect. Husband, Farewell

J. F. Culver

---

1   While J.F.C. was at Frankfort, General Buell, learning that the Confederate armies had passed beyond London, started McCook's and Gilbert's corps for Lebanon, the first stop on their march to Nashville. The Lebanon Branch Railroad linked Lebanon with the

Louisville & Nashville Railroad, 40 miles to the northwest. The Frankfort & Lexington Railroad connected Frankfort with Louisville. General Buell, like other Civil War leaders, whenever possible employed railroads to ease the problem of supplying his army.

The 129th Illinois broke camp at Crab Orchard the morning of Oct. 19, 1862, and started for Lebanon by way of Harrodsburg, Danville, and Perryville. On the night of the 21st, the regiment camped on the Perryville battlefield, and one of the soldiers observed, "It was a horrible site. Our men were well buried but the secesh some were covered with straw, some with brush and some was pretended to be buried but there heads and feet were sticking out." Letter Books, 129th Illinois Infantry, NA; *Through the South with a Union Soldier*, p. 31; Grunert, *History of the 129th Illinois,* pp. 9-10.

2   The reference is to the photographs of their son, which Mary Culver had promised to forward.

3   Brother Sammy was Mary Culver's youngest brother. It has been impossible to identify further the prospective renter, Mr. McClary.

4   Dr. John B. Hulsey was a 37-year-old Fairbury physician. In 1860 the Kentucky-born doctor was living with his wife, Bell. Eighth Census, Livingston County, State of Illinois, NA.

5   John B. Perry, a 24-year-old Livingston County farmer, had been mustered into federal service at Camp Pontiac on Sept. 8, 1862, as captain of Company C, 129th Illinois Infantry. Captain Perry, having received a surgeon's certificate that he was suffering from chronic diarrhea, resigned his commission on Nov. 21, 1864. Isaac G. Mott, a 38-year-old Pontiac attorney, was mustered into federal service on Sept. 8, 1862, as a private in Company C, 129th Illinois Infantry. He was promoted to hospital steward on Sept. 9, 1862, and assigned to regimental headquarters. Hospital Steward Mott died on April 12, 1863, at South Tunnel, Tenn., of pneumonia. Compiled Service Records of Union Soldiers, NA.

 20 

Head Quarters, Company A, 129th Ills.
Camp near Bowling Green, Ky.
Nov. 1st 1862

My Dear Wife

I wrote to you from Frankfort & mailed, or sent my letter by Express, with my watch which I hope ere this you have received. I arrived in Camp last night after two weeks absence though in the mean time I spent one night with the Company.[1] It seems much more pleasant to be with the company again than fighting R. R. Companies for transportation, & I feel glad that my mission is ended.

I find the men in much better condition than I expected to find them after so severe a march. Some few are sick in the hospitals but none seriously ill. I saw Alex McDonald yesterday; he came down on the train, he has been quite sick but is getting better. I feel better than I have for two weeks. I feel quite comfortable; I do not think we will remain here long but expect Nashville will be our destination. There are no rebels in this part of the country & no reason that I can see why one should remain here.[2]

The Brigade was mustered yesterday for pay. I do not know when the paymaster will be around, but hope it will be soon. It may be two months or more. Many of the Regts. have recd. no pay for six or eight months. I have no news from home later than the 21st Octr. The 3rd of this month is my birth-day, 28 years have almost passed away as a dream.

I will now try & write to the S. School. I have wished to do so for a long time but have had no opportunity.[3] What has become of the heifer I bought of Sammy? Unless you wish to keep her, you had better sell her this fall as you have no opportunity of wintering her. If you wish to keep her, try & make arrangements soon to have her kept. Will your cow pay her keeping or is she dry? I hope I shall be able to send you some money soon. I presume ere this Bro. Johnnie [Murphy] is much better. Please tell him for me not to be in a hurry to leave home. I feel anxious to know what disposition you have made of our house & what arrangements for yourself; tell me all about it when you write.

To-morrow is Sunday. Bro. Cotton came down with me, & we will have preaching. I hope we will not be compelled to march as I anticipate a very pleasant time.

I should be happy to hear from Bro. Johnnie as soon as he is able to write. We get no papers as they cumber the mails too much, so we have to depend upon our letters for all the news.

A sad accident happened in Miller's Battery a few days ago; by some act of Carelessness fire was communicated to one of the Caissons: it exploded injuring some six men, one died in a few hours afterward, & the other five are very seriously wounded. I was not acquainted with any of them & did not learn their names.[4]

One man of the Fairbury Company, named Cumpston, died in the Hospital at Louisville last week;[5] this is the only man we have lost thus far.

Has Henry Greenbaum, Russell & Peter gone with Lace to form a Brigade Band yet?[6] They intended to leave sometime ago. Give my love to Mother, Maggie, & all the rest. I saw a short paragraph from Hetty

Autrim in her Cousin's letter saying that little Frankie was doing remarkably well. I am happy to hear it, & hope his mother is quite as well. Remember me kindly to all our friends. May the riches of God's Grace rest upon you all & ever keep you, my Dear Wife, preserve you & our babe's health &, if in accordance with His will, hasten the time when we may again enjoy each other's society & in all things keep us resigned to His will. Let us pray for it.

Hoping soon to hear from you, I remain, as ever,

Your affect. Husband

J. F. Culver

---

1  The 129th Illinois had reached Lebanon on the 23d. There the regiment camped for several days, being subjected to a snowstorm on the 25th. From Lebanon, the regiment marched to Bowling Green, where it went into bivouac on Oct. 31. Grunert, *History of the 129th Illinois,* p. 10; *Through the South with a Union Soldier,* p. 37; Letter Books, 129th Illinois, NA.

2  The Confederate force nearest Bowling Green was Col. John H. Morgan's cavalry at Huntsville, Tennessee, more than 50 miles to the south. *O. R.,* Ser. I, Vol. XX, pt. I, pp. 3-4.

3  Mary Culver, in her letter of Oct. 21, had asked her husband to find time to write to the children of his Sunday school class, as "they would like it amazingly." Mary Culver to J.F.C., October 21, 1862, Culver Collection.

4  On October 24, while Company M, 1st Illinois Light Artillery (Miller's battery) was being drilled at a gallop at Louisville, a caisson exploded, killing two men and severely wounding several others. Killed in the accident were Pvts. Adam Gerbert and August Kellerman, both of Chicago. *Report of the Adjutant General of Illinois,* Vol. VIII, pp. 653-655.

5  John Cumpston, a 29-year-old Livingston County farmer, was mustered into federal service on Sept. 8, 1862, as a sergeant in Company D, 129th Illinois Infantry. Sergeant Cumpston died in a Louisville hospital on Oct. 23, 1862, of typhoid pneumonia. Compiled Service Records of Union Soldiers, NA.

6  Henry G. Greenebaum was born in Hesse, Germany, in 1837, and emigrated in 1854 to the United States with his brothers, Joseph and Samuel. Moving to Pontiac in 1856, Henry and Joseph opened a dry goods store, known as Greenebaum Bros. William T. Russell in 1857 had been elected the first supervisor of Pontiac Township. He had been J.F.C.'s partner in an insurance business in 1862. It has been impossible to further identify Peter. Philip H. Lace had entered service as a member of the regimental band of the 39th Illinois Infantry. J.F.C. and these men had played in the Pontiac band in the years before the Civil War. *History of Livingston County,* pp. 307-308, 633.

## 21

Head Quarters, Company A, 129th Ills. Vols.
Camp Near Bowling Green, Ky., Nov. 6th 1862

My Dear Wife

I write to you to-night from the fact that I have just been informed that I shall be sent out on Picket duty to-morrow & perhaps be absent a couple of days. I intended to wait until Sunday [the 11th], but you know how uncertain our movements are.

I am in the enjoyment of excellent health & trust Providence has bestowed the same blessing upon you. We anticipate marching orders in a few days; we know not how soon. Genrl. Rosseau's division was inspected & reviewed to-day by General Rosecrans, which nearly completed his duties here, & we will immediately be ordered forward.[1] As yet we do not know our destination.

We have had considerable rejoicing over the election returns received from every part of the North. Under Democratic rule the country must be sane??[2] We have nothing yet from Livingston. I should like to see Job Dye elected, but hope the bal. of the ticket elected is democratic.[3]

I am not well posted, but, judging from what I hear, I think Abolitionism has died out in the Army, if in fact it ever existed.

I was in Bowling Green a short time to-day on business. The City has been almost destroyed, almost all the good citizens have been compelled to leave. That class that remain can be fully illustrated by the saying of the old woman in the Revolution, when called upon by some soldier & not knowing who they were, she replied, "If you're Whig, I'm Whig; if you're Tory, I'm Tory." The Rebels held the city for many months;[4] very many of its finest buildings are in ruins.

We get mail daily now. The cars run through from Louisville. Lieut. Smith has just retired. Have you any idea how we sleep? In the first place, I could not tell when I undressed unless to wash or change clothes. I put my overcoat on, draw the cape over my head for a night cap, & roll over. I would give considerable to-night to occupy my old place by your side.

The weather has been quite cold for a few days. It was trying to snow all day but is more calm to-night. I very frequently get too cold & have to hunt the fire. We have plenty of wood, however, & get along very well.

I shall look for Gagan [sutler] in a few days with those pictures. I intended to write to the S. School on Sunday but shall not now have an opportunity. I have been somewhat disappointed in not hearing from any one in Pontiac. I thought I had a few friends left there. Give my love to all. Write as often as you can. I love very much to hear often from you. May the richest of Heaven's blessings rest upon you.

Farewell.

Your affect. Husband

Frank

---

1  Brig. Gen. Lovell H. Rousseau commanded one of five divisions assigned to General Thomas' center wing of the Army of the Cumberland. General Rosecrans maintained his headquarters at Bowling Green until Nov. 11, when he transferred his headquarters to Nashville. *O. R.*, Ser. I, Vol. XX, pp. 11, 31, 35.

2  Congressional elections held in Iowa, Ohio, Indiana, and Pennsylvania on Tuesday, October 14, had resulted in gains for Democrats, except in Iowa, where the Republicans carried the state. Three weeks later, when the voters went to the polls in more Union states, the Democrats made more gains at the expense of the Lincoln administration. They elected a governor in New York, and registered significant successes in New Jersey, Illinois, and Wisconsin. The Republicans, however, retained control of the House of Representatives, with victories in New England, the border states, California, and Michigan. E. P. Long, *The Civil War Day by Day: An Almanac, 1861-1865* (New York, 1971), 278, 284.

3  Job E. Dye was the Republican candidate for sheriff of Livingston County to succeed Edwin Maples. *History of Livingston County*, p. 266.

4  Bowling Green had been occupied by Confederate forces in early September 1861. It had anchored the Confederate center of the defense line in the West until its evacuation in mid-February 1862. Union victory at Mill Creek in January, the capture of Fort Henry on February 6, & the investment of Fort Donalson made the Confederate position at Bowling Green untenable.

22

Head Quarters, Co. A, 129th Ills. Vols.<br/>Camp near Bowling Green, Ky., Nov. 9th 1862

Dear Mary

I arrived in Camp from Picket Duty about 11 o'clock to-day & after dinner went to attend the funeral of a young man in the 111th Ohio Regt., who died last night.[1] After which I set down to write, but scarcely had commenced when the Bugle sounded for Dress Parade. I

*33*

now hastily pen a line before preaching. I am in the enjoyment of good health, [also] Lieut. Smith. Capt. [Hoskins] has been complaining some to-day but is not very sick. We have had more on the sick list since in camp than when on the march, in fact more than 2 to 1 in one company. I cannot account for it, unless it be from want of exercise.

There is a camp rumor here to-day that we will go into Garrison for the Winter in Bowling Green. I hope it may be so, for, should we be paid off any time this fall, I think you would like to spend the winter with me. It would be a matter, however, of weighty consideration with you. Your own & the babe's health must be carefully considered. However, it is as yet so uncertain that nothing should be concluded upon, & I should not be at all surprised at any moment to receive marching orders.[2]

You might think the matter over, but lay no plans or say anything until we know definitely. I hope to hear from you very soon. I had a letter from Chas. McGregor yesterday; kin folks are all well & Jennie & the babies doing well. Give my love to all.

Your affect. Husband

Frank

---

1   The 111th Ohio Infantry was one of the four regiments constituting Colonel Chapin's 38th Infantry Brigade. *O.R.*, Ser. I, Vol. XVI, pt. II, p. 595.

2   To protect the Louisville & Nashville Railroad, the army's supply line, from raids by Confederate cavalry, required a large force which would be drawn from Thomas' corps and Granger's division. This information provided grist for the rumor that the 129th Illinois might spend the winter in and around Bowling Green. *O. R.*, Ser. I, Vol. XX, pt. II, pp. 9, 11, 20, 31.

 23

Head Quarters, Co. A, 129th Ills. Vols.
Bowling Green, Ky., Nov. 11th 1862

**Dear Wife**

I am happy to inform you this morning that I am in good health. I rather expected to hear from you by yesterday's mail, but presume you had not time to write.

It is generally believed that we will go into Winter Quarters here in a few days. Lieut. Smith & myself will, as soon as the thing is surely known, make arrangements for you & Mrs. Smith if you should conclude to come.[1] It might be well if you have any preparation to make in the way of clothing & have any money to get them. We rather expect to be paid off soon, when I will be able to send you sufficient. If not, I shall try to borrow some. I will write more in a few days.

Lieut. Smith with a squad of men went out last night & stole an officer's tent so that [we] will be comfortable until we get into houses. Should we be sent into town, houses will be furnished; if sent any other place, we will immediately build so that if you come, you can enjoy the sight of an entire village of log cabins.

Bro. Cotton will send for his wife, & a great many of the officers will do likewise. I am satisfied that we can live thus much cheaper than to board.

Write soon. Give my love to all.

Your affect. Husband

J. F. Culver

---

1  It was common practice during the Civil War for officers' wives to visit their husbands when the armies were in winter quarters or during seasons of prolonged inactivity. For example, Mrs. Ulysses Grant frequently visited her husband. She was in Holly Springs, Mississippi, when that important supply depot was captured by Confederate raiders on Dec. 20, 1862. Every courtesy was extended to Mrs. Grant by the Confederate horse-soldiers, and guards posted to insure her privacy. Bearss, *Decision in Mississippi* (Little Rock, 1962), pp. 110-111.

 24

Head Quarters, Company A, 129th Ills. Vols.
Camp Near Bowling Green, Ky., Nov. 12th 1862

Dear Wife

Maples is going home this morning & will see you perhaps before my last letter reaches you.[1] I am quite well & getting along well. Write soon.

We have not recd. the election returns yet.[2] We are yet in Camp & do not know where or when we will go into Winter Quarters.

Give my love to all. Hoping that God will be with & bless you, I am in haste,

Your affect. Husband

J. F. Culver

---

1 Sheriff Maples of Livingston County, on his frequent visits to the regiment, served as a volunteer mail carrier. This was common practice. Undoubtedly the most famous mail carrier, North or South, was Absalom C. Grimes. To learn more about Civil War mail carriers, the reader is referred to *Absalom Grimes: Confederate Mail Runner,* edited by Milo M. Quaife (New Haven, 1926).

2 On November 4 voters had gone to the polls in most Northern states to elect representatives to Congress and to state and local offices.

 25

Head Quarters, Co. A., 129th Ills. Vols.
Camp near Bowling Green, Ky., Nov. 16th 1862

My dear Mary

Yours of the 8th inst. I recd. on Friday evening last & yours of 3 inst. by politeness of Gagan on yesterday evening, with one from Maggie & Mother, Abbie Remick & Henry Greenebaum; also the pictures, socks & papers. Dear Wife, accept my thanks.

I am led to believe from the tenor of your last letter that the last three letters I wrote have never reached you, but hope they soon will. I shall answer your letters according to their date only remarking that I am surprised to find no notice of the long letter I wrote to the S. School in any of your letters & further that [Lt.] Smith is cutting meat for Supper on one end of the table & I can hardly write, but he is disposed to bother me & I shall have to grin & bear it. He is getting quite Saucy of late.

Bro. Johnny [Murphy] need have no fears about the Battery getting very far from Louisville. I apprehend they will go into Winter Quarters there.[1]

I have no idea how the report could originate that I was "coming home." I should be very happy to do so but have no idea that such a thing will happen until we all return. Looking at the matter from this point, it is simply impossible.[2]

We are still in Camp. The Col. [Chapin] commanding the Brigade is dangerously ill, & we shall receive no orders until there is a change in affairs.

I did not see your letters until after I had opened the picture & to tell you what I said after opening the pictures I cannot save that I was surrounded by the whole Company & made no remark to any one, but thought all I can better tell you perhaps what I thought.[3] It was that God had been very good to bestow such health & so dear a tie to comfort you at home. Having read your last letter first, it is not unnatural that I should look carefully at him, who has so largely engrossed your affections. I thank God to-day that he has so kindly Ordered all things & feel satisfied that your affection for me has not diminished. I pray that God may bless you both. He is generally supposed to resemble his father very much. I hope he may inherit his mother's good disposition.

I have not forgotten what you wrote about baptism, but I have been resolving the matter over in my mind. I think I would like to be present when the rite is performed. If God spares my life to return, I should prefer waiting until that time; if not, you may use your own pleasure. I have always felt the pledges of infant baptism most solemn & responsible.[4]

Tell Mother [Murphy] she has my thanks for her kindness. I have the socks on to-day & like them very much. I shall endeavor at my earliest opportunity to answer her kind letter. I am well supplied with gloves, sufficient I think for the winter.[5]

The letters pertaining to the Boyer Estate should all go to Wolgamott, Justice. All other business letters give to Fleming. I hope the letter from Mr. Saul will soon be forwarded, please attend to it. Has Bro. Utley examined the dockets in J. R. Wolgamott's hands? I think there must surely be some money there for you.[6] I shall be happy to hear from him [Utley] soon. I have never had the least intimation of how my business is progressing. I hope he may be successful in buying horses as it is a very risky business, especially for the Army.[7] I was rather at a loss to determine what the mark on the extra sheet of paper was, but by the assistance of Capt. Hoskins & Lieut. Smith we solved the problem.[8]

Now for letter No. 2 dated Nov. 8th

In the first place I enjoy excellent health & shall not overtask myself or expose myself unnecessarily. I do no more than my share of the labor I presume.[9]

I am very happy to hear of baby's good health. I am not sufficient posted on ("infantry tactics") to divine what disposition he evinces by his exceeding gravity. I am sure he can improve largely on his father & be saved from many difficulties.[10]

I admire your wisdom in your conclusions. I have rejoiced ever since my Enlistment at the probability of your having strong attachments to bind you at home & afterward at the Goodness of God in bestowing so rich a gift. Into your hands is committed the precious charge until I return to assist, & I feel that God has well endowed you for the performance of those duties. Should I never return, I pray that he [the baby] may be a consolation to you in his infancy, an honor to you in his youth, & your supporter & Comforter in his manhood & your old age. I feel willing to trust all to that God who has dealt so bountifully with us.[11]

You must dispose of your hogs & cattle as you see fit. I hope you may be able to realize some money out of them.[12] With regard to the furniture, you must exercise your own judgment. I would rather sell it at a sacrifice now than have it abused. Get Benj. Fisher to break open my desk & put a new lock on it if you have not found the key. It will not cost much.[13] Get a wagon for the baby by all means. After your careful consideration for me, I do hope you will not over exert yourself. If your back is in any way weak, be very careful. It may cost you years of pain & suffering should you receive any injury.[14] From Mother's letter, I should judge it most prudent to board with her.

I am glad to hear that you have had such fine weather.[15] We have suffered much from the dust. To-night it is raining. I hope it will not rain very much until we get into Winter Quarters.

I had a letter from Henry Greenebaum with the package. I find the Band are all there, but aside from that he gives but little news; & now I have occupied every spare moment for more than half a day, for though it is Sunday we have many duties to perform. I received an invitation this morning to take dinner with several officers at a Mr. Ewings' who lives near our Camp.[16] We had a very fine dinner. I did not see any white people about the house & judge he has no family. Lieut. Smith tells me that his wife has a baby which accounts for her absence.

I have not learned what you intend to do with Sis. Remember me kindly to her. I shall write to her as soon as you answer the letter relating to her I wrote several days ago.

Bro. Cotton preached the funeral sermon of 3 of our Regiment who died in the Hospitals since we left Home. I do not know their names: they belonged to the Scott County companies.[17] I fear we shall lose a member of our company; his name is Marion Rush from Reading.[18] R. Syphers, who was sick when we left Pontiac, has been discharged, & I presume is at home. Rockwell is in Louisville trying for a discharge, & I think will soon be home. I do not think he will ever be of any use in the Army.[19] Several others of our Regiment have been discharged & have gone home.

Give my love to Mother, Maggie & all the family. Tell all our friends we are getting along well. I learn Job Dye is elected & am glad to hear it.[20] Tell Father [Murphy] to Congratulate him for me. Tell Bro. John to write me all the changes that have taken place since I left. I fear he is needing money, & I have borrowed $50 of him. Please let me know.

Tell Sis to write to me if she gets into trouble & tell her it is my earnest desire that she'll serve God with her whole heart. She knows the dangers of temptation. May God in his mercy protect her. I shall answer Sister Maggie's letter as soon as possible.

Write soon & now, Dear Mary, I wish you to consult your comfort in all your arrangements. Try & be happy & may the richest of Heaven's blessings rest upon you all. Kiss baby for me & if I never see him, when he is old enough, tell him I desire him above all things to be a servant of God & strive in every way to do good; that whatever should be his calling or profession not to forget his God.

Hoping that God will preserve us, I remain

Your affect. Husband

J. F. Culver

---

1 William John Murphy, a quartermaster sergeant in Company M, 1st Illinois Light Artillery, and Mary Culver's brother, had been invalided home when his unit was ordered from Camp Douglas to Louisville. He was suffering from hepatitis, and in mid-October it was feared that he would die. His condition had taken a turn for the better, and on the 4th, he had gone to the polls.

Unknown to J.F.C., the battery had been transferred on Nov. 11 to Lebanon and assigned to the 34th Brigade. From Lebanon, the battery was marched to Columbia to guard against the raids of Colonel Morgan and other Rebel cavalrymen. Mary Culver to J.F.C., Nov. 3, 1862, Culver Collection; *Report of the Adjutant General of Illinois,* Vol. VIII, p. 665.

2 Mary Culver had written in her letter of Nov. 3, "The report is all over town that you are coming home, you and Capt. Perry. I tell them I know nothing of it, but I think it is not so." Mary Culver to J.F.C., Nov. 3, 1862, Culver Collection.

3   The photograph mentioned is the one Mary Culver had forwarded of their son, Frank, born on September 21, 1862, 22 hours before J.F.C. had left Pontiac. In her letter of the 3d, Mrs. Culver had observed, the baby "looks larger than he really is . . . I want you to tell me just what you say when you first see" the photograph. "Even the children recognize the likeness of our baby to you." *Ibid.*

4   Mary Culver, in her letter of Oct. 6, 1862, had inquired, "What was it Frank I heard you say once about having the baby baptized? Did you say, you thought you would not have him baptized in his infancy." Mary Culver to J.F.C., October 6, 1862, Culver Collection.

5   Mary Culver had discussed plans to knit her husband gloves, as opposed to her brother's suggestion that buckskin gloves would be more appropriate. Mary Culver to J.F.C., Nov. 3, 1862, Culver Collection.

6   J. R. Wolgamott was a wealthy retired Pontiac merchant. In 1860 the 39-year-old Wolgamott valued his real and personal estate at $48,000. Eighth Census, Livingston County, State of Illinois, NA.

7   Leander Utley, according to Mary Culver, was "so busy he hardly knows how to spend a moment in his spare time and at night he is too tired [to write]. He has no help & are having plastering and painting done and corncribs and woodshed built. He is going to furnish the army with some horses." Mary Culver to J.F.C., Nov. 3, 1862, Culver Collection.

8   The mark referred to had been made by the baby. In her letter, Mary Culver had written, "Baby wants to write a letter on my page but I tell him he must take one of his own." *Ibid.*

9   Mary Culver, in her letter of the 8th, acknowledging J.F.C.'s of Nov. 1, had expressed anxiety about his health. She was "afraid" that he was not taking care of himself and "overtasking" his strength. Mary Culver to J.F.C., Nov. 8, 1862, Culver Collection.

10   Referring to their son, Mary Culver had observed, he was "well as usual," but hardly ever laughed, and was going to be "very grave and thoughtful." *Ibid.*

11   This paragraph was generated by Mary Culver's statement that she used to think that she would want to die if her husband failed to return, but since the birth of their son she now thought that she "must live for my baby." Continuing she wrote, "You did not know how sorry I used to be because we expected a little one. I thought it prevented my going with you. I now see how wisely all things were ordered." *Ibid.*

12   Mary Culver had decided to rent their house and go live with her mother. She had discussed with the butcher the sale of their large hog, and he had quoted her a price of $3 a hundredweight. The smaller hog she would give to her brother Sammy. As for the cows, they would probably be sold. *Ibid.*

13   Mary Culver had locked her husband's roll-top desk and had misplaced the keys. *Ibid.* Burton Fisher was a 27-year-old Pontiac painter. Eighth Census, Livingston County, State of Illinois, NA.

14   The baby was so heavy that Mary Culver found that it hurt her back to carry him any distance. She had suggested that they buy a baby wagon from Mrs. George Wolgamott. Mary Culver to J.F.C., Nov. 8, 1862, Culver Collection. George Wolgamott was a 38-year old Pontiac carpenter.

15   They were experiencing a beautiful Indian summer in Livingston County. *Ibid.*

16   There were several Ewings living in Warren County, Ky., in 1860. The one who entertained the Union officers at dinner was either John H. or James F. Both were wealthy farmers. Eighth Census, Warren County, State of Kentucky, NA.

17   The deceased Scott County soldiers were: Alexander Ridenbark, a 24-year-old farmer, mustered into federal service on Sept. 8, 1862, as a private in Company I, 129th Illinois Infantry. Private Ridenbark died of pneumonia at Danville, Ky., Nov. 3, 1862. Jacob Topper, a 29-year-old- blacksmith, was mustered into federal service on Sept. 8, 1862, as a private in Company H, 129th Illinois Infantry. Private Topper died of diarrhea at a Bowling Green hospital on Nov. 4, 1862. It has been impossible to identify the third Scott County soldier eulogized by Chaplain Cotton. Compiled Service Records of Union Troops, NA.

18   Marion Rush, a 21-year-old Reading farmer, was mustered into federal service on Sept. 8, 1862, as a private in Company A, 129th Illinois Infantry. Private Rush died of typhoid fever in Bowling Green Hospital No. 1 on Nov. 19, 1862. *Ibid.*

19   Pvt. Almon A. Rockwell was given a medical discharge at Louisville on Nov. 21, 1862. *Ibid.*

20   Job Dye, a 43-year-old Pontiac merchant, was elected sheriff of Livingston County on Nov. 4, 1862, defeating S. H. Putnam, his Democratic opponent, by a vote of 1,036 to 902. *History of Livingston County*, p. 266.

 26

Head Quarters, Company A, 129th Ills. Vols.
Camp Near Bowling Green, Ky. Nov. 20th 1862

Dear Wife

Yours of the 10th inst. came to me while out on Picket night before last. It was raining, & I was very happy to receive it. I am glad to learn that you are all well. I should indeed be most happy to step in when you feel lonely & cheer you up.

I am not prepared to divine what the future of our country will be, I get so little news. The proclamation of Lincoln looks to me very much like a sham affair, & I should not be a bit surprised to find him out-generaled, but I have no disposition to discuss the matter.[1]

I do not understand why you are not receiving letters every few days. I always write twice a week & often more. There was another Bill against the Corporation of two dollars. Get some one to see if the Bill was allowed. It certainly should be.

You wish me to make some suggestions to assist you in writing. All the suggestions I can make is to give me every change in affairs & every little thing you can mention. All is interesting to me. I am glad my letter to the S. School has been received. I shall write again as soon as I can & shall also endeavor to write to the S. S. prayer-meeting.

We are just informed that we will leave here within a few days for Mitchelville, some 30 or 40 miles farther south.[2] As we will be very busy preparing for the march, so you may not hear from me for a few days.

Marion Rush of our company died yesterday & was buried this morning. He was one of the best men in our company. My health is very good, & we are all getting along well. Mr. Rush, Marion's father, arrived here yesterday evening & left to-day. He has promised to call & see you the first time he gets to Pontiac.

I must be brief. I have considerable Company writing to do to-night. Write to me as often as you can conveniently. I cannot answer your letter in full. I recd. a letter from Sister Hannah [Culver] very similar to the one you recd. Give my love to all. Be sure & make yourself comfortable. If necessary sell off the furniture. I hope to hear from Duff & Fleming soon in relation to some business in their hands. Continue to direct [mail] as before. Kiss baby for me. Get him the wagon if you can.

Remember me to all our friends.

Farewell,

J. F. Culver

---

1 On September 24, 1862, President Lincoln issued his preliminary Emancipation Proclamation warning that on January 1, 1863, all slaves in states or parts of states in rebellion against the United States "shall be then, thenceforward and forever free," and the federal government would "recognize and maintain the freedom of such persons." This was a war measure and, as Mr. Lincoln's critics have pointed out, it did not free a single slave in territory under jurisdiction of the United States. A wave of fury swept the South. Lincoln was breaking the law of civilized warfare, outraging private property rights, and inviting a servile insurrection. Carl Sandburg, *Abraham Lincoln: The Prairie Years and the War Years* (New York, 1954), pp. 319-321.

2 Late in the third week of November, troops of General Rousseau's division of Thomas' corps, which were responsible for guarding Union supply lines between Mitchellville and Cumberland River, were ordered to concentrate at Nashville. To relieve Starkweather's brigade, posted at Mitchellville, General Granger was ordered to send a regiment to that point. *O. R.*, Ser. I, Vol. XX, pt. II, p. 75.

Granger accordingly on the afternoon of Nov. 20 issued orders for the 129th Illinois to "take post at Mitchelville and relieve the brigade there now guarding stores and loading and unloading them, as soon as the trains ran through to Nashville, which will probably be within three days. This regiment had better make its camp at that place, some two miles out of Mitchelville, where there is said to be plenty of water. Their duty will be to protect the country around Mitchelville." Letter Books, 129th Illinois, NA.

Head Quarters, Company A, 129th Ills.
Camp near Mitchellville, Tenn. Nov. 24th 1862

Dear Mary

I wrote to you on Thursday Evening informing you that there was a probability of our leaving Bowling Green. We commenced the march about 3 o'clock P.M. of Friday [the 21st] & arrived here yesterday morning about 10 o'clock, the distance 27 miles.[1]

We are now in Dixie, how long we shall remain here I do not know. We flattered ourselves with the hope of remaining in Bowling Green all winter but were disappointed. This is the most God forsaken place I ever saw, but we can make ourselves very comfortable.

We have two small tents to ourselves, & I got a stove from Louisville just before we left Bowling Green. [Lt.] Smith & Sidney Arnold have been cooking, & we do finely.[2] If we could only draw our pay, we could supply ourselves with all we need by sending to Bowling Green.

My health is very good. I received a letter from Henry Greenebaum this morning containing some little news. I am several letters behind but will answer them as soon as possible. I shall expect a letter from you by to-night's mail. Give my love to all the family. I write in haste. Kiss baby for me. With love for yourself.

I remain, as ever, your affect. Husband

J. F. Culver

---

1  Lt. Col. Henry Case had commanded the regiment on the march south from Bowling Green. On his arrival at Mitchellville, on the morning of the 23d, he found the post in charge of Col. Henry A. Hambright of the 79th Pennsylvania Infantry, the brigade commander John C. Starkweather being absent. Colonel Hambright was surprised to find that the 129th Illinois had been directed to relieve his command, as he had received no orders in this respect from his immediate superior, General Rousseau, to proceed to Nashville. Colonel Case was placed in an embarrassing situation when Colonel Hambright declined to accept his offer of assistance in guarding or unloading supplies. Hambright predicated his refusal on the probability that his brigade would be ordered to Nashville within several days, and "it would only introduce confusion" if the 129th participated in this activity. He would, however, allow the 129th Illinois to help picket the area. Case to Granger, Nov. 30, 1862, Letter Books, 129th Illinois, NA.

2  Sidney Arnold had been hired by the officers of Company A to be their cook and orderly.

Head Quarters, Company A, 129th Ills. Vols.
Camp Near Mitchellville, Tenn. Nov. 26th 1862

Dear Wife

I am somewhat disappointed in not having heard from you before this. I earnestly hoped to have a letter to help spend Thanksgiving to-morrow. We will have no duty to perform, except to guard our camp, but I shall have to spend most of the day in getting the company books & papers straightened.

We are gathered around our little stove tonight. Capt. Hoskins has just arrived.[1] He was detained in Bowling Green, setting in a court martial. Smith is talking to Sidney about the sin of war; he is trying to make him believe that it would be wrong to shoot a rebel because he might not be prepared to die, but Sidney thinks Rebels are all wicked & so the argument goes on. I do not know how it will terminate.

We have two tents, one to cook, & one to sleep in. Our sleeping tent is double & quite warm.

We got a chicken & some potatoes for Thanksgiving to-morrow. We will also have a ration of flour issued in the morning, & Lieut. Smith thinks he can make some cakes so we will have a fine dinner. I shall wonder what you have at home. Quite a number of the Officers have turkies for dinner, but we are not quite so lavish.

My health is very good, & we are getting along well. Col. Smith is expected here in a few days; he has been absent sick over a month. Bro. Gaff will be here to-morrow night; he is much better.[2] Rockwell has gone home, & I presume is in Pontiac now. It is late. I have been often interrupted & must close. Give my love to all. Write soon, May God bless you all.

Farewell,

Your affect. Husband

J. F. Culver

---

1 Capt. John A. Hoskins had been on special duty, sitting on court martials at Bowling

Green, from Nov. 4-28, 1862. Compiled Service Records of Union Soldiers, NA. With Hoskins on detached duty, J.F.C. commanded Company A.

2   James H. Gaff, a 35-year-old blacksmith, was mustered into service on Sept. 8, 1862, as a corporal in Company G, 129th Illinois Infantry, and immediately promoted to sergeant. Sergeant Gaff was detailed to the division ambulance corps on May 23, 1864, and was mustered out at Washington, D.C., June 8, 1865. *Ibid.*

 29

Thanksgiving morning Nov. 27/62

Dear Mary

I have got up quite early this morning & made a fire, & as all is quiet I felt like talking with you. Lieut. Smith is expecting his wife here soon. He wrote for her to come to Bowling Green, then expecting to remain all winter there; & when the news came of our removal, it was too late to notify her. While we remain here, he may possibly find fair accommodations for her. I thought if we spent the winter in Bowling Green, I should like to have you with us.[1] But I could not think of your coming here with your babe, &, as you made no mention of it in your last letter, I concluded you did not contemplate it.

I have not heard from Duff or Fleming yet, neither have I received the letter from Saul. I am not sure that our mail will be at all regular. This [Mitchellville] is but a Small Station about the size of Cayuga,[2] but for some time has been the terminus of the R. Road. There is an immense amount of Army supplies here making it very necessary to have a large force here.[3] The cars went through to Nashville & returned yesterday for the first time. As soon as possible these stores will be shipped there, & then I presume we will be sent to some other post.

One of General Fuller's aids from Springfield is now passing through this State inspecting the condition of the troops. He will be with us a few days the first of next week, & we expect to get some changes made for the better. The affairs of our Regt. have been rather loosely conducted, & we have suffered some for it.[4]

The health of the Regt. is improving, especially that of Company A. We had quite a large number sick a few days ago, none are seriously ill but David Higbee of Reading.[5] There is some doubt of his recovery; he is lying in Hospital No. 2 in Bowling Green.

I should be very happy to spend Thanksgiving with you to-day & hope before another year rolls round we may to-gether give thanks for a Union restored & the restoration of Peace & prosperity in the Land. I feel anxious to know what is being done, we get no news here at all reliable. I shall try and answer Mother [Murphy], Maggie [Utley] & Abbie's [Remick] letters to-day if possible.

The mail goes North early this morning, & we receive our mails in the evening. I shall look for a letter from *My Dear Wife*. May the richest of God's blessings rest upon you all. I hope you are getting along well. I have hoped to hear from Bro. Johnie before this & hope he is getting Strong. Why has Bro. Sammy not written? Tell all to write. And now, again, Dear Mary, I must say *Adieu* for a short time. Write to me as often as you find it convenient & believe me true until death.

Your Affect. Husband

J. F. Culver

---

1   In letters written Nov. 9 and 11, from Bowling Green, J.F.C. had broached the subject of his wife traveling south for a visit, provided the regiment went into winter quarters at that point.

2   Cayuga is a village several miles northeast of Pontiac.

3   Confederate raiders during the Kentucky Campaign had wreaked havoc on the Louisville & Nashville Railroad. Except for the tunnel midway between Mitchellville and Gallatin, which had been caved in, crews quickly effected repairs. Until the tunnel was reopened to traffic, Mitchellville was the railhead. All supplies for General Rosecrans' army in and around Nashville had to be unloaded there and forwarded the remaining 35 miles by wagon train. *O. R.,* Ser. I, Vol. XX, pt. II, p. 9; Cist, *The Army of the Cumberland,* p. 81.

4   Allen C. Fuller had been named adjutant general of the state of Illinois on Nov. 11, 1861. Colonel Smith's poor health had caused him to be absent from the regiment most of the time since its muster in. Moreover, his failure to personally drill the regiment and his ignorance of tactics caused many of his officers to question his fitness to command. Proceedings of a Board of Examiners, held at Gallatin, Tenn., by Order of SO 63, March 7, 1863, Regimental Papers, 129th Illinois, NA.

5   David Higbee, a 27-year-old farmer, was mustered into service as a private in Company A, 129th Illinois, on Sept. 8, 1862. Private Higbee was hospitalized at Bowling Green on Nov. 1, 1862, with chronic bronchitis, and given a medical discharge at Louisville on Jan. 9, 1863. Compiled Service Records of Union Soldiers, NA.

## 30

Head Quarters, Co. A, 129th Ills. Vols.
Camp Near Mitchellville, Tennessee, Nov. 30th 1862

Dear Wife

As Mr. Jos. Reeder of Dwight is here & returns home to-morrow, I am happy to have another opportunity to write to you, as you will receive it much sooner than you would by mail.[1] Smith & Capt. Hoskins both recd. letters from home. Mrs. Hoskins says you are well which is the best news I could receive. I would like to have recd. a letter also but hope better of the next mail.

I wrote quite a lengthy letter to-day to the monthly S. S. Prayer-meeting, & as all our letters will reach Pontiac on Saturday, please see that the letter is recd. & read on Sunday, it being the regular day for Prayer-meeting. I sent the letter in care of Mr. Strawell; they will be handed to the mail carrier at Pontiac.[2]

I am at a loss to know what to say about your coming down here.[3] I should like very much if you could spend a few weeks & was so happy at the thought of spending the Winter in Bowling Green, but I tremble at the thought of your coming here. There are scarcely any houses inside our Picket lines, & I cannot venture beyond them while in and around camp. There are so many lying with the measles that I fear it would cost our babe's life if you brought him,[4] besides we have no guarantee of staying here even one week. I presume Mrs. Smith will come. I do not know; & it would be an excellent opportunity for you both.

We have been looking for orders to go into Winter Quarters, but it looks more doubtful now than it did at Bowling Green. Perhaps after a few weeks we shall know our fate, at least I hope so.[5] I believe much as I would love to have you here, I dare not risk the responsibility of advising you to come just now. I sometimes think it was all wrong for me to ask you to come, but I had thought the matter over & felt sure I could keep you both safe & comfortable in or near Bowling Green. But I hope our hearts are prepared for the uncertainties of War. May God make you happy & keep you both in the enjoyment of good health. Perhaps before long things may change for the better.

Col. Smith & his wife arrived here yesterday evening; he is better but quite weak yet.[6] I understand they intend to return to Bowling Green, as they can find no place to stop here & his health will not permit his staying in camp.

My health is quite good. It has been raining hard this afternoon & is very damp & getting quite cold to-night. We may expect winter in earnest soon. The fall has been very favorable.

I presume ere this you have gone home, as Mrs. Hoskins writes that you would do so last week. I hope you are comfortable. Enclose find five dollars I succeeded in borrowing yesterday. I wish it was much more but can do but little until pay day. By selling the cow, you will have a little at least; sell all if necessary.

Our mails come very irregularly since we are here, most of it goes to Nashville first. We sent to Bowling Green last night for the mail we recd. this Evening. We are getting along very well, I presume full as well as any Regt. in the field & have suffered less from disease. Bro. Cotton preached to us to-day & would have done so to-night, but it rained too hard.

Give my love to all. I wrote to you, Mother & Maggie a few days ago. Kiss baby for me. Write as often as convenient. You speak of Hoskins not writing, he has written at least one letter a week ever since we left home. He wrote immediately when I told him what you said. He recd. a letter tonight & was much pleased.[7] May the blessings of Heaven rest upon you all, try & be cheerful & happy. God rules all things well.

Your affect. Husband

J. F. Culver

---

1 Joseph Reeder was a 39-year-old Dwight Township farmer. In 1860 he valued his real estate at $4,000 and was living with his three sons, Levi 13, George 8, and James 5. Eighth Census, Livingston County, State of Illinois, NA.

2 Jason W. Strawell was a 31-year-old Pontiac hardware merchant. Strawell in 1860 was living with his wife Elizabeth. *Ibid.*

3 On Nov. 16, 1862, Mary Culver had written, "Oh, Frank do you think I can come to you: I'm afraid almost to think of it lest I be disappointed. I am so well and the baby too that if you stay there [at Bowling Green] this winter, I must come pay or no pay. I will sell the cow and every thing else I have to pay my expenses there and if I can have tea to make dinner for my baby, I can live on almost nothing, at least I can live on anything you do, and I know my husband will share with me. How soon will we know whether you go

into winter quarters or not. I shall dread to open your letters." Mary Culver to J.F.C., Nov. 16, 1862, Culver Collection.

4   Like many regiments recruited from a rural environment, the 129th Illinois experienced a measles epidemic. These epidemics were virulent and claimed many lives.

5   Two days before, on Nov. 28, there had been a confrontation between Colonels Hambright and Case. It was precipitated when Hambright called on Case to send two companies of the 129th to Nashville as train guards. Case refused as this was contradictory to his orders from General Granger. Hambright said that if this were true, he would not call on the 129th for details in the future, as Case had refused to obey orders.

When he notified General Granger of his difficulties with Colonel Hambright, Case pointed out that although his regiment was encamped within the picket line manned by Hambright's command, he, for his own protection, would send out the same number of pickets as heretofore. In view of Hambright's intransigence, the 129th's only duties for the time being were to provide for the security of their camp and to drill in the afternoons. Case to Granger, Nov. 30, 1862, Letter Books, 129th Illinois Regiment, NA.

6   Colonel Smith, having secured a surgeon's certificate attesting to his illness, had left the regiment in the fourth week of October at Lebanon. Proceedings of a Board of Examiners, Held at Gallatin, Tenn., by Order of SO 63, March 7, 1863, Regimental Papers, 129th Illinois, NA, RG 94.

7   Mrs. Hoskins had complained to Mary Culver that she had only received two letters from her husband since he had left Pontiac on Sept. 23, 1862. J.F.C. was to tell Captain Hoskins that "he ought to be ashamed of himself." Mary Culver to J.F.C., November 16, 1862, Culver Collection.

 31

Head Quarters, Company A 129th Ills. Vols.
Camp Near Mitchellville, Tenn. Dec. 2nd 1862

My Dear Wife

Yours of Nov. 25th came by to-day's mail. I am very happy to learn that you are all so well but feel sorry at your disappointment when you learn that we are no longer at Bowling Green & with no prospect of going into Winter Quarters. You cannot experience a greater disappointment than myself; for it was a matter I contemplated for some time & even now, did I not feel so thoroughly convinced that the risk was too great, I would urge your coming but under the circumstances I dare not do it.[1]

I recd. a day or two ago the "Pontiac News" containing a letter dangerous in its effects & alarming were it true. I am sorry that such falsities should for a moment gain credence. I hope you will not allow them to disturb you. I wish you could see things as they are. I know you would be better satisfied.

You ask me to state such business as I feel anxious about. As I have written several letters & recd. no answer, I wish you would get definite answers to the following questions: Have I been properly discharged from the Boyer and DeWitt Estates?[2] If so, let the certificates of discharge in all such cases granted under the Seal of the Court be given to you. Has the "Home" & "Winneshiek" Insurance Companies accepted of my final accounts and acknowledged the same in any way?[3] Call on S. S. Fleming for answers. Ask M. E. Collins if C. J. Beattie has paid the amount due me to him, & if the same has been forwarded to the heirs of J. H. Dart and their receipts secured?[4] Also whether any settlement has been had with Salathiel Hallam, & if so the amount paid to him.[5] If Bro. Johnnie's health will permit, he can readily get replies, & further I wish to know how Wolgamott has succeeded in collecting & if there has been sufficient in his hands to meet all the demands against me. If there is any overplus, you ought to have it. I have never recd. Saul's letter yet & feel quite anxious to see it.[6] I wrote to J. Duff & Fleming both but have never recd. an answer.[7] I do not know why, as both promised to attend Strictly & inform me of my affairs. I presume however they are busy.

I shall submit to Bro. Johnie's judgment in renting the house as you seem to have referred the matter to him. For many reasons I am glad Sis has succeeded in getting so good a place. I only hope she will have the moral courage to resist the influences brought to bear against her staying.[8] I shall write to her soon, perhaps tonight; I have been intending to do so for sometime.

I conclude from your last letter that you have broken up house-keeping. I feel sure that some of your letters have gone astray, or I should have a fuller history. The date of the last before this was 16th Nov. I sent a letter yesterday by Mr. Jos. Reader which you will receive, I presume, long before this. I also wrote to the Monthly Union S. S. Prayermeeting & hope it may be acceptable. I was interrupted so often that I could not write that which I had premeditated. My health is quite good. Lieut. Smith looks for his wife next week. I presume she will come with Maples, & now, Dear Mary, I most earnestly pray God to bless and comfort you. I know it would be a lasting pleasure to both of us could you come, but God I believe wills it otherwise. I can give no assurance of coming home, but trust in God that in his good time he will allow us to meet. Let us pray that we may receive Grace to discharge our whole duty.

Give my love to all the family. I do not understand what you mean by Sammy's having an operation performed upon his throat.[9] I have never heard of any difficulty. Tell both to write. Remember me kindly to all our friends & Hoping that God will ever bless, I remain as ever,

Your affect. Husband

J. F. Culver

---

1   Mary Culver had not received the letters from her husband, telling of the regiment's change of station to Mitchellville and discouraging her visit. In her letter of the 23d, she had written, "Oh how I long to read from you, 'you may come.' " Mary Culver to J.F.C., Nov. 23, 1862, Culver Collection.

2   The Boyer estate refers to the property that had belonged to the late George W. Boyer, a Pontiac furniture merchant. It has been impossible to further identify the principals involved in the Simeon DeWitt estate. Eighth Census, Livingston County, State of Illinois, NA; *History of Livingston County*, p. 306.

3   Before entering service, Culver had served as Livingston County agent for the Winneshiek Insurance Company of Freeport, Illinois.

4   Marcellus E. Collins was a 30-year-old Pontiac lawyer. In 1860 Collins was living with his wife, Elizabeth, and valued his real and personal property at $2,500. Charles J. Beattie, a 32-year-old Pontiac lawyer, was born in New York. In 1860 Beattie was living with his wife, Eliza, and their two sons. He valued his real and personal property at $11,675. It has been impossible to further identify the principals involved in the J. H. Dart estate. Dart had been a pioneer Pontiac attorney. Eighth Census, Livingston County, State of Illinois, NA.

5   It has been impossible to further identify Salathiel Hallam.

6   Samuel S. Saul, born in 1832 in Pennsylvania, had moved to Livingston County in 1854, where he taught school, until being elected county clerk in 1857. Saul had been instrumental in prevailing upon J.F.C. to settle in Pontiac. In 1860 he was living with his wife, Kate, and their four children: Charles S., Rodman, Charlotte, and Eugene. *Ibid.; History of Livingston County*, p. 324.

7   Jonathan Duff was a 32-year-old Pontiac lawyer and had been J.F.C.'s partner. In 1860 the Pennsylvania-born Duff was living with his wife, Hannah, and their daughter, Emma. Eighth Census, Livingston County, State of Illinois, NA.

8   Mary Culver had written, "Mary [sis] is coming down to stay all next week. Mother is going to wean her Johnie." Mary Culver to J.F.C., Nov. 23d, 1862, Culver Collection.

9   Mary Culver had written that her brother, Sammy, had gone to Chicago to have enlarged tonsils removed. *Ibid.*

Mitchellsville - Dec. 3rd/62

Dear Wife

I just saw Mr. Crull at the Depot, who returns to Pontiac immediately being discharged.[1] We are expecting marching orders for Nashville, but all is uncertain. The troops were [to] leave to-day.[2]

I wrote you a long letter & sent [it] by Mr. Reader on Monday. He thought he would get to Pontiac by Saturday. I also wrote to monthly S. S. Prayermeeting & sent both by him.

My health is good. I should like to say come as per your letter recd. yesterday but cannot. If we had any assurance of staying here any time, I should wish you to come. But Col. Case just tells me that our Brigade at Bowling Green has most of it been ordered on, & he expects we will go with it.[3]

May God Bless & keep you all. Give my love to all. Write soon to your affect. Husband.

J. F. Culver

---

1 James L. Crull, a 37-year-old Fairbury farmer, was mustered into service as a private in Company E, 129th Illinois Infantry, on Sept. 8, 1862. Private Crull was medically discharged at Bowling Green, Nov. 25, 1862. Compiled Service Records of Union Soldiers, NA.

2 With trains running between Mitchellville and Nashville, the supplies stockpiled at the former were forwarded to the army. General Rousseau accordingly alerted his brigade commanders to put their units in motion for Nashville. At the last minute, however, it was decided not to move Hambright's brigade until more troops were brought down from Bowling Green to guard the railroad north and south of Mitchellville, because Colonel Morgan had sent raiders across the Cumberland attired in "citizens' dress to loaf around and injure the railroad." O. R., Ser. I, Vol. XX, pt. II, pp. 108, 116, 127.

3 There was a dispute between General Rosecrans and Maj. Gen. Horatio G. Wright, the commander of the Department of the Ohio, over control of General Granger's troops. As Wright was responsible for protecting the railroad between Louisville and the Tennessee line, he was unwilling for Rosecrans to pull the 38th Brigade out of Bowling Green, until he could replace it with one of his brigades. On the 2d, after much bickering, Wright finally agreed to release the 38th Brigade, but on the following day he changed his mind. Ibid., pp. 74, 76, 110, 116.

Mitchellsville, Tenn. - Dec. 11th 1862

Dear Wife

As a leisure moment offers opportunity, I cannot better reconcile myself to wait for your letters than by writing. I recollect in Abbott's life of Josephine, he gives many sketches from Napoleon's letters, while she was his wife, stating that so great was his attachment to her that scarce a day passed, while on the march or battlefield, but what a courier was dispatched with some missive of love.[1] I am happy therefore that the disposition to love & manifest it is not only displayed in greatness, for then I could not be a partaker of its bliss.

I wrote quite a lengthy letter to Friend Russell to-night, which I hope will elicit an answer.[2] I had the pleasure of enjoying a real Pontiac dinner day before yesterday [with] Mess No. 2 of Company G, & I was tempted to wish that the distance were not quite so great & expressage so far beyond reason that I might elicit a similar favor of my friends. But I could scarcely deem it practical.[3]

Christmas & New Year's are approaching. I wish you all a merry time & all the comforts & blessings this life can give.

I believe I forgot in my letter of yesterday to mention that I recd. a letter from Sister Jennie & Bro. Charley on Saturday.[4] All at home are well. Jennie says you have not answered her letter yet. Mother [Culver] promised to write soon. Sister [Hannah] is preparing to go to Harrisburg to teach, & Chas. McGregor was well & flourishing.[5] She also informs me of the very sudden death of Mrs. Postlethwaithe (Mary's mother) while on a visit.[6] Bro. Wes is Assistant Surgeon in the 56th Regt. Penna. Vols. & is stationed near Washington, D. C.[7] I believe that is all the news.

My health is quite good; I am gaining rapidly. I presume Maples & Mrs. Smith will be here by to-morrow evening. Many besides myself are looking anxiously for their arrival.

Lucian Perry got as far as Louisville, but I believe failed to get a pass through & could not come any farther.[8] The Orders are very Strict, yet almost any business man may succeed. Quite a number go through on the road every day.[9]

Nothing new has occurred since I last wrote. All is going on well. Bro. Cotton & myself are bunking together for a few nights. We have a large comfortable fire on the hearth & are quite pleasantly situated. The floor get[s] rather hard sometimes before morning,but it is as good as we could wish under the circumstances. I shall expect to hear from you to-morrow night. Give my love to all. Write soon. For the present — Good night. May God protect and bless you.

Your affect. Husband

J. F. Culver

---

1   John S. Abbott (1805-1877) was a prolific American writer, best known for his many biographies. His *History of Josephine* was published in New York City in 1851.

2   William L. Russell was born in Ohio in 1821, and in 1860 he was sheriff of Livingston County. A widower in the latter year, he boarded and roomed in Pontiac with Rufus and Elizabeth Babcock. Eighth Census, Livingston County, State of Illinois, NA.

3   Company G, one of five Livingston County companies, was commanded by Capt. Henry B. Reed of Pontiac.

4   J.F.C.'s letter to his wife of Dec. 10, 1862 is missing. Jennie Culver Cheston and Charles Culver were the writer's younger sister and brother. Jennie was 22 and Charles 15. In 1860 both were living with their mother and father in dwelling 597, the East Ward, Carlisle, Pa. Eighth Census, Cumberland County, State of Pennsylvania, NA.

5   Charles McGregor was a student at Carlisle's Dickinson College. In 1860 the Ohio-born McGregor was living in Pontiac with his mother, Mary J. McGregor, a school teacher. Eighth Census, Livingston County, State of Illinois, NA; *History of Livingston County*, pp. 642-643.

6   It has been impossible to further identify Mrs. Postlethwaite.

7   W. Wesley Culver had been mustered into service in November 1862, as assistant surgeon of the 56th Pennsylvania Volunteer Infantry. Compiled Service Records of Union Soldiers, NA.

8   Lucien B. Perry, born in Virginia in 1836, was the son of Dr. James M. and Hannah Perry. In 1860 he clerked in a Pontiac store, and he was en route to visit his brother, Pvt. W. W. Perry of Company A. Eighth Census, Livingston County, State of Illinois, NA.

9   In a futile effort to control illegal trading with the enemy, General Rosecrans on Nov. 27 issued a general order providing that: (a) all army sutlers must report to their regiments and not make any sales to any persons except those connected with the army; (b) no sutler could ship boots, shoes, or clothing to his regiment, unless he first secured a certificate from the regimental commander; (c) no persons, except sutlers, would be permitted to follow the army and establish themselves within its lines; (d) in towns or cities within the army's lines, no person would be allowed to sell goods unless he was a resident trader, with a permit signed by the provost marshal attesting to his loyalty and fidelity; and (e) any person or persons found shopping, selling, or attempting to sell goods in violation of these orders would be arrested and their goods confiscated. But where large profits could be made by trading with the enemy, many ways were found to evade regulations. Consumer goods were smuggled through the Union lines to be bartered for cotton which commanded premium prices in the North. *O. R.*, Ser. I. Vol. XX, pt. II, pp. 104-105.

## 34

Head Quarters, 129th Illinois Volunteers
Mitchellsville, Tenn., Dec. 12th 1862

My Dear Wife:

May the richest of Heaven's blessings rest upon you today. On this the first Anniversary of our marriage, let me present my compliments first to you, my own love, secondly, to the fine boy you hold in your arms. I imagine I can see a blush mantle the cheek of the maiden of one year ago at the thought or anticipation of the result now realized. God has been merciful and gracious, full of love, & we have reaped, largely at his hands, health & happiness. My heart is filled with gratitude: Oh Lord, continue thy loving kindness to us.

My memory is crowded this morning with recollections of the past: hours spent in joy & gladness, hours of trial & temptation, yet few of the latter in comparison, so good has been "Our Father in Heaven," I know of no surer method of interesting you to-day than by a rehearsal of events, some of which we have spoken, yet many bright to memory yet never mentioned. In this I must be allowed to play the lover once more. I do not mean in the literal meaning of that word for I have never ceased to be your lover, but I mean in the general acceptation of the term, & it was in earlier life somewhat of a mystery to me why it should be thus. I trust, however, & believe it has been reciprocal in its most literal meaning.

I recollect a year ago this morning, surrounded with business, endeavoring to accomplish the task before me, while my mind was in another part of the town, friend Russell came to pay me a visit: Smiling & casting some very knowing glances, expressing much that he dare not audibly express, for the Office was crowded, but stepping aside, we had quite a lengthy conversation over "Coming Events." After he retired, a thousand thoughts came into my mind. The step I was about to take must tell on my whole life for weal or woe. If our tastes be congenial, if we succeed in contributing to each other's happiness, if we are led together by the hand of God, all is well; if not, have I the strength to stand the trial, if my wife be unhappy, discontented & fretful as many I have known, what would become of me? & then this other burning thought—if I fall below the estimate my intended has placed upon me, if she be disappointed, her hopes gone, her prospects blasted for life, what may be the result? All these things engaged my mind while to a casual observer I was busy examining records & doing general office business: thus the greater part of the day passed & evening drawing nigh, then thoughts of the past seemed to solve in part the future. How we have loved & expressed the same to each other, of our first acquaintance growing into friendship & then love, of hours so happily spent in each other's society.

I confess I came to you in the evening, strong in hope & purpose, fortified by the promises of God. I found you calm, trusting, confident, & thus together we pledged ourselves to love & cherish each other so long as we both shall live. One year has passed; to-day we are far separated from each other, surrounded by circumstances not the most flattering, yet in joy I give my testimony. You have for me solved the whole problem: faithful, true affection, & in every way worthy. You are my wife; you have made me happy. My most sanguine anticipations have been more than realized & rejoice in God that so great blessings have been vouchsafed to me. How I wonder this morning what the past has developed to you, what prospects in the future lie before you. I shall expect to hear when I secure from you the result of to-day's reflection.

I just received by this morning's mail yours of Dec. 3rd & am most happy to learn that you are all well. I expect Maples here this evening or to-morrow if he does not stop in Louisville. As you say nothing about Mrs. Smith coming, I presume she will not come.[1] No women are allowed to travel South of Bowling Green, Ky., & even passing through Louisville are liable to be searched unless they have a pass. I shall feel quite sorry for both him & her should she come, as it will be quite difficult for him to get to Bowling Green to see her & then only for a short time.

We have had no mail trains for two days until this morning. Company A, F, D, & K are posted some eight miles south of Mitchellsville on the R. Road.[2] I am informed this morning that they have been relieved & will return to-day or to-morrow. I have not been with the Company since Monday last [8th]. I have been ailing with the Jaundice for almost two weeks & returned to this place to take care of myself. I have not been confined to bed any part of the time & before you receive this, I shall be entirely recovered. My Complexion has been so yellow most of the time that I could scarcely recognize myself, but it is fast leaving. I have received very kind attention ever since I returned here & have enjoyed myself very much.

I wrote to you on your first intimation that the Small-Pox was in the neighborhood to have the babe vaccinated & hope ere this it has been done.[3] It will do no harm to have it tried on yourself. I shall be happy if the disease proves to be other than the Small-Pox. I presume friend Russell is sorely tried. I should love to hear the prattle of our little one as you desire, but you will have to act my part. Kiss him for me.

The two School Orders you refer to were both paid to Dr. Johnson (then school treasurer) about the 4th or 6th of August, as he wished to credit them on a judgment vs. Rollings in favor of the school Trustees.[4] I will go & see him now & have his explanation. Dr. Johnson, I understand, went to Bowling Green this morning & will not be home before to-morrow or next day.[5] They were merely left in my hands for Johnson who at first refused to take them unless sufficient was paid to cancel the judgment, but he afterward accepted them, &, as I had no interest in the matter, & paid them as per Rollings' order. I took no receipt: I think the judgment is on See's Docket. I shall write, however, as soon as I can see Johnson.

It is now almost night. I have written at intervals through the day, having nothing else to do. I have kept it sacred to thoughts & reflections of our life as you requested me: 1st by anew consecrating myself to God & committing you & our little one to his tender mercies; then I spent some time in reading His word & afterward commenced this letter. Could I have written all my thoughts it would fill a volume. My plans for the future thus far developed are to lead a more consistent life, trusting in God for help; to contribute all in my power to the comfort & happiness of my family, & trust them in the hands of a kind Providence endeavoring to be resigned to the will of God. Many times to-day I have almost longed for Home, but these thoughts do not trouble me when I am well & strong. I shall move forward in the discharge of what I believe to be the path of duty. If I fall, heaven will be my home where I shall meet you both ere long. But my hopes are bouyant; I fully expect to spend many years with you. I have believed God would spare us to gather our children around us & teach them the way to Heaven.

I think I have received all your letters. I shall expect one by the hand of E. R. Maples. Gagan tells me that friend Russell expects to pay us a visit. How happy I should be to see him. I hope he will come.

There is a rumor in camp that we will be paid off next week. I do hope it is so. I know you must need money very much. I sent you $5 in a letter a few days ago. Did you get it? I shall now leave my letter until after dark, or if no opportunity offers I will finish in the morning before the mail closes. I shall spend the evening, however, as the day, devoted to you. Since I last wrote, I have finished a letter to the Sunday School which I will enclose in yours.

As I came into camp from supper, Bro. Cotton invited me to his tent to have a season of prayer. We have held our prayer-meeting, & I feel that God is ever with those that call upon him. Let us, my dear wife, strive to be holy. O, there is so much real happiness in the full enjoyment of God's Love.

It is now about the hour in which with friends gathered around us, we commenced our life together. Can we make any improvement? I hope to hear many suggestions from you, &, if we are not both permitted to see another anniversary like to-day, I believe the day is coming when together in Heaven we shall be most happy forever.

I can add no more of interest. I may dream of home & wife, but it will add nothing to my enjoyment for it is all gone in a moment. I shall look anxiously for your letter. Give my love to Mother & all.

A man in Company G told me yesterday he had received a letter from your Father & that all were well. I think he said his name was Collins.[6] I never knew him before. Allen Fellows is rather downcast that he receives no letters from his wife; he has had none for over a month save the one you sent. Kiss baby for me. Remember me kindly to all our friends & may the blessings of Heaven so plentifully bestowed upon us be continued.

Farewell,

Your Affect. Husband

J. F. Culver

---

1  Mary Culver had written on Dec. 2, in a letter which had been delayed, that Mrs. Smith had decided not to visit her husband. Mary Culver to J.F.C., Dec. 2, 1862, Culver Collection.

2  Captain Hoskins with Companies A, F, and K, 129th Illinois, had taken position on Dec. 7 at the stockade eight miles south of Mitchellville. Here his men guarded the water tank and two railroad bridges spanning Drakes Creek to prevent their destruction by Rebel raiders. Two days later, on the 9th, Company D reinforced Hoskins' battalion at the stockade. Case to Hoskins, Dec. 6, and Smith to Case, Dec. 9, 1862, Regimental Papers, 129th Illinois, NA.

3  A smallpox epidemic was sweeping Pontiac. Mary Culver had reported that several families had been stricken, and Lura Russell and her boys "are a complete sore from head to foot." Other neighbors who had been vaccinated and had been stricken had very few sores, so Mary Culver would have their baby vaccinated as soon as Dr. Elisha Capron returned. Mary Culver to J.F.C., Dec. 3, 1862, Culver Collection.

4  Bro. Utley had asked Mary Culver to inquire about a county order for $9 which Phillip Rollings had given her husband. *Ibid.*

Rollings was a 48-year-old Livingston County farmer.

5  Dr. Darius Johnson of Pontiac was the regiment's assistant surgeon.

6  There was no soldier in Company G named Collins.

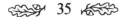 

Mitchellsville, Tenn., Dec. 16th 1862

Dear Wife

I have consulted Dr. Johnson with regard to the School Orders in question. He acknowledges the receipt of them & says that their amount is properly credited as interest on a note or notes in his hands of which Mr. Rollings is one of the payors.

I cannot describe the notes other than that Messrs. Ladd & Rollings joined in a note or notes with some other party which are payable to Johnson either as original payee or by endorsement & that he had the right & power to so appropriate it.[1] If necessary I will ford. Immediately his receipt of the amount. The date of receipt is August 4th or 6th, I am not positive which. Please hand this to Mr. Utley, Wolgamott or Fleming, wherever the inquiry arose.

Yours &c.

J. F. Culver

P.S. In returning for further evidence, get if possible the date & amount of the order, also to whom payable & by whom made.

J. F. Culver

---

1 Samuel C. Ladd was a 47-year-old Livingston County farmer. In 1860 he was living with his wife, Mary, and their son, and he valued his estate at $18,000. Eighth Census, Livingston County, State of Illinois, NA.

 36

Head Quarters, Co. A, 129th Ills. Vols.
Mitchellsville, Tenn., Dec. 16th 1862

Dear Mary

I anticipated the arrival of E. R. Maples with several letters from you before this, but notice by the "Pontiac News" that he will leave Pontiac to-morrow. I shall look quite anxiously for him, as I scarcely expect any more letters by mail before he comes. My letter of Dec. 12th will not, I presume, reach you in time to get an answer by him.[1]

I am enjoying quite good health & think I shall feel better & stronger from my slight attack of sickness. I have had no letter since the 12th, which indeed is a very short time, but you have by your frequent writing led me to expect one every few days, & I am not fully satisfied without.

Francis A. Gorbet of our Company died this morning in the Hospital here;[2] he was sick but a few days.

I recd. a letter from Scott McDowell to-day.[3] They are all well as usual. He said he saw your smiling face but a short time ago & that all was well, which gave a degree of comfort at least in the absence of better authority from yourself.

All your friends & acquaintances, I believe, are well. I saw Sam Mc [Goodin] and McCartney; they are well. Jim Morrow is flourishing as usual.[4]

Give my love to all. Kiss baby for me. Write soon. I think my letters will go full as well with stamps.[5] Please send me a few if convenient. May God bless & keep you all.

In haste.

Your affect. Husband

J. F. Culver

---

1   The Dec. 12 letter is the one J.F.C. wrote his wife on their first wedding anniversary.

2   Francis A. Gorbet, a 41-year-old Rook's Creek farmer, was mustered into service on Sept. 8, 1862, as a private in Company A, 129th Illinois Infantry. Private Gorbet died of pneumonia in the regimental hospital at Mitchellville, Tenn., on Dec. 16, 1862. Compiled Service Records of Union Soldiers, NA.

3   It has been impossible to further identify Scott McDowell. Eighth Census, Livingston County, State of Illinois, NA.

4   James E. Morrow, a 26-year-old clerk, was mustered into service on Sept. 8, 1862, as a corporal in Company G, 129th Illinois Infantry, and immediately promoted to sergeant. On Feb. 23, 1864, Sergeant Morrow was detached and returned to Illinois on recruiting duty. He rejoined the regiment in the summer of 1864 and was mustered out at Washington, D.C., June 8, 1865. Compiled Service Records of Union Soldiers, NA.

5   Mary Culver had written on Dec. 2, "Don't put any stamps on your next letters, perhaps they will be more likely to come." Mary Culver to J.F.C., Dec. 2, 1862, Culver Collection.

Mitchellsville, Tenn., Dec. 18th 1862

Dear Wife

I received yours of the 7th & 8th this morning, rather unexpectedly, as I scarcely expected a letter before the arrival of Maples. I am happy & thankful that you all enjoy such good health.

I can readily inform you what I was doing on the Sunday you were writing as you wondered.[1] About 4 oclock in the morning [of the 7th] we started & marched about 14 miles halting about 1 o'clock P.M., pitched our tents, & arranged for the night. I was quite sick & as I have already told you, I returned to this place on Monday [the 8th].[2] I am most happy to say I am quite well now.

I have quite a good opinion of Rev. Pearce as a preacher & man & am very glad you like him. I do not know Mr. Pollard.[3] I feel sorry my letter to the S.S.U. Prayermeeting had not arrived in time, as I hoped it would. I am also glad the Schools have united in their celebration of Christmas.[4] If I can get time, I shall write a letter as my contribution to the tree, but cannot promise definitely.

I cannot express the joy I feel that you manifest so much zeal for the Sabbath School. I feared that losing so many it might lag in interest & lose its numbers. I scarcely dared hope that under the circumstances you would feel interested. I do not pretend & I hope have no desire in my heart to even make a suggestion directing your actions. But my love & zeal for the prosperity of the School for which I have labored so hard & hoped for so much are a sufficient reason for the gratitude I feel.[5]

I expect that boy of ours will grow beyond all bounds if he keeps on; he must be quite large.[6] I hope your health may not be impaired carrying & caring for him.

I should be full as happy to have you here as you possibly could be, & if I thought it practicable at all, I would urge you to come, but I dare not do it. The risk is too great.

I heard of the marriage of Mr. Foote a few days ago but scarcely credit it. I hope he may be happy & prosperous. If I had his address, I would write to him.[7] You seem to think that your letters do not reach me. I think I have received all. Sometimes they come by way of Nashville, & are thus delayed but invariably reach me.

I was appointed to-day upon the Board of Survey for this post, which will occupy my time probably for several weeks.[8] The nature of the business coming before us will give it much the nature of a court of inquiry. Our business will be to inquire into the loyalty of those persons asking indemnification from the government. The advantage will be that all our business will be in a comfortable room, a comfort I will relish very much.

I have never received Mr. Saul's letter; I fear it is lost. Josiah Wood of Pontiac is lying dangerously ill.[9] I think he will die but may recover. We are all doing well. Lieut. Smith is expecting his wife soon. A letter from Maples to-day informs us that he will not start before the 22nd. Mrs. Blackburn & Mrs. Fitch of Fairbury will arrive here to-morrow.[10] Give my love to all & now committing you to the hands of Providence for the present, Farewell.

Your Affect. Husband

J. F. Culver

---

1  Mary Culver had written on the 7th, "I have thought much of you today and often wondered where you were and what you were doing." Mary Culver to J.F.C., Dec. 7, 1862, Culver Collection.

2  The march described by J.F.C. was that of Hoskins' battalion from Mitchellville to the Drakes Creek stockade, and the distance covered was about 8, not 14, miles. As Culver had explained in his letter of the 12th, he was suffering from jaundice.

3  Mary Culver had informed her husband that the Reverend Pearce had preached the funeral sermon for Mr. and Mrs. James H. Herbert's child. It had been a good sermon, and she had liked "him much better than Mr. Pollard though he is far inferior in looks and others in the church do not like him." Mary Culver to J.F.C., Dec. 7, 1862, Culver Collection. Herbert was a 49-year-old Pontiac saloon keeper. In 1860 he and his wife were living with their four children. Eighth Census, Livingston County, State of Illinois, NA.

4  According to Mary Culver, the Presbyterian and Methodist Sunday schools had united and would have one big Christmas tree. Mary Culver to J.F.C., Dec. 7, 1862, Culver Collection.

5  Mary Culver had written, "I have thought lately Dear Frank and it struck me very forceably today that perhaps the reason I was not permitted to go away from here this winter was that God wanted me to work here and do what I could to make good your place [in the Sunday school]." Ibid.

6  Their son, born Sept. 21, weighed in December between 16 and 17 pounds. Ibid.

7  Mary Culver had met Morgan Foote on the street, and he had shown her a photograph of his wife, "a nice looking woman about 38 years old." They had been married in Wisconsin and would soon go there to live. Ibid.

8  Colonel Smith, on Dec. 18, issued a special order assigning three of his officers—Maj. Andrew J. Cropsey, Capt. John B. Perry, and Lt. Joseph F. Culver—to a board of survey to "examine and audit the claims of loyal citizens in this vicinity against the United States Government." SO 12, Dec. 18, 1862, Letter Books, 129th Illinois, NA.

9   Josiah Wood, a 21-year-old Pontiac blacksmith, was mustered into service on Sept. 8, 1862, as a private in Company A, 129th Illinois Infantry. He was hospitalized in December in the regimental hospital at Mitchellville and died at Fountain Head, Tenn., Jan. 7, 1863, of typhoid fever. Compiled Service Records of Union Soldiers, NA.

10   Benjamin F. Fitch, a 34-year-old Livingston County farmer, was mustered into service on Sept. 8, 1862, as 2d lieutenant of Company E, 129th Illinois Infantry. He was promoted to 1st lieutenant on April 17, 1863, and was mustered out at Washington, D.C., June 8, 1865. John F. Blackburn, a 26-year-old Fairbury druggist, was mustered into service as 1st lieutenant of Company E, 129th Illinois Infantry, on Sept. 8, 1862. He resigned his commission on Feb. 25, 1863, having received a certificate of disability signed by the regimental surgeon. On Sept. 5, 1863, Blackburn was elected regimental sutler. *Ibid.*

 38

Bucks Lodge, Dec. 22nd 1862

Dear Wife

We left Mitchellsville on Saturday [the 20th] about 3 P.M. & arrived on the ground about 1/4 mile from here after dark & camped.[1] Yesterday (Sunday) we moved to where we now are encamped & pitched our tents which occupied all the day. We are in the woods on a high hill.[2] I have not yet been out of the timber to see what view is afforded from our position.

Mrs. Blackburn & Mrs. Fitch of Fairbury arrived in Mitchellsville on Friday evening. I feel truly sorry for them. Mrs. Blackburn's baby was quite sick, & in the excitement of Saturday, they must all have suffered severely. They were brought through in an ambulance, but as we have been threatened with an attack every day they cannot enjoy themselves. The probability [is] that we will fall back from this point very soon to some other place. I understand the ladies will start home immediately, &, as they came with the intention of staying all winter, they must be sorely disappointed. They lost their trunks & all their clothes on the way, & no one here has any opportunity to look for them.

My health is much better. I feel almost as well as ever though the Jaundice has not entirely left me.

I recd. a letter from Duff Saturday with Saul's letter enclosed. I find C. J. Beattie has gone to Chicago without paying as he promised. Employ some one to attend to it immediately. If Mr. Utley goes to

Chicago, he will perhaps attend to it. I believe the amt. is $29.21. M. E. Collins has his receipt given to me for the note. Something must be done immediately. The money I am under bonds for & must be paid. It should have been paid the 1st of August & is due the heirs of J. H. Dart, decd. The Amt. to make up the balance is in the hands of M. E. Collins, & I fear has never been forwarded. I feel alarmed as it is a matter of more than ordinary urgency, & I must know if there is any possibility.[3] Please do all you can.

Mrs. Smith & Maples are expected soon.

Give my love to all. It seems a long time since I have heard from home. Write soon

Your affect. Husband

J. F. Culver

---

1  The 129th Illinois had been ordered from Mitchellville to Buck Lodge on Dec. 20. There they would guard the Drakes Creek railroad bridges and the water tank.

2  There were several high hills, both over 900 feet, on either side of the railroad at Buck Lodge. USGS—Fountain Head Quadrangle—7.5 Series.

3  J.F.C. had been bonded as an executor of the Dart Estate. Duff had been his law partner, while Beattie and Collins were other Pontiac attorneys.

 39

Bucks Lodge, Tenn., Dec. 25th 62

My dear Wife

Sixteen days have elapsed since the date of your last letter,[1] & with the news of the prevalence of the Small-Pox all around you, I feel unusually anxious to hear. I have lived in hope for the past ten days expecting Maples by to-day at farthest. This morning we received the unwelcome news that on account of the Small-Pox, he has indefinitely postponed his coming.

Letters were received here today announcing his intention, & I feel alarmed because I believe if you were well you would be among the first to write. I shall be under apprehension of the worst news I can learn until I can hear from you. May God take care of you.

By late advice from Pontiac, we are informed that Wm. J. Russell, J. P. Garner, Dr. Croswell, Mrs. Strawell, Mrs. Stevens & others have the Small-Pox[2] & that it continues to spread. I am sorry that I did not advise you at the earliest intimations of the disease to sell all & go east to Father's until Spring; now I fear it is too late. If you think not, go if possible. If we only had received our pay, you now might have sufficient money to go on.

I have but little more to say save that I am well. I am just informed that S. Bennet will go home to-morrow.[3] I shall therefore wait until after the evening mail & finish to-night.

Christmas Evening!

The day has passed & no mail. I am informed that communication is cut of[f] by the Rebels some place North of Bowling Green. If it be so, it may be a long time before this reaches you, or before I hear from you.[4] Rumors are so plenty[iful], however, that I do not credit it.

Mrs. Blackburn & Mrs. Fitch go home on Monday [the 29th] if they can get through, but as they will not risk going to Pontiac or seeing any one from there I shall not send by them.

We have but little news here, a few of the Companies regaled themselves of the good things from home today. I am indebted to Mrs. Blackburn for a piece of very nice cake. We had a can of oysters for supper to-night, making quite a palatable fare.

I wrote to you a few days ago, soon after our arrival in this place.[5] I cannot boast of being mentally very bright to-night. Our company were up all night last night. The weather is very pleasant. We scarcely ever have fire unless to cook for the past week. It looks a little like rain just now & a prospect of its getting colder.

I should have been happy to have been present at the S. School gathering to-day, yet have feared that but few could assemble under the circumstances [the small-pox epidemic]. Tell me all about it.

I have not recd. the letter from Bro. Johnie yet. I should have written sooner & now feel sorry that I did not. I must now close with the hope that I shall soon hear from you. May God in his infinite mercy keep you from harm. If you can save yourself & babe by leaving, do not hesitate to sacrifice everything & go.

Give my love to all. I commit all unto the hands of God believing all is for the best & shall ever pray,

Your affect Husband

J. F. Culver

---

1 The reference is to Mary Culver's letter of Dec. 7 and 8, 1862.

2 Jerome P. Garner was a 48-year-old Pontiac lawyer. In 1860 he was living with his

wife, Mary, and his three children by a previous marriage. Thomas Croswell was a 40-year-old Pontiac druggist. In 1860 Thomas and Martha Croswell were living with their two children, Augustus and Henrietta. Mrs. Elizabeth Strawell was the wife of Jason W. Strawell, owner and operator of a hardware store. Mrs. Sophia Stevens was the 22-year-old wife of Pontiac carpenter William H. Stevens. Eighth Census, Livingston County, State of Illinois, NA.

3   Seymour Bennett was a 32-year-old Pontiac clerk. In 1860 he was living with his wife, Polly, and their two-year-old son Eddie. *Ibid.*

4   John Hunt Morgan, having been promoted to brigadier general by the Confederate Congress in recognition of past successes, had left Alexandria, Tenn., on Dec. 22 with 3,100 Rebel cavalrymen. Striking north into Kentucky by way of Glasgow, Morgan's raiders on Christmas Day, threatened the Louisville & Nashville Railroad near Munfordville. Next day the Confederate horse-soldiers struck the railroad, capturing stockades at Bacon Creek and Nolin. Vital bridges and trestles were destroyed. Morgan's column on the 27th and 28th advanced up the Louisville & Nashville Railroad through Elizabethtown and destroyed the two long Muldraugh Hills trestles. *O. R.*, Ser. I, Vol. XX, pt. I, pp. 154-156.

5   This reference is to J.F.C.'s letter of the 22nd.

 40

Letter No. 2
Hd. Qrs., Co. A, 129th Ills. Vols. Inft.
Buck Lodge, Tenn. Dec. 25th 1862

Dear Wife

I commenced [a] letter hastily this afternoon & closed it this evening, & as I have still a few leisure moments I will try & give you a short description of our present situation.

We left Mitchellsville rather hastily last Saturday evening [the 20th] having learned that Morgan with a large force was intending an attack here.[1] We were well fortified & felt quite secure. We have just fairly commenced our fortifications here. Bucks Lodge is nothing more than a tank which supplies the Rail-Road with water. There are two bridges & over 3/4 mile of trestle work under the road which if destroyed would take a long time to repair, hence the importance of the place.

It is a wild country all around & a few years ago a favorite haunt for deer, hence the name Buck Lodge. Our Camp composed of the 79th Ohio & 129th Ills. occupy three hills, one north, South, & west, all of which we are fortifying. The little valley is not more than a mile either way.[2] Our main camp is on the west side & commands the tank & bridge, the other two command the R. Road. When our fortifications are completed, we will be able to cope with much more than an equal force unless they bring Artillery upon us.

We are all hard at work. Last night we lay in readiness to fight all night, & the entire forces were in line of battle from 4 o'clock till after day-light. Our company was stationed about 1 mile north of camp, & we were in the woods near the road all night, but no enemy came. Tonight all is quiet; rumor says the enemy has fled.[3]

The country about 2 miles west & South of this, I am informed, is very thickly settled. I have never had an opportunity of seeing it as yet, however. All around Camp it is quite romantic. Quite a number of the Officers were invited out to dinner to-day & talk very largely of the good things. I am not one of the fortunate ones, however. They tell me there are quite a number of Union families in the neighborhood.[4]

It has commenced to rain a little, but we are located so high & dry that I do not feel much uneasy[iness] but what we will be comfortable.

We organized a Regimental Church tonight & were pleased to receive 30 names. I think by Sunday it will reach 100. A very good feeling prevails, & the nightly meetings are well attended. There has been one conversion this week, a young man from Scott County. I do not recollect his name. We hope for a general revival soon. Pray for us.

The health of the Regt., with the exception of a number of cases of measles, is quite good. None of the latter cases have proven fatal. I rather think Lieut. Smith is getting them. He feels much like it to-night, but you need not mention it. As it is growing quite late, I will close with [a] kiss for yourself & baby & much love to all.

Your affect. Husband

J. F. Culver

---

1 On the 19th General Granger had telegraphed Colonel Smith to "hold yourself in readiness to march, if required, at a moment's notice. Meantime fortify strongly to resist a superior force, be vigilant. Keep pickets out to the east and southeast." Granger to Smith, Dec. 19, 1862, Regimental Papers, 129th Illinois, NA.

This alert had been triggered by a message from General Rosecrans warning, "John H. Morgan started today from his camp, below Lebanon, with between 5,000 and 6,000 cavalry . . . and a few small batteries, for the purpose of breaking up the railroad." Orders soon followed for the force at Mitchellville to reinforce the regiment at Buck Lodge. *O. R., Ser.* I, Vol. XX, pt. II, pp. 200, 202, 212.

2   The 79th Ohio had been posted at Buck Lodge previous to the arrival of the 129th Illinois. On Dec. 21 Colonel Smith had notified General Rosecrans that when his regiment reached Buck Lodge the previous evening he found the 79th Ohio, "with only about 200 men fit for duty, and no fortifications." To hold the area, he needed a section of artillery. *Ibid.*, p. 214.

3   On Christmas Eve, while J.F.C. and the soldiers of the 129th Illinois guarded the approaches to Buck Lodge, General Morgan and his raiders camped six miles south of Glasgow. As Glasgow is 50 miles northeast of Buck Lodge, this demonstrates that Morgan, as he drove toward the Louisville & Nashville Railroad on his Christmas Raid had hoodwinked Rosecrans and his subordinates. *O. R., Ser.* I, Vol. XX, pt. I, p. 154.

4   Private Dunham, on Dec. 23, had written his parents, "Thare is some good Union people heare. Thare is one good old lady that brings something in every day for the sick." *Through the South with a Union Soldier*, p. 50.

 41

Hd. Qrs., Co. A, 129th Ills. Vols. Inft.
Bucks Lodge, Tenn., Dec. 28th 1862

Dear Wife

I see but little prospect of this communication reaching you for some time, but as soon as opportunity offers, will ford. it. This is Sunday & a beautiful day, though for the past two days it has been raining hard & is yet quite damp.

My health is quite good, all thanks to a kind Providence. We are rather sorely afflicted. Otis Taylor is very low with scarcely a hope of recovery.[1] He has had the measles & was doing well, but the dampness has driven them in, & they have settled in his lungs. I wish it was possible to send word to his family, but all communication is cut off.[2] I hope to be able to tell of his recovery soon, but it is at present highly improbable. Lieut. Smith has the measles but is doing well, & if nothing happens will soon recover. Earl H. Kenyon is very low with typhoid fever & congestion of the brain;³ he may recover. He was married while our Company was at Kankakee & lived in Dwight. I am informed that J. Wood is getting better; he is back at Mitchellsville.

3 o clock P.M. Kenyon is better but Taylor worse. Smith is still doing well.

The Chaplain of the 79th Ohio preached for us to-day. How often I have thought of home. Quite a large pack of letters are awaiting the mail. We have no late news concerning the amt. of damage done to the Rail Road. The last we heard was that two miles of track & two bridges were destroyed. It will take at least a week to repair. We may have telegraph communication in a few days.⁴

We have a very pleasant place for camp, but are almost out of provisions. We have depended on the R. Road for supplies, & I presume will have to forage soon unless the Road is repaired.

We have had no papers for ten days, consequently no news. I expect S. Bennet will get home before New Year's Day. We are still most anxious to hear from home & know to what extent the Small Pox is raging. As I intend to write each day until the mail goes out, I will close for the evening.

Your affect. Husband

J. F. Culver

Dec. 30th 1862

Dear Wife

Amid the cares & business surrounding me, I did not write yesterday, but, as I shall have an opportunity of sending my letter by a gentleman going North to-morrow. Otis B. Taylor died this morning about three o'clock, & by intelligence from Bowling Green just recd. I learn that Uriah Springer of our Company died on Christmas.⁵ E. A. Kenyon is rather better but still bad. Lieut. Smith is getting well fast & is, I think, beyond danger.

Mrs. Blackburn & Mrs. Fitch are still here but are heartily tired of their visit. There is no knowing at present when they will be able to go home, while their accommodations are very poor.

Quite a number of letters have been received, but I have not been so fortunate. I hope, however, to receive one as a New Year's gift. I wrote to you & sent by Bennet. I understand he did not get from Bowling Green until this morning. My letter will not reach you in time to wish you a "Happy New Year," but I will hope that it may be so.

I almost dread to hear from Pontiac for fear some of you have been infected with the Small-Pox, yet I pray God for better things. I have never received the promised letter from Johny, but hope he is entirely well.

We have no news of Maples yet. I was hoping he would arrive before New Year's so that I might have my budget of letters. I am wholly at a loss what news to write without any letter to answer. The last is dated Dec. 8th. I shall commence to read the old ones over soon.

I shall try & write to Mr. Taylor to-night and scarcely know how to tell them of his death.[6] I know they will be almost disconsolate. Otis was among our best boys, exemplary in conduct & died in a hope full of immortality beyond the grave. His was truly the Christian's death; he was much beloved by all. And now Dear Wife, I most earnestly pray that God continue to be with you, protect & preserve you from harm & disease. Give my love to all, &, if Maples has not yet started, send me letters by mail.

With much love, I remain, as ever

Your affect. Husband

Kiss baby for me.                                            J. F. Culver

---

1   Otis Taylor, a 22-year-old Pontiac Township farmer, was mustered into service Sept. 8, 1862, as a private in Company A, 129th Illinois Infantry. Private Taylor died of measles on Dec. 30, 1862, in the regimental hospital at Buck Lodge, Tenn. Compiled Service Records of Union soldiers, NA.

2   General Morgan and his horse-soldiers between Dec. 26 and 29 wreaked havoc on the Louisville & Nashville Railroad. A number of weeks would pass before there would again be through traffic between Louisville and Nashville.

3   Earl H. Kenyon, a 22-year-old surveyor, was mustered into service on Sept. 8, 1862, as a sergeant in Company A, 129th Illinois Infantry. Sergeant Kenyon died of pneumonia on Jan. 6, 1863, in the regimental hospital at Fountain Head, Tenn. *Ibid.*

4   Morgan's Confederates had destroyed four trestles— the two long Muldraugh's Hill structures and the ones spanning Bacon and Nolin Creeks. Several miles of track had been torn up at Upton and the rails warped and twisted. The telegraph also had been cut. *O. R.,* Ser. I, Vol. XX, pt. I, pp. 154-156.

5   Uriah Springer, a 27-year-old farmer, was mustered into service Sept. 8, 1862, as a private in Company A, 129th Illinois Infantry. Private Springer died on Christmas 1862 of

measles in Hospital No. 5 at Bowling Green, Ky. Compiled Service Records of Union Soldiers, NA.

6   The deceased's parents were George and Uretta Taylor. In addition to Otis, they had two other sons—John and George. The father was a 45-year-old Pontiac Township farmer. Eighth Census, Livingston county, State of Illinois, NA.

 42

Head Quarters, Co. A, 129th Ills. Vols. Infty.
Bucks Lodge, Tenn. Dec. 31st 1862

My Dear Wife

In a very short time the old year will have passed into eternity & the "New Year" ushered in. Let me say "Happy New Year," & God grant that it may be a happy one to you.

The night thus far has been beautiful, clear and calm; the moon is shining brightly & the Heavens are dotted with Stars. I feel to-night that had I the assurance that you were well and happy, nothing would be wanting to make me supremely happy. I feel at Peace with the whole world.

I have been unusually busy for the past few days making out Muster & pay rolls. To-day we were mustered for pay, & this evening I finished my monthly reports so that I had but little to trouble my mind.[1]

The weather is cool, & we built a large log fire in front of the Quarters where we have been singing & talking for some time. I came into the tent to get something to eat & found some pickeled beef's tongue & some light Bread just out of the oven with some good Tennessee butter. The bread Capt. Hoskins got baked by a young lady not far from Camp, & the same family promised to let me have some buttermilk & Yeast to-morrow morning. So you see we are trying to live.

We have engaged a new cook, Henry Fisher, who used to live at Mrs. Camp's at Odell.[2] Sid [Arnold] will go home as soon as we can raise money to send him. He has got tired &, I think, homesick.

Lieut. Smith is almost well but will not be permitted to go out for several days yet. The measles are almost dried up. We buried Otis

Taylor this morning, & I wrote to his Father last night. Kenyon is getting worse & will not probably recover. He is a noble fellow, & I feel exceedingly sorry to lose him.

By the Nashville papers of to-day, we learn that some 18 miles of the Rail Road has been torn up, and it will take several weeks to repair it.[3] In the meantime we shall get but little mail, I presume.

The boys are having considerable fun around the Quarters trying to sell each other. I expect all will have a good time to-morrow if we do not get orders to move. I believe nothing has been heard from Pontiac for ten days or two weeks. There are several citizens here from Scott County, Ills. who intended to go home to-day, but are not going till tomorrow.

I hope S. Bennett has got home by this time so that you may have an opportunity of hearing from me. It is now almost midnight, the close of the old year. What the new year has in store for us as individuals, what joys & fears, trials & encouragement remains to us undeveloped. Let us try & prepare our hearts by calling upon God for assistance. We have the blessed assurance that a sufficiency of grace will be supplied.

God has been pleased to bless us abundantly. As far as I know, neither disease or excessive troubles have taken hold upon us. The first half of it [the year] has been replete with pleasure, &, though during the last few months we have had some trials, yet God has abundantly blessed. Let us live then in the hope of usefulness in the future that whenever or wherever our Master may call our work may be done and well done.

I shall live in the hope of hearing from you soon. I half expected E. R. Maples might get here by to-day. Communication is still open by water to Bowling Green, Ky., & from there by Rail Road through this place to Nashville, Tenn., though no mails are sent by that route.[4] I understand it takes some five days to go by water.

We learn but little of the movement of the Army here. Tomorrow is the commencement of a new era in the History of the War unless Lincoln has modified his proclamation.[5] I tremble for the results. We have thousands of Tennessee & Kentucky troops in this branch of the service, & should they refuse to fight we might be overwhelmed with superior numbers. I confess that to honestly express myself, I do not like the idea of giving over the reconstruction of the government upon the constitutional basis, yet under my oath I shall fight under any approved policy. I have seen an instance of this new policy to me trying & disgusting, the way is or will be open for large abuses of power. Let us hope God will be with us & control the affairs of the Nation. I should like just now to read the Northern sentiment.[6]

Give my love to all the family & remember me kindly to all our friends. Hoping that the richest of Heaven's blessings may rest upon you, for which I shall ever pray, I subscribe myself as ever.

Your affect. Husband

J. F. Culver

---

1   Colonel Smith, at 2 P.M. on the 31st, had reviewed and inspected the regiment, when it was mustered for pay. Smith to Case, Dec. 31, 1861, Regimental Papers, 129th Illinois, NA.

2   Mary Camp was the wife of Edgar Camp, a 38-year-old Odell farmer. In 1860 the Camps were living with their three children. It has been impossible to further identify Henry Fisher, other than that he had worked on the Camp's farm. Eighth Census, Livingston County, State of Illinois, NA.

3   This refers to damage done the Louisville & Nashville Railroad by Morgan's cavalry.

4   With the Louisville & Nashville Railroad out of operation between Bacon Creek and the Muldraugh's Hill, lightdraft steamboats were pressed into service and ascended the Green and Barren Rivers to Bowling Green. There they were unloaded and supplies destined for Rosecrans' army loaded on railroad cars. *O. R.,* Ser. I, Vol. XX, pt. II, pp. 275, 291, 296.

5   The Confederate states having ignored his preliminary proclamation of Sept. 22, 1862, President Lincoln on January 1, 1863, issued his Emancipation Proclamation, declaring that "all persons held as slaves" within certain designated "states, and parts of states, are henceforward" free.

6   J.F.C., as a constitutional lawyer and Democrat, questioned President Lincoln's use of his war powers to effect such a sweeping economic and social change. Like most people from the "Old Northwest," Culver was fighting for preservation of the Union, and if slavery was to be abolished it should be done by a constitutional amendment, not an executive proclamation. The Northern press was divided in its views. Pro-administration editors supported the president, while those in the opposite camp agreed with the New York *Herald,* "While the Proclamation leaves slavery untouched where his decree can be enforced, he emancipates slaves where his decree cannot be enforced. Friends of human rights will be at a loss to understand this discrimination." Sandburg, *Abraham Lincoln, The Prairie Years and the War Years,* pp. 345-346.

 43

Mitchellsville, Tenn., January 4th 1863

My Dear Wife

In four more days one month will have elapsed since the date of your last letter. We have no communication with the North yet. I notice by late papers from Nashville that this R. Road has refused to carry the mail, &, if the mail from the distributing office at Cairo has been sent by water as I presume it has, we have no prospect of mail for some time to come.[1] I did not anticipate so long a delay & especially at a time when I should feel unusually anxious to hear from you.

I sent a couple of letters by persons going North to be mailed. I hope they have reached you. I am happy to say I enjoy excellent health. If I could only know that you were all well, I should be fully satisfied. But it is ordered otherwise, & without murmering it is our duty to submit.

We were ordered back to this place on Friday, Jan 2nd, & are in good comfortable Quarters. There is none but our Company.[2] The men are in a large Shed and have beds & straw. We [the officers] have a Harness shop which with our stove makes it very comfortable. It is the best accommodation we have had since we left home.

Lieut. Smith has wholly recovered from the measles & is looking well. We are all doing quite well. I wrote to Mr. Taylor concerning the death of his son the same time I wrote to you. I also wrote quite a lengthy letter to you on New Year's Eve, all of which I hope you have received. I sent them by some gentlemen from Scott County. I cannot account for Maples' delay unless he has taken the Small-Pox. Earl Kenyon is getting better slowly, & I hope with care will soon recover.

After writing to you on New Year's Eve, I sat down & read all your letters recd. since I left home. They gave me much pleasure, so many evidences of your love and affection cheer my heart. I am not so sure but that this Separation will give us an opportunity of learning much of each other, which amid prosperity we might never have learned. I feel that I never appreciated your worth so fully as now, & I never realized how very dear you were to me as now, amid fears of the dangers that surround you.[3] Oh, if I only knew all, anything would be preferable to this suspense. Yet I shall hope for the best. "God rules all things well." He will not try us above what we are able to bear. We are not alone; alas! very many others suffer with us, some bereft of all in this world most dear. I feel thankful for the hope of good tidings, when so many live on without any hope of meeting their loved ones in this life.

The battle is still raging at Murfreesboro. The News are meagre but sufficient to inform us that thousands of our brave men are cold in death & many thousands more are lying on the battle field wounded & uncared for. We cannot determine the result yet, but it looks rather favorable. Our men are driving the rebels slowly yet surely before them.[4] It is the most hotly contested battle ever fought on the Continent, & more lives lost than ever was dreamed of in one battle. This is the Sixth day. These are about all the reports that we have received.[5]

Just now we received news from Cave City. Col. Duke is killed & Morgan badly wounded & his troops dispersed.[6] This is good news for us, as we have no other force to fear at this point. I hope we will be ordered to move forward.

I shall try & send my letter by some one going North, if the train will stop long enough. I shall not close my letter until to-morrow. As I am on duty all night, I may write more before morning, & I wish to devote part of the night if possible to reading. I got a bible of Henry Fisher, &, as I but seldom have one, I wish to improve the opportunity. Hoping that God will bless & keep you & our babe from harm & bestow the riches of his grace upon us, I bid you

Good Night

Your Husband in affection & love

J. F. Culver

---

1  With no traffic over the railroad north of Munfordville, mail was loaded on steamboats at Cairo, Illinois, and sent up the Ohio, Green, and Barren Rivers to Bowling Green. From Bowling Green, it came south to Mitchellville and Nashville by rail.

2  Morgan and his raiders, having accomplished their mission, were en route back to their base in Middle Tennessee, and Colonel Smith had redeployed his command. Captain Hoskins was ordered on the 2d to take post at Mitchellville with Company A. His duties were to guard the railroad and the countryside around Mitchellville. Supplies, except forage which was to be requisitioned from disloyal citizens, were to be drawn from Fountain Head, where Colonel Smith had established regimental headquarters. Smith to Hoskins, Jan. 2 & 3, 1863, Regimental Papers, 129th Illinois, NA.

3  This refers to the smallpox epidemic at Pontiac.

4  General Rosecrans had advanced from Nashville on Dec. 26, 1862, with eight divisions of his Army of the Cumberland. General Bragg had massed his Army of Tennessee and had taken position three miles northwest of Murfreesboro, covering the bridges across Stones River. On the 30th there had been heavy skirmishing, as the bluecoats drove in Confederate outposts. At daybreak, on the 31st, Bragg attacked and routed the Union right. There was savage fighting, as Rosecrans' troops retired through the cedars and re-formed covering the Nashville Pike. Here they held. On New Year's Day, the armies regrouped, and on the 2d Bragg assailed Rosecrans' left and was repulsed with terrible casualties.

On the night of the 3d, Bragg's Army of Tennessee abandoned its position in front of Murfreesboro and retired about 30 miles to Tullahoma and Shelbyville. The Federals occupied Murfreesboro but were too exhausted to press the pursuit.

5  Union casualties at Stones River (Murfreesboro) were 1,730 killed, 7,802 wounded, and 3,717 captured or missing. General Bragg listed Confederate losses at 1,236 killed, 7,766 wounded, and 868 missing. Stones River, for the numbers engaged, was the bloodiest battle between white armies yet fought on the North American continent. O.R., Ser. I, Vol. XX, pt. I, pp. 215, 681.

6  There was no truth to the report that Col. Basil Duke had been killed, General Morgan wounded, and Morgan's division dispersed. On New Year's Day, Morgan had started his

withdrawal from Kentucky by way of Columbia and Burkesville, and on the 5th he reached Smithville, Tenn., within the Confederate lines. Morgan's Christmas Raid was one of the Civil War's most successful cavalry operations. *Ibid.*, pp. 157-158.

 44

Mitchellsville, Tenn., January 6th 1863

My Dear Wife

I sent a letter yesterday morning by a gentleman on the train going north, with the request to mail it at Louisville, &, as opportunity may offer to send again soon, I sit me down to write to-night. I returned from Fountain Head just before night, where I had been to sit upon the "Board of Survey."[1]

I found the Regiment in good Spirits over the late glorious news from Murfreesboro and generally doing well. The probabilities are that we will be left here to guard the R. Road, while others more fortunate will share the glories of the success in southern Tennessee.[2] Perhaps it is all for the best, but this is rather dry work.

The news are almost too good to believe & not sufficiently confirmed, but we have evidently achieved a glorious victory. I know you have a much fuller account of the battles in the Northern Papers than we can possibly get here, & we are waiting anxiously to get some Northern papers.

We have neither mail or tidings from the North, nothing of home or friends. How eagerly all look for the arrival of the trains, & yet they pass us day after day without bringing any news. Everything is contraband of war, nothing can be taken off the wires & nothing allowed to be published. Yet we are all well, for which all thanks to a kind Providence.

Much has been said about the war closing after this battle, but I anticipate many more before the consumation of that happy event while I hope the crisis will soon be passed.

We have rumors of a battle at Vicksburg[3] & also in Arkansas[4] but nothing reliable. No news from the Potomac since the 28th December.[5]

I saw McCartney to-day, he was quite well. Every person was enquiring the news from home, &, though I have been absent from the Regt. but two days, very many hoped that some tidings from home might have reached me. As I can form no idea when I shall hear or receive any letters, I shall look daily.

I want you to write all the same as if you were sure I received them, so that when they do arrive I shall have a full history of all that has transpired. I feel more confident to-night that you are all well than I have since communication was cut off. So much for the presentiment, I hope it may be true. Smith & Hoskins are both quite well. The time passes rather slowly on our hands here. I wish I could get hold of something good to read, but it is at present impossible. Perhaps we may be called into more active service soon.

I took breakfast with Lieuts. Blackburn & Fitch & their wives this morning. The ladies seem quite anxious to get home.

We have very comfortable accommodations at present. Let me urge you not to neglect to write. Give my love to all the family. What has become of Bro. Johny? Is he still at home? Tell me all the news as they transpire.

May the blessings of Heaven rest upon you, my Dear Wife, & upon our babe. May our Father keep you safe from danger & bestow upon you the riches of his grace.

Farewell,

Your Affect. Husband

J. F. Culver

---

1  Regimental headquarters, along with most of the 129th Illinois Infantry, was at Fountain Head, on the railroad six miles southeast of Mitchellville.

2  Although the Federals had gained a victory at Stones River (Murfreesboro), they had suffered such frightful losses that Rosecrans failed to capitalize on the Confederate withdrawal. Instead of pushing after Bragg's retreating columns, Rosecrans ordered the Army of the Cumberland into winter quarters in and around Murfreesboro.

3  Maj. Gen. William T. Sherman had left Memphis on Dec. 20, 1862, with a powerful amphibious force. Descending the Mississippi, the convoy turned into the Yazoo River, and on the 26th Sherman's 32,000 men went ashore, seven miles north of Vicksburg. The Federals spent two days feeling their way toward the Confederate rifle pits covering Chickasaw Bayou. On Dec. 29 Sherman assaulted the Rebel defenses and was repulsed with heavy losses. He then evacuated his army and returned to the Mississippi.

4  At Prairie Grove, in northwest Arkansas, on Dec. 7, 1862, a Union army led by Maj. Gen. James G. Blunt defeated Maj. Gen. Thomas C. Hindman's Confederates. Hindman's troops, hounded by Union cavalry, had retreated across the Boston Mountains to Fort Smith.

5  General Lee's Army of Northern Virginia on Dec. 13, 1862, at Fredericksburg, Va., had repulsed with grievous losses the poorly coordinated assaults of Maj. Gen. Ambrose E. Burnside's Army of the Potomac. Burnside had withdrawn his army to the north side of the Rappahannock and a stalemate ensued. The terrible casualties suffered by Union armies at Stones River, Fredericksburg, Chickasaw Bayou, and Prairie Grove cast a pall of gloom across the North.

 45

Mitchellsville, Tenn., Jan. 8th 1862

My dear Wife

The first mail from the North reached us yesterday evening but brought no news from Pontiac. I recd. a letter from Cousin Lucy Dunmire of Burbank, Ohio, being the extent of my mail matter.[1] I hope, however, by to-day's mail to hear from you.

I am quite well, & we are doing well. I sent a letter yesterday by a gentleman going to Louisville to be mailed, & hope you will receive all I have written in due time.

Hoping that God has blessed you all with health and happiness, & with much love to all, I subscribe myself in haste. Dear Mary, as ever,

Your Affect. Husband

J. F. Culver

---

1  Cousin Lucy Dunmire was a niece of Martha Dunmire Culver, J.F.C.'s mother.

 46

Mitchellsville, Tenn., Jany. 10th 1862[3]

My dear Wife

An opportunity offers to get a letter mailed at Louisville, & with the hope of letting you hear from me I eagerly embrace it.

Unable to bear the suspense any longer, I telegraphed yesterday from Fountain Head & this morning am awaiting your reply. Lieut. Smith remains there to bring up your answer to-day.

My health is as good as ever; in fact, I do not know that I ever enjoyed better health. We are still at Mitchellsville with excellent accommodations. E. H. Kenyon & Josiah Wood were buried yesterday. A. S. Bradford & John B. Lucas, all of our company, died in Bowling Green a few days ago.[1]

Hoping soon to hear from you, I remain, in haste,

Your affect. Husband

J. F. Culver

---

1  Andrew J. Bradford, a 28-year-old Pontiac merchant, was mustered into service Sept. 8, 1862, as 1st sergeant of Company A, 129th Illinois Infantry. He died of chronic diarrhea on Jan. 2, 1863, in Hospital No. 4 at Bowling Green, Ky. John B. Lucas, a 20-year-old farmer, was mustered into service Sept. 8, 1862, as a private in Company A, 129th Illinois Infantry. Private Lucas died Jan. 2, 1862, of consumption in Hospital No. 4 at Bowling Green, Ky. Compiled Service Records of Union Soldiers, NA.

 47

Mitchellsville, Tenn., January 12th 1863

My dear Wife

I was made most happy yesterday and to-day by the reception of all your letters, dating from the 10th to the 26th of Dec. I thank God that you have been spared. On Friday last, unable to bear suspense longer from the rumors in camp, I telegraphed to you asking you to answer for yourself & Mrs. Smith. I have as yet received no reply & presume the dispatch never reached you. I am informed this evening that Park Loomis starts for Pontiac to-morrow morning & will carry letters through.[1] I have been very busy until a late hour this evening, &, as I have one or two business letters to write yet, I shall be unable to write a full answer to all your letters.

I am happy to inform you that I am well & perhaps never enjoyed better health in my life than at present. Lieut. Smith has been ailing since yesterday with the diarrhea, but we hope he will be better to-morrow. In former letters I have told you of all who have died & seriously ill. As a general thing, we are improving in health. Capt. Hoskins is well, but in the large amt. of mail recd. the last two days, recd. no tidings from home. He feels disappointed, I know, for he has written very often.[2] I received yours of the 26th this evening with stamps & $5 enclosed.[3]

You only mention in your letters $2 sent. If you can make yourself comfortable without it, I am most happy to acknowledge its receipt, but you must not rob yourself for me. I can get a living without money, while it affords many comforts. You may be needy before I can assist you. We do not know when to look for pay & must make all our calculations accordingly.

The boots are high priced & I hope good. I do need them very much & almost wish I had not sent, as I could have bought a pair not so cheap but might have used them for some time. They will come good, however, in the muddy spring.[4]

We have had large accounts of the Small-Pox in Pontiac, and I hope it may soon subside. Fleming in his letter of Dec. 25th writes quite encouragingly, & I hope it may be so. The most important & sure preventative is dieting. Use as little salt as possible & no strong meats, could salt be wholly extracted from the system, there would be no marks left. I have had considerable experience & with equal chances would as soon risk the Small-Pox as the measles. There is no danger if care is taken. I have had varioloid several years ago & with the above precaution suffered but a short time.[5] The same teas &c. that drive out measles will apply with the same effect in Small-Pox. But do not expose yourself. Keep out of Town if possible, & may God preserve you & baby from its deleterious effects.

I recd. a letter from Bros. Johny and Leander.[6] I should like to answer both to-night but shall not be able. I will do by mail very soon. I presume from the tenor of Bro. Johny's letter he has joined the Battery ere this. I shall feel grateful for the oysters when they arrive.

We had the honor of a visit today from Col. Smith & wife, Adgt. Plattenburg, Dr. Johns, Capt. Martin, & Lieut. Gilchrist, & had a very pleasant time.[7] We were fortunate enough this morning to trade an old axe we had for some eggs, or we would have had a very slim dinner.

You inquire if Bro. Gaff is discharged; he is not. His health is very good, & I understand has been promoted to sergeant. Bro. Lee has not been discharged; I wish he was.[8] I fear he will never be quite well. His back has failed him, & he looks quite bad; yet he has great courage & will not complain.

I am not prepared to-night & have not the time to answer your fair proposition with regard to Methodism, but, as you have opened up the way, I will consider myself invited to give my opinion. To say that you need my forgiveness for any act or remark is scarcely fair. I have no recollection of any "unkind words" & certainly never felt that you were in any way erring by clinging to the denomination of your choice. I am not a respector of denominations, &, while I feel more at home in a Methodist Church, God forbid that I should [word omitted] souls for personal prejudice. To say that I should be happy to have you think & feel as I do would not be sufficiently expressed, & I dare not flatter myself that it is wholly so. I would not have you for a moment espouse a doctrine unless you fully endorsed it, but I shall write at length of this shortly. May God abundantly bless and help you in investigating this matter.[9]

Your letters of 12th gave me much pleasure. I feared that in a careful retrospect of the past, you might long for those pleasant hours of earlier years. If you have been this happy I can scarcely fear aught for the future, for certainly the past year has been rather inauspicious. May God grant us a glorious future.

I shall feel more confident of the prosperity of the S. School with its present corps of officers, without a desire to applaud & do feel unbounded faith in your success if enlisted in the cause. May God help & bless all your efforts. And now, Dear Wife, I have written at far greater length than I intended, but your letters will afford opportunity for several letters. You can use your own judgment about renting the house. I am not at liberty to say anything about "Fisher of Reeds Company." Please not talk of it to any one.

Give my love to all. Kiss baby for me. I am glad he is so much comfort to me [you?]. Did Mother [Murphy] ever receive my answer to her letter? Remember me kindly to all our friends. I hope you will write each day as you have done. It gives me much pleasure, and now committing all I love most to the kind care of our Heavenly Father, invoking his blessings to rest upon you, I remain as ever,

Your affect. Husband

J. F. Culver

P.S. Mrs. Blackburn has her babe here. Her & Mrs. Fitch both long for an opportunity to get home. They are well.

J.F.C.

1   Park Loomis was a 26-year-old Reading clerk and had been employed by the regimental sutler Gagan as his clerk. On Jan. 13, 1863, Loomis was convicted of vending spiritous liquors to the men of the 129th Illinois and was expelled from camp. Loomis, on Feb. 11, formally apologized to Colonel Smith for his misconduct, and the colonel revoked the expulsion order and permitted him to return to and remain in camp, subject to all military rules and regulations. SO 16, Jan. 16, 1863, Regimental Papers, 129th Illinois, NA.

2   Earlier Mrs. Hoskins had complained to Mary Culver that her husband wrote infrequently.

3   Mary Culver's letter of Dec. 26 is missing from the Culver Collection. On the 27th she wrote, "In my letter of yesterday, I enclosed one dollar's worth of Postage stamps and a five dollar bill." Mary Culver to J.F.C., Dec. 27, 1862, Culver Collection.

4   As the local bootmaker had declared that he could not make the boots in less than two weeks, Mary Culver had ordered them from Chicago. Mary Culver to J.F.C., Dec. 3, 1862, Culver Collection.

5   Varioloid is a mild form of small pox. Among Civil War soldiers, especially those from rural areas, measles had a high mortality rate.

6   Johnny Murphy, a sergeant in Company M, 1st Illinois Light Artillery, was Mrs. Culver's brother, while Leander Utley was married to her sister Margaret.

7   Henry C. Johns, a 43-year-old physician, was commissioned surgeon of the 129th Illinois on Nov. 18, 1862, and ordered to report to the regiment. Having been found incompetent by a medical board on Dec. 18, 1863, Surgeon Johns resigned his commission on Jan. 19, 1864. George W. Gilchrist, a 37-year-old Dwight farmer, was mustered into service on Sept. 8, 1862, as 1st lieutenant of Company B, 129th Illinois Infantry. On April 29, 1864, Gilchrist was detailed to the Pioneer Brigade, and on Aug. 3, 1864, he was placed in charge of the Third Division Pioneers, XX Army Corps. Lieutenant Gilchrist, on April 24, 1865, was detailed as an aide-de-camp at headquarters, 1st Brigade, Third Division. He was mustered out on June 8, 1865, at Washington, D.C. George W. Martin, a 35-year-old Winchester farmer, was mustered into service Sept. 8, 1862, as captain of Company H, 129th Illinois Infantry. Captain Martin resigned Sept. 13, 1864, because of disabilities brought on by a severe attack of typhoid fever. Compiled Service Records of Union Soldiers, NA.

8   John S. Lee, a 36-year-old blacksmith, was mustered into service Sept. 8, 1862, as a private in Company G, 129th Illinois Infantry. Private Lee was severely wounded in the shoulder at the battle of Peachtree Creek, July 20, 1864, and on his recovery, on Jan. 1, 1865, he was assigned to duty as a blacksmith in the ambulance corps, Third Division, XX Corps. He was mustered out at Washington, D.C., June 8, 1865. *Ibid.*

9   Mary Culver had been raised a Presbyterian. The letter in which she raised the question regarding Methodism has been lost.

Mitchellsville, Tenn., Jan. 14th 63

Dear Wife

All well this morning. Loomis goes North by 10 o'clock train. It is raining but quite warm. I have not had opportunity to write more since my last.

Was at the Regt. yesterday & found all well. Lieut. Smith is better.

In haste,

Your affect. Husband

J. F. Culver

 49

Monday Morning, 19th Jan./63

Dear Mary

As an opportunity may possibly offer to-day to send letters North, I haste to add some matters of business. There are some laths standing in the corner of our hen house. Please get some one to put them in the wood shed, else they will all be destroyed. See that all the doors are securely fastened of the house, &, if Foote did not put in those window glass, close up the place so that the snow & rain will not get in or it will destroy all the ceilings & paper. I have some fear of the kitchen sinking when the frost comes out of the ground. The foundation is very insecure. If some of our friends will give it a little attention in time, that part of the building can be saved. I had hoped to be able to have made it secure before this.[1]

Ask Bro. Utley to get you the amount of tax due on the NW 1/4 of Block 74, Original town of Pontiac, also the amount of my personal tax now due.[2] Also in a memorandum book of mine marked "address of correspondents," you will find a list of lands purchased by me and assigned to James Longdon, J. H. Case, & Charles Zug.[3] I want a list of those tracts assigned to Charles Zug with the amount of tax due on them. They are all in town 30, Range 5, I think.

Tell me who the Town collector for the Town of Pontiac is, &, if the legislature postpones the time for the payment of taxes, I wish to know it immediately.[4] Please see that all the gates around our lot are securely fastened & the fence in a good condition, a very little opening may cause us serious damage. You never gave me any account of our sweet potato crop. You know it was an experiment, & I should like to hear the result.[5]

Harrington wrote to me about some matters of business with Workman Hickman;[6] I referred him to my letters in your possession. It occurs to me that I possibly copied my answers to Workman Hickman in my copying press. Please look in that, & if it throws any light on the matter, show it to him. I leave him to explain its nature. It is unaccountable to me. I was sure it was all settled & hardly think I am mistaken, yet I done a large amount of that business & there is a possibility of a mistake.

Look among all my papers & give him every information you can. I do not wish you to run the risk of contracting disease to accomplish it. He can wait until danger is over. It also occurs to me that the letter acknowledging the receipt of the certificates may be in the drawer containing my receipts among them. Please look there also. I am better today. The train is coming,

Good Bye

J. F. Culver

---

1   On Jan. 31 Mary Culver informed her husband that "every thing is right over at the house." Her brother Sammy had attended to the laths and reported the kitchen secure, while Mr. Foote had put in the window glass before he moved to Wisconsin. Mary Culver to J.F.C., Jan. 31, 1863, Culver Collection.

2   The tax due on the NW 1/4 of Block 74 was $7.18, and Culver's personal tax for 1862 was $1.66. *Ibid.*

3   It has been impossible to further identify James Longdon and Charles Zug. For further identification of J. H. Case, see letter of July 2, 1863.

4   Mary Culver wrote her husband on Feb. 1, 1863, that James G. Albe was the Pontiac tax collector, and the legislature had not changed the date for payment of taxes. Mary Culver to J.F.C., Feb. 1, 1863, Culver Collection.

5   The sweet potato crop had not thrived, most of the hills producing not more "than three or four potatoes." Mary Culver to J.F.C., Jan. 31, 1863, Culver Collection.

6   It has been impossible to further identify Harrington and Workman Hickman. Mary Culver wrote her husband on Feb. 1, "I called on Harrington this p.m. but could give me no help, on the business. I have looked through your papers and can find but one letter from Hickman and that casts no light on the subject." Mary Culver to J.F.C., Feb. 1, 1863, Culver Collection.

Cumberland Gap near Gallatin, Tenn.
June 2nd 1863

Dear Mary

I requested Mrs. King to write to you & tell you to come to Gallatin. I
will be in to-morrow or next day. There is but poor chance for you to
stay out here, yet I know you would like to see the place. You can stay
in Gallatin as long as you wish, &, as the Dr. will be out every few
days, he will bring you out.

Hoping both you & Frankie are quite well, & I will see you soon, I
remain as ever.

Your Affect. Husband

J. F. Culver

In haste.

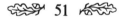 

## 51

Head Qurs., Co. "A", 129th Ills. Vol. Infty.
Gallatin, Tenn., June 22nd 1863

Dear Mary

I delayed writing all day Saturday [the 20th] thinking that on Sunday I
would write you a long letter, but just as I was preparing to go to church

I received orders to go on a Scout. I was in the saddle all day & thus had no opportunity to write. This morning I am detailed as Judge Advocate on a Board of Commission which meets at 9 o'clock.[1] My health is good. Your shawl & a letter from Maggie [Utley] arrived on Thursday, so I presume I heard the news of the birth of the great heir before you did.[2] They say he looks like Frankie, so he must be a wonderful *boy*. You will please give my hearty congratulations & a kiss to Maggie. (I wonder if she gets a new dress.)

I will send your shawl this morning by Mr. J. F. Earnhart.[3] He stops at Chenoa but will send it along immediately.[4]

I gave Mrs. King part of the cake sent by Mr. Byrne.[5] I have not seen the girls since you left, but the whole family are well.

[General] Morgan has been near Gallatin with a large force for a few days.[6] It is hard to tell whether he will attack the Town or not. He is anxious to save his friends in it & knows we will burn it up.

We are all enjoying good health. I feel somewhat lonely but you know that is scarcely admissable in a Soldier's life, so I am compelled to overcome it. I wished to write to the Liv[ingston] Co. S. S. Union yesterday, but failed the same as I did in writing to you. I thought of several matters of business on Saturday but cannot call them to mind this morning.

The weather is beautiful & not so warm as it was last week. We hear every day that we will march soon but know nothing definite. I have no word from Bro. Johnie yet.[7] I am waiting anxiously to hear from you.

Mrs. Smith has been sick ever since you left & talks of going home.[8] Lou [Allen] is well & talks also of going home.[9] Mrs. Folks has gone.[10] There is considerable danger, & I feel very much more like fighting since Frankie & you are out of harm's way. I can shoot up Town if necessary, you don't know how easy.

I had an opportunity to go to Louisville on duty the next day after you left, so if you had been one day later I should have gone with you. But I must close.

I heard of the body of Luther Vandoren.[11] It floated down the river on Thursday last, but there being no boats the citizens would not venture in. We may possibly recover it at an Island some ten miles below where we spent yesterday.

The mail has gone, & I must go to the Depot. Give my love to all, remember me to the S. S. I will write soon again. Write to

Your affect. Husband

J. F. Culver

1   The "Board of Commission" referred to was the one to which J.F.C. had been appointed on Dec. 18, 1862. It was charged with examining and auditing claims of loyal citizens against the United States. Regimental Papers, 129th Illinois, NA.

2   A second child, their first son, had been born to Leander and Margaret Utley. Culver, "Robert Murphy and Some of His Descendants," p. 99.

3   James F. Earnhart, a 29-year-old gunsmith, had been mustered into service on Sept. 8, 1862, as a private in Company E, 129th Illinois. He was detailed as regimental gunsmith and called Fairbury his home. Compiled Service Records of Union Soldiers, NA.

4   Chenoa is in Livingston County, about 10 miles southwest of Pontiac.

5   Mrs. Mary King was the 35-year-old wife of Charles B. King, the Gallatin undertaker, from whom Mary Culver had rented a room during her four-month visit. It has been impossible to further identify Mr. Byrne.

6   Brig. Gen. John H. Morgan with 3,000 to 4,000 horse-soldiers was camped near Alexandria, reportedly getting ready for a dash on Carthage or to raid into Kentucky. Alexandria was 35 miles southeast of Gallatin. O. R., Ser. I, Vol. XXIII, pt. II, pp. 440-441.

7   Brother John Murphy, a quartermaster sergeant in Company M, 1st Illinois Light Artillery, was stationed at Triune, Tenn., 20 miles southeast of Nashville.

8   Mrs. Margaret Smith was the 27-year-old wife of Lt. John W. Smith of Company A. She had traveled from Pontiac in February for a visit with her husband, which had been prolonged by illness.

9   Lou Allen of Newton was the wife of Pvt. Joseph Allen of Company A. Eighth Census, Livingston County, State of Illinois, NA.

10   Mrs. Elmira Folks of Pontiac was the 19-year-old wife of Sgt. Richard D. Folks of Company G. *Ibid.*

11   Pvt. Luther Vandoren had drowned in the Cumberland River, near Gallatin, on June 10. Compiled Service Records of Union Soldiers, NA.

 52

Head Quarters, Co. "A", 129th Ills. Vol.
Gallatin, Tenn., June 27th 1863.

My dear Wife

I recd. your letter of Monday last night.[1] I hope you will give yourself no uneasiness about your trunks. I think they will get through all safe.[2] I telegraphed to Louisville & Jeffersonville last evening, &, if they are not found there, I will telegraph to Indianapolis & Chicago to-day.[3] I will order them forward[ed] by Express when they are found.

I am glad you have got through safe & hope you may both soon be rested & well. I did not think you would get through your visit so soon, but you will take much pleasure I hope in your trip East.[4]

It has been raining very hard for the past 4 or 5 days, & the ground is very wet. I was detailed to go Scouting again last night but fortunately was relieved. Capt. Hoskins was quite sick the past two days but is much better today.

I have had no letters since you left except yours. The Post master is about to leave with the mail so I must close. We are all well. Give my love to all. Tell Maggie I think *Frank Culver* a very good name for her boy.[5] With many kind remembrances for all our friends & the prayer that God may abundantly bless you, I am, as ever,

Your affect. Husband

J. F. Culver

---

1   Mary Culver's letter of June 22, along with others written between June 22 and Aug. 6, 1863, are missing from the Culver Collection.

2   On her return from Gallatin to Pontiac, Mary Culver's trunks had gone astray.

3   As the trunks traveled separately, J.F.C. correctly deduced that they had been misdirected at one of the transfer points. Louisville was the terminus of the Louisville & Nashville Railroad, while Jeffersonville, Indianapolis, and Chicago were other transfer points on the route by which Mary Culver had returned to Pontiac.

4   Mary Culver planned a trip after a brief rest to New York and Pennsylvania to visit friends and relatives.

5   The Utleys named the baby Albert Allen. Culver, "Robert Murphy and Some of His Descendants," p. 99.

## 53

Head Quarters, Co. "A", 129th Ills.
Gallatin, Tenn., June 27th 1863

Dear Mary

I have been on duty to-day & am to-night. I see by the papers this evening that Carlisle is in possession of the Rebels,[1] & I greatly fear the shock will be too great for Father to bear.[2] I feel very anxious to hear from home which at present is impossible.

The invasion need not interfere with your visit to New York.[3] &, as soon as the way is open, you can go from there to Carlisle if you can make up your mind to go there at all. Do not let the loss of your trunks interfere with your arrangements if they should not be found in time, as I presume you can easily replenish your wardrobe in Pontiac. I telegraphed to Louisville & received information that the trunks were not in the Depot there. I have also written to Jeffersonville & will write to Indianapolis & Chicago. Tell me where you lost track of them.

I hope you will not worry about them. I have no papers that are of sufficient importance as to cause you any uneasiness; while I feel quite sure that they will be found. I feel happy that you have got home safe, & I hope you will soon feel fresh & blooming as ever.

While up-town [Gallatin] to-day I called at Kings. The family are all well. I did not see any one but Mrs. King, Maggie & Marion.[4] The latter looks rather worse than when you left & is quite sick.

I shall try if I have time to-morrow & write to the S. Schools. I hope to hear soon from you about the condition of ours. I hope Sister Maggie has sufficiently recovered as to be able to get around.[5] Give her my love & a kiss also [for] little Mary.[6]

I wonder if Frankie has forgotten me yet. I should like to see him. Will it become necessary to wean him soon? What did Mother [Mrs. Murphy] say of your *case*? When does she expect to start East? Tell me all the news. Tell Abba Remick I directed the letter I wrote to her & Lida to Evanston.

I thought as your last letter was so long on the way I should receive another to-day. Don't forget your resolution to write every day. You see I am doing well as this is the second letter today.

I often think now of many things I might have spoken of while you were here, but while you were here I thought so little of Pontiac that I forgot to ask you all I wanted to know. Now that you are there, my mind is with you all the time.

What is the condition of the Churches there? Do not forget to remind

Bro. Fisher of the renewal of my license.[7] Oh, how I would like to be with you to-morrow; we would go to S. School & Church. I seem to live old times over again, & the recollection of the last year with you makes me very happy. May God bless you.

I lament my inability to render your stay with me here more comfortable. No opportunities to get away from the dull camp, [so] your life must have been most intolerable. You do not know how often I felt grieved over the condition of affairs, of the time I had to leave you at Richland all alone, & often was absent for days, & all the time you alone.

Dear Mary, if God spares my life to return, I will strive to make your life very happy that you may forget your grievances in this land of Dixie. May God give us a long & happy reunion. I hope you will pray for me. I think of it almost every night when I go to bed, & I love to feel that my wife has prayed for me.

Kiss Frankie for me. I wish I could give you the kiss to give him. Write soon & often. May God keep your heart pure as he ever has & make you supremely happy & keep us all under his kind protecting care for continual usefulness in this life & the full enjoyment of a "Home in Heaven."

Good night.

Your Affect. Husband

J. F. Culver

---

1  In the first week of May 1863, General Lee and his Army of Northern Virginia had defeated the Army of the Potomac at Chancellorsville. To capitalize on this success, General Lee in the second week of June put his columns in motion toward Pennsylvania. Lee's II Corps, sweeping up the Shenandoah Valley, defeated the Federals at Winchester on June 14-15, crossed the Potomac at Williamsport, and, advancing by way of Chambersburg, entered Carlisle on June 27. Wilbur S. Nye, *Here Come the Rebels* (Baton Rouge, 1965), pp. 301-310.

2  Joseph Culver, J.F.C.'s father, was 72 years old. He was a retired farmer, living in Carlisle's East Ward, and in 1860 valued his real estate at $25,000 and his personal property at $5,000. Eighth Census, Cumberland County, State of Pennsylvania, NA.

3  Mary Culver's New York State goal was New Hartford, in Oneida County, several hundred miles northeast of Lee's invasion route.

4  Maggie (Margarette) and Marion were two of the children of Charles and Mary King. Eighth Census, Sumner County, State of Tennessee, NA.

5  Maggie Utley had recently given birth to a son. Culver, "Robert Murphy and Some of His Descendants," p. 99.

6  Mary was the Utleys' one-year-old daughter. *Ibid.*

7  Bro. Fisher may have been Samuel Fisher, a 53-year-old resident of Pontiac Township. A widower, Fisher in 1860 was living with his three children. Eighth Census, Livingston County, State of Illinois, NA.

## 54

Head Quarters, Co. "A", 129th Ills. Vol. Infty.
Gallatin, Tenn., June 28th 1863

Dear Wife

Sunday has passed. I hoped to have time to write to the S. S. Pic Nic
to-day, but was disappointed. After being relieved from guard it was
time for church, & after church I found some blanks on my desk
waiting for me. I made them out & spent a short time looking up a
sermon & then Dress Parade.[1]

I preached to-night from Isaiah, 26th Chap. & 4th verse to a very
large congregation, house full to overflowing & had unusual liberty. I
hope done some good. Oh, how I wished to be in the pulpit at Pontiac
to-night with your eyes looking up into mine. I tried to imagine you
were here. Bill Russell went with me.[2] I feel very happy; God has been
good. I always feel well after trying to preach. I thought to-night of the
little children who were wont to gather around the alter & say "Our
Father Who Art in Heaven," a type of angelic purity; of the time
standing by my Mother's knee I first learned to love Jesus. Dear Mary,
those are among the fondest recollections of my youth. As soon as our
boy can comprehend, teach him to love Jesus. I know you will. May
God help us to do our duty & make him obedient & loving. Let our
prayers ascend in his behalf.

No word yet from Father, I feel very anxious to hear from him.[3] Mrs.
Smith is not enjoying good health. Allen heard from Lou yesterday; she
arrived home safe. How is Sis & Mrs. Remick getting along Spiritually?
Is Sis punctual in attendance at S. School, Church & class? Use your
influence to help her along. I feel some anxiety for her. Tell me how
Abba & Lida are?[4] Are they study [studious] or are they carried away
with fashion & self importance? I feel a very deep interest in their
spiritual welfare & have prayed for them much. Remember me to all the
little ones.

Give me all the information about the result of the Pic Nic. I will send
my Gold Watch home by the first opportunity; one of the wheels is
broken. If you wish to carry it with you, get it fixed, & I would rather it
were running than not. I bought another yesterday.

As it is getting late, I must get my light out. May God bless you all. Give my love to all the family. I hope to hear from you soon. Kiss Frankie for me.

Good night.

Yours Ever,

J. F. Culver

1 Beginning on Tuesday, June 23, the regiment fell out for reveille at 4 A.M., guard mount at 7:30 A.M., dinner at 12 noon, retreat at 7 P.M., and tattoo at 8 P.M. Dress parades were held twice a week, on Saturdays and Sundays, at 6:30 P.M. There were two weekly battalion drills, held from 4:30 to 6 P.M. on Mondays and Fridays. Regimental Papers, 129th Illinois, NA.

2 William Russell, the former sheriff of Livingston County, had been employed by the regimental sutler Edwin Maples as his assistant.

3 Soldiers of Lt. Gen. Richard S. Ewell's II Corps, Army of Northern Virginia, had been in occupation of Carlisle, Mr. Culver's home town, since June 27. Hannah Culver on July 9 reported, "Father's health is not improving. He is better one day and worse the next. He seems to be wearing away. He is very weak and does not eat more than necessary to sustain life." Hannah Culver to J.F.C., July 9, 1863, Culver Collection.

4 Abba (Abigail) and Lida were the teenage daughters of J. W. and Sarah DeNormandie Remick. Their father was a prosperous farmer and clerk of the Livingston County Circuit Court, while their mother was a superintendent of the Methodist Sunday School. Eighth Census, Livingston County, State of Illinois, NA; *History of Livingston County,* pp. 315, 648-649.

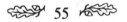 55

Head Quarters, Co. "A" 129th Ills.
Gallatin, Tenn., July 1st 1863

Dear Wife

An old adage says that disappointments never come single handed, & so it has proven as three or four mails from the North have been distributed & no letter for me. I presume now I shall receive none until the arrival of Sergt. Gaff when I anticipate a long one.

As it is quite late to-night, I shall not write at any great length. I was out all of last night on a scout, & it was too warm to sleep to-day so that I feel somewhat sleepy. I have failed from the amount of duty to write to the County Pic-Nic.

The Rebels made an attack on a scout from Richland near Fountain Head yesterday noon; killed one Lieut., two men, wounded several & took 12 prisoners.[1] They number about 75 or 80 men. A Scout of 100 men are just leaving here commanded by Capts. Hoskins & Perry & Lieuts. Smith & McKnight.[2] I hope they may succeed.

I know of no reason why the trains have not been captured, as there are several large forces near Mitchellsville & Richland. We learned this evening that a force of some 75 Rebels were within 8 miles. Just now reports are coming in from the Pickets who have been fired on. There may be a show for some fun.[3] A little fight would be very acceptable just now.

We are all quite well. I feel anxious to know how you & Frankie are getting along. Nathan Hill [a private in Company A] is setting here blowing about having taken you out buggy riding at some time or other. Christ Yetter sends his respects.[4] He is anxious to get home to see Jennie Gutherie.[5] You might intercede for him a little. The boys are all in good spirits; Christ & Nathan Hill are trying to be funny & make me laugh so that it is difficult to write.

Remember me kindly to all our friends & Give my love to Mother & Maggie & all the rest. I have received no letters from any one yet.

I notice in the papers to-night that the Rebels are falling back from Carlisle, so that I may possibly here from there soon.[6] I fear Bro. Charlie has joined the Army & left Father all alone. I hope it may not be so.[7] Write soon

Good night — a kiss for yourself & Frankie.

Your Affect. Husband

J. F. Culver

---

1 On June 28 a report reached Buck Lodge, the headquarters of the 106th Ohio Infantry, that guerrillas had robbed a Union sympathizer. A 12-man mounted patrol was sent to investigate, and soon located a trail left by the raiders. The Ohioans followed the trail but lost it during the night. As they were returning to Buck Lodge on the morning of the 29th, they were bushwhacked near Butler's Mill, and Lt. Gustavus Bertgold and one soldier were killed, and three wounded. Whitelaw Reid, *Ohio in the War: Her Statesmen, Her Generals, and Soldiers*, 2 Vols. (Cincinnati, 1868), Vol. II, pp. 572-575.

2 John P. McKnight, a 23-year-old farmer, was mustered into service on Sept. 8, 1862, as 2d lieutenant of Company G, 129th Illinois Infantry. On April 19, 1864, Lieutenant McKnight was appointed aide-de-camp to Brig. Gen. W. I. Ward, and on Nov. 1, 1864, he was detailed for special duty with the Signal Corps, Department of the Cumberland, and

was mustered out on June 8, 1865, at Washington, D.C. Compiled Service Records of Union Soldiers, NA.

3  The regimental papers of the 129th Illinois do not contain "After Action Reports" filed by members of the patrol, or any information from the "pickets who have been fired on." Regimental Papers, 129th Illinois, NA.

4  Christopher C. Yetter, a 22-year-old farmer, was mustered into service on Sept. 8, 1862, as a sergeant in Company A, 129th Illinois Infantry. Sergeant Yetter was wounded in the chin at New Hope Church, Georgia, May 27, 1864, and was commissioned 1st lieutenant of Company A on Nov. 9, 1864. He was mustered out near Washington, D.C., June 8, 1865. Compiled Service Records of Union Soldiers, NA.

5  Jennie Gutherie was the 17-year-old daughter of George and Sarah Gutherie, prosperous Pontiac Township farmers. Eighth Census, Livingston County, State of Illinois, NA.

6  Ewell's II Corps, Army of Northern Virginia, evacuated Carlisle on the morning of June 30, leaving by the Baltimore Pike. Part of the corps was engaged the next day at Gettysburg. While in Carlisle, the Confederates had sacked the grocery, drug, clothing, and shoe stores. Joseph Culver was fortunate not to lose anything to Rebel foraging parties. Sister Hannah wrote on July 9, "We have escaped almost miraculously having lost nothing."

7  J.F.C.'s fears that 16-year-old Charlie had joined the army were groundless. He was still at home. After the Battle of Gettysburg, he and a number of friends visited the battlefield. Hannah Culver to J.F.C., July 9, 1863, Culver Collection.

 56

Head Quarters, Co. "A", 129th Ills.
Gallatin, Tenn., July 2nd 1863

My Dear Wife

By the arrival of Bro. Gaff this evening, I received news of your departure for New York, where I presume this letter will find you, I hope, safe & well. I have filled your proposition on my part quite well as I have written almost every day since you left. I think surely there must be some letters that I have not received, as only two short notes have reached me, one in pencil on your arrival & one written on Monday following.

I was very anxious to learn the news from Pontiac. I have succeeded in gathering some things from Sergt. Gaff. I am glad your trunks have arrived safe, & am much obliged for the "Initial G."

I am unable to learn anything about the condition of our property, as Gaff was not there. I received a letter from Bro. Remick containing Statement of the disposition of monies in his hands. All very satisfactory. Mrs. Remick is very dangerously ill.

What disposition did you make of the articles Laurence wished to buy? & what condition did you find the property in? Please give me all the information you can, & I can suggest such changes as may be necessary.

I hope you have a delightful trip on the lakes.[1] I should like to have been with you very much. Why has Bro. Thomas not written.[2] Is he in want of money; if so, I earnestly hope you will inform me, as I think I can procure the amount at anytime if he needs it. I have only deferred because I thought he would as soon have it out at 10 per ct as not if he feels secure.

I received a letter from Bro. Sammy this evening. He acknowledges the receipt of a letter from Bro. John but does not say where he is.[3] I also recd. a letter from Henry Greenebaum in which he says he has a cap for Frankie. I presume he has received it.

I have in the several letters I wrote to you at Pontiac mentioned matters of business which I cannot call to mind just now. I have sent at least 6 or 8 letters. I shall have time to-morrow, however, to think them up & will write soon again.

Did you get your shawl? I sent it by Mr. Earnheart a few days after you left. I shall be on duty to-morrow & have no opportunity to write. Among other items of interest from Pontiac, I am informed that a report is in circulation that I have been drinking hard & gambling heavy. How much credence has it claimed?

You have not told me how Mother [Murphy] received you. Is she with you? Give many messages of Love to our friends in New York.

I do not remember whether I ever answered Mary & Sarah Williams' letters, & yet it seems to me I did but when I do not recollect.

I preached to a large congregation on Sunday night from Isaiah, 26th Chap. & 4th verse, a lengthy account of which I have written in a former letter.

Late advices from Carlisle report Lee's entire Army there, & it is very probable it will soon witness one of the most terrible battles of the war.[4] I tremble for the result. I greatly fear Father's health will not stand the shock. I have no word from them & all communication is cut off. I shall write soon to Harrisburg & perhaps may get advices by private sources.

Write soon & give me all the news. I hope you will have a very pleasant visit. I came nearer being homesick since you left than any time since I have been in the service.

The cloud that overhangs the Country is growing darker. The news from Port Hudson to-night is the repulse of Banks' entire army and the loss of 8000 prisoners.[5] At Vicksburg I see no advance; heavy losses to our Army are reported.[6] Harry McDowell recd. intelligence this morning of the death of his Bro. James in the army at Vicksburg.[7] Nothing cheering from the East. Rosecrans army is in motion; several hundred prisoners were sent to Nashville from the front yesterday.[8] He is within 2 miles of Talahoma & finds a large army entrenched there & there is heavy fighting in progress.[9]

A party of 60 guerillas made an attack on a mounted force of the 106th Ohio at Richland day before yesterday; killed one Lieut, two men & took several prisoners. Col. Case, Capts. Hoskins & Perry & Lieuts. Smith & McKnight started for Richland with over 100 mounted men last night to capture them if possible. I learn that they sent in 7 prisoners this evening, & five captured by the troop stationed there this morning.[10] The Union people are all fleeing. I saw Carrie Rodomore's brother on the train this evening on his way to Nashville.[11] He is afraid to remain at home longer. He reports the family all well, but their house sacked & everything destroyed by the Rebels. All the Union families are suffering, but I think our force will drive out the invaders.

Our duties are growing heavier. A Negro Regiment is being raised here.[12] Tom, Henry & Joe have enlisted so we are again without a cook, also Col. Case and Lt. Col. Cropsey.[13]

Ed Maples is on a visit to Troy, New York, & Bill [Russell] did not get home the 4th. I presume you have gone to New Hartford, & I will direct [my mail] in care of J. H. Case, Esq. as I do not know Mr. Williams' name.[14]

Remember me kindly to all. May God bless & prosper you; Give you all good health & a warm reception.

Should that other event you anticipate not transpire, I shall try & make a visit to Father's with you before you return if I can possibly get leave of absence.[15] But should you be compelled to hasten home, you [might] prefer that I should be in Pontiac in January. I cannot expect to go twice. Tell me which you wish me to do & whether I will be required to furnish the new dress. I must have some notice beforehand.

Kiss Frankie for me & as many of the others as you desire or would desire me to kiss were I there. Did you stop in Cleveland?

With an earnest prayer for you, my dear wife & our Boy, I remain,

Your Affect. Husband

J. F. Culver

1 Mary Culver was traveling to New Hartford by way of Chicago, Detroit, Cleveland and Buffalo. She and her mother had booked passage on a steamboat between Detroit and Buffalo.

2 Thomas Murphy, Mary Culver's oldest brother, was a Cleveland, Ohio machinist and boat builder.

3 Brother Johnny Murphy's unit (Company M, 1st Illinois Light Artillery) was currently assigned to the First Division, Reserve Corps, Army of the Cumberland. The battery had participated in Rosecrans' Middle Tennessee Campaign and was posted at Shelbyville, Tenn., from June 29-September 6, 1863. *Report of the Adjutant General of Illinois.* Vol. VIII, p. 665.

4 Two divisions of General Ewell's II Corps of Lee's Army of Northern Virginia had occupied Carlisle from June 27-30. J.F.C.'s forecast of "a most terrible battle" was correct. On July 1 at Gettysburg, 30 miles south of Carlisle, commenced the bloodiest three-day battle of the Civil War.

5 Maj. Gen. Nathaniel P. Banks' Army of the Gulf on May 23 had invested a small Confederate army led by Maj. Gen. Franklin Gardner at Port Hudson, La. Banks' troops on May 27 and again on June 14 had attempted to storm this stronghold on the Mississippi, 250 river-miles south of Vicksburg. In these assaults Banks lost 3,800 in killed, wounded, and missing. There was no truth to the report that Banks had lost 8,000 prisoners. Edward Cunningham, *The Port Hudson Campaign: 1862-1863* (Baton Rouge, 1963), pp. 43-93.

6 General Grant's Army of the Tennessee, after being checkmated during the winter of 1862-63 on the western approaches to Vicksburg, had crossed the Mississippi at Bruinsburg on April 30. Striking northeastward and then wheeling his army to the west, Grant, in an 18-day campaign that earned him recognition as one of the "Great Captains of History," defeated the Confederate armies of Gen. Joseph E. Johnston and Lt. Gen. John C. Pemberton. Pemberton's army had been invested in Vicksburg. On May 19 and 22, Grant's heretofore victorious troops had charged the Vicksburg earthworks to be hurled back with more than 4,100 casualties. Siege operations had commenced on May 25 and dragged on through June into the first week of July. Francis V. Greene, *The Mississippi* (New York, 1882), pp. 135-192.

7 William H. H. McDowell, a 21-year-old farmer, was mustered into service on Sept. 8, 1862, as sergeant major of the 129th Illinois Infantry, and was commissioned 2d lieutenant of Company E on April 17, 1863. On Feb. 22, 1864, he was detached and sent to Illinois on recruiting duty, rejoining the regiment on May 29. Lieutenant McDowell on Nov. 13, 1864, was detailed to the brigade ambulance corps, and was mustered out near Washington, June 8, 1865. Compiled Service Records of Union Soldiers, NA.

8 Goaded by the War Department, General Rosecrans had put his Army of the Cumberland in motion on June 24. Soldiers of Maj. Gen. Alexander McD. McCook's XX Corps drove the Confederates from Liberty Gap, while Maj. Gen. George H. Thomas' XIV Corps cleared the Rebels out of Hoover Gap. Heavy rains slowed the bluecoats, as their long columns pushed deep into Middle Tennessee. Cist, *The Army of the Cumberland,* pp. 154-156.

9 General Bragg, his army weakened by the detachment of five infantry brigades and a cavalry division to Mississippi in a futile effort by the Confederates to relieve Vicksburg, permitted himself to be outmaneuvered by Rosecrans. The Federals, after forcing the gaps, had advanced on Manchester. Finding that his right had been outflanked, Bragg was compelled to abandon his fortified position at Tullahoma without firing a shot. Reports that the enemy was evacuating Tullahoma had reached General Thomas on July 1, and he ordered a forced reconnaissance. Feeling its way forward, a reinforced brigade entered Tullahoma and found the Confederates gone. *Ibid.,* pp. 156-166.

10   Colonel Case filed no report, so J.F.C.'s letter constitutes the only information we have about this patrol. Regimental Papers, 129th Illinois, NA.

11   Carrie (Caroline) Rodamore was the 21-year-old daughter of Ann Rodamore, a Gallatin widow. Carrie's brother, Jacob, was a conductor on the Louisville & Nashville Railroad. Eighth Census, Sumner County, State of Tennessee, NA.

12   Early in 1863 the Lincoln administration adopted as its policy the organization of black regiments to be officered by whites. Adjutant General Lorenzo Thomas was sent to the Western armies to explain and rally support for this policy. In 1862, prior to President Lincoln's preliminary Emancipation Proclamation, the administration had discouraged efforts of several departmental commanders to organize black units. J. G. Randall, *The Civil War and Reconstruction* (Boston, 1953), pp. 503-505. The 13th U.S. Colored Infantry (2d U.S. Infantry Regiment [Colored]) was organized in July 1863 from laborers in the staff departments at Gallatin, Clarksville, Murfreesboro, etc. *Tennesseans in the Civil War* . . . 2 parts (Nashville, 1964), pt. I, p. 398.

13   Tom, Henry, and Joe were former slaves  freed by the Emancipation Proclamation, employed by officers of Company A to cook for them and to keep their quarters policed. A special order had been issued by Rosecrans' headquarters permitting each regiment in the Department of the Cumberland to employ for use by the government about 40 blacks as teamsters, cooks, etc. Regimental Papers, 129th Illinois, NA.

14   J. H. Case was a prosperous New Hartford farmer. In 1860, the 41-year-old Case was living with his wife, Charlotte, and their 5-year-old son Herbert. It has been impossible to further identify Mr. Williams, as there were a number of families with that surname in and around New Hartford. Eighth Census, Oneida County, State of New York, NA.

15   J.F.C. refers to the possibility that his wife was pregnant; if she were, she would give birth to a second child in January 1864.

 57

Head Quarters, Co. "A", 129th Regt. Ills.
Gallatin, Tenn., July 6th 1863

My Dear Wife

We have had no train through yet & consequently no word from you. The news reached us, however, of a glorious victory in Pennsylvania.[1] Longstreet & Hill killed, Lee seriously wounded & 20,000 prisoners.[2] It is almost too much to believe, with the entire Rebel Army in full retreat. I hope it is all true, however.

I presume none of my letters have reached you. We are all doing well, Russell is rapidly improving & thinks he will be able to get to Camp tomorrow.

2500 Rebels have taken possession of the Rail Road near Shepherdstown[3] & report says some 15,000 are advancing from Cumberland Gap.[4] If it be true, I cannot say when we may have communication with the North. All their Efforts cannot affect us, however, at the present stages of high water.[5] The Army of the Cumberland is advancing but with what results we cannot tell.[6] Our force here has been considerably augmented since you left, & I think we should be able to hold our position against a very considerable force.[7]

We are all very anxious for News from the North. I shall expect quite a number of letters by the first mail. I have no news from Bro. Johnie yet, nor do I know where he is. Report says there is a hard fight at Franklin, Ky., but with what forces I did not learn.[8] Our Cavalry are making a scout in that direction now.

I hope to hear that you are all well & enjoying yourselves. Frank will be quite busy hunting up his relations. I should like to be favored with a copy of his notes on Board the Propeller from Chicago. Give him a kiss for me.

I wrote a letter to my Mother to-day. I have no word from home since the invasion of Pennsylvania but hope to hear soon. If Lee's Army is in retreat as represented, with a moderate effort I feel sure it might be routed before reaching the Potomac.[9] I hope the final result will reach that position.

I have no word from Pontiac since Gaff returned. I shall be on duty to-morrow & shall not likely find time to write. Do not forget your promise to write every day. You see I have kept mine. May the Blessings of Heaven rest upon you, & the Establishment of National Peace give us an early opportunity to repair to our home to enjoy its comforts. I have tried to comply with your request to Pray. "Trust Thou in God for we shall yet praise him for his Wondrous Love."

Remember me to all our friends

Your Affect. Husband

J. F. Culver

---

1   In a 3-day battle at Gettysburg, July 1-3, the Union Army of the Potomac defeated General Lee's Army of Northern Virginia. On the night of July 4, Lee's army commenced its retreat to Virginia.

2 Confederate losses in the battle, the bloodiest of the Civil War, were 2,592 killed, 12,709 wounded, and 5,150 missing or prisoners. Although five Confederate generals were killed or mortally wounded in the struggle, Lt. Gens. James Longstreet and A. P. Hill were not among the slain. The story that General Lee had been seriously wounded was unfounded.

3 General Bragg, in a futile effort to check the advance of Rosecrans' Army of the Cumberland, sent General Morgan to destroy Union supply lines in Kentucky. Morgan was to enter Kentucky at or near Burkesville, on the Cumberland River, proceed northward to the Ohio River, and then retreat out of the state by the route which the exigencies of the moment dictated.

On July 2 Morgan's division crossed the Cumberland near Burkesville and started north. Riding by way of Columbia and Lebanon, the raiders passed through Bardstown on the 6th and effected a brief lodgment on the Louisville & Nashville Railroad near Shepherdstown. A train was captured near Lebanon Junction and the passengers robbed. Vigorous pursuit by the Federals prevented much damage to the railroad, and on the 7th, Morgan and his raiders started for Brandenburg, where on the 8th they crossed to the Indiana side of the Ohio River. *O. R.,* Ser., I. Vol. XXIII, pt. I, pp. 700-703; Bennett H. Young, *Confederate Wizards of the Saddle* (Kennesaw, 1958), pp. 367-379.

4 There was no substance to the rumor that 15,000 Confederates had advanced into Kentucky by way of Cumberland Gap. This story probably was released by some of Morgan's men who had tapped the telegraph line, sending out messages calculated to cloud the situation and spread confusion.

5 Recent rains had caused the rivers and streams of the region to flood and had turned unimproved roads into ribbons of mud. *O. R.,* Ser. I, Vol. XXIII, pt. II, p. 518.

6 Bragg's army, having been flanked out of its fortified position at Tullahoma, was retiring on Chattanooga, closely pursued by the Army of the Cumberland. On July 4 the Federals crossed Elk River on a broad front, occupying Cowan, and learning that Bragg's columns had withdrawn across the Cumberland Plateau. *Ibid.,* pp. 512-515.

7 On July 6 General Paine, post commander at Gallatin, wired Rosecrans that a large force of Rebels was in the area and that he should be reinforced by two infantry regiments and 300 cavalry. To hold Gallatin and guard 30 miles of railroad, he had 900 men, and if attacked could only hold the Gallatin earthworks. *Ibid.,* p. 516.

8 A company of Confederates on the 5th had attacked the details posted at Woodburn and Franklin in a futile effort to burn the depots and cut the telegraph. *O. R.,* Ser. I, Vol. XXIII, pt. I, pp. 5, 820-821.

9 The Army of the Potomac had also suffered frightful casualties at Gettysburg, and Maj. Gen. George G. Meade's pursuit of Lee's Army of Northern Virginia was not vigorously pressed.

 58

Head Quarters, Co. "A", 129th Regt. Ills. Vols.
Gallatin, Tenn., July 8th 1863

My Dear Wife

As communication is not yet open, I have received no letters from you, & I presume none of mine have reached you. I wrote a long letter on Friday evening [the 3d], but the train & mail was captured so that someone else will peruse it than my wife. I hope it may do them good. Some of the men of this Regiment were captured with the train, but I have not yet learned who.[1] If the train coming South was captured, which is probable, Daniel Graff is likely among the number, as he was to have returned by it.[2]

We have had no papers, but several dispatches sent as we think by Morgan, as he had a Battery attached to the lines:[3] one was of the entire overthrow of Lee's Army in Penna; the other, the fall of Vicksburg on the 4th inst. with 24,000 prisoners.[4] Report says that Morgan has retreated & that the road will be repaired in a few days.[5] But we dare not rely on the reports not knowing who works the wires. Morgan evidently has in his employ some operative of the Road, as a stranger could easily be detected. Instead of destroying the train he captured, he sent it back to Nashville with all the ladies aboard, telegraphing at the same time that it was the regular train from Louisville. We have no news from any part of the Army that is reliable.

Lt. Culver left here for his regiment at the front yesterday.[6] He promised to hunt up Bro. Johnnie & let me know where he is. I cannot understand why he has not answered any of my letters. You cannot imagine with what anxiety we await the first train for news from friends & loved ones & the Armies.

Russell's health is improving; but he is not able to be about much yet. I have been reading during my leisure hours a history of the war by E. A. Pollard.[7] I am sorry to say I never read such a collection of falsehood in my life. I wish very much to get a true, well written history. Perhaps in your travels you may find one; if so purchase & read it, & I can get it should I succeed in getting home this fall. Another thing I want very much is a pocket map of the U.S., reliable. Should you see any of Floyd's [*sic*] Newspaper maps of the seat of War, please send me one by mail.[8]

I had a short ride in the country this evening with Col. Cropsey. This country is looking beautiful & reminds me so forcibly of Cumberland Valley that I long to see the old home once more.[9]

We are plodding on in the even tenor of our way lately; duties heavy but health good. I am getting quite fat lately which is *unaccountable*. I think I shall soon be up to my old weight. We are having quite a feast on blackberries, which are ripe & plentiful. I should like to have a mess of whortleberries. They are ripe now. I hope you will enjoy them. I presume you have ripe apples, eat a few for me. I hope you are enjoying yourself visiting the old haunts of pleasure.

I thought this evening while riding through the grove that perhaps you were roaming around those old hills, visiting old friends & thinking of the change the few years of absence has effected in your own condition

& that of others. I earnestly hope you may have no regrets for the result & that your cup of happiness may be full.

I have not forgotten my tramp from New Hartford to Mr. Case's through mud ankle deep; of the pleasant acquaintances I made while there. Indeed, had I been single, I am not sure that it would have been a wise policy to send me among those lady friends of yours there. As one of them has very large lustrous eyes that are quite captivating, I do not deem it prudent to mention names. Yet an initial acrostic may not be inappropriate such as:

Songs of Minstrels fill the air

While Nature blooming ever fair &, &c, &c

Do not get alarmed at my poetry for I never wrote a line correctly in my life, & I am rather far advanced in life now to be effected by the muses.

Remember me kindly to all our friends. I set down to have a little chat with you and have almost exhausted all the subjects at my command. I have written punctually almost every day. Indeed, I think I have not missed more than three or four since you left. I can hardly expect you to do as much as you will be very frequently without facilities to write.

Capt. Hoskins has been quite sick to-day. Mrs. Smith requests me to say that she would like to hear from you. She is well.

I hope Frankie is making good use of his time & opportunities; that he is enjoying good health & giving you little trouble. I wish I could encircle you both in my arms & get a sweet kiss in return. Sometimes I feel sorry that you are gone, yet I must confess that I could not wish you surrounded with the dangers we are liable to encounter here. I hope the time will soon come when separation will no longer be a necessity, & we in our quiet home can enjoy the greater sweets from our long absence, when our country will no longer need the sacrifice of all that is so dear to our hearts. Let us devoutly pray for a glorious future. I could not enumerate all the dreams of future happiness I have had should God in His Infinite Goodness prosper us.

I feel very sanguine that the great dark clouds will soon disappear & the reign of Peace be ushered in. May it come speedily.

Let us trust wholly in the promises of God & earnestly strive to do his will. I feel unusually buoyant & happy tonight, whether it is the precursor of a fit of the blues or the dawning of a glorious reality, I cannot tell; yet I will not forego the pleasures of present realities. Trusting in God for your happiness, I remain,

Your Affect Husband

J. F. Culver

---

1  The train had been captured at Bardstown Junction on the 6th. After destroying the

mail and robbing the express company safe and a number of passengers, Morgan released the train and sent it back to Elizabethtown. *O. R.,* Ser. I, Vol. XXIII, pt. I, pp. 659, 702.

2  Daniel Graff, a 33-year-old farmer, was mustered into service on Sept. 8, 1862, as a private in Company A, 129th Illinois. Graff was promoted to corporal on May 9, 1863, and was mustered out at Washington, D.C., June 8, 1865. Compiled Service Records of Union Soldiers, NA.

3  Morgan's command included several skilled telegraphers, equipped with keys and batteries, who would tap into telegraph lines and send dispatches calculated to confuse the Federals.

4  The messages detailing Lee's defeat at Gettysburg and of the surrender of Vicksburg were legitimate and had not been sent by Morgan's scouts. On the 7th Secretary of War Stanton had telegraphed General Rosecrans, "Vicksburg surrendered to General Grant on the 4th of July. Lee's army overthrown; Grant victorious." *O. R.,* Ser. I, Vol. XXIII, pt. II, p. 518. At Vicksburg 29,500 Confederates had been surrendered by General Pemberton.

5  Morgan and his raiders had been dislodged from their brief grip on the Louisville & Nashville Railroad, and on the 8th, having seized a steamboat at Brandenburg, crossed the Ohio and carried the war into Indiana. *O. R.,* Ser. I, Vol. XXIII, pt. I, p. 705.

6  Lt. Charles Culver had been mustered into service as 2d lieutenant of Company H, 105th Illinois Infantry. He was currently serving on General Paine's staff. Compiled Service Records of Union Soldiers, NA.

7  E. A. Pollard, editor of the *Richmond Examiner* and caustic critic of President Jefferson Davis, in 1862 wrote *The First Year of the War.* This book, while critical of President Davis, was sympathetic to the Confederacy.

8  H. H. Lloyd & Co. of 25 Howard Street, New York City, in 1863 published a "New Military Map of the Border and Southern States." The popular 33 x 92 inch map sold for fifty cents.

9  Reference is to the Cumberland Valley of Pennsylvania where J.F.C. had spent his youth.

 59

Head Quarters, Co. "A" 129th Regt. Ills.
Gallatin, Tenn., July 9th 1863

My Dear Wife

Another day has passed without any mail, with the usual promise that it will come to-morrow. Morgan has gone with a portion of his command to Indiana. Should he venture any considerable distance his capture is certain.[1] Reports still confirm of the fall of Vicksburg & the rout of Lee's Army in Penna., but we scarcely believe it all.

By the time we get reliable news, great changes will doubtless have been effected. It looks to me much like the last struggle before their [the Confederates] final overthrow.[2] Some 5000 deserters from Bragg's Army have come into Rosecrans' Camp.[3] They are rapidly evacuating Tennessee.[4]

We may look for stirring times where small detachments are stationed. We are expecting reinforcements here daily of an entire brigade, even now within striking distance of the place, so that our duties if we remain here will have lighter duties to perform.[5]

Our health is still good. Russell is rapidly improving & is able to be about most of the time. I have nothing new to communicate. How I wish for some word from you. Kiss Frankie for me.

May God bless my Dear Wife

Your Affect. Husband

J. F. Culver

---

1 Morgan and his division after crossing the Ohio had struck northward into Indiana, and on the 9th passed through Croydon. J.F.C.'s forecast was correct. Morgan's raid north of the Ohio caused thousands of militia to turn out, and with the Ohio and other rivers and streams of the region at or near flood stage, it made a recrossing of the Ohio problematical.

2 Most Union leaders would have echoed J.F.C.'s estimate of the situation. The Confederates, however, fought on and the war continued until the spring of 1865.

3 The figure (5,000) given by J.F.C. as the number of Confederates who had abandoned the fight and had surrendered to Rosecrans' army during the Middle Tennessee Campaign (June 24-July 7), is greatly exaggerated. During this period, 1,634 Confederates were captured, of whom 616 claimed "to have delivered themselves" voluntarily, being "conscripts or tired of the war." *O. R.,* Ser. I, Vol. XXIII, pt. I, p. 425.

4 General Bragg's Army of Tennessee had evacuated Middle Tennessee, crossing to the south bank of the Tennessee River at Shellmount and Kelly's Ford on July 6-7. General Rosecrans now halted his pursuit to bring up supplies and consolidate his gains, preparatory to advancing on Chattanooga. *O. R.,* Ser. I, Vol. XXIII, pt. II, pp. 900-902.

5 On July 7 Rosecrans directed Maj. Gen. Gordon Granger, commander of his reserve corps, to send one or two regiments to strengthen the force at Gallatin. This was in response to General Paine's plea for reinforcements. *Ibid.,* p. 518.

Head Quarters, Co. "A" 129th Regt. Ills. Vols.
Gallatin, Tenn., July 10th 1863

My Dear Wife

If you have ever anticipated without presuming to doubt the arrival of glad tidings & being delayed day after day with bright hopes for the morrow (when anticipated pleasure brings but blank disappointment & you are left in doubt & uncertainty with great fears for the result). If you have experienced all this, you can sympathize with me to-night.

The mail arrived for the first time this evening for 9 days, bringing a large number of letters for a large majority of the Company, but none for me. No news from my wife. No knowledge of where you are, whether you have reached your destination & are in good health, & a great many things that I expected to hear. No news from home, not a letter or paper.

To say that I am disappointed is scarcely half. I fear something has happened but what I cannot determine. I pray God my fears may be groundless & all be well. Oh, how anxiously I have looked for this mail. I shall most earnestly hope for some news to-morrow. If you were near where a telegram would reach you, I should not wait for the train for word from you, & yet if anything has happened I hope our friends would be considerate enough to let me know immediately. I shall hope on; hope that you are well & Frankie also.

My health is quite good. We were reinforced to-day by the 71st Ohio Regt.[1] Two more regts. are expected with a Batallion of Cavalry.[2] I can but close & wait. My God bless & keep you both, fill you with love & grace divine.

Good Night

Your affect. Husband

J. F. Culver

1   The 71st Ohio Infantry had spent the winter of 1862-63 at Fort Henry, Tenn., and was ordered from Fort Donelson, on the Cumberland River, to Gallatin in the first week of July. There it was to help guard the railroad between Nashville and Mitchellville. Reid, *Ohio in the War,* Vol. II, p. 410.

2   There was no substance to the rumor that the force at Gallatin was to be further reinforced. General Rosecrans had decided that three infantry regiments (the 129th Illinois, and the 71st and 106th Ohio) and one battery of artillery (the 13th Indiana) were sufficient to hold Gallatin and guard the railroad.

 61

Head Quarters, 129th Regt. Ills. Vols. Infty.
Gallatin, Tenn., July 11th 1863

My Dear Wife

Another day has passed without any word from you. I leave at 10 o'clock to-night on a scout of 100 cavalry, 200 infantry & 2 pieces of Artillery. Will be absent for two days,[1] but as the trains do not run north of Louisville, I can hardly expect to hear for several days. Morgan has possession of the Rail Road from Jeffersonville to Indianapolis.[2]

We are all well. Capt. Reed, Sergt. Quakenbush, Lacy McFee & Bob McIntyre came near being captured at Spradling's to-day by some 30 Rebels but succeeded in making their Escape.[3]

I expected to have several letters to answer to-morrow (Sunday). Hoping that God's blessings may rest upon you & Frankie, I remain,

Ever Your Affect. Husband

J. F. Culver

1   Private Dunham of Company C wrote his parents on July 12, "I am heare alone [at Gallatin] most of the boys went out last nite on a scout. They took two peces of artilery with them", *Through the South with a Union Soldier,* p. 76.

2   Morgan and his raiders on the 10th swept through Salem on the New Albany & Salem Railroad, and on the 11th slashed across the Indianapolis-Jeffersonville Railroad near

Vienna and the Madison, Indianapolis & Peru Railroad at Vernon. *O. R.,* Ser. I, Vol. XXIII, pt. I, pp. 719-726.

3  Henry B. Reed, a 30-year-old farmer, was mustered into service on Sept. 8, 1862, as captain of Company G, 129th Illinois. From Feb. 17-April 18, 1864, he was detailed on court martial duty in Nashville. Captain Reed was mustered out on June 8, 1865, at Washington, D.C. George M. Quackenbush, a 27-year-old saddler, was mustered into service on Sept. 8, 1862, as a sergeant in Company D, 129th Illinois, and was appointed regimental quartermaster sergeant two days later. Sergeant Quackenbush was mustered out at Washington, D.C., June 8, 1865. Robert M. McIntyre, a 24-year-old tinsmith, was mustered into service on Sept. 8, 1862, as a private in Company G, 129th Illinois. Private McIntyre was hospitalized at Gallatin on April 14, 1863, and on his release from the hospital was detailed as provost clerk. On Dec. 7, 1863, he was assigned to duty with the Nashville Quartermaster Depot, and on April 28, 1864, he was ordered to report for naval service at Chattanooga. Henry L. McFee, a 28-year-old farmer, was mustered into Company B, 129th Illinois, as a private on Sept. 8, 1862. He was appointed wagon master on Feb. 4, 1863, and on Dec. 21, 1863, was detailed as a clerk to the Nashville Quartermaster Depot. Compiled Service Records of Union Soldiers, NA.

 62

Head Quarters, Co. "A", 129th Regt. Ills.
Gallatin, Tenn., July 15th 1863

My Dear Wife

I have received no intelligence of you yet nor any from home. I recd. a letter from Bro. Johnie yesterday. He is quite well & in Camp at Shelbyville, Tenn. He writes for money, & I will send him $20 by mail this evening, though it is a great risk.

It still continues to rain. I found some of the small streams yesterday almost impassible. A continuous fog overhangs the Country.

We are all well. My anxiety to hear from you has become alarm for your Safety, and yet I cannot believe that if anything serious has happened our friends would not  telegraph. May God's blessings rest upon you. Kiss Frankie for me. I must close for this morning's mail. Farewell,

Your Affect. Husband

J. F. Culver

Head Quarters, Co. "A" 129th Regt. Ills. Vols.
Gallatin, Tenn., July 21st 1863

My Dear Wife

I have delayed writing for four days hoping to be able to answer your last two letters in person. An old Proverb says "That whom the Gods would destroy they first make mad." Whether it will apply in my case or not cannot be determined, except as time may solve the problem.

Last week Genrl. Rosecrans was in Nashville[1] & a few of the fortunate ones got permission to visit him & secured leave of absence to visit home. Flattered with a hope of success, I immediately sent in my petition but it arrived too late, as he spent but one day there, & I have been waiting very impatiently for it to reach him & receive his decision. After this long delay I can hardly hope for success, as it will fall into the hands of his aid whose orders prohibit the issue of any such document. I cannot say that I have no hope, but rather that the chances are growing very small in my favor. Let us wait & see.

I am sorry to inform you that Mrs. Smith is no better & but very little hope is entertained of her recovery.[2] She is occupying the room you had at Kings. I saw her at noon to-day. She was scarcely able to speak & is entirely helpless. Everything is proceeding as usual.

I recd. a letter from Sister Hannah which I will enclose.[3] They had not received my last letter & do not know where you are.

I will write as soon as my fate is decided if I am still to wait for the favorable opportunity. I hope you have entirely recovered from your illness & are enjoying yourself. I cannot write at length, but will either be with you soon or write a long letter. Till then Goodbye. May the richest of Heaven's blessings rest upon you. Kiss Frankie & Mother [Murphy] for me & love to all.

Your affect. Husband

J. F. Culver

---

1 General Rosecrans' field headquarters were at Tullahoma. On July 18 the general was in Nashville. *O. R.*, Ser. I, Vol. XXIII, pt. II, p. 542.

2  Mrs. Margaret Smith was an invalid.

3  Hannah Culver, in her six-page letter of July 9, had described in detail the occupation of Carlisle by Ewell's corps, and the engagement on July 1 between the Rebel cavalry and Union militia. Hannah Culver to J.F.C., July 9, 1863, Culver Collection.

 64

Head Quarters, Co. "A" 129th Regt. Illinois, Vols. Infty.
Gallatin, Tennessee July 26th 1863

My Dear Wife

Yours of the 16th reached me yesterday evening and of the 14th a few days ago.[1] I am very Sorry to hear that you do not enjoy good health. I hoped the climate would produce good results & that you would gain rather than lose Strength. I wish Frankie could be weaned for I think he is the principal cause of it, but you know best; only be careful of your health.

I have almost despaired of getting leave of Absence. It is ten days since my petition was forwarded & no answer yet. I dare not look for a favorable return & have almost given up the anticipated pleasure. When the time will come, I cannot divine but earnestly hope it may be soon.

Russell is almost entirely well; he will start home to-morrow. He comes as near being homesick as any one I ever saw. Maples returned yesterday. He brought a letter for me from Abbie [Remick]. Our friends in Pontiac are all well. Your shawl is at Dehner's; Mrs. Smith is getting better, & if she does not relapse may get well. She is very poorly. Her father arrived here Friday evening. I shall write to the S. School to-day & send by Russell.

He [Russell] denies having sent Mrs. Green any present. He is smitten with Fanny Mott, & says he is going home to see her.[2] I am of the opinion that he is becoming anxious to get a wife. When you married, he said he would never try again (such is life).

I wrote you an account of Jim Abbe & Soph (Frost) Stephen's Elopement. They have been caught & are now awaiting trial.[3]

I recd. a letter from Bro. Wes [Culver] a few days ago. Father is no better. All the rest are well. When do you expect to visit Carlisle? Mother is very anxious for you to come. Jennie was on a visit with her husband. Annie Zug['s] sister, Lizzie's oldest daughter, was married recently. Bro. Charlie [Culver] got a fine horse & equipments from the Rebels while they were in Carlisle.

Frankie, you say, will soon be able to walk alone. I wonder if he would know me; how much I should like to see you both, I presume ere this you have recd. my letters anticipating my visit home. I am sorry for the disappointment.

Our Chaplain [Reverend Cotton] has resigned. He would have gained credit by doing so long ago. We had some Company Records printed. I will send one to Pontiac & have it framed by the time you return, also one to mother.[4] They make quite a handsome picture.

Dr. Moore was here yesterday; his family are well.[5] Mike Collins is editor of the Sentinel.[6] Gagan has gone to California.[7] There were none of our Regt. captured on the train Morgan took; it was only a report.

I must close or I will not get my letter in the mail this morning. My health is quite good. We got new tents on Friday & the Camp looks very nice. Write to me often as you can. Remember me kindly to all our friends. Kiss Babie & Mother for me. Let me know when you go to Carlisle. I shall write to Mother to-day if possible. May God bless and keep you and hasten our return to home. Let us praise him for all his goodness thus far.

Farewell,

Your Affect. Husband

J. F. Culver

---

1  General Morgan and his raiders on July 13 had invaded Ohio. The pursuit was vigorous, as the Confederates rode eastward, in search of a way to recross the Ohio into Kentucky. There were frequent skirmishes. Many of the Confederates straggled, and on the 26th Morgan with the remnant of his once-feared division surrendered near New Lisbon, Ohio. With Morgan hard-pressed and unable to halt long enough to seriously damage the railroads, communication lines south to the army leading through Louisville were promptly reopened. *O. R.*, Ser. I, Vol. XXIII, pt. I, pp. 632-633.

2  Fanny Mott was a recent widow, her husband the regimental hospital steward Isaac Mott having died at South Tunnel, April 12, 1863. Sarah Green was Silas Green's 25-year-old widow. Eighth Census, Livingston County, State of Illinois, NA.

3  Jim Abbe, the Pontiac city clerk, had deserted his wife and family for the charms of Sophia Stephens, the 23-year-old wife of William Stephens, a Pontiac carpenter. *Ibid.*

4  A Civil War fad was for a unit, usually a company, to have its roster engraved on parchment and reproduced. J.F.C. was mistaken about Chaplain Cotton's resignation. Cotton would remain with the unit another year before resigning.

5   It has been impossible to further identify Dr. Moore.

6   Mike (Marcellus) Collins was a 31-year-old Pontiac attorney, and he had purchased the *Sentinel* from Cook & Gagan. Eighth Census, Livingston County, State of Illinois, NA; *History of Livingston County,* p. 317.

7   William Gagan had resigned as regimental sutler on March 27, 1863. His replacement was Ed Maples, a former sheriff of Livingston County. Regimental Papers, 129th Illinois, NA.

 65

Head Quarters, Co. "A" 129th Regt. Ills. Vol. Infty.
Gallatin, Tenn., July 28th 1863

My Dear Wife

Yours of July 22nd is duly received.[1] I hoped to hear that you were quite well & feel sorry to hear that you do not enjoy good health.

I have hoped for a favorable return of my last petition until now. I dare not anticipate the granting of a leave of Absence any longer for the present at least. I intended yesterday to try & go to Nashville to-day & press my suit with General Rosecrans, but Orders have been received forbidding any Officer to go without permission from the Post Commander at Nashville.[2] I feel disappointed & I know you will, but let us conclude that all is for the best.

I have been sick myself to-day with strong symtoms of a Billious Attack. I am taking medicine to-night & hope to be much better in the morning.

If it becomes essential to your health to wean Frankie, you must not hesitate to do it. The weather will soon be getting cooler, & with his good health I think there would be but little danger.

In answer to your letter, I saw Dr. Moore on Saturday; he was here a couple of hours. His family are all well & were seemingly glad to hear from you. I have written to Bro. Fisher about the matter you forgot, thinking that in your hasty departure you might have forgotten it. It was not of much importance, probably would have been attended to without saying anything.

I am happy to hear that Frankie has such a good appetite, as it denotes good health. I hope in taking "after his Papa," he may improve on the Example set him.

I am unable to say how long Beer has been in use, but probably something of its nature has been used even in our Savior's time. I have used more of it during the past month than I have for years. I think it does me good, but it is not palatable.[3]

I presumed that you would consult Mother about your condition before this, & conclude that if nothing has been developed by this time, or within a very few days at least, that I have won the bet.[4] I have never thought of laughing at you, nor am I much surprised if you are mistaken. I earnestly hope that you are gaining Strength, as you seem to think in closing your letter that you are improving. Tell Frankie that Papa sends a kiss to him & Mother inside this ring ⟨Kiss.⟩

I am inclined to believe that all your letters have reached me but some of them are at a very late date. I have letters from New Hartford mailed on the 10th, 11th, 14th, 17th, 21st, 22nd of July. You can tell if that is all. You wrote in one of your letters for my opinion of your going to Carlisle. I hope if you are able you will go if it is only for a short visit. I had planned to meet you & go with you, but all is past for this time. Do not let my failure depress you, for you will need the more courage. I presume ere this if my letter has been received, that you have heard from Mother [Culver] perhaps through Hannah or Jennie. You need fear nothing. Yet I know I could have added materially to your enjoyment if I could have been with you.

I regret very much that I did not know that Mother [Murphy] was with you when I wrote home. I told my Mother that I thought it probable she was, but I did not know as you did not mention it, either in your letter from Pontiac or Detroit. I shall write again to Mother to-night.

I recd. another letter from Bro. Wes. Father is no better but declining. I would ask Bro. Charlie to meet you in Harrisburg, if I thought you had fully fixed upon a time to go, but I presume after receiving my last letters you will wait for my coming. If you will write to him the time of your coming, he will be happy to meet you.

I wish both Mother & you a very pleasant visit. I know our Mothers will enjoy each other's society. Tell Mother M. not to feel any hesitancy in making herself at home there for my sake. It is my old home & very dear. There are so many things I intended to show you & tell you about that I should fail to Enumerate all in a letter. I shall write to you at Carlisle as soon as you let me know the time you will start & try & open the way for you. You must not get frightened at the host of Bros.,

Sisters, Nephews & Nieces you will meet. The girls will take delight in showing you around.[5]

Christ Yetter is enjoying good health. He said yesterday that he was going to write to you. Alf Huetson says that if you come again, he will take Frankie & make him a bed beside his.[6] Mrs. Smith is growing better slowly & hopes are entertained of her speedy recover. Her Father is here.

Bill Russell started for Pontiac yesterday morning. I am sure I never saw any one so homesick. He could hardly stand the prospect of being once more in Pontiac & talked & acted like a little *Boy*. He told us how he intended to conduct himself, & all he intended to say. He is determined to flirt with Miss Turner, Mrs. Green, and Mrs. Mott if he can, but professes no desire to go farther. If he were beseiged by all three at once (*as he fears*), I do not know what he would do. Miss Turner has kept up a regular correspondence. You must be discreet with my secrets, I do not wish to be in the least compromised in any way or event. But Bill & I have been confidents for a long time, & it is not improper that I should see & read for myself. I shall surely use my influence to secure his happiness. Though I may have been guilty once of looking after my own happiness in antagonism to what might have been strictly proper, I have surely no interests at stake now. I hope he may be as happy as I am in possessing the love of a noble, pure, & good wife.

May God bless you, my Wife, and make you happy always & never allow anything to transpire to mar your happiness. I wrote a long letter to the S. School on Sunday night. I have been waiting for a letter from Maggie [Utley] for sometime. I fear she has forgotten her promise to you. I have not heard from Bro. Johnnie [Murphy] yet. I must write again to-morrow. I should not be disappointed much if the money I sent him was lost. Bro. Thomas [Murphy] has not written yet.

I shall look for a full account of your Visit soon. How did you find your old haunts of pleasure. I hope beautiful as ever. Kiss Frankie & Mother for me & accept very many for yourself. I shall add a line in the morning informing you how I feel. Remember me kindly to all our friends. Hoping that God will bless you with health & happiness for which I shall ever pray, I will say Good Night

Your Affect. Husband

J. F. Culver

Dearest Wife

I feel much better, & I think before night I shall be well as ever. I dreamed of seeing Frankie & you last night. I thought we were on our way to Carlisle. May God bless my Wife and child - Farewell -

J. F. Culver

1 Mary Culver's letter of July 22 is missing from the Culver Collection.

2 General Rosecrans was in Nashville from July 22-25, and on the 26th he returned to the front, establishing his headquarters at Winchester, Tenn. *O. R.*, Ser. I, Vol. XXIII, pt. II, pp. 550-560.

3 In her letter of the 22d, Mary Culver must have broached the question of beer drinking.

4 J.F.C. is alluding to the possibility that his wife might be pregnant.

5 This would be Mary Culver's first visit to Carlisle, and she had misgivings over meeting her in-laws for the first time.

6 Alfred C. Huetson, a 22-year-old farmer, was mustered into service on Sept. 8, 1862, as a private in Company A, 129th Illinois. He was promoted to corporal on May 9, 1863, and on March 21, 1864, was detached as brigade topographical engineer. On April 6, 1865, Corporal Huetson was placed on duty at headquarters, Army of Georgia. Compiled Service Records of Union Soldiers, NA.

 66

Head Quarters, Co. "A" 129th Regt. Ills. Vol. Infty.
Gallatin, Tenn. July 30th 1863

My Dear Wife

Yours of the 28th inst. came to hand this evening. I felt somewhat surprised before opening your letter to find it Post Marked Clinton, a name not at all familiar,[1] & I feared you had removed where my letters would not reach you. I was very agreeably disappointed upon opening it, however, & finding you still among warm friends. I have felt great anxiety about your health & hope you will not hesitate to make use of any means to restore you to your accustomed good health.

I wrote to you two days ago but as the trains were employed in transporting troops, the mails were necessarily detained. Wean Frankie by all means. I apprehend no serious results in his case, while it may prove very serious in yours to delay longer, especially if the surmises of Dr. Griswold are correct.[2] I did not encourage it here [weaning Frankie] because I thought you entirely mistaken in your conjectures, & I hope you will run no risks in the matter. If it should still prove a mistake, no harm will result, and if not, much good to yourself.

I was not aware that Frankie was so heathenish as to debar him from the privilege of attending church. I hope, however, he may improve in manners, as he grows in years.[3]

Do not let your expenses debar your pleasure in any way. I want you to enjoy yourself & get well as soon as possible, & you have the greater need of it if the early part of the winter should find you (winning your dress). May God bless you & speedily restore your health.

I am very thankful to Mr. Scott for his kindness, & hope some day to have the pleasure of taking a ride myself on the S. D. Caldwell.[4]

Thomas [Murphy] has not written, neither have I heard from Johnie lately. I have a perfect understanding of how matters stand with Sis & also Miss Turner, as I saw Miss Turner's letter on the subject. (Mum).

You will Remember me kindly to Mrs. Williams & all the family. I dare not think of the pleasure it would give me to accept her kind wishes & assist to make your Visit a happy one. Perhaps when my duty is done here I may be permitted to see them all.

I am under obligations to Miss Sarah for a very kind & interesting letter which I will try and answer. I am sorry that my letter never reached her as I wrote quite a lengthy one as you can testify. Remember me also to Miss Aggie Davidson. Perhaps she will recollect my Visit at Utica; though short, it was very pleasant. I am exceedingly sorry to hear of the death of Miss Reed. My recollection is that she played the Organ when I was there. Am I correct?

It has been raining hard for the past 24 hours, leaving everything very wet & damp. We have scarcely got well dried since you left, almost continual rains. Pegram with 2000 men went into Kentucky on Monday to help Morgan not having heard that he was Captured.[5] He is rapidly retreating with some 6 or 7,000 troops on his flank & rear.

I have had no news from home since I last wrote. I expect to hear from Russell very soon.

It was one year ago on Wednesday [the 28th] since I left you on the little porch to attend the meeting in which I signed my name as a recruit. Do you recollect it? I shall never forget your look when I returned & told you what I had done. How easily I read your thoughts, & oh, how I thanked God for so noble [&] self sacrificing a heart, as he had given me in my wife. When all the anticipated pleasures of a life were placed in the balance, with a dark prospective future and on the other hand duty, she had no remonstrance but cheerfully yielded all to the cause of right & Country. Few men have greater incentives to deeds of bravery than I have. May God abundantly reward you.

Very many times have all these circumstances recurred to my mind, & I have always felt that I should ever strive to be worthy [of] the confidence reposed in me, & give you no reason to regret your resolution. Pray for me.

Christ Yetter promised to write to you but has not done so yet. He came off duty this morning wet to the skin & has not been feeling very well to-day. Mrs. Smith is much better & expects to be able to travel home in ten days. Capt. Reed will return from Pontiac by Monday, & we will get the news.

Charlie Paige is in Pontiac & report says he has been appointed Brig. Genrl. of [a] negro Brigade. I doubt it very much. I hope he may be useful for once.

Alf Huetson has been experimenting in vaccination on himself & has a very sore arm; I think the bins [?] he used must have been impure. He has several large boils which are quite painful.

Phil Plattenburg [Regimental Adjutant] has been sick for several days, & I have been assisting him some. I made out the Consolidated Monthlies for him today & find the total sick in the Regt. only 48; a very small list, indeed, which tells well for the health of the Regiment.

Dr. Johnson & Bob Edgington are in Louisville to see their wives, who are there but could not get through the lines. I do not know whether they intend to bring them here or not.

Nelson has put up a tent, & his wife expects to stay in camp.[6] We received a dispatch from Genrl. Rosecrans, inquiring if Nelson was dangerously ill. It seems his wife telegraphed for a pass, stating that he was; but she got through & it did not become necessary to answer it. He has not been sick at all. I intended to answer Sarah's letter to-night, but it is getting very late & I think I shall defer it until to-morrow evening.

I have written a much longer letter to you than I expected & laughed at myself for selecting so large a sheet. My health is quite good. We have apples plenty. Peaches and plums are ripening, but are not plenty [iful] yet.

If I could step into Mrs. Williams' Parlor to-morrow morning, I would give you one of the sweetest kisses you ever had. Please accept it, at any rate; & perhaps I shall be able to make it good someday. I want you to be well enough to come & see me this fall if I cannot get home & we remain here.

Read at your leisure the 25th and 35th chaps. of Isaiah. Give my love to Mother, Frankie & all our dear friends. I shall look anxiously for another letter soon. The paper you sent has not yet come to hand. "Do not be discouraged" but persevere. I must say Good-night, praying that God will be with & bless you all.

Your Affect. Husband

J. F. Culver

---

1  Mary Culver's letter of July 25 is missing from the Culver Collection. Clinton, another Oneida County town, is about five miles west of New Hartford.

2  Dr. Walter R. Griswold was a 44-year-old New Hartford, New York, physician. Eighth Census, Oneida County, State of New York, NA.

3  Apparently Frankie had acted ill-manneredly in church.

4  Captain Scott was master of the screw steamer *S.D. Caldwell* of 757 tons. Mary Culver had booked passage on the *S.D. Caldwell* from Detroit to Buffalo. *Merchant Steam Vessels of the United States, 1807-1868, "The Lytle List"* (Mystic, 1952), p. 167.

5  Morgan with the remnant of his command had been captured on July 26, 1863 near New Lisbon, Ohio. Col. John S. Scott, not Brig. Gen. John Pegram, had crossed from East Tennessee into Kentucky through Big Creek Gap on Saturday, July 25. Advancing rapidly by way of Williamsburg, London, and Big Hill, Scott's brigade engaged the Federals at Rogersville on the 28th and occupied Richmond. There Colonel Scott learned of Morgan's capture. On the 29th Scott's troopers pushed on to Winchester, and, on learning of the approach of strong Union columns, abandoned their toehold in the Bluegrass region and started back to East Tennessee. *O. R.*, Ser. I, Vol. XXIII, pt. I, pp. 839-840.

6  Erastus J. Nelson, a 27-year-old painter, was mustered into service on Sept. 8, 1862, as a corporal in Company A, 129th Illinois. Nelson was reduced to private on Jan. 12, 1863, and was wounded in the chest at Peachtree Creek, Georgia, on July 20, 1864, and hospitalized at Nashville until Oct. 8, when he was given a medical discharge. Compiled Service Records of Union Soldiers, NA.

 67

Head Quarters, Co. "A" 129th Regt. Ills. Vol. Infty.<br>Gallatin, Tenn., Aug. 2nd 1863

My Dear Wife

I am disappointed in not hearing from you to-day & earnestly hope the state of your health has not prevented your writing. I hope that I may be more successful to-morrow.

*117*

I received my petition for leave of Absence to-day returned rejected. I have still another in the hands of Dr. Heermans, who went to the front on Friday Evening. I have but little hopes of success, however, & will not base any expectations upon it. My last petition has been three weeks getting through. I shall in all probability try again, the first opportunity that offers, but you must not allow any prospect of my success enter into your arrangements. If possible I shall be with you before your return home, unless I am assured that there will be necessity for my waiting until Winter. Your letters intimate such a contingency & perhaps you may soon be able fully to determine.[1]

I wrote to you on Thursday Evening & a long letter to Sarah on Friday. I rec'd. a letter from Sister Hannah stating that Father was slowly declining & they fear he will not live much longer, & also Stating that she had written to you to visit them, & as I feared Mother's name [Mrs. Murphy's] was not mentioned.[2] My last letter had not been received. I am exceedingly sorry as Mother will undoubtedly feel slighted & not feel at liberty to go. I hope she will not feel so, & you can explain fully how it has happened. I am confident it will be rectified if you acknowledge the receipt of Hannah's letter, so that she may know hers has been received.

If I had been successful [in obtaining a leave] & could have been with you, all would have been well. As it is, I shall hope for the best.

You intimate in your last letter that you are almost done visting in New York. When do you expect to leave it? I have no clue to your intentions, but you could not determine your course, I presume, until you heard from Carlisle.

I shall wait anxiously to hear from you & especially to learn the state of your health. I do not know that I can add any suggestions to my former letter except that cheerfullness is a great aid to health. Bilious diseases almost always produce a morbid state of mind which requires great effort at times to throw off. I have been so often afflicted that I am conversant with its effects. Do not allow anything to give you trouble. If even your surmises as to your condition are correct, there is no reason for depression. I shall feel thankful to God for all blessings, & though I know you may have some severe trials, which I would be most happy to alleviate if in my power by my presence; yet I cannot deny that I should look with pleasure for the event, if my dear Wife only enjoys good health.

I hope much from the weaning of Frankie in the regaining [of] your health. I am inclined to believe that you have suffered much more than your letter intimates & have felt considerable uneasiness. If your health should prevent your writing, be sure & get some friend to write & give me your true condition. Do not hesitate to tell me the worst, I shall certainly expect it & rely upon your letters.

Nothing of interest has transpired since I last wrote. Capt. Reed has returned from Pontiac but brings but little news, save that all are well. I do not understand why Sister Maggie [Utley] has not kept her promise to write to me. I have heard nothing of Bro. Johnie yet, nor from Thomas or Sammy.[3] I presume they are all busy. Russell has not written yet & had not arrived when Capt. Reed left. I presume he is having a happy time.

I learn through Reed that the reports in circulation in Pontiac [of Russell's romantic interests] have lost nothing, but are becoming more serious. I apprehend but little evil from them, however, while they will furnish food for the minds of many, who always knew that it would be so. I shall trust still in God. Pray for me.

Mrs. Smith is slowly improving but is very far from being able to travel. She can sit up in bed for half an hour at a time but that is all. She will regain strength but slowly until she is able to move about. My health is quite good.

Your papers have not yet arrived. We have no exciting war news. The Rebels have left Kentucky, & our troops hold undisputed possession.[4] Dr. Johnson & Lt. Edgington have returned from Louisville & their wives gone home. It was late when they got into the city, & Doc's [Johnson's] children had gone to bed. In the morning the youngest wakened earl[y] & not knowing his father, alarmed his mother by his cries saying there was a man in bed. You know Doc's disposition, & Jo[?] enjoys the joke very much.

I shall try & write to-morrow evening if I hear from you. To-day, one year ago, I was sworn into the *service*. Who knows what the coming year may bring forth? I hope we may see the inauguration of a permanent Peace. The Rebels are as determined as ever & will not yield except as they are overcome.[5]

May God in mercy bless you, my dear Wife, & keep us ever from evil. Kiss Frankie & Mother for me & Give my love to all our Kind Friends. Write to me as often as you can. With a kiss & much love to you, I remain, as ever,

Yours till Death,

J. F. Culver

---

1 J.F.C. is alluding to the possibility that his wife might be pregnant.

2 Hannah Culver in her letter of July 27 had written, "Father's health is not improving any. He infrequently suffers with pain in his stomach, besides his rheumatism in his back and limbs and of course is growing weaker." She also reported that she had written Mary Culver, inviting her to "spend the remainder of the summer with us." Hannah Culver to J.F.C., July 27, 1863, Culver Collection.

3   Johnny, Thomas, and Sammy Murphy were J.F.C.'s brothers-in-law.

4   Colonel Scott, in retreating from Kentucky, had divided his brigade. Col. G. W. McKenzie with his regiment withdrew through Fulkerson's Gap, while Scott with the main column retired by way of Big Hill, Lancaster, and Stanford, and recrossed the Cumberland River at Smith Shoals on August 1. When Scott reassembled his brigade at Concord, Tenn., he found that his raid into East Kentucky had cost 350 casualties. *O.R.*, Ser. I, Vol. XXIII, pt. I, pp. 840-843.

5   Northern euphoria caused by Lee's repulse at Gettysburg, the surrenders of Vicksburg and Port Hudson, and the withdrawal of Bragg's army from Middle Tennessee had evaporated. In the days immediately following Lee's retreat from Gettysburg and news that Vicksburg had fallen, most Northern leaders, as well as the people, believed that the war was about over. President Jefferson Davis and his generals, however, rallied their soldiers and civilians and the war continued another 22 months.

 68

Head Quarters, Co. "A" 129th Ills. Vols.
Gallatin, Tenn., Aug. 4th 1863

My Dear Wife

The mails have been quite irregular of late, & I have recd. no letter since Friday [July 31]. However, I feel assured that if anything serious had happened you would have telegraphed.

I wrote to you night before last informing you that my petition for Leave of Absence had been rejected. I have not yet heard from the one Doc. Heermans took for me, &, in the event it also fails, I have prepared another to go up through the regular military channels again. I am not altogether hopeless as Col. Case & Capt. Lamb both leave for home in the morning having been successful.[1] My former one was missent in some way, &, although I do not feel very confident of Success, I shall have done all that was in my power.

My health is quite good, &, if I had the assurance that your health was improving, I should be happy. While you have not written discouragingly, I am led to believe from the tenor of your letters that you feel much depressed. This is one reason why I have looked so anxiously for a letter for the last few days. I hope most earnestly to hear, my Dear Wife, that your health is improving & that you are happy. I am blessed with excellent health at present for which I hope I am sufficiently thankful.

Mrs. Smith is rapidly improving and will be able to start home next week if she continues to mend. Bill, the oldest of our cooks, died in the hospital this morning.[2] He has been quite sick for some time. Lt. McKnight is very sick; he has been growing worse for some ten days. I do not think the Drs. consider him very dangerously ill. Uncle Bart. Allen is not well yet, & we have on the sick list Leonard, Chritten & Shellenbarger.[3]

Christ Yetter was detailed in the Mounted Squad & is acting Orderly for Co. M. We are sorry to lose him, but he can do more in that capacity.

I have recd. no letters since I last wrote. I shall surely expect a letter from you to-morrow. Remember me kindly to all our friends. Give my love to Mother & kiss Frankie for me. I shall trust all in the hands of a kind Providence & hope for your speedy recovery of health. Pray that God may assist me & keep me through Grace Divine. I shall write as soon as I hear from you & report progress every other day as I have done to-night. "May holy angels guard thee"

Good night

Your Affect. Husband

J. F. Culver

---

1   On July 30 leaves of absence for 15 days, with permission to travel outside the Department of the Cumberland, had been granted to Col. Henry Case and Capt. Albert Lamb. Regimental Papers, 129th Illinois, NA.

2   Bill, a freedman, had been employed as a regimental cook.

3   Christopher C. Leonard, 27-year-old farmer, was mustered into service on September 8, 1862, as a private in Company A, 129th Illinois. He was promoted to corporal on May 9, 1863, and was mustered out on June 8, 1865, at Washington, D.C. James M. Chritten, a 20-year-old farmer, was mustered into service on Sept. 8, 1862, as a private in Company A, 129th Illinois. Private Chritten was promoted to corporal on May 9, 1863, and on July 4, 1864, he was detailed to the U.S. Sanitary Commission at Kingston, Ga. Joseph Shellenbarger, a 19-year-old horticulturist, was mustered into service on Sept. 8, 1862, as a private in Company A, 129th Illinois Volunteers. Private Shellenbarger died March 31, 1864, in the brigade hospital at Wauhatchie, Tenn., of pneumonia. Compiled Service Records of Union Soldiers, NA.

## 69

Head Quarters, Co. "A" 129th Ills. Vol. Infty.
Gallatin, Tenn., Aug. 7th 1863

My Dear Wife

Your letter commenced July 27th & mailed Aug. 1st came duly to
hand by this evening's mail.[1] I am surprised that so long a time should
elapse without your receiving a letter from me, as I have written
regularly every other day, with but two exceptions, & very frequently
every day. Our mails have been very irregular for two weeks past which
accounts for the delay of our letters I presume.

I hoped to hear that your health was improving, &, if a change for the
better does not soon commence, I shall feel seriously alarmed. I should
be desirous to obtain Leave of Absence, even if you should not be able
to make the visit with me, as I have business of grave importance both
at Pontiac & Carlisle.

Harrington has expressed a desire to have me pay $15 which he thinks
he is due and which I feel sure I could satisfy him was paid if I could
gain access to my papers & see him.[2]

I have not heard from home since Hannah wrote, which letter you
have received. You have not acknowledged the receipt of any letter
from Mother [Culver] or any of the family, & I fear have not received
any. I shall write home again immediately.

How earnestly I wish your health was good. I know Frankie must be
a severe trial to you, yet feel very thankful that he enjoys good health.
By this time you have weaned him; I hope his health may not be
seriously effected. The weather is severe, but I hope much from his
good health. I think if his teeth do not trouble him, he will do very well.
Mother [Murphy] understands well how to care for him, & I feel
satisfied nothing will be wanting. Your necessary absence from him for
a short time will also be a severe trial under the existing state of your
health, but it is all for the best. I pray God to restore you speedily to the
enjoyment of vigorous health.

I have not heard from the petition I sent by Doc. Heermans for Leave
of Absence yet, but do not expect it will be successful. I have given up

all hope for the present, as the Col. comdg. refuses to sign any more [leaves] until the other officers have had a chance.

Col. Case passed through Utica [N.Y.] yesterday if nothing happened on his way to visit his mother in Connecticut. I thought it barely possible you might be in Town, &, as the train stops there for dinner, he will look around to see you. But your letter precludes the possibility of his seeing you. Your health would prevent your being in the City.

My health is very good. I was prevented from writing last night. I was sent out on a scout shortly after dark & did not get back until 7 o'clock this morning, & was so sleepy that I could not write before mail time.

Mrs. Smith is improving slowly. She is able to sit up a couple of hours at a time. Lieut. McKnight is dangerously ill with chronic diarrhea but hopes are still entertained for his recovery. His wife is still here. Thompson Laycock is very ill with inflammation of the bowels but may recover.

We all received a severe shock from lightning day before yesterday evening. It struck the little tent beside our cook tent in which Tom sleeps & tore it all to pieces.[3] We had just finished supper, & I had got into my tent some ten steps distant. [Lt.] Smith & Maples & the two negroes were still in the cook tent. They were thrown some six or eight feet from the tent but not hurt much. Nelson, his wife, & both children were knocked down. I was standing in my tent near the bed. My legs gave way, & I fell on the bed. The shock was very severe all over camp, yet no one was hurt though Lt. Smith & Maples made a very narrow escape.

The report that Mary Snyder had fallen into the hands of Harper & Berryman was untrue. She has thus far kept out of their way though they have been after her several times.

Yesterday was "Thanksgiving Day." We observed it by having chicken & some few other nice things for dinner.[4]

I received a letter from Bro. Johnie yesterday, which I have enclosed thinking you would all like to hear from him.[5] I recd. a letter from F. H. Bond this evening. He says all are well.[6] I have no word from Maggie [Utley] yet. I fear she has forgotten me altogether.

We are performing about the same routine of duties. There are no bodies of troops on this side of the Cumberland River. Guerrillas are plenty, however, and give us some long rides. [The] Kings have heard from their son (Francis). He writes that he "is confined in the Ohio Penitentiary with the balance of Morgans horse-thieves."[7] They are lamenting his fate very much, yet are as strong REBELS as ever. I have not seen Carrie [Rodamore] for a month or more. I believe she is in Nashville. The family are well.

Give my love to Mother & all our friends. Kiss Frankie for me. Has he learned to say MAMA yet? I long very much to see you all and I hope to hear that you are getting health. May God make you happy & bless you abundantly. Your letters portray the state of your mind much more than you imagine, & I read them closely. I shall be very happy to hear good news from you soon, and, if I do not succeed in my contemplated visit, I shall believe still that our Heavenly Father has some wise end in view. Let us praise him.

Write to me as often as the state of your health will permit.

I presume the letter written to Sarah had not been recd. You have not yet told me the value of the note on the Canada Bank I sent you. Please don't forget it as the old negro may accuse me of trying to cheat him.

Trusting that God will restore you to health and happiness, I remain, Dear Wife,

Your Affect. Husband

J. F. Culver

P.S. Preserve Bro. Johnie's letter carefully, as it is the only acknowledgement of the money paid him I have.[8] Put it among my receipts in the desk when you get home.

J.F.C.

---

1   Mary Culver's letter of July 27 is missing from the Culver Collection.

2   Robert B. Harrington had defeated J.F.C. in November, 1861 for the office of Livingston County Clerk. He held this office for the next eight years. *History of Livingston County,* p. 266.

3   Tom, a black, was employed by the officers of the 129th Illinois as a cook.

4   President Lincoln had issued a proclamation declaring Thursday, Aug. 6, as "a day of Thanksgiving for the signal advances made by the Union armies toward the suppression of rebellion and of prayer that they be continued, to the speedy restoration of peace with a once more united country." *O. R.,* Ser. I, Vol. XXIII, pt. II, pp. 592-593.

5   Sergt. John Murphy's letter was dated Aug. 1, 1863, from a camp near Shelbyville, Tenn. W. J. Murphy to J.F.C., Aug. 1, 1863, Culver Collection.

6   F. H. Bond was clerk of the Pontiac Township. *History of Livingston County,* p. 308.

7   General Morgan and his officers, following their capture, had been turned over by the military to the warden of the Ohio State Prison at Columbus. Their hair had been trimmed and their beards shaved for cleanliness. They were placed in separate cells, and allowed two hours in the morning and two in the afternoon for exercise and conversation, and were segregated from the convicted felons. *O. R.,* Ser. I, Vol. XXIII, pt. I, p. 815.

8   J.F.C. had loaned his brother-in-law $20. W. J. Murphy to J.F.C., August 1, 1863, Culver Collection.

## 70

Hd. Qr. 129th Ills. Vol.
Gallatin, Tenn., Aug 10th 1863

My Dear Wife

I recd. your letter of the 2nd inst., bringing me the news of Frankie's misfortune & your health scarcely improving.[1] I hope Frankie may prove not to be seriously injured. Your letter, though several days later than your last, does not intimate that you have weaned Frankie yet. I expect to hear that your health is rapidly improving after he is weaned.

Mrs. Smith has taken a relapse, and all this day they have been looking for her to die. She was easier this evening. You would scarcely know her. Mrs. McKnight is still here with her husband; he is very low but may recover. Lou [Allen] left for home about 10 days after you left. I informed you [of this] in a former letter. Allen says she is quite well. Mrs. Ray went home about two weeks ago. Mrs. Fisher is still here in good health; also Mrs. Coppage & Mrs. Soir.[2] Mr. Kay is still here & expected to be able to start home with Mrs. Smith by to-morrow or next day.[3] Saml. McGoodin is in the enjoyment of good [health] & assigns as the reason of his not writing that he cannot write. I have offered to write for him if he calls on me. I have been interrupted & shall close for to-night, so Good night, may holy angels guard you.

Morning Aug 11th/63: I am in excellent health this morning. The weather is excessively warm. I can scarcely tell you which [rail] road is preferable to go to Harrisburg. You can go through New York & Philadelphia. It is about as cheap as any & gives you a chance to see the cities, but is somewhat difficult for you alone. The easiest rout[e] for you is to go to Rochester & take the [rail] road to Harrisburg, direct through Elmira & Williamsport. The fare either way is about the same & will cost from 10 to 15 dollars. If you go by way of New York, you will be compelled to stay there all night, get to Philadelphia about 2 o'clock next day, leave Philad. at 11 P.M., & get to Harrisburg at 3 A.M. next day, leave Harrisburg at 8 A.M. & get to Carlisle at 10. By the other rout[e], you will have fewer changes & at smaller towns. Try & take the train from Rochester in the evening, & you will get to Harrisburg in time for the train to Carlisle next day.

I have not heard what has been done with Allbe & Soph. Gagan took his whole family [to California] with him. We have got Bell tents similar to the one the sergeants used.[4] I wish you had returned the Canada Bill to me. I could have returned it & satisfied the old man; as it is, I do not know how to convince him. I sent you a letter from Bro. Johnie by last mail. He is still at Shelbyville, Tenn.

I have been act. adjutant of [for] a week. Phil (Plattenburg) is in the Hospital but will be back by to-morrow. I was interrupted last night, & now it is mail time. I will enclose a letter from Sis giving the Pontiac news. With love to all, I must haste to say, good bye. May God bless you.

Your Affect. Husband

J. F. Culver

---

1 Mary Culver's letter of Aug. 2 is missing from the Culver Collection.

2 Mrs. Bay of Pontiac was the wife of Pvt. George W. Bay of Company G; Mrs. Fisher of Pontiac the wife of Sergt. Augustus F. Fisher of Company G; Mrs. Coppage of Scott County the wife of Capt. Joseph W. Coppage of Company I; and Mrs. Loir (Lore) of Joliet the wife of Pvt. Robert C. Lore of Company B.

3 Mrs. Smith was the eldest daughter of John and Joanna Kay, prosperous Pontiac Township farmers. In 1860 the Kays were living with their other nine children. Eighth Census, Livingston County, State of Illinois, NA.

4 Colonel Case on June 12 had complained to the post commander that his troops were "sadly wanting in tents." Although the officers had wall tents, the enlisted men had been issued worthless second-hand tents or had picked up tents abandoned by other units. He accordingly wished to requisition Sibley tents for the regiment, as it would be stationed at Gallatin for some time. His efforts to secure Sibley tents for the regiment were unsuccessful, as orders were given by the chief quartermaster, Department of the Cumberland, to have the troops turn in their old canvas and draw "shelter tents." Case to Sweet, June 12, 1863, Regimental Papers, 129th Illinois, NA.

 71

Hd. Qr., 129th Ills. Vol.<br>Gallatin, Tenn., Aug. 14th 1863

My Dear Wife

No letter from you yet. It is four days since I recd. your last letter. I have continued to write every other day, & I presume you have done the same, but the irregularity of the mails prevent their coming.

We received a dispatch from Bill Russell; he will be here this evening. Scott McDowell is with him. I anticipate a very pleasant time for a few days, & a host of News from Pontiac. I shall send you everything of importance by next mail.

I shall be really happy if I but receive a letter from you assuring me of your good health and Frankie's. As soon as you get quite well, I shall expect a full history of your visit. I want to know all that transpired during your stay in New York. Will you go to Niagara? If you go to Harrisburg by way of Rochester, it will not be very far out of your way to go to the falls. I hope to see them some day, &, if you can do so, I should advise you to go & see them.

I have not received one particle of News of any kind since I sent you the letters I recd. I will write to Sis [Maggie Utley] this morning to send me 3 or 4 white shirts by [Alfred] Huetson. She can easily find them; can she not? I shall direct her to look in the desk drawers; all I fear is that they may be locked.

Rumor says that the 129th will leave Gallatin this week.[1] I have no reason to believe that it is true, yet it is not improbable. Mrs. Smith is no better; 'tis a bitter Struggle with death. God alone knows which will conquer; she is resigned to her fate. Her disease has been of so long duration and so severe as to almost make death desirable; she has expressed such desires I am told. She is utterly helpless.

I saw Mrs. Laurence & Mrs. Loir [Lore] yesterday evening, they are both quite well.[2] I tried to get permission to go to Bowling Green Ky., to meet Bill & Scott but had my usual luck in refusal. I have no cause to complain. God has given me excellent health, &, if I could but know that you were well & happy, I should be fully satisfied. It is hard to be so far away from those we love when sickness or troubles intervene.

I fear I am a dreamer, but I have tasted of realities. I have often thought how happy we will be in Heaven. "There will be no sorrow there." We will not be separated but to all eternity enjoy each other's society. Let us try hard to take Frankie with us. Teach him of Jesus as soon as he can understand. Perhaps I shall be with you by another year, when together we will teach him & pray for him.

Have you any further evidence of your former anticipations? You must not fail to tell me of all your hopes and fears, joys & troubles. I hope to receive a long letter from you this evening.

I sent you a coral & gold embroidered Masonic Pin. I have not yet seen a fitting pin, or I should buy you one. Give my love to Mother [Murphy] & all our friends. Kiss Frankie for me. I have never heard of the letter I wrote to *Sarah*. Tell me whether it was received. May God bless you, My Dear Wife, & bless our child. Keep us all in health &

restore us speedily to our homes & each other's society. Let us continue to pray. I shall very probably write to-night, so till then, Farewell.

Your Affect. Husband

J. F. Culver

---

1 With the destruction of Morgan's command and the withdrawal of Bragg's Confederate army from Middle Tennessee, the danger of a raid by an organized Rebel force on the Louisville & Nashville Railroad had been alleviated. Partisans would have to be guarded against, but to cope with these required less troops. General Rosecrans could now redeploy some of his troops guarding that vital railroad.

2 Mrs. Laurence of Pontiac was the wife of Pvt. Reuben E. Laurence of Company G.

 72

Hd. Qrs. 129th Ills. Vol.
Gallatin, Tenn., Aug. 14th 1863

My Dear Wife

Yours of the 6th & 9th Inst. came to hand this evening.[1] I am very happy to hear that there is a fair prospect of your speedy recovery to health. If you should start early in next week for Carlisle, my letter may not reach you.[2]

I am sorry to hear that Mother [Murphy] has not yet concluded to go with you.[3] I should like very much to have her go. Tell her I think it very probable I shall be in Carlisle in three or four weeks, & if she remains in New York or goes to Pontiac I shall not probably have an opportunity of seeing her. I could get a leave of absence now without doubt, but I gave my chance to Lt. Smith to-night.[4] Col. Cropsey gave me the assurance to-day that I should go,[5] but Mrs. Smith is beyond the hope of recovery & will not probably live more than a few days. Lt. Smith wants to bury her at home, & my going would prevent him. I can therefore cheerfully wait, & if no circumstances transpire to materially change the state of affairs here, my chances will be equally good on his return, & I feel that it is but justice to do so. The time furnished, however, will not give me an opportunity to go any out of my way, as only 15 days are granted.

I hope if you can content yourself & be happy, you will remain in Carlisle 5 or 6 weeks at least. If you cannot, I should be sorry to have you stay, & I will come to you wherever you are.

I surely never recd. any of your letters stating that Mother [Murphy] was with you. The letter you refer to says that Thomas was unwilling to return without you but Mother is not mentioned.

I cannot deliver your message to Alf. Huetson.[6] He is at home, & I presume supremely happy.

You continue to write, "We shall wean Frankie next week." I hope, my Dear Wife, you will not delay until your own health is sacrificed. I want to hear of your speedy recovery. I am happy to hear that Frankie is growing so rapidly in size, & I hope also in good qualities. I am afraid from the vast changes you find in your old home during your absence, that all the assistance I might be able to render you will be of no avail, as so many changes in my old home have taken place that you would not recognize it as the same place.[7]

I accept all the kisses in letter no. 1, and now for no. 2, You will be under the necessity of writing every day & sometimes twice a day to "catch up with me." I have been writing every day lately. I am much obliged for the correction; I now recollect both Miss Root & Miss Reed. It was not my intention to give you pain for mentioning the noble self-sacrifice you made, & you will forgive me for repeating that whatever internal struggle you had, you never intimated anything to me. Let us praise God for your victory over yourself. I cannot see that any retraction of my former assertions are necessary, & I love you all the more for all your fortitude. None but God knew whether I would be with you in your severest trial as a wife, yet he ordered all so well that I hope I may never cease to feel grateful.

I shall be careful to eat none but ripe fruit and plenty of it. We have apples & peaches in abundance. Oh, how I wish I could send you some.

I should fully appreciate those kisses you wish to kiss & feel myself fully competent to return them with good interest. I perceive by your letter you have not yet decided whether I shall furnish a dress or receive a neck-tie, but as usual you expect soon to know. I should have no hesitancy in promising two dresses, believing that even possibility is in my favor.

Five days have elapsed since the date of your last letter, & Frankie by this time has almost learned to gain a living by eating. Write to me very soon, I shall feel very anxious to hear the result. I am happy for the assurance that you will not attempt to conceal from me the worst if at any time either of you should be sick.

I greatly fear I shall never have an opportunity to deliver your message of love to Mrs. Smith. She is unable to speak & in great pain. I spent about an hour with her this morning in company with Col. Cropsey. She was very happy & ready to die. God has bountifully blessed her. This evening she is much worse, several Drs. held a consultation in her case & have decided that she will die. I scarcely expect to see her again alive. King's whole family have been very kind, & the girls sit up almost every night.[8]

Bill Russell & Scott McDowell arrived this evening. Bill is enjoying good health. He brought me a letter from Abbie [Remick] which I have enclosed to you. They report all our friends well. Mrs. McDowell is at Magnolia, Ills., with her mother counselling with a physician.[9] Trudy is no better, & I fear will never be much better in this world. I saw a picture of their baby. It looks very healthy & quite pretty.

Many changes have taken place in Pontiac, but generally for the better. I am led to believe from Bill's talk that he has been trifling with Miss Turner. If I knew her, I could determine. I hope most earnestly it is not so, for I heartily despise anything of the kind. Henry Greenebaum sent me a pint of unadulterated English Brandy, sealed up, with the request that it should not be opened until I took sick. I hope to be able to carry it back to Pontiac with me, don't you? You have as yet made no mention of the letter I wrote in answer to Sarah's letter; is it possible that it, too, is lost?

Lt. McKnight is no better but is in a very critical condition. We hope for his recovery. The rest of our sick are rapidly improving. Plattenburg has not yet returned to duty but will very soon. I believe he is quite well again but is still resting. The duties have not been very heavy here this week, but this office [the Adjutant's] is very confining. Scott McDowell will remain here for some time, I do not know how long.

I have written quite a long letter & must close, else I shall have nothing to write to-morrow. I do not believe you will be able to keep up with me but do all you can. Write very often, your letters make me happy. If mine are equally as interesting, I shall take pleasure in multiplying them. Give my love to Mother & all our friends. I hope to hear of Mother in Carlisle. You can draw on Remick at any time for $75. I shall be compelled to get a little back if pay-day is delayed. Kiss

Frankie for me  May God in Mercy bless you, for which I shall ever pray.

Your Affect. Husband

J. F. Culver

1 Mary Culver's letter of Aug. 9 is missing from the Culver Collection.

2 Mary Culver had written, "My health continues to improve and if nothing happens to prevent, I will go to Carlisle week after next." Mary Culver to J.F.C., Aug. 6, 1863, Culver Collection.

3 Mother Murphy did not plan to go to Carlisle, as she had not finished her visit in New Hartford. *Ibid.*

4 On Aug. 20, 1863, Lt. John W. Smith was granted a ten-day leave, with permission to return to Illinois. Regimental Papers, 129th Illinois, NA.

5 With Colonel Case on a 15-day furlough, Colonel Cropsey commanded the regiment. *Ibid.*

6 Mary Culver had directed her husband to tell Alf "to prepare Frankie's bed and be sure and have it large enough, he is growing amazingly, a few feet longer than his own will do." Mary Culver to J.F.C., Aug. 6, 1863, Culver Collection.

7 Mary Culver had complained, "I have been so poorly since I have been here, I have walked no where; and it does not seem as if I had seen many things that was once familiar, everything is so changed, it does not look like the place I used to know as New Hartford." *Ibid.*

8 Mrs. Smith occupied a room in Gallatin at the Kings', where Mrs. Culver had stayed during her visit.

9 Mary T. McDowell was the 26-year-old wife of J. Scott McDowell, a Fairbury farmer. Eighth Census, Livingston County, State of Illinois, NA.

73

Hd. Qrs., 129th Ills. Vol.
Gallatin, Tenn., Aug. 16th 1863

My Dear Wife

I was uptown with Mrs. Smith & did not take time to write, so I can but send a few lines this morning. Mrs. Smith is still very low. I did not deliver your message. She is not able to Speak. I have very little hope for her recovery.

I ford. a petition yesterday for a Leave of Absence for Smith, & as [Captain] Hoskins will claim the next chance, I shall not make any effort for 5 or 6 weeks, but then I think I shall succeed.[1] It may be so far advanced by that time as to be safe for you & Frankie here.

I have been Studying whether to send this letter to Carlisle but concluded not to. I expect to hear from you to-day and shall then know when to write to Carlisle.

My health is very good. It was my intention to write a long letter last night, but I will try & write some this afternoon. With much love to all, I close, praying that God will bless & keep you.

Your Affect. Husband

J. F. Culver

P.S. King's family requested last night to be remembered to you.

1 Lieutenant Smith's 10-day leave was approved by headquarters, Army of the Cumberland, on Aug. 20, 1863. Regimental Papers, 129th Illinois, NA.

 74

Hd. Qrs. Co. "A" 129th Ills. Vol.
Gallatin, Tenn., Aug. 19th 1863

My Dear Wife

I have been disappointed in not hearing from you for the last five days. I have written three letters since the receipt of your last to New Hartford & have concluded to write to Carlisle to-night in anticipation of your arrival there.

I received a letter from Sister Hannah this evening, informing me of the sudden death of Sister Jennie's children,[1] & Mother's earnest desire for your presence [in Carlisle], which, together with your intention of visiting there this week, has induced me to write to you at Carlisle, believing my letter will find you there.

I am reminded of my promise to write you a long letter, but find myself at a loss to know what to write that will contribute to your enjoyment. There are a great many things I desire to write, more than either time or Space will admit. I sympathize deeply with Sister in her bereavement. How often I think of Frankie and you both so far away from me that in sudden or dangerous illness I could scarcely expect to see. But we have trusted ourselves to God, & we must not doubt his wisdom and goodness. I hope to hear soon that you are both quite well.

Mrs. Smith is still alive but no better. Every person is excluded from her room. I have been up every day but have not seen her. She suffers very much but is quite happy.

Hannah says Father [Culver] is no better. Quite a number of my old acquaintances have been drafted, among the number, Sister Beccie's husband & Annie Good's sister Lizzie's oldest daughter's husband.[2] They have only been married a few weeks, & it will be hard to part. I think much more so than if he had voluntarily enlisted from a sense of duty. I do not know whether either of them will be able to find a Substitute.

Mother [Culver] expresses so great desire to have you with her that I feel almost certain you will be happy. You will meet so many of my old friends and companions that I scarcely know how to make mention of them.

Sister Beccie [Pague] still lives on the old homestead farm, a place endeared by very many hallowed associations. I have built almost all the fences, planted a large majority of the trees, and ploughed time & time again every acre of the land. My room was just over the kitchen, opening on the balcony. My bed is still there, or was when I was last at home. At the South East corner of the front porch stands a cedar planted by Sister Beccie & myself, many years ago. It was broken down once, but has after buffeting, storm, & accident, grown into a good sized tree.

In front of the kitchen, on the slope of the hill, stands a cherry tree under whose shade I have had many an hour's rest at Noon in harvest time. In the garden stands a fine pear tree; we were never permitted to pull them, & we always tried to be first up in the morning to get what had fallen during the night. Then there are the flowers, the Lawton blackberries. I paid $3 for the six roots first planted but never got a berry. Perhaps they are not all over yet. It is now just pear time, & I hope you may find them plentiful.

In the rear of the Kitchen is a Willow. I recollect many years ago of carrying a switch from the old fish pond below Miller's & planting it there. I wattered it every time I washed for 3 or 4 years, & now it has grown into a large tree. Sister will take pleasure in showing you all that I took particular pleasure in.

At the east end of the porch are two large Stone Steps, where the whole family congregated every Sunday evening. Father & Mother generally had their chairs. The older girls occupied the Steps, but my place was invariably on the grass. Very many times have I rolled over the little mound there. Many years ago the house in which I was born stood there. I recollect it well though I was quite small. It now stands at the lower end of the farm on the road going East. The oleander that was given to me when I was *married* is at Father's.

Among the old friends of mine will be Miss Sistie Johnson, I know you will be pleased with the whole family. Dr. Johnson is one of my best friends.[3] You will also very probably meet Miss Annie Underwood.[4] You will remember I corresponded with her for a year or more after our marriage. If her temper is not soured by long teaching, you will find her very companionable. The whole family have shown me very many kindnesses. Miss Sarah Stewart, with whom I boarded while at College & the family Milliner,[5] quite old but a true friend of mine; Mr. Martin's family, also proprietors of the Farmers' Hotel.[6] I do not know whether Jennie is married yet or not. Tom Greenfield was reported once to have married her, but I never heard it confirmed.[7]

You will meet many dear friends, & I hope you will be very happy. You may find some old family relics, too, that are very dear to memory: Mother's Bible & the old Family Bible. You will find both on a little red stand covered with oil cloth. Mother's chair and the old arm chair in which I sat many weary months while recovering from an attack of rheumatism. There is an old wooden chest either at Father's or at Sister Beccie's that has a large number of papers belonging to me, also a desk in one of the drawers of which I left many little things. I always thought I would preserve them for my children if God ever gave me any, believing they would prove interesting to them. How I would like to look over them once more & think of "days gone by."

Even while I write, memory is busy with recollections of the past, & I bless God that I find all pleasure and no pain in reviewing them. Oh, I have been so very happy amid those fields and flowers, those trees and rocks, that the recollection of them will never fade. If I could only be with you, for I fear there has been so many changes that you will fail to recognize my description of the old place.

Get Hannah & Charlie to write to me more frequently. I feel so anxious to hear from them all very often. I feel so certain you will love Mother, & she will be so happy to have you with her. Kiss her for me.

I hope Mother Murphy is with you, for I know she will enjoy the visit. I hope to hear from you very soon after you get there. Give my love to all. Charlie [Culver] will be very happy to have Frankie with him, and I know will show him all the sights. He will take you wherever you wish to go.

I hope you will be able to visit Mount Holley gap; it is only 2 miles from Sister Lizzie's [Elizabeth Culver Zug's] & Bro. Jacob Zug will furnish you all the assistance you desire.[8] Give my love to all of his family. Then there is Bro. John's wife & children,[9] & Millers, a large family.[10] Fanny must be almost a woman by this time. I feel confident you will have a happy time. Remember me kindly to Bro. Wes & his family.

In one of the Secret Drawers of Father's desk, there is one or two pieces of California gold sent me by Bro. James.[11] If not lost, I wish Mother would give it to you to take home & put in one of my little drawers. I wish very much to preserve it. Father knows where it is.

I believe you will find Sister Hannah a good companion, & I know she will take pleasure in going around with you, & Sister Jennie, try and console her in her great loss. I hope God will sustain her. Cheer up Father. I should like so much to see him once more & talk with him. I could write much more but must give you the news & will commence another sheet.

There is a rumor afloat that we will be sent [to] Nashville in a few days, but it lacks confirmation.[12] I was relieved this morning from duty as adjutant & have returned to the Company. Phil [Plattenburg] will be able to resume his duties in a few days. Capt. Hoskins is sitting in a Court-Marshall so that I am alone. Alf. Huetson has not yet returned. Bill [Russell] is enjoying good health. He & Maples are about selling out to Scott McDowell & John Blackburn, they are both here.[13]

I expected Russell would not remain with us long but did not think of Maples leaving. I promised to write to Trudy (Scott's wife) but have not yet had time.

I received a long letter from Mrs. Custer two days ago.[14] Mr. Lawrence has left our house, and a family by the name of Coe now occupy it. They are from LaSalle County. I do not know them. I forwarded Abbie Remick's & Emily Johnson's letters in my former letters of this week, thinking they would be of interest to you. I will write a short letter to Mother [Culver] to-night, requesting her to ford. this letter to you should you have been unable to get there.

I shall wait anxiously for some word from you. I cannot promise anything from leave of Absence at present but hope to be able to see you in Carlisle. We are all in the enjoyment of good health. Allen heard from Lou a few days ago when she was quite well. Can Frankie talk any yet? Which did he learn to say first, *Mama* or *Papa*? Do you recollect your prediction? What prospect is there of its fulfillment? Give me all the news. May God in his Infinite Mercy bless and keep you. Oh, how much I desire to hear of your enjoying good health. May you ever be happy.

Farewell

Your Affectionate Husband

J. F. Culver

1   Hannah Culver's letter, conveying news of the death of the Rev. H. C. and Jennie Culver Cheston's two oldest children, is missing from the Culver Collection.

2   On March 3, 1863, the federal government enacted a national conscription law. By this act all able-bodied male citizens between 20 and 45 were "to constitute the national forces" and were declared liable to military service. By harking back to practices employed in old militia systems, two provisions of a questionable nature were included — those pertaining to substitutes and commutation money. If a drafted man furnished an acceptable substitute he might be exempt from service; such exemption could also be bought outright for $300. Randall, *Civil War and Reconstruction,* pp. 410-411.

J.F.C.'s sister Rebecca (Beccie) was married to S. Augustus Pague, a Middlesex Township farmer. Pague and his wife were 29, and in 1860 they were living on the family farm with their one-year-old son Franklin. Eighth Census, Cumberland County, State of Pennsylvania, NA.

3   Dr. Herman M. Johnson was a 47-year-old professor of English literature at Dickinson College and Lucena (Ludy) was his wife. Living with the Johnsons in 1860 were their seven children and two domestics. *Ibid.*

4   Miss Annie Underwood was a 29-year-old school teacher. In 1860 she was living with her mother and three sisters. *Ibid.*

5   Miss Sara B. Stewart was a 53-year-old Carlisle milliner. *Ibid.*

6   David Martin and his wife Rebecca owned and operated the Farmers' Hotel in Carlisle. In 1860 their four children, two boys and two girls, were living with them. The oldest boy, Samuel, tended bar for his parents. *Ibid.*

7   It has been impossible to further identify Tom Greenfield.

8   Jacob Zug, the 42-year-old husband of Elizabeth Culver, was a wealthy South Middleton Township farmer. In 1860 the Zugs were living with their seven children, ranging in ages from 7 to 16. *Ibid.*

9   Mrs. Elizabeth Zug Culver, the widow of John Culver, with three of her children (Clara, Ira, and John) was living in 1860 with Jacob Zug and his family. *Ibid.*

10   It has been impossible to further identify the Miller family.

11   James Culver, the eldest son of Joseph Culver and his first wife (Elizabeth Cary Culver) had emigrated to California in 1849. James died there in 1863. Jennie Culver Cheston, "History of the Joseph Culver Family within the Memory of Mrs. Jennie Culver Cheston," Ms., Culver Collection.

12   The rumored transfer of the 129th Illinois from Gallatin to Nashville was verified on Aug. 21, 1863. On that date, Col. B. J. Sweet issued a post order, announcing that the regiment had been relieved from duty at Gallatin. Commending the regiment for its service, Colonel Sweet pointed out that "circumstances" had made him "intimately acquainted with the organization and history" of the 129th.

"The duties which have been assigned to it have been arduous and peculiar, requiring much of their time, its separation by detachments and details. They have been of such character that their performance required judgment, tact, alertness and decision. Taking part in no battles, officers and men have yet been tried by fire in numerous skirmishes; in scouting it has been diligent and always trusted by its commanders; it has developed the highest capacity to successfully circumvent and destroy guerrillas, doing duty equally well as infantry or mounted men showing a ready adaptability and quick courage to meet all emergencies. At times the Colonel commanding the Post has been obliged to require exhausting, constant and unpleasant duty of this regiment and found it failing never. He has therefore the fullest confidence in its new command and relations. It will make a history honorable to officers and men as that formed for itself in and around Gallatin." Regimental Papers, 129th Illinois, NA.

13 Ed Maples, who had held the position of regimental sutler since March 27, was thinking of selling out to John Blackburn and Scott McDowell. Blackburn had resigned his commission as lieutenant of Company E on Feb. 26, 1863. Bill Russell had been in partnership with Maples. *Ibid.*

14 Rebecca Custer was the wife of Israel Custer, a Pontiac flour miller. In 1860 the Custers had two children, Charles and Laura. Eighth Census, Livingston County, State of Illinois, NA.

 75

Head Quarters, Co. "A" 129th Ills. Vol.
Nashville, Tenn., Aug. 24th 1863

My Dear Wife

We arrived in Nashville yesterday morning [the 23d] after a tedious march.[1] The weather is excessively warm. We are camped on the South side of the city & have a fair prospect of remaining some time. We are all very busy to-day fixing up our tents & cleaning up. I have not got my desk up yet & am occupying the adjt's. [adjutant's] desk to write a few lines.

I recd. your letter of the 18th on the march & am very happy to hear that your health is improving.[2] I have written twice to Carlisle, as you informed me in a former letter that you would start for that place at farthest on Tuesday of last week. Your last letter indicates indecision as to the time you will go, & hints lightly at your not going at all. I directed, however, in a letter to Mother that my letters should be ford. to you in the event of your not arriving,[3] & I presume ere this you have received them.

I am enjoying very good health. The boys all stood the march very well, but we are not anxious for a repetition of it very soon. We are on a hill & have some pleasant breezes, but it is still very warm. I will try & write at length for to-morrow's mail. Give my love to Mother & all the friends & kiss Frankie for me. May God bless & make you happy.

Your Affect. Husband

J. F. Culver

1   The 129th Illinois left Gallatin at 5 P.M., on August 21, and reached Nashville at 9 A.M., on the 23d. The distance marched was 30 miles. Regimental Papers, 129th Illinois, NA.

2   Mary Culver's letter of August 18, 1863, is missing from the Culver Collection.

3   This letter to J.F.C.'s mother is missing from the Culver Collection.

 76

Head Quarters, Co. "A" 129th Ills. Vol.
Nashville, Tenn., Aug. 27th 1863

My Dear Wife

I have not had the pleasure of hearing from you since our arrival here, but hope very soon to be made happy by a letter. I am in the enjoyment of excellent health. Our duty thus far has been very pleasant.[1] I went out on Picket on Monday [the 24th] & had a very pleasant time. Our post was in a very pleasant grove quite near a house, the ladies of which supplied us with some fine music, both instrumental & vocal.

We made an exchange of Arms yesterday & have all new guns (rifled).[2]

The last time I wrote to you, I directed my letter to New Hartford, as you requested, but think there must be letters sent that have never reached me. We have recd. two large mails from the North this week but nothing for me. We heard from Mrs. Smith on Sunday. She was much better than when we left & still improving.[3]

The weather was very cold on Tuesday, so much so that it required an overcoat to be comfortable. It is quite cool & pleasant to-day.

Rumor says Sumpter has fallen & that Charleston is besieged.[4] Rosecrans is advancing & Burnside descending through East Tennessee.[5] The war is progressing finely, & we may hope for stirring events.

If I could only determine where a letter would find you, there are many things I wish to write, but I will wait until I hear from you. Wherever you are, I hope you are well & happy. Kiss Frankie for me. May God abundantly bless you & keep you from all harm. Write soon & often.

Your Affect. Husband

J. F. Culver

---

1　On reaching Nashville, Colonel Case of the 129th Illinois reported to Maj. Gen. Gordon Granger, who was charged with responsibility of protecting the Army of the Cumberland's depots and lines of communication. General Granger assigned the 129th Illinois to the 2d Brigade of Brig. Gen. Robert S. Granger's Third Division of the Reserve Corps, and the men were turned to pitching tents, between Fort Negley and the Murfreesboro Pike, near the southeastern outskirts of the city. *O.R.,* Ser. I, Vol. XXX, pt. III, pp. 37, 372; Grunert, *History of the 129th Illinois,* p. 34.

2　Col. Case on May 30, 1863 had notified General Paine that the regiment's caliber .69 muskets were obsolete. These weapons, manufactured more than 30 years before, had been altered from flintlock to percussion, and could not "be relied upon except at close quarters." While they "would do a great deal of execution at one hundred yards if directed upon troops *en masse,*" at ranges in excess of 150 yards they were "very uncertain even in the hands of good marksmen, if fired upon an enemy deployed as skirmishers." At a range of 300 yards, they were practically worthless. If the regiment were attacked by "an inferior force" armed with the Springfield rifle musket, the "only salvation would be to advance rapidly upon the enemy in his own chosen position, and come at close quarters at once." Case to Paine, May 30, 1863, Regimental Papers, 129th Illinois, NA.

When no action was taken on this request, Colonel Case on July 27 addressed a communication to General Gordon Granger. Besides repeating his former arguments, he pointed out that the caliber .69 muskets were "constantly getting out of repair," and he had been "compelled to turn over so many as broken and damaged that we have not enough now to arm our men. " Case to Granger, July 27, 1863, Regimental Papers, 129th Illinois, NA.

3　Lieutenant Smith had remained with his wife at Gallatin when the regiment marched to Nashville.

4　The rumor that Fort Sumter had fallen was false. On August 17, Union batteries emplaced in Morris Island had opened fire on Fort Sumter. Simultaneously, Union monitors and ironclad attacked Battery Wagner. Although Fort Sumter was wrecked by the bombardment and most of its guns dismounted, the Confederates held onto the pile of rubble. Battery Wagner was abandoned by its defenders on the night of September 6, and on the night of the 8th a small boat expedition from the fleet attempted an amphibious assault on Fort Sumter but was repulsed.

Union land and sea forces on July 10, 1863 had launched a campaign aimed at capturing Charleston. The Confederates, though dislodged from Folly and Morris Islands to the south of Charleston Harbor, fought on, and Charleston and Fort Sumter were not abandoned until the third week of February 1865. Daniel Ammen, *The Atlantic Coast* (New York, 1883), pp. 125-138.

5 General Rosecrans' Army of the Cumberland, having brought up supplies and consolidated its position, resumed the offensive on August 16. The Cumberland Plateau was crossed, and by the 20th Crittenden's corps on the left had moved through Sequatchie Valley; Thomas' XIV Corps in the center had reached the Tennessee River on a broad front extending from Battle to Crow Creeks; and McCook's corps on the right was massed near Stevenson. One of Crittenden's columns on the 21st made a forced reconnaissance to Harrison's Landing, and on the 27th Union artillery was unlimbered and opened fire, shelling Chattanooga on the south side of the Tennessee River. Confederate General Bragg withdrew his troops from the city and prepared to defend the commanding ground beyond. *O.R.*, Ser. I, Vol. XXX, pt. III, p. 217; Cist, *Army of the Cumberland*, p. 178.

Maj. Gen. Ambrose E. Burnside on August 15 had started his columns south from bases in eastern Kentucky. His goal was to drive the Confederates from East Tennessee. Advancing by way of Stanford, Somerset, and Monticello, Burnside's troops were in possession of Chitwood's, 15 miles into Tennessee and 55 miles northwest of Knoxville, by the 27th. *O. R.*, Ser. I, Vol. XXX, pt. III, pp. 22, 195.

 77

Head Qurs. Co. "A", 129th Ills. Vol.
Nashville, Tenn., Aug. 28th 1863

My Dear Wife

I recd. two letters from you this morning dated the 22nd & 23rd & am happy to hear that you enjoy such good health.[1] I presume ere this you have arrived in Carlisle & have recd. my former letters. I have not recd. Sister Hannah's letter yet of which she speaks.[2] I recd. a letter from Bro. Sammy this morning, dated the 22nd; he was quite well & enjoys himself finely. He was after Morgan & gives quite a glowing description of his marching.[3]

I am not aware that I owe Sister Maggie [Utley] a letter. I wrote to her twice & never recd. but one letter from her. I will write, however, in a few days. I wrote to Mrs. McDowell this morning. She is at Magnolia, Ills. & is improving in health.

Lt. Smith has Leave of Absence for 10 days & is expected to start for home to-morrow. He is still in Gallatin with his wife. She is so much better that she will be able to travel.

We are all enjoying good health. I have almost reached my old weight, 186; I weighed 182 about two weeks ago. I believe I never enjoyed better health in my life.

You talk of coming down here, &, if we remain at this place, you would find it very pleasant. I think board could be obtained very convenient to camp though prices are very high & would almost alarm you. The city is quiet & is but a Village compared to most of our Eastern cities.[4]

I hope you are happy & enjoying yourself. I shall direct all my letters to Carlisle & shall expect to hear from you soon after your arrival there. New Hartford has been very attractive to detain you there so long. Frankie, it seems, has not yet forgotten his dinner; he must have a good memory.[5]

I am sorry that you will not have the pleasure of seeing me in Carlisle. No leaves of Absence are granted from this Post. While we remained at Gallatin, I had good hope but here I cannot expect it. [Lt.] Smith only got 10 days, & his wife was supposed to be dying. I shall expect a letter from Sarah very soon.

I have heard of the change of tenants in our house but not one word from Fleming; I wrote to Remick to take the matter in hand & hope to hear from him soon.[6] I will send for your pistol if opportunity offers but understand that no Furloughs will be granted. The papers you sent have not yet arrived. I hope you had a very pleasant ride with Cousin Thomas. I can scarcely realize that Frankie can say anything, he must almost be able to walk. I think he will find it very pleasant at Carlisle. I feel very anxious to hear how you like the place & our friends there.

Russell & Scott [McDowell] are both here yet & in good health. I have no late news from Pontiac except by Capt. Baird yesterday evening,[7] & he saw no one but Chas. McGregor. Francis Van Doren had a letter from Hetty Antrim a few days ago. She was in Cincinnatti & quite well.[8] Alf. Huetson will return to-day or to-morrow, when I shall have some news I presume. [Christ] Yetter has not written yet to you. He writes a great many letters mostly to Jennie [Gutherie] & Lib. Mr. Hill's family are all well. Col. Cropsey's wife is expected here to-day;[9] she has been several days on the way from Louisville, not being able to get through.

I must close as I have considerable Company writing to do to-day. Huetson & Jo. Allen both being away, I shall be very busy for a few days closing up the monthly accounts.

I hope God may continue to bless us with health & keep us from all evil. May his blessings rest especially upon you & our dear Boy. Give my love to all the family. I expect you to be very happy during your stay at Father's. Remember me kindly to all the friends that may inquire of me. Let us hope that the present success of our Armies is a harbinger of Speedy Peace,[10] and live happy in the prospect of soon being united at "Home again."

What has become of Mother [Murphy]? Give my love to her. I did hope she would go with you to Carlisle & feel disappointed. Will she remain in New Hartford or go home? Have you sent to Remick for money yet & how are you off? Will you need more soon? We will be paid off in a few days again. I believe I could write all day if nothing prevented. It seems I never get through talking to you. Farewell, May God bless My Dear Wife,

J. F. Culver

---

1   Mary Culver's letters of August 22 and 23 are missing from the Culver Collection.

2   Hannah Culver's letter is also missing from the Culver Collection.

3   Samuel Alexander Murphy, Mary Culver's youngest brother, like thousands of others had been called up to oppose Morgan's raid north of the Ohio. Like most of these, he never got within 100 miles of the raiders.

4   In 1860 there were about 37,000 people living in Nashville and its suburbs, and the city embraced an area of about six square miles.

5   Frankie was proving difficult to wean.

6   Fleming had been designated J.F.C.'s agent and placed in charge of renting their house and collecting and forwarding the rent.

7   Cyrus N. Baird, a 29-year-old Fairbury "vocal music teacher," was mustered into service on Sept. 8, 1862, as captain of Company E, 129th Illinois. Captain Baird led his company throughout the war, and was mustered out near Washington, D. C., June 8, 1865. Citing ill health, Captain Baird in August had returned to Livingston County on a 20-day-leave. Compiled Service Records of Union Soldiers, NA.

8   Francis M. Vandoren, a 24-year-old farmer, was mustered into service on Sept. 8, 1862, as a private in Company A, 129th Illinois. On April 27, 1864, Private Vandoren was detailed as a teamster in the supply train of the Third Division, XX Corps. He rejoined the regiment in August 1864. Private Vandoren was wounded at Averysboro, N. C., March 16, 1865. *Ibid.* It has been impossible to further identify Hetty Antrim.

9   Maria J. Cropsey was born in Ohio in 1826. In 1860 she and her husband were living in Fairbury with their five children, all boys. Eighth Census, Livingston County, State of Illinois, NA.

10   In the weeks following the surrender of Vicksburg and General Lee's retreat from Gettysburg, Northern armies had continued to make headway. General Rosecrans' Army of the Cumberland had swept the Confederates out of Middle Tennessee and was threatening Chattanooga, and General Burnside's columns were striking toward Knoxville. At Charleston, the Confederates were under heavy pressure, while General Meade's Army of the Potomac was again in Northern Virginia.

*142*

## 78

Head Qrs. Co. "A" 129th Ills. Vols.
Nashville, Tenn., Aug. 30th 1863

My Dear Wife

I have been prevented from writing regularly, or at any great length for several days, owing to the press of business. We have been preparing for Inspection & Review which takes place to-morrow, also muster for Pay & the closing up of our monthly accounts. Jos. Allen was left sick in Gallatin, & Alf Huetson has been home on Furlough, leaving all the writing on my hands. Huetson returned yesterday evening. He has been sick all the time he was home but is improving rapidly & will be well soon.

I was disappointed this morning in not hearing from you, as I expected to receive my first letter from you dated at Carlisle containing very interesting information. I hope I shall be made happy to-morrow by the receipt of it.

My health is quite good as it ever was, for which I hope I am duly thankful. Mrs. Cropsey arrived here yesterday evening; she is quite well & will remain a week. Maples, Russell & Scott McDowell will start for home in the morning; they have gone into the city to be ready for the morning train. They sold out to John Blackburn. Scott intended to go in with him but got home-sick & backed out.[1]

Lieut. Smith & his wife will start for Pontiac day after to-morrow if her health continues to improve. She is very much better. They are still in Gallatin.

I received a short note from Abbie Remick by Alf Huetson yesterday. She intended to start for school on the 29th for 5 months. Lida [Remick] is not going at present. Our friends are all well. I wish to send for my overcoat by Smith but do not know where to direct him to find it. I shall therefore direct him to Sis, presuming that she will know where it is.

I intended to write Sister Maggie [Utley] to-day but did not succeed. I will try and do so soon & will send for your pistol as you wish it. Orlin Converse returned from Pontiac yesterday evening.[2] He saw Mr. Utley who told him the family are all well. I shall enquire more fully at the first opportunity.

*143*

The weather is unusually cool for this season of the year but healthy. We have but very few sick in the Regiment. I have had no letters except the one I have mentioned from Abbie since I last wrote. Abbie informs me that she would send me her photograph on the 28th, so I shall look for it in a few days.

Mrs. Laurence is assisting at the Boarding home where we board; Mrs. Nelson is keeping house, or rather room, in a little house near camp; Mrs. Loir & Mrs. Fisher have a tent in rear of the camp; Lt. McKnight & his wife board down [the] street.[3] He is improving rapidly in health and will be able for duty in 10 days or two weeks. His sister has been here & returns home to-morrow morning. I believe I have accounted for all the ladies that are here except Mrs. McDonald. She is still here; I met her this evening but did not think of asking her where she stops. Little Mary Nelson comes to my tent every day & is quite pleasant company.[4]

I have made the acquaintance of several little boys & girls that congregate around the camp, & the first Sunday that I am free I shall go to Sabbath School. I was at church just a few rods from camp to-night & heard a very good sermon *(Baptist)*. The Quoir sang "Hendon" at close, & it seemed much like old times.[5] I have heard much better singing in Pontiac, however.

I should have liked very much to have written to the Sabbath School to-day, if I had had the time, & I must try & write soon. I have not received Sarah Williams' promised letter yet & fear she has forgotten to write. I received the [news]papers you sent & am very much obliged. Send again when convenient. You can scarcely imagine how anxious I am to receive your first letter from Carlisle. I know you have felt a degree of hesitancy in going, & I wish to know whether your first impressions are favorable or unfavorable. In your old home you had the assistance of old familiar scenes & faces to render the influences around you happy, but none of these things will be of any assistance in Carlisle. All will be new & strange, & I feel exceedingly anxious to learn whether our relatives & friends possess sufficient cordiality to fill your heart with joyous welcome. Tell me honestly all about your estimation of the many you may meet. You will pardon me for alluding to these things so often, and, if you knew how much of my thoughts your visit to Father's has occupied my mind, you would not wonder at my anxiety. I have feared that you might feel embarrassed & lonely, & my old home fail to throw around you that charm which has so engulfed myself. But I shall wait patiently for your letter.

Give my love to all. Kiss Frankie for me. Make the best use of your time, & I pray God you may be very happy. Write as often as you can. May Our Father in Heaven keep you and surround you with every comfort and blessing. May we be saved from Sin by Grace Divine and finally be at rest in a "Home in Heaven."

Good Night

Your Affect. Husband

J. F. Culver

---

1   John F. Blackburn, who had resigned his commission as 1st lieutenant of Company E on February 26, 1863, had contracted to replace Ed Maples as regimental sutler. Colonel Case appointed him to that position on September 5, 1863. William Russell and Scott McDowell had been partners with Maples. Compiled Service Records of Union Soldiers, NA.

2   Orlin Converse, a 28-year-old farmer, was mustered into service on Sept. 8, 1862, as a private in Company G, 129th Illinois Infantry. He was promoted to sergeant on Oct. 26, 1862, and was mustered out near Washington, D.C., on June 8, 1865. *Ibid.*

3   Mrs. Laurence of Pontiac was the wife of Pvt. Reuben Laurence of Company G; Mrs. Fisher of Pontiac was the wife of Sergt. Augustus R. F. Fisher of Company G; Mrs. Lore of Joliet was the wife of Pvt. Robert C. Lore of Company B; Mrs. Sarah Nelson of Pontiac was the wife of Cpl. Erastus Nelson of Company A; and Mrs. McKnight of Chenoa was the wife of 2d Lt. John P. McKnight of Company G. Eighth Census, Livingston County, State of Illinois, NA.

4   Mrs. MacDonald of Dwight was the wife of Pvt. Joseph D. MacDonald of Company B. Four-year-old Mary Nelson was the oldest child of Erastus and Sarah Nelson. *Ibid.*

5   "Hendon" was a popular hymn of the 1860's.

 79

Head Qrs. Co. "A" 129th Ills. Vol.
Nashville, Tenn., Sept. 3rd 1863

My Dear Wife

Yours of Aug. 28th, dated at Carlisle, reached me this morning, informing me of your tedious & unpleasant journey, also of your safe arrival in Carlisle.[1] I have not written since Sunday as I have been absent & without opportunity to write. I found on my return two letters from you & one from Sarah Williams; a very long & interesting one, indeed. If I don't forget it, I will send it to you when answered.[2]

You will be happy to know that Bro. Johnie [Murphy] spent last night with me & is in good health. My letter will explain itself, as I think the incidents connected with a long journey into Dixie will prove interesting.

I left this place on Monday morning [the 21st] at 6:30 A.M., as Military Conductor of Freight Train loaded with commissary stores, with 25 men as train guard.[3] About 9 o'clock A.M. we were stopped by the wreck of two cars of the train preceeding us, and lay there about 7 hours. We got to Christiana at about 7 o'clock & found ourselves out of water, & none to be had. We ran on a side track & put up for the night.[4]

We had lain there but a short time, when our ears were greeted with the sound of music. So the Conductor of the train & myself took a lantern & set out to find from whence it came. In a grove a few hundred yards from the Rail Road, we found a very handsome cottage from which the music proceeded. We cast about us to devise some way to introduce ourselves & finally hit upon the happy expedient of seeking lodging for the night. We went boldly to the door & knocked, not knowing what fate might have decreed, and asked for the Gentleman of the house. The darkies not knowing what our business might be, at first refused to listen to us & was about to close the door on us, when a little girl about 8 years old happened to come into the hall. With her we were more successful, & soon a gentleman made his appearance.

We made known our wishes & was referred to the Mistress of the cottage, who soon made her appearance & invited us in. After making ourselves known, we were duly introduced into the parlor, where we found a very old lady, three young ladies, a gentleman, a piano & melodeon. We found during our conversation that the family were originally from New York & latterly from Pennsylvania & have been residing in Tennessee for the past eight years. Two of the ladies were of the ages of 14 & 15, the beauties of the house, & the other perhaps 18 several years ago & exceedingly anxious for a BEAUX.[5] She found out I was married, I presume, as she made a furious onsett after the Conductor & almost annihilated him.

In the meantime I succeeded in getting the two young ladies to the melodeon, & we sang & played till midnight, & then retired to a very handsomely furnished room & bed. I cannot boast of a very excellent night's rest for the feather bed, as usual, prevented my resting well. I believe I much prefer a floor & carpet. We got a good breakfast in the morning, and, after repeated invitations to call again, we bid them adieu & departed.

I sent a note the night before to Jack Lothrop, military operator at Wartrace, to telegraph to Bro. Johnnie to meet me on Wednesday [Sept. 2] at that place.[6]

We got started from Christiana at 7 o'clock, & about 8½ o'clock A.M. were again stopped by the wreck of two cars of a train that passed us during the night. We got off at about 11 A.M. and passed over the battle field of Stone River about noon. It would be impossible to give an accurate description of it from the hasty glance I got of the place. There are a large number of fortifications, some of them very extensive. There are but few troops there.[7]

We arrived at Wartrace about 2 o'clock P.M. & laid there about one hour. I found that Lothrop, in addition to the dispatch, had written to Johnie & also to the officer commanding the Battery. Shelbyville is eight miles from Wartrace on a branch road, one section of the Battery is at Wartrace & the balance at Shelbyville.[8]

We passed on out of Tennessee into Alabama. I was not very favorably impressed with the appearance of the country. It is much more devastated than any place north of Nashville, vast numbers of houses destroyed, & all the mills, factories & manufactories. The soil looks very sterile & what little produce has been raised looks stunted and imperfect. The most prepossessing aspects are the groves, many of which are beautiful. Tallahoma, the first place of note after leaving Wartrace, was a short time ago the front of our Army.[9] There are a few troops only left, & the country bears trace of the presence of a large Army.

About half way between Tallahoma & Cowan we stopped in a forest for wood.[10] There I saw a sight that I hope I may never behold again. I have read many accounts of the destitution of the poor whites of the South, but never even conceived their real condition. I have seen on this trip many families who scarcely seemed to possess intelligence above the brutes & scarcely were their equals in instinct & self preservation. In a little hovel, a few feet from the wood yard, live one young man, three women, and several children. One of the women is a raving maniac & lay upon the floor amid all kinds of filth, tossing about & making a very hideous noise. Outside of the hut sat another woman, afflicted with disease & looking the picture of misery. The younger, a woman of about twenty-five to thirty, & the mother, I should judge, of the children, was very pregnant, & the whole party almost entirely naked; the mother without a husband & never had any, & all the children fatherless. It was a horrid sight, & I hope I may never behold the like again.

At Decherd I saw the first armed negro soldiers I have ever seen, an entire Brigade drilling. They made a fine appearance & had a beautiful camp. There was but few white troops.[11]

At Cowan the Army had just left a few weeks, and the camp equippage was being removed. At this place we commenced the ascent of the Cumberland mountains. The grade is very heavy & with the assistance of an additional engine, we got along at a good speed. There is a tunnel on the mountain 2800 feet long, & the descent on the other side is steep and long. At various points through the mountains, detachments of troops are posted, but it would be a small task to get on the cliffs beyond the reach of the guns & roll rocks sufficient to crush a train & escape without harm.[12] I am surprised that it has not often been done.

At Anderson at the foot of the mountains, there was two divisions of troops, Genl. Rousseau's division and a large number of Regulars.[13] The first named Division were making preparations to leave the next day.

We arrived at Stevenson, *Alabama*, at about 8 o'clock, the end of our journey, making 113 miles in two days. After the train stopped, I looked around for something to eat, my rations being all consumed by our delay on the route, & finally found a tent in which meals were served. I succeeded in getting a couple of eggs, a little piece of meat, some bread, butter & a cup of coffee, for which I was charged the moderate sum of 75 cents.

After supper, I took a guard & started for General Rosecrans' Head Quarters to report myself. It is about a mile south of Stevenson in the direction of the [Tennessee] river. General Negley's & Sheridan's Divisions were marching on Chattanooga, & the men were singing, laughing & hallooing, seeming to be very lively.[14] You could scarcely conceive of the noise & confusion occasioned by the moving of 15 or 20,000 troops.

Two Divisions crossed the river last week, & part of the Army is in Chattanooga.[15] The Rebels fled without making any attempt to defend the place & have fallen back to Atlanta.[16] I must request that the present positions of our Army are not made public. I do not know whether the news are contraband or not, but, having seen nothing in the papers, I am somewhat suspicious. In fact many of the papers have denied that our Army have possession of Chattanooga.

A large number of deserters from the Rebel Army have been brought over the river, & will average, I am told, from 50 to 100 per day.[17] Many days they amount to 2 or 300. The Rebel Army is badly scattered. Burnside's Army is at Knoxville & pressing steadily East.[18]

I arrived at Hd. Qrs. at 10 P.M. & after transacting my business returned to Stevenson, succeeded in buying some rations, & after waking up the guards to cook their breakfast, I lay down on a little bench in the car & slept about 2 hours. At 4 A.M. of Wednesday [the 2d] we left Stevenson for home, & arrived at Wartrace at about 11 o'clock.

I found Bro. Johnie just arrived. He came from Shelbyville on horseback & came aboard the train with us. He is enjoying better health than at any time since he has been in the service & looks well. He is in good spirits & enjoys himself very well. Shelbyville has more *Union* families than any part of the South, and they are generally very kind. We had a pleasant time. He says he recd. a letter from you a short time ago which he answered. He has had no letters from Pontiac for two months. I am sorry his stay was so limited; he returned this morning. There is to be an election for Lieutenant in the Battery in a few days, & he is busy engineering for the position.[19] One of the sergeants that I met in Wartrace tells me that his chances are very flattering; I earnestly hope he may succeed.

I have some idea of the difficulties you had to encounter in your travels, & wish very much I could have been with you to relieve you of your burden. I am happy to learn that no accident befell you & hope you have ere this recovered from the effects of your journey & are enjoying your visit. I fear I shall not be able to answer your letter to-night; it is very late, but as I cannot get my letter off before 2 o'clock to-morrow, I will try & write in the morning. If I should fail, I will write again to-morrow night. May God help you, dearest, & keep both Frankie & you in perfect health. Good night.

Morning 5-1/2 o'clock; Dear Mary. The first thing that proposed itself to my mind this morning was the finishing of my letter, for by walking to the Depot, about 2 miles, I can get my letter off to-day; otherwise it must wait until to-morrow &, believing that you will be happy to hear from me, I will try & make the trip. I will not attempt to answer in full.

I cannot perceive any reason to be alarmed in your letter, yet I have trembled for fear you might not enjoy yourself.[20] I hope you will not feel diffident nor hesitate to enter into the full enjoyment of every pleasure afforded. Recollect I went among your friends in New York once, a perfect stranger, & made a very happy visit.

I feel kindly for the man though he is black who had gallantry enough to offer his seat. May his shadow never grow less & the smiles of the one he loves best ever be sweet & abundant.[21]

I am surprised to learn of Jennie's fix, but it will be some little consolation to YOU. It ought to make you friends forever.[22] I never was in the room you occupy. I spent two nights in the little room in the south east corner of the building fronting toward Carlisle Barracks.[23] You will find the heighth of the mountains increases as you near them,

& very rapidly if you commence to ascend them.²⁴ I believe I could enjoy a cup of cider very much if I were with you.²⁵

I never learned why Mother [Murphy] returned home & certainly never received the letter you allude to as informing me. I shall write to her to-day.

Lt. Smith & his wife started for Pontiac on Tuesday [the 1st], & I presume are there by this time. Alf Huetson has returned. He was sick all the time he was home. He informs me that his wife was thrown from her horse last spring & lost her babe from the injury. He never knew that he was about to be a FATHER until he went home. He walks about six feet 4 in. now. Christ Yetter & Johnie [Murphy] had a long talk about Jennie Gutherie. I had forgotten that they both corresponded with her.

I must close. Give my love to all the family. Write to me very often & take notes of all that you find interesting. Kiss Frankie for me. He must be growing into a large boy. What did grandfather & grandmother think of him?

Remember me kindly to all our friends. I will write soon again. May God give you health & happiness & your visit prove very pleasant. I shall be so happy to know that you enjoy yourself & that nothing mars your happiness. Until I hear from you again, Farewell,

Your Affect Husband,

J. F. Culver

---

1   Mary Culver had written, "I reached this place [Carlisle] safely and in health yesterday afternoon [the 27th]. I had rather a tedious journey and do not think I shall ever travel this road again alone, with a baby. I would tell you of a host of troubles, I had on the way, but I think would occupy too much time and space to enumerate. Suffice to say I had to change cars five times and get my baggage checked as many, and with one exception the only attention or politness I received from a *man* was from a black who got up and offered me his narrow front seat rather than see me stand up with a baby in my arms, while his *white brethren* comfortably kept their seats. I sat down and cried. I could not help it, I believe they thought I was a *bad woman*, as they would not have treated me so.

"I found no one at the [Carlisle] Depot, who knew me, so sent a boy with my card to the house, and Hannah and Charlie came right down after me. I had written them when I would come, but they have never received the letter.

"Mrs. Zug was at the Depot when the cars came but there was so great a crowd she did not see me, or if she did, failed to recognize me." Mary Culver to J.F.C., Aug. 28, 1863, Culver Collection.

2   Sarah Williams was a New Hartford friend of Joseph and Mary Culver.

3   To supply his army as it thrust deep into the Confederacy, General Rosecrans employed the Nashville & Chattanooga Railroad. By August 31, the railroad had been reopened to traffic as far as Stevenson, Alabama. To protect supplies  while in transit to forward depots  General Robert Granger called upon commanders of units stationed in and around Nashville for necessary manpower.

During September and October, the 129th Illinois was ordered to provide daily two officers and 50 enlisted men for duty as train guards; two officers, nine noncommissioned officers, and 50 enlisted men as pickets; one noncommissioned officer and 12 enlisted men for extra duty; and one noncommissioned officer and five enlisted men for fatigue details. Speed to Case, Sept. 1, 1863, Regimental Papers, 129th Illinois, NA.

4   Christiana was a station on the Nashville & Chattanooga Railroad, 12 miles south of Murfreesboro.

5   The family visited by J.F.C. near Christiana may have been that of J. H. Grant, an engineer. Grant, a native of Maine, had lived in New York and Pennsylvania before moving to Rutherford County, Tenn. In 1860, Grant was living with his wife and three daughters (Mary, Sophia, and Emma) and two sons. Eighth Census, Rutherford County, State of Tennessee, NA.

6   John P. Lothrop of Pontiac had been mustered into service on Sept. 8, 1862, as commissary sergeant of the 129th Illinois. Lothrop had been reduced to private and had been transferred to the military telegraph service. Compiled Service Records of Union Soldiers, NA.

7   The train would have passed the Stones River battlefield on the previous day as the site of that bloody battle, fought December 31, 1862, and January 1-2, 1863, is several miles northwest of Murfreesboro. In the months following the battle and before resuming the offensive in the fourth week of June, General Rosecrans' troops had erected a number of earthworks. These fortifications, centering on the Stones River railroad bridge, were known as Fortress Rosecrans.

8   John Murphy's unit (Company M, 1st Illinois Light Artillery) had been headquartered at Shelbyville since June 29. The battery commander at this time was 2d Lt. Thomas Burton. *Adjutant General's Report, State of Illinois*, Vol. VIII, p. 665.

9   General Bragg's Army of Tennessee  had evacuated Tullahoma on June 30, and the town had been occupied by Rosecrans' soldiers the next day. Rosecrans' columns had pushed on, and during the period August 29-September 4 crossed the Tennessee River at four points. Cist, *Army of the Cumberland*, pp. 179-180.

10   The stop for wood was made near Elk River Bridge.

11   One white regiment (the 69th Ohio) from General Thomas' XIV Corps had been detached and detailed to guard the depots at Decherd and Cowan, the tunnel, and the bridge across Boiling Fork. *O.R.*, Ser. I, Vol. XXX, pt. III, pp. 35, 268.

The 12th U.S. Colored Infantry Regiment commanded by Col. Charles R. Thompson had been organized in July and August and was posted at Elk River Bridge. *Tennesseans in the Civil War*, Vol. I, p. 397.

12   The 69th Ohio, reinforced by 650 casuals, guarded the railroad between Elk River Bridge and Anderson. On September 1 orders were issued for General Gordon Granger to relieve the Ohioans with a regiment from Fayetteville, so they could rejoin their brigade. *O.R.*, Ser. I, Vol. XXX, pt. III, pp. 289-290.

13   Brig. Gen. Absalom Baird  on August 23 had assumed command of the division of the XIV Corps formerly led by Maj. Gen. Lovell H. Rousseau. Included in Baird's First Division was Brig. Gen. John H. King's brigade of regulars. There were one, not two, divisions camped along the railroad between Anderson and Stevenson.

General Thomas on the 1st  had issued orders for Baird's division to march from Anderson to Taylor's Store, crossing the Tennessee River at Bridgeport. *Ibid.*, pp. 132, 267-268, 282.

14   Maj. Gen. James S. Negley's division of Thomas' XIV Corps had crossed the Tennessee River at Caperton's Ferry during the afternoon. Maj. Gen. Philip H. Sheridan's

division of McCook's XX Corps was at Bridgeport. It would cross the Tennessee River as soon as the engineers had completed the pontoon bridge. *Ibid.*, pp. 282, 285-286.

15  Although General Bragg was pulling his troops and supplies out of Chattanooga, the Federals had not occupied that key transportation center. It was September 9 before units of General Crittenden's XXI Corps crossed the Tennessee River and occupied Chattanooga. Cist, *The Army of the Cumberland*, p. 183.

16  Stories that the Confederate Army of Tennessee was abandoning the region and falling back on Atlanta had been spread by "deserters" sent into the Union lines. Bragg and his generals hoped that Rosecrans would be taken in by these stories and lunge into the rugged hills and hollows of northwest Georgia. Rosecrans on September 9 telegraphed General in Chief Halleck, "The army has retreated to Rome. If we pursue vigorously they will not stop short of Atlanta." Horn, *Army of Tennessee*, p. 248.

17  The number of Rebel deserters is exaggerated. Between September 1 and October 7 the number of deserters tabulated by Rosecrans' provost marshal was 750. *O.R.*, Ser. I, Vol. XXX, pt. I, p. 232.

18  General Burnside's vanguard had reached Montgomery, Tennessee, on August 30, and the next day found his cavalry skirmishing with Confederate horse-soldiers on the Knoxville and Kingston roads, 14 miles east of Montgomery. Knoxville, which had been evacuated, was occupied by units from Burnside's XXIII Corps on September 3. *O.R.*, Ser. I, Vol. XXX, pt. III, pp. 267, 333.

19  Commissary Sergeant John Murphy was campaigning for the vacant 2d lieutenancy created by promotion of Thomas Burton from 2d lieutenant to 1st lieutenant on August 5, 1863. *Adjutant General's Report, State of Illinois*, Vol. VIII, p. 653.

20  Mary Culver had written, "I was very kindly received by the whole family, and think I shall love them very much and enjoy my visit exceedingly." Mary Culver to J.F.C., Aug. 28, 1863, Culver Collection.

21  On the roundabout ride from New Hartford to Carlisle, a black man had given up his seat to Mrs. Culver and her baby. See note 1.

22  J.F.C.'s sister, Jennie Cheston, was pregnant and would give birth to another child in November. On October 24, 1862, she had given birth to twins, both of whom had since died. Mary Culver to J.F.C., Aug. 28, 1863, Culver Collection.

23  Mary Culver had written, "I occupy the room over the sitting room. I believe I am turned around for I cannot tell whether it is East or West." *Ibid.*

24  The "Cumberland valley," Mary Culver had written, is "very beautiful . . . so different from the monotonous scenery of our Prairie State." *Ibid.*

25  Father Culver was making cider from apples blown during a recent hail storm. *Ibid.*

 80

Head Qrs. Co. "A" 129th Ills. Vol. Infty.
Nashville, Tenn., Sept. 7th 1863

My Dear Wife

I intended to write on Saturday night [the 5th], but before I got fairly seated was called out on the Picket line & did not get in until 10 o'clock

A.M. of yesterday. Immediately on my return, I started for church & afterward hoped to be able to find Sabbath School somewhere in the city but failed.

Last night I went to church again, making the first Sabbath at church since I have been in the Service. I am sorry to say that I did not realize the pleasure I anticipated. The feeling existing still in the hearts of the people manifests itself in all their actions, and but a few minutes sufficed to satisfy me that my presence was not wanted & that my appearance destroyed the pleasure of others. In the evening I had the most positive evidence of their ill feeling: Noses turned up in scorn & I was left in undisputed possession of several feet of space on all sides.

I hoped to receive a letter from you this morning but was disappointed. My health is quite good. Our duties are very heavy at present. Capt. Hoskins started to Alabama this morning. We furnish two train guards each day, & my turn will return very soon. Our daily details amount to about 180, almost as heavy as our first month at Gallatin.[1]

Lieut. Smith is due here on Thursday. All furloughs & Leaves of Absence are stopped here, so that the hopes we entertained of visiting home must be indefinitely deferred. The health of the Regt. is good. The man in Co. "K" whose wife & child have been here all summer lost their child last week. I did not learn what disease. Nelson's youngest child is very ill & not expected to live.

The weather is almost insufferably warm to-day & was yesterday. The nights, however, are very cool & comfortable.

I have not yet had an opportunity of answering Sarah Williams' letter. I wrote to Mother [Murphy] a few days ago, directing to Pontiac. No late news from any source has reached me.

I hope you are enjoying yourself among our friends. I hope you will be punctual in reporting progress. You need not be surprised at Sister Jennie's success after your own fears.[2] I believe I gave you due warning that you had married into a *prolific* family, did I not?

The hour for Battalion Drill has arrived, &, as the mail leaves before I return, I must close.[3] I earnestly hope to hear from you soon. Kiss Frankie for me. Give my love to all the family. Write to me very often. May God Bless & keep you both in the enjoyment of health. I shall write again very soon.

  Farewell,

         Your Affect Husband

         J. F. Culver

---

1 J.F.C. overstated the number of men required for these details. The number of men

detailed daily was four officers, "11 noncommissioned officers, and 117 privates, a total of 132." Speed to Case, Sept. 1, 1863, Regimental Papers, 129th Illinois, NA.

2  Reference is to the expected birth of a child to Jennie and H. C. Cheston in November. Mary Culver to J.F.C., Aug. 28, 1863, Culver Collection.

3  Battalion drill was held from 4:30 to 6 P.M. twice a week on Tuesdays and Thursdays. Brigade drill was held at 3:30 P.M. three times a week on Mondays, Wednesdays and Fridays, in a field to the right of the Granny White Pike. Ward to Case, Sept. 17, 1863, Regimental Papers, 129th Illinois, NA.

 81

Head Qrs. Co. "A" 129th Ills. Vol. Infty.
Nashville, Tenn., Sept. 7th 1863

My Dear Wife

I wrote to you to-day but was so frequently interrupted that I fear my letter was very much disconnected. I commenced it just after Reveille roll-call & did not get it sealed until a few moments before Drill this afternoon. I sit down therefore to-night to talk to you a while.

I believe I could make my conversation more interesting if I could sit by your side & tell you what I have to say, in a manner as in days gone by, when upon the sofa we sat & chatted of those things most interesting to ourselves. Do you remember? And when we lacked sufficient matter of interest to engage our time, we filled up the interim with music. It may be considered by many silly to speak or even to allow one's thoughts to linger amid recollections of past & happy experience when the great future stands open before us, but I am not proof against recollections of past happiness.

I shall ever remember what joy filled my heart when, after the day's arduous labors were completed, I sat by your side in Mother's [Mrs. Murphy's] little parlor. I am confident that your mind will readily recall those hours of happiness which I am sure are indelibly impressed there. Your smile of contentment and happiness then expressed betokened a long remembrance. I hope you are equally happy now & ever may be all through life until you are permitted to enter upon joys Celestial in Heaven.

A letter from you would be very joyfully received to-night—a long letter informing me of the various methods by which you consume your time. Tell me who has called to make your acquaintance & how you have succeeded in making the acquaintance of our numerous relatives.

I have just received notice to be ready for picket duty at 7 A.M. to-morrow, so that I shall not be able to hear from you until the day after to-morrow even if a letter should arrive. We receive our mail at about 8 o'clock generally, & I shall be gone. [Cpl. Erastus] Nelson has sent for me to come & see his child, who they think is dying.[1] I will write more on my return.

I have returned. Charlie Nelson is very low, but I hope not beyond recovery.

Thompson Laycock returned from Furlough this evening. He is the last sent from Gallatin. He says the corn crop is entirely destroyed in Illinois, Indiana, & the Northern part of Kentucky by frost. I did not gather any other important news.

Co. "F" has been detailed to-night for some special duty & are just loading up to leave.[2] Another Regiment is to be sent forward in the morning, making our duties so much heavier.[3] We are among the unfortunate ones, being the very tail end of the Army.[4] We will in all probability remain here for some time. I see no prospect of our ever seeing a battle unless the Rebels should gather sufficient courage to flank our Army & strike in the rear, which does not look probable at present.

Mrs. Cropsey is still here. She only intended to remain a few days, but has lengthened out the time & shows no disposition to return. The Army seems to possess a strange fascination for some women. I am strongly tempted to believe that COFFEE has a SERIOUS effect upon HER in some UNACCOUNTABLE way.

I did intend to write to Sarah Williams to-night & send her letter to you, but it has grown too late. If I was not going on duty in the morning, I should attempt it but under the circumstances must defer it. I would send the letter [Sarah's] but will wish to refer to it in my answer. I am sorry to say I have got very far behind with my correspondents, except one with whom I think I am somewhat ahead of, &, I expect to be able to keep ahead, if I have a fair chance. But I have been interrupted several times until it has grown late.

Have you made the acquaintance of Miss Annie Underwood or Dr. Johnson's family? Have you been to the old homestead yet? I intended to make this a continuation of a former letter, describing persons & things as they occurred to my mind, but I must defer it, & who knows when another opportunity will offer.[5] I shall find sufficient time, however, to answer your letter at length, & if possible shall devise some means to have your letter sent to me to-morrow.

Kiss Frankie for me. I should like to take him in my arms & kiss him myself. May God keep you both in health & secure to you perfect happiness. Oh, how earnestly I desire to know that you are happy. It lessens materially every difficulty & gives me perfect contentment. There is nothing gives me more pleasure than a knowledge of your condition & satisfactory evidence of your happiness; & now, as the continuous conversation of different persons continually interrupts, I must close. Hoping to hear from you very soon. Remember me kindly to all

Good night—

Your affect. Husband

J. F. Culver

P.S. Sept. 8th/63 Dear Mary, I am well this morning & am about to start on duty. May God bless you.

J.F.C.

---

1   Cpl. Erastus J. Nelson of Company A, a resident of Pontiac, had brought his wife and two children to Nashville.

2   Company F, 129th Illinois Infantry, was to escort a supply train to Stevenson.

3   The 80th Illinois Infantry, which had been brigaded with the 129th, was detached on the 7th, and next morning sent to Bridgeport by rail. *O.R.*, Ser. I, Vol. XXX, pt. III, pp. 274, 431.

4   With the Army of the Cumberland across the Tennessee River and thrusting into the ridges and hollows of northwest Georgia, General Gordon Granger in the period September 4-8 redeployed his troops responsible for protecting the army's supply line. Garrisons were pared to the minimum, as Granger collected and forwarded units of his reserve corps to the front. By September 6 two regiments, the 22d Michigan and 108th Ohio, had left Nashville by rail for the front. Granger proposed to have 8,500 men at Bridgeport by the 9th. *Ibid.*, pp. 351-352, 372-373.

5   J.F.C.'s reference is to his letter of August 19, 1863.

 82

Head Qrs. Co. "A" 129th Ills. Vol. Infty.
Nashville, Tenn., Sept. 10th 1863

My Dear Wife

I shall start for Stevenson at 6 A.M. to-morrow if nothing happens & shall not receive the letter I expect is in the mail for me until I return, which will most probably be Monday evening [the 14th]. I wrote a long letter this morning & have but little more to write.[1] I am quite well. I intended to write to Sister Maggie [Utley] & Sarah Williams to-day, but have failed after I concluded the one to you. It was so warm, & this evening we were out on drill until after dark. I don't know why it is, but, aside from the letters I write to you, I find but little time to write.

I am generally on duty 4 days in the week, & when in Camp we have generally about 6 hours drill each day,[2] which with the company writing & Board of Survey consumes nearly all my time. I get a glance at a paper occasionally.

I did not answer your letter as fully this morning as I intended but am not able to-night to do it. I am tired, & my feet are very sore & painful. I shall be happy always to receive your letters so full of interest. If I could sit down a few hours & reflect, I could find very much that I should love to write about, but I shall continue to hope that I may get home before your visit is ended.

Nelson's child is still living, & the Dr. thinks it may live a few days longer. It suffers intensely, & they would be happy if death would relieve it from misery.

It is quite late, & I must close. Give my love to all the family & Remember me kindly to all our friends. May Our Father in Heaven Keep you from all harm & preserve you in health & happiness. Farewell.

Your Affect Husband

J. F. Culver

---

1  J.F.C.'s letter to his wife, written on the morning of the 10th, is missing from the Culver Collection.

2  In September reveille sounded at 5 A.M.; guard mount at 7 A.M.; company drill at 7:30 A.M.; dinner 12 noon; retreat at 7 P.M.; and tattoo at 8 P.M. There were either battalion or brigade drills in the afternoons Mondays through Fridays, and dress parades on Sundays at 5 P.M. Regimental Papers, 129th Illinois, NA.

Head Qrs. Co. "A" 129th Regt. Ills. Vol. Infty.
Nashville, Tenn., Sept. 14th 1863

My Dear Wife:

I have before me a photograph of Frankie & you, & I try to imagine
you both here, but it is hard work & poor success. I was made the
happy recipient of three letters this morning on my return [from
Stevenson] mailed on the 5th, 9th & 7th inst. The photograph is
excellent, though I can plainly see the result of your sickness. I hope,
however, from the assurance your letters give that you have recovered
good health. Frankie looks wide awake with mouth & eyes open. I
apprehend he attempted to exhibit his teeth but failed, not even the half
tooth is visable.[1] He will persist in prophecying & *Mamma* is to be
gratified, so says the adage, & I can cheerfully say Amen!

I never knew that Father [Culver] wore a truss or that he ever had
occasion to use one.[2] I have a very distinct recollection of the
conversation between Bro. Wes & myself on the wood pile, & also of
the Tomatoe pies of which he spoke.[3] Sister Kate has not assisted in
household duties for many years at home, & I am not surprised that she
does not assist now.[4] She has for several years spent but a small portion
of her vacation at Father's & never entertained much friendly feeling
toward Mother. I never understood why.

Your second letter was commenced on the 6th & mailed on the 9th. I
am sorry that the performance of duty will prevent my writing regularly,
& I may often fail to get a letter for you on Saturday.[5] To-morrow
morning I must go on Picket & will likely go south again on Thursday.
The short time alloted for rest is consumed almost entirely in keeping
the Company Books & papers in order. The old gentleman to whom you
allude as having assisted in the administration of the Sacrament was
Father Squires.[6] I know him well.

You have seen Mary Postlethwaite. I should be happy to hear that her
sister Charlotte has married agreeably.[7] I have still hoped that my old
friend *Troxel* to whom she was engaged would yet return for her.[8] I
received a letter from him just before the mails were stopped [in 1861] in
the south mailed at Atlanta, Georgia, in which he made many inquiries

about her. I gave him all the information I could, but rather think my letter never reached him.

You say it is rumored that Mary is about to marry Alf Sponsler.[9] I can scarcely believe it, yet would scarcely be surprised at anything she might do. When I was home last, she was engaged to a Mr. Lee, a Lawyer, who has since enlisted & is now either Lt. Col. or Major in the Army of the Potomac. I wish her no harm yet have but little hope, with her volatile disposition, she will ever realize much happiness in this life. It is perhaps my duty to warn you to be a little careful; I believe she would not hesitate to compromise your happiness in any way she might find convenient should opportunity offer. Sisters Jennie & Hannah know her well & will, I know, be discreet.

I never received even an intimation that Lucy Dunmire was married.[10] I wrote to her & also to her Father in the early part of the winter but never received an answer & presume they never received it as the mails were very irregular at the time.

I should be very happy to see both Mrs. Caldwell & Mrs. Lynch & wish to be kindly remembered to them & also to their Mother, Mrs. Roney.[11] I hope you will see their mother, she always was a very warm friend of mine &, like Charlotte Postlethwaite, a devoted Christian. They live by prayer & possess faith in an eminent degree.

I would like to know the name of the gentleman to whom Sister Kate was once engaged.[12] I was aware that such a circumstance transpired but never could learn the man's name. Perhaps I may have known him; please tell me the name.

Alf Huetson brought my shirts & among them the one Mrs. Remick gave me which I wished to preserve. I am sorry that Frankie does not deport himself better but hope his mouth will soon be well, & then I think he will be less cross.[13]

I am sorry to hear of the sad condition of Harry Cheston's sister-in-law. None know the full realization of blasted hopes & the crushing weight of sorrow occasioned by such irreparable loss except those who have been afflicted.[14] Luther Van Doren's body never was found; his poor mother has become almost entirely insane.[15] Do you recollect John Horie? His Brother David deserted at Richland Station while you were there, & John died shortly after he got home.[16] You saw him in the hospital at Gallatin. They were Brothers of Alf Huetson's wife. Their mother, after John's death & learning of David's desertion, has become hopelessly insane. Huetson says he did not dare go near where she was while at home.

I had a letter from Mother [Murphy] this morning which I will enclose. I have not seen Lt. Smith since his return [from furlough]. He left with a train [for Stevenson] before I got home this morning. I learn that his wife is rapidly recovering.

*Letter No. 3*: I have written letters every time I was in camp & do not understand why you have not received them.[17] I am sorry to hear that Father [Culver] is no better in health.[18] He must suffer intensely. Does he ever speak of me & what? Tell him I will be home to see him this fall if possible.

I hope that your Crab-apple jellie will be "Grafted into" "this portion of the Army."[19] I hope the next letter will inform me of your good health.

I have almost consumed this entire sheet in answering your three letters, though I aimed to be brief. The early part of the evening was consumed in signing muster & pay rolls, preparatory to receiving our pay to-morrow; & the time has passed swiftly by till it is now ten o'clock.

Charlie Nelson died on Saturday morning [the 12th] & was buried here. I have not seen either Nelson or his wife to-day but heard that they are very much depressed. Sergt. Lemmon of Co. "D" died on Sunday morning.[20] His wife was telegraphed for but has not yet arrived. He was home on Furlough but a few weeks ago & returned in excellent health. His disease was very similar to that of DeWitt's, Perforation of the bowels.[21]

There is a revival in progress about half a mile from here among the Kentucky troops. I have heard them singing & praying all evening. Quite a number from the Regiment went over, but Capt. [Hoskins & Lt.] Smith both being absent, I could not go. I received the notice of the renewal of my [minister's] license this morning. It is much more complimentary than I deserve, & I fear I have sadly degenerated. I shall try for the future, & live better. I have felt it a duty to preach occasionally but have had so little time to read that I have always concluded it was improper. I shall have to do something soon, or I fear I shall be lost beyond recovery. Pray for me.

Miller's Battery is in the vicinty of Chattanooga.[22] Rumor says that a battle is raging between General Thomas' Division & Johnson's forces, but it lacks confirmation.[23] There is also a report that our troops have taken 11,000 prisoners.[24] Deserters continue to come in; over 600 passed through our lines on Sunday morning. While I was in Stevenson, I brought 25 [deserters] up on the train with me whose homes are in Kentucky & Northern Tennessee.

Miss[es] Paines have returned home.[25] They send many kind messages. The weather is becoming quite cool in the night, but is still intensely warm in the middle of the day.

If I do not get home this fall, I think you will find pleasure in a visit here when the climate becomes settled & cool. It is just about the sickly season. Our Regt. is in very good health though the cases of disentery & flux are increasing. Several of the boys are complaining.

I will have some photographs taken soon & send you some. I have recd. no word from Sammy or Thomas [Murphy] lately. I wrote to Mother [Murphy] again a few days ago for some things. I have no word from Remick or Russell yet about the rent of the house or the disposition of the furniture.[26] Mother [Murphy] informs me that Mr. Wm. B. Lyons has taken possession, & I think he will take good care of it.[27]

I was at John Harper again to-day to sell me his Quarter Block, but scarcely think I can effect a purchase.[28] I should like very much to have them as we might raise some fruit.

Connelly has just arrived from Sevenson; he brings additional news of the battle.[29] Our Army is moving steadily forward, & the Rebels are slowly retreating & fighting as they fall back. Their train brought quite a number of prisoners.

I must close. It is almost eleven o'clock, & I must get up early to get my letter off. The boys are just returning from church. Give my love to all the family & Remember me kindly to all our friends. Kiss Frankie for me. Write as often as you can & tell me all the news. Every name you mention brings with it some recollections of the past, and every object has its interest in memory. May Our Father in Heaven preserve you in health & the enjoyment of life. The war will soon be over, & we can be at home once more. Let us continue to pray.

Farewell,

Your Affect. Husband

J. F. Culver

1 Mary Culver had forwarded a picture taken of her and Frankie by a Utica, N. Y., photographer. Commenting on it, she had observed, "It was taken just after I was able to get about and being very weary the expression of my countenance is anything but intelligent." Mary Culver to J.F.C., September 7, 1863, Culver Collection.

2 On September 4 Mary Culver had written that Mother Culver's "time is wholly occupied with" your father. "He was suffering a great deal this morning, but is better this afternoon, and walked outdoors a few minutes. A new difficulty has arisen. You probably know he has a rupture, and has worn a truss for the last ten years. The one he has been wearing does not help him now, and thus far they have found none which does him any good." Mary Culver to J.F.C., Sept. 4, 1863, Culver Collection.

3 One day while the boys were at the wood pile, Frank had exclaimed, "Wes, I like to chop wood better than I do any other kind of work, don't you?" Wes replied, "No sir, I like tomato pie a great deal better." *Ibid.*

4  J.F.C.'s comments regarding his half-sister Katherine were triggered by Mary Culver's statement that Hannah "has too much to do for such a little body. There are seven of a family beside so much company. It makes me feel miserable to see her work so hard knowing that I add to her cares and not able to assist her any. Kate might help her but don't seem inclined. She is a strange genius." *Ibid.*

5  Mary Culver began her letter, mailed on the 7th, "I received no interesting letter yesterday. I expect it will come tomorrow." Mary Culver to J.F.C., Sept. 7, 1863, Culver Collection.

6  On Sunday, the 6th, Mary Culver had attended church with Hannah and Wes' wife. "It was communion service and I enjoyed it very much. The minister, Mr. Black, reminded me very much of Mr. Pierce of Pontiac. He was assisted by an aged . . . preacher. I have forgotten his name but I presume you know him, he lives in this place." *Ibid.* The "aged preacher" was Father Squires.

7  Mary and Charlotte were the daughters of James or Charles Postlethwaite, Carlisle wagon makers. Charlotte, who was 24 and three years older than her sister, was a teacher. Mary was a seamstress. Eighth Census, Cumberland County, State of Pennsylvania, NA. In her letter Mary Culver had written, "It is rumored that the Postlethwaite girls are to be married. Charlotte to a gentleman from Baltimore at the Holiday's and Mary to some one who lives here in town." Mary Culver to J.F.C., Sept. 7, 1863, Culver Collection.

8  It has been impossible to further identify Troxel.

9  Alf Sponsler was a cripple and had been injured in a railroad accident. His legs had been crushed, and he wheeled himself about Carlisle "in a chair made for the purpose." He was a 40-year-old real estate agent. Mary Culver to J.F.C., Sept. 7, 1863, Culver Collection; Eighth Census, Cumberland County, State of Pennsylvania, NA.

10  Mrs. Culver had written, "Did you know Lucy Dunmire was married?" Lucy Dunmire was a Culver cousin.

11  Hannah Caldwell was the 44-year-old wife of Samuel Caldwell, a Carlisle chandler. Mrs. Mary Rowney was a 68-year-old widow, and in 1860 she lived with the G. W. Parks family. It has been impossible to further identify Mrs. Lynch. Eighth Census, Cumberland County, State of Pennsylvania, NA.

12  Jennie Cheston had told Mary Culver "that among the rebels who made the raid into Cumberland Valley was the gentleman to whom Kate [Culver] was once engaged . . . He was chaplain of a Regiment." Mary Culver to J.F.C., Sept. 7, 1863, Culver Collection.

13  Mary Culver had informed her husband that Frankie "has lost his reputation entirely of being a good-natured baby since he came to Carlisle. Some days I hardly know what to do with him. His mouth is very sore [with an ulcer]." *Ibid.*

14  Harry Cheston was the husband of Jennie, one of J.F.C.'s sisters. Mary Culver had written that Harry's brother's death had caused the widow, a recent bride, to lose her reason, and it was feared she would be sent to an asylum. *Ibid.*

15  Luther Vandoren had drowned near Gallatin on June 10, 1863.

16  David Horie, a 29-year-old Woodford farmer, was mustered into service on Sept. 8, 1862, as a private in Company A, 129th Illinois. He deserted at Richland, Tennessee, April 29, 1863. John Horie, a 22-year-old farmer, was mustered into service on Sept. 8, 1862, as a private in Company A, 129th Illinois. Private Horie was discharged at Gallatin, Tenn., on April 22, on a surgeon's certificate. Compiled Service Records of Union Soldiers, NA.

17 Mary Culver had complained in her letter postmarked the 9th, "I did not receive a letter from you today and feel somewhat disappointed." Mary Culver to J.F.C., Sept. 7, 1863, Culver Collection.

18 Mary Culver had written, "Father [Culver] suffered intensely all last night and a greater part of this forenoon, to-night he is easier. Dr. said this morning that he was better than he was a month ago. But Mother [Culver] does not seem to think so." *Ibid.*

19 "I have been making crab apply jelly this afternoon," Mary Culver had written. "I have two quarts and am going to graft it into the army, Providence permitting." *Ibid.*

20 William S. Lemon, a 27-year-old Scott County laborer, had been mustered into service on Sept. 8, 1862, as 1st sergeant of Company D, 129th Illinois. 1st Sergeant Lemon died of dysentery in the regimental hospital at Nashville on Sept. 13, 1863. Compiled Service Records of Union Soldiers, NA.

21 It has been impossible to further identify DeWitt.

22 Miller's battery (M, 1st Illinois) had left Shelbyville on September 6, and on the 12th was posted with Brig. Gen. James B. Steedman's division, near Ringgold, Georgia. *Adjutant General's Report, State of Illinois,* Vol. VIII, p. 665.

23 Soldiers of General Crittenden's XXI Corps had occupied Chattanooga on the 9th, and had pushed on toward Lee and Gordon's Mills; meanwhile, Rosecrans' other corps, satisfied that the Confederates were abandoning the region, had forged ahead. McCook's XXII Corps on the right drove for Alpine, while Thomas' XIV Corps lunged toward McLemore's Cove. General Bragg, after evacuating Chattanooga, massed his army near Lafayette, ready to take advantage of Rosecrans' blunder and beat his army in detail. Orders were issued for an attack on Negley's and Baird's divisions which had thrust into McLemore's Cove. By the afternoon of the 10th, 30,000 Rebels were closing in on the Federals. Negley learned of his peril, and, when the Confederate generals failed to coordinate their movements, he delayed the advance of one of the Rebel columns and extricated his troops from the Cove and retired to Stevens' Gap. Cist, *Army of the Cumberland,* pp. 185-186; *O.R.,* Ser. I, Vol. XXX, pt. III, pp. 564-567.

24 There was no truth to the report that Rosecrans had taken 11,000 prisoners in the fighting on the 11th. Union casualties in this engagement were 11 killed and 27 wounded. While the Confederates made no report of their losses, they could not have exceeded 100. *O.R.,* Ser. I, Vol. XXX, pt. I, p. 259.

25 It has been impossible to identify further the Misses Paines.

26 His tenants having moved out of their house, J.F.C. had authorized James W. Remick and Willam Russell to find new renters. As the tenants had damaged their furniture, J.F.C. was hopeful of either selling or storing it.

27 For additional data on William B. Lyons see J.F.C. to Mrs. Nancy Murphy, March 27, 1862, Culver Collection.

28 John A. Harper, a 26-year-old farmer, was mustered into service on Sept. 8, 1862, as private in Company G, 129th Illinois, and was promoted to corporal in November 1862. Corporal Harper was captured on March 16, 1865, at Averysboro, N. C. and paroled by the Confederates at Aiken's Landing, Va., April 2, 1865. He was mustered out at Springfield, Ill., June 11, 1865. Compiled Service Records of Union Soldiers, NA.

29 Joseph B. Connelly, a 36-year-old Pontiac farmer, was mustered into Company A, 129th Illinois, as a private on Sept. 8, 1862. Private Connelly was mustered out near Washington, D. C., June 8, 1865. *Ibid.*

Head Qrs. Co. "A" 129th Regt. Ills. Vol. Intry.
Nashville, Tenn., Sept. 16th 1863

My Dear Wife

I rather expected to be greeted on my return this morning with a letter but was disappointed. We had rather a gloomy night of it on picket. It rained very hard & the lightning & thunder was terrific. One house in the vicinity of Camp was struck, but I have heard of no further accident. Nearly all the tents were blown down & many of our things spoiled. My health is quite good.

I met [Lt.] Smith this morning for the first time since his return & have been trying to gather news from Pontiac, the most that I learn is that all our friends are well. I fear the people have almost forgotten us. They seem to be very intent upon all matters of business & politics. They may be suddenly awakened some of these days. I shall try & write this evening at length, for the present I must close.

Give my love to all & a kiss to Frankie. Hoping that Our Father in Heaven will keep you,

I am, as ever,

Your Affect. Husband

J. F. Culver

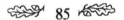 85

Head Qrs., Co. "A" 129th Regt. Ills. Vol. Inft.
Nashville. Tenn., Sept. 16th 1863

My Dear Wife

I attempted to write to you to-day but signally failed, yet, for fear that opportunity might not be given to-night, I sent the few lines I had written. It is seldom that I find myself in no state of mind to write, but it so happened. I can explain in a few words. While on duty last night, Corp. J. M. Chritten was taken suddenly ill, & I sent a messenger for the Dr. & an ambulance,[1] but Dr. Johns refused to allow either, & Chritten lay all night in an old shed. I felt angry, &, when I came in this morning, made a written statement to the Col. [Case], &, for myself, I must confess I was not in any mood for writing.

The weather continues cloudy & threatens rain. It has required considerable labor to clean up & repair after the storm last night. The camp presented a rather ludicrous appearance, I am told, as the boys had to hold their tents to keep them from blowing away & did not have sufficient notice to dress themselves.

We have news this evening from the front which have evidence of truth: Gen. McCook's Division is in the rear of Bragg's Army & have been retreating south & fighting since Sunday. Rosecrans is urging his Army forward, & we hope to hear in a few days that Bragg's entire army has been captured, though it is not impossible that the Rebels may fall with such force upon McCooks Division as to rout them.[2] If the plan succeeds, the war will virtually be ended in this department. Should it fail, there will be a demand for more troops. Let us hope for the best.

Deserters are still joining, over 800 arrived on Monday.[3] Some of them say that Bragg will fight, others say not; but he is evidently fighting now.

Day after to-morrow I shall probably have to go to Stevenson again. I have not heard from Bro. Johnie since he left Shelbyville. I heard, however, that the Battery [Miller's] was near Chattanooga.

I have been thinking since the receipt of your letters that perhaps your visit [to Carlisle] was not as agreeable as it might be. Father must require all of Mother & Sister Hannah's time, leaving but little to devote to you. I hope that you will not grow weary. I am very anxious to spend a short time with you there. I believe I can find items of interest after you have completed your searches. After thinking the matter over, I believe that I occupied the same room you now occupy. How many troops are there at Carlisle Barracks, & what troops are they?[4]

I have not yet had an opportunity of attending Sabbath School here. I hope I may be more successful next Sabbath. I shall expect a letter to-morrow morning from you.

[Lt.] Smith saw Leander Utley & says all the family are well. I am sorry to say I have not written to Maggie [Utley] yet.

How I should like to be in Carlisle to-night. Let us hope that at some day not far distant I may succeed in getting *home*. Give my love to all the family. Write all the news. I have not written to Mother [Murphy] since your arrival but should be happy to hear from her.

May God bless both Frankie & you, preserve you in health, & give you perfect happiness.

Good night

Your Affect. Husband

J. F. Culver

---

1   James M. Chritten, a 20-year-old Pontiac farmer, was mustered into service on Sept. 8,1862, as a private in Company A, 129th Illinois, and was promoted to corporal, May 9, 1863. Corporal Chritten was mustered out near Washington, D.C., June 8, 1865. Compiled Service Records of Union Soldiers, NA.

2   General Bragg, having failed to trap two divisions of Thomas' corps in McLemore's Cove, determined to hurl his columns against Crittenden's divided corps, which was advancing south and southeast from Chattanooga. Before he could do so, Crittenden had concentrated his corps at Lee and Gordon's Mills. Having failed again to strike Rosecrans' army in detail, Bragg ordered his generals to take position east of the Chickamauga and be prepared to take the offensive as soon as Lt. Gen. James Longstreet arrived from Virginia with two divisions of his corps.

General Rosecrans now realized that he had been hoodwinked by Bragg. The Confederates were not in wild retreat as he had believed but massing and threatening to destroy his army. Rosecrans, on the 12th, to concentrate his army to cope with this menace, ordered Thomas' and McCook's corps to close to the left. Thomas' troops held their ground, and on the 13th McCook put his divisions in motion from Alpine by way of Valley Head into Lookout Valley. Cist, *Army of the Cumberland,* pp. 189-191.

3   The number of Confederate deserters is exaggerated. Rosecrans' provost marshal, in the period September 1-October 7, 1863, reported that about 750 Rebel deserters were counted. *O.R.*, Ser. I, Vol. XXX, pt. I, p. 232.

4   Mary Culver had written on September 2, "The ruins of the Barracks are plainly to be seen from my window and it looks quite natural to see the white tents of the soldiers clustered around them." Mary Culver to J.F.C., Sept. 2, 1863, Culver Collection. The Confederates had burned the Carlisle Barracks during the Gettysburg Campaign.

 86

Head Qrs. "A" 129th Regt. Ills. Vol. Infty.
Nashville, Tenn., Sept. 18th 1863

My Dear Wife

Yours of the 11th inst. came to hand this morning, also a catalogue & 3 [news]papers for which I am much obliged.[1] I recd. the Philad. Ledger a few days ago.

I know exactly where you are, as I boarded nearly a year at Mrs. McGary's in that same house.[2] Please remember me to them kindly; I am indebted to them for many favors. Are the girls married yet? I have not seen or heard of any of them for years.

I shall take great pleasure in sending you long letters whenever I have opportunity; it is no tax upon me to write to YOU.[3] I try to imagine myself talking with you, telling you all I know that I think would be interesting, and then waiting patiently for your reply. We often talk about you here & Alf Huetson invariably, whenever he sees me do or hears me say anything out of the way, reminds me that it is not consistent with my wife's views. I have, therefore, a good monitor, & it has become a fixed rule to comply with your wishes in all matters. It is a happy thought to be in possession of a loving, true & noble hearted Wife. It alleviates our sufferings, gives strength in trial and temptation, & joy & happiness in all the walks of life. My heart is filled with gratitude to God for his abundant mercy & so great a blessing.

I am sorry to hear of Father's declining health. I am much afraid that before my opportunity for getting home arrives, he will have passed away. I am sorry Bro. Wes. does not exercise more energy in securing so good a position,[4] but inactivity is his characteristic. I was in hopes that his accumulating a family would be an incentive to energy; if that fails, I fear nothing will arouse him. Allen Fellows recd. a letter from his Wife this morning. She is quite well.

I am well acquainted with Mary Moore & Annie Brady, but they were only little girls when I was home & went to Sabbath School.[5] Annie Brady was a very bright scholar & won many honors in the public schools in Carlisle.

How do you like Mrs. Proff. Johnson?[6] You will find her very intelligent. I hope your acquaintance with the family may prove pleasant. I am not acquainted with Proff. Boswell's family.[7] Annie (Van Horn) Davis has been quite successful, or rather prolific.[8] Give Lizzie Zug a kiss for me, she is an especial favorite of mine.

I believe I could guess in three times who made the remark to her about Frankie. It was either Mary Rheem, Em. Ensiminger, or Ell. _____, the last named lives on the corner of the Alley west of Sister Jennie, at the lumber yard.[9] I have forgotten her last name though it is very familiar. I recollect it now, it is Ell. Armstrong. The language is very like either of them. It is not very singular that either of them should recognize him [Frankie].

[Lt.] Smith has not heard from his wife since his return [from furlough] & feels quite uneasy. The weather is so cool this morning that my fingers are quite numb. Every body is wearing overcoats. I presume it will last until after the 21st, [equinox]: If it should continue long, we will be compelled to get a stove. The changes in the weather are full as severe and sudden as in Illinois.

Frank Long has just been here requesting a recommendation for a position in a negro Regiment, & it has broken into my thoughts considerably.[10] I must finish my letter now, or it will miss to-morrow's mail.

I had thought of a number of things I wished to write, but fear they have gone out of my mind entirely. I have received no letters since I last wrote to you from any source, but have been expecting to hear from Pontiac daily. Henry Greenebaum [a friend and Pontiac dry goods merchant] sent me another package of Collars, so that I am well provided. I am much in need of my boots & hope they will not forget to send them by McIntyre.[11]

I am sorry to say that I have not answered either Maggie [Utley's] or Sarah Williams' letters yet, though I am strongly impressed that I wrote to Maggie last. If there was no drill this afternoon, I would write to both of them; as it is, I fear I shall not be able.

The health of the men is generally good. I sent you a Nashville paper yesterday containing an undeserved compliment. The troops were from the different companies & not all of Co. "A", & we had no idea of eliciting any encomium.[12] I shall in all probability be on duty on Sunday again, it seems to be my misfortune.

The boys are crying at some Provost Guards passing, "White Gloves." They have a holy horror of all style. I fear it would require a great effort for us to comply with the regulations of the "Army of the Potomac." The men complain now of being too much of a band-box Regt, yet our style falls far short of the requirements of some portions of the Army.[13]

I have not heard from Bro. Johnie yet. I presume he is quite busy. There has been some hard fighting at the front for the last four days, but we have not learned the result though the papers report Rosecrans driven back this morning.[14] Yet it is not generally believed. We shall hear definitely in a few days, I presume.

Give my love to all the family. I should like very much to hear from Mother & the rest of my Bros. & Sisters, but they apparently expect you to do their writing. Kiss Frankie for me. I am happy to hear that you both enjoy such good health. I shall look anxiously for the *music,* we need something of the kind very much.

We have not yet been paid off but are promised to-morrow. I do not know why it is delayed. Write as often, your letters are not less interesting to me than mine are to you. Though I should be far happier to communicate more directly with you, yet I rejoice at this opportunity still left for communication & earnestly hope though distant to hear very often.

Remember me kindly to all our friends in Carlisle. Tell me all you hear & see, for rest assured that everything and almost every person are familiar to memory.

May Our Father in Heaven bless you & preserve you in health and happiness. I remain, Dear Mary,

Your Affect. Husband

J. F. Culver

---

1 Mary Culver's letter of Sept. 11 is missing from the Culver Collection.

2 Mary Culver evidently had written J.F.C., describing a visit to Mrs. McGary's.

3 Mary Culver had expressed appreciation for the long letters her husband frequently wrote, contrasting them to her briefer ones.

4 In an earlier letter, dated September 2, Mary Culver had written, "Wes and Little Willie was up this afternoon. Wes expects to report to Washington soon. He is quite lame yet and Mother thinks he never will entirely recover the use of his ankle." Mary Culver to J.F.C., Sept. 2, 1863, Culver Collection. Wes Culver had fractured a small ankle bone by falling out of a tree the previous autumn.

5 Anna Brady was the 19-year-old daughter of Ernest and Margaret Brady. The father was an agent for a Bible society. Mary Moore was the 17-year-old daughter of Robert and Ann Moore. The father was a Carlisle Township farmer. Eighth Census, Cumberland County, State of Pennsylvania, NA.

6 Lucena Johnson, to whom Mary Culver had been introduced, was the wife of Professor Herman M. Johnson of Dickinson College. *Ibid.*

7 W. A. Boswell was a 35-year-old professor of mathematics at Dickinson College. In 1860 he was living with his wife, Frances, and their three children. *Ibid.*

8 It has been impossible to identify Annie Van Dorn Davis.

9 Mary Rheem was the 25-year-old daughter of Jacob and Susan Rheem. The father was a wealthy Cumberland County speculator. Elizabeth Ensiminger was the 24-year-old daughter of Samuel and Frances Ensiminger. Her father was a Carlisle saddler. Ellen Armstrong was the 21-year-old daughter of Mrs. Mary Armstrong. She and her mother lived in Carlisle with her brother, a well-to-do lumber merchant. *Ibid.*

10 Frank M. Long, a 20-year-old Pontiac blacksmith, had been mustered into the army on Sept. 8, 1862, as corporal in Company A, 129th Illinois. Long was promoted to sergeant on Jan. 20, 1863, and reduced to private on May 20, 1864, for repeated misbehavior in face of the enemy. On June 20, 1864, at Kennesaw Mountain, Ga., he deserted. He was arrested at Gallatin, rejoined the regiment near Vining's Station, Ga., on Sept. 15, 1864,

and placed in arrest. Compiled Service Records of Union Soldiers, NA. The black regiments being organized by the United States were officered by whites.

11  There were two McIntyre brothers in Company G, 129th Illinois, both of whom had been tinsmiths in civil life. Eighteen-year-old Charles and 24-year-old Robert M. McIntyre were mustered into service as privates on Sept. 8, 1862. Charles, while posted at Chattanooga, on April 19, 1864, was ordered to report to General Steedman for transfer to naval service. Robert, on June 17, 1863, was detailed as a provost clerk at Gallatin, Tenn., and on December 7, 1863, was detailed for duty at the Nashville Quartermaster Depot. On April 28, 1864, Private McIntyre was ordered to report to General Steedman at Chattanooga for transfer to naval service. Compiled Service Records of Union Soldiers, NA.

12  The *Nashville Union* for September 17 carried this article. "I witnessed an incident while attending a funeral today, that made a deep impression on me.

"Company A, 129th Illinois, on picket duty under command of a lieutenant, presented arms as a funeral cortege passed. The little girl who was going to her long home could not know it, but it thrilled the hearts of her parents that strangers thus saluted their darling.

"Such instinctive courtesy notes this gentleman eyewitness; and courtesy and valor have ever gone together. Those men will not be found wanting wherever they may be. In camp and field, in life and death may God bless them."

13  The 129th Illinois was not a "spit and polish" unit. On July 27, 1863, Lt. G. W. Morris of the Inspector General's Department had directed Colonel Case to have his adjutant inspect the guard detail before marching it to the parade ground. He would see that the muskets were loaded, and that they were "free from dirt, rust, grease, pieces of tape, string or other unnecessary appendages," and that their "equipments are in good order and properly adjusted." No clothing other than that prescribed by regulations would be worn. Trouser legs would not be stuffed into boots; coats and blouses were to be buttoned up to the chin; blankets compactly rolled and slung across the right shoulder. Sergeants were to fall out with their muskets and sidearms. Inspector General to Case, July 27, 1863, Regimental Papers, 129th Illinois, NA.

On August 3 Lieutenant Morris had reported that the 129th, "although well commanded did not come up to the standard even of volunteers. There is that *lack of pride or interest* that should exist, and which is necessary to the maintenance of Good Order and Military Discipline. All of which may be attributed to the fact that the officers are both negligent as to their own personal appearance and to the enforcement of the regulations among the men." Granger to Case, Aug. 5, 1863, Regimental Papers, 129th Illinois, NA.

These complaints caused Colonel Case to take corrective measures, and General Gordon Granger soon observed a "decided improvement" in the military appearance, discipline, and drill (both company and battalion). Granger was especially pleased to see the company officers were stimulating that "feeling of pride so necessary to advancement in everything pertaining to the soldier." Morris to Case, Aug. 6, 1863, Regimental Papers, 129th Illinois, NA.

14  General Thomas' XIV Corps in the period September 13-16 had held its ground in McLemore's Cove, awaiting arrival of McCook's XX Corps on its right. Forced reconnaissances were made to Catlett's Gap and toward Blue Bird and Dug Gaps, and on the 17th Thomas put his corps in motion and closed up on Crittenden's right along Chickamauga Creek. McCook by nightfall was in position on Thomas' right at Pond Spring, and Rosecrans had massed his army along a 12-mile front.

General Bragg in the meantime had marshaled his Army of Tennessee east of the Chickamauga, with its right near Reed's Bridge and its left under Lt. Gen. D. H. Hill south of Lee and Gordon's Mills. Wheeler's cavalry guarded Bragg's left and Forrest's horse-soldiers his right. Cist, *Army of the Cumberland*, pp. 188-190.

*170*

## 87

Head Qrs. Co. "A" 129th Ills. Vol.
Nashville, Tenn., Sept. 19th 1863

My Dear Wife

We are notified to be prepared for marching orders, an indication at least that we will soon leave here, & though we have no definite idea of where we are going, yet, as the whole Brigade is to move, we anticipate being sent to the front.[1] As I shall probably be on duty to-morrow & not have another opportunity, I wish to-night to give you a full understanding of our business affairs at home. Our communication will be necessarily less frequent & should we cross the Tennessee River, it will doubtless be very irregular. I have often thought that I should have embraced the opportunity while we were to-gether to make you fully acquainted with all our affairs, yet [I] postponed [it] from time to time until it was entirely neglected.

I regret exceedingly the additional expenditure caused by our removal to this place, & by a late order of Genrl. Rosecrans which compels "a report of the appearance of each officer 4 times a month." I have spent considerable for clothing.

I have never yet been able to get any definite information of the condition of affairs at Pontiac. [William] Russell promised me he would write, but I have never recd. any word from him. Mrs. Custer, in a letter written some two months ago, informed me that our carpet was almost destroyed & the furniture very much damaged. I may not be wholly excusable for not informing you, but I feared it would mar your pleasure & possibly interfere with your visit. I accordingly wrote to Mr. Remick to attend to it, &, when Russell went home, authorized him to make sale of such articles as were likely to be injured, & if he could effect a good sale to dispose of all of it.

I am wholly unable to determine what amount of money is in Remick's hands. I had over $40 in Company Records sent to McCleary for sale & $100 sent to him in money. Out of that you have drawn but $25. I ford. by express to-day $25, & ordered him [Remick] to pay $50 to the church, which they tell me will cancel the last of my notes there; & also pay Maples $11 [to] Bond for a pair of boots I ordered; also Fisher amt. due him, which does not exceed $10. So that there should be a balance in his [Remick's] hands of $30, aside from the Records and whatever has been realized from rent or the sale of furniture.

My liabilities on the house yet is $450 due; $150 which will be due next month & $300 int. due next March. I could, if nothing happens, meet all the liabilities on it, if I was sure Bro. Thomas [Murphy] would not call or want the amount due him next spring which will be $600. In addition to our home, I have paid $50 on those 2 lots in Mott & Collins' addition.

My matters have become quite seriously damaged since I left. I had sufficient collections well secured, placed in Fleming & Collins' hands, to have met all my obligations as they became due had I been there to attend to them. I can gather no information from them [Fleming & Collins] & am left to infer that nothing has been done & consequently all has been lost. The interest I had in Tax lands, which promised a good harvest, has all been forfeited in my absence & lost.

We have nothing left then but our share in our home & those lots [in Mott & Collins' Addition], & yet I could cheerfully resign all were there any prospects of affairs changing for the better. In addition to the other settlements, I placed in Collins' hands vouchers to complete the payment of my note to McDonald for Spurlock.[2] The man by whom the vouchers were payable has left the country, so that there remains $40 & interest to be paid there, which with the amt. lost by Beattie makes the whole of my indebtedness save $25 here [Nashville]. I am very bare, however, & shall probably have to borrow some before next pay day, not exceeding $25, however.

Will you pardon me, my dear Wife, for not informing you more fully on these matters before this? When I left home, my affairs were in a very prosperous condition, & had all been quiet & prosperity continued, all my obligations would have been cancelled before this. Out of the justices's office I have never heard of any money being paid over, except the little you recd. I do not wish to be unkind, but I do feel that Utley has not done the part of a friend, much less a Brother.

You will perceive that my letter was commenced on the evening of the 19th & this is now the 22nd. Since that time I have been two days & nights on [picket] duty. Great changes have taken place. I am not sure that there is cause for dispondency, but things look somewhat gloomy. The news from our Army informs us of a severe battle & heavy losses,[3] & the recognition of the Confederacy by the French.[4] I apprehend no serious results finally, but an indefinite prolongation of the war. If the North remains united, we are still safe.

It is with all these things in view that I have written at such length, so that if our communication should be cut off, you might be able possibly to arrange affairs in my absence & in that worse contingency, my death.

Do not think I feel any despondency, but I think it wise to provide for any contingency that could possibly happen.

I have a request to make. You recollect I placed in one of the little drawers a sealed package [my will] with the request that it should not be opened during my life time. I wish the document destroyed, but it cannot be done legally except by myself & that in the presence of witnesses. Try & think of it when you go home & send it to me. Should any thing happen to prevent its reaching me; John Wolgamott is witness to it, & this letter shown to him shall be my warrant to him for its destruction. Yet should anything still happen to make all doubly sure, I will make another *will* revoking all former ones, & retain it until that one is destroyed & then destroy it.

And now, my dear Wife, though misfortune & heavy loss has been the result of my leaving home, yet our country was in danger & is not yet safe. I entered conscientiously upon what I felt to be the discharge of duty, &, if you can yield so great a sacrifice, I shall be perfectly satisfied if it be God's will to commence the world again. It may not have been most wise to base so much on so Sandy a basis, yet I am confident that with ordinary diligence nearly all my liabilities would to-day have been cancelled. Let us bid farewell to business & talk a little of ourselves.

I recd. your letter of the 13th inst.,[5] day before yesterday, while out on [picket] duty, & I am happy to hear that you are so well. You ask me to guess what you gave Bro. Harry [Cheston] for acting as your Post Boy. I should guess a "Kiss." Am I right?

It is a year ago to-day that we left Pontiac. Yesterday was Frankie's birthday. I suppose it was celebrated with due solemnity. I hope when his next arrives, I may have the pleasure of joining in the celebration when you may realize your anticipated joys in the knowledge that we are all *at home* once more to remain. I am happy to hear that Jennie and Harry [Cheston] are so happy. If it be God's will, we will one day be very happy. I doubt not in the Providence of God, all will be for the best.

There is no Ohio Regt. here. I may possibly meet your Cousin, &, if so, I will try & make his acquaintance.

I set for some Photographs on Saturday but on examining them to-day did not like them. I will sit again to-morrow. The number is 448, &, if you should wish at anytime within a year to get any by sending for the number & this date, you can have them copied. The negative is kept on hand for a year. I will send you one as soon as I can get it.

Enclosed find $10 to be preserved for Frankie as birthday present. If Gold comes down, buy gold as it will be surer. If I get home, I will invest it for him. Kiss him for me. I have been until a late hour writing to-night, being interrupted very often.

Christ Yetter took very sick while on [ picket ] duty last night [the 21st]. I sent him to Camp, but he is much better this morning & was walking around. The health of the Company is generally good. Quite a number of the men have been drinking too much to-day; they seem to fear that their money will not be spent soon enough. It generally happens after pay day, but is much worse this time, being in the city.[6]

I came very near losing the package of money I sent to Remick to-day. I put it up, but could not find the Col. to get a pass to go to the express office, & lay down on the bed to wait & fell asleep. Little Mary Nelson came into my tent, as she frequently does, & attracted by the red seals upon it, I presume, took it out of my hands & carried it out & in playing in an adjoining yard with another little girl lost it. [Adjutant] Plattenburg, happening to pass, found it, & returned it to me, after I had concluded it was gone. Had many a one found it, I should doubtless been the loser of $25. She knew she had taken it, but could not tell where she had lost it.

I will try and write to Harry [Cheston], but I am so busy that I find but little time to devote to correspondence. I owe a large number of letters.

We are on duty much more than half the time & but seldom in camp; when here drill consumes nearly all our time or leaves us so tired that it requires considerable effort. I went on duty Sunday morning [the 20th] & was relieved about 9 A.M. to-day, besides [having] 3 hours' drill this afternoon. I had a little time to go to the express office & that was all.

The papers will give you an account of the Battle [of Chickamauga]. We have but few particulars yet. Our loss in killed & wounded is at least 10,000, & I shall feel glad if in the summing up it does not reach 15,000 or over.[7] The Slaughter is terrible. We expect almost every hour to be ordered forward. One division of our Corps [Grangers's ] was in the battle, either the 1st or 2nd, we have not yet learned which.[8] Bro. Johnie is in the 2nd Division & was at last accounts at Chattanooga, & probably not in the battle. I will write to you as soon as I learn. His is Morgan's division of Granger's Corps.[9]

Send me a paper with the account of the French recognition. We are waiting anxiously to learn what England & Russia are doing or intend to do.[10] Will the North stand a draft of 600,000 more?[11] If so, we are yet safe. I think this interference will have a tendency to arouse & unite them. I hope so at least.

I am sorry to learn of Father's condition.[12] I dare not hope or do I wish for leave of Absence while affairs are in so critical a condition. Let us trust all to God. In his love & protecting care our best interests will be preserved. Do not grieve over past misfortunes but look hopefully to the future. Whatever God directs is for the best.

I have received no letters for some time from any source. My friends seem to be waiting for me to write. Neither Mother [Culver] or Hannah have written since you arrived there. Give my love to all. Believing that God will bless & preserve us, yet committing all to his hands,

I remain, as ever,

Your Affect. Husband

J. F. Culver

---

1  On September 17 General Rosecrans, to strengthen his army at the front, suggested to General Gordon Granger that it would be possible to reduce further the garrisons and posts guarding the supply lines and depots in Middle Tennessee. Rosecrans urged that one infantry regiment be withdrawn from Fort Donelson and Clarksville; one cavalry regiment from Nashville; three battalions of infantry and one of cavalry from the Murfreesboro area; and three infantry regiments from the ten currently posted at Caperton's, Stevenson, Bridgeport, and Jasper. If Granger knew of any garrisons which could be pared further to provide troops for the army at the front, he was to do so. *O. R.*, Ser. I, Vol. XXX, pt. III, pp. 713-714.

2  It has been impossible to further identify MacDonald and Spurlock.

3  General Bragg's Army of Tennessee, reinforced by General Longstreet with two divisions from the Army of Northern Virginia, crossed Chickamauga Creek on September 19 and attacked Rosecrans' Army of the Cumberland. The Federals more than held their own in the first day's fighting, but on the 20th several of their generals blundered. As the armies fought and maneuvered through the woods and clearings, a gap opened in the Union front. Through it surged a powerful Confederate column, spearheaded by Longstreet's veterans. Two of Rosecrans' four corps (McCook's and Crittenden's) collapsed and fled for Chattanooga. Fortunately for the North, Thomas' XIV Corps and one of Granger's divisions held their ground. Instead of pursuing the routed corps, Bragg hurled his divisions against Thomas' and Granger's bluecoats. A terrible struggle ensued as the Confederates vainly sought to drive Thomas from Snodgrass Hill. Under cover of darkness on the evening of the 20th, Thomas, having won for himself the name "Rock of Chickamauga" and time to enable Rosecrans to rally and re-form McCook's and Crittenden's corps, evacuated his position and retired into the Chattanooga defenses.

Chickamauga was the bloodiest two-day battle of the Civil War. Union casualties were 1,657 killed, 9,756 wounded, and 4,757 missing, out of 58,000 engaged. General Bragg listed his losses as 2,312 killed, 14,674 wounded, and 1,468 missing, out of a force of 66,000. The casualty rate for both sides was about 28 percent. E. B. Long, *The Civil War Day by Day: An Almanac, 1861-1865.* (New York, 1971), p. 412; Cist, *Army of the Cumberland*, pp. 193-229.

4  There was no truth to the report that France had recognized the Confederacy. Although Louis Napoleon's government favored such action, it would not act unilaterally. Napoleon and his ministers would be guided by Great Britain's actions.

5  Mary Culver's letter of September 13 is missing from the Culver Collection.

6  The 129th Illinois was a typical unit in this respect. Public drunkeness has always plagued military units whenever the men receive their pay.

7  See note #3 for a brief account of the battle of Chickamauga. Union casualties (dead, wounded, and missing) numbered 16,170.

8  General Granger with two brigades of the First Division (Steedman's) had marched from Rossville to General Thomas' assistance. He reached Snodgrass Hill at 3 P.M. on the 20th, and employed Steedman's troops in a counterattack routing the Confederates from a gorge from which they were threatening to turn Thomas' right. Cist, *Army of the Cumberland,* pp. 209-210. Brig. Gen. James D. Morgan's division of Granger's Reserve Corps guarded the crossings of the Tennessee River and the forward supply depots at Bridgeport and Stevenson. *O. R.,* Ser. I, Vol. XXX, pt. III, pp. 742-743.

9  J.F.C. was mistaken. Company M, 1st Illinois Light Artillery, was assigned to Steedman's, not Morgan's division, and had participated in the battle on September 20, losing 2 killed and 14 wounded. *Adjutant General's Report, State of Illinois,* Vol. III, p. 665.

10  In the summer of 1863 the Roebuck resolution urging joint recognition of the Confederacy by Great Britain and France had been debated in Parliament, but, when it failed to elicit sufficient support, it was withdrawn. Napoleon was ready to act but would not do so unilaterally. Randall, *Civil War and Reconstruction,* pp. 646-647.

11  In June President Lincoln had called on the governors of Pennsylvania, Ohio, Maryland, and West Virginia for 100,000 men for six months. Three months before, on March 3, the Congress had enacted a national conscription law, declaring all able-bodied male citizens between 20 and 45 liable to military service. The draft aroused bitter opposition in parts of the North, culminating in the New York City draft riots of July 13-16. *Ibid.,* pp. 410-416.

12  Father Culver's health had continued to deteriorate.

 88

Head Qrs. Co. "A" 129th Ills. Vol. Infty.
Nashville, Tenn., Sept. 24th 1863

My Dear Wife

Yours of the 18th & 19th came to hand to-day.[1] I am truly happy to hear that you & Frankie enjoy such good health. I wrote a long letter to you night before last, but forgot to tell you to draw on Remick whenever you are in need of money.[2] There is at least $30 in his hands & should be $60 or $70. I will inform you of the Amount as soon as I learn. Should it fall short of your necessities, write to me; I have made arrangements here to borrow if I need it.

I cannot write a very long letter to-night, as I leave in charge of train at 3 P.M. in the morning [*sic*]. My health is very good.

I did not mean to be impertinent in my question about your winning a silk dress & sincerely beg your pardon for any offence I may have given.[3] I will give you an explanation of the other bet. I may & doubtless was indiscreet, but it was not intentional, I assure you. While at Richland Station [in the spring] in a conversation one day with Lieut.

Smith & Capt. Hoskins, they both insisted that you might regret your visit South, & offered to bet on it.[4] I took the bet, & when they raised the question some time ago, I assured them that they had lost & they paid up. My assurance was based upon your letter admitting that you had lost the dress. That was all. I cannot say whether I was glad or sorry. I should, for my own part, have been happy had I lost the bets; but, knowing your fears, I should have dreaded even the consummation of so happy an event. It is all well, however.

I am unable to tell yet what our lot will be, whether to remain here or move forward. There is a Brigade forming to go to the front, sometimes we are included & then again left out.[5] We shall know probably on my return.

My Photographs will be done when I return, & I will forward them. I should have been very happy to have made the visit to the old homestead with you. Those old places are very dear to memory. I could tell you of many things were I there that are indelibly impressed upon my memory, besides the association would assist me to recall much that I have doubtless forgotten. The meadows are all drained but they must have filled up if it has overflowed. I am sorry that Gustie [Pague] has not been more fortunate; I would like to see him prospering.[6]

Large numbers of wounded have arrived & are still arriving on the trains from the front. We know nothing definite from the battle yet. Great secrecy is observed for some cause.[7] I have not yet been able to learn whether Bro. Johnie was in the battle or not.

I am sorry that Ira & John have gone into the service. I fear the temptations will be too great for them. Why has Wes [Culver] not gone to duty? Is he not able?

I have recd. no news from Pontiac except a short letter from Utley. Maggie, Mary, the babie, & Mother [Murphy] are well. He says considerable about the pleasures of home, but he forgot that a very little effort on his part might have proved very beneficial to us. Let us not judge him harshly, however, & hope that all will yet end well.

But I must close. I hope to have some news for you on my return. If we remain here, I would be happy to have the music, & I think it safe if you will send it. Give my love to all the family. My last letter contained ten dollars, please tell me if you received it. Kiss Frankie for me. Trusting that God will bless & keep you, I remain,

Your Affect. Husband

J. F. Culver

---

1   Mary Culver's letters of September 18 and 19 are missing from the Culver Collection.

2   In the missing letters, Mary Culver undoubtedly called attention to her need for money.

3   Reference is to the wager the Culvers had made as to the possibility that Mary had become pregnant during her March-June visit. Mary was not with child and had lost the wager.

4   J.F.C.'s bet with Captain Hoskins and Lieutenant Smith concerned the possibility that Mary might be pregnant.

5   General Rosecrans in the fourth week of September determined to withdraw additional troops from the Nashville garrison to guard the vital Nashville & Chattanooga Railroad. Their places would be taken by two regiments of infantry rushed south by rail from Glasgow, Ky. *O. R.*, Ser. I, Vol. XXX, pt. III, p. 839.

6   Mary Culver had visited her husband's boyhood home in southern Middlesex Township, several miles east of Carlisle, occupied by J.F.C.'s sister and brother-in-law, Mr. and Mrs. Augustus Pague. The house still stands.

7   By September 22 Rosecrans' Army of the Cumberland had retired into Chattanooga and had taken position with its back against the Tennessee River. Rifle pits were thrown up and artillery emplaced. Bragg's columns moved up and, occupying Missionary Ridge and Lookout Mountain, partially invested Rosecrans' army. Confederate cavalry crossed the Tennessee River to attack wagon trains employed to supply Rosecrans' troops from the advance depot at Stevenson. Cist, *Army of the Cumberland*, pp. 230-233.

89

Head Qrs. Co. "A" 129th Ills. Vol.
Nashville, Tenn., Sept. 29th 1863

My Dear Wife

I recd. a letter from you on my return yesterday from Stevenson & looked for another this morning but was disappointed.[1] I am happy to know that you continue to enjoy such good health. You wrote upon the eve of Frankie's first birthday, I doubt not, as your letter intimates you have upon reflection found the past year full of trial, care & trouble.

I have very often thought of your difficulties & wished that the exigencies of the case were not so urgent, so that I could in some way justify myself in returning home. But at present that must not be; & I believe God in his manifestations of love and mercy has given no evidence of his approbation. May we always prove deserving.

I had a rather tedious journey through this time but no accidents. I learned but little; it appears the farther one gets from a battlefield the more they can learn. The report of killed, wounded, and missing reported falls far short of the true amount. The lowest estimate is little short of 15,000.[2] Another battle is impending. New troops are being sent forward, and, while thousands pass through here, we are still left behind.[3] It is doubtless best so, but we feel that we are able to do more than stand guard all the time. It is possible that our opportunity will yet come; when we hope to be found among the first in our Country's Cause.

I have not learned anything from Bro. Johny yet, save that the Battery was on the Battlefield, & that is only surmise.[4] I know nothing definite. The Artillery took but little part in the action; the nature of the country would not permit them. It is reported that Seigel's [sic] Corps will pass through the city this evening on their way to reinforce Rosecrans.[5] I hope it is true. Another great Battle is impending. The Rebels must either fight or retreat.

My health is quite good. I am happy to hear that Frankie is improving in disposition.[6] I will try and pray that God will give us wisdom to train him aright. I know your responsibilities are great, but I feel assured that you will be happy in the efforts you may make to lead our dear boy to Jesus. May God give you grace & strength.

I have received no letters from any source since I last wrote. My friends seem to have forgotten me. I intend to write to Sister Maggie [Utley] this evening. I wrote to Sarah Williams this afternoon & sent her a Photograph. I will send one to Maggie also.

I informed you in two former letters that Luther Van Doren's body never was found. We made diligent search for it. Christ Yetter has not been on duty yet, but I think is quite well. All the rest enjoy good health.

I hope your visit to Lizzie's [Zug's] may be pleasant. Tell me all you know about Anna's husband.[7] How is Mother's health? Why has she not written? Write to me as often as you can. I am always very happy to hear from you. Give my love to all the family & Remember me kindly to all our friends.

May the riches of God's grace dwell with you & his blessings ever rest upon you.

Your Affect. Husband

J. F. Culver

---

1 The letter referred to, written on September 20, is missing from the Culver Collection.

2 See J.F.C.'s letter of September 19, 1863, for data on Union casualties at Chickamauga.

3   To recover the initiative and drive the Confederates from the approaches to Chattanooga from where they invested Rosecrans' Army of the Cumberland, the War Department on the 22d called on General Grant at Vicksburg and General Meade in Virginia to rush reinforcements to the point of danger. General Grant was to send four divisions by boat from Vicksburg to Memphis. The troops would then be shuttled by rail to Corinth, Miss., and from there to march east to Bridgeport, repairing the Memphis & Charleston Railroad as they advanced. General Meade was to detach two corps, the XI and XII, from his Army of the Potomac and send them by rail from Manassas, Virginia, to Bridgeport by way of Washington, Louisville, and Nashville. This latter massive troop movement was carried out with efficiency and dispatch. The first of the 15,000 men being rushed to Middle Tennessee from the Army of the Potomac left Washington, D.C., on September 25, and the first four troop trains with units of Maj. Gen. O. O. Howard's XI Corps rumbled through Nashville on the evening of the 29th. *O. R.,* Ser. I, Vol. XXX, pt. III, pp. 812, 841-842, 862, 920, 947.

4   Company M, 1st Illinois Light Artillery, had supported Steedman's division in the fight for the gorge on the afternoon of the 20th, and the next day was engaged near Rossville, where it shelled Rebel cavalry that appeared in the valley beyond. On the 22d the battery had retreated into Chattanooga, closely followed by the Confederates. *Adjutant General's Report, State of Illinois,* Vol. VIII, p. 665.

5   Maj. Gen. Franz Sigel, a popular figure in Missouri and Illinois and with the Germans, had formerly led the XI Corps. General Howard had commanded the corps since late spring, having led it at Chancellorsville and Gettysburg.

6   Mary Culver in her letter of September 7 had complained of Frankie's conduct. In her letter of the 20th, she must have made reference to an improvement in his behavior.

7   Annie was the 19-year-old daughter of Jacob and Elizabeth Zug of South Middleton Township, Cumberland County. She had recently married. Eighth Census, Cumberland County, State of Pennsylvania, NA.

 90

Head Qrs. Co. "A" 129th Ills. Vol.
Nashville, Tenn., Octr. 2nd 1863

My Dear Wife

The music you sent me arrived this morning with your letter of the 24th inst.,[1] & one from Bro. Johnie which you will find enclosed.[2] I will write to Mother [Murphy] immediately & tell her that he is safe & well.

I hope Frankie may not be as bad as anticipated. May God in his good providence soon restore him to health. I shall await anxiously for further news.

The Drum is beating for drill. Good bye.

May God bless & Keep you,

Your Affect. Husband

J. F. Culver

---

1  Mary Culver's letter of September 24 is mssing from the Culver Collection.

2  Brother John Murphy's letter was dated Chattanooga, Sept. 25, 1863. Sergeant Murphy had written, "This is the first opportunity I have had of writing you since the receipt of the papers, as we have been in very active service in the field away from our baggage. Rosecrans has been driven back to this place. Our Brig. participated in the battle of Sunday last [the 20th]. It was very severe during the afternoon. We lost 14 men. I am well." W. J. Murphy to J.F.C., September 25, 1863, Culver Collection.

 91

Head Qrs. Co. "A" 129th Ills. Vol. Infty.
Nashville, Tenn., Octr. 2nd 1863

My Dear Wife

I wrote a note hastily to-day & intended to enclose Bro. Johnie's letter, but the drum beat for drill, &, in my haste, I neglected to put it in. Please find it enclosed herein. ,

I wrote a short note to Mother [Murphy] to-day, informing her that he [Brother Johnny] was well, thinking that she would feel uneasy.

I shall look anxiously for a letter from you every day until Frankie gets better. You cannot imagine [how glad] I was this morning to receive your second letter dated but one day after your other informing me of his illness.¹ I know you are taxed heavily, but if you can only write a line to tell me how he is. I hope to be able to get this into to-night's mail; I am not sure of success but will try. I must therefore be brief.

Troops are still passing through here in large numbers.² I saw Maj. Genrl. Hooker to-day. He is on his way to the front to take some command.³ It is reported Burnside's, but we hope that is not true.⁴

We are all enjoying good health. It has rained quite hard for two days. It is quite cool at present. I will write to Bro. Johnie to-night. He requested me to send him some of your letters which I will do. They will give him pleasure.

In my distribution of photographs, I did not have enough & could not send Mother one. I will get more as soon as I am able. I sent one to Maggie [Utley] which I had long ago promised. Enclosed find Capt. Reed's which he gave me this evening on promise that I would return the compliment. [Lt.] Smith claimed one for his wife which I promised, & Capt. Hoskins one in return for his. I sent one to Sarah Williams, & Christ Yetter took one, & another disappeared.

The Boys are all in good Spirits. Alf [Huetson] is singing the songs you sent, & waiting for this letter to go to the office with it. He wants to get the *Ledger*. You never mentioned the receipt of the "Nashville Union" I sent you. Did you receive it? We have no late news; everything from the front is contraband. Our Landlady had an opportunity to let the room I engaged to-day, & I told her to let it go.⁵ There are others to be had in the vicinity. When Frankie gets well, & you determine the time you will come I will make arrangements.

Give my love to all the family & Remember me to all our friends. Mrs. Smith is still quite poorly but talks of returning soon. If she gets able to travel, she will surely come. Kiss Frankie for me. May God grant him speedy health. I shall not forget to pray for you both. I have written in haste. Good night.

Your Affect. Husband

J. F. Culver

---

1   Mary Culver's letter of September 25 is missing from the Culver Collection.

2   The last of the trains with General Howard's XI Corps infantry having passed through Nashville on the 30th, those with foot-soldiers of Maj. Gen. Henry C. Slocum's XII Corps were now traveling through the city. *O. R.*, Ser. I, Vol. XXX, pt. IV, p. 49.

3   Maj. Gen. Joseph Hooker commanded the two corps from the Army of the Potomac en route to help drive the Confederates from the approaches to Chattanooga. Hooker left Nashville late on the 2d, and reached Stevenson early next morning. *Ibid.*

4   There was no truth to the rumor that General Hooker was to replace General Burnside as commander of the Department of the Ohio. Burnside was at Knoxville with most of his field army.

5   In anticipation of an early visit by his wife and son, J.F.C. had engaged a room for them near the camp of the 129th Illinois.

 92

Head Qrs. Co. "A" 129th Ills. Vol.
Nashville, Tenn., Octr. 5th 1863

My Dear Wife

Yours of the 27th Sept. came to hand this morning & relieved my mind of much anxiety about Frankie.[1] I hope he may soon recover. Consult Dr. Heermans about your bringing him down here. I believe it will prove to be very beneficial especially if his lungs remain weak for a long time. The climate here is very much milder than at the North; though for the latitude it is at present very cold & bids fair for a healthy season.

I do not believe I ever felt the cold more at this season of the year in the North. We keep a constant fire, & it requires considerable effort to keep comfortable. It will not remain so, I presume, but it will ward off the fever that infests this country during this month generally.

I am very happy to hear that you have received so much kind attention. You have not informed me whether you are at Mother's or Jennie's, yet I judge at the former place from your allusions to the clock.

I have been off duty to-day. The first Sunday I have had entirely to myself since we left Richland Station. Our duties have not been so heavy for the past week. After Inspection this morning, I started down street to look up a Sabbath School & found one in a Cumberland

Presbyterian Church.[2] I am not able to describe my feelings as I entered it, the first since I left home. The sight of the children recalled the most vivid recollections of the happy hours I spent in them at home. I looked eagerly around the room, & my heart yearned for some token of recognition, either from officers, teachers, or children, but found none. The hymn books were distributed to the school all around me. The Superintendent & teachers passed & repassed me, but not even a bow or smile. I scanned carefully the face of every child in the room but could not elicit a smile from a single one.

You cannot imagine my feelings when the truth flashed upon my mind that I was not wanted there & was an intruder. The same expression of scorn I have before witnessed was again expressed here, & I [my] heart was filled with pity for the miserable principles imbibed by the children from their teachers and parents.[3] I fear it will be many years before a Northern man will even be tolerated among them, &, unless the children learn to forget their present teachings, God alone knows the misery that awaits them.

Oh, how I longed for a short time in some Sabbath School at home that I might forget the grief & sorrow that filled my heart. We have preaching occasionally in Camp but have not had a prayer meeting for long months. I do not pretend to justify myself for not being more active in the performance of religious duties; but I long for you to come that we may commune together with God. That is a cheering thought embodied in the words you have quoted, "Though sundered far by *Faith* we meet; Around one common mercy-seat." We will sing it when you come.

Mrs. Fitch came last night & intends to spend the winter if we remain here.[4] I entertain no fear of a defeat at Chattanooga; some 30,000 reinforcements have arrived.[5]

I presume ere this you have recd. Bro. Johnie's letter. He drew a pair of Artillery boots for me, but they are at Chattanooga & I can see no way of getting them. I also sent to Bond [in Pontiac] for a pair over two months ago, but they have not come yet.

Which of the Miss Porters did Will Mullin marry? Is Jos. Mullin married yet? We were Chums together at College for over a year. I believe I am not acquainted with the Miss Parsons that Charlie Mullin married, unless it be a daughter of the old man who formerly kept the "Mansion House."[6] I wish Sister Jennie may be fully as successful as before. Remember me kindly to her & Harry.

I have sat many an hour with the little clock before me, trying to master some knotty problem in Trigonomotry or in the translation of Greek or Latin.[7] I love those relics of earlier life, & often wished when at home I had more of them around me. If you inquire of Mother, you can learn perhaps what has become of my old manuscripts. I left them in an old wooden chest in my room. You might find matters of interest perhaps among them; & also among my first Compositions. I wrote a long story once for print & put it in a secret drawer of the old chest under the till. I do not know what ever became of it; I often wished I had it. It was in part an autobiography of myself & contains many things I should like to read now.

Sergeant Howard of Co. "H" died on Friday night.[8] I did not learn his disease.

You will find enclosed 4 Photographs to put in your Album. I shall go on Picket duty in the morning. Unless the weather changes, it will be quite a cold job.

There is no prospect of our moving to the front or leaving this place. We are fixing up in anticipation of a winter's stay.

I wish you would write to Mother [Murphy] to send me the sealed package in the little drawer of which I wrote in a former letter.[9] I do not know where to direct her to find the key, or I would write to her.

Will you come directly here or by the way of Pontiac?[10] If you come by Pontiac, I have some things I wish you to do. I have thought you would be compelled to go there perhaps for your winter clothing. Let me know the amount of money Remick sends you upon my order. It will assist me to determine possibly how affairs stand there.

My health is very good. I hope Frankie will very soon be able to be around. May God bless you both abundantly.

Did you get the Album & pictures? Christ Yetter has promised me one soon, also Nathan Hill.[11]

Give my love to all the family, & Remember me kindly to all our friends. Hoping very soon to hear that you will be able to come, I remain as ever,

Your Affect. Husband

J. F. Culver

---

1 Mary Culver's letter of September 27 is missing from the Culver Collection.

2 The First Cumberland Presbyterian Church was on the west side of Summer Street, between Church and Broad.

3 See J.F.C.'s letter of September 7, 1863, for an account of the way he was received by a different congregation.

4 Mrs. Eliza Fitch of Fairbury was the 30-year-old wife of 1st Lieutenant Benjamin F. Fitch of Company E. She had previously visited her husband when the regiment was camped at Mitchellville in the winter of 1862-63.

5 General Hooker was at Stevenson. His XI Corps was at Bridgeport, while units of the XII Corps guarded the railroad between Stevenson and Wartrace against raids by Rebel

cavalry. General Sherman, with four divisions 17,000-strong from Grant's Army of the Tennessee, had reached Memphis from Vicksburg. As fast as the troops disembarked from steamboats, they were shuttled to Corinth, Miss., by rail. *O. R.,* Ser. I, Vol. XXX, pt. IV, pp. 49, 52, 90-91, 111.

6  In her letter of Sept. 27, Mary Culver discussed the marital affairs of the Mullin brothers. Sarah, Fannie, Martha, and Ida were the daughters of William and Martha Porter. The father was editor of one of the Carlisle newspapers. Sarah was 25 and Fannie 23. Charles H. (30), William A. (28), and Alfred F. (26) Mullin were residents of South Middleton Township. The two older men helped their father manage and operate the Union Paper Mill. Alfred "Fos" Mullin was a teacher. It has been impossible to identify further Miss Parsons. Eighth Census, Cumberland County, State of Pennsylvania. NA.

7  Mary Culver, in her letter of the 27th, must have referred to a clock at her mother-in-law's, of which J.F.C. had fond memories.

8  Newton Howard, a 27-year-old Winchester attorney, had been mustered into service on Sept. 8, 1862, as a sergeant in Company H, 129th Illinois. Sergeant Howard died in the regimental hospital at Nashville on Oct. 2, 1863 of typhoid fever. Compiled Service Records of Union Soldiers, NA.

9  The sealed package contained a will J.F.C. had drafted before his September 1862 departure from Pontiac. For additional information on the will see J.F.C.'s letter of September 19.

10  In her letter of the 27th, Mary Culver had written of plans to visit her husband at an early date.

11  Nathan W. Hill of Pontiac was a private in Company A.

 93

Head Qrs. Co. "A" 129th Ills. Vol. Infty.
Nashville, Tenn., Octr. 14th 1863

My Dear Wife

I felt very much disappointed in not hearing from you this morning, not having recd. any word from you yesterday. My mind has been ill at ease all day to-day, yet I earnestly look for a letter to-morrow morning.

I recd. a letter from Sister Maggie [Utley] this morning; her family and mother [Murphy] are quite well. Leander is in Bureau County but well when last heard from.

I requested Lt. Smith to ask his wife to send one of the Photographs to Mother. I cannot get more until after pay-day. I will try then & send a few home if you have not sufficient. [Lt. Col.] Cropsey says he will give his whenever I furnish him with one of mine. Christ Yetter has not had his taken yet.

I would give a great deal to know to-night how Frankie is and earnestly pray your letter to-morrow may bring good news.

It has been very wet to-day, raining most of the day. We recd. the news of the defeat of Valandigham in Ohio and Woodward in Pennsylvania to-night, & I hope it is all true.[1] I hope they are so completely beaten that their supporters may hide their faces for shame. The contest is raging in Livingston County, but I feel satisfied the Copperheads will be defeated.

How does Bratton feel now?[2] God will surely bring to judgment such foul traitors to their Country. It makes my blood boil to think of it: Has he ever been to Father since?

I have not heard from Bro. Johnie since I sent you his letter. Report says the Rail-Road will be completed to within 9 miles of Chattanooga this week, after which communication will be more frequent.[3]

Thursday, Octr. 15th 1863

Dear Wife

Unfortunately I have recd. no letter to-day. I have been working on some Ordnance reports, trying to keep my mind engaged but with little effect. I do feel sadly disappointed and very uneasy. I feel assured, however, that had anything serious happened you would have telegraphed to me, yet I cannot account for this long silence.

I very much fear that I shall be sent out on train guard to-night or in the morning, & thus two or three days more will elapse before I hear from you & Frankie. It is very probable, but I will hope for better things. I felt so certain that I should hear from you every day. I know you must be almost worn out with care & watching [over Frankie]. May God give you health and strength.

The papers you sent me were recd. yesterday, mailed the 8th. I think the letter sent with them must have miscarried. My health is good. It has quit raining but is still very muddy. I cannot compose myself to write much. Give my love to all. Kiss Frankie for me. I earnestly hope he may be better.

May God bless & Keep you both.

Your affect. Husband

J. F. Culver

---

1 Clement L. Vallandigham was a Democratic congressman from Ohio who opposed the

war. His strong and able opposition to all measures for national defense proposed in the House directed upon him the intense hatred of the Lincoln administration. After his defeat for reelection to Congress in 1862, he was regarded as leader of the Peace Democrats or "Copperheads" in Ohio. For defiance of General Burnside's GO No. 38, he was arrested in Dayton, Ohio, and tried in Cincinnati for treason. He was convicted and banished to the Confederacy. Running the blockade, he made his way to Canada, and from there ran for governor of Ohio. He was defeated in the October 13, 1863, general election by John Brough. Judge George W. Woodward was the Democratic candidate for governor in Pennsylvania. On October 13, the Pennsylvania voters reelected Republican Andrew G. Curtin governor by a majority of more than 60,000.

2   John B. Bratton was editor of a Democratic newspaper critical of the administration's conduct of the war.

3   Reports reaching the camp of the 129th Illinois that the railroad would be operating to within nine miles of Chattanooga by October 21 were overly optimistic. By that date the railroad was only as far as Bridgeport, 23 miles by rail from Chattanooga. *O. R.*, Ser. I, Vol. XXXI, pt. I, pp. 693-694.

 94

Head Qrs. Co. "A" 129th Regt. Ills. Vol. Infty.
Nashville, Tenn., October 16th/63

My Dear Wife

Yours of the 9th & 10th inst. reached me this morning.[1] The past two days have been almost insupportable. The last letter was recd. on Monday, dated the 8th, & this is Friday with no intelligence.[2] I could not imagine what had happened. I tried to keep myself busily employed all day yesterday, but failed to keep my mind from reaching out into the future. I feared that the care and anxiety attending Frankie's illness had brought disease upon you, & the improbability of my getting leave of Absence seemed unendurable. I feel better satisfied now, however, & earnestly hope and pray that Frankie's health may continue to improve and yours be preserved. God is still good and merciful to us. Let us praise him.

I wrote to Sarah Williams & Maggie [Utley] last night — but fear my tone was not very cheerful. I requested Sister Maggie to send me the package in my drawer & told her where to find the key. I will notify you when it is received.

How are you off for money? Did Remick send you any more?

I am happy to hear that Father's health is better & hope it will continue to improve.

It has been raining almost incessantly for several days past. I fear it will prove disastrous to our Army, as the roads are becoming impassible, and the Army is solely dependent upon wagon trains for Supplies.[3]

I have no news from Bro. Johnie since the last I sent you. My health continues to be good for which I have great reason to be thankful. Lt. Smith heard from his wife this morning. She has been very poorly again but is slowly recovering. The health of the Regiment is good. Lt. McKnight & his wife have returned [from Livingston County]. He was home on a leave of Absence from the Hospital for 20 days, & she went with him. His health is much improved, but he is still feeble.

I will send you a copy of the [Pontiac] Sentinel. Do you still receive it, or has father [Murphy] ordered it stopped?

The news from the elections in Ohio & Pennsylvania are favorable, but not so large as we hoped. Valandigham will be defeated by a large majority, & I hope Woodward also. How does Father [Culver] feel about affairs now?

Are all our friends strong in the faith? We must have more troops. What will Pennsylvania do?

I hope Frankie's health has so far improved that you will get rest. You will please accept my warmest thanks for writing so punctually every day. May God bless & keep you both. Write to me as often as you can. Give my love to all the family. Kiss Frankie for me.

Your Affect. Husband

J. F. Culver

P.S. I expect to leave on train guard for Stevenson this afternoon & shall not probably hear from you for a few days.

1 Mary Culver's letters of October 9 and 10 are missing from the Culver Collection.

2 Mary Culver's letter of October 8 is missing from the Culver Collection.

3   Confederate horse-soldiers led by Maj. Gen. Joseph Wheeler had forded the Tennessee on October 1 and, advancing up Sequatchie Valley, had captured and destroyed over 300 wagons. To add to the Federals' difficulties, torrential rains turned the 60-mile road from Bridgeport to Chattanooga by which the Army of the Cumberland was supplied into a ribbon of mud. Rations ran short. There was grave danger that Bragg's army would starve the Federals out of Chattanooga before relieving columns under Generals Hooker and Sherman could swing into action. Cist, *Army of the Cumberland,* p. 231.

～～ッ 95 ⚬⚬⚬

Head. Qrs. Co. "A" 129th Ills. Vol. Infty.<br>
Nashville, Tenn., Octr. 19th 1863

My Dear Wife

On my return from Stevenson last night, I found your letter of the 11th, one from Sister Lizzie [Zug], one from Bro. Wes [Culver] & Bro. Johnie [Murphy], & this morning recd. yours of the 12th.[1] I am very happy to learn that there is some hope of Frankie.

Bro. Wes gave me a history of his disease from which I conclude that it will take great care and attention to save him. A slight cold will prove fatal, & this is a season of the year in which colds are very easily contracted. I see but little prospect of his safe removal before Spring, &, though the trial for you will be severe and the sacrifice great, yet it will save our child. His lungs are very seriously affected and without the greatest care will remain defective for life.

I know, my dear wife, that your trials have been & will be severe; yet doubt not God has some wise purpose in view. I am very thankful for your kind sympathy in my behalf & always feel assured that whatever may befall me, one loving heart at least beats in harmony with my own. I looked forward with much pleasure to your Stay with me, yet to save Frankie I can forego that pleasure & trust to God for his blessings.

I should be happy to act upon Bro. Wes' suggestions & get a leave of Absence if it were among the possibilities. Perhaps by and by it will succeed, we will live in hope.

My health is very good. My trip to Stevenson was very pleasant. I had the passenger train & was only absent two days. I met Capt. West of Genl. Smith's staff,[2] who was in Carlisle at the time the Rebels were throwing shells into the town. He says that it was him who cut those fine shade trees down in front of Judge Hepbrun's, Martin's Hotel, and Judge Watts'.[3] They were cut down to barricade the street.

I heard of quite a number of my old acquaintances in the service in the Potomac Army. General Knipe was formerly a shoemaker in Harrisburg;[4] I knew him but not intimately. He commands a Brigade in the 11th Corps.

I hope Father's health may continue to improve. Bro. Wes does not speak very hopefully of his case. I will try and answer Sister Lizzie's letter to-day or at least very soon.

I sent several papers to Bro. Johnie by Captain West & will answer his letter the first opportunity. There is a gentleman going to the front on Wednesday with whom I think I can send the money. I do not like to risk it by mail, as they are very uncertain & irregular. I also sent Bro. Johnie your two letters of the 8th & 9th, which I happened to have in my pocket.

You ask what overcoat I sent for. It was my black one. I intended to get a cape & military buttons put on it & wear it, but I do not think I will go to the trouble now. My boots came in a box sent to Company "C" on Friday evening.

We all live together again & have ever since we came to Nashville. I boarded for several weeks, but we are now messing. It is the only way we can get our meals regularly & get rations to take with us when on duty. The hours for meals at a boarding house are regular & very often we could not go.

I will enclose Bro. Johnie's letter. The weather is very pleasant to-day but has been cold and very wet for a long time. The waters are high. The news from our front are cheering.[5] The papers anticipate a raid into Maryland again, but it looks very improbable.[6] I hope the Call for 300,000 will be promptly answered.[7]

I am grieved to learn of Sophie Emmet's sad fate.[8] She was a very *intimate* friend of mine long ago & was a very fine girl.

I informed you that I had written to Sister Maggie [Utley] for the package [containing the will] in my drawer. I requested [Lt.] Smith to ask his wife to give Mother [Murphy] one of my pictures, as she has two. The health is generally good. Sergt. Godfrey was sick for a short time but is almost well again.[9] Capt. Culver of the 105th Ills. was in to see me this morning and has promised me his photograph.[10] I will send it to you when I receive it. I do not recollect whether you met him or not in Gallatin. He was there on General Paine's Staff, but is now a Captain in the 105th Ills.

I must try and write to Wes to-day as he expects to leave so soon. Kiss Frankie for me. I earnestly hope he may speedily regain health and Strength. Should Father's health improve, as I hope it will, Mother & Sister Hannah will be able to assist you in caring for him. I presume you all anticipate accessions to Jennie's family. Sister Lizzie informs me that they all love you very much. I am truly happy, & I believe they will try to make your Stay pleasant.

Mother [Murphy] is very anxious to have you home, & I know she must be lonely, but the condition of society in Pontiac is such that I fear you would not enjoy yourself there. You can better judge of that, however, than I. The drum is beating for 12 o'clock roll call. I will have to hasten to write two letters before 2 o'clock drill. Give my love to all the family & remember me kindly to all our friends. Tell Charlie [Culver] to write, &, if he has any fears about the cost of a postage stamp, give him one.

May the blessings of Heaven rest upon you & Frankie. I feel that God will continue his goodness to us. Continue to write as often as convenient.

Farewell,

Your Affect. Husband

J. F. Culver

---

1   All the letters referred to are missing from the Culver Collection except the one from Sister Lizzie Zug.

2   Capt. P.C.F. West of the U.S. Coast Survey was on the staff of Brig. Gen. William F. "Baldy" Smith, the Army of the Cumberland's chief engineer. *O. R.*, Ser. I, Vol. XXXI, pt. I, p. 78.

3   Martin's Hotel was better known as the Farmer's Hotel. Judges F. Watts and Samuel Hepburn owned lots on opposite sides of East High Street, between Bedford and Hanover Streets.

4   Brig. Gen. Joseph F. Knipe commanded the 1st Brigade, First Division, XII Corps. Knipe's brigade until October 22, when it was ordered to Bridgeport, was stationed at Decherd. *O. R.*, Ser. I, Vol. XXXI, pt. I, p. 696.

5   On October 16 the Departments of the Ohio, the Cumberland, and the Tennessee were consolidated and constituted "The Military Division of the Mississippi," to which command Maj. Gen. Ulysses S. Grant was assigned. By the same order General Rosecrans was sacked and General Thomas named to lead the Army of the Cumberland.

General Hooker's two corps were still at Stevenson and guarding the railroad between Bridgeport and Wartrace. General Sherman with his four divisions had left Corinth, and by the 21st his advance guard had reached Tuscumbia, Ala., on its march east. Grant on taking command had ordered Thomas "to hold Chattanooga at all hazard," and Thomas had replied, "I will hold the town till we starve." *Ibid.*, p. 666; Cist, *Army of the Cumberland*, pp. 233-234.

6 General Lee on October 9 had crossed the Rapidan with two corps. His goal was to flank Meade's Army of the Potomac out of its position north of Culpepper. The Confederates were successful, but when they sought to intercept Meade's columns, as they retired up the Orange & Alexandria Railroad on the 14th, one of Lee's corps was mauled at Bristoe Station. Lee then abandoned his limited offensive and retired behind the Rappahannock. Douglas S. Freeman, *R. E. Lee,* 4 vols. (New York, 1935), Vol. III, pp. 171-185.

7 President Lincoln on Saturday, October 17, had issued a proclamation calling for 300,000 additional volunteers for the Union armies. Long, *Civil War, Day by Day,* p. 423.

8 It has been impossible to further identify Sophia Emmet.

9 William H. Godfrey, a 35-year-old carpenter, was mustered into service on Sept. 8, 1862, as a corporal in Company A, 129th Illinois, and was promoted 1st sergeant of his company on January 20, 1863. 1st Sergeant Godfrey was mustered out on June 8, 1865, near Washington, D.C. Compiled Service Records of Union Soldiers, NA.

10 Charles C. Culver of Sandwich, Illinois, had been mustered into service on September 2, 1862, as 2d lieutenant of Company H, 105th Illinois Infantry, and promoted to 1st lieutenant on December 30, 1862. He was promoted to captain and transferred to Company C, August 3, 1863. The 105th Illinois had been stationed at Gallatin from Feb. 1, 1863 to June 1, 1863, when it had been transferred to Lavergne. The regiment had been ordered to Nashville on Aug. 19, 1863. *Adjutant General's Report, State of Illinois,* Vol. V, pp. 670-679.

 96

Headqrs. Co. "A" 129th Ills. Vol. Infty.
Nashville, Tenn., Octr. 23rd 1863

My Dear Wife

Your letters of the 15th & 16th inst. came to hand this morning.[1] I must confess that I had a severe fit of the blues yesterday, but with the night they have disappeared. Though I cannot glean much hope for Frankie, yet it is a satisfaction to know even the worst.

I expected to be in Gallatin this morning, when I wrote yesterday, but was disappointed.[2] I shall probably go up to-morrow evening. I sent a petition to General Paine for the release of Lorin O. Cooley, & I wish to back it by entreaty if perchance it may succeed.[3] His wife is in a very destitute condition & has been sick for almost a year. We have furnished her money out of our Company fund, and she is not aware of his condition; & I think that his further punishment will result in no good either to himself or the service.

I can fully realize your trials, & very often wish I could be with you to assist and support you. We can only trust to the wisdom and mercy of an overruling Providence, and though his judgments seem severe, and your trials weigh heavily upon your mind, doubt not his goodness, which has always vouchedsafe so many blessings and protected us from so many evils. I have at times, I fear, given up too much to repining, but when I reflect upon the goodness of God so long interposed in my behalf and the many blessings I have received, I am led to forget all my light afflictions and trust still in the unbounded wisdom and mercy, of our Heavenly Father.

I still hope that sometime during this fall or winter I may succeed in getting leave of absence. Everything now implies that we will remain here this winter, &, if so after the fall campaign has closed, I hope to spend a short time with you. Yet should all my efforts fail, let us not repine for in less than two years my time of service will expire, and then we will go home again.

I informed Mother [Murphy], in one of my letters, of her mistake, & I doubt not she will be surprised, as she wrote so positively that she knew what was the matter. I have had quite a laugh at her expense & would enjoy an opportunity to tease her about her long experience in such matters very much.[4]

I recd. your letter to Bro. Johnie after I wrote to you. By some misfortune it had got into some of the other companies; I sent it forward immediately. You will find his address in full in his letter which I sent you a few days ago. You told him I sent you all important letters, but I have sent you every letter I received but one, & I mislaid that one some way & could not find it. I took the liberty to add a post-script to your letter.

You wish to know if the contention in Pontiac is only political. It was at first but has grown into personal hatred and enmity.[5] The people do not associate as formerly, and the sources of quarrel[ing] and wrangling are interminable. It shows a disposition of base cowardice or else unpardonable duplicity. They are either afraid to stand out boldly for the right or else pecuniary interests are allowed to embarrass them. Either is a despicable excuse, and the kind of spirit manifested will surely result in a total degeneration of the moral tone of society there. May God open their eyes and enlighten their minds to the dangers that lie before them.

I really fear that I did not sufficiently weigh the matter of your visit to Carlisle. It never occurred to my mind that you would ever meet with anything that could impress you unfavorably. But, My Dear Wife, let me assure you from a full knowledge of the persons, and all that could be brought into comparison, you have nothing to fear. Will Mullin I know well, far better than sister Lizzie [Zug] can. His wife, formerly Fanny Porter, was the most intimate friend of Mary P[ostlethwaite] & doubtless is fully acquainted with all that ever transpired, while Will's Bro., Jos. Mullin, was my room-mate for over a year, &, though not a confidante of mine, was doubtless well posted. I was often in company with all the Boys & knew their estimate of Mary P[ostlethwaite] which was never very flattering.

Even Will Mullin's wife, warmly as she was attached to her, attempted to convince me very many times that I was deceived.[6] Thus I feel assured that you have nothing to fear while you may justly feel proud of conscious superiority. I am not surprised that he [she] [Mary P.] should feel anxious to make your acquaintance for many reasons of which I do not deem myself justified in speaking. I might have told you, but the persons were all unknown to you, & I feared I should not be able to explain sufficiently to make it interesting. I hope to have an opportunity some time, however, & a knowledge of the persons will aid materially. It was all, however, only those little things in which boys & girls so often engage. Each trying to outdo the other in their attentions to the greatest number, or to have exclusive rights over the other. I had almost forgotten them in the cares of the past few years & the enjoyment of present happiness. I will be able to tell you in a few weeks.

Should you meet with Fanny Mullin, Will's wife, you will find her not only agreeable but of a very sweet disposition and one of the finest singers in the East. She was very beautiful as a girl of 16 & 18, but when I last saw her she had faded considerably. Remember me kindly to her & also her husband if you meet them.

Miss Laura Keene of New York is in the city & playing at the New Theatre.[7] I went to hear her night before last in the "Blind Heiress" or "Eleanor Mowbry." She has lost none of her old style & power. I heard her in the same play several years ago. I do not know that I ever felt the same power in her rendition of the play as on that night, and it brought to mind so many incidents of my own eventful life that I believe it proved very profitable.

It has been raining very hard all morning and is quite gloomy out of doors, yet I have felt happy. My health is good for which I have great reason to be thankful.

I have not been able to write as often of late from some cause, we have been almost constantly on duty. The war news are very cheering.

Burnside's demonstration in the rear of Lee's Army is drawing off troops from our front, & our Army is preparing to move.[8] We hope soon to hear of glorious victories.

Abbie Remick has never furnished the [promised] pictures yet. I shall remind both her & Lida of their promised New Year's present if I don't forget it. I have received no letters & have not written to either Sister Lizzie or Bro. Wes. yet.

Give my love to all the family & Remember me kindly to all our friends. Kiss Frankie for me. I accept the kiss sent. How much I wish I could be with him to assist in caring for him. Do not let his illness prey upon your own health. Long confinement to a sick Room will seriously effect your health without great care and abundant exercise in the open air. If you can only be contented and happy, I shall not regret your long visit at Father's.

How is Mother's health, & Why does not Sister Hannah write? She has not written one word since you went there. I must write to her & find out why it is.

And now, my Dear Wife, do not let our sore trials weigh so heavily upon your mind. God intends this chastening for our good. Let us not doubt his goodness or mercy but trusting implicitly in his wisdom resign all to his Will. Let my love for you console you in all that worldly things afford, and for all else let us trust to Jesus. May He bless & Keep you, preserve us for the enjoyment of each other's society in life, and finally give us Sweet rest in Heaven.

Your Affect. Husband

J. F. Culver

---

1    Mary Culver's letters of October 15 and 16 are missing from the Culver Collection.

2    J.F.C.'s letter of October 22 is missing from the Culver Collection.

3    Lorin O. Cooley, a 25-year-old farmer, was mustered into service on Sept. 8, 1862, as a private in Company A, 129th Illinois. Private Cooley was placed under arrest for getting "beastly drunk" and deserting his post to watch a cock fight, and was confined to the guardhouse at Gallatin, Tenn., June 29, 1863. Court martialed, he was sentenced on July 20 to stoppage of pay and to be confined at hard labor for six months in the Nashville penitentiary. His sentence was commuted Oct. 23, 1863, by order of General Paine, and he rejoined his unit. Private Cooley was mustered out near Washington, D.C., June 8, 1865. Compiled Service Records of Union Soldiers, NA.

4    Mrs. Murphy had mistakenly suspected that her daughter was pregnant, and J.F.C.'s comment about "her long experience" refers to her having given birth to three sons and two daughters.

5    With an election at hand, the Livingston County Republicans and Democrats were at each others' throats. The question of the administration's conduct of the war and emancipation of the blacks had inflamed passions.

6  Although Mary Culver's letter in which she broached that subject is missing, it is apparent that J.F.C. courted Mary Postlethwaite while a student at Dickinson College.

7  Laura Keene, a British actress trained in Mme. Vestris' Company, came to the United States in 1852 as a member of James W. Wallack's New York Company. She enjoyed brilliant success as a comedy star. She starred in "Our American Cousin" at Ford's Theater on the night President Lincoln was assassinated. Miss Keene was appearing at the New Theatre, at the corner of Union and Summer Streets.

8  The report that General Bragg had detached troops from his army investing Chattanooga to send against Burnside's command at Knoxville was premature. Twelve days later, on November 4, Bragg sent General Longstreet with two divisions to operate against Burnside in East Tennessee. This was a blunder on the Confederates' part which Grant exploited. Long, *Civil War, Day by Day*, p. 430.

 97

Head Qrs. Co. "A" 129th Ills. Vol. Infty.
Nashville, Tenn., Octr. 28th 1863

My Dear Wife

I have just been ordered to Stevenson again though scarcely rested from my last trip. I intended to write a long letter to-day but must wait until my return. I am very well & earnestly hope on my return to hear good news from you. May God bless you both. Yours of the 21st reached me yesterday evening.[1]

I shall probably be back in 3 or 4 days but may be gone a week or more, as there is no regularity in the trains. Give my love to all. Committing you to the protecting care of our Father in Heaven, I must say,

Farewell.

Your Affect. Husband

J. F. Culver

_____

1  Mary Culver's letter of October 21 is missing from the Culver Collection.

Headqrs. Co. "A" 129th Ills. Vol. Infty.
Nashville, Tenn., Octr. 28th 1863

My Dear Wife

I wrote a hasty note to you this morning before I left, expecting to be absent several days, but fortune favored me for once, & I went to Columbia, instead of Stevenson, & consequently got home to-night.[1] I have desired ever since the receipt of yours of the 19th inst. to write you a long letter[2] but have signally failed. I shall possibly accomplish it to-night if sitting up late will do it. As I am on detail for the first extra train sent out, I may have to go in the morning; no one can tell, but to-night is my own if nothing happens. I will try at least to interest you, and if I can be instrumental in relieving your care or in anyway alleviating your trials, I will be happy indeed.

You told me in your letters of the 20th that you "live on my letters," & I feel sorry that what few you have received since that time are short & unimportant. Your last received yesterday evening looks more hopeful than any late news, & I pray God that Frankie's health may improve and your cares grow lighter. We cannot tell what the future may develop to us of joy or sorrow; yet the opportunity is offered for the strengthening of our Faith in Jesus, and the enlargement of our hopes. Two years ago we did not anticipate this sorrow. Then all looked prosperous, but are we less happy now? Had God in the dispensation of his Providence so ordered our affairs that I were yet at home, who can tell but that some greater trial would have come to us. My heart responds to the sentiment expressed in your letter that in view of all the manifestations of God's mercy & his goodness ever exercised toward me, with his promises and assurances for the future, I feel that I should not repine or murmer though the hand of affliction be laid heavily upon me. It would be well for me perhaps, if I were with you, not only to relieve you of a portion of your care but to profit by the chastisement God has doubtless wisely intended for our good.

My duties have been so unremitting and severe as to allow but little time for reflection. I feel very much worn down, both in mind and body, yet enjoy excellent health. The guarding of the trains was a light job at first. We made a trip in 3 days & both nights were spent within the lines of our troops where we could lay down and sleep. But of late our engines have become so much out of repair as to require from 4 to 8 days & running almost every night, which keeps us on constant watch.

Our trip to-day was very pleasant. The country through which the [rail]road passes is not thickly settled, but is very beautiful. Franklin is on the rout[e], which I described in a former letter.[3] My guards were all of our own Company [A], which makes it very pleasant. Cooley was among the number, and it is the first duty he has done [since his release from the guard house]. He seems to be very happy.

I hear some trains coming in [from Stevenson], & I presume some of the boys will soon be in. Lt. McMurray has been out since last Tuesday, over a week, & Lt. Fitch has been gone a full week.[4] His wife is very uneasy about him. She has been ordered to vacate the room they had rented & did not know where to go till his return. I think she is stopping with Mrs. Love.

I have no late news from Johnie, none since the last I sent you. I have not had time to answer the [Remick] girls' letters yet, but will enclose some of them, as I cannot tell when I shall have opportunity to answer them. If I am so fortunate as to remain in camp to-morrow, I will try & write some. I recd. a letter this morning from Cousin Lucy J. Baker (formerly Dunmire).[5] She is married to a gentleman who formerly went to school to me. He is a fine man & will make her a good husband though he was a widower & must have had quite a large family. She does not speak of having any family, however.

Quite a number of my scholars have gone to war, & many have died. Oh, what a record the closing of this war will present: of homes made desolate, families broken up, & of widows & orphans. All our relatives there are well. I will send you the letter as soon as answered.

I have not yet had time to write to Mother or Maggie. Lt. Smith says his wife is exceedingly anxious to see you. She regrets that she did not see things in their true light long ago & desires to make some reparation for her former conduct. I hope it may be lasting. Smith seems determined to keep up a constant broil in the company ever since his return [from furlough]. I am tried at times almost beyond measure, while I see no present remedy. He seems to forget everything that belongs to others' happiness in his grasping ambition for promotion, & places himself only in a more disgusting position.

I have just recd. orders to report at the North R. R. Bridge to take charge of a forage train at 5 o'clock, A.M., which will be quite an early start. I cannot tell when I shall get home but possibly to-morrow night. I have not yet heard where the guard comes from.

We have no news from the front. Genl. Hooker has crossed the [Tennessee] river with his Army.[6] We may possibly hear of him soon.

Give my love to all the family. I hope father's health may continue to improve. When will Mother or Hannah write?

Let us, my Dear Wife, repose full confidence in the wisdom and mercy of our Heavenly Father. Though he chastise us, we will still love him. Though our trials be severe, yet we are hastening to our eternal home in Heaven. May God bless & keep you and continue his manifold blessings to us. Accept the sincere love

Your Affect. Husband

J. F. Culver

I shall devote a portion of the 3rd of next month to writing to you if I am in camp. By reference to the family record you can tell why.[7] I have forgotten upon what day I may commemorate a like event for you. Please inform me in your next. I am looking anxiously for news from you.

Farewell,

J.F.C.

---

1   The Central Alabama Railroad was operating south from Nashville to Columbia, and the 13th Wisconsin and 14th Michigan were posted at Franklin and Columbia. Magazines were being stockpiled by the Quartermaster Department should it be determined to reopen the railroad between Columbia and the Tennessee River, as a means of supplying General Sherman's columns as they marched east from Cherokee and Eastport. Detachments from the 129th Illinois were required to guard the trains operating between Nashville and Columbia, as they were those running between Nashville and Stevenson. *O. R.*, Ser. I, Vol. XXXI, pt. I, pp. 685, 755, 765.

2   Mary Culver's letter of October 19 is missing from the Culver Collection.

3   J.F.C.'s letter describing Franklin is missing from the Culver Collection.

On October 4, with Confederate cavalry striking toward the Nashville & Chattanooga Railroad, Colonel Case had been directed to hold the regiment ready to march at a moment's notice: the men to carry three days' rations in their haversacks and 100 rounds of ammunition. Three days later, with Wheeler's column advancing west from Shelbyville, General Robert Granger ordered Colonel Case to march his regiment to the Chattanooga Depot and entrain his troops. One battalion was to take position at Franklin and the other would report to Col. Henry R. Mizner at Columbia.

The train with the 129th aboard pulled out of the yards at 10 P.M., on the 7th and started south. One battalion detrained at Franklin about midnight and the second battalion, which included Company A, was run down to within eight miles of Columbia. There J.F.C. and his comrades got off the cars and marched to Columbia. When they arrived, they found the garrison preparing to resist an attack by Wheeler's cavalry. The Rebels failed to appear, and the battalion on the 9th marched back to Franklin. On the 10th the entire regiment entrained and returned to Nashville. Grunert, *History of the 129th Illinois,* p. 37; *Through the South with a Union Soldier,* p. 86; Ward to Case, October 4, and Speed to Case, October 7, 1863, Regimental Papers, 129th Illinois, NA.

4   Albert A. McMurray, a 36-year-old farmer, was mustered into service on Sept. 8, 1862, as a sergeant in Company C, 129th Illinois Infantry. Sergeant McMurray was commissioned 2d lieutenant of his company on March 25, 1863, at South Tunnel, Tennessee, and on May 25, 1865, he was promoted to captain. McMurray was wounded in the head at Lost Mountain, Ga., on June 15, 1864, and in the right leg at Peachtree Creek, Ga., July 20, 1864. Compiled Service Records of Union Soldiers, NA.

5   The subject letter is missing from the Culver Collection.

6   General Hooker had crossed the Tennessee River by the pontoon bridge at Bridgeport, on the morning of October 26, with most of the XI Corps and part of the XII Corps, and, pushing rapidly forward, occupied Lookout Valley. Meanwhile, General "Baldy" Smith had organized a force from the Army of the Cumberland. Fifteen-hundred soldiers were embarked at Chattanooga in small boats at 3 A.M. on the 27th, and dropped down the Tennessee nine miles to Brown's Ferry. A second column, camped north of the river opposite Chattanooga, had marched across Moccasin Bend. The small boat party took the Confederates by surprise. A successful landing was made, reinforcements ferried across the Tennessee, a Confederate attack repulsed, and the Brown's Ferry bridgehead secured. By 4 P.M. a pontoon bridge was in position and Smith's troops confidently awaited the arrival of Hooker's columns from Lookout Valley. Cist, *Army of the Cumberland,* pp. 238-241; *O. R.,* Ser. I, Vol. XXXI, pt. I, pp. 77-78, 92-93.

7   J.F.C.'s birthday.

 99

Headqrs. Co. "A", 129th Regt. Ills. Vol. Infty.
Nashville, Tenn., Octr. 29th 1863

My Dear Wife

Through good luck or by mistake, I am in camp this morning. I reported myself at 5 o'clock this morning in accordance with my orders, but no one came near me; so, after spending a couple of hours sitting upon a stump, I returned to camp to await another detail which I will not be surprised to see any minute.

While awaiting orders this morning, I stepped to the tent of Capt. Wilson, 79th Ohio, which is encamped at the north side of the R. R.

Bridge.[1] And, as it was some time after Reveille, I walked thoughtlessly in & saw a sight that reminded me of old times. His wife was with him, both in bed, sound asleep, his arms around her & her head pillowed on his bosom. I was almost selfish enough to envy them & turned around hastily and left the tent.

Both your letters of the 21st & 23rd with Charlie's arrived this morning.[2] Dr. Johnson tells me that those "Critical Eruptions" are very favorable omens, & that Frankie, unless he takes a relapse, is beyond danger; that, after the matter is all drawn out of his system, he will speedily recover. This is the best news I have had for a long time. I earnestly hope that you may ere this be relieved of the burden of your care & have opportunity to recruit your own health.

Charlie wishes me to understand that he has no friendly feeling towards "old Abe & his dear nigger." I will write to him when I get opportunity & try and correct his opinions. I fear, if the sentiments expressed in his letter and Sister Lizzie's are general among our relatives there, it may prove unpleasant for a Soldier's wife.[3] Yet as you never made any mention of expressed opinions there, I felt Satisfied that all was right. I felt somewhat alarmed on reading Charlie's letter & wish to know now how my relatives stand. The task for you would be unpleasant and very unprofitable, so I will not ask it of you, but I formerly had correspondents in Carlisle which I know to be loyal, & I shall find out through them. If my Surmises are correct and any of them from enmity to the administration stand aloof from the interests of the Government, I want to know it, & woe be to them if I have the power to make them feel their willful error.

Smith got a photograph this morning, about the size of mine at home, for his wife & paid $7 for it. It is not good in my opinion.

The weather to-day is beautiful and pleasant. All the train guards but one that have been out over a week have returned last night. Mrs. Fitch is happy again.

The election in Livingston County is for County Treasurer, School Commr., and Surveyor. The Union candidates are Collins for Treas., Pearre for Commr., & Buck for Surveyor. The Copperheads are Maxwell for Treas. & the others I forget, & nobody seems to know which is no matter.[4]

The Army of the Cumberland, though devotedly attached to Rosecrans, feel that at least in the emergency at Chickamauga he was not adequate, & they will readily yield to another, hoping that in the coming Campaign, which is on an immense scale, Grant may be more successful. No one will ever replace Rosecrans in our affections, and, in all his associations with the Army up to Chattanooga, he will ever receive the highest commendations of praise. I cannot give you any extended history of affairs. At some other time I can say more.

I will send you the "Sentinel." I sent one over a week ago. When you write to Remick, tell him to get Collins to continue the paper to your address. It has been paid for, & you may as well get it as not.

I gave you an account of the accident on the Rail Road in a former letter.[5] I put the letter I wrote last night on the train this morning. I hope you will not yield to blues or homesickness. Happiness is very essential to health. I must close for drill. Give my love to all the family, and accept my heart's best love for yourself. Kiss Frankie for me. May God bless you.

Your Affect. Husband
J. F. Culver

Tell me how Sister Lizzie likes her letter.[6]

---

1 Capt. William Wilson had been mustered into service at Camp Dennison, Ohio, on Aug. 23, 1862, as captain of Company A, 79th Ohio. The regiment had been stationed at Gallatin, Buck Lodge, Lavergne, and Edgefield before being ordered to Nashville. The 79th Ohio was one of the five infantry and two cavalry regiments currently assigned to the Nashville garrison. *O. R.*, Ser. I, Vol. XXXI, pt. I, p. 754; Reid, *Ohio in the War*, Vol. II, p. 455.

2 Mary Culver's letters of October 22 and 23, as well as Charlie's, are missing from the Culver Collection.

3 Sister Lizzie Zug had written, "We all love your wife very much, but I must tell you if you have changed your polaticks and gone with the Woolly heads as I have heard, I am affraid I will have to quarll with you." At a recent Republican rally, a "man made a speech and said the war would not be over until we would all be made equil. Is this what you are fiting for? This very idea is disgusting?" Lizzie Zug to J.F.C., undated, Culver Collection.

4 Marcellus E. Collins was a Pontiac lawyer; Nelson Buck, a 55-year-old, New York-born, Livingston County surveyor; Robert Maxwell, a 54-year-old, Virginia-born Livingston County farmer; and O. F. Pearre an Ohio-born attorney. When the voters went to the polls on Nov. 3, 1863, they elected the Republican candidates. *History of Livingston County*, p. 267.

5 J.F.C.'s letter describing the train wreck is missing from the Culver Collection.

6 J.F.C. had answered Sister Lizzie Zug's letter, in which she had voiced her "disloyal sentiments," on October 23.

 100

Headqrs. Co., "A" 129th Regt. Ills. Vol. Infty.
Nashville, Tenn., Octr. 31st 1863

My Dear Wife

I was somewhat disappointed this morning in not receiving a letter from you, though the last came through in so short a time that unless the others were equally fortunate, they could not reach me within two or three days.

We had a bad night on picket last night & have just got fairly dried out. It rained almost incessantly and was very cold. I was for once rather fortunate last night, and had the use of a lounge & fire, where I rested very comfortably. We intend to make shelters on each of the picket posts, so that it will at least protect us from the wet during the few hours we are off duty.

It is clear and cold to-day. We have just been notified to appear for Brigade Drill at 12 o clock which, in addition to the amt. of duty we perform, is beyond all reason. We get no rest at all. A heavy guard was detailed this morning to guard Boats to Carthage.[1] I presume it will be a pleasant trip; we shall learn when the guard returns. If, in addition to the duties on hand, we have to guard them [the boats], we need not expect to spend any time in camp this winter.

I have written no letters since my last to you nor received any. I anticipate more hopeful news from you next time.

We were mustered for pay this fore noon & expect to be paid off in a few days, yet cannot tell. [Lt.] Smith is off on train guard. Christ Yetter recd. a letter from Miss Hill this morning. All are well. I feel very tired & will lay down until drill which will be in an hour. May God abundantly bless you & speedily restore Frankie & Father to health. Kiss Frankie for me & give my love to all the family. Farewell.

Your Affect. Husband

J. F. Culver

---

1 By the end of the third week of October, Burnside's Army of the Ohio found itself running short of clothing and certain other quartermaster stores. Great difficulty was encountered in supplying the army by wagon trains from the depots at Camp Nelson, 160 miles to the northwest in Kentucky. A road was accordingly opened from the railhead at Clinton to the mouth of Big South Fork of the Cumberland. During high water steamboats could ascend the Cumberland to that point. With the Cumberland on a rise because of heavy autumn rains, the Quartermaster Department was employing steamboats to stockpile supplies at Carthage, preparatory to forwarding them to the mouth of Big South Fork. *O. R.*, Ser. I, Vol. XXXI, pt. I, pp. 680, 756.

Headqrs. Co. "A" 129th Ills. Vol. Infty.
Nashville, Tenn., Octr. 31st 1863

My Dear Wife

I recd. your despatch this evening informing me of Frankie's death.[1] Let us cheerfully Submit to the will of him who doeth all things well. I telegraphed in reply to bury him in a zinc lined coffin, so that if we should ever wish to remove him, it could easily be done.[2] If my despatch arrives too late, do not be worried about it.

I send you a pass from Louisville here to the United States Hotel. It is good for 20 days from this date. I thought you might wish to come immediately. If not and you come within the 20 days, it will still be good.

You will be short of money unless Remick has sent more. If so, tell Father or Mother to give you $50 or more if necessary, & I will forward it as soon as we are paid off, which I think, will be very soon. It is past due, & the paymaster has promised to pay in a few days. If he should fail, I will still send it shortly after your arrival if necessary.

I will write to Mother [Murphy] that in the event you wish to come direct here to express what things you need, waiting for you to name the articles.

I must go on duty in the morning again & will be absent a couple of days. I have made arrangements for you should you arrive during my absence at Mrs. Wilkinson's.[3] It is the next to the last house on the right hand side, on the South end, of Summer Street & easily found. Take a hack at the Depot. Telegraph to me from Louisville what train you come on.

Should you wish to go to Pontiac first, you will have time to hear from me again. Though God's ways are mysterious, yet he has given us so many evidences of his love and mercy that we should not murmur. Give my love to all. I should like to get your letter which I think will come in the morning, but must wait until my return. May God abundantly bless you.

Your Affect. Husband

J. F. Culver

---

1 Mary Culver's telegram read, "Frank C. died last night, eleven o'clock. Bury here on Sunday [November 1]." Mary Culver to J.F.C., October 31, 1863, Culver Collection.

2  The telegram sent by J.F.C. to his wife on October 31 is missing from the Culver Collection.

3  Mrs. Wilkinson's house was within a few feet of regimental headquarters. Mrs. Culver was to take her meals with the officers until J.F.C. could make other arrangements.

 102

Headqrs. Co. "A" 129th Ills. Vol. Infty.
Nashville, Tenn., Octr. 31st 1863

My Dear Wife

Enclosed find your pass from Louisville to Nashville. Telegraph from Louisville to me telling upon what train you will come. Should you arrive here in my absence, which is very probable, take a carriage at the Depot and go to the next to the last house on the right hand side of the South End of Summer Street (Mrs. Wilkinson's). It is within a few feet of the Col's. Headqrs. If either of our Co. officers are in camp, I will request them to meet you in my absence. You will board at our Headqrs. till I can make other arrangements.

Let us put our trust in God and submit cheerfully to his wise decrees. May he bless you.

Your Affect. Husband

J. F. Culver

P.S.  By mistake the pass is for Mrs. Capt. Culver instead of Lieut. The Provost Marshall said it would pass thus.

J.F.C.

## 103

Head Qrs. 1st Brig., 1st Div., 11th A.C.[1]
Nashville, Tenn., Jany. 30th 1864

My Dear Wife

I imagine to-night you are at the wharf in Cairo. I hope well and enjoying yourself.[2] I wish I had requested you to telegraph from Cairo, for I feel considerable anxiety to learn whether you have arrived safe. Yet trusting in God's protecting care and the fair prospect of your safe and pleasant trip, I do not intend to borrow trouble, though it seems to me, and in all probability will be, a long time before I hear from you.

I have been very busy ever since you left, so much so that I spent but a few moments at the house yesterday evening removing the things. Mrs. Drake sent me word about noon by Green that she wanted the room cleaned immediately.[3] I sent her word back that I would give "it up when I was ready and no sooner." She got angry at Green for locking the door and said, "We'll not steal the things." So when I went down, I was not in the humor to bandy words very long. I gave her the cook stove & pipe and called the account square. I found a sheet that she said did not belong to her, so I sent it to Mrs. [John W.] Smith & told her if it was not hers to take it home with her for you.

I paid Mrs. [Erastus] Nelson the $25 borrowed, & loaned Capt. Hoskins $25 and [Lt.] Smith $30—as Hoskins expects to go home soon after we leave, he will pay you. I loaned all the money I could spare, thinking you would find sufficient in Remick's hands to meet your present needs. I had to buy a saddle & bridle as [Chaplain ] Cotton's did not come. I got a very handsome bridle & saddle for $34—much finer than Dr. Johnson's was when new, & he asked $30 for his old one.

Mrs. Harrison starts for Home on Monday morning.[4] Our present orders are to commence the march at 7 A.M. on Monday morning [the 1st].[5] It is doubtful, however, whether we get off before Tuesday. We are all packed up here & ready. The Regiments turned over their tents to-day, and to-night the Boys are trying the virtue of "dog tents" (shelter). I wished very much to see how they looked but could not get time to go up to camp.

I received a letter from Bro. Johnie this morning, also one from Bro. Sammy,[6] the former I have enclosed. I hope I shall get to see Sammy, as he passes through here, as he will have to stop all night & till 4 P.M.

the next day.[7] I am very sorry I cannot deliver the kiss Bro. Johnie sends. It would give me great pleasure.

I feel more lonely to-night than I have since you left. I am all alone just now. Col. [Harrison] has just gone to bed, and all the rest are in the City.[8] I feel glad you had so good an opportunity to get home, however, and had you remained, you would have had but little pleasure for I have been so constantly employed in the office here that you would have seen but little of me. I expect the box of butter tomorrow. Sammy writes that it was forwarded on the 22nd.

Nate Hill [of Company A] got home yesterday evening. He was very sorry you were gone; I told him you sent much love & he was very much pleased. I saw Christ Yetter [of Company A] this morning, but he was very busy packing up so that I did not get a chance to speak to him.

It rained very hard last night and this morning, and the weather is still cloudy but much colder. Old Uncle Sam (who lives at Drake's) was here this evening. He said he expected his two sons in Town (runaways, I presume) & wanted them to go with me. I got them positions as Brigade teamsters & will do what I can for Them.[9] My horse is much better & will be able to stand the march, so I will keep him. I forgot to get "Green" the book I promised him to-day & will probably not have another chance. If so, I will get you to send one by mail.

I recd. no letters but the two referred to since you left. Old Nancy [a black servant] seemed anxious to talk to me yesterday evening, but Mrs. Drake kept close to her all the time I was there, so she had no opportunity. Little Mary Harrison presented to me a very nice little needle case & pin cushion yesterday.[10]

I could not think of much to have you say for me at home; I am somewhat unfortunate in that respect. When I wish to send most, I am at a loss out of the multitude of my thoughts what to say & invariably end by saying nothing. But I will trust to you to act as spokesman, for I feel that you are acquainted with my thoughts and feelings towards my friends. (The clock strikes ten). R. D. Folks is much better.[11] I will try and get out to see him tomorrow. Give my love to all the family. Kiss Mother [Murphy] & Maggie [Utley] and the babies for me.

I bought a pair of Dr.'s Pill bags to-day, &, by cutting out the fixings inside, I have an excellent place to carry some paper and ink & rations. I intend to write on the march, and mail a letter whenever I have opportunities. Don't forget to write to Mother Culver as soon as you have an opportunity. I wrote a short note before the mail closed requesting her to forward all your things. That if she was compelled to prepay the expressage to notify you of the amount so you could forward it to her.

I got those pants washed to-day that I spilled the oysters on & had gold lace sewed on them; they look as well as new ones. I cannot find my [books on] tactics & think they must be in your trunk. Take care of them; I can easily get another set out of this office. Did you take my slippers? I could not find them.

I spent for all the articles I purchased $48.90. I paid old debts amtg. to $72. I loaned $57, and for rations for the march and mess chest—my share about $10, leaving me about $25 dollars on hand which will I think be amply sufficient. I think my expenses at the front will be much lighter; I hope so at least.

I will look very anxiously for your letters and especially the first one. Remember me in much love to the Sabbath School, do not let the children forget me. Tell me how they are getting along. I pray most earnestly that God's blessings may rest upon you. Try and be happy, & you will enjoy much better health than if you keep brooding over your trials and privations. Keep me posted in regard to your *condition* as it progresses.[12]

Write to me when you feel inclined to the "Blues."

We have no late war news, except the report that a reconnisance made a few days ago before Chattanooga developed the fact that all the Rebs had left.[13] It may portend some hand fighting at Knoxville.[14] Large bodies of troops are moving to the front daily. But it is eleven o'clock, & I must close. I wish to write a few lines to Bro. Johnie to-night & also to Lt. Donaldson.

May Holy Angels guard you.     Farewell,

Your Affect. Husband

J. F. Culver

---

1   By Special Order No. 4, 1st Brigade, First Division, XI Army Corps, January 11, 1864, J.F.C. had been detached from the regiment and assigned as an aide-de-camp to the brigade commander. The First Division, XI Corps, commanded by Brig. Gen. W. T. Ward, was organized in early January 1864. Five infantry regiments (the 70th Indiana, the 78th Ohio, and the 102d, 105th, and 129th Illinois), constituted the division's 1st Brigade. Compiled Service Records of Union Soldiers, NA; *O.R,* Ser. I, Vol. XXXII, pt. II, p. 11.

2   Mary Culver had taken a steamboat from Nashville to Cairo, where she would board the Illinois Central Railroad.

3   Albert Green, a freedman, had been employed by J.F.C. as a "servant" during the autumn of 1863. He remained with J.F.C. throughout the war, and then accompanied him home to Pontiac. Green lived with the Culvers until he married.

The Culvers had rented a room from Mrs. Drake during Mrs. Culver's three-month visit.

4   Mrs. Caroline (Scott) Harrison was the wife of the brigade commander, Col. Benjamin Harrison. Twenty-four years later she would enter the White House as First Lady.

5 General Hooker on January 24 issued orders for General Ward's division, currently guarding the railroad between Nashville and Christiana, to advance and relieve the division led by Brig. Gen. David M. Stanley, then protecting the railroad from Whitesides to Bridgeport. Stanley's troops were to be redeployed on the line of the East Tennessee & Georgia Railroad, between the Chickamauga and Charleston. *O.R.*, Ser. I, Vol. XXXII, pt. II, pp. 196-197.

6 The subject letters are missing from the Culver Collection.

7 Samuel A. Murphy had enlisted in Company M, 1st Illinois Artillery, and was en route from Pontiac to the Camp Yates, Ill., reception center. Although J.F.C. could not know it, several months were to pass before Sammy was sent South to join his unit. *Adjutant General's Report, State of Illinois*, Vol. VIII, p. 656.

8 Benjamin Harrison was a grandson of William Henry Harrison, 9th President of the United States, and destined, himself, to be elected to the Presidency in 1888. Born in August 1833, on his grandfather's estate at North Bend, Ohio, Ben Harrison was graduated from Ohio's Miami University with distinction in 1852, and the following year married Caroline Scott. Harrison moved to Indianapolis in 1854, where he practiced law, and in 1857 was elected city attorney as a Republican. At Governor Oliver P. Morton's request in 1862, he recruited the 70th Indiana Infantry and became its colonel. On January 9,1864, Harrison assumed command of the 1st Brigade, General Ward having been named to lead the newly constituted First Division. Grunert, *History of the 129th Illinois*, p. 42.

9 It has been impossible to further identify "Old Uncle Sam" or his two sons beyond their being freedmen.

10 Mary was the little daughter of Benjamin and Caroline Harrison.

11 R. D. Folks, a 24-year-old carpenter, was mustered into service on Sept. 8, 1862, as 1st sergeant of Company G, 129th Illinois. He was mustered out near Washington, D.C., on June 8, 1865. Compiled Service Records of Union Soldiers, NA.

12 Mary Culver had become pregnant during her visit, and J.F.C. wished to be kept posted as to her condition.

13 A 450-man patrol led by Col. William P. Boone had left Rossville, Georgia, on the 21st, and, traveling by way of McLemore's Cove, had crossed Lookout Mountain and Taylor's Ridge, to attack and destroy a camp occupied by Georgia militia. A flag of truce party had left Chattanooga on the 22d, and by the 24th reached a point ten miles south of La Fayette, without encountering any Confederates. *O.R.*, Ser. I, Vol. XXXII, pt. II, p. 233.

14 The Confederate Army of Tennessee now commanded by Gen. Joseph E. Johnston was camped in and around Dalton, Georgia, on the Western & Atlantic Railroad, 30 miles southeast of Chattanooga. Lt. Gen. James Longstreet with his corps was headquartered at Morristown, Tennessee, 40 miles northeast of Knoxville.

 104

Head Qrs. 1st Brig., 1st Div. 11th A.C.
Nashville February 1st 1864

My Dear Wife

We are still here, all packed and ready to march. Mrs. Harrison &

Mrs. Merrell went home this morning.[1] A large portion of our train is out on the Murfreesboro Pike. We have had several orders to start and as many to wait. We are now held in readiness to move at an hour's notice.[2] We are all tired waiting. I had to unpack part of the boxes to get at some blanks. The boys commenced rebuilding their walls to cover with their "Dog Tents."[3] We will not probably move until Wednesday morning [the 3d].

I received a letter from J. B. McClean to-day, stating that he has not sold any of the Company records.[4] [At] the next festival for the soldiers, hand in about ten of them, perhaps they may do a little good in that way. I rec'd. a letter from Jennie [Cheston] to-day which you will find enclosed. I am sorry she writes so about Mother & cannot understand it.[5]

We have a constant rush of business on hand. I wrote an entire ream of letter paper yesterday & almost a half one to-day. The orders are not long but a great many of them. I have some reports to make to-night yet.

Capt. Hoskins is better and has gone to a boarding house. I have not seen any of the women since I last wrote. I have not heard whether any have gone home or not. R. D. Folks is better; he was removed to the hospital.

We recd. the "Sentinel" yesterday & the "Ledger" last night. The Scorpions with Aaron have been despersed, and the papers of this evening announce that Lt. Farragut (now Commodore) has taken Mobile, Alabama.[6] I hope it is true.

I must close & get at my reports. I will try and drop a line before we start. If I am to do all that is laid out for me on the march, I fear I will be able to write but little. I feel a little home-sick to get back to the company to-night; in fact, I am very tired. Keep up good heart. All will yet be well. Trust in God.

Give my love to all. I expect to get my box in the morning.

Your Affect. Husband

J. F. Culver

---

1  Mrs. Merrill was the wife of Maj. Samuel Merrill, the acting commander of the 70th Indiana.

2  General Rousseau, commander of the District of Nashville, had complained on the 31st that when Colonel Harrison's brigade took the field, there would be insufficient soldiers to guard the railroad between Nashville and Chattanooga. When apprised of this, General

Thomas issued instructions for Harrison's brigade "to remain at Nashville until troops can be obtained to relieve it." *O. R.*, Ser. I, Vol. XXXII, pt. II, pp. 270, 320.

3   Private Grunert of Company D noted in his diary, "The tents were again erected and the camp made as commodious as possible." Grunert, *History of the 129th Illinois*, p. 43.

4   J. B. McClean, a Pontiac businessman, had taken it upon himself to sell the engraved company rosters J.F.C. had referred to in his letter to his wife of July 26, 1863.

5   The subject letter is missing from the Culver Collection, so it is impossible to ascertain what Sister Jennie had written about Mother Culver.

6   There was no truth to the report that R. A. David G. Farragut's fleet had forced its way into Mobile Bay capturing Mobile. It would be August 5, 1864, before Farragut's warships passed the forts at the mouth of Mobile Bay, and another nine months before Union forces captured the city.

 105

Head Quarters 1st Brig., 1st Div., 11th A.C.
Nashville  February 3rd 1864

My Dear Wife

You will be surprised on looking at the date of my letter to find it written at Nashville, but such are the fortunes of War. We are still here. This morning we were ordered out at 10 o'clock, loaded up, & were ready to start when the order came for us to remain here for the present, so we have unpacked and set down to work again.[1] How long we will remain here we cannot tell. I am almost sorry you went home. The Col.'s family were hurried off at short notice & have scarcely more than reached home.

I presume as I recd. nothing by telegraph you are safe at home. There is just the least bit of a possibility that I may be at home a few days soon but not enough to base a hope upon. Col. [Harrison] told me to-day that as I am in command of the Band it would devolve upon me to go North to purchase their instruments.[2] It sounds too much like a joke, but I will try & make it do me all the good I can. But do not expect anything, and you will not be disappointed, & be sure and say nothing about it.

There is nothing new. I bid some of the ladies goodbye this morning, expecting that to-night we would be on the road to Bridgeport. I presume, however, all the women here are happy. It is rather unpleasant to be held in readiness to move & just when you have succeeded in reconciling yourself, to find all reversed. It is the general opinion still that we will leave as soon as more troops arrive, which are reported on their way here.

I was to see Capt. Hoskins this morning. He is some better. Enclosed is a photograph which you will not fail to recognize. I have not seen the boys [of Company A] since the order to move was countermanded, but presume they are satisfied. It seems quite lonely. I would like to walk over to "Drake's" to-night and find you there. Would it not be pleasant?

I am waiting anxiously for a letter from you, which will certainly arrive before the week is out. I have recd. no letters since I last wrote, neither have I had time to answer those on hand. I was at the Express office to-day, but the box of butter had not yet arrived.

I had a very agreeable visit to-day from R. D. & A. A. McDonald.[3] They are on their way to visit some friends at Decherd and also at Chattanooga. The latter are in the 125th Ills.,[4] the former are relatives and Rebel citizens. They both look well. Alex was discharged last May, and both are doing business in Danville, Illinois. They took dinner with me & started out this afternoon.

We are all well. May God bless you with good health and surround you with innumerable blessings and comforts. Give my love to all the family.

Good night,

Your Affect. Husband

J. F. Culver

---

1   For the background to these orders and countermanded orders see J.F.C.'s letter of February 1, 1864.

2   One of J.F.C.'s duties as aide-de-camp to Colonel Harrison was to serve as commander of the brigade band.

3   Robert D. McDonald had been a 30-year-old Pontiac merchant. In 1860 he was a bachelor and listed the value of his real estate at $1,500 and his personal estate at $4,000. Eighth Census, Livingston County, State of Illinois, NA.

4   The 125th Illinois was assigned to the Second Division, XIV Corps, Army of the Cumberland, and was camped near Rossville, Georgia.

## 106

Head Qrs., 1st Brig., 1st Div., 11th A.C.
Nashville Feby. 7th 1864

My Dear Wife

Enclosed is a letter to the Sunday School, which you will please deliver to some one to read.[1] I have been interrupted so often that I fear very much it will not prove interesting.

I have a very bad cold & a constant tickling in my throat & as the room is getting cold, & it is growing late, I do not deem it prudent to write much. It has just struck ten.

To-morrow will be a busy day, so that I shall not have time to write before the next mail goes out. Give my love to all. Do not forget to remember me to a throne of Grace. May God bless you. I feel very anxious to hear from you. Good night.

Your Affect. Husband

J. F. Culver

---

1  J.F.C.'s letter of February 7 to the Sunday school is missing from the Culver Collection.

## 107

Head Qrs. 1st Brig., 1st Div., 11th A.C.
Nashville Febry. 9th 1864

My Dear Wife

I set down to write to you last night, after finishing my letter to [James W.] Remick, but was interrupted; and, no opportunity offering to-day, I sent it thinking that even the short note would be acceptable. We recd. no mail to-day, but to-morrow morning I hope to receive a letter from you dated at Pontiac. I enclosed Remick's letter to you, so that you might become acquainted with its contents & thus be able to give those matters a little attention.[1] Neither Fleming or Wolgamott have paid over anything, & Remick writes that the amount due him is $28.[2] I will send some money home soon to apply on those notes; in the meantime, collect all you can.

I am not well to-night. I have had a very bad cold for several days, and I got so cold on Brigade Drill this afternoon that I have a fever to-night. The cook is making up a stew for me which I will take & go to bed, & I hope to be well in the morning. I was not up to the Regt. to-day, but presume all are well. Hoskins was much better yesterday.

I enclosed a letter from Bro. Thomas [Murphy] day before yesterday, with his Photograph, requesting mine. If you have one to spare, send it; I have none here. I will write to Bro. Johnie & him soon. I have no communications from home [Carlisle] since you left. I must write to Mother [Culver] again to-morrow. Sammy [Murphy] has not called here yet. I fear he has gone through without an opportunity of coming to see me.[3]

I wrote several days ago that the box of butter had arrived. We have tried it & found it excellent. I am waiting anxiously for news from Pontiac. Give my love to all. I know Mother [Murphy] will be rejoiced to see you. Remember me kindly to all our friends. May God bless and keep you

Your Affect. Husband

J. F. Culver

Feby. 10th 1864

Dear Mary

I left my letter open thinking I would write more if I got time, but I overlooked it to-day & it missed the mail. I recd. a letter from Sister Hannah [Culver] this morning, which I will enclose.[4] I also commenced a letter to Mother this morning, but did not get it finished in time for the mail.

Hannah has ere this gone to Williamsport [Pa.] to school. My health is somewhat better to-day, yet my cold is troublesome. I coughed almost all last night, & I am almost afraid to go to bed for fear of the same to-night. I believe it is caused by having too warm coal fire in our bedroom.

The rumor is afloat again that we will march. Genl. Hooker's Chief of Staff is here, & says we will immediately be sent forward.[5] I hope I shall get a letter to-morrow. Give my love to all.

May God bless you.

Your Affect. Husband

J. F. Culver

1   The Remick letter is missing from the Culver Collection.

2   For additional information about J. R. Wolgamott, see J.F.C.'s letter of Nov. 16, 1862. Efforts to secure more data on Fleming have been unsuccessful.

3   J.F.C.'s fear was unfounded. Pvt. Sam Murphy was still at Camp Yates, Ill. *Adjutant General's Report, State of Illinois,* Vol. VIII, p. 656.

4   The subject letter from Hannah Culver is missing from the Culver Collection.

5   General Hooker commanded the XI and XII Corps, Army of the Cumberland. Maj. Gen. Daniel Butterfield, Hooker's chief of staff, was in Nashville to learn why Ward's division was detained. From General Ward he learned that, exclusive of his command, there were about 16,000 troops in and around Nashville. In Butterfield's opinion, the interest of the service would be promoted by moving Harrison's brigade, if not the entire division, to the front. When he made this recommendation to General Hooker on the 12th, Butterfield observed, "Their present condition near Nashville, with its temptations to soldiers, will not be improved. The command [Harrison's] is represented in a very high state of discipline and perfection in drill. Their permanent camps are broken up, and they are not comfortably situated." *O. R.,* Ser. I, Vol. XXXII, pt. II, p. 376.

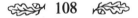 108

Head Quarters 1st Brig., 1st Div., 11th A.C.
Nashville, Tenn., February 11th 1864

My Dear Wife

I hoped very eagerly to receive a letter from you this morning, but the mail brought me nothing. I feel satisfied, however, that nothing serious has happened, or else the telegraph would have informed me. I have also looked in vain for Bro. Sammy. He must have taken the other route or else passed through here without stopping. I have received no letters since I last wrote. I wrote to Mother [Culver] to-day & will write to Sister Hannah soon.

I am trying hard to raise money for the Band, still hoping to be sent to purchase them instruments. I would in that event be able to spend a few days at least at home with you. Don't you wish for it, too? Yet it is not sure enough to base much hope upon. Col. Cropsey has sent in his resignation. I feel very sorry, as we shall miss him very much. Yet his health will fully justify him. It will be well, perhaps, to say nothing about it, as I think he wishes to keep it quiet, especially as it may not be accepted.[1]

We are all getting along quietly here. Almost every day we hear rumors about moving. The pay-master is busy paying the Brigade. I have not seen Capt. Hoskins to-day, but he was better yesterday. I hope he will succeed in getting a leave of Absence. I have enclosed Cordie Dunmire's letter, thinking you would like to read it. I wrote to Joe Culver to-day. I believe you saw his letter to me.[2] Alf. Huetson was down to see me to-day and drew my horse upon the wall. It was so well done that the Col. [Harrison] says he will prove invaluable in the Engineer Corps, and he will probably be included in its organization.[3] Christ [Yetter] & Nate [Hill] were out this morning, they are both in good health. My health is good, except a constant tickling in my throat. I am taking some medicine to-night.

I earnestly hope to-morrow's mail may bring me a letter from you. Give my love to all. Write often. May the blessings of Heaven rest upon you. Remember me kindly to all our friends. You need not be surprised if I make my appearance there some night. Will you let me in?

Your Affectionate Husband

J. F. Culver

---

1 Andrew J. Cropsey's resignation as lieutenant colonel of the 129th Illinois Infantry was accepted February 27, 1864. Compiled Service Records of Union Soldiers, NA.

2 The letter from Joseph Z. Culver is missing from the Culver Collection.

3 On March 21, Corporal Huetson was detached to headquarters, 1st Brigade, First Division, XI Corps, as topographical engineer.

## 109

Head Qrs. 1st Brig., 1st Div., 11th A.C.
Nashville, Tenn., Febry. 12th 1864

My Dear Wife

Your letter of the 6th inst. came to hand this evening.[1] I am very happy to hear that you have arrived Safe at home. I judge from the tenor of your letter that this is not the first letter you have written since you arrived at home, but it is the first I received except your letter from Decatur.[2]

I am sorry to hear that you find it dull and uninteresting in Pontiac, yet it has been full as much so here. It is with difficulty that I can reconcile myself to your absence & were it not that we have considerable business on hand, I do not know how I should pass the time. I do not know how many times I have wished you back.

You say nothing about receiving any letters from me, and yet I have missed but one mail since you left, & once I sent two which would make a letter every day since you left. I have not seen Bro. Sammy yet. I feel sorry that you did not get to see him, but you would probably have been fully as unfortunate. I should be glad to meet my old friends in Pontiac, but think you will not find a very great number so over-anxious as Mrs. Murphy [J.F.C.'s mother-in-law].

We are still laying on our oars in Nashville. We had Battalion drill to-day & we have Brigade School to-night. I look every moment for a summons to attend it. I did not see Hoskins to-day, but learn he is still improving. We are unable to learn how long we will remain here. It look[s] as if it might be several weeks unless the Rebs. make some demonstration on our Front.

How much I wish you were back here. We have been urging Col. Harrison to send for his wife, but he refuses to do so. If he does, I will get you a pass also. If I do not succeed in raising money enough for to purchase instruments for the Band, I will try & send enough money to pay the interest on all the notes due besides what you will require.

I can in a measure realize how dull it must be for you there. If I was there, it might be better, but I fear we will both find it dull after the excitement of Army life. You say "none of the outsiders suspect" you.

Have you any good reasons to doubt it yourself, or have you still as tangible evidence as you had before you left.[3] I am called to school; good-bye, until I return.

9 o'clock. I sit me down to finish my letter. I have had a bad cold for several days and my head aches wofully to-night. I took some blue mass last night, but it seems not enough. I feel very billious. I will get some more to-morrow if I am not better.

I wrote a letter to Remick a few days ago & enclosed it to you. I cannot account for the delay of your letters, unless they have been sent forward to Corps Hd. Qrs., which is very probable.[4] I presume they are full of news. While I have been anxiously waiting for them, they are making a fruitless journey to Chattanooga. They will get back here, however, soon. I fear the Post master's clerks here are in the habit of sending all the mail to the front that they are not familiar with, and, as this Brigade always went by the name of Ward's Brigade, frequent errors occur.[5]

You have not mentioned either Mother or Maggie in your letter, yet I presume they are well. I wrote to Sister Hannah [Culver] to-day. I recd. a letter from [Marcellus] Collins this morning on business. The claim due McDonald has not yet been paid & nothing has been collected of Hallam. Bro. Thomas' claim is $100 less than I thought. Please send me his letter after you have read it. I wish to refer to it occasionally.

Remember me kindly to all the friends and especially the Sabbath School. Give my love to the family. Tell Maggie & Mother to write. Will you please copy for me, if you have an opportunity, the Song, "Mother Dear, Oh! pray for me."[6] I have forgotten what book it was in, but I think the "Thanksgiving."

Write to me often. I would be pleased to attend the meetings in progress & hope they may result in great good.[7] Write to me often. When you find the time hanging heavily on your hands, write to me, or when you are happy, write. At all times write & tell me how you are getting along. And may our Father in Heaven who has ever been so bountiful in blessings to us keep you by his grace and abundantly bless you. Hoping that I may hear from you soon & very often, I remain, as ever,

Your Affectionate Husband

J. F. Culver

---

1   Mary Culver's letter of February 6 is missing from the Culver Collection.

2   While en route north by rail from Cairo to Pontiac, Mary Culver had a layover at Decatur. The Decatur letter is missing from the Culver Collection.

3   This is a reference to Mary's pregnancy.

4   Headquarters, XI Army Corps, were in Lookout Valley, near Chattanooga.

5   Brig. Gen. William T. Ward had led the brigade from the summer of 1863 until January 9, 1864, when he assumed command of the First Division, XI Army Corps. Grunert, *History of the 129th Illinois*, p. 42.

6   "Mother Dear, Oh! Pray for Me" was a popular hymn of the mid-nineteenth century.

7   A series of revivals or camp meetings were being held by the Pontiac churches.

 **110**

Head Quarters, 1st Brigade, 1st Division, 11th Army Corps
Nashville  February 13th 1864

My Dear Wife

Your letter of the 6th & 7th of February came to hand this evening and made me both happy and Sad.[1] Very happy to learn that you are safe at home and in good health and Sad that you are at home instead of here. Pontiac seems to have but few charms for you, and I have felt such a longing desire to be with you to settle down in our quiet home once more and enjoy the bliss of a "Home Circle" again. Bright visions of comfort and happiness are constantly flitting before my fancy, whether waking or sleeping, while at my desk or in my leisure hours, they still come. The pleasures of the Winter have brought everything back afresh, & I feel as if I was without a home. And your utter loneliness is continually in my mind.

I have been trying to make myself believe for some days past that you would be happy amidst friends and acquaintances, but Bro. Harry Cheston's letter came this evening and dispelled all my delusions. I feel in my heart that nothing but the peril of our Country could keep me from you, and even that at times seems a gross strain of Patriotism. There is doubtless truth in the quotation you have made. In my experience I have felt "Sweetness" even "in deep woe" from the sympathy of the true loving heart God has given me in my wife.

*220*

Since I commenced the sentence, I have sat over an hour in conversation and in listening to others. What would you think of returning to Nashville? The prospects is very favorable to our remaining here all Spring & perhaps through the summer. Col. [Harrison] & I have been talking of sending for our wives. We will know more & perhaps definitely in a few days. But it is nearly 12 o clock, & I must close for to-night.

I commenced about ten, but just as I finished the first page, several of the Staff came in & we have been talking over our prospects. So I will bid you good night and will write to-morrow if all goes well. May our Heavenly Father bless you, keep in health, and make you happy. Please accept the good night kiss I would be only too happy to impress upon your lips did the opportunity offer. May your dreams be sweet.

Sunday morning: Dear Mary

I lay abed rather late this morning. It looks very gloomy outside & has been raining some during the night. The probabilities of our moving have been fading away, day by day, until I think only one thing will ever get us away from this city: that is a strong attack on the Front by the Rebels. Genl. Thomas' Chief of Staff & Inspector General have been here for a week, but are gone without helping us any.[2]

If I thought you could get a pass in Louisville, I would advise you to come on, &, should you not find us here, you could wait until you heard from me. Genl. Ward is satisfied that even should we succeed in getting out of the city, we could get no further forward than Murfreesboro, & we all prefer staying here to going there. But if I can succeed in raising money enough for instruments for the Band, I will be home for a few days & will then bring you with me. For fear you may not have succeeded in collecting any money [owed by persons in debt to J.F.C.] I will enclose an order on Wm. B. Lyon [a Pontiac merchant] for $30, which you can draw & use if you need it. I have not sent any money, because I have still some hope of getting home before the 1st of March.

Enclosed you will find a pencil sketch by Huetson & a Photograph of (Sergt. James H.) Gaff & one of Corp. Chritten. Please put all the sketches of Huetson's together. Have you the one of "our home" at Richland [Tenn.]? Alf has promised to make me some more, so that by & by we may have a small collection.

I have also enclosed Bro. Harry's letter. Do not forget to write to our friends in Carlisle. Sister Hannah's address is Dickinson Seminary, Williamsport, Penna. The institution is remotely connected with the College in Carlisle and bears the same name. I will write to Harry and Jennie to-day. Sister Kate [Zug] has not answered my letter yet.

The Adjt. wishes to go out to-day, so I shall not get to church.[3] I may possibly to-night.

I look for some of those letters of yours to-day that were written immediately after you got home. I will write to Bro. Johnie to-day if I have time. I saw Captain Hoskins yesterday evening; he is getting much better. I shall be sorry not to find the same old familiar faces in Sabbath School, but I must expect changes.

Allen Fellows will not be sent home on a recruiting expedition.[4] The appointment comes from Genl. Thomas. A petition will be sent forward in a few days. I do not know who will be recommended. Genl. Fuller [the Adjutant General of Illinois] has no control over troops in the field. You were correct.

Remember me kindly to all our friends. Give my love to all the family. May God bless and keep you. Let us hope for the future and trust in God. All will be well. Farewell.

Your Affectionate Husband

J. F. Culver

---

1   Mary Culver's letter of February 6th & 7th is missing from the Culver Collection.

2   General Thomas' chief of staff was Brig. Gen. William D. Whipple and his inspector general was Lt. Col. Arthur C. Ducat. As Whipple was at Chattanooga throughout this period, it is presumed that J.F.C. was referring to Hooker's chief of staff, General Butterfield, who spent most of the second week of February in Nashville, gathering information to be used to secure the release of Ward's division for duty at the front. *O. R.*, Ser. I, Vol. XXXII, pt. II, pp. 376-381.

3   Colonel Harrison's adjutant was Lt. James L. Mitchell of the 70th Indiana. Compiled Service Records of Union Soldiers, NA.

4   A special field order was issued on Feb. 19, 1864, detailing Lt. W.H.H. McDowell, and Sergts. James Morrow, George W. August, Homer A. Kenyon and John C. Burger "to proceed at once to report to Brig. Gen. [John M.] Corse at Springfield for the purpose of taking charge & bringing forward to this army all recruits belonging to their regiment." Regimental Papers, 129th Illinois, NA.

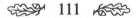

111

Head Quarters, 1st Brigade, 1st Division, 11th Army Corps
Nashville, Tenn., Febry. 16th 1864

My Dear Wife

Your letter of the 9th inst. was placed in my private drawer yesterday afternoon in my absence,[1] & I did not get to see it until this evening. I am very happy to hear that you are in good health, & I hope from the tenor of your letter that you are trying to enjoy yourself. Do not allow yourself to feel uneasy about the danger of my position. I do not think the danger is any greater than in the command of a Company.

Bro. Johnie [Murphy] is not "chief of artillery." He is doing the duties of Junior 2nd Lieut. but has no commission. Should the Battery be recruited to the number entitling them to another officer, he will doubtless be commissioned.[2] I sent you the last letter I received from him.

Col. Harrison sent for his family to-night, so I procured a pass for you at the same time. I will send it, but ask you not to start until you hear from me. If I can raise sufficient money for instruments, I will be home, & I now think it can be done. If not, I will telegraph for you to come on. Do not say anything about my going home or your coming but get ready quietly. I feel, oh, so lonely.

Col. [Harrison] & I went to Genl. Rousseau's to-night to get his opinion, & he said we should send for you as we will remain here for weeks yet.[3] Yet all things in Army life are so uncertain that there is still a possibility of our hopes being disappointed. I feel happy in the thought of having you with me once more. If we were on the march or at the front, I could perhaps in the excitement of business overcome my feelings; but if we are compelled to lie here for weeks, it would be insufferable without you.

I sent you an order on Wm. B. Lyons a few days ago for $30, which, with what you may gather there, will bring you safely through. If I get home, I will bring you with me. What things you need, get. If you have not money enough, borrow some of Bro. Remick. I have about $100 on hand, & I will return it to him by Express. I do not like to send money in a letter.

You will conclude from the tenor of my letter that I make no allowance for your not coming. I have tried hard to give up the idea but have failed, so I have given myself up to anticipated pleasure of your Society.

I have recd. no letters since I last wrote. I sent to Sarah Williams [at New Hartford] for another dozen of your & Frankie's pictures to be sent to you at Pontiac. Mother's was spoiled, & some of the rest of the family did not receive theirs.

Your last letter contains much news, but I do not feel like writing about them. I do not know any very late news here. I saw Capt. Hoskins this morning. He is much better, & I think will be home on leave of absence in a few weeks. I have not seen either Chris [Yetter] or

Nate [Hill] since I opened your letter, but I will convey your message to them to-morrow.

I will close. Let us pray for our success. Give my love to Mother and all the family, & Remember me kindly to all our friends. May God bless & keep you. I will not forget to pray. May your prayers in my behalf be answered.

Your Affectionate Husband

J. F. Culver

P.S. I have enclosed $20 for fear you would be short of funds.

---

1  Mary Culver's letter of February 9 is missing from the Culver Collection.

2  Sergt. John Murphy was not promoted to 2d lieutenant until August 8, 1864, although he had acted in that capacity for almost one year. *Adjutant General's Report, State of Illinois,* Vol. XIII, p. 653.

3  Maj. Gen. Lovell H. Rousseau commanded the District of Nashville. His protest that the dispatch of Harrison's brigade to the front would gravely weaken the force charged with defense of the city had led to cancellation of the orders to march. *O. R.,* Ser. I, Vol. XXXII, pt. II, p. 378.

 112

Head Qrs. 1st Brigade, 1st Division, 11th A.C.<br/>Nashville Febry. 17th 1864

My Dear Wife

I wrote to you last night, enclosing Pass & twenty dollars, also in a letter a few days previous I enclosed an order on Wm. B. Lyon for $30. I hope they will arrive safe.

I feel very well to-night. Col. Harrison telegraphed his wife to start on Friday, so that she will be here Saturday evening [the 20th].

I am living in the expectation of getting to see you soon. All is prospering finely. We are all well.

I expect a letter to-morrow certain. I have recd. but three since you returned, & one of them was from Decatur. It is midnight. We had [Brigade] school to-night till after ten, & then I had a letter to write for Davy Jones to his little boy.[1] Enclosed you will find his Photograph. I have not been in camp since day before yesterday. Good night. May God bless you. Write often to

Your Affect. Husband

J. F. Culver

---

1 David Jones, a 37-year-old miner, was mustered into service on Sept. 8, 1862, as a private in Company A, 129th Illinois. Private Jones died at Chesterfield Courthouse, S.C., on March 3, 1865, of a congestive chill. Compiled Service Records of Union Soldiers, NA.

 113

Head Qrs., 1st Brig., 1st Div., 11th A.C.
Nashville Febry. 19th 1864

My Dear Wife

I recd. no letter to-day; it is just one week since your last arrived. I cannot divine the reason. [Pvt. Joseph] Allen recd. a letter from Lou, dated the 14th, in which she says you are well.[1]

You wrote in one of your letters for me to send a [black] servant for Mrs. Remick and one for Maggie [Utley]. I would be happy to comply if it were possible, but every negro captured in Kentucky is sold into Slavery.[2] None are allowed to cross the Ohio River. The only way is to get a permit to take your servants home with you, as Dr. Johns did, & then go up the river to Cairo.[3] I cannot take time to go by water, & therefore will not be able to take them with me.

I am unable to tell how soon I may be ready to start home, or whether it is certain or not. I have succeeded well in my own Regt., but some of the others are slow.[4]

My health is good. If I could only hear from you, but I feel fearful that your health may not be good. I have recd. no letter from any source since I last wrote. I wrote to Bro. Charlie [Culver], Johnie [Murphy], & Scott McDowell last night. I have not been able to sleep for the cold for several nights.[5] Mrs. Harrison will be here to-morrow. How I wish you were here, but wishing is in vain. Give my love to Mother & Maggie. May God bless & keep you. Good night.

Febry. 20th/64

Dear Mary

No letter yet; I am wholly at a loss to account for it. I am quite well. I saw Capt. Hoskins this morning, he is much better, & will be home in ten days or two weeks. I also saw Lt. [Benjamin F.] Fitch, his wife is well. I close in haste.
May God bless you.

Your Affect. Husband

J. F. Culver

---

1   Lou Allen was the wife of Pvt. Joseph Allen of Company A, 129th Illinois Infantry. Eighth Census, Livingston County, State of Illinois, NA.

2   Thousands of blacks freed by President Lincoln's Emancipation Proclamation, dated January 1, 1863, had refugeed to the Nashville area and were living in camps in and around the city. According to terms of the Emancipation, Union slave states—including Kentucky, all of Tennessee, and sections of Virginia and Louisiana—had been excluded from its provisions. Slave owners, legal residents of these states or regions, could identify and claim the return of their blacks. Randall, *Civil War & Reconstruction*, pp. 490-498.

3   Dr. Harvey S. Johns' resignation as surgeon of the 129th Illinois had been accepted January 19, 1864. Compiled Service Records of Union Soldiers, NA.

4   J.F.C.'s reference is to the collection of funds from the troops to purchase instruments for the brigade band.

5   Private Grunert noted in his diary for February 18, "intensely cold weather today." On February 17, Private Dunham had written his mother, "We are having splendid wether heare now but rather cool. People are plowing." Grunert, *History of the 129th Illinois*, p. 44; *Through the South with a Union Soldier*, p. 104.

## 114

Head Qrs., 1st Brig., 1st Div., 11th A. C.
Nashville, Febry. 21st 1864

My Dear Wife

I recd. two letters from you yesterday evening, both mailed on the 12th, but one written on the 6th & 7th & the other on the 12th.[1] I am happy to learn that you enjoy such good health. I will not undertake to answer the questions you have asked, for I feel rather certain that I shall get home this Spring. If not, I will telegraph for you.

If you get an opportunity to see Thomas Hill, ask him what he can do to assist me.[2] The money of Tom Smith's & Joe Shellebarger's that I expected to borrow is in his hands.[3]

Mrs. Harrison will be here this evening; the Col. recd. a dispatch from her to-day. My going home will be delayed on Mitchel's account.[4] He has sent in an application for leave to go home & get married. I will cheerfully wait on him. I think he is more nervous about it than I was. He will probably bring his *bride* here.

I was at church to-day & heard a very good sermon. It was late when we got back, & now it is mail time & my letter very brief. I have been almost tempted to telegraph for you & give up the idea of getting home. I am afraid by the time Jim returns, which will be full one month, we will have marching orders. If I succeed in being sent for the instruments, it will not interfere with my getting a leave of absence next fall, but to get a leave of absence now would prevent it.

If I do not get home, I will write in full about the matters of which you write. Hoskins will be home next week; I will send by him. He is ordered to Chicago to appear against C. J. Beattie.[5]

You want me to tell you the next prettiest name to Mary. For dark eyes & dark hair, brunnette, I like *Ellen,* & for light hair & complexion, *Jennie.*[6] Give my love to all. I must close. I hope to get home. May God bless you.

Your Affect. Husband

J. F. Culver

---

1   Mary Culver's letters of February 7 & 12 are missing from the Culver Collection.

2 Thomas Hill was a 43-year-old Pontiac Township farmer. In 1860 he valued his real estate at $13,000, his personal estate at $1,400, and lived with his wife, Mary, and four children. One of his four farm hands had been Chris Yetter. Eighth Census, Livingston County, State of Illinois, NA.

3 Joseph Shellenbarger, a 19-year-old fruit tree agent, was mustered into service on Sept. 8, 1862, as a private in Company A, 129th Illinois. Private Shellenbarger died in the brigade hospital on March 31, 1864, at Wauhatchie of pneumonia. Thomas R. Smith, a 23-year-old farmer, was mustered into service on Sept. 8, 1862, as a private in Company A, 129th Illinois. Private Smith was hospitalized at Quincy, Ill., with wounds to the left arm received at New Hope Church, Ga., May 27, 1864. He received a medical discharge on May 18, 1865. Compiled Service Records of Union Soldiers, NA.

4 Adjutant Mitchell of Harrison's staff was granted a 10-day leave on February 19, 1864, "to attend to personal business" in Bloomington, Ind. *Ibid.*

5 Charles J. Beattie, a Livingston County lawyer, had been indicted for forgery in the U.S. District Court for the Northern District of Illinois. *Ibid.*

6 Mary Culver had written J.F.C. of her hope that their next child would be a girl and had asked his preference for a name.

 115

Head Quarters, 1st Brig., 1st Div., 11th A.C.
Nashville Febry. 22nd 1864

My Dear Wife

Your letter of the 15th came to hand this evening.[1] I am happy to hear that you enjoy such good health. I telegraphed to you this morning informing you that we would leave here to-morrow.[2] We are loaded & the train has started, so that there is not much probability of our not going this time.

Mrs. Harrison arrived yesterday evening. The train was several hours behind time. She had not been in bed a half hour before the orders came to march. How would you have enjoyed it? She will remain in the city a couple of weeks.

Harry McDowell starts home in the morning, & Jim Morrow.[3] I will write to you as often as I can on the march.

You wrote to me as to what you should do. I have still some hope of getting home. Since I set down we recd. orders to send out our Pickets again. Another sell. It is now so late that I cannot write more, or I will not get to see McDowell. I am well. Harry will give you all the news.

Chris [Yetter] & Alf [Huetson] were here to-night. I will write more by mail. May God bless you.
Good night,

Your Affect. Husband

J. F. Culver

1 Mary Culver's letter of February 15 is missing from the Culver Collection.

2 To prevent Confederate General Johnston from rushing soldiers from his Army of Tennessee to Demopolis, Ala., to oppose General Sherman's columns which had advanced east from Vicksburg to Meridian, Miss., General Grant directed General Thomas to employ two corps of his Army of the Cumberland to make a forced reconnaissance toward Dalton. This movement was to begin not later than Monday morning, the 22d.

In conjunction with this movement, orders were received by General Ward to start Harrison's brigade for Bridgeport, Ala., where it would report to General Howard. On the departure of Harrison's brigade, Ward's 2d Brigade would report to General Rousseau and take post at Nashville, Lavergne, and McMinnville. *O. R.,* Ser. I, Vol. XXXII, pt. I, p. 25; pt. II, p. 435.

3 Lieutenant McDowell and Sergeant Morrow were to return to Illinois on recruiting duty. William H. H. McDowell, a 21-year-old farmer, was mustered into service on Sept. 8, 1862, as sergeant major of the 129th Illinois, and on April 17, 1863 he was commissioned 2d lieutenant of Company E. On Feb. 22, 1864, he started for Illinois to bring up a detail of recruits from Camp Yates, and rejoined the regiment in April. In August 1864 McDowell was detailed to the XX Corps' ambulance corps, and in January was assigned to duty with the Pioneer Corps. He was mustered out with the regiment on June 8, 1865, near Washington, D.C. James Morrow, a 26-year-old clerk, was mustered into service on Sept. 8, 1862, as a sergeant in Company G, 129th Illinois Infantry. Sergeant Morrow accompanied Lieutenant McDowell to Illinois on recruiting duty, but did not rejoin the regiment until mid-summer. He was mustered out on June 8, 1865, near Washington, D.C. Compiled Service Records of Union Soldiers, NA.

 116

Head Qrs. 1st Brig., 1st Div., 11th A.C.
Nashville Febry. 24th 1864

My Dear Wife

We have just finished breakfast, & it is six o clock. In another hour, we will be on the march. The Column will be in motion out the Murfreesboro Pike at 8 o clock.

Our wagon is waiting to be loaded, & I have embraced this leisure moment to say good bye. Write to me often. We will get mail on the route, so I hope to hear from you. We are all in good health.

I have deferred writing in answer to your question because I thought I would get home. If you prefer, go to Mrs. McGregor's.[1] Make yourself comfortable by all means & try & be contented and happy. May God bless & keep you.

Give my love to all,

Good Bye.

Your Affect. Husband

J. F. Culver

---

1  In one of her letters to J.F.C., Mary Culver had broached the subject of leaving her parents' home and taking a room at Mrs. M. J. McGregor's. Mrs. McGregor was a 45-year-old widow. *History of Livingston County*, p. 642.

 117

Head Qrs., 1st Brig., 1st Div., 11th A.C.
In Camp, 11 miles South of Nashville
Febry. 24th 1864

My Dear Wife

We are on the road at last. We went into camp at 2 o'clock this afternoon, making a short day's march; we purpose marching only 10 miles a day for the first few days.[1] All are in good spirits. The Band of the 79th Ohio are playing Marseillaise hymn, & the sun is setting. The day has been very beautiful. All nature seems most happy. It is seldom that everything seems so beautiful.

My health is very good. I feel anxious to hear from you. We will get mail at Lavergne to-morrow & at Murfreesboro the day after, also at Tullahoma, Decherd & Stevenson, so that I hope to hear from you.

We left Nashville at 8 A.M. The roads are very good thus far.[2] Give my love to all. May God bless & keep you. Pray for me. I love to feel that it is so — Accept much love.

Your Affect. Husband

J. F. Culver

In camp at Stewarts Creek — Febry. 25th 1864

Dear Mary

We did not get an opportunity to send letters at Lavergne to-day, so I have opened this to add a few lines. We have marched only 10 miles to-day & went into camp at 12 o clock. The men are in excellent spirits.

There is a Fort on the south side of the creek, & just outside of it, we have our Head Qurs.[3] The 129th are camped on the West of us. I have just come from the Company. All are well & in good spirits.

On the East side of us there was a year or two ago a very dense cedar thicket, which was cut down for to give range for the guns of the fort. There is about 10 acres of dead brush which the boys have set on fire to drive out the Rabbits. There are about 500 men around it, & they have caught more than 100. They are having a fine time, & you could hear them yell for miles when a Rabbit appears. The fire looks as if a city were in flame.

We will get mail to-morrow at Murfreesboro. We recd. orders by telegraph to-day to report to [General] Hooker, so we will not stop this side of Chattanooga.[4]

The Rabbit hunt is getting exciting. There must be over 1,000 men & officers out just now. The chaplain of the 79th Ohio is going to [the] train, so we may get some papers this evening. We are having beautiful weather.

I hope you are making yourself comfortable. Do not forget what I told you in a former letter. Make yourself happy. It is my earnest desire that you so dispose of your time & use all the money you need to secure your comfort & happiness. Give my love to all. Write often. May God bless & protect you. Accept love and a kiss.

Your Affect. Husband

J. F. Culver

---

1 Colonel Harrison had been told that: (a) there was no "necessity for making hurried or long marches"; (b) it was advisable to make detours from "the usually traveled highway,

if by doing so a better road could be found, having in mind always supplies of rations and forage"; and (c) his brigade was to reach the front "in serviceable condition." It was suggested that the brigade march from Decherd, by way of Tracy City, to Bridgeport instead of taking the road paralleling the railroad. *O. R.*, Ser. I, Vol. XXXII, pt. II, pp. 276-277.

2   Private Grunert of Company D provides additional details of the day's march. He reported that after breakfast the troops fell into line, and that "many of the citizens, with whom we became intimately acquainted during our six months' stay in Nashville, accompanied us to the suburbs of the city, until the command 'forward' was given and the band of the 79th Ohio played a beautiful march." We turned our "backs to Nashville, the friends we had won there, and our sick in the hospitals." Camp was made in a field "of a rebel, and in order to have a good remembrance we burned a considerable number of fence rails in the camp fires which kept us warm." Grunert, *History of the 129th Illinois,* pp. 44-45.

3   An earthen fort had been thrown up by the Federals in the winter of 1862-63 to guard the vital railroad and highway bridges crossing Stewarts Creek.

4   General Hooker's headquarters were in Lookout Valley, southwest of Chattanooga.

 118

Head Quarters, 1st Brig., 1st Div., 11th A.C.
In Camp on Big Flat Creek, 5 miles South of Shelbyville
Febry. 28th 1864

My Dear Wife

Though this is [the] Sabbath, we have marched 16 miles.[1] It rained sufficient to lay the dust & marching is very pleasant. The Post Office in Shelbyville was closed, so that we had no opportunity to mail letters.

To-morrow we will reach Tullahoma, if nothing happens, where we can send our letters back, & I hope we will get some mail. Everything passed off very pleasantly. The men are tired. The roads since we left Shelbyville are not good. We will have no more pike & may expect some bad roads.

My health is good. The country through which we passed to-day north of Shelbyville was very fine; on this side, it is very broken. I should have been pleased to call & see Bro. Johnie's lady friends there [at Shelbyville], but I have forgotten their names.[2] We got into camp about two o'clock.

Write to me often. May God bless you with health and happiness. Be cheerful; all things work to gether for our good. Give love to all & accept the most ardent for yourself.

Your Affect. Husb.

J. F. Culver

---

1   On the 26th Harrison's brigade broke camp at sunrise, and by 10 o'clock halted on the Stones River battlefield. The soldiers visited the graves, paled at the sight of bleaching bones, and shook their heads at the way the storm of canister and exploding shells had shredded the cedars near Round Forest. The march was resumed and, passing through Murfreesboro, the troops halted and camped alongside the Shelbyville Pike south of town.

A 13-mile march was made on the 27th, but it was fatiguing because several streams, the bridges of which had been destroyed, had to be forded, and the road "was either covered with several inches of dust, or led through a rocky, hill country." Grunert, *History of the 129th Illinois*, pp. 45-46.

2   Sergt. John Murphy had been stationed at Shelbyville from June 29 to September 6, 1863. While there he had courted several local girls.

119

Head Qurs., 1st Brig. 1st Div. 11th A.C.<br>In the Field near Tullahoma<br>March 1st 1864

My Dear Wife

We reached this place yesterday evening amid one of the worst rain storms I ever was in. It rained very hard from noon yesterday until noon to-day. It has been so cold that we almost perished. The ground is all mud, & in mud & water we are encamped. It was impossible to march to-day. Part of our train has just got in, some 15 wagons together with the rear guard were in the mud all night. I went out with Col. Harrison to bring them up. In coming the last 2-1/2 miles, five of our mules died in the wagons. Several died last night.

All are in good spirits, & the boys are cheering each other up. Since it has quit raining, we are beginning to get dry.

I recd. your letter this morning, dated the 22nd, but mailed the 21st [*sic*]. I am most happy to learn that you are well. I would rather you would not engage in teaching if you can otherwise content yourself.[1] I will try hard to keep my pledge to protect & provide for you while my life & health is spared. Yet as I cannot be with you, I wish you to use your own pleasure in the disposition of your time. You have not been a dead weight on my hands. You are all the world to me, and the thoughts of you comfort me amid all the trials of life. May God bless you and spare us.

I recd. letters this morning from Bro. Johnie, H. C. Cheston, J. M. Barr & Cordelia Dunmire. All are well. I will enclose some.[2]

My hands get so cold I cannot write. I will try & write every day. We will leave here to-morrow. I have not seen the Company to-day but last night all were well.

Give my love to all. Write as often as you can. We have collected $600 for the Band. I do not know whether I will be sent home or not, I think it doubtful. Pray for me. May our Heavenly Father keep you in health & happiness.

Farewell,

Your Affect. Husband

J. F. Culver

---

1 Mary Culver's letter of February 22 is missing from the Culver Collection. In this letter, Mary had raised the subject of securing a position as teacher in the Pontiac school system.

2 The letter from Sergt. John Murphy was dated February 19 and mailed from Loudon, Tenn. Sergt. Murphy had written of his surprise at learning that Brother Sammy had enlisted. When Sammy had raised the subject, John had told "him to go to school two or three years, and then if necessity required it, to get into the army." John Murphy to J.F.C., Feb. 19, 1864, Culver Collection. H. C. Cheston's letter was postmarked Carlisle, Feb. 20, 1864, and Cordelia Dunmire's (illegible), Feb. 15, 1864.

Head Qurs., 1st Brig., 1st Div., 11th A.C.
In the Field March 3rd 1864

My Dear Wife

We are as far as Cowan Station at the foot of the mountains;[1] we will cross to-morrow if nothing happens. We are all well. We will receive no letters till we get to Stevenson, two days more. I shall anticipate a letter there.

I hope you are well. Give my love to all. May our Father in Heaven keep you.

Your Affect. Husband

J. F. Culver

1  The sky having cleared, the brigade broke camp on March 2 and travelled ten miles, halting after crossing Elk River. On the 3d a similar distance was logged. Grunert, *History of the 129th Illinois*, pp. 46-47.

Head Quarters, 1st Brig., 1st Div., 11th A.C.
In the Field March 5th 1864

My Dear Wife

We left Tantalon at one o'clock this afternoon. We are now in camp about 5 miles south of Tantalon and 4 miles north of Anderson. We expect to reach Stevenson, Alabama, to-morrow. The [wagon] train just got up as we Started.[1] All right. We are still among the mountains. Our Head Qurs. to-night are upon a little island, about 50 feet wide & perhaps two hundred long. It is "a sweet little nook by the babbling brook." The moss is growing all around us, & we found some very beautiful flowers, one which contains the colors beautifully blended, red, white and blue.

My health never was better. We have not lost a man crossing the mountains. The valley [of Big Crow Creek] through which we are passing is very narrow. The troops marched all the way upon the Rail Road track. We will break camp at 6 o'clock to-morrow morning. Reveille sounds at 4-1/2 o'clock. It is 14 miles to Stevenson.

I hope you are well and happy. I expect a letter to-morrow night. The roads to-day have been quite good. Give my love to all. May God bless you. Accept much love from

Your Affect. Husband

J. F. Culver

---

1  On the 4th the 129th Illinois had been detailed to guard the wagon train as it climbed up over the Cumberland Plateau. It was hard pulling for the horses and mules, and soldiers were detailed to help the teams get the wagons up the steeper grades. Darkness overtook the train before it reached Tantalon, where the brigade camped and the wagons were corralled. Grunert, *History of the 129th Illinois*, pp. 46-47.

122

Head Quarters, 1st Brig. 1st Div., 11th A.C.<br/>In the Field near Stevenson, Alabama<br/>March 6th 1864

My Dear Wife

We arrived at Stevenson this evening. I recd. your letters of the 23rd and 24th, came to hand by mail, and of the 25th by Dr. Wood who joined us here.[1] I also recd. a very handsome Masonic pin, for which you will please accept my thanks. I am most happy to hear of your good health and that you are trying to enjoy yourself. Three days' mail has gone forward to Corps Head Qurs., so that I shall get your former letters when we arrive there [in Lookout Valley]. I am also glad to learn that the money I forwarded went safely through.

You wish to know whether you may teach school.[2] If you can pass your time better in that way, I have no objections; while I would prefer it otherwise, it is for your sake. I fear it will be a severe tax on you, and I wish you to enjoy as much of life as possible. I am afraid also that your health will not admit of it. You must try and prepare yourself for coming events.[3]

It is barely possible I may get home, but the prospects are not flattering. We have got along thus far on our march very well. To-morrow we expect to reach Bridgeport, Ala., and the day after we will cross the Tennessee River. Where our destination will be next, we cannot tell. Should we be sent to Mobile, we will have no mail facilities for months.[4] It is still only a rumor as yet & perhaps without foundation.

I forgot all day that it was Sunday. I feel ashamed of myself, but it does sometimes happen so. We have been on the march almost two weeks. The weather is beautiful & the roads good. We marched 14 miles to-day, started at 6 o'clock this morning & went into camp about 2 this P.M.

Chris [Yetter] and Nate [Hill] are looking anxiously for a letter from you. I presume Harry McDowell & Jim Morrow are having a grand time. Remember me kindly to all our friends and give my love to all the family. I will send this letter to Capt. Hoskins & request him to take it home with him. He is still in Nashville.

I have written every day but one since we started. May our Father in Heaven bless you and keep you by Divine Grace. Continue to pray for me. God has been merciful to us; let us hope for a continuance of his favor and in all things praise Him.

Accept all the love and affection of your

Husband,

J. F. Culver

P.S. A very serious Collision occurred on the Rail Road at Anderson in which a Paymaster's daughter, two soldiers' wives, and one little babe were killed and several wounded.

1   Mary Culver's letters of Feb. 23, 24, & 25 are missing from the Culver Collection. Orlando S. Wood, a 25-year-old physician, was mustered in as assistant surgeon at Stevenson, Ala., on March 6, 1864. He was promoted to regimental surgeon on April 9, 1865, and mustered out near Washington, D.C., June 8, 1865. Compiled Service Records of Union Soldiers, NA.

2   See J.F.C.'s letter of March 1, 1864.

3   Mary Culver was three months  pregnant.

4   There was no substance to rumors that a powerful column was to be sent southwest from Chattanooga to attack Mobile. This story was triggered by news that General Sherman with two corps had advanced east from Vicksburg and had captured Meridian and that Farragut's squadron was anchored off the entrance to Mobile Bay. Sherman's army by March 6 had returned to Vicksburg, and on the 4th General Grant had directed him to transfer most of his troops to Memphis, and be ready to join Grant at Chattanooga for the spring campaign. *O. R.*, Ser. I, Vol. XXXII, pt. III, p. 19.

 123

Head Qurs., 1st Brig., 1st Div., 11th A.C.
Lookout Valley, March 13th 1864[1]

My Dear Wife

I recd. two letters from you this morning dated the 3rd & 4th of March.[2] I am sorry to hear that you are suffering with Neuralgia, for, if it is anything like I had at Nashville, it places you in a most uncomfortable position. I am much obliged for the copy of the Song sent me.[3]

I cannot answer your letters at length this morning, though it is Sabbath and the day very fine, yet I have a large amount of business that must be attended to immediately. I may possibly find time to write this afternoon, but the mail goes out at 12 M.

We recd. a letter from [Jim] Mitchell this morning. He started back, but, by an accident on the Rail-Road at Columbia, Ind. he was very seriously injured and may not be here for weeks.[4] Some 8 or 10 were killed in the same car & a great many injured. I shall have no opportunity to try for a leave until he returns. My health is good, though

I feel very tired being so constantly at the Desk. I will make an effort to get some help to-morrow; I want to visit Lookout point as soon as I can.

Give my love to all. May God bless & keep you.

Your Affect. Husband

J. F. Culver

---

1 Harrison's brigade marched to Bridgeport on March 7, remained there one day, and crossed the Tennessee River pontoon bridge on the 9th. At noon on the 10th, the brigade halted at Whiteside Station and at dusk camped in Lookout Valley, where Colonel Harrison reported to General Howard, commander of the XI Corps. The day's march had been through rugged terrain and a number of mules had died. The next day the brigade moved a short distance to a better camp site. Grunert, *History of the 129th Illinois*, pp. 47-48.

2 Mary Culver's letters of March 3 & 4 are missing from the Culver Collection.

3 Mary Culver, as requested on February 12, had forwarded a copy of "Mother Dear, Oh! Pray for Me."

4 Lieutenant Mitchell had been injured on March 8, when several cars of the Indianapolis & Jeffersonville Railroad had jumped the track. His injuries consisted of a severely sprained ankle, fractured ribs, and internal injuries. Dr. S. Davis of the 10th Indiana Infantry certified that Mitchell would be unfit for duty for at least four weeks. Compiled Service Records of Union Soldiers, NA.

ﾃﾟﾟ 124 ﾃﾟﾟ

Head Quarters, 1st Brigade, 1st Division, 11th Army Corps
Lookout Vallie, March 17th 1864

My Dear Wife

Yours of the 11th inst. came to hand to-night.[1] I am very happy to learn that your "health is pretty good," which I suppose to mean that it is as well as could be expected under existing circumstances.

The weather here has been very cold for the past three days. The first day [the 15th] it was spitting snow, blowing and freezing, & I thought it would not last over one day, but next morning (yesterday) it was still freezing and much colder than the day before so that I had to suspend work & fix up a place to write in. I procured some timbers and built a house about 3-1/2 feet high, & set my tent on top. I have a fireplace in it, & by noon to-day I commenced operations again. This will account for my not writing for the last three days.

I am quite comfortably situated now, and though it is ten o'clock and all the Staff have gone to bed, I have set down to chat with you. I know there is a great deal in the letters I have on hand that remains unanswered, yet the number is so great that were I to undertake to overlook them to-night, I would have no time left to write. So I will promise to attend to every one of them soon, and ask your indulgence for this one time more. I have besides a host of other letters, all unanswered. You wished to know why I have not sent Sister Beccie's [letter],[2] & I am almost ashamed to tell you that aside from a very hasty glance when it came to hand amid the rain & cold at Tullahoma, I have neither read or seen it. I know you would pardon me if you knew how busy I have been. You know how well I love to be busy, and my health was never better than now, for which I feel very thankful.

The fire on the hearth looks so cheerful that I can almost imagine *you* present here. You will feel a great disappointment in my not getting home, but God orders all things for the best. Let me caution you against any disposition to fret or allow anything to bear heavily upon your mind. Be cheerful and, if possible, make yourself happy. Despondency, aside from affecting your own person seriously, may possibly live after you, & I feel anxious for you also on that account. You give me assurance, however, that you are happy, & I earnestly hope you will use every means to secure it. May God bless you. I shall try to pray for myself & you, as you request, & shall feel happy in the knowledge of the aid of your prayers. Bro. Johnie in his last letter wished to know how I was getting along spiritually.[3] I have only had time to send him a few lines in answer as yet, telling him where I was. I have never heard from Lt. Donaldson yet.

All your friends here are well. Alf Huetson has been recommended for appointments as Topographical Engineer of this Brigade, & he will without doubt be appointed and I think before long get a commission. I do not yet know what his rank will be; I have not been around any yet. I can see the Camp of the 129th from here, and it looks very fine. The boys are all still busy fixing up.[4] To-morrow we will have a Brigade Inspection & Review, and on Saturday we will be Inspected & Reviewed by Maj. Genl. Howard. Everybody is anxious to have it come off well, as most of the troops here think us "green," "conscripts,"

&c.[5] I feel assured, however, that we will make a good impression. Our Brigade is larger than any Division I have seen yet.[6]

We hear no news from the front, except what we see in the Louisville and Nashville papers. One of the trains was captured and burnt yesterday near Estill Springs, & the train did not come in till this evening.[7] We have not learned the particulars yet.

The Chicago Tribune has not come to hand yet. I shall be glad to get it. And now I must close; I do not think I can answer your letters before Sunday or Monday, but I will try.

Mitchell is so badly injured that I do not know when to expect him back. Give my love to all the family. Remember me kindly to Lou [Allen]. I am glad she is getting well so rapidly. Also remember me to all our friends. Good night my *Love,* good night, & may holy angels guard you.

Your Affect. Husband

J. F. Culver

---

1  Mary Culver's letter of March 11 is missing from the Culver Collection.

2  Sister Rebecca Culver was married to S. Augustus Pague, and they lived on the family farm in northern Cumberland County.

3  Sergt. John Murphy, on February 19, had written, "How is it with your soul, Frank? Are you prospering spiritually? I am not doing very well now. The circumstances with which I am surrounded are very untoward." W. J. Murphy to J.F.C., Feb. 19, 1864, Culver Collection.

4  Private Grunert noted in his diary on the 12th that the soldiers were chopping wood for huts and shebangs, while on the 20th, Private Dunham wrote, "We have got settled down again but don't know how long we will stay, so we have got tip top houses maid. Four in a house." Grunert, *History of the 129th Illinois,* p. 48; *Through the South with a Union Soldier,* p. 109.

5  Unlike the regiments of Harrison's brigade, most of the units constituting the XI and XII Corps had participated in a number of battles, including Lookout Mountain, Wauhatchie, Gettysburg, Chancellorsville, Fredericksburg, etc.

6  General Ward's two-brigade division numbered almost as many effectives as the other two XI Corps divisions combined. *O. R.,* Ser. I, Vol. XXXII, pt. III, p. 207.

7  On March 16, near Estill Springs, a southbound train was derailed by Confederate partisans led by Col. John M. Hughs. Before being driven off by a detachment of the 123d New York, the partisans burned three cars, robbed the passengers, and killed several non-combatants. *O. R.,* Ser. I, Vol. XXXII, pt. I, pp. 56, 499-501.

Head Quarters, 1st Brigade, 1st Division, 11th Army Corps
Lookout Valley, March 20th 1864

My Dear Wife

I have sat down this morning to answer your letters which have
accumulated since we left Nashville. I may have answered some of
them, but do not now recollect which. Yours of the 12th inst., one
enclosing Bro. Tom's [Thomas Murphy's] letter, came to hand
yesterday.[1]

I am very glad to hear that you are well and trying to enjoy life. Capt.
Hoskins has reached home. I sent you a letter by him from Cowan or
Bridgeport which you do not mention. I suppose that Mrs. Folks went
home when her husband was sent to the Hospital. She was not allowed
to go with him, & he was full two miles from where she was stopping. I
presume also that they had not the means of living when no rations were
furnished.

I am not much surprised at Mrs. Smith's statements, for I think [Lt.
John W.] Smith was always of that opinion. I cannot tell how he is
getting along, except as remarks are made by the boys [of Company A],
from which I judge that things do not move very pleasantly. I never go
near him.[2] I sent your letter to Chris [Yetter] yesterday evening by Alf.
[Huetson].

I do not know what is going on in the Regt. in regard to the vacancy
occasioned by [Lt. Col.] Cropsey's resignation. I have been far too busy
here to think much about it. It is my impression, however, that Hoskins
will be made Major, in which event I shall get the Captaincy of the
Company.

Bro. Gaff recd. a letter from his wife on Friday.[3] He was very much
alarmed, as he had not heard from her for a month. I do not understand
why Jim Morrow & Harry McDowell should act so shabbily; I will call
them to an account when they return. I will send Bro. Thomas' Letter
to Johnie tomorrow.

In several of your letters you speak of having headache, from which I
judge that it is a very constant companion. Cannot you get something to
relieve you? You say you have not collected anything of Fleming yet. I

want the matter attended to immediately. If not soon collected, you will never get it. You can learn through Remick the amount. I understand his [Fleming's] business is assuming a rather doubtful shape. Employ an attorney if necessary.[4]

I cannot tell what to do for Lawrence; ask Thomas Hill to arrange matters as well as he can.[5] As there is no prospect of pay here, I dare not spare the little money I have on hand. You can say to Thomas Hill that if he has no use for the money sent him by Tom Smith, Joe Shellenbarger, and Chris [Yetter], I can borrow it; or, if he prefers, he can use it in lifting my notes & waiting awhile. Do the best you can.

I am doing what I never done before. I am compelled to burn your letters, as I have no way to take care of them. My desk is a public one & open to every one, & my valise is too small for my clothing. I am reading them & then consigning them to the flames. It seems almost Sacrilegious; 11 are already gone. I wrote to you some time ago to get the amount of the order on Lyons; it will be safer to do so. I have just finished reading and destroying your letters. There was 27 in all. I wonder whether your list is as large. The train has just come in, & I expect a couple of letters. The mails have been very irregular last week caused by the raid on the road at Estell Springs. The weather is very fine to-day. We had a general Review and Inspection at Genl. Howard's Hd. Qurs. yesterday.[6] The Brigade looked very fine & was as large as the 2nd Division of this Corps.[7]

I intended to go to church this morning, but my clerk wished to go to Lookout Point; &, as he has been very faithful, I preferred to let him go. I shall try & get out to preaching this evening.

A few days ago an artist, who has a gallery on the top of Lookout [Point], was fixing something on the edge of the cliff, was approached by some ladies and in attempting to bow to them, he lost his balance, went over, and was instantly killed. His gallantry cost him his life.

Adgt. Mitchell, it is said, will not be able for duty for two months. I am now Acting A. A. Genl. of the Brigade & will be until his return.

Here is the mail: two letters for me, one from you, and one from Carlisle. Your letter is dated Mch. 13th but mailed Mch. 14th; it notices the death of Jay Pratt.[8] I am sorry to hear of Mrs. Capron's danger.[9] You say nothing of your own health. The other letter is from Jennie & Harry [Cheston]. All are well.

I intended to look over Beccie's letter and send it, but I have been all forenoon reading your letters & now it is nearly mail time. I will answer some this afternoon & send them to you to-morrow.

Some one sent me the "Ledger" from Nashville yesterday of Mch. 8th. I think it was [Pvt.] Joe Allen. Alf Huetson is now on duty at these Hd. Qurs. as Top. Engineer, & is recommended for appointment and also for a Commission. The latter may be a long time getting around. He is much pleased with his prospects.

I have not seen either Chris [Yetter] or Nate [Hill] to-day. All the Camps are fixed up very comfortably. I have not heard from Bro. Johnie yet. I will try & write to him again soon.

Capt. Hoskins will be returning soon. Send me a few pounds of fine cut chewing tobacco by him if convenient. I will try & write this evening for to-morrow's mail. May God bless you, my Dear Wife, & keep you in health and strength. Give my love to all the family & Remember me kindly to all our friends.

Your Affect. Husband

J. F. Culver

---

1   Mary Culver's letter of March 12 is missing from the Culver Collection.

2   J.F.C. and Lieutenant Smith had had a disagreement and were no longer close friends. With Captain Hoskins on leave and J.F.C. on staff duty, Lieutenant Smith commanded Company A.

3   James H. Gaff of Pontiac was a sergeant in Company G, 129th Illinois Infantry. Compiled Service Records of Union Soldiers, NA.

4   It has been impossible to determine how Fleming made his living.

5   Thomas Hill was a wealthy Livingston County farmer. See J.F.C.'s letter to his wife of Feb. 21, 1864, for additional details concerning this transaction.

6   Private Grunert reported that at 8 A.M., on the 19th, the brigade was assembled and marched to the parade ground two miles away, "where the regiments were posted according to their number, and had to await the arrival of the commanding General. At the appointed hour some cannon shots announced the arrival of Major Generals Hooker and Howard, who, after having passed along the front and rear of the column, took their places, and the column moved forward, delighted by the excellent music of the 33d Massachusetts regiment. The parade went off fine, and both Generals seemed well pleased with the maneuvers of the brigade." Grunert, *History of the 129th Illinois*, p. 48.

7   The Second Division, XI Corps, commanded by Brig. Gen. Adolph von Steinwehr, numbered 2,726 present for duty on March 31, 1864. *O. R.*, Ser. I, Vol. XXXII, pt. III, p. 207.

8   Andrew J. Pratt had been a 24-year-old Pontiac livery stable operator. In 1860 he was living with his wife and three children, and valued his real estate at $600 and his personal estate at $800. Eighth Census, Livingston County, State of Illinois, NA.

9   Mary E. Capron was the 36-year-old wife of Pontiac physician E. W. Capron. *Ibid.*

## 126

Head Quarters, 1st Brig., 1st Div., 11th A.C.
Lookout Valley, Sunday Evening 11 o'clock
March 20th 1864

Dear Mary

In fulfillment of my promise made this morning, I should set down to write, and, were that the only incentive, I might send an apology and go to bed. But I wish to talk with you, & then I think I shall be ready for Sleep.

I did not write all the letters to-day I intended. After writing to you, which occupied my time till dinner, I wrote a long letter to my mother, which, with the little business I had to transact, occupied my time until 3 o'clock, when Col. Harrison came into the office and invited me to ride with him to Corps Hd. Qurs. to attend services there. I accepted, of course. We heard a very profitable sermon by the Chaplain of the 33rd Massachusetts Regt. from this text, "If a man die, shall he live again?"[1] There was no singing, but one of the Regtl. Bands was present which played three very beautiful hymns. The ride was very pleasant.

Chris [Yetter] was here this afternoon. He brought over a letter which he wishes me to enclose.

In your letter recd. to-day, you remarked that Capt. Hoskins [is] looking very well. I think you were aware that he had stopped drinking. I hope he has not indulged since he got home. I intended to write to him to-day, & I may possibly enclose a short note to him in this letter.

It is quite cold out, but my fire is burning very cheerfully. If you only were here, so that I could look into your eyes & see them sparkle with love as they always do, & have your head on my shoulder, I believe I should be supremely happy. But as that cannot be to-night, I will trust in God for a happy reunion as soon as He in his good Providence sees fit. I shall look for a long letter to-morrow.

Chris [Yetter], Nate [Hill], and several of the boys were on Lookout Mountain to-day. They all give a glowing account of the sights to be seen.

I did not get Sister Beccie's letter answered, and, as I wish to answer it at length, I will not send it for a day or two. I am really ashamed to send it to you, for it is so very strongly tinctured with disloyalty that you may lose all respect for the writer.[2]

A young man by the name of Small from Grundy County called on me to-day & said that James Murphy, a cousin of my wife's, wished me to call & see him when I went to Chattanooga.[3] I sent him word that my business was such that I could see no probability of my getting there, but I would be pleased to see him at my office. I could not think who he was, but it occurred to me just now that it must be the same James Murphy, through whom W. J. Murphy passed his property. If he is, I am not very anxious to make his acquaintance. It may be a son of his, however, & I will let you know when I find out.

I have heard nothing of [Pvt.] Sammy [Murphy] yet. If he has not started [from Springfield] yet, you can tell him that our Head Qurs. are on the right hand side of the Rail Road at Wauhatchie Station on his way coming down.

I must close & write a short note to Hoskins. If he is gone, you can retain or destroy it. You are also at liberty to read it. Give my love to all the family. Tell Mother [Murphy] I expect her to take good care of my WIFE. Kiss her for me. Remember me kindly to all our friends. May our Heavenly Father bless & keep you. I shall continue to pray for my loving wife. Live close to God, and may you ever be happy.

Tell me how your health is. Have you still those pains in your hip? I think you should advise with Dr. Capron.[4] Perhaps he can cure it, & I fear sometimes that they are not caused only by your condition. Do not let any disease run too long before applying a remedy.

Good night, May Angels guard thee,

Your Affect. Husband

J. F. Culver

---

1   The chaplain of the 33d Massachusetts at this time was Isaac S. Cushman. Compiled Service Records of Union Soldiers, NA.

2   Sister Rebecca Pague, like Sister Lizzie Zug and Brother Charlie Culver, was opposed to the Emancipation Proclamation and the premise that all men are free and equal.

3   James Murphy, a son of William and Ann Courtney Murphy, was born in 1824 near Belfast, and emigrated to America with his parents in 1835. The family settled near Utica, New York, where James learned the carpenter's trade. In 1850 James, having married, moved west and settled on a farm in Grundy County, Illinois. W. J. Murphy was James' older brother. Culver, "Robert Murphy and Some of his Descendants," pp. 71-72.

4   E. W. Capron was a 37-year-old Pontiac physician. A native of New York, Dr. Capron in 1860 valued his personal estate at $600, and owned no real estate. Eighth Census, Livingston County, State of Illinois, NA.

Head Qurs., 1st Brig., 1st Div., 11th A.C.
Lookout Valley, Mch. 22nd 1864

My Dear Wife

We were very much surprised on getting up this morning to find snow eleven & 1/2 inches deep. This "Sunny South" passes all understanding; ever since we came here it has been extremely cold.[1] We may look for mud of course. The train has just worked its way through.

I have not recd. my mail for this morning yet. As I recd. no letters yesterday I hope for some to-day. I just recd. yours of the 16th inst., and am most happy to hear that you were well.[2] I had forgotten when your birth day was, but will try and remember it hereafter.[3]

I do not understand why Capt. Hoskins has not given you the letter I sent. I enclosed a letter to you with his leave of Absence, & he surely received it. The papers you sent have not come to hand yet. My health is very good. We are trying to make ourselves comfortable & it requires a good deal of effort.[4] Write to me often. May God bless you.

Your Affect. Husband

J. F. Culver

---

1   Private Dunham of Company C, writing his mother on the 22d, reported, "It has been very cold heare for several days. It snowed all last night and all day today and the snow is now all of a foot deep. I have hurd people talk about the suny South but for my part I have seen enough of it to satisfy my appetite." *Through the South with a Union Soldier*, p. 110.

2   Mary Culver's letter of March 16 is missing from the Culver Collection.

3   Mary Culver's 22d birthday had occurred on March 17. Culver, "Robert Murphy and Some of His Descendants," p. 107.

4   According to Private Dunham, the enlisted men of the 129th had built comfortable four-man log huts. Fireplaces had been erected, but the one in his hut "smokes so that we can hardly stand it some times." *Through the South with a Union Soldier*, p. 110.

Head Quarters, 1st Brigade, 1st Division, 11th Army Corps
Wauhatchie, Tenn., March 27th 1864

My Dear Wife

This morning opened out very beautiful, and all nature seems to be praising God for his goodness. I had the blues yesterday badly but succeeded in driving them away before I went to bed. I feel very happy and contented this morning.

I returned from a visit to Joe Shellenbarger & just finished writing to his mother.[1] I am very much afraid he will not recover. The Dr. allows no conversation with him, so that I do not know how he feels about it. I intend to visit him this afternoon & talk a little with him if I can get permission. All the rest are well.

I expect Capt. Hoskins in a few days and look for a letter and all the news. I wish to write to the Sabbath School this afternoon.

The train came this morning without any mail, so that I shall get no letter to-day. The roads are drying up & in a few days will be in a passable condition. Our snow has nearly all disappeared, except on the mountains we can still see it.

We heard from [Lieutenant] Mitchell yesterday, he is improving rapidly and will soon return to duty. If the campaign does not open very shortly after his return, I will try for a leave, though I see no probability of my getting it.

There is a report afloat here this morning that Hoskins is commissioned Major and that Plattenburg has been recommended for the Captaincy of Company "A."[2] It is only an alarm I think among the boys. The news reached me from the Company this morning.

I am so closely confined to the office here that I gather but little information. Alf Huetson is appointed Topographical Engineer of this Brigade and is now on duty here. An effort is being made to get him a Commission. McCartney is expecting James Murphy here to-day.[3] I do not know why Bro. Johnie has not written to me. I have written twice or three times since we went into Camp. I have recd. no letters lately from any source.

I heard singing in the Camp of the 129th Ills. this morning & think there was preaching there. I may possibly take time to write to Sis. this afternoon. I shall look for a long letter from you written to-day. The mail is just going & I must close. Give my love to All. May God bless you & help you to enjoy this holy Sabbath.

Ever your Affectionate Husband

J. F. Culver

---

1   Private Shellenbarger was confined in the brigade hospital with pneumonia. Compiled Service Records of Union Soldiers, NA.

2   Captain Hoskins was not promoted major of the 129th until June 28, 1864, but he was to rank from February 27. He would occupy the billet vacated by promotion of Thomas H. Flynn to lieutenant colonel. There was no truth to the rumor that Adjutant Plattenburg was to replace Hoskins as captain of Company A. *Ibid.*

3   Edward McCartney, a 44-year-old farmer, was mustered into service as a private in Company B, 129th Illinois, on Sept. 8, 1862. He was detached as a musician in the brigade brass band on Feb. 2, 1864, and was mustered out near Washington, D.C., June 8, 1864. *Ibid.*

⧉⧉ 129 ⧉⧉

Head Qurs., 1st Brig., 1st Div., 11th A.C.<br>Wauhatchie, Tenn., March 27th 1864

My Dear Wife

I have spent the evening thus far very pleasantly, and it seemed more like old times than usual. If you had been one of our number, I think I could have easily imagined us all at home once more.

Shortly after dark Col. Harrison called Alf. Huetson, Bradbury (my clerk) & myself into his house to sing.[1] He selected out of the "Golden Shower" those pieces with which he was familiar, & we all sang with him. The first piece was one "There is sweet rest in Heaven." I could not enumerate all, but most of them were very intimately associated with recollections of the past. We have been thus employed for over three hours. It was very pleasant for me, and I hope also profitable.

I visited the Company this afternoon & found all well, and also spent a half hour with Joe Shellenbarger. The Dr. thinks him a very little

249

better, but he is still very dangerously ill. I would have liked very much to have talked with him, but the Dr. forbid it. We still hope earnestly for his recovery.

I did not see Chris [Yetter], but he is well. Henry Polk was over to see me this evening.[2] He says his Mother called on Mr. Lyon to see if the order had been paid, &, when she found it had not been, she directed him to pay it when the order was presented.

I have enclosed a photograph of Park Pemberton which he handed me to-day.[3]

I recd. a letter from Joe Z. Culver, formerly of the 10th Penna. Vols., and now a 2nd Lieut. of the 39th U. S. Cold. Troops.[4] He says the folks at home are rather opposed to his position; if they are of the same persuasion as Sister Beccie [Pague], I have no doubt they are.

The mail got here to-day shortly after dinner but brought no letter from you. I read a letter this evening written by Mrs. Hyndman to Mrs. [James] Gaff giving a detailed account of the meetings in Pontiac.[5] They seem to have been very successful.

I did not get to church to-day, nor can I expect to have very many opportunities for going while I am in the office alone. I did not write either to the Sabbath School or to Sis. as I intended to do to-day. I have a slight headache to-night, caused, I presume, in part by singing so much. The day was so fine, & I have been so closely confined ever since we arrived here that I could not resist the temptation of sitting out of doors and consequently neglected my writing. I sat down once to write to Sis., & some business matters interrupted me. It is very doubtful whether if I delay it to-night I shall have an opportunity before next Sabbath; I will study over it while I am writing to you. I have also a letter unanswered from Sarah Williams recd. on the march.

You asked me once to whom I wished to send your likeness. Joe [Culver] has written for one, and I should be pleased if you would write to him and enclose one. I will enclose his address.

The Chicago Times you sent came to hand day before yesterday. I have read the N.Y. Ledger up to No. 4. The story is making a very interesting change. The boys have concluded that Ishmael & Claudia will yet make a match.

I ran across one of my Sabbath School scholars to-day. He has been in the regiment for over two months, & I never saw him to know him before. His name is James Funk.[6] Did you know him? He says he tried to speak to me once on the march, but I did not stop. I presume I was busy.

I have enclosed the last letter I recd. from Sister Jennie [Cheston]. Write to me often. I have not been able to write every day but never omit more than one day, & sometimes I write two. I hope for a good long one. I have concluded not to mail any other letters to-night, as it is quite late, & I wish to get rid of this headache before morning. May our Heavenly Father bless you. Give my love to Mother and Maggie, and remember me kindly to all our friends. Neither Mother or Maggie have answered my last letters. Why don't they write? I earnestly hope you are enjoying good health. Let us pray for each other. I have enjoyed much of the presence of God to-day, & I feel that this has been a good day for me. I hope you have been richly with the presence of our God. May we in his good Providence soon be permitted to mingle our voices together in praise and supplication, sweet rest and peaceful slumbers. May holy angels guard thee.

Good night,

Your Affect. Husband

J. F. Culver

---

1   William H. Bradbury, a 33-year-old lawyer, was mustered into service on Sept. 8, 1862, as a private in Company B, 129th Illinois. He was mustered out on June 8, 1865, near Washington, D.C. *Ibid.*

2   Henry P. Polk, a 21-year-old farmer, was mustered into service on Sept. 8, 1862, as a private in Company A, 129th Illinois. Private Polk, while on a foraging expedition near Averysboro, N.C., on March 15, 1865, was captured and paroled by the Confederates. He was mustered out of service at Springfield, Illinois, June 11, 1865. Compiled Service Records of Union Soldiers, NA.

3   Allson P. Pemberton, a 20-year-old farmer, enlisted as a private in Company A, 129th Illinois Infantry on Sept. 19, 1862. Private Pemberton was wounded in the right arm at New Hope Church, Ga., May 28, 1864, and hospitalized at Murfreesboro, Tenn. that summer. He rejoined the unit in September and was mustered out near Washington, D.C., June 8, 1865. *Ibid.*

4   Twenty-one-year-old Joseph Z. Culver was mustered into federal service at Pittsburgh, Pa., for three years as a private in Company D, 10th Pennsylvania Reserves, on Sept. 11, 1862. He was honorably discharged on Feb. 28, 1864, to accept a commission as 2d lieutenant in the 39th U.S. Colored Troops. Culver was mustered in as 2d lieutenant, Company C, 39th U.S.C.T., at Baltimore on Feb. 29, 1864. He was promoted to 1st lieutenant on Sept. 13, 1864, and transferred to Company K. *Ibid.*

5   Mrs. Hyndman of Pontiac had described in her letter the revivals being held by the local churches.

6   James R. Funk, an 18-year-old student, was recruited into service on Dec. 17, 1863, at Springfield, Ill., as a private in Company C, 129th Illinois. Private Funk was hospitalized at Chattanooga from May 23, 1864, until mid-September. He was mustered out with the regiment near Washington, D.C., June 8, 1865. Compiled Service Records of Union Soldiers, NA.

Head Quarters, 1st Brigade, 1st Division, 11th Army Corps
Wauhatchie, Tenn., March 30th 1864

My Dear Wife

Your letter of the 22nd inst. came to hand this morning.[1] It was my intention to write you a long letter last night, but my tent smoked so that I could not keep a fire in it. I went in the early part of the evening to see Joe Shellenbarger; I found him getting better.[2] He is so much better this morning that I feel confident of his recovery. Afterward I went to see Capt. Hoskins & had a long talk with him about the sights he saw at Pontiac.

When I got back to my Quarters it was midnight & several papers awaiting me, so I went to bed without writing. We will be so very busy for the next week that I cannot promise you any very lengthy letters. I feel provoked that I did not write for some things that I need very much and have no opportunity of getting down here. I want some socks badly. If you get another chance, send me at least a dozen pairs of cotton socks.

I have not heard from Bro. Johnie; I can't see why. To-morrow evening Sis is to be married. I will try and bear it in mind if I am not too busy.

I judge the hour to be about 3 o'clock, as the train goes North about 4 or 5. Chris [Yetter] has been sick for a few days but not seriously; he was walking around this morning.

I am glad to hear of the "extremely interesting, substantially, unfashionably &c."[3] You can give them my hearty congratulations. I would like to hear of the progress Mrs. Culver is making in the same direction. Capt. Hoskins says you are looking well. I do not know whether [Lt.] Smith hears from his wife or not; I never asked him & have not heard.

I told you that your idea of working in Strevell's store was distasteful to me.[4] I presume that it is not very much more so than any other pursuit in which you might engage; for, under the circumstances, I earnestly hope you will not bind yourself to any employment. I must confess, however, to some unpleasant recollections in connection with your suggestion.

My health is excellent. The weather is still very cold, not more so than it is in Illinois, I presume. I have been trying to gather all the news from Hoskins, much relates to strangers & is not so interesting.

Send me a couple pounds of fine cut chewing to-bacco if you get a chance. Some of Dehner's is preferable. I will write to Thomas Hill as soon as I can get time.[5] The mail is about to close. Alf [Huetson] just recd. Ledger No. 5 in which Bee and Ishmael have opened a Bee-hive. He seems much pleased. Alf is becoming quite famous in his new profession [topographical engineer]. His prospects for promotion are quite flattering. I believe he is the best Engineer in the Department, & he will soon reap the reward of his industry and perserverance. Every body not mentioned is well.

Write to me often and long letters.

May God bless you and make you supremely happy. Give my love to all & accept my heart's best and warmest affections for yourself.

Very affectly.,

Your Husband,

J. F. Culver

---

1  Mary Culver's letter of March 22 is missing from the Culver Collection.

2  This was a rally before a fatal relapse. Private Shellenbarger died the next day, March 31, 1864. Compiled Service Records of Union Soldiers, NA.

3  This phrase refers to the marriage of a Livingston County couple with whom the Culvers were acquainted.

4  Jason W. Strevell owned a general store and had hired Mary Culver as a part-time clerk.

5  For additional information on Thomas Hill, see J.F.C.'s letter of February 21, 1864.

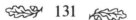 131

Head Quarters, 1st Brigade, 1st Division, 11th Army Corps
Wauhatchie, Tenn., Sunday, April 3rd 1864

My Dear Wife

Your letter of 29th March came to hand this morning.[1] I am very happy to hear that you are well. This day opened very beautiful. I was on my way to the Company when I recd. your letter, & have just returned. I intended to delay writing until this evening, but I have an opportunity to send it by a man going home on furlough. I haste to write before the train goes north.

I found the Company all well. I did not see Chris [Yetter] or Nate [Hill] but heard they were well. There is still considerable uneasiness about the promotion to major. Nothing definite is yet known.

I cannot understand why Cox is making inquiries about his policy.[2] I will write to him, however, and also to the Insurance Company. It occurs to my mind that the policy on our house may have expired. I think it runs for three years from May, 1862, but it is barely possible that it is for only two years. I wish you would make inquiry. The policy is in John Dehner's hands, and is assigned to Dehner and Russell.[3]

I recd. a letter from [Lieutenant] Mitchell yesterday; he is improving slowly but will not be able to come up for some time yet. My health is very good. I recd. a letter from Bro. Johnie yesterday & will write to him to-day.[4] I have his letter. I am glad to hear from Bro. Sammy, & will inform Bro. Johnie.[5] Sis will have returned by the time this letter reaches you. Give her my hearty congratulations; I may possibly get time to write to her to-day.

A private of Co. "E" of our Regt. named Hildreth, went home on furlough yesterday.[6] I did not know he was going until just before the train started, or I would have sent a letter by him. He promised to call and see you & bring such things as I want. I need badly about a dozen prs. cotton socks & two shirts. Get the longest shirts you can. I think Henry [Greenebaum] will give you some good ones. I will enclose a note to him. If the man does not come, you can send them by first opportunity.

Give my love to all. I am very happy that you write so often. I will write again, possibly this afternoon. May our Father in Heaven keep you in perfect health and make you happy. Give my love to Mother and Maggie.

Your Affect. Husband

J. F. Culver

---

1 Mary Culver's letter of March 29 is missing from the Culver Collection.

2 David Cox was a 47-year-old Pontiac Township farmer. In 1860 he was living with his wife, Gracie, and their six children, and valued his real estate at $6,000 and his personal estate at $600. Eighth Census, Livingston County, State of Illinois, NA.

3 John Dehner, a Pontiac merchant, was born in Germany in 1808. In 1860 he was living with his wife, Jane, and valued his real estate at $16,000 and his personal estate at $12,000. *Ibid.*

4   Sergt. John Murphy, whose unit was camped at Loudon, Tennessee, had written, "I have been anxious to hear from you on Sammy's account. I vainly hoped to hear of his whereabouts through you. I can get nothing definite about him. About a month ago he was in Springfield. We have received the descriptive rolls of some 14 or 15 recruits and only three of them arrived at the Battery. Some of them have been a month and a half on the road and one young men . . . died in Indiana on his way to our company. I wish Sammy could get here. It is two-fold harder and more unpleasant for a new soldier to be knocking around in barracks than to go at once into the field."

Sergeant Murphy reported that all was quiet in East Tennessee, and the battery was "preparing with all possible dispatch for the Spring Campaign. We are temporarily in the Dept. of the Ohio, and the only Battery in this department that is equipped for marching and as a consequence if there is a movement made soon in this section of country, we will be called out. I hope that we may have from 30 to 60 days longer in which to prepare. It is quite difficult to get the necessary equipment here. We are pretty well supplied with horses." John Murphy to J.F.C., March 22, 1864, Culver Collection.

5   Pvt. Sammy Murphy had written J.F.C. from Camp Yates, Springfield, Ill., on March 22. Sammy explained that he would have written sooner, but he "expected to leave here soon and thought I'd wait and write when I got to another place. They have sent away the Inft. and Cav. recruits and I think the Art. will leave soon, but I have thought so for some time. I am the only one for Battery 'M' that is here, and I would rather be with it than here.

"The weather has been cold here for a few days past, but it is getting warmer now, and begins to look like spring. Camp Yates is situated one mile west of Springfield. It is a pretty nice place for a camp, and we have pretty good water. The Governor's mansion is just a little ways from camp." Sam Murphy to J.F.C., March 22, 1864, Culver Collection.

6   Joshua T. Hildreth, a 30-year-old farmer, was mustered into service on Sept. 8, 1862, as a private in Company E, 129th Illinois. He was mustered out near Washington, D.C., on June 8, 1865. Compiled Service Records of Union Soldiers, NA.

 132

Head Quarters, 1st Brigade, 1st Div., 11th A.C.
Wauhatchie, April 6th 1864

My Dear Wife

Yours of March 26th 1864 came to hand two days ago, but the one I recd. by Capt. Hoskins was three days later, Mch. 29th.[1] I looked for a letter to-day, but it did not come. I expect it in the morning but will not delay writing for fear I may not have an opportunity before the mail goes out.

Unless you can get someone to collect the amount due from Fleming, there is but little prospect of your ever getting it.[2] It would not be policy for you to attempt to approach him if he is so constantly drunk. Can Remick do nothing with him?

I have not seen Chris [Yetter] since I recd. your letter. I read both letters. I told him I thought you would not understand him, but he felt so sure that you would "only think it was him" that I consented to let it go. He is more deeply interested than he wishes to make known, & he wished to surprise you at guessing so near the truth.

I recd. a very good letter from Joe Shellenbarger's sister to-day.[3] It was dated the same day I telegraphed to them & was sent before my dispatch reached them. I sympathize with them. They wrote so affectionately of him that the affliction will be deep and lasting. May God comfort their hearts.

I recd. a letter from Bro. Wes [Culver] to-day.[4] He tries to explain Sister Beccie's letter. Mother was not at home. I will send you his letter when I get time to answer it. I do not fully understand what school exhibition you speak of and who had charge of it.

My health is very good. I moved into the new house yesterday evening. It is very pleasant for office purposes; we have six desks and tables in it, all occupied so that there is but little room left. Ben Thompson, Henry Polk, the two Pembertons, Billy Sheets, and Charlie Peck built it. Ira Ong helped a few days.[5] The boys are now planting Pine trees and making gravel walks.[6] The weather has been very pleasant to-day.

We received information unofficially this evening that the 11th & 12th Army Corps will be consolidated and form the 1st Army Corps to be commanded by Genl. Hooker.[7] Another rumor says that as soon as the balance of the troops come up, we will advance by way of Knoxville on Richmond.[8] This last is most probably unfounded & unreliable. The former is probably correct.

Everything is quiet here. A soldier's wife of the 102th Ills. arrived here to-day on the cars. I did not see her but heard of her arrival. There are some of the soldier's wives of the Eastern Regts. here. I saw one or two in the neighborhood of Genl. Howard's Hd. Qrs. I cannot imagine how they stay here, but almost everything is possible now-a-days.

It has drawn near midnight. Dr. Reagan has been here for the last hour.[9] I let him read Miss Shellenbarger's letter, & our conversation has been directed by it to religion. He was very much interested in Joe Shellenbarger & done all for him that could be done. It is said still water runs deep, so it proves in his case. He was always so quiet & seemed to be moved by nothing, but to-night I was permitted to look into his heart & I find it full of love and sympathy. He was called away to attend a patient but requested another opportunity to talk about heartfelt religion. I feel very much benefited by his company. He is a very learned man & is our Brigade Surgeon.

May God bless you, my Dear Wife, and keep you in health and strength. Late as it is, I think it my duty to answer Joe's sister's letter, so good night. May Heaven's blessings rest upon you.

Your Affect. Husband

J. F. Culver

Lieut

I almost signed my official signature.

---

1  Mary Culver's letter of March 26 is missing from the Culver Collection.

2  Fleming's debt to J.F.C. dated to before his muster into service on Sept. 8, 1862.

3  Delia Shellenbarger of Covington, Ill., had written J.F.C. on March 31, the day her brother died. Delia thanked J.F.C. for his letters of the 24th, 26th, and 27th, and expressed regret to learn of her brother's illness. "How thankful we are," she wrote, "that he has friends there to take care of him. Oh! that he were near that we might take care of him. But God wills it otherwise and we must submit. You say he may get well, if he *does* get better, we would like so much to have him brought home. Can you? Will you? do all in your power to have him get a furlough?" Delia Shellenbarger to J.F.C., March 31, 1864, Culver Collection.

4  The subject letter from Wes Culver is missing from the Culver Collection.

5  James Pemberton, a 23-year-old farmer, was mustered into service on Sept. 8, 1862, as a private in Company A, 129th Illinois. Private Pemberton was killed in action at Averysboro, N.C., March 16, 1865. William H. Sheets, a 20-year-old farmer, was mustered into service on Sept. 8, 1862, as a private in Company A, 129th Illinois. Private Sheets was slightly wounded in the back at Resaca, May 15, 1864, and was mustered out with the regiment on June 8, 1865, near Washington, D.C. Ira Ong, a 28-year-old farmer, was mustered into service on Sept. 8, 1862, as a private in Company A, 129th Illinois, and mustered out on June 8, 1865, near Washington, D.C. Benjamin Thompson, a 31-year-old farmer, was mustered into service on Sept. 8, 1862, as a private in Company A, 129th Illinois. Thompson was promoted to corporal on May 9, 1863, and to sergeant on March 1, 1865. He was mustered out with the regiment on June 8, 1865, near Washington, D.C. Compiled Service Records of Union Soldiers, NA.

6  Like other Civil War soldiers, the men of the 129th Illinois beautified their camps. Private Grunert reported that on April 6 "some decorations were added to the camp of Company D." Grunert, *History of the 129th Illinois*, p. 50.

7  On April 4, 1864, the War Department issued G.O. 144 consolidating the XI and XII Corps, and designating the new unit the XX Corps. Maj. Gen. Joseph Hooker would lead the XX Corps; Maj. Gen. Oliver O. Howard, former commander of the XI Corps, would

relieve Maj. Gen. Gordon Granger as leader of the IV Corps; and Maj. Gen. Henry Slocum, commander of the XII Corps, would report to Maj. Gen. William T. Sherman for reassignment. *O.R.*, Ser. I, Vol. XXXII, pt. III, p. 258.

8  There was no substance to the rumor that the "army group" being massed by General Sherman in and around Chattanooga would advance on Richmond, Va., by way of East Tennessee and Knoxville. When the spring campaign opened, Sherman's "army group" would advance into northwest Georgia—its mission to be the destruction of the Confederate Army of Tennessee.

9  Amos W. Ragan was mustered into federal service as surgeon of the 70th Indiana Infantry on Aug. 11, 1862. On Jan. 12, 1864, Ragan was detailed as brigade surgeon of the 1st Brigade, First Division, XI Corps, and when the XI and XII Corps were consolidated, he was appointed brigade surgeon, 1st Brigade, Third Division, XX Corps. Compiled Service Records of Union Soldiers, NA.

 133

Head Quarters, 1st Brigade, 1st Division, 11th Army Corps
Wauhatchie, Tenn., April 10th 1864

My Dear Wife

I delayed writing last night hoping to hear from you by this morning's mail. The train did not get in until just before noon, but it brought me no letter. I felt so much disappointed that I did not attempt to write before the mail went North.

I recd. the New York Observer and Ledger for which I am much obliged. I wrote to Mr. Remick last night. My health is good. I am sorry to learn in your letters of March 30th & 31st, the last I received, that you were again contending with the blues.[1] I hope, however, you succeeded in speedily dispelling them.

You must have been mistaken in Capt. Hoskins' Commission as no news of that kind has yet reached us; besides his appointment could not be made until Flynn's commission arrives here and he is mustered, making a vacancy in the next in rank.[2] I have given myself very little trouble about the matter, though I think still that Hoskins will receive the promotion.

The weather to-day has been April like—both sunshine and clouds; it sprinkled rain once or twice but not much. Rev. Mr. Ruter of Chicago

(Universalist) preached in the camp of the 102th Ills. I did not go to hear him; I saw a great many going from some of the Regts.

The 11th & 12th Corps have been consolidated and now form the 20th Army Corps, commd. by Genl. Hooker; Genl. Howard, who commanded our Corps, has been assigned to the 4th A.C.[3] No orders have been yet received announcing the change, but Genl. Howard started for Loudon yesterday to assume command. We regret his loss very much.

I saw Chris [Yetter] to-day. He said he would write to you making an explanation of his last letter. I advised him to do so immediately as I thought you did not understand him. Nate [Hill] has been on picket for two days and has not yet returned. I expected during the week to talk to the Company to-day, but the boys were all on Picket. I have received no letters lately. I will try and write a letter to Sis to-night and will also add more to this if I am not disturbed. For the present, I hope God will bless you.

April 10th, 11 o'clock night

Dearest—I have been out riding this evening, visiting the Picket Lines & feel much refreshed. It was a great change to get from close confinement out amid nature. Everything is green, fresh and beautiful. Desolate as the Country [is], yet nature succeeds in wearing a Smile.

Shortly after I returned, Chris Yetter called in, and after conversing with him about an hour, I walked over to the Company. I did not get back until nearly ten o'clock & found the officers here discussing the war. All have gone to bed now, & I have sat down to finish my letter, as I shall have no time to-morrow before the mail closes. I feel thankful to God to-night for all his mercies and also feel encouraged to apply myself diligently to the performance of every duty. I commenced a letter to Sis at dark, but was interrupted, & it is doubtful whether it gets finished, and yet I feel it is my duty to write something to her.

Allen Fellows sent me a piece of maple sugar this evening and sent word that he would tell me about it the first time he saw me. Yetter wrote a letter to you which he handed me to read, but he took it back to modify it somewhat. We have no further news to-night. I am hoping anxiously to hear from you by to-morrow's mail. May our Father in Heaven bless you. Give my love to Mother [Murphy] and Maggie and Remember me kindly to all our friends. I think I will add a few lines to Sis's letter and enclose it to you. Please hand it to her after you read it. Be of good cheer and trust still in God who is able to keep us. Give me a particular account of the state of your health. I have felt a vague presentment to-day that you are not well; I know not why. Pray for me. Write often. Good night.

Your Affect. Husband

J. F. Culver

P.S.
Please enclose a few stamps. I find it very difficult to get them here. I am very thankful for those already received. I hope we may be paid off soon. I fear you are short of funds.

---

1   Mary Culver's letters of March 30 and 31 are missing from the Culver Collection.

2   Andrew Cropsey, the regiment's lieutenant colonel, had resigned his commission on Feb. 27, 1864, and had returned to Illinois. It was May 1 before Maj. Thomas H. Flynn of Winchester was promoted to fill the billet vacated by Cropsey, and June 28 before Captain Hoskins was commissioned major. Some of the soldiers preferred Captain Perry of Company C to be promoted to major rather than Captain Hoskins. *Through the South with a Union Soldier*, p. 113.

3   General Howard on April 8 issued a general order formally taking leave of the XI Corps. *O.R.*, Ser. I, Vol. XXXII, pt. III, p. 303.

 134

Head Qurs., 1st Brig., 1st Div., 11th A.C.<br/>Wauhatchie, Tenn., April 12th 1864

My Dear Wife

Yours of April 2nd came to hand yesterday, also one from Mother [Murphy].[1] I am very happy to learn of your good health. Your letter had been torn open by some one. Tell Mother I will write to her very soon.

I expect an opportunity to visit Chattanooga and Point Lookout to-day, so that I can only write a line or two. I understand that some member of Co. "E" goes home on furlough to-day, & I wish to send this with him.

I will have a long letter to write soon, giving you a description of my visit. Do not allow yourself to feel uneasy for me when the wind blows for I am in a very comfortable house. We are all well and getting along well. I look for another letter from you this morning. Kiss Mother for me and Remember me kindly to all. May God bless you and make you happy.

Your Affect. Husband

J. F. Culver

---

1 The subject letters are missing from the Culver Collection.

꿏꿏 135 ꙩꙩ

Head. Qurs., 1st Brigade, 1st Division, 11th A.C.
Wauhatchie, Tenn., April 13th 1864

My Dear Wife

I did not have the pleasure of hearing from you to-day as I expected, nor did I write last night as I promised. I felt very confident yesterday morning of getting an opportunity to visit Lookout Point but was disappointed.

My time was occupied in getting the yard fixed up. I planted cedar all around the yard; it looks more like a fancy garden now than anything else. We have four good comfortable houses with a gravel walk along the front for a pavement and a gravel walk to the road. We have also built a fence around our yard with pine and cedar around the border and on both sides of the walks, with an arch over the gate.

Co. "A" have just completed one of the finest Arches I ever saw. I cannot fully describe it. It is after the gothic style, with one principal and four smaller entrances. It is about 20 feet high. The center is full of strange devices, on one side is the mall and wedge, the weapons of Abe Lincoln; on the other side, a bundle of sticks, a symbol of strength. Over the center piece, the letter "A" made of mountain moss, and on each side:

*261*

129 Regt. Ills.

A

Just above the word Regt. is another gothic structure, which I cannot describe. The design was made by Alf. [Huetson], & he has promised to make a sketch of it for me.

Genl. Hooker inspected the Camps to-day, with Genl. Ward & Col. Harrison. All say it is the finest Structure of the kind they ever saw. The boys are very proud of it. I was over this evening; all are well.

Maj. Genl. [George H.] Thomas will review our Division to-morrow.[1] Great preparations are being made. We expect to make a good impression and will try hard to.

My health is very good. I have been working around the Head Qurs. all day to-day & feel a little tired to-night, yet I could spend a few hours talking with you if you were here to sit on my lap to-night. I can think of a great deal to say that would appear foolish on paper perhaps. There is no news. Nothing has been heard concerning promotions in the Regt. yet; at least, I have heard nothing. I wish very much you would see our place now; everything seems so pleasant.

Last night the Band of the 79th Ohio serenaded us; it was delicious. They also sang several airs. I hear one of the members of our Band playing on an old horn out at the Band Quarters. It sounds very sweet. We are expecting our instruments every day. I hear that the party that went North for them, sent to New-York for them & went home to wait for them. It would have been an excellent chance for me. As their order was unlimited, they have been away about 23 days already. But I hope to get home, if God Spares my life, to stay by and by; until then let us ask God for patience. May he bless you with health and happiness. I often muse thinking over our life from our first acquaintance. Has it not been very happy even amid our sorrows? May "Our Father in Heaven" continue his blessings to us.

I intended to write to Mother [Murphy] to-night, but it has got very late & I must be up very early. I detailed 50 men to clean off the Review ground, & they will report before I can get up unless I get to bed soon. It is now nearly 11 o'clock.

Tell me if you are happy. My heart yearns to-night for communion with you. Tell me all your troubles; do not fear to trouble me, I will try and cheer you. I often long for an opportunity to contribute to your happiness and comfort. Rest assured that you have my heart's best affections.

Next to God and my Country, I love my wife. Do you not know it? If I thought you did not, I would not say so, and yet I know you love to hear it. In you is centered all my desire of life, and I believe to secure your happiness is my highest Ambition outside of duty, and I believe you feel it so. Kiss Mother for me; I will certainly write to her soon. Remember me kindly to all. May Holy angels guard thee to-night, and may "Our Father in Heaven" keep you.

Farewell,

Your Affectionate Husband

J. F. Culver

---

1 General Hooker's newly constituted XX Corps belonged to General Thomas' Army of the Cumberland.

 136

Head Qurs., 1st Brig., 1st Div., 11th A.C.<br/>Wauhatchie, Tenn., April 15th 1864

My Dear Wife

I recd. three letters since I last wrote: two yesterday and one to-day, mailed, respectively, Apr. 7th, 9th & 11th.[1] I am very happy to hear from you so frequently & am sorry that I have not written more regularly. I will try and answer all of your letters to-night if I am not interrupted.

We received information of the consolidation of the 11th & 12th Corps; the order announcing it will appear to-morrow, I presume. We are 1st Brig., 3rd Div., 20th A.C. Genl. Ward commands the Brigade, & Genl. Butterfield the Division.[2] As a matter of course, the present Brigade Commander [Col. Benjamin Harrison] and *Staff* will be sent back to their Regts., so that in a few days at farthest, I will be with Co. "A" again. It is not known what changes will be made, as the Staff of Genl. Butterfield will be selected from this Division.

Col. Harrison was called to Corps Hd. Qurs. this evening to give counsel in the selection of Staff Officers. He asked me if I desired a position, but I had not thought of it and deferred giving an answer at

*263*

present. There are very few positions that I prefer over my position in the Company, especially with my present prospects of promotion [to Captain]. Nothing has yet been learned concerning the promotions in the Regts. There must be something wrong, but where we cannot tell. We will soon hear the decision be it what it may. We regret very much the change from Harrison to Ward's command, but time will rectify all things.[3]

Col. Harrison has just informed me that he has recommended me as A.D.C. on the Division Staff (Maj. Genl. Butterfield's).[4] I do not know that I should refuse if I were selected, but I feel as if I would prefer staying with the Company. Staff duty costs much more, & I feel the necessity of Saving until our home is paid for. It has cost me nearly all I made in two months to keep me three, & that is a very heavy tax. There are many advantages it is true, and I presume more honor, but not more pleasure and much more responsibility. Besides I have the impression that Genl. Butterfield is inclined to be a little fast, and fear my qualifications would not come up to his standard.

I was at the Company this evening. All are well. The boys seem very glad at the prospect of my returning.

I am sorry to hear of so much sickness in Pontiac. I hope to hear soon of Bro. Johnson's recovery.[5] Mrs. Shellenbarger is a widow. I recd. a letter yesterday from Mrs. Minton, a married sister of Joe's; she has besides a Brother in the Army of the Ohio at Knoxville and another sister, the one who wrote the letter sent you. Mr. Paige has not yet returned.

I bought a pair of shirts of Capt. Hoskins thinking you might not have an opportunity to send any very soon, & I was much in need of them. The socks will be very acceptable, as those I have are much worn.

You say "Mrs. Culver is beginning to make a little progress in her present study," but I do not know what the study is. I am very happy that your headaches disapper so readily. Hoskins said nothing "of our circumstances," what could he say?[6] I hope Bro. Sammy may soon get to the Battery; it will be much more pleasant for him. I would have written to him but expected him along almost daily.

I fear you will not be able to get Fleming to settle. If I thought it would do any [good], I would write to him.

I am happy to hear that Sis. enjoys life so well & hope it may continue so. Remember me kindly to her. I hope your Sabbath School class may prove interesting. I am sorry, however, to hear that Bro. Fisher has left.[7] What has become of his shop? Is the Boyer Estate settled up yet?

I was surprised to hear of Bob Edgington's ill health.[8] He has been around all the time and looks well and hearty, and I never heard that he was sick. Harry McDowell can very easily get an order returning him to his Regt. if he will report his desire to Col. Case. I am certainly surprised to hear of his treatment of Miss Thayer and cannot understand it.[9] I supposed he was more gallant and gentlemanly.

Our review came off yesterday but was not as good as those we had at Nashville which you saw.[10] I was much pleased with the appearance of Maj. Genl. Thomas; he is quite an old man and very pleasant looking.[11]

The balance of the staff [Harrison's] have been discussing their prospects under the new organization, and I have been writing at intervals until I have occupied nearly 4 hours in producing this letter. I fear you will find it disconnected and uninteresting. Continue to write often. I am very happy to hear from you so often. It is five minutes past 12 o'clock, & I must go to bed. I will send this letter by Mr. Amos Clark who is going home on furlough to-morrow.[12]

May God in his infinite Mercy bless you with health and bestow upon you the richest of his Grace. Remember me to all. Accept the love and affection with a kiss from

Your Affect. Husband

J. F. Culver

Direct as before until I can safely notify you of the change [of address].

---

1  Mary Culver's letters of April 7, 9, and 11 are missing from the Culver Collection.

2  General Thomas' order announcing consolidation of the XI and XII Corps and organization of the XX Corps was dated April 14, 1864. Maj. Gen. Daniel Butterfield, before assuming command of the Third Division, had served as chief of staff to Generals Hooker and George G. Meade. He had accompanied Hooker to the west. General Thomas on April 8 had suggested to General Sherman that Butterfield be assigned a division in Hooker's corps. Today, Butterfield is best remembered as composer of the bugle call "Taps".

Brigaded with the 129th Illinois in General Ward's 1st Brigade would be the 70th Indiana, 79th Ohio, and the 102d and 105th Illinois Infantry Regiments. *O.R.*, Ser. I, Vol. XXXII, pt. III, pp. 292, 364; Warner, *Generals in Blue*, pp. 62-63.

3  A number of soldiers in the brigade had even stronger opinions regarding General Ward. Lt. Charles H. Cox of the 70th Indiana had written on July 22, 1863, "Genl. Ward has gone to Nashville and will probably go home on a furlough (if he can get one) which I hope he can and will go home and *stay*, it would be for the 'good of the service' if he should. He is the *ranking* Brigadier in this Dept., but by his incompetency, has been continually kept in the *rear. Confound* such a General as Ward!" "The Civil War Letters of Charles Harding Cox," edited by Lorma Luter Sylvester, *Indiana Magazine of History*, Vol. LXVIII, No. 1, p. 62.

4  A.D.C. is the abbreviation for aide-de-camp.

5  Morris Johnson had moved in 1859 to Livingston County from Virginia. He and his wife, Minerva Ellir Johnson, were the parents of two children. Johnson was engaged in merchandising. *History of Livingston County*, p. 637.

6   This is a reference to Mrs. Culver being five months pregnant.

7   It has been impossible to further identify Bro. Fisher.

8.  Twenty-eight-year-old Robert P. Edgington was mustered into service on Sept. 8, 1862, as 1st lieutenant of Company C, 129th Illinois Infantry. Lieutenant Edgington was placed on detached duty on Nov. 14, 1864, as quartermaster of the Third Division Hospital, XX Corps. He was mustered out near Washington, D.C., June 8, 1865. Compiled Service Records of Union Soldiers, NA.

9   Lt. Harry McDowell, who had returned to Illinois on recruiting detail, had jilted Emma Thayer, a local belle.

10   Private Grunert reported, "At 8 o'clock the brigade marched to the parade ground and soon after General Thomas appeared. Generals Hooker, Ward, Butterfield, &c. were present. The parade was one of the finest we had ever witnessed." According to Private Dunham, "there was something like eight thousand soldiers present," and it was a grand review. Grunert, *History of the 129th Illinois*, p. 50; *Through the South with a Union Soldier*, p. 115.

11   General Thomas at 47 was prematurely gray which made him appear much older than his years.

12   Amos Clark, a 39-year-old farmer, was mustered into service on Sept. 8, 1862, as a private in Company G, 129th Illinois Infantry. Private Clark was granted a 30-day furlough on April 16, 1864. He rejoined the regiment in January 1865 and was mustered out near Washington, D.C., June 8, 1865. Compiled Service Records of Union Soldiers, NA.

 137

Hd. Qurs. Co. "A", 129th Ills. Vols.[1]
Wauhatchie, Tenn., April 20th 1864

My Dear Wife

I recd. a pass this evening with recommend[ation] to get pass from Chattanooga to Cleveland.[2] I will start on the 5 o'clock train to-morrow morning, & will try to get to Bro. Johnie & Sammy to-morrow if possible. My pass is only for three days.

Your letter of 13th & 14th arrived this evening.[3] I am happy to hear that you are well. May God preserve your health.

There is a rumor here of a battle at Cleveland to-day.[4] If it be true, I may not get through to-morrow. I will write again in a few days. Give my love to all. May our Father in Heaven keep you, and so endow you by grace Divine that you may be continually happy.

Good night,

Your Affect. Husband

J. F. Culver

_____

1  On April 18 Lieutenant Culver was detailed for temporary duty as an aide-de-camp to General Butterfield, and 48 hours later he was relieved from that assignment and rejoined Company A, 129th Illinois. Compiled Service Records of Union Soldiers, NA.

2  Company M, 1st Illinois Artillery, the unit to which Sergt. John Murphy was assigned, had left Loudon, Tenn., on April 18 for Cleveland, Tenn. *Adjutant General's Report, State of Illinois*, Vol. VIII, p. 666.

3  The subject letter is missing from the Culver Collection.

4  There was no truth to the story that there had been a battle at Cleveland. Reports reaching General Thomas' Chattanooga headquarters indicated that General Johnston's Army of Tennessee was in its camp in and around Dalton, Ga. *O.R.*, Ser. I, Vol. XXXII, pt. III, pp. 411-12.

 138

Head Qurs. Co. "A", 129th Ills, Vols.
Wauhatchie, Tenn., April 24th 1864

My dear Wife

I arrived here safe on yesterday evening. Bro. Johnie came with me & is now here.[1] We went to church this forenoon, & this afternoon we will take a walk to see some of his acquaintances. He will leave for his Battery this evening or in the morning.

Yours of the 14th I recd. on my return last night.[2] I cannot understand why my letters do not reach you regularly; I have certainly written. I will write a long letter to-night if Bro. Johnie leaves, &, if not, I will write to-morrow.

We left Bro. Sammy very well. All are well here. I recd. a letter from W. O. Russell & A. J. Cropsey this morning, also from Lieut. H. H. McDowell.

I hope to hear from you soon again. I close in haste. May God bless you with the riches of his Grace. Give my love to all.

Your Affect. Husband

J. F. Culver

---

1  Sergt. John Murphy, having received a three-day pass, accompanied J.F.C. on his return to Wauhatchie from Cleveland.

2  Mary Culver's letter of April 14 is missing from the Culver Collection.

 139

Head Qurs., Company "A", 129th Ills, Vols.
Wauhatchie, Tenn., April 24th 1864

My Dear Wife

This has been a Holy Day, & I feel much refreshed. We had preaching at 10 A.M. Bro. Cotton preached the funeral of Jos. Shellenbarger & 4 others who died since we left Nashville.[1]

At 1 o'clock there was a Sabbath School organized. I took Bro. Johnie around to see some of his acquaintances, as he leaves very early in the morning, intending to go as soon as the Officers were elected & thus evade occupying an Official position,[2] but on entering, was informed that I was elected superintendent. I did not wish by any means to evade my duty, but I thought there were others who were more capable & I preferred to receive instruction rather than teach. I talked a short time this afternoon, and by request exhorted to-night from Ephesians, 2nd chap. & 8th verse. I had good liberty and feel rejoiced in spirit.

Bro. Johnie & Chris [Yetter] have been so busily engaged in talking over their private affairs that I am in my tent alone to talk a while with you; I will write until they come in. Bro. Johnie's visit has been very pleasant, & I am very sorry that he is compelled to return so soon.

In your last letter, you express great uneasiness over the rumor of our leaving this valley. I hope you will not allow any movements we may make [to] give you any alarm. There is a prospect of a forward movement but none of a battle.[3] It is so absolutely necessary that you should rest easy & be happy under your present circumstances.

I offered Sergt. Gaff my congratulations on his prospects, but he said it was stale news. Harry McDowell has much to say about Miss Emma Thayer in his letter; he eulogizes her very highly.

I hope you recd. the letter for Sunday you were expecting. About the time I was closing up my official business as A.A.A.G., I did not write as often as I was very busy and had but meagre opportunities.[4] I did intend to write a considerable length, but Johnie & Chris came in & several others, & I have been detained until it is almost midnight. So I will close & embrace the earliest opportunity to give you full particulars of my visit. We are all well. May Holy Angels guard thee to-night. I may possibly be able to add a few lines to-morrow. Give my love to all. Write often.

Your Affect. Husband

J. F. Culver

Monday morning — April 25th

My Dear Wife

Bro. Johnie has not got up yet, & I will add a few lines. Here comes Alf. [Huetson] with my mail, two letters from you, both dated the 19th, one containing stamps.[5] The one of the 18th aluded to has not yet arrived.

I am very happy to hear that you are in such good health and spirits. May God continue his blessings. I have now on hand four or five letters, unanswered. I ought to answer them this morning, but John has remained here to-day in order to visit Lookout Point; &, as I have not been there yet, I desire to go with him. I have only written a short note at a time for two weeks, & I feel that I ought to write a long letter soon. I am glad you are taking music lessons & hope it may give you many hours of pleasure. I am of the same opinion you are concerning the Union League & will talk more at length in my next letter.[6] Billy Perry is calling to breakfast, & after that I have some business to attend to before we start, so I must say Good Bye. Your letter makes me happy, I hope nothing may mar your happiness.

Your Affect. Husband

J. F. Culver

---

1  Pvt. James C. Monday of Company H had died of pneumonia at Bridgeport, Ala., on March 9; Pvt. John R. Phillips of Company E had died of smallpox at Tullahoma, Tenn., on March 17; Cpl. William M. Scott of Company K had died of smallpox at Bridgeport on March 21; and Pvt. James Burk of Company H had died at Louisville, Ky., on March 24. Compiled Service Records of Union Soldiers, NA.

2  Chaplain Cotton wrote the Sunday school of the Pontiac Methodist Episcopal Church, "Last Sabbath [the 24th] we organized a Soldiers' Sunday School, and your old friend, Lieut. Culver is the Superintendent. Of course, it is a very different looking affair to what it would be if the children and ladies were present, but we can sing quite well, and pray and study the good word of God." Cotton to Sunday school, undated, Culver Collection.

3  General Grant in March had been called to Washington, promoted to lieutenant general, and placed in command of all Union armies. To destroy the two major Southern armies and crush the Confederacy, Grant planned a spring campaign. He would establish his headquarters in northern Virginia with General Meade's Army of the Potomac and direct the campaign aimed at destroying General Lee's Army of Northern Virginia. General Sherman with an "army group" which included General Thomas' Army of the Cumberland was to hammer General Johnston's Army of Tennessee.

4  J.F.C. from Jan. 13, 1864, until April 18, had served first as Colonel Harrison's aide-de-camp and, following Lieutenant Mitchell's departure, as his acting assistant adjutant general. Compiled Service Records of Union Soldiers, NA.

5  The subject letters are missing from the Culver Collection.

6  Beginning in Philadelphia in November 1862, Union Leagues, which served as rallying points for citizen support of the Northern cause, proliferated. As the months passed, activities of the league became increasingly political, the very word "Union," denoting the cause of the Northern people, having been appropriated by a party. Randall, *Civil War and Reconstruction,* pp. 637-38.

 140

Hd. Qurs., 129th Ills, Vols.
Wauhatchie, Tenn., April 27th 1864

My Dear Wife

I was detailed this afternoon as Adjt. of the Regt. to act in the absence of Phil [Plattenburg]. He went to Louisville this afternoon to purchase a horse to be presented to Col. Case by the officers of the

Regt.[1] The duties will not be very heavy as there are two clerks on duty. To-morrow we have Division Drill.

I made a purchase of a barrel of green apples to-day from the Commissary Department for $3.50; about 1/2 were rotten, but still I think I got a good bargain. They will keep off scurvy.

We are all well. My health is very good except that I had a slight Head-ache to-day. Lieut. [Benjamin F.] Fitch & I had a few games of chess to-night after roll-call. I shall look for a letter to-morrow morning, though I have recd. four this week already.

May God bless you. I feel unusually happy to-night and hope you are well and happy. Remember me kindly to all.

I wrote to Thomas Hill some time ago to pay the $100 in his hand to Lawrence, also to get the amt. due from Fleming and Lyons, and add to it. I wrote at the time you informed me that you did not intend to draw it. If you see him [Hill], you can tell him that I will be able to pay $100 more shortly after the 1st of May. It was all right for you to use it. I wished it so at first & did not think at the time that you would have sufficient without it. I will answer Thomas Hill's letter soon. May Holy Angels guard thee this night.

Your Affect. Husband

J. F. Culver

---

1   The money collected would also be used by Adjutant Plattenburg to purchase a saddle and bridle for the gift horse. Grunert, *History of the 129th Illinois*, p. 56.

 141

Head Qurs., 129th Regt. Ills. Vols.<br>Wauhatchie, Tenn., April 29th 1864

My Dear Wife

Your letter of the 23rd and 24th was received just now, & I haste to reply.[1] I am very happy to hear that you enjoy good health, a blessing for which we should be very thankful. I presume you have received the letter I sent by [Amos] Clark before this. George Bay returned to his

Company to-day but brought no news for me;[2] he says he did not see you. You have learned all about Bros. Johnie and Sammy before this from my former letters.

I received a letter to-day from Joe Shellenbarger's sister with hers and her mother's Photographs.[3] I will send them with the letter to you. She requests a Photograph of Frankie and you; please write to her & send one. I am very busy and may not get time for a long time. They will be glad to hear from you.

The weather is very dry and hot; drilling is almost unbearable.[4] Yesterday we had Division Drill. We took 30 rounds blank cartridges. After forming two lines of skirmishers & two lines of battle, we commenced advancing up the valley; after proceeding about a mile, the front line engaged the enemy and commenced firing. They compelled them to retreat when the skirmish line was called in and the line of battle advanced about 1/2 mile and changed direction to the right. We had two Batteries and about 6 or 7000 men. The fight at Nashville was no circumstance.[5] We fought bravely for about an hour. We drove the enemy from every point and retired without the loss of a man, covered with glory. We got into camp at dark, tired and dirty, but well satisfied with what we learned. Gens. Thomas and Hooker were present with their Staffs.

Lum Hill is no better to-day.[6] All the rest of us are well. [James H.] Gaff came up to the office much excited this morning to get my opinion on a matter of discussion in Co. "G", as to whether the babies born of Soldiers' wives while they were on a visit to Dixie would necessarily [be] "Butternuts."[7] I referred the matter to Geo. Bay, but he said that his own Specimen was so small when he left that he could not determine. What is your opinion?

I must hasten to close. We go on drill in a few moments, and I am interrupted so frequently that I cannot write connectedly. I am so busy on reports that I cannot promise to write regularly for a few days. Give my love to all. May Our Father in Heaven bless and keep you. I will try and write soon. May you ever be happy.

Your Affect. Husband

J. F. Culver

---

1  Mary Culver's letter of April 23 and 24 is missing from the Culver Collection.

2  George Bay, a 34-year-old carpenter, was mustered into service on Sept. 8, 1862, as a corporal in Company G, 129th Illinois Infantry. He was sent to the General Hospital at Nashville on April 30, 1864, and did not rejoin the regiment, being mustered out at Keokuk, Iowa, May 3, 1865. Compiled Service Records of Union Soldiers, NA.

3 Delia Shellenbarger had written J.F.C., "I would like so much to have your [photograph] . . ., also your little boy's, if you have any to spare. I want to get an Album and want them to put in it. Joe was going to buy me one but never did." Delia Shellenbarger to J.F.C., April 1864, Culver Collection.

4 Private Dunham on April 26 had written his parents, "We have three drills a day, Company, Battalion, Briggade and once a week Division drill. That don't give us much time for play." *Through the South with a Union Soldier*, p. 116.

5 This is a reference to maneuvers in which the regiment had participated during Mary Culver's November-January stay in Nashville.

6 William C. "Lum" Hill had enlisted in Company A, 129th Illinois, on Nov. 24, 1863. Compiled Service Records of Union Soldiers, NA.

7 Sergeant Gaff of Company G was an expectant father. His wife was pregnant with a child conceived on a visit to her husband, while the regiment was stationed at Gallatin, Tennessee. "Butternuts" was a term Union soldiers used for Confederates.

 142

Head Qurs., 129th Regt. Ills. Vols.
Wauhatchie, Tenn., April 30th 1864

My Dear Wife

I recd. no letter from you this morning, but recd. one from Henry Greenebaum in which he says you are well. My health is very good. Dr. [Darius] Johnson is quite sick with dysentery. Lum Hill is much better. We are mustering for pay to-day and expect pay next week.

I have but a moment to write before the call sounds for muster. I will try and give you a long letter to-morrow (Sunday). Connelly handed me an ambrotype of himself taken on horseback;[1] I will send it as soon as I get time to put it up carefully. Bro. Johnie gave me a set of sleeve buttons which I will send you to have them fixed; get a gold link and some device on the top.

You must not feel any uneasiness if you receive no letters from me for several weeks. The Army is expected to move soon, and all mails going North will be stopped.[2] I look for it every day. In the meantime, keep a brave heart and write often. Your letters will still reach me. I may get an opportunity occasionally to send a letter by private sources to be mailed north of the lines, but you must take it for granted that all is well and trust in God. May he bless you with health and happiness and kindly watch over you.

We are forbidden henceforth to furnish any army news, and we feel that it is all right and proper. You may confidently expect to hear a good account of us if an opportunity offers. Remember [me] in love to Mother [Murphy] and Maggie and kindly to all our friends. May holy Angels guard thee and peace and contentment dwell with thee. With much love, I remain,

Your Affectionate Husband

J. F. Culver

---

1  Joseph B. Connelly, a 30-year-old farmer, was mustered into service on Sept. 8, 1862, as a private in Company A, 129th Illinois. He was detailed to headquarters, 1st Brigade, Third Division, XX Army Corps, in April 1864, and mustered out near Washington, D. C., June 8, 1865. Compiled Service Records of Union Soldiers, NA.

2  General Sherman on April 26 had alerted General Thomas to have his Army of the Cumberland ready to move out from its camps on May 2, 1864. When Sherman's "army group" advanced against Johnston's Army of Tennessee, Thomas' Army of the Cumberland would constitute the center; Maj. Gen. John M. Schofield's Army of the Ohio the left wing; and Maj. Gen. James B. McPherson's Army of the Tennessee the right wing. *O.R.*, Ser. I, Vol. XXXII, pt. III, pp. 496, 498-99.

 143

Head Qurs., 129th Regt., Ills. Vols.
Wauhatchie, Tenn. May 1st 1864

My Dear Wife

I feared when I wrote this morning that I might not be able to write much to-day.[1] We are almost ready to move, and will commence the march at 6 1/2 A.M. to-morrow.[2] I am not allowed to tell our destination but you will hear from me before very long if the mails are not stopped. Do not allow yourself to be troubled. Trust in God. All will be well in any event.

My health is excellent. I am furnished with a horse as I am still acting Adgt. There is much that I would like to say, but I have not the time. I will endeavor to give you satisfactory accounts of all our marches whenever opportunity offers, but let me urge upon you the necessity of being contented. It is possible you may not hear from me for a month or even two months, and, though you may feel lonely, still try and be happy. May our Father in Heaven deal kindly with us.

We are 1st Brig., 3rd Division, 20th A.C. You may hear from us through the papers. Give my love to Mother [Murphy] & Maggie and Remember me kindly to all. May God in his mercy keep you and bless you, so that whether we meet again in this world or not, we may have the assurance of a Home in Heaven. Pray for me that God may sustain me by his Grace. Good bye, Dearest.

Your Affectionate Husband

J. F. Culver

---

1  The subject letter is missing from the Culver Collection.

2  During the morning the brigade received its long expected marching orders. Rations for three days were issued, and the officers alerted to have their men ready to take the field early on the 2d. All equipment not prescribed, including the officers' writing desks, was stored. A final dress parade was held during the afternoon, and the troops retired early, sleeping for "the last time at the foot of grand lookout, whose peak towers high toward heaven." Grunert, *History of the 129th Illinois*, p. 53.

 144

Hd. Qurs., 129th Ills. Vols.
Gordon's Mill, May 3d 1864[1]

My Dear Wife

The mail will leave here for Chattanooga this evening. Rumor says that no mail goes North of Nashville now, but I will write anyhow.

Yours of April 28th came to hand last night.[2] You do not say that you are well, but I feel assured that you are else you would have told me. I grant that 20 days' Leave of Absence would have been very acceptable, but I am not so fortunate. I think at the close of this Campaign, if my life is spared, I shall surely get home. It is possible that "August" with its trials may be over and I hope abundantly blessed.[3]

Allen Fellows is well and doing well.[4] I am sorry to hear of Bro. Johnson's continued ill health. We recd. the "Louisville dailies" regularly at Wauhatchie. I have seen no papers here yet, but they will soon come along. Haldeman has not been heard from for a long time.[5] I am surprised to hear of Harry McDowell's intention to resign.[6] I have had no opportunity to answer his letter.

We have but little paper with us, and, if we are to be kept in the field in this way, I fear I shall soon have to stop writing for want of paper. I cannot spare any to write to anyone except my *Wife*, so all my letters must remain unanswered. Write to Mother [Culver] often. Tell her that I have to carry all the paper and envelopes for the campaign in a haversack and the supply is very limited.

I wrote to you yesterday from Lieut. Donaldson's tent;[7] his Brigade left this morning for Ringold. We will probably stay here a few days. We are just notified that a train leaves in an hour, & the mail must be sent in immediately.

Chris [Yetter] is sick lying on my bed; he is not bad and will be all right as soon as he is rested. Bart Allen is very sick. Co."A" were sent out on Picket last night after the march.

We have a very pleasant camp. It was very cold last night, and we had a heavy frost. It is quite cool to-day. This climate is unaccountable, the nights are very cold and the days hot.

I hope to get another letter by the wagon train to-morrow. The nearest place to Rail Road here is Ringold, 8 miles. This is the first time we have been off the Rail Road since we left Bowling Green. "Buzzard's Roost," a Rebel stronghold, is 10 miles front of us. There are about 35,000 troops there.[8]

I must close for the mail. Allen [Fellows] is setting here and wishes you to tell her [his wife] he is well and that he has not felt better since he has been in the service and where we are. May God bless you and keep you amid all your trials. I hope you may be happy. Do not allow yourself to feel uneasy about me. Trust all to God. Give my Love to all the family. I burnt all my letters before leaving Wauhatchie, as I do not much expect ever to see my trunk again. Write often, good long cheerful letters. Accept my Love and my heart's warmest affection.

Your Husband

J. F. Culver

1   Reveille was beaten at 4 A.M. on the 2d. After roll call a "hasty breakfast" was eaten,

and "the haversacks filled with bread, meat, etc. for three days." Preparatory to taking up the march at 6:30 o'clock, the shelter tents used as roofs on the huts were taken down, rolled up, and buckled to the knapsacks. At the designated hour the regiment fell in to the beat of the drums and marched to the parade ground, where the brigade rendezvoused.

General Butterfield gave the command to move out, and the 1st and 3rd Brigades, along with the division artillery, ordnance and supply trains, took up the march. Passing to the southwest of Chattanooga, the column marched through Rossville Gap and across the Chickamauga battlefield, going into camp at Gordon's Mills. Grunert, *History of the 129th Illinois,* pp. 53-54; *O.R.,* Ser. I, Vol. XXXVIII, pt. IV, pp. 11-12.

2   Mary Culver's letter of April 28 is missing from the Culver Collection.

3   Mary Culver was five months pregnant and the couple's second child would be born in August.

4   John Allen Fellows of Pontiac was the regiment's hospital steward.

5   John Halderman, a 30-year-old miller, was mustered into service on Sept. 8, 1862, as a sergeant in Company D, 129th Illinois Infantry. He was promoted to 1st lieutenant two days later. Lieutenant Halderman was captured at Richland, Tenn., on June 4, 1863, and sent to Libby Prison. Transferred to Camp Oglethorpe, Ga., on May 1864, he was subsequently sent to a prison camp near Columbia, S.C., where he died of fever on Nov. 15, 1864. Compiled Service Records of Union Soldiers, NA.

6   Lt. W.H.H. McDowell reconsidered and served with the regiment until it was mustered out near Washington on June 8, 1865.

7   The subject letter is missing from the Culver Collection.

8   On May 2 Union cavalry had advanced, and driving Confederate outposts from Ringgold Gap, forced them back on Tunnel Hill. Camped in and around Dalton, Ga., and braced to oppose the Union advance, was General Johnston's 44,000-man Army of Tennessee. *O.R.,* Ser. I, Vol. XXXII, pt. II, p. 866.

 145

Head Qurs., 129th Regt. Ills. Vol. Infty.
Pleasant Grove near Ringold, Tenn. [*sic*], May 4th 1864

My Dear Wife

Yours of the 25th March [*sic*] I recd. at Gordon's Mill.[1] We left that place at 9 o clock A.M. and arrived here at 4 P.M., 15 miles.[2] We are now at the foot of Taylor's Ridge, 2 1/2 miles from Ringold, about 10 miles from Tunnel Hill, and from 15 to 20 miles from Dalton. One column is moving by Ringold, Tunnel Hill, and Buzzard Roost; another from Cleveland, and ours, making in all three columns.[3] We are close on the enemy's lines. The weather is warm but pleasant during the day and quite cool at night.

Plattenburg has not yet returned, & I am still acting Adgt. & get to ride. [Captain] Hoskins was last night detailed to act as Major until further orders and is also mounted. [Lieutenant] Smith is in command of the Company. Chris [Yetter] was sick last night but is quite well to-night. Bart Allen is better.

I would like very much to give you a full history of our movements, but it is unsafe. The capture of a mail would furnish too much information.

I am happy to hear that you are making such good progress in music. Learn "Fairy Bell" and "Laurina" for me; I shall be happy to hear it when I return. Do not allow yourself to feel the least uneasy about us. We never felt in better spirits. All will be well.

I hope your effort at gardening may prove more successful than my last one. Have any of the Grape lived? And the roses should be in bloom.

We are so far in the field that I fear that there will be no pay forthcoming until the close of the Campaign. No pay since Dec. 31st. We can easily get along here. If you get short, call on Remick or Henry [Greenebaum], either of them will advance all you need.

Give my love to all. Tell Henry and Russell and all the rest I will write as soon as paper becomes more plentiful; our transportation is too limited. We have plenty of meat and hard bread & get along finely.

May God bless and keep you in health and happiness. Live in hope "God doeth all things well." Kiss Mother [Murphy] for me and Maggie. Remember me kindly to all. May Holy Angels guard thee. With much love, I remain,

Your Affectionate Husband

J. F. Culver

---

1  The subject letter is missing from the Culver Collection.

2  The division had struck its tents and moved out at an early hour. Butterfield's orders were to take position near Pleasant Grove Church, with his left in contact with Brig. Gen. Jefferson C. Davis' division. *O. R.*, Ser. I, Vol. XXXVIII, pt. IV, p. 29.

3  Maj. Gen. John Palmer's XIV Corps, Army of the Cumberland, had marched from Graysville on the road paralleling the Western & Atlantic Railroad, and by the 4th had occupied Ringgold, Ga. General Howard's IV Corps, advancing on Palmer's left, had left

Cleveland, Tenn., on the 3d, and reached Catoosa Springs on May 4. Hooker's XX Corps constituted the Army of the Cumberland's right. General Schofield's Army of the Ohio had followed Howard's corps south from Cleveland and was camped in and around Red Clay. General McPherson's Army of the Tennessee was being concentrated at Chattanooga, preparatory to following the route pioneered by Hooker's columns. *Ibid.*, pp. 25-33.

 146

Nickajack Trace, Georgia[1]
May 6th 1864

My Dear Wife

We have had no mail for several days, so that I have not heard from you, but earnestly hope you are in good health. Phil [Plattenburg] joined us to-day, and I have returned to my Company.[2] We are on Picket to-night but will commence the march before morning.

Hoping that this may find its way to you, I am happy to say that my health is excellent. Keep a brave heart. All will be well.

The health of the Company is good. May our Father in Heaven keep you in health and ever make you happy. Kiss Mother [Murphy] and Maggie for me and remember me kindly to all. I have every reason to be thankful for the many blessings I enjoy. God has been very bountiful in mercy, and I feel content to suffer his will. Heaven is all bright and glorious. Pray for us. Write often; it may be several days before I have another opportunity to write.

May Holy Angels guard thee, and all our hopes of happiness be centered in Heaven. Accept all the love of an affect. heart.

Good bye.

Your Husband

J. F. Culver

---

1   The division remained in camp at Pleasant Grove Church on the 5th, and late in the day soldiers of the 129th drew three days' rations. On May 6, the division broke camp at an early hour and turning south halted on the Nickajack Trace, east of Leet's Tanyard. *O. R.,* Ser. I, Vol. XXXVIII, pt. IV, p. 44.

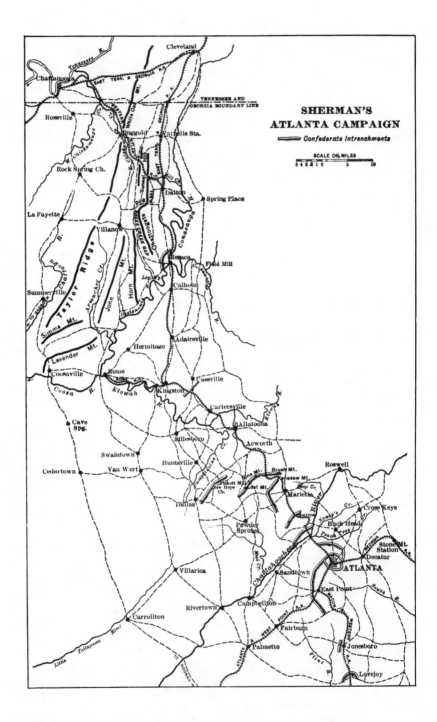

General Johnston on the 5th had ordered his infantry and artillery out of their camps and into defensive positions along the rugged ridges and in the gaps. Lt. Gen. William J. Hardee's corps was on the left with his men holding Rocky Face; Lt. Gen. John B. Hood's corps guarded the right, where the line bent down to the east of Dalton; and Maj. Gen. Joseph Wheeler's cavalry covered the flanks, guarded the gaps through Taylor's Ridge, and observed the advance of the Union columns as they felt their way forward. Gilbert E. Govan & James W. Livingood, *A Different Valor: The Story of General Joseph E. Johnston, C.S.A.* (Indianapolis, 1956), p. 262.

2   Adjutant Plattenburg had been sent to Louisville with money contributed by the officers and men of the 129th to purchase a gift horse and saddle and bridle for Colonel Case.

 147

Hd. Qurs., Co. "A" 129th Ills.
In the Field Near Tunnel Hill[1]
May 9th 1864

My Dear Wife

Yours of May [*sic*] 30th has just come to hand.[2] I am very happy to learn that your health is good. That dream of yours was doubtless very agreeable yet very far from the reality. I am glad to learn that Sis & Bro. Johnson are better. I hope you may have many opportunities to ride out during the summer months.

I have never heard of any of Co. "G" dying of Small Pox. It is certainly a mistake.[3] The 4th Corps to which Bro. Johnie belongs is in our rear, or was yesterday.[4]

The cannon are booming in our front this morning. The fight has commenced.[5] We were called into line yesterday to move out and support a column in our advance, but our services were not needed.[6] We may go to-day. We are lying here in readiness. The rumors from the Army of the Potomac and also from our front are glorious but too good to believe.[7]

We are all well but [Cpt. Erastus] Nelson, he has a slight attack of ague. Mrs. Smith [the wife of Lt. John W. Smith] is at Felicity, Clearmont County, Ohio. Tell Bro. Thomas [Murphy] when you write to him that I have no opportunity to write. My health is most excellent for which I feel thankful.

Yesterday was a blessed day [Sunday]. I felt very happy all day and do this morning. God has been very bountiful in blessings. May he bless you likewise.

Did you write to Dehlia Shellenburger and send your photograph? I did not have an opportunity to answer her letter. Capt. Hoskins is not very well but has a horse. The horse purchased for Col. Case was presented in presence of the Regt. yesterday evening. It is a very fine animal. Capt. Perry made the presentation Speech. It was good. Col's. response was very fine. The Regt. is in good health and spirits.

I have written nearly every day since we left Wauhatchie. I think it's doubtful whether any mail has gone North for the past few weeks. I think of you *very, very* many times during each day but am consoled by Faith in God. I know he will care for you and our child if anything befalls me. Be cheerful. We have a "Home in Heaven." This life is but short, and Heaven is an "Eternal Home." I have no presentiments of the approaching battle and feel perfectly willing to suffer God's will. What I most desire is Wisdom and understanding to perform my duty well. I feel that God will help me and take care of me.

Kiss Mother and Maggie for me and remember me kindly to all. Enclosed find a kiss for my *Wife,* my *love.* May our Heavenly Father deal kindly with you and take care of you, and, if consistent with his will, spare our lives that I may again enjoy the happiness your presence and society affords and for which my heart is thankful. My past life spent with you has been so *happy* and full of joy that I feel God has specially cared for me. ⟨kiss⟩

In thinking over all this morning, I can recall no hour since our lives have been so intimately associated together that my heart did not feel grateful for God's blessing. You may feel satisfied with your performance of the vow you voluntarily assumed. It has been most faithfully performed, and I feel a consciousness this morning that I have tried to perform mine. I still "love and cherish" if possible more than ever. My only regret is that my time was so much preoccupied that I could not devote more of it to your comfort and happiness. Trust still in God and praise him for all his mercies and blessings, and, under whatever circumstances we may be placed, praise Him ever. With much Love, I remain until it is God's will to call me away,

Your Affect. Husband

J. F. Culver

---

1  The XX Corps broke camp shortly after daybreak on the 7th and, marching by way of Gordon's Gap, crossed Taylor's Ridge, and took position in front of Buzzard Roost. The First Division was posted at Trickum's Post Office; Butterfield's Third Division on the Dalton and Gordon's Springs road; and the Second Division on the Ringgold and Villanow

roads about three miles from Trickum's, with its picket line connecting with the right of Butterfield's division. *O. R.*, Ser. I, Vol. XXXVIII, pt.IV, pp. 45, 61.

Private Grunert recalled the day's march as an unpleasant one, "over narrow, dusty or rocky roads." The weather was terribly hot. When the regiment took a break during the afternoon in a field, the troops quenched their thirst "in a milky, dirty creek, in which higher up some were bathing, others washing their feet." The sun was setting when the 129th, after a 20-mile march, went into camp near Mrs. Swain's. Grunert, *History of the 129th Illinois*, p. 55.

2　Mary Culver's letter of April 30 is missing from the Culver Collection.

3　Mary Culver had mistakenly assumed that the two soldiers (Private Phillips and Corporal Scott) who had died of smallpox in March were members of Company G, 129th Illinois.

4　Troops from General Howard's IV Corps on the 7th occupied Tunnel Hill, four miles north of the position held by the 129th Illinois. On the night of the 8th, cannoneers of Company M, 1st Illinois Light Artillery, manhandled two guns into battery atop Rocky Face, where the Rebels "thought no gun could be put." *Adjutant General's Report, State of Illinois*, Vol. VIII, p. 666.

5　On May 9 General Butterfield made a forced reconnaissance of the Confederate lines on Rocky Face. Mill Creek was bridged and crossed. Soon thereafter his skirmish line was shelled and orders were received from General Thomas to return to camp. *O. R.*, Ser. I, Vol. XXXVIII, pt. II, pp. 320-321.

6　General Hooker's Second Division led by Brig. Gen. John W. Geary on May 8 attempted to force its way through Dug Gap. Confederate cavalry, reinforced by units from Maj. Gen. Pat Cleburne's division, held their ground in face of slashing attacks. After suffering 357 casualties, Geary recalled his brigades and retired to the foot of Rocky Face. The attack at Dug Gap was made to divert the Confederates' attention from General McPherson's Army of the Tennessee which was advancing through Snake Creek Gap with the goal of capturing Resaca. *Ibid.*, pp. 114-117; *O. R.*, Ser. I, Vol. XXXVIII, pt. III, p. 721.

7　The Army of the Potomac on May 4 had advanced against General Lee's Army of Northern Virginia. A terrible battle had been fought in the wilderness, south of the Rappahannock, on the 5th and 6th. Although Meade's army suffered more than 18,000 casualties, General Grant did not turn back. The Army of the Potomac broke contact with Lee's troops on May 6 and advanced to the southeast. A forced march was made by Lee, and he intercepted the Federals at Spotsylvania. From May 7 to 18 the two armies battled in front of Spotsylvania.

 148

Hd. Qurs. Co. "A" 129th Ills.
[Near Cassville, Ga., May 20th 1864]

My Dear Wife

I wrote a line this morning & have just learned that another mail goes out shortly. Yours of the 10th & 11th I recd. to-day.[1] I am very happy to hear that your health is so good. God be praised for all his mercies.

We have lay in camp all day. I heard from Lt. Smith yesterday, his wound is not dangerous.[2] The other boys are doing well; Fred Huetson is worst.[3] I had my Company under the enemy's fire yesterday about 4 hours,[4] and on last Sunday [the 15th] about 6 hours of a most murderous fire, none faltered except Frank Long (Sergt.) & I had him reduced to the ranks to-day for cowardice.[5] I have a noble Company & my earnest wish so long cherished has been granted. I have been permitted to lead them in all their battles. We will again advance upon the enemy, & I fear no danger. We will end this Campaign with brilliant and permanent success.

Continue to write often. A letter is a great treat. I scarcely think our letters yet go beyond Chattanooga or Nashville, but you will get them by & by. May God bless you and keep you by his Grace. Remember me to all and accept the love of

Your Affect. Husband

J. F. Culver

Much obliged for the stamps. I have recd. all.

---

1 Mary Culver's letter of May 10 & 11 is missing fron the Culver Collection.

2 General Sherman's "army group" had outflanked Johnston's Army of Tennessee, compelling it to abandon its Rocky Face line and retire into the defenses covering Resaca. The 129th Illinois had marched south by way of Snake Creek Gap, and on the 13th approached Resaca from the west. On May 15 General Butterfield's division moved to the left and took position in front of the earthworks east of the Dalton road defended by Maj. Gen. Carter L. Stevenson's division of General Hood's corps. Orders were issued for Ward's brigade to attack and storm the redoubt and rifle pits to its front with bayonets. The units formed in battalion column at intervals of 44 paces between regiments—the 129th being the fourth regiment in the column—and prepared to advance. The soldiers shucked their knapsacks and fixed bayonets, and Colonel Case gave the command "forward!"

Much of the ground across which the brigade advanced to reach the works defended by Brig. Gen. John C. Brown's Tennessee Brigade of Stevenson's division was grown up in dense underbrush. Cannoneers of the Cherokee Georgia Artillery, who had unlimbered their four 12-pounder Napoleons about 80 yards in advance of the breastworks, opened fire on the Federal column with shell at a range of 800 yards. Soon thereafter the bluecoats entered a dense cedar thicket which screened them from view. As the Illinoisans ascended a "small hill about 400 yards" from the Georgians' guns, they were fired upon by Brown's Tennesseans posted in the rifle pits.

The column charged at the double-quick, the men cheering. There was a change of direction to the right, and the companies on the right, having a shorter distance to go, approached the battery first. General Ward shouted, "Go in boys, give them the devil!"

and the soldiers stormed into the "redoubt, which was simply a natural basin on the ridge, with formidable breastworks flanking it on the right and left, and on higher ground." Sergt. Frederick Hess of Company H, 129th Illinois, placed the colors near the guns of the Cherokee's Artillery. Brown's Tennesseans, from their breastworks, blazed away, forcing the storming party to retreat a few steps and take cover in front of the "redoubt." The four cannon, abandoned by their gunners, were between the lines, and a desperate struggle ensued for their possession. In this fight casualties were heavy; General Ward was wounded; and the Confederates called up reinforcements. Soldiers of Ward's brigade held the ground gained for five hours, until relieved by General Geary's division on the night of May 15.

Rolls were called. It was found that in the charge and fight for the "redoubt" that the 129th Illinois had lost 9 killed and 39 wounded. The dead were buried on the field next day. Lieutenant Smith had been wounded in the abdomen and shoulder. He was hospitalized until June 4, when he was released from the hospital and given a 20-day furlough. *O. R.,* Ser. I, Vol. XXXVIII, pt. II, pp. 322-323, 340-341, 365-366, *Ibid.,* pt. III, pp. 812-813; Compiled Service Records of Union Soldiers, NA; Grunert, *History of the 129th Illinois,* pp. 60-62.

3  Frederick G. Huetson, a 20-year-old farmer, was mustered into service on Sept. 8, 1862, as a private in Company A, 129th Illinois Infantry. Private Huetson was wounded in the left leg at Resaca, May 15, 1864, hospitalized at Madison, Ind., and medically discharged at Quincy, Ill., March 25, 1865. Compiled Service Records of Union Soldiers, NA.

4  On the 15th, while the 129th was engaged east of the Dalton road, other Union troops advanced on Lay's Ferry to the Confederates' left and rear. With his position at Resaca outflanked, General Johnston, under the cover of darkness, abandoned the works successfully defended for two days and retired south of the Oostenaula. Soldiers of Ward's brigade on the 16th policed the battlefield, buried the dead, and succored the wounded. The Union dead were buried on a knoll, "the bodies wrapped in blankets and laid along side of each other. Some green twigs were put over the dead, several chaplains addressed the listeners, the grave closed . . . and a board, bearing an inscription the name, number of brigade, regiment, and company of the dead, was placed at the head of each corpse."

That evening the brigade started in pursuit. Next morning the 129th Illinois crossed the Coosawatee, five miles east of Resaca, and turned south. On the 18th an exhausting 20-mile march was made, the column passing east of Adairsville. The day was terribly hot, and many soldiers straggled. Near Cassville, on the 19th, General Johnston prepared to turn on Sherman's pursuing columns. The Confederate corps commanders botched their assignments, and Johnston pulled back, posting his Army of Tennessee south and east of Cassville.

On the morning of the 19th General Ward's brigade, with other units of Hooker's XX Corps, formed into line of battle and advanced on Cassville. Ward employed the 105th Illinois, deployed as skirmishers, to cover his battle line. Confederate skirmishers were encountered and forced to retire. The Union advance came to a halt when shelled by a Rebel battery. Taking cover in the timber, the troops threw up breastworks. Here they remained until ordered by General Hooker to move by the right flank to Price's farm and support the artillery.

About 2 p.m., the advance on Cassville was resumed, and four companies of the 129th, one of which was Company A, advanced as skirmishers. Supported by the other six companies, they pressed forward, "driving the enemy from their ambushes and entrenchments until they reached a point less than 1/4 mile from town, and would have penetrated the town had they not been ordered by Gen. (Joseph F.) Knipe to advance no further." The gallant conduct of the 129th called "forth repeatedly very flattering compliments . . . from Gen. Knipe." Here they were relieved at dark. *O. R.,* Ser. I, Vol. XXXVIII, pt. II, pp. 341-342, 366; Case to Thomas, May 21, 1864, Regimental Papers, 129th Illinois, NA.

5 Sergeant Long was reduced to the ranks on May 20 and deserted one month later. Compiled Service Records of Union Soldiers, NA.

 149

Hd. Qurs. Co. "A" 129th Ills.
In the Hills near Allatoona
May 24th 1864

My Dear Wife

After a severe day's marching, we have turned the flank of the enemy again & are fortifying ourselves among the hills south west of Allatoona. The Rebs seem to understand retreating to perfection, & it is probable we will not get an opportunity to do more than shell them a few minutes.[1] The present Campaign thus far has been a perfect success.

We expect a mail to-night & news from home. The troops endure the hardships of the Campaign with great fortitude. There has been a great many cases of sun stroke within the last two days, but I think none have resulted seriously. Co. "A" were deployed as flankers to-day, & we came in this evening very weary.[2]

My health is very good and seems to improve rather than diminish. I heard from [Lt.] Smith yesterday; he is getting along finely. Allen Fellows is well.

I do not think there will be much fighting this side of Atlanta which we are nearing rapidly. If the Rebs cannot fight through this country, they will surely not stand long any place. We captured two more cannon yesterday. We carry our bridges with us. The Rail Road bridge across Etowah River, I understand, was saved without any serious damage.[3]

All the boys are well & in good spirits. The country through which we are passing is very fine and promises fine crops. Everything is pleasing. The fruit will soon ripen, & berries are coloring.

I must close as the mail leaves shortly. We have built quite a formidable fortification in front of our guns to prevent a surprise.[4]

There was some cannonading on our right & light skirmishing on our front as we came in, but that has been an every day occurrence for so long that we have ceased to notice it. Write often. Our mail goes and comes quite regularly.

Genl. Sherman issued an order urging soldiers to write to their families and friends but forbidding newspaper correspondence.[5] I will write every opportunity. May Our Father in Heaven preserve you in health & bless us with all things needful. Give my love to Mother and Maggie, Chris [Yetter] & Nate [Hill] are well. May Holy Angels guard thee.

Your Affect. Husband

J. F. Culver

---

1 The 129th Illinois remained near Cassville until 4 A.M. on May 23. When it moved out, Butterfield's division marched to the southwest, crossing the Etowah at Milum's Bridge shortly before sundown. To guard against sunstrokes, Colonel Case had his men "put fresh leaves in our hats."

Nightfall on the 24th found the 129th Illinois camped in the hills near Burnt Hickory. One of the soldiers, echoing Lieutenant Culver, reported, "Many of our men suffered so much from the sun and heat that they could not assist" in erecting breastworks, and "threw themselves on the cold ground to sleep and rest, not caring for any supper." Grunert, *History of the 129th Illinois,* pp. 65-66; *O. R.,* Ser. I, Vol. XXXVIII, pt. II, p. 382.

General Johnston, after abandoning his position in front of Cassville on the 19th, had posted his army astride the Western & Atlantic Railroad at Allatoona. General Sherman wisely determined to flank Johnston's position. After establishing his base at Kingston, his "army group" crossed the Etowah on a broad front and, abandoning the railroad, struck toward the southeast, flanking Johnston's fortified Allatoona line, with Marietta as their goal. Horn, *Army of Tennessee,* p. 320.

2 During the day the vanguard skirmished with Confederate cavalry, the greyclads capturing some of Hooker's foot-soldiers. *O. R.,* Ser. I, Vol. XXXVIII, pt. II, p. 382; *Ibid.,* pt. IV, p. 742.

3 The XX Corps had crossed the Etowah on May 23 on a pontoon bridge laid by the army's Pioneers. Culver was mistaken. On May 20, Maj. Gen. Joseph Wheeler's cavalry division, covering the Confederate retreat from Cassville into the Allatoona lines, had crossed the Etowah, burning the railroad bridge. *O. R.,* Ser. I, Vol. XXXVIII, pt. III, p. 946.

4 The opposing armies no longer disdained throwing up breastworks whenever they halted for the night. The Confederates grew so adept at it that the Federals said, "The Rebels must carry their breastworks with them." But so well did they emulate this example that the Confederates countered, "Sherman's men march with a rifle in one hand and a spade in the other." Horn, *Army of Tennessee,* p. 331.

5 General Sherman on May 20 had notified the troops there was no truth to the rumors that he had "prohibited the mails to and from this army." On the contrary, he wished to encourage them "to keep up the most unreserved correspondence with their family and friends wherever they may be. Army, Corps and Division Commanders should perfect their arrangements to receive and transmit mails, and all Chaplains, Staff Officers & Captains of Companies shall assist the soldiers in communicating with their families."

Sherman, however, discouraged "the maintenance of that class of men who will not take a musket & fight but follow an army to pick up news for sale, speculating on a species of information which is dangerous to the army and our cause, and who are more used to bolster up worthless and idle officers, than to notice the hardworking and meritorious whose modesty is generally equal to their courage and who scorn to seek the cheap flattery of the press." Circular, May 20, 1864, Mil. Div. of Miss., Regimental Papers, 129th Illinois, NA.

⧯⧯ 150 ⧯⧯

Hd. Qurs., Co. "A" 129th Ills. Behind the
fortifications in front of Dallas, May 27th 1864

My Dear Wife

Yours of the 17th has just come to hand.[1] I am very happy to hear that you were well. We moved up to this place on the evening of the 25th about 5 p.m. The enemy were concealed in the woods and opened a terrific fire upon the head of the column. The 1st Div. of our Corps was in advance & commenced skirmishing immediately. The 1st Div. drove the enemy back about 1 1/2 miles into their fortifications, & our Div. formed line of battle & moved up to their support.[2] Coming up through the woods, the shell and shot fell thick around us. Walter Good, orderly of Co. "C", had his right hand shot off.[3] George Conner of my Company lost the index finger of his left hand.[4] Only a few others in our Regt. were wounded & those but slightly.[5]

The firing on the front line was very heavy, & the loss of our 1st & 2nd Divisions, I understand, was severe.[6] We moved up to within 30 yds of the 1st line & lay down. The fighting on our left was equally severe. The enemy, after attacking our front, attempted to turn our left flank, but the 4th Corps were in readiness to receive them & they were handsomely repulsed.[7] I heard that the 4th Corps took 2 cannon but do not know it.[8]

Yesterday we were all day finding the position of the enemy & no hard fighting was done. We are told this morning that 2 Corps have already passed the enemy's left flank, & we can hear cannonading far on our right.[9] Also that 2 Corps are pushing the enemy's Right-flank, & we can also hear cannonading far to our left. The object is to make the enemy fight a decisive battle here if possible. We now hold the fortifications on our right centre.[10] If they will fight at all, we can whip them easily. We are supported by line after line & fortification after fortification for miles in our rear. Those that have just come up from the rear say that there is no end to our Army.

There has been heavy cannonading on the line we occupied yesterday but no response from the enemy. My health is excellent, & I feel very thankful God has specially preserved & blessed me. Chris [Yetter], Nate [Hill], Allen Fellows, & all are well. [Lt.] Bob Edgington was slightly injured by the falling of a limb cut off by a cannon ball on the evening of the 25th, but he is up all right again. I have never felt in better spirits. I can trust all consequences to God, & I feel that I have tried to discharge my whole duty. By this time you have full particulars of our battles. We feel very sanguine of success. We have from 40 to 60,000 troops coming that have not yet got up.[11]

I heard from Lt. Smith & our boys left at Resaca this morning. All are doing well; they have gone to Chatanooga & Smith to Nashville, from there he will either go home or have his wife come to him.

Still trust in God; He is caring for us & will preserve us. Let us praise and magnify him & strive diligently to do our duty. The Company are doing nobly, & I believe I love them more & more each day. Give my love to Mother & Maggie & Remember me to all our friends.

The heavy rains have cooled the atmosphere, & the weather is pleasant.[12] Alf [Huetson] is busy making maps; he is well. I have not seen or heard from John or Sammy in three or 4 days, but, as no batteries have been engaged, I presume they are all right. May our Heavenly Father keep and bless you, and Holy Angels guard you. Watch & pray. Let us thank God for all his mercies. Accept much love,

from your Affect. Husband,

J. F. Culver

---

1 Mary Culver's letter of May 19 is missing from the Culver Collection.

2 General Hooker's XXX Corps advanced from Burnt Hickory in three columns on the 25th. The day was hot and humid and there were hundreds of stragglers. General Johnston, having learned from his cavalry that Sherman's "army group" was across the Etowah and threatening to outflank his Allatoona line, started his army for Dallas. On the 25th Hood's corps took position at New Hope Church, with Hindman's division on the left, Stewart's in the center, and Stevenson's on the right. When the First Division of Hooker's corps drove in Hood's skirmishers, Butterfield's Third Division diverged toward the right. The earthworks assailed by the Federals were defended by Maj. Gen. A. P. Stewart's division. *O. R.*, Ser. I, Vol. XXXVIII, pt. II, pp. 30, 123, 324; *Ibid.*, pt. III, p. 761.

3  Walter Good, a 28-year-old farmer, was mustered into service on Sept. 8, 1862, as a private in Company C, 129th Illinois Infantry, and was promoted 1st sergeant on Dec. 6, 1862. 1st Sergeant Good was wounded in the right hand at New Hope Church on May 25, 1864, and hospitalized at Chicago's Marine Hospital. His hand was amputated, and he was given a medical discharge on Nov. 10, 1864. Compiled Service Records of Union Soldiers, NA.

4  George W. Conner, a 21-year-old farmer, was mustered into service on Sept. 8, 1862, as a private in Company A, 129th Illinois Infantry. Private Conner was wounded, one of the fingers on his left hand being shot off, at New Hope Church on May 25, 1864. He returned to duty and was mustered out near Washington on June 8, 1865. *Ibid.*

5  Casualties in the 129th for the day were 5 wounded. *O. R.,* Ser. I, Vol. XXXVIII, pt. II, p. 366.

6  In the fighting at New Hope Church on the 25th, the First Division had 102 killed, 639 wounded, and 4 missing; the Second Division on the 25th and 26th lost 52 killed, 439 wounded, and 18 missing. *Ibid.,* pp. 30, 125.

7  One division of General Howard's IV Corps (Newton's) reached the area at 6 P.M. and went into action on Hooker's left. J. D. Cox, *Atlanta* (New York, 1882), p. 73.

8  There was no truth to the report that the IV Corps had captured two Rebel cannon on the 26th. During the day Schofield's Army of the Ohio had taken position on the left of Howard's IV Corps, his left extending to and covering the road from Allatoona to Dallas, via New Hope Church. *O. R.,* Ser. I, Vol. XXXVIII, pt. I, p. 144.

9  General McPherson's Army of the Tennessee, early on the 26th, arrived from Van Wirt and occupied and fortified a line covering the approaches to Dallas. Confronting McPherson's two corps was Lt. Gen. William J. Hardee's Confederate corps. Cox, *Atlanta,* p. 74.

10  On the 26th there was skirmishing along the entire 8-mile front. Sherman proposed to pin the Confederates in their earthworks and employ his superior numbers to turn Johnston's right. *Ibid.,* pp. 75-76.

11  Culver overstated the number of men en route to reinforce Sherman's "army group" as it thrust deeper into northwest Georgia. About 30,000 men from the Army of the Tennessee were currently under orders to report to General Sherman. Of these about 19,000 did, but the 11,000 men of Maj. Gen. A. J. Smith's detachment, currently en route from Red River, were detained at Memphis to operate against Confederate cavalry in northeast Mississippi.

12  There had been a severe thunderstorm on the night of the 25th, with the soldiers being drenched by a "cold, pelting rain." This broke the heat wave which had gripped the region. *O. R.,* Ser. I, Vol. XXXVIII, pt. II, p. 124.

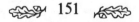 151

Hd. Qurs. Co. "A" 129th Regt. Ills. Vol. Infty.
1 Brig. 3rd Div., 20th A.C. In front of Dallas, Ga.
Monday Eve. May 31st [*sic*] 1864

My Dear Wife

I have a few moments (10) to write, & the mail is just going. My health is excellent for which my heart is thankful. We have recd. no mail yet.

We occupy the front line on the right centre to-day.[1] We were out supporting a "Battery" & have just returned.[2] We lost no men since Saturday [the 28th] morning in my Company and but few in the Brigade.

Harry McDowell is setting beside me writing too. There has been no very heavy fighting to-day, only one light attack on our lines last night. Everything is very favorably; no skirmishing on our front.

We hear that there will be a mail up to-night. I feel anxious to hear from you. I fell asleep just before dinner behind the fortifications and dreamed of home & you. I presume it is because my mind has been so much occupied with Home thoughts since Harry's return.[3] I waked up imagining your arms around my neck & your head resting on my breast. May our Father in Heaven bless and keep you, preserve you in health and strength. I am very well contented & feel happy in the discharge of duty.

Give my respects to Miss Emma Thayer, Harry's friend. Give my Love to Mother [Murphy] and Maggie & Remember me kindly to all. Write to Mother Culver often & let her know that I am well. May God keep you by Grace and bless us as we need, and hasten the day when we may unite our hearts with our voices in his praise and enjoy the pleasures and comforts of Home. Good bye.

Your Affect. Husband

J. F. Culver

---

1 On the 27th, General Sherman had sent General Howard, reinforced by units from the Army of the Ohio, to feel for the Confederate right. The Federals found the Rebels at Pickett's Mill and were repulsed with a loss of about 1,500. General Hardee's corps on the Confederate left on the 28th made a forced reconnaissance of the position held by McPherson's Army of the Tennessee east of Dallas and was repulsed with heavy casualties. Cox, *Atlanta*, pp. 76-87.

Ward's brigade on the 27th advanced its lines under a heavy fire to within a few hundred yards of the Confederate breastworks at New Hope Church and entrenched. In the day's skirmishing, the 129th Illinois lost one killed and 10 wounded. Next day the brigade was relieved by the 2d Brigade, and on going to the rear was posted near a battery, "at which the enemy's guns were firing. . ., every moment a shell exploding over or near us and cutting off the branches of the trees." Grunert, *History of the 129th Illinois*, pp. 68-70; *O.R.*, Ser. I, Vol. XXXVIII, pt. II, p. 366.

2 The 129th was on picket on May 31, and was fired on by Rebel sharpshooters posted in the upper story of a house. To discourage the greyclads, two cannon were advanced to the picket line, and "a few shots from them stopped the mad firing of the Rebels." Grunert, *History of the 129th Illinois*, p. 70.

3 Lt. Harry McDowell had rejoined the regiment after a three-month absence in Illinois on recruiting duty. Compiled Service Records of Union Soldiers, NA.

Hd. Qurs. Co. "A" 129th Ills. Vols., 1st Brig. 3rd Div. 20th A.C.
on the Battle field, Ga., June 3rd 1864

My Dear Wife

We commenced moving from the centre to the left of our lines June 1st. The first evening we spent very pleasantly being sufficiently in the rear not to be disturbed by the roar of cannon or the roll of musketry.[1]

At 2 o'clock P.M. yesterday [the 2nd], we moved to the rear of a Fort to repel an attack by the enemy who had made two charges at that place. Just as we broke camp, the rain came down in torrents and soaked us to the skin. We lay about two hours in position, but no attack was made.[2] We were then moved to the left of the 23rd Corps, where we are now lying in line of Battle.[3]

Shortly after taking our position here, the enemy opened a Battery & commenced shelling us. Most of the shells passed over us and no one of our Regt. was injured. Dr. Potter of the 105th Ills. & Brig. Surgeon at Nashville was killed by a shell.[4] There was no other casualties. It was very wet & damp last night, but we are all getting along finely this morning.

We left Corpl. Chritten back sick June 1st. From all I can learn everything is going full as well as was anticipated. The enemy is still losing ground, while we are steadily gaining. This is the 9th day of the Battle. It would be a great relief to get beyond the noise & tumult of the Battle Field and rest for a short time, but all seem perfectly willing and anxious to stand up to duty. A few days will make a vast change in the aspect of affairs, and I confidently expect to give you the joyful news of the enemy's complete defeat and route before many days. The Troops are rapidly coming up, and the line of Battle is being so rapidly changed that the Enemy will not have time to fortify.

My health is still good, for which I feel very thankful. God has been very good to me and has bestowed upon me all needful blessings. He has been truly "My Father."

I have recd. no letters from you since Harry's [McDowell] return on Sunday last though we have had one mail since. Let us unite our voices in praise to God for his numerous blessings and for so specially caring for us. Kiss Mother and Maggie for me. Remember me kindly to all. Be of good cheer and trust all to "Our Father" who doeth all things well.

May his grace richly abound in our hearts and prepare us for the discharge of every duty and every change that awaits us. Committing ourselves with all we have and love to Him, I remain as ever

Your Affect Husband

J. F. Culver

P.S. Nate [Hill] wishes you to tell his mother that he is well. Allen Fellows is still at Kingston. I have not heard from the wounded since I last wrote.

1  General Sherman, finding his way barred by the Confederates, employed his superior forces to begin a gradual shift to the east toward the Western & Atlantic Railroad. General Johnston's Army of Tennessee moved in the same direction to keep between Sherman's "army group" and Atlanta.

On the afternoon of June 1, troops of Maj. Gen. John A. Logan's XV Corps, which had been posted on the Union right, relieved Hooker's corps in front of New Hope Church. The 129th Illinois, along with other units of Butterfield's division, pulled out of the line and marched to the northeast several miles, halting for the night in rear of the sector held by the XIV Corps. Grunert, *History of the 129th Illinois,* pp. 70-71;  *O.R.,* Ser. I, Vol. XXXVIII, pt. IV, p. 362.

2  Hooker's corps on June 2 took position in support of General Schofield's XXIII Corps, which was deployed in line of battle and had crossed Allatoona Creek. Here the Federals encountered Confederates behind breastworks covering the forks of the Dallas-Acworth road. Cox, *Atlanta,* pp. 89-92.

3  Butterfield's division on the 2d marched to the northeast toward Acworth in support of Hovey's division, the XXIII Corps., and camped for the night near Morris Church on the army's left. *O. R.,* Ser. I,Vol. XXXVIII, pt. II, pp. 324, 383.

4  Surgeon Horace S. Potter was killed on June 2, while selecting a site for a field hospital. *Ibid.,* pp. 26, 358.

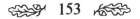 153

Head Qurs. Co. "A" 129th Regt. Ills. Vol. Infty.
In the Field June 5th 1864

My Dear Wife

We are lying behind the 3rd or 4th line of fortifications in the mud to-day.[1] It has rained very hard for several days and the mud is, as a matter of course, plenty. We keep out of it in our tents by laying limbs of trees, first, and leaves upon them, with our rubber blankets on top of them, our tents over us, and two woolen blankets to cover us.

We have thus great reason to be thankful for the comforts we enjoy on this Holy Sabbath. It has just ceased raining, &, hoping that some opportunity may offer to send mail back, I have sat down to write to you.

Our supplies come to Kingston by Rail Road and from there by wagon, so that this weather may prove a serious hindrance to our forward movement. We have been so long on the extreme front lines that we know but little of what is transpiring in the rear, yet our rations come regularly and in abundance.

We are about 2 or 3 miles further to our left than when I wrote on the 3rd inst. We have heard but little heavy firing since, though there is still the constant roar of artillery on our right and left & some little on our front. We are now about 1-1/2 miles behind the skirmish line, and everything seems quiet to-day. A little bird is singing near, a very sweet strain, and there are some indications of its clearing up.

Nate Hill & I bunk to-gether; he is well. Harry McDowell spent a couple of hours with us this morning. We have heard nothing of the sick and wounded lately, except that some of their names are mentioned in the Chatanooga papers as having been among the wounded.

I have not heard from Bros. John or Sammy since last Monday [May 30]. They were both well then. Saml. McGoodin is well.

I have recd. no letter since the one brought by Harry last Sunday [the 29th]. There has been but one mail since. The Leader of the Brig. Band started to Chicago with the body of Dr. Potter this morning. If I had known it, I might possibly have sent a letter with him. If we remain here all day, there will probably be an opportunity to send mail out. I saw John Lee yesterday, he was well.[2]

I know but little of the progress we are making. Rumor says that our lines on the left are advance[d] to within 4 or 5 miles of Marietta on the Rail Road.[3] What the design is I do not know, but we repose confidence in our Leaders and trust all to God.[4] Our Campaign thus far has been a complete success. The enemy on retiring have gathered up everything that could be of any use to them, and the entire country through which we pass is almost deserted. We see but few citizens, and prisoners say that all have been conscripted into the Rebel ranks.[5] Our Army is full as large to-day as it was when we left Resaca and is rapidly increasing by reinforcements.[6] I presume ere this the 100,000 new tendered by the North West are all in the field. Most of them were out the last accounts we had from the North.

We had a Chattanooga paper of the 2d yesterday, but no Northern papers since last Sunday. The latest I have had was the New York Herald of the 23rd May. This state of things will not last long, however.

I have every reason to feel thankful for the kind care "Our Father" has exercised for me. My Faith is still strong as ever in His doing for me all that is necessary for my protection and happiness, and much more than I deserve. If you are in good health, you are doubtless at this hour in the Sanctuary of God hearing his word expounded. My mind reverts to the time when to-gether we listened to the ministrations of the Gospel of Christ, and also to the many times that in much meakness I attempted to expound God's word to the people of Pontiac. I often imagine myself there again and think of much I might have done to bring others to Christ that I neglected. And the dear children of my Sabbath school, many of them have passed from youth to manhood and womanhood and are scattered far and wide. I shall never see all of them again this side of Eternity, but my heart still yearns after them, and I earnestly hope all may be brought into the fold of Christ.

Remember me kindly to all that remain. The many new scholars that have been gathered in will not know me, yet I feel a very warm interest in all of them. Perhaps when the Campaign is over, if God spares my life, I may get to see them. It seems a long time since I was at Home, almost two years, and it will be fully that perhaps before I get there. Do you write to Mother [Culver]? I have not written since we left Wauhatchie and have depended entirely upon your keeping her informed of my whereabouts. My health continues to be very good, and for which I try to be very thankful.

May the riches of God's Grace ever [be] upon our hearts. Let us strive to live aright that we may be acceptable in Our Father's sight. He will care for us and protect us, and under whatever circumstances we may be placed still be assured that "He doeth all things well." If in your power, render Mrs. Burns [Byrne] & others, the wives of the men of my Company, some assistance.[7] Do not let them suffer. If we had been paid off before the Campaign opened, they would have plenty; as it is, do what can be done for them. Give my love to Mother and Maggie and Remember me kindly to all. May Holy Angels guard thee.

Your Affect. Husband

J. F. Culver

---

1   Sherman's cavalry on the 3d had occupied Acworth on the Western & Atlantic Railroad. On June 4 Butterfield's division, including the 129th Illinois, was called to the front to occupy the breastworks erected the previous day by Hovey's soldiers. That night the Confederate army abandoned its New Hope Church line, and retired to the new

positions selected by General Johnston's engineers, covering an 8-mile front from Lost Mountain on their left to Brush Mountain on their right. *O.R.*, Ser. I, Vol. XXXVIII, pt. II, p. 384; Cox, *Atlanta*, pp. 92-93.

2  John S. Lee, a 38-year-old blacksmith, was mustered into service on Sept. 8, 1862, as a private in Company G, 129th Illinois Infantry. Private Lee was severely wounded in the shoulder at Peachtree Creek, Ga., July 20, 1864. On returning to duty in the winter of 1864-65, he was detached to the ambulance corps, 3d Brigade, Third Division, XX Corps, as a blacksmith. Private Lee was mustered out with the regiment near Washington, D.C., June 8, 1865. Compiled Service Records of Union Soldiers, NA.

3  Sherman's cavalry at Acworth, on the railroad, was within 12 miles of Marietta.

4  General Sherman's primary mission was to destroy the Confederate Army of Tennessee. A secondary assignment was to capture Atlanta, a key railroad, industrial and supply center. Rather than attempt costly frontal assaults on Confederate breastworks, Sherman had skillfully employed superior numbers to flank the Rebels out of a succession of fortified positions. General Johnston each time had succeeded in disengaging his army and redeploying it across Sherman's line of advance.

5  In addition to large numbers of Georgians who had either volunteered or been conscripted into Confederate service, many of the remaining local men between 17 and 18 and 45 and 50 had been called up in late April and sent to camps of instruction to be organized into regiments of Georgia reserves.

6  On May 31 the effective strength of Sherman's "army group" was about 112,000, whereas on April 30 this figure had been about 135,000. Maj. Gen. Frank Blair's XVII Corps, 10,000 strong, was en route to reinforce Sherman, and on June 5, it reached Rome, Ga., having marched from Decatur, Ala., on May 27.

7  Mrs. Byrne was the wife of Pvt. Francis Byrne of Pontiac.

 154

> Hd. Qurs. Co. "A" 129th Regt. Ills. Vols.
> In the Field, Ga., June 7th 1864

My Dear Wife

Your letters of 22d, 25th & 27th have just come to hand[1] with the Sentinel of 20th May, and 3 New York Tribune & 3 Nashville Times, with a letter from Sarah Williams. I have read none but your letters yet, as I am informed we can send our mail at 5 P.M. We have Genl. Inspection at 3 P.M., &, as I do not know how long it may last, I hasten to write before.

*296*

I am most happy to hear that you are well. Our Father has been very kind to us. The God of Battles is truly our God. I dare not attempt to answer your letters at length, for I have not time. I wrote to you on Sunday, [the 5th] & sent it back yesterday.

We have moved to a new line and fortified, but I find it impossible to locate myself.[2] No one seems to know where we are, but it is not over 7 or 8 miles to Marietta.[3] We have heard nothing of the Enemy since they fell back on Saturday night and Sunday, except by rumor, & I do not put sufficient reliance in them to give them as news.[4] We are strongly fortified here, & it would facilitate matters very much if the Rebs would attack us.

I was on Picket with my Company last night & had Harry McDowell with me. He is in a terrible way about the mail, as this is the first we have had since his return. I hope it has brought him all he has anticipated.

Our men are all out of sorts about all the newspaper accounts of our Battles. The New York Tribune says, "Ward's Brigade of Indiana Troops" and also, "Col. Case's Regt. of Hovey's Indiana Troops."[5] No paper except the Nashville Times has given anything like a true statement. When the Campaign is over, I may have an opportunity to give you a full account.

I have been interrupted, & the hour of INSPECTION has arrived. Harry Mc[Dowell] wishes me to say that he is well & hearty, "never was better." The Brig. Band is playing. The weather for the past week has been constantly wet, & I wonder that more of us have not been sick. Nate [Hill] & I had a good dinner, beef & vegetable soup, but we have gone hungry several times since we left Wauhatchie. You can scarcely believe that the boys could work on 2 & 3 of those small Hardtack with the small pittance of meat allowed, & yet we are very well. We are on 2/3 rations, & sometimes much less.

I can give you but little news. We know nothing, except that everything moves along as well as was anticipated. We will undoubtedly have a severe Battle before we reach Atlanta.

I heard from Chris [Yetter] yesterday. He is acting Ward Master in one of the Hospitals at Kingston. His face is still quite sore, but he sent me word he would be up with us as soon as he could get away from the Hospital. I do not know where Lt. Smith is; the last I heard of him, he was expecting to go Home & was improving very rapidly. Harry recd. a letter from Mrs. Smith to-day making inquiry about him. If he is not at home, he is most probably at Nashville. I felt certain I should get a letter from him to-day. We have a number of letters for him, but do not know where to send them. I have not heard from any other of our wounded boys. They were sent to Chattanooga & Nashville.

Nate is waiting for the portfolio to write. I regret very much to hear of Mr. Barr's degeneracy,[6] & hope most earnestly it may not have a serious effect upon the Sabbath School. May our Father in Heaven bless the children. I will write to them as soon as I can. Kiss little Mary & the baby for me & give my Love to Mother & Maggie. Continue to write often. God has been most bountiful in his blessings to me. Let us still praise Him & continue to trust Him. May his richest blessings rest upon you.

Your Affect. Husband

J. F. Culver

1  Mary Culver's letters of May 22, 25 and 27 are missing from the Culver Collection.

2  General Thomas on June 5 ordered the XX Corps to cross Allatoona Creek at Mason's Bridge and take position on the ridges "in the angle between the road to Big Shanty and the one leading south, to the east of Lost Mountain," its right to rest on Allatoona Creek. Hooker's corps marched as ordered on the 6th, and, after advancing about five miles, Butterfield's division took post on the Sandtown road at Mt. Olivet Church. From the ground occupied and fortified by the 129th Illinois, Pine Mountain on the left and Lost Mountain on the right could be seen. *O.R.*, Ser. I, Vol. XXXVIII, pt.II, pp. 324, 367,387; *Ibid.*, pt. IV, p. 415.

3  Marietta was eight miles southeast of Mt. Olivet Church.

4  The Confederate Army of Tennessee since the morning of the 5th had been posted with its left at Lost Mountain, its center near Gilgal Church, and its right anchored near the Western & Atlantic Railroad. The Southerners were throwing up breastworks and felling timber. Prisoners captured by Butterfield's pickets identified the enemy to their front as belonging to Cheatham's Tennessee division of Hardee's corps. *O.R.*, Ser. I, Vol. XXXVIII, pt. III, pp. 616-617; *Ibid.*, pt. IV, pp. 428-429.

5  Units constituting Ward's brigade in addition to the 129th Illinois were: the 102d and 105th Illinois, 70th Indiana, and 79th Ohio. Brig. Gen. Alvin P. Hovey commanded the First Division, XXIII Army Corps, a unit in Schofield's Army of the Ohio.

6  Samuel Barr was a 31-year-old Pontiac baker. In 1860 he was living with his wife Emma and their one-year-old daughter, Eva. Eighth Census, Livingston County, State of Illinois, NA.

 155

The first page (or pages) of this letter is (are) missing. [June 10, 1864]*

I apprehend that for bold, daring, and careful and successful

*Internal evidence suggests that J.F.C. wrote this letter on or about June 10, while the 129th Illinois was posted at Mt. Olivet Church.

*298*

movement, it [Sherman's Atlanta campaign] has never been equaled.[1] We have advanced our lines over 100 miles through the heart of the Enemy's country, through some of the strongest natural fortifications in this country, in a period of 40 days.[2] To guard a base of supplies from Louisville, Ky. to this place is of itself a herculean task, it being very nearly 500 miles.[3]

The next mail will bring us the result of the Baltimore Convention.[4] We have but little doubt, however, but what it will present the name of Lincoln for the Presidency. Illinois has by her Legislature denied us the privilege of suffrage at the coming Election. I ought not to murmur, perhaps, as the members of the party to which I have so long subscribed [the Democratic] were wholly instrumental in withholding from us the right to vote. We will certainly remember their charity should we be permitted to exercise the rights of citizenship again.

The Cleveland Convention has proved itself a mere farce.[5] I did not think the North contained such a body of arrant political knaves. They have made no pretensions to either truth or consistency.

I feel very anxious to hear from Mother [Culver], & know what arrangements have been made for her comfort. The only word I have had from home was through Bro. Wes, who had opened my letter in Mother's absence and answered hastily.

I am sorry to hear that Miss Shellenbarger is not in good health. I have not yet been able to learn definitely anything about Bronson.[6] I fear the report of his death is too true. We have no further news of our wounded. I feel very anxious to learn where they are that I may send them their descriptive Rolls, so that they can draw the pay due them.

I expect Chris Yetter up shortly unless he should get a furlough home, I need him very much, as I am so very closely confined. I have to depend on Green to procure our rations;[7] he does very well, but a great deal is wasted.

I have not learned yet whether Thomas Hill has paid the $100 due me from Shellenbarger on my notes in Lawrence's hands. Please give it a little attention. I presume the letter of the Freeport Insurance Co. will set the transaction with David Cox all straight. We should know something by this time of the settlement of Father's estate. I will write to Mother to-day if I get time. I would also like very much to write to the Sabbath School & to a number of friends in Pontiac, but I will have to wait until the close of the Campaign.

I do not often have as good opportunity for writing as I have this morning. I found a cracker box & the Orderly furnished me some ink. My pen I have carried thus far safely.

In a letter Nate [Hill] recd. from his Bro. a few days ago, he says

Henry Greenebaum is married. I wish him much happiness if it be true. I think it is a mistake, however, as he did not expect to be married before summer.[8] Perhaps his intended decided, as a lady I could name, that "summer was too warm," &, not willing to wait til fall, they have hastened their nuptials.

Rumor says Lida Remick & Mr. Crook or Brook are to be married very soon.[9] "May I be there to see." I am glad that Sis and Remick have settled. I have feared that should she marry a man who was disposed to examine closely into the settlement of her estate, there might be some serious trouble. The settlement is as nearly right as it can be made, & I feel satisfied she has lost nothing. I hope she enjoys married life and may be ever happy. Abbie [Remick] seems to be surrounded with a world of trouble. The trials may make her a better woman.

I hear cannon booming off to our right and occasionally to the front. I have heard no reply from the enemy yet. It is singular the Rebs use so few cannon.[10] Some of their prisoners say that every time they open a Battery we either knock it all to pieces or capture it.

Alf Huetson was here yesterday. He is now first Asst. Topr. Engr. at Corps Hd. Qurs. He enjoys life finely & has a very pleasant position. Nate [Hill] has lay down and is fast asleep. Cannonading is becoming more general all along the line. It is the time of day for the ball to open if they intend to do anything.

Bro. John's Battery [M, 1st Illinois] moved to the front of our line last night, but they have not gone to the front yet. They have been in reserve ever since Resaca.[11] I think probably it is our turn now for awhile. We have been on the front line ever since the Campaign opened.

The Band have been playing almost constantly for the past few days, making it very pleasant. And the evenings are so beautiful, the moon & stars have shined brightly; music on earth and music in Heaven. How natural and easy for the mind to wander upward for the thoughts to centre around the throne of Grace. God has been most bountiful in blessings to us. Let our hearts praise him.

Night before last, we sat upon the fortifications singing until quite a late hour. The Chaplain came up, & we invited him to pray. It brought back so many dear remembrances of by-gone times. I have enjoyed very much of God's presence and love in my heart, & I hope by his Grace to do his will and carry out His design in placing me here. The pleasures & comforts of Home often cross my mind. The Love of a Dear Wife and friend are ever present with me, but God will in his own good time restore me to them if consistent with his will. I will work on, cheerfully trusting to him alone for results.

I feel much anxiety at times for your approaching trial.[12] May God be with you and deal kindly with you. I would that circumstances were such that I could be with you, but there is no certainty of that. "Trust in God. He will never leave thee or forsake thee." "Sorrow endureth through a night, but joy cometh in the morning." I earnestly hope that the pleasures of maternity may more than counterbalance all your trials. May the desires of your heart be granted and the richest blessings of Heaven rest upon you.

Kiss Mother & Maggie for me. I know Mother [Murphy] will take good care of you; be cheerful and, if possible, contented. In my letter of yesterday, I told you of the arrangement I have made with Allen Fellows to furnish you with what money you may need.[13] He wrote to his wife also, but I think did not get his letter off. Remember me kindly to all.

Here comes the news that Richmond is taken.[14] A dispatch, it is said, to Genl. Sherman. All the Bands of this Corps are assembling. There will be a tumult here shortly; the boys are dancing already. We will know certainly very soon, but we hear so many rumors that I cannot credit them. The taking of Richmond was only a question of time, but we did not expect it so soon. Our latest news from there, however, was the 28th of May, & there has been time enough since to fight several hard battles.

It is dinner time. I have endeavered during the forenoon to write while at leisure, with the hope to contribute to your happiness and add pleasure, and, if possible, profit to the perusal of my letter. You have already received assurance of my love and desire for your happiness. You have still as ever the confidence and affection of a true heart. Accept therefore all I have to give, and may we under the blessings and direction of Our Heavenly Father live to enjoy each other's society, [&] be useful to all around us in being the instruments in His hands of leading many to Christ, and when life is over meet with all our love around His throne in Heaven.

"There shall be no night there." Rev. 21-25

And I will betroth thee unto me forever. Hosea 2-19

The Lord will give grace and glory. Psalm 84-11

Also - Rom. 8-28, Psalm 25-10, Matthew 12-20, Gal. 6-9, Isaiah 9-20, Rev. 3-11, John 14-3, 1st Peter 5-4, Rev. 21-3&4.

Your Affect. Husband

J. F. Culver

---

1  Sherman's Atlanta Campaign is considered a classic by many military historians.

Sherman's skill in employing a superior force to flank a foe out of a succession of formidable defense lines and Johnston's ability to conduct a successful retrograde are still studied in military schools and colleges.

2   The 129th Illinois had broken camp at Wauhatchie, Tenn., on May 2.

3   Sherman's greatest fear was that Maj. Gen. Nathan B. Forrest's cavalry corps, based in northeast Mississippi, would raid into Middle Tennessee and destroy the single track Nashville & Chattanooga Railroad, severing his supply line. To keep Forrest occupied in Mississippi, Sherman ordered out a series of expeditions from Memphis.

4   The regular Republican (Union) party met at Baltimore on June 7, and nominated President Lincoln for a second term. Andrew Johnson of Tennessee was selected to replace Hannibal Hamlin of Maine as Lincoln's running mate. The platform was broad enough to accommodate the diverse elements constituting the party. Randall, *Civil War & Reconstruction*, pp. 612-13.

5   In Cleveland, Ohio, a convention convened on May 31 attended by a few disaffected Radical Republicans under the sponsorship of B. Gratz Brown and Wendell Phillips. Maj. Gen. John C. Fremont was nominated for the Presidency and John Cockrane for the Vice-Presidency on a radical platform. In accepting the nomination, Fremont violently criticized the Lincoln administration. *Ibid.*, pp. 611-12.

6   William H. Bronson, a 25-year-old jeweller, was mustered into service on Sept. 8, 1862, as a private in Company A, 129th Illinois Infantry. He was detailed as company nurse, rejoining the unit on Jan. 25, 1863. In the spring of 1864 he was hospitalized with tuberculosis at Chattanooga and was given a medical discharge on April 10, 1865. Compiled Service Records of Union Soldiers, NA.

7   Albert Green, a freedman, had attached himself to J.F.C.'s mess. This was a common practice during the Civil War.

8   Henry Greenebaum on Aug. 14, 1864, married Carrie Hart of Chicago. *History of Livingston County*, p. 633.

9   Lida E. Remick, the daughter of J. W. and Sarah DeNormandie Remick, married Edgar Cook of Pontiac. *Ibid.*, p. 649.

10   Private Grunert noted in his diary that on the 10th there was heavy firing "in the afternoon, and that on the 11th, firing was heard throughout the day." Grunert, *History of the 129th Illinois*, p. 72.

Union artillery with its better equipment, superior organization, and customary inexhaustible supply of ammunition usually more than held its own against Rebel cannoneers.

11   General Howard's IV Corps, to which Company M was attached, on June 10 took position on the left of Hooker's XX Corps, occupying ground in front of Pine Mountain. General Schofield's XXIII Corps was on Hooker's right, and General McPherson's Army of the Tennessee was being deployed on Sherman's extreme left across the Western & Atlantic Railroad.

Company M had last been engaged near New Hope Church on June 1, when a Rebel battery sent several shells through the embrasures into the emplacements. *Adjutant General's Report, State of Illinois*, Vol. VIII, p. 666.

12   Mary Culver was seven months pregnant.

13   The subject letter is missing from the Culver Collection.

14   There was no truth to the report that Richmond had been taken. On May 26 the Army of the Potomac crossed the Pamunkey River to find General Lee's Army of Northern

Virginia awaiting it behind the Totopotomoy. Grant then moved to Old Cold Harbor and, reinforced by a corps from the Army of the James, the Army of the Potomac assailed Lee's troops on June 3. Repulsed with frightful losses, the Federals had entrenched. From June 1 until the 12th, the two armies faced each other along the Cold Harbor lines, 10 miles northeast of Richmond.

~~~ 156 ~~~

</div>

Head Qurs. Co. "A" 129th Regt. Ills. Vols.
In the Field, Near Marietta, Georgia
June 14th 1864

My Dear Wife

As an opportunity offers to send mail to the rear, I am happy to be able to write. We are still lying behind the fortifications on the same line we occupied a week ago. The army has been in motion and fighting, but the centre has not advanced over two miles.[1] We have heard fighting all along the line each day. It has rained almost incessantly for 13 days, so that you can imagine the conditions of the roads, almost impassible. We are still held in readiness to move at a moment's notice.

The weather is clear and pleasant to-day & very beautiful after the season of cloud and storm we have had. The wet weather has produced some sickness, as must be expected, mostly diarrhea. I was quite unwell yesterday but am much better to-day. The most I can complain of is weakness; I hope to be all right to-morrow. There is only one or two sick in my Company, & they will soon be well. Harry McDowell, Allen Fellows, Capt. Hoskins, Dr. Johnson, and Lt. McKnight have been here for a little while, but all have gone to write home. Allen's health is much improved. We have no late reliable news; I look for a mail to-day with news from Home.

I recd. notice yesterday that Lt. Smith has recd. a Leave of Absence for 20 days, and I presume he is Home ere this. It is very probable that Tom Wilson will see a long term of service in some penitentiary, if, indeed, he is not shot.[2]

It was so wet all day Sabbath [the 12th] that we had no services of any kind. The mail came in the afternoon and brought your letters of the

30th May & 1st June.³ I was very happy to learn that you are well. Chaplain Cotton is liked much better than he was a year ago. I have not seen or heard from Bros. John or Sammy since I last wrote, but presume they are well. I hope the Sabbath school is still prospering. I wrote a long letter to them on Sunday and enclosed it to you; I hope it may reach you.

McCartney of Co. "B" was not wounded,⁴ both he and Saml. McGoodin are well. I should like to see Bro. Tom [Murphy] & hope he will spend the summer with you. I am happy to hear that Mother [Murphy], Maggie and the children are well. Kiss them for me.

Col. Case was not injured in any of our battles. Wm. F. Miller fills Frank Long's place as sergt.⁵ Hoskins has never recd. his commission [as major] yet. I wrote to John Dehner on Saturday last about it, & hope he may be able to give it some attention.

There has been some fighting all along the line this morning. We learn nothing here and have to depend on the papers for our knowledge of results. Our troops hold Marietta.⁶ The cars came through Sunday, & we hear their welcome whistle daily now, about three miles to our left. If our communication with the rear and our supplies can be kept uninterrupted, we will soon see Atlanta. The enemy have tried to break our lines several times but have been every time repulsed.⁷

Nate [Hill] is well. We have not heard from [Chris] Yetter lately; I would not be surprised to hear that he is home. Nate wishes to write, & I must hasten to close as we have only one portfolio between us. Remember me kindly to all. Let us praise God for his continued mercy. May our Father in Heaven preserve you in health and bestow upon you all needful blessings. Tell Bro. Joe Dehner I shall expect to hear a good account from him in regard to the Sabbath School.⁸ May God give him Grace & make him instrumental in doing much good. May all the efforts made in that direction be signally blessed of God.

I feel that God is doing a great work in the hearts of many of my Company. Oh, may he help me to discharge my duty and set a Godly example before them. I most earnestly desire their conversion. Pray for them and ask the churches to pray for them, also the Sabbath Schools. May Holy angels watch over thee, and our Father keep thee in perfect peace.

I remain through Christ, as ever

Your Affect. Husband

J. F. Culver

P.S. Get the Bible Society to send me a dozen testaments by Lt. Smith. We need them very much. Many have been lost during the Campaign.

J.F.C.

---

1 Reinforced by Blair's XVII Corps which had arrived from Decatur, Ala., General McPherson's Army of the Tennessee of the left advanced, occupied Big Shanty on the railroad, and found the Confederates strongly posted on Brush Mountain, with Noonday Creek to their front. General Thomas had divided his Army of the Cumberland into three columns. Palmer's XIV Corps on the left, in contact with McPherson, inched its way ahead on the road to Newton's Mill; Howard's IV Corps in the center and Hooker's on the right felt their way toward Pine Mountain. Schofield's Army of the Ohio was on Sherman's right and pressing slowly closer to Gilgal Church. Brig. Gen. George Stoneman's cavalry guarded the "army group's" right toward Lost Mountain.

General Johnston to cope with Sherman's move to the east had massed his infantry on the Gilgal Church-Brush Mountain line. Hardee's left was at the church, Polk's corps extended from Pine Mountain across the railroad to the Acworth-Marietta wagon road, and Hood's on the right was massed behind Noonday Creek and along the foot of Brush Mountain. Cox, *Atlanta,* pp. 95-96.

2 Thomas J. Wilson, a 22-year-old farmer, had been mustered into service on Sept. 8, 1862, as a private in Company A, 129th Illinois Infantry. Private Wilson was detached on Jan. 30, 1864, and detailed as a teamster in the ordnance train, Third Division, XX Corps. Private Wilson was mustered out near Washington, D.C., June 8, 1865. Compiled Service Records of Union Soldiers, NA.

3 The subject letters are missing from the Culver Collection.

4 William McCartney, a 44-year-old farmer, was mustered into service on Sept. 8,1862, as a private in Company B, 129th Illinois Infantry. He was detailed to the brigade brass band on Feb. 2, 1864, and was mustered out with the regiment on June 8, 1865, near Washington, D. C. *Ibid.*

5 William E. Miller, a 24-year-old farmer, was mustered into service on Sept. 8, 1862, as a private in Company A, 129th Illinois Infantry. He was promoted to corporal on Jan. 20, 1843, and to sergeant to rank from May 20, 1864. Sergeant Miller was mustered out with the regiment on June 8, 1865, near Washington, D.C. *Ibid.*

6 J.F.C. was mistaken about the occupation of Marietta by Union troops. What he should have written was that Union troops held Big Shanty on the Western & Atlanta Railroad. On June 11 the Etowah bridge was opened for traffic, and next day "the whistle of the locomotive was heard at Big Shanty, notifying friend and foe that Sherman's supplies were now close in rear of his line." Cox, *Atlanta,* p. 97.

7 The only major counterattack made by the Confederates since the beginning of the campaign had occurred at Dallas on May 28. This thrust started as a forced reconnaissance, and the Confederates were repulsed with heavy losses. The key to General Johnston's strategy was to goad Sherman into making suicidal assaults on fortified positions.

8 Joe Dehner was a 24-year-old clerk in his father's Pontiac store. In 1860 Joe was living with his wife and infant daughter. Eighth Census, Livingston County, State of Illinois, NA.

## 157

Hd. Qurs. Co. "A" 129th Regt. Ills. Vols.
Behind the Fortifications, June 17th 1864

My Dear Wife

Yours of June 9th came to hand last night, & I read it this morning.[1] As I may possibly get an opportunity to send a letter to-day, I hasten to write.

I am most happy to learn of your good health. Do not think it hard that our mails are not regular. Could you but know the difficulties that have to be surmounted, you would be surprised that any letters reach you.

We moved forward at noon on the 15th about two miles, & sent out a Regt. of skirmishers and commenced to drive the Rebel lines. We advanced our lines about 1-1/2 miles, the left of our Regt. resting within 150 paces of the Enemy's works and the right protected by a ravine & hill in front about 200 paces, the 79th Ohio & 70th Ind. on our right.[2] The 70th [Ind.] was not so well protected, & they lost about 70 killed & wounded. The 79th Ohio lost about 40, & our loss was about 20.[3] I did not learn the loss in the 102nd & 105th [Illinois], but it was not heavy.[4] Our Division has lost heavily again. The loss in our Regt. was all on the left: Henry Hornder of Co. "G" killed; Hoffman, Co. "B" killed & Stahl, Co. "B" mortally wounded; & Sergt. Deborn, Co. "K" killed.[5] A few of the wounded are serious but most of them slight. I have not learned all their names. Col. [F. C.] Smith, 102nd Ills., slightly wounded; Major [Z. S.] Reagan, 70th Ind., severely.

We fortified all night on the 15th & all day yesterday. We were ready for a hard fight to-day, but last night the enemy withdrew, how far no one knows, but their rear guard throws solid shot nearly to our lines.[6] Our skirmishers are 1-1/2 miles in advance.

The Lord has again signally cared for us. On the evening of the 15th, the shot & shell fell all around us in torrents. The bursting of the shell was close enough to burn the faces of the men, & yet none were hurt. Let us thank God for his mercies. We are all well, & will probably advance this morning. There is heavy cannonading on our left in the direction of Marietta and the river. Alf [Huetson] has just come, & I will close & send by him. May God bless you. Give my love to all. Good bye.

Your Affect. Husband

J. F. Culver

---

1   Mary Culver's letter of June 9 is missing from the Culver Collection.

2   On the 14th, with a cessation of the rain, Sherman ordered his army commanders to advance skirmish lines and crowd the enemy, but not to assault them in their fortifications unless "some specially favorable opportunity should occur."

Thomas pushed forward the right of Palmer's corps and the left of Howard's into the re-entrant angle between Pine Mountain and the Confederate works to the east. Next day, the Rebels having evacuated Pine Mountain, Thomas sent Hooker's corps forward. Butterfield's division was deployed into the line of battle at Gilgal Church, forming east of the Sandtown road. Covered by a strong skirmish line, General Ward advanced his brigade, took possession of two hills to his front, and thrust into the woods beyond, driving pickets and sharpshooters from Cleburne's division before him. Ward was now ordered to attack and hurl the Confederates from the breastworks pinpointed by his scouts 600 yards to his front. The bluecoats surged forward with fixed bayonets and dislodged the Rebels from their advance line of rifle pits, but were unable to carry their main line of works. *O. R.*, Ser. I, Vol. XXXVIII, pt. II, pp. 324-325, 367.

3   In this fight, known as the battle of Gilgal Church, the 70th Indiana lost three killed and 46 wounded; the 79th Ohio 16 wounded; and the 129th Illinois three killed and 15 wounded. *Ibid.*, pp. 367, 374, 377.

4   The 102d Illinois lost 13 wounded and the 105th Illinois had seven killed, 40 wounded, and one missing in the action of June 15. *Ibid.*, pp. 355, 361.

5   Henry K. Handler enlisted in Company G, 129th Illinois Infantry, on Sept. 22, 1862, as a private. He was killed near Kennesaw Mountain on June 15, 1864. Compiled Service Records of Union Soldiers, NA. William Hoffman, a 23-year-old farmer, was mustered into service on Sept. 8, 1862, as a private in Company B, 129th Illinois Infantry. He was killed in action near Kennesaw Mountain, Ga., June 15,1864. August Stahl, a 26-year-old farmer, was mustered into service on Sept. 8, 1862, as a private in Company B, 129th Illinois Infantry. Wounded near Kennesaw Mountain on June 15,1864, Private Stahl died in a military hospital at Resaca, Ga., five days later. Henry F. Dibbern, a 29-year-old millwright, was mustered into service on Sept. 8, 1862, as a corporal in Company K, 129th Illinois Infantry. He was promoted to sergeant on May 13, 1863, and was wounded in the arm on June 15, 1864, dying the next day in a field hospital at Burnt Hickory, Ga.

6   The Confederates' left (Hardee's corps) found its position untenable, and on the night of the 16th abandoned its position and retired into a new line of earthworks behind Mud Creek, three miles to the east. Schofield and Thomas followed Hardee, their skirmishers clashing frequently with Rebel cavalry seeking to slow their advance. Cox, *Atlanta*, p. 100.

## 158

Hd. Qurs. Co. "A" 129th Regt. Ills. Vols.
In the Field Near Marietta, Ga., June 22nd 1864

My Dear Wife

Yours of 11th, mailed 13th inst., came to hand yesterday.[1] I am most happy to learn of your good health, may God ever preserve it. Since I last wrote, we have moved several miles to the right. The enemy evacuated their fortifications on Saturday night [the 18th], & on Sunday morning we commenced to move.[2] It rained very hard, and the Streams became swollen so rapidly that it was difficult to pass them. We got into position amidst the rain about 4 P.M. and advanced our line. There was some little Skirmishing, but we moved up and fortified during the night. We had two seriously & two slightly wounded.[3] It continued to rain through the night. On Monday evening [the 20th] we advanced the right of our Brig. & fortified, which occupied most of the night & a portion of the day yesterday.[4] We have no news reliable from any portions of the army, but everything seems to move right though slowly. We are still gaining ground.

I have not seen or heard from Bros. John or Sammy for two weeks though they are not far from us.[5] There has been considerable hard fighting around the lines, but none of it has fallen to our lot. My health has been excellent for which I feel that I have great reason to be thankful. The Lord who has been always so bountiful in blessings is still with us. May he keep our hearts from sin & fill us with Love Divine.

I am much obliged for the extracts from the papers. Our mails are not regular, but yet much more so than we could expect. The boys are all well. I am much obliged for the prospect you offer for Strawberries, & hope I may have the privilege to enjoy them with you. We get no fruit.

I presume [Lt.] Smith is enjoying himself. I should like very much to have attended the S.S. celebration at Peoria, yet I trust through the kind Providence of Our Father to attend many in time to come. Allen Fellows is still back at the Hospital with Dr. Johnson. Harry McDowell is wondering why Mr. Ladd's family do not write. Chris [Yetter] & Nate [Hill] are well. The weather is much more pleasant this morning than it has been for several days. I am in hope of its clearing up for a few days, at least.

The Rebs have been throwing shells in the direction of our fortifications this morning, but all of them fall short. They will get the range, & we may find this a warm place before noon.[6]

I got my face poisoned night before last among the brush [poison ivy or oak], and my left eye is considerably swollen. It has commenced drying up & will soon be well.

We cannot see the close of this Campaign yet, but we will trust in God and fight on. He will rule all things well. Give my love to all the family. I have heard nothing from Carlisle yet; I cannot imagine why.

The Regt. on our right have just recd. orders to pack up ready to move.[7] I presume we will move also in a few moments. Let us still trust in God, "He will keep us in perfect peace." May our hearts be always ready for any change that may await us. God who has always cared for us will still be with us.

Good bye

Your Affect. Husband

J. F. Culver

---

1 Mary Culver's letter of June 11 is missing from the Culver Collection.

2 Hardee's Mud Creek line was subjected to heavy pressure on June 17-18. While Hooker threatened the front, Schofield gained the ridge between Mud and Noses Creeks, and Hardee was compelled to pull back his left. On Hardee's right, where his Mud Creek line joined the breastworks held by Loring's corps (formerly Polk's), there was a salient angle enfiladed by artillery. General Johnston therefore abandoned his Mud Creek-Brush Mountain defenses and retired into the Kennesaw Mountain line. Big and Little Kennesaw Mountains were occupied by Loring's corps, Hood's held the high ground east of the Western & Atlantic Railroad, and Hardee's corps was on the left, its right connecting with Loring's on the Stilesboro road and its left entrenched on the high ground commanding a branch of Noses Creek. Cox, *Atlanta*, pp. 101-104.

3 Butterfield's division followed the Lost Mountain road as it advanced on the 19th. Ward's brigade deployed south of the road, as it pressed ahead skirmishing with the Rebel rear guard. In the day's fighting, Colonel Case's horse, the one given him by the regiment, was wounded. *O. R.*, Ser. I, Vol. XXXVIII, pt. II, pp. 367, 385-386, 439; Grunert, *History of the 129th Illinois*, p. 76.

4 Butterfield's division, along with other units of Hooker's corps, on the evening of the 20th shifted to the right, occupying positions on Kolb's Farm near the Powder Springs road. Cox, *Atlanta*, pp. 106-109.

5 Howard's corps, to which Company M was attached, was the next corps to the left of Hooker's.

6 General Johnston on the night of June 21 shifted Hood's corps from his right to the left. Hood's people marched through Marietta and out the Powder Springs road. Forming

his divisions near Zion Church, one mile northeast of Kolb's Farm, Hood on the afternoon of the 22d advanced to attack Hooker's and Schofield's commands. The Powder Springs road separated Hooker's right (Williams' division) from Schofield's left. Cox, *Atlanta,* pp. 108-109.

7  Butterfield's division was on Hooker's left some distance from the Powder Springs road. To repulse Hood's assault, Hooker called on Butterfield for reinforcements. *O. R.,* Ser. I, Vol. XXXVIII, pt. II, pp. 387, 440.

〰️ 159 〰️

Hd. Qurs. Co. "A" 129th Regt. Ills. Vols.
In the Field Near Marietta, Ga.
June 25th 1864

My Dear Wife

We occupy the same position we have held for the past few days. The weather is very warm, but by planting bushes in the ground we manage to keep in the shade & comparatively comfortable. The Enemy's balls still keep flying over our heads, at times quite close to us. No one has been injured since yesterday morning, & only one in our Regt. since we came here.[1]

We are all in good health with plenty to eat for which we have every reason to be thankful. This Campaign is becoming very tiresome, & all would be glad for a short respite in which to rest. It is now almost 60 days since we left Wauhatchie, &, during that time, it has been almost one incessant roll of musketry & cannonading. Though tired we are still determined to carry out as near as possible the original intention of the Campaign.[2] We have heard heavy cannonading in the direction of Kenesaw mountains all morning.[3] With what result we cannot tell.

We have no late news from Grant's Army, except that they were rapidly crossing James River.[4] Of course, none can tell the final result of all our efforts, but, trusting in God, all will be well. If I could see anything but misery in any other than a complete victory to our arms, I might doubt the intentions of Our Father. I therefore feel Satisfied that he will not sacrifice this great nation & people without the

*310*

accomplishment of some great design. Victory must then be ours, & while we wish no evil to our erring enemy, yet we pray God that their eyes may be opened & that right and truth may prevail.

We have been looking for Jim Morrow for several days, but he has not yet arrived.[5] Judd was back to Chattanooga & returned yesterday.[6] The Rebs succeeded in destroying the R. R. Bridge near Tilton, but it was rebuilt & the trains running in 24 hours afterward.[7] Green saw Sergt. Gaff this morning; he was well.

There is heavy skirmishing on our right, &, as we may have work to do here,[8] I must close. I have not heard from Bros. John or Sammy for some time. Give my love to all. May the richest of Heaven's blessings rest upon you. Trust ye in the Lord forever, for in the Lord Jehova is everlasting strength.

Your Affect. Husband

J. F. Culver

P.S. Nate [Hill] & Chris [Yetter] are well.

1 On June 22d the division's infantry was too far north of the Powder Springs road to participate in the repulse of Hood's corps at Kolb's Farm. During the night, Butterfield's division was relieved by Stanley's division of Howard's corps and marched south, camping north of the Powder Springs road in the rear of Williams' XX Corps division. Next morning the 2d Brigade (Coburn's) was advanced and took position north of the road, within musket range of the foe's breastworks, and entrenched. South of the road was a line of works occupied by the XXIII Corps. The 129th Illinois, along with other units of the 1st Brigade, was posted in support of Coburn's soldiers. On June 24 a number of men from the 129th were sent forward to man the picket line, and one of them was killed. *O. R.*, Ser. I, Vol. XXXVIII, pt. II, pp. 326, 367, 382, 440; Grunert, *History of the 129th Illinois*, p. 78.

2 The mission given Sherman's "army group" by General Grant was the destruction of the Confederate Army of Tennessee.

3 Big and Little Kennesaw Mountains were four miles north of the camp of the 129th Illinois, and during the day there was a "heavy cannonade from [a] Rebel battery on the mountain." *O. R.*, Ser. I, Vol. XXXVIII, pt. IV, p. 594.

4 Checkmated by General Lee's Army of Northern Virginia at Cold Harbor, General Grant skillfully disengaged Meade's Army of the Potomac. Stealing a march on Lee, the Army of the Potomac crossed the James River on a pontoon bridge.

On June 15 the Army of the James, supported by one corps from the Army of the Potomac, attacked and captured a section of the fortifications guarding the eastern approaches to Petersburg. The Federals were unable to exploit this success, and the Confederates pulled back, dug in, and held.

5 Sergeant Morrow had been sent to Illinois in February on recruiting duty. Regimental Papers, 129th Illinois, NA.

6 Curtis J. Judd, a 24-year-old clerk, was mustered into service on Sept. 8, 1862, as a private in Company B, 129th Illinois Infantry, and was detached as the colonel's clerk

seven days later. Judd was promoted regimental sergeant major on April 17, 1863. Sergeant Major Judd was mustered out near Washington, D.C., June 8, 1865. Compiled Service Records of Union Soldiers, NA.

7   On the night of June 23, 300 Confederate horse-soldiers struck the Western & Atlantic Railroad near Dalton. One bridge was burned and a second heavily damaged by the raiders. *O.R.*, Ser. I, Vol. XXXVIII, pt. IV, p. 587.

8   General Schofield's troops, south of the Powder Springs road, sought to outflank Hood's corps by extending their right. *O.R.*, Ser. I, Vol. XXXVIII, pt. II, p. 514.

 160

Hd. Qurs. Co. "A" 129th Regt. Ills. Vols.
In the Field Near Marietta, Ga.
June 28th 1864

My Dear Wife

I am a little disappointed in not having heard from you by yesterday's mail. Some were recd. from Pontiac of as late a date as the 21st. I presume, however, mine has been sent by Sergt. Jim Morrow, and he has not yet arrived.

The weather is excessively warm, but we are all in good health for which all thanks to a kind Providence. There has been some hard fighting in which only one Division of our Corps was engaged, also one Div. of the 4th and one Div. of the 14th Corps.[1] The last two Divisions were repulsed, but the 2nd Div. [Geary's] of our Corps held its ground with a very small loss. The loss in the Divisions of the 4th & 14th Corps was somewhat heavier.[2] The ground over which they charged was very much against us. There has been very heavy cannonading for the greater part of two days which must have punished the Enemy severely.

We leave here to-night or in the morning for some new point.[3] Where our destination will be, we do not know definitely, but we can form a very good idea. I hope therefore that we may get mail this evening, as we will in all probability have no opportunity for several days to get mail.

The 13th and 19th Corps have arrived and are in position.[4] Every one is in high hopes. Our trust is all in God; truth and justice must prevail. The news from the Potomac Army is good, & we look for a glorious victory there in a few weeks.[5] Let us still trust in God. He will bring us off more than conquerors through Christ our Lord.

I have not heard from Bro. John or Sammy since about the 10th inst. I am told the 4th and 14th Corps go with us, & I hope it is true. Chris [Yetter] is writing to Thos. Hill, & Nate [Hill] is intending to write when I get done. We have built very strong fortifications here & would be very well satisfied if the enemy would undertake to break through our lines here, but that is very improbable.

Subscribe for the Chicago Tribune for me & have it sent along as soon as possible. The Semi-weekly will answer. I have not recd. any copies of the "Sentinel" for some time, please inquire about it. Lt. Smith subscribed for the New York semi-weekly Tribune which I now receive regularly. I hope he is mending rapidly. Alf Huetson was here this afternoon; he is well. Harry McDowell is also well, and all your acquaintances as far as I know. There is a prospect of dry weather now, & we anticipate very warm weather.

I should like very much to spend the 4th in Pontiac. I hope you may have a happy time. Give my love to Mother and Maggie. Kiss the children for me. Remember me kindly to all our friends. "Continue instant in prayer," and exercise unbounded Faith in Christ. "All things work to-gether for Good to those who trust in God." May the riches of his Grace rest upon your heart and his blessings be abundantly bestowed upon you. Write often.

Your Affectionate Husband

J. F. Culver

---

1 Frustrated in his efforts to flank Johnston's Army of Tennessee out of its Kennesaw Mountain line, General Sherman at 8 A.M. on June 27 made a frontal assault. McPherson's army on the left advanced against the breastworks on Little Kennesaw and Pigeon Hill defended by Loring's corps; Newton's division of Howard's corps and Davis' of Palmer's corps assailed the rifle-pits held by Hardee's corps on Cheatham Hill; Geary's division of Hooker's corps advanced on Palmer's right; and units of Schofield's army crossed Olley Creek and rolled up the Confederate cavalry screening Hood's left. McPherson's, Howard's and Palmer's bluecoats, although they drove in the Confederate pickets, were unable to cross the breastworks and were driven back with heavy losses. Cox, *Atlanta*, pp. 116-127.

2 Geary's division, advancing in support of Palmer's corps on its left, routed the Rebels from a line of rifle pits. To hold these gains, breastworks were erected and artillery advanced. *O.R.*, Ser. I, vol. XXXVIII, pt. II, p. 134.

3 On the 26th the 1st Brigade, including the 129th Illinois, had relieved Coburn's brigade in the advance rifle pits, north of the Powder Springs road. There was no truth to the

report that the XX Corps was going to "leave here to-night or in the morning for some new point." *Ibid.*, pp. 326, 387, 440.

4   The story that Sherman's "army group" had been reinforced by the XIII and XIX Corps was a wild rumor. The XIII Corps, currently assigned to the Department of the Gulf, was serving in Louisiana, and the XIX Corps was being transferred from New Orleans to Washington, D.C., by ship.

5   The Armies of the Potomac and the James had been checkmated in front of Petersburg. In the fourth week of June, the Army of the Potomac suffered a reverse in the battle of the Jerusalem Plank road.

 161

> Hd. Qurs. Co. "A" 129th Regt. Ills. Vols. Inftry.
> In the Field Near Marietta, Ga.
> July 1st 1864

My Dear Wife

Sergt. Jim Morrow arrived this morning bringing your letter of the 17th June and the box of cherries, the latter were all rotten. I am most happy to learn that your health is good. I gave Saml. McGooden his sister's letter, but have had no opportunity to send to Bro. John [Murphy]. There is a soldier here visiting belonging to the 44th Ills., and I will try & get him to carry the letter & will also send a note by him.[1]

The weather is clear and very warm. I am reaping the result of my promotion by acting "Brig. Off. of the Day."[2] I will try and write to Hill's S. School soon, & will do so to-day if I get time. We are drawing clothing to-day. I have not had a chance to talk with Jim [Morrow] yet, so many have been gathered around him gleaning news of Home that I did not wish to disturb him, much as I wish to learn all that he knows.

The men are all gathered around and talking so much that it is difficult to write. We have been on the rear line of fortifications for two days past but will probably be put in front to-night.[3] Col. Ben Harrison is again in command of the Brig. & Jim Mitchell is A.A.A.G.[4] The latter is rapidly improving in health but will probably never be quite well.

Chaplain Cotten has just passed around with some papers and tracts of which I got several. He has been quite ill for several days but is still able to be around. Harry McDowell has been sent to the Hospital sick with the fever; I think he will be around in a few days. My health is quite good for which I have every reason to be thankful.

We had a very excellent prayer-meeting last night and also two evenings ago. The boys are all very prompt in attendance, & I hope are striving earnestly to be Christians.

There has been no news of importance since I last wrote. We hear very little that is reliable, except what we get from the papers, all of which you have before it reaches [us]. Our losses in the series of charges made on last Monday & Tuesday will reach over 2,000.[5] We are still slowly but surely gaining ground. I have not heard from Allen Fellows since he left. I recd. a letter from Henry Greenebaum by Jim this morning. Saml. McGooden is well. Mrs. Baird and Mrs. Fitch have been on a visit to Lieut. Smith and have written that he is slowly improving.

I must make the round of the skirmish lines & must close. I recd. the stamps. Give my love to all. May Our Father in Heaven bless and preserve you. Good bye.

Your Affect. Husband

J. F. Culver

---

1   The 44th Illinois Infantry was assigned to the IV Corps division commanded by Brig. Gen. John Newton, the unit to which Company M, 1st Illinois Light Artillery, was attached. *O.R.*, Ser. I, Vol. XXXII, pt. III, pp. 551-552.

2   J.F.C. had been notified that he had been promoted to captain of Company A, 129th Illinois, to rank from Feb. 24, 1864, the date of Captain Hoskins' promotion to major. Compiled Service Records of Union Soldiers, NA.

3   The 3d Brigade (Wood's) on June 29 had relieved the 1st Brigade (Ward's) in the advance line of rifle pits north of the Powder Springs road. *O.R.*, Ser. I, Vol. XXXVIII, pt. II, p. 440.

4   General Butterfield on June 29 had received a leave to return to his home in New York and General Ward had assumed command of the Third Division, XX Army Corps. Colonel Harrison as senior colonel had resumed command of the 1st Brigade. *Ibid.*, p. 326.

5   Union casualties in the June 27 assaults on the Kennesaw Mountain line were 1,999 killed and wounded and 52 missing, while the Confederates lost about 500, of whom 270 were killed or wounded. Long, *The Civil War Day by Day,* p. 529.

 162

Hd. Qurs. 129th Regt. Ills. Vols. Infty.

In the Field 8 miles South West of Marietta,

Ga., July 4th 1864

My Dear Wife

Yours of the 23rd June came to hand yesterday evening, & I am most happy to learn of your good health. All thanks to our Father in Heaven.

About 8 P.M. on Saturday evening [the 2d], it was known that the enemy were falling back, & we were ordered to be in readiness to move at day-light next morning.[1] We moved out on the Marietta road at Sunrise through the enemy's fortifications. We came upon the rear of their columns & opened upon them with two Batteries to which they replied with Energy.[2]

Thos. Moran of my Company was killed.[3] It will devolve upon you to convey the painful intelligence to his family; they live near you. He was a noble man & excellent soldier. He has gone to rest. The affliction will be very severe to his widow and orphans. May God care for them. Tell his wife that if my life is spared I will write to her as soon as we get quieted down. He neither moved or spoke after he was struck; his head was broken in on the right side. We buried him & marked the grave. He lies on the road leading from Marietta to Powder Springs, about one mile from Marietta.

No one else was injured in the Company. We moved about 12 to 16 miles yesterday, but most of the time were hunting the enemy's position. We are now on the right flank.[4] The weather is very warm & it is difficult to make a march.

This the 4th. All our Bands are playing but the day bears but little aspect to the festivities of the day, the booming of the cannon can be heard to our left, & probably before night we will be fighting our way into position. It is supposed that the enemy will not make a determined stand on this side of the [Chattahoochie] river.

Give my love to Mother & Maggie. Tell Mary I accept the Kiss & wish to return it. May our Father in Heaven bless and keep you. He has thus far been with us. Let us trust all to him.

Committing all to God, Good bye,

Your Affect. Husband

J. F. Culver

---

1 In the days following the battle of Kennesaw Mountain, General Sherman pushed his right flank units to the southeast. Hooker's soldiers occupied rifle pits on both sides of the Powder Spring road, and General Schofield's Army of the Ohio was massed south of Olley Creek. This grave threat to his left compelled General Johnston on the night of July 2 to evacuate his Kennesaw Mountain line and retire into the entrenchments behind Nickajack Creek. Cox, *Atlanta*, p. 132.

2 General Ward reported that as his column advanced on Marietta, via the Powder Springs road, it encountered Rebel cavalry. He called up Battery I, 1st Michigan, which engaged two Confederate batteries unlimbered to the southeast, near the railroad, in a spirited duel. *O.R.*, Ser. I, Vol. XXXVIII, pt. II, pp. 326, 388.

3   Thomas Moran, a 27-year-old farmer, was mustered into service on Sept. 8, 1862, as a private in Company A, 129th Illinois Infantry. Private Grunert reported that the projectile scattered Moran's "brains in every direction." Grunert, *History of the 129th Illinois*, pp. 80-81; Compiled Service Records of Union Soldiers, NA.

4   On the 4th General Ward's division took position on the right of Hooker's corps, near Mill Grove. The Army of the Ohio was on Ward's right. *O.R.*, Ser. I, Vol. XXXVIII, pt. II, pp. 327, 388.

 163

Hd. Qurs. Co. "A" 129th Ills. Vol. Infty.
On Picket 6 o'clock A.M., July 9th 1864

My Dear Wife

I intended to write you a long letter yesterday but was so busy laying out a camp and fixing up that I deferred it until to-day, and last night I was detailed for Picket. I sent in at daylight this morning for the portfolio to write to you, but, before it arrived, we recd. orders to advance. Cris Yetter brought out my breakfast, & I hasten to write a line while we are waiting as it is probable the army may advance to-day, and I may have no other opportunity soon.

We recd. the news this morning that the right wing of our army has crossed the river (official) & it is probable the whole army will move rapidly forward. We were in hopes that a few days would be allowed for rest, but we will be content to submit cheerfully to the better judgment of others.

I am very happy to be able to tell you that my health is excellent for which let us praise God. All the Company are in good health. Harry McDowell has come up to the Regt., his health is much improved.

We are now ordered to move. God bless you. Good bye.

Your affect. Husband

J. F.Culver

8 A.M. I closed my letter hastily & gave it to Chris Yetter to mail, but he waited until we advanced our lines thus giving me an opportunity to resume. It is very warm this morning and indicates a hot day; all will be gratified if it does not become necessary to march to-day.

Yesterday evening's mail brought me no letters, yet I have recd. so many of late that I should be satisfied. Nate Hill has had a very sore foot, but it is improving rapidly. We rather expected to get pay before crossing the river, but it is probable now that we will have to wait till the close of the Campaign.

We had a very pleasant and profitable prayer meeting at Hd. Qurs. Co. "A" night before last, & I hope we may lay quiet to-morrow that we may enjoy the privileges of one more Holy Sabbath. We have been marching or fighting on every Sabbath of late, but I presume the necessities of the case demanded it. God has still dealt very kindly with us. Let us be thankful.

I have not heard yet from Bros. John or Sammy. Alf Huetson promised to go around and see them yesterday, but I have had no opportunity of seeing him since. I may learn of them after I am relieved this evening or to-morrow. I have had no opportunity to see Sergt. Gaff lately. John Lee was up to see me yesterday; he is well. I also saw Robinson (son of Warren Robinson) of the 20th Ills. yesterday; he says that all the boys that are left are well. All the non-veterans have gone home.

I must close as Yetter is anxious to return. If we do not move to-morrow, I will write. Give my love to all. Trust all to God. May his blessings rest upon you.

Your affect. Husband

J. F. Culver

 164

Hd. Qurs. Co. "A" 129th Regt. Ills., Vols. Infty.
In the Field Near Chattahoochie River July 10th 1864

My Dear Wife

Yours of June 30th has just come to hand. I am most happy to learn that you enjoy such a good degree of health. May our Father in Heaven bless you with a continuance of the same. My health continues to be very good for which I feel very thankful. I am sorry to learn that Lt. Smith improves so slowly, as we certainly expected him to be with us soon.[1] I hope, however, that he may soon recover. The health of the Company is very good.

Last night the enemy evacuated all their works on this side of the river, and our lines of Skirmishers were advanced to the river bank.[2] The 23rd Corps are on the other side on the enemy's right flank and probably to-morrow the whole army will advance. Rumor says the Rebs destroyed the R. R. Bridge which is very probable.[3]

I am sorry that Mathis is disposed to give you any trouble; I will write to Mr. Lyons and Mathis on the subject. Do not allow the matter to give you any unnecessary trouble. The well is not worth repairing and must remain until I get home, if it be God's will to spare my life.[4] If Mathis desires to leave the premises, he will probably give you notice, &, if you cannot readily rent it, it can remain empty. I cannot make any arrangements at present to regulate the matter. If you need money, try and borrow of Mrs. Fellows or Mr. Remick until pay-day.[5]

We packed up & moved out of camp this morning but were brought back again & now occupy the same ground we have occupied for the last three days.[6] I have heard nothing from Bros. John or Sammy yet; they are about 3 miles to the left of us.[7] I have enclosed a letter to Mrs. Moran and Wm. B. Lyons in this as I have no ink to back envelopes, though if I can succeed in getting any, I will mail them separately.

I have no desire to sell our property at present, though if Mathis offers you $1,250.00 cash, you can tell him he can have it for that if you desire to part with it. I am very glad you have told me of it, an early knowledge of such things may save me a great deal of trouble. I can very easily settle the matter. All matters relating to business should be known to me. I wish for your sake we could receive our pay, but that is improbable until after the Campaign closes.

I am much obliged for the extracts from the Chicago Tribune. It is always much later than any papers we get.

We had our S. School this morning, and it was a very profitable meeting to me, & I hope to all the rest of the Company present. Chris Yetter and Nate Hill are well. I will write a short note to the aid-society in behalf of Mrs. Moran. Unless they assist her, she will undoubtedly suffer. Her husband recd. no pay since Dec. 31st, 1863, & it will be 6 or 7 months before she gets back pay and bounty due him. Try & get the people interested in behalf of the needy soldiers' wives. They are doing all they can for the country, & the thought that their loved ones at home may suffer is a great barrier to their enjoyment and a source of constant sorrow.

I should write to the  Hill S. School  to-day,  but it is drawing near mail  time, & I  think of so much I  would like to write as tnis may be the last  opportunity for several days.

Give my love to Mother and Maggie and kiss the children for me. I have enjoyed much of the presence of God; let us praise his name and trust all to him.

The weather is very warm but the health of the troops good. Remember us in your prayers. We live in hopes that the time will soon come where we can mingle our voices with those we love in praise to God for a Country saved from intestine war and in peace and prosperity. Pray for our Country. Now is the day of trial, but, God being with us, all will be well. May the richest of Heaven's blessings rest upon you.

Your affect. Husband

J. F. Culver

P.S. Tell Remick Hume Tuckerman has just come into my tent — that he is well & looks well. He belongs to the 20th Ills.[8]

1   Lieutenant Smith was at home, recovering from the wound received at Resaca in mid-May.

2   The Confederates, on the night of July 4, evacuated their lines behind Nickajack Creek and retired into previously prepared defenses covering the crossings of the Chattahoochie River. On the 5th, Ward crossed Nickajack Creek and advanced his division along Turner's Ferry road. It was an exhausting march, and on the 6th the division took position "confronting the enemy's fortifications on the Chattahoochie." The camps were on a high ridge overlooking the river. *O.R.*, Ser. I, Vol. XXXVIII, pt. II, pp. 327, 388.

3   General Sherman, in a successful effort to flank the Confederates out of their Chattahoochie line, pulled General Schofield's Army of the Ohio (the XXIII Corps) out of its position on the right of the Army of the Cumberland and marched it to Smyrna Camp Ground, near the Western & Atlantic Railroad. On the 8th Schofield's divisions, with the army's pontoon train, marched northeast and forced its way across the Chattahoochie at a lightly defended crossing at Phillip's Ferry. Confederate efforts to destroy Schofield's bridgehead failed, and on the night of the 9th, General Johnston withdrew to the south bank of the Chattahoochie. Next morning Rebel engineers removed their pontoon bridges. and Johnston's rear guard retired, burning the railroad and highway bridges. Cox, *Atlanta*, pp. 134-140.

4   Mathis was renting the Culver property. Apparently, the well had failed and Mathis was demanding its repair.

5   Mrs. Fellows was either the wife or mother of the hospital steward J. Allen Fellows of the 129th Illinois Infantry.

6   In a futile effort to cut off and capture Confederate stragglers, Ward advanced a line of skirmishers to the Chattahoochie. After establishing a picket line, the troops returned to their camps to rest and wait for the Pioneers to bridge the river. *O.R.*, Ser. I, Vol. XXXVIII, pt. II, p. 327.

7   Company M, 1st Illinois Light Artillery, on the 5th had unlimbered its six guns on high ground, near Pace's Ferry, from where could be seen the spires of Atlanta, eight miles to the southeast. Next day a number of ranking officers, including Generals Sherman and Howard, visited the battery and watched as the gunners engaged Rebel cannon on the opposite side of the Chattahoochie. *Report of the Adjutant General of Illinois,* Vol. XIII, p. 668.

8   Hume Tuckerman, a 21-year-old farmer, was mustered into service on June 13, 1861, at Joliet, Ill., as a private in Company D, 20th Illinois Infantry. Wounded at Shiloh in April 1862, he was detailed in June as regimental teamster. On Jan. 5, 1864, he reenlisted as a veteran volunteer at Big Black Bridge, Miss., and in June 1864 was detailed as brigade wagonmaster. Private Tuckerman was mustered out at Louisville, Ky., July 16, 1865. Compiled Service Records of Union Soldiers, NA.

 165

Hd. Qurs. Co. "A" 129th Regt. Ills. Vol. Infty.
In the Field Near Chattahoochie River
July 11th 1864

My Dear Wife

Contrary to expectation, we are still laying in Camp resting. Alf [Heutson] was here a short time ago, & he thinks there is a prospect of our remaining here several days.

The mail has generally gone out at 4 o clock, but I have just learned that it goes out to-day at 2, so I have only a few minutes to write in. I just finished a letter to the Hill Sunday School, but I was interrupted so often that I fear it will not be interesting.

We are all well to-day and the weather very warm. There is light Skirmishing along the river bank, but it is three miles distant and we seldom hear it.[1] We had prayer-meeting last evening and a very profitable time. Alf drew a sketch of the burning of a cotton factory by our Cavalry and left it at my tent when I was on picket, but someone stole it before I got to see it.[2] He intended it for you. I sent you a map of our position two days ago.[3]

The mail has just arrived, and I hope has brought a letter for me, but I must send this out or it will be too late. Give my love to all. May our Father in Heaven bless and preserve you.

Your affect. Husband

J. F. Culver

---

1   Historian Grunert reported that in the skirmishing on July 11, Private William F. Dermund of Company E was killed. Grunert, *History of the 129th Illinois*, p. 82.

2   Union cavalry had occupied Roswell on July 7, where there were "extensive cotton, wool and paper mills, running at their full capacity and till this last moment turning out supplies for the Confederate government." The owners in a futile effort to protect their property claimed their ownership was French and raised the tricolor. Sherman did not recognize this subterfuge, and they were burned. Cox, *Atlanta*, p. 137.

3   This map is missing from the Culver Collection.

 166

Head Qurs. Co. "A" 129th Regt. Ills. Vols.
In the Field Near Chattahoochie River
July 16th 1864

My Dear Wife

The mail came in twice yesterday but brought no letter from you. I heard from you, however, up to July 5th through Mrs. McDowell; she writes to Harry that you are well. I am indeed happy to hear it.

My health continues to be good. Col. Case recd. a letter from Lieut. Smith yesterday, in which he says he expects to be able to return to the Company in a few days. Major Hoskins recd. a letter from his wife yesterday of date the 5th in which she says you are well.

We still remain in Camp, while the rest of the army is working its way rapidly toward Atlanta.[1] We have heard no news lately, except that some 2,000 prisoners have been forwarded to the North.[2] The health of the Regiment is good, and all the boys are full of life. We have not been able yet to determine what disposition will be made of us. Some conjecture that we will be left to guard the rear, while McPherson's army moves to the front to do the fighting for awhile.[3]

The pay-master is expected in a few days. Chris [Yetter] went out for blackberries this afternoon; we have had them quite plenty for a few days past. Nate [Hill] is well and enjoying himself. We had a very excellent meeting last night and anticipate a good day to-morrow. Quite a number of our Regt. are seeking the Savior. I will try and write a short letter to the Sabbath School to-morrow if I am not sent on duty. Give my love to all the family and remember me kindly to all our friends. May our Heavenly Father bless you.

Good bye,

Your Affect. Husband

J. F. Culver

---

1 Howard's IV Corps had been rushed to Schofield's support at Phillips' Ferry; Dodge's XVI Corps, reinforced by Newton's IV Corps division, bridged the Chattahoochie at Roswell; and Thomas' Pioneers on the night of the 12th laid a pontoon bridge at Powers' Ferry.

Sherman's plans called for Schofield's Army of the Ohio to advance from its bridgehead at Phillips' Ferry by way of Cross Keys toward Decatur. McPherson's Army of the Tennessee, having been moved from the right, would cross the Chattahoochie at Roswell, and, covered by a cavalry division, take position on the extreme left and strike the Georgia Railroad between Decatur and Stone Mountain. Thomas' Army of the Cumberland was to cross the Chattahoochie at Pace's and Phillips' Ferries and approach Atlanta from the north. Cox, *Atlanta,* pp. 142-147.

2 During July, Sherman's "army group" captured 3,200 Confederates and paroled 732 deserters. Of this number, the Army of the Cumberland had captured 2,722 Rebels and counted 576 deserters. *O.R.,* Ser. I, Vol. XXXVIII, pt. I, p. 159.

3 General McPherson's Army of the Tennessee in the second week of July was withdrawn from its position on the right of Hooker's corps and marched northeast to Roswell, where Dodge's XVI Corps had established a bridgehead. By the morning of the 17th, the last of McPherson's soldiers had crossed the 700-foot pontoon bridge and were south of the Chattahoochie. In the advance on Atlanta, McPherson's army would be on the left, Schofield's in the center, and Thomas' on the right. *O.R.,* Ser. I, Vol. XXXVIII, pt. III, p. 38.

 167

Head Qurs. Co. "A" 129th Regt. Ills. Vols.<br/>July 17 1864 - 2 o clock P.M.

My Dear Wife

I wrote a short note this forenoon & sent by Alf Huetson to the mail,[1]

*323*

at which time we had orders to march at 3 o clock P.M. The orders have been countermanded just now, though we are held in readiness to move at a moment's notice.[2] I therefore am happy to have an opportunity to write to you as I promised in my letter yesterday, so until the orders come I am wholly yours.

I have felt a desire which is daily increasing to be with you during your anticipated trial in August.[3] If there was any probability of the Campaign closing very soon, I should make an effort. I was almost persuaded a few days ago when it was rumored that we would spend a month here, but, now as we commence the advance upon Atlanta, I could not expect to succeed. We will hope, however, that if God spares my life and health through the balance of this Campaign, we may have the joy of greeting each other again. We live in hope and trust all to God.

While engaged in marching and fighting, I do not think of Home so constantly, but, for the last eleven days laying here, it has been constantly in my mind. I have felt considerable uneasiness during the past few days as no letters have arrived. The last one received was dated June 30th. To most men who seldom receive more than two or three letters a month, there would be no alarm, but you have written so punctually every few days that I have feared you were sick. You do not know, perhaps, how dependent I am upon the knowledge of your good health and happiness for my own happiness and contentment.

The greatest desire I have after the performance of the duty I owe to God and my country is to be worthy of your Love and Confidence, and to contribute all in my power to your happiness. Nothing but a full conviction of duty could have induced me to leave you thus alone for so long a time. I know you feel lonely and desolate at times and especially under your present trying circumstances, but I feel that "Our Father in Heaven" will sustain you and deal kindly with you. Did I not feel so confident that Mother [Murphy] will do all she can for you, and knowing her thorough knowledge and ability to do more for you than I could, I should feel very uneasy. But it is almost an impossibility, and I do not even anticipate my ability to be with you so soon, even should everything here move rapidly and victoriously forward.

The 14th Corps is crossing the river to-day, & I think all the army is over except the Cavalry and our corps.[4] Quite a large body of troops have been left at Marietta & vicinity to guard our communications, while troops are almost daily arriving from the rear.[5] Lieut. Scott arrived on Friday last;[6] he was wounded at Resaca & has been home. Quite a number of those slightly wounded are returning.

The weather to-day has been very pleasant. It rained last night, and the air to-day is quite cool. This climate is not as severe as I expected, though it is very warm some days. We feel very much refreshed by our rest here; this makes the 11th day we have been in camp. Our supplies have been abundant. Rations of beans have been issued every few days, also dessicated potatoes & rice. The men have been troubled with diarrhea caused by eating berries and green fruit, I presume, but they will soon get over it when we get to marching again.

All are in good spirits. Our Sunday School this morning was very profitable, there were about 30 present. Lt. Scott preached a very good sermon. We have been holding meetings every evening for some time past, and a very excellent state of feeling exists. I did hope to have an opportunity to-day to write to the Sabbath School, but unless we receive orders to remain here for the night I could not undertake it.

There has been very heavy cannonading over the river all day.[7] Rumor says the Enemy made a desperate chase on Friday night-last [the 15th] but were repulsed with very heavy loss.[8] Everything in this department has been entirely successful. God has been with us and signally blessed every effort we have made.

I have not heard from Bro. John or Sammy yet, but may meet them over the river. The mail will be in by 5 o clock, & I hope will bring a letter for me. Remember me kindly to all the S. School children and all our friends. Give my Love to Mother and Maggie. Why is it they never write? Do you ever hear from Carlisle? I presume the raid into Cumberland Valley will cause considerable excitement there.[9] I have written several letters but get no reply.

Write as often as you can. May our Father in Heaven bless you. Please accept all the love and affection of my heart and be assured that you are dearer to me than all of Earth beside.

Your Affect. Husband

J. F. Culver

---

1 The "short note" is missing from the Culver Collection.

2 General Thomas, on the morning of the 17th, ordered General Hooker's XX Corps to cross the Chattahoochie at Pace's Ferry. As the XIV Corps was crossing, Hooker was to regulate his movements accordingly. This was the reason for the delay. *O.R.,* Ser. I, Vol. XXXVIII, pt. V, p. 161.

3 Mary Culver was eight months pregnant.

4 General McPherson's and Schofield's armies were south of the Chattahoochie and feeling their way toward Decatur. General Howard's IV Corps of Thomas' army, having crossed the Chattahoochie at Power's Ferry, covered the crossing of the XIV Corps at Pace's Ferry. J. F. C. was mistaken on one point; Brig. Gen. Kenner Garrard's cavalry

division was across the Chattahoochie, screening McPherson's left flank, and preparing for a dash on the Georgia Railroad, east of Decatur. *Ibid.*, p. 158.

5  A brigade of infantry was posted at Kennesaw Mountain and Big Shanty to protect the railroad near Marietta. Three regiments, one from each army, were posted at Marietta to unload cars. Brig. Gen. John E. Smith's division of McPherson's army guarded the railroad from Allatoona to Cartersville. *Ibid.*, pp. 112-113.

6  Abel H. Scott, a 37-year-old minister, was mustered into service on Sept. 8, 1862, as a sergeant in Company F, 129th Illinois Infantry. He was promoted to sergeant major on March 7, 1863, and three months later, he was commissioned 2d lieutenant. Lieutenant Scott was wounded in the left hip at Resaca on May 15, 1864, and was hospitalized until mid-July when he rejoined his company. On Dec. 29, 1864, Scott was mustered in as regimental chaplain to replace Brother Cotton. Compiled Service Records of Union Soldiers, NA.

7  McPherson's and Schofield's columns, as they forged ahead, skirmished with Confederate cavalry. A Rebel battery, supported by infantry and emplaced in a redoubt north of the railroad, engaged in a duel with cannoneers of the 11th Indiana Battery. During the afternoon, the Southerners limbered up their pieces and retired across Peachtree Creek. *O.R.*, Ser. I, Vol. XXXVIII, pt. V, pp. 158, 160.

8  There was no substance to this rumor. On July 16 the regimental historian reported, "Not a single shot was fired by the pickets of our brigade at the Rebels, or by those at us, but the Rebels were prohibited from speaking a single word to our men and would not allow them to go into the water. Our men were generally out of tobacco and continually asked the Rebels for some, who did not answer, but now and then tied a piece of tobacco on a stone, and threw it over the river." Grunert, *History of the 129th Illinois,* p. 83.

9  A powerful column led by Lt. Gen. Jubal A. Early had advanced up the Shenandoah Valley, crossed the Potomac, and on July 9 occupied Frederick, Md., defeating a small Union army in the battle of Monocacy. Early's army then threatened Washington. But on finding that the force holding the capital city had been heavily reinforced, Early, after demonstrating against Fort Stevens, retired and recrossed the Potomac into Virginia.

 168

Hd. Qrs. Co. "A" 129th Reg. Ills. Vols.
In the Field Near Atlanta, Ga., July 19th 1864

My Dear Wife

We crossed the river Sunday evening & are now in front of Atlanta.[1] I recd. two letters yesterday, dated the 6th & 7th, and was very happy to learn of your good health. May our Father fill our hearts with gratitude for all his mercies and blessings.

I saw Jim Rawlins yesterday evening just as we were forming our lines.[2] He says Bros. John & Sammy are both well; they lie about 1-1/2 miles to our left. I may get to see them to-day, but it is probable that our lines will be advanced to-day which may keep us all very busy.[3]

The greater part of our army has crossed the river and Rumor says our left rests on the railroad running from Atlanta to Richmond.[4] If it is true, we may gain Stone Mountain without any very hard fighting, and thus compel the evacuation of Atlanta.

The weather yesterday afternoon & this morning has been quite pleasant, a cool breeze is stirring. We are all well with the exception of a few cases of diarrhea. I recd. a letter from Tom Smith yesterday,[5] & he is improving rapidly. I am happy to hear that Lt. Smith is improving. Mrs. Fellows sent Allen two lbs. of tobacco by mail at a cost of only 8 cts. per lb. It is very difficult to get here. If convenient, send me 2 or 3 lbs. of plug tobacco (natural leaf). Fine cut would all dry up before it reached here.

Jesse Massey is at home but will have started for the Company before this reaches you.[6] Tell Lt. Smith we have used all his letter paper & envelopes and to bring a large supply with him. If convenient send me by him a tin plate or two, a tin cup, and knife & fork, also a couple of towels.

May God keep you in health and make you happy. Trust all to him; He has kept us thus far & will still be with us. His Grace is all sufficient for us. I will pray for you as I always have done. In all my prayers you have been remembered, and will always be. Let us hope and pray for a speedy reunion. Give my love to all the family. I accept the kisses. Committing all our interests to God, and trusting in our acceptance of Him through Christ, I remain, as ever, in Love,

Your Affect. Husband

J. F. Culver

---

1   Hooker's corps had crossed the Chattahoochie at Pace's Ferry on the evening of the 17th and halted for the night within one mile of Nancy Creek. This stream was bridged the next morning, and the corps advanced and took position on the right of General Howard's IV Corps. Ward's division was on the left. Before going into camp, the troops entrenched. *O.R.,* Ser. I, Vol. XXXVIII, pt. II, p. 327.

2   James Rollins of Pontiac had been mustered into service on July 9, 1862, as a private in Company M, 1st Illinois Light Artillery. *Report of the Adjutant General of Illinois,* Vol. VIII, p. 655.

3   Company M had crossed the Chattahoochie on July 13 with General Howard's IV Corps. On the 18th it had engaged and silenced a Rebel battery on Nancy Creek. *Ibid.,* p. 666.

4 Soldiers of McPherson's Army of the Tennessee, on July 18, had reached the Georgia Railroad, seven miles east of Decatur and four miles from Stone Mountain. Garrard's cavalry was burning trestles and twisting rails. *O.R.*, Ser. I, Vol. XXXVIII, pt. V, pp. 169-170.

5 Thomas R. Smith, a 23-year-old farmer, had been mustered into service on Sept. 8, 1862, as a private in Company A, 129th Illinois Infantry. Private Smith was shot in the left arm at New Hope Church on May 27, 1864, and hospitalized at Quincy, Ill., until discharged on May 18, 1865. Compiled Service Records of Union Soldiers, NA.

6 Jesse Massey, a 30-year-old miner, was mustered into service on Sept. 8, 1862, as a private in Company A, 129th Illinois Infantry. Private Massey was wounded in the hand at Resaca on May 15, 1864, and while hospitalized deserted on June 28, 1864. He rejoined the company on Jan. 22, 1865, and was mustered out with the regiment on June 8, 1865, near Washington, D.C. *Ibid.*

⟨⟨⟨ 169 ⟩⟩⟩

Head Quarters Co. "A" 129th Regt. Ills. Vols.
In the field in front of Atlanta, Ga.
July 23rd 1864

My Dear Wife

I have had no opportunity to answer fully your letters of the 9th, 10th & 12th, & shall not be able to do so to-day, I presume. You must have gathered a large quantity of Sanitary Stores judging from the quantities mentioned in your several letters.[1] I hope I may have an opportunity to assist in consuming them. Your health has been much better than I anticipated, & I am very happy. God has dealt very kindly with us.

I am very much obliged for the papers you sent. I have recd. some 5 or 6 within a very few days. I have understood all along that Henry Greenebaum was strong for the union & am surprised to learn that he has any sentiments in common with the Copperheads.[2]

The Sentinel notices a tornado which passed through town lately, but I see it did not do much damage.[3] I spoke to Chris Yetter about not writing, but he gave no satisfactory answer. I presume it is negligence more than anything else.

I have no doubt the ride with Maggie to Mr. Russell's was very pleasant & wish you could enjoy very many like it. I wrote a short letter and enclosed my Commission.[4] I hope it has reached you.

Genl. Ward was not arrested but is commanding the Division; Genl. Butterfield went east about the 20th of June.[5]

You wish to know who of the boys are regular attendants at prayer meeting. Almost all of the Company attend. Poor Tom Moran is dead. John McDermit is often near when our prayer-meetings are held but never takes part.[6]

Because all the questions you have asked have not been answered, you must not conclude that you do not receive all of mine. I have but seldom attempted to answer a letter fully during the Campaign, as my opportunities and time has been very limited. I can see no occasion for any reserve on your part in writing about yourself. I do not think what you have written at all silly & am very happy to hear thus from you. May our Father in Heaven deal kindly with you. I should like very much to have read those letters you thought unfit to send me & tore up.

I am still hoping that the Campaign may end, and my life and health be spared to get home by the middle of August, though it is scarcely probable just now. The Rebs have had a fine time shelling us this morning, & I hope they enjoyed it, as they done us no injury.[7]

The fighting along McPherson's line was very severe yesterday. The enemy made three assaults. At the fiirst, they succeeded in driving a portion of his line but they soon regained their position. The other two assaults were successfully repulsed. The enemy's loss must have been heavy.[8] During the afternoon a body of Rebel Cavalry turned his [McPherson's] left flank and attacked a wagon train in the rear. Genl. McPherson & his staff rode back to see what was the matter, and he was killed, also several of his Staff.[9] The Enemy captured a Battery & destroyed a large train.[10]

Last night, just after dark, the enemy got up a great noise & fired heavily on our pickets, but the pickets held their position & the night passed off quietly.[11] We are strongly entrenched here & the enemy are welcome to charge if they wish. We can certainly hold ten lines at bay as easily as we did five in the open field on the 20th.[12] Dinner is ready, two hardtack, coffee, & a piece of meat.

My dinner was very unceremoniously interrupted by a charge of the enemy upon our Skirmish line. They drove our line back about 20 rods, but the rallying soon regained their line.[13] They cut our dinner very short and are now treating us to another serenade of Shell. We have a great deal of artillery on our line, & when they open, they generally make the Johnies hush up.

It is very pleasant in the trenches to-day. The boys found a large quantity of blackberries in their advance yesterday. I will try and copy you a list of the casualties of the 20th.[14] I had no opportunity to get former lists.

I just now succeeded in getting a bottle filled with ink; I have been begging for a month past as mine was all spilled. This is blue but is better than none. I hear just now that our boys are 200 yds. in rear of their line & cannot retake it. The hill on which our pickets were posted gives a fine view of both the enemy's line and ours & was very valuable. The enemy can thus cover an advance for over half a mile. We may regain it again and will probably try.

All the boys are well. I recd. notice to-day that my Subscription to the Sentinel has expired. I would like to have the paper continued but cannot send the money now. I hear that we have no mail going out to-day & I may write more, but for the present I must close. Let us praise God for all his blessings and trust him for the future. "He doeth all things well."

Everything progresses finely thus far in this department. May God still be with us and give us victory. Give my love to Mother [Murphy] and Maggie and remember me kindly to all our friends. May the richest of Heaven's blessings rest upon you. Pray for Grace and Faith. I feel that God has been with me constantly and can safely trust all to His care. May He in his good Providence preserve our lives for the enjoyment of the future in commingling our voices in songs of praise.

Good bye.

Your Affect. Husband

J. F. Culver

P.S. Our boys charged the enemy and now hold their old line. Capt. Horton of Co. "F" commands the Skirmishers of our Brigade.[15] He is very brave and will do all that man can do. Chris [Yetter] & Nate [Hill] are well. Send me a few Stamps.

---

1 The Sanitary Commission, employing funds raised by voluntary donations and fund-raising "Sanitary Fairs," provided food, medicine, clothing, and other necessities for Union soldiers. Among popular items were lemons, oranges, other fruits and vegetables to provide a balanced diet for men who needed such items to combat scurvy. Francis A. Lord, *Civil War Sutlers and Their Wares* (New York, 1969), p. 65.

2 "Copperheads" were Democrats outspoken in their opposition to the Lincoln administration and its conduct of the war.

3 A tornado had struck Pontiac in early July.

4 J.F.C.'s commission as captain of Company A, 129th Illinois Infantry, was dated June 29, 1864.

5 Brig. Gen. William T. Ward had replaced Maj. Gen. Daniel Butterfield as commander of the Third Division, XX Corps, on June 29, 1864. *O.R.*, Ser. I, Vol. XXXVIII, pt. II, p. 321.

6   John McDermitt, a 25-year-old miner, was mustered into service on Sept. 8, 1862, as a private in Company A, 129th Illinois Infantry. Private McDermitt was mustered out on June 8, 1865, near Washington, D.C. Compiled Service Records of Union Soldiers, NA.

7   On July 21, the day after the battle of Peachtree Creek, soldiers of the Third Division spent the day burying the dead and caring for the wounded. On the 22d General Ward's division felt its way closer to Atlanta, its line of advance the Buck Head road. After advancing about three miles, the foe was encountered, and General Ward deployed his division, Colonel Harrison's brigade taking position and entrenching on a ridge south of the road. To the front, not more than 1,000 yards distant, were the Rebel fortifications. A shell from one of the Confederate cannon exploded in the rifle pits occupied by Company A, 129th Illinois, but fortunately caused no casualties. *O.R.*, Ser. I, Vol. XXXVIII, pt. II, p. 348; Grunert, *History of the 129th Illinois*, p. 88.

8   Gen. John B. Hood had replaced General Johnston as commander of the Army of Tennessee on July 18. On the 22d as McPherson's army was closing in on Atlanta from the east, Hood marched one of his corps to assail McPherson's exposed left flank. Confederates of Lt. Gen. William J. Hardee's corps, attacking with their characteristic elan, swept forward. While Hardee's divisions were driving back McPherson's left, Maj. Gen. B. Franklin Cheatham's corps advanced and assaulted McPherson's center at Leggett's Hill. Cheatham's brigades were beaten back by the bluecoats in savage fighting. McPherson's left, after giving ground, rallied and checked Hardee's onslaught, and the tide of battle shifted. Repulsed, Hardee's and Cheatham's corps withdrew into the Atlanta defenses. Confederate casualties in this fight, known as the battle of Atlanta, were more than 8,000, while Union losses numbered 3,521. Cox, *Atlanta*, pp. 163-176.

9   J.F.C. had been misinformed as to details of General McPherson's death. On learning of the assault on his left, McPherson had left Sherman's headquarters and had ridden to the point of danger. After ordering his trains to be moved to a less exposed position, McPherson and one aide encountered a Confederate skirmish line, advancing into a gap torn in the Union line. When he refused to heed their call to surrender, the Confederates opened fire, killing McPherson and wounding and capturing his aide. *Ibid.*, p. 169.

10   The Confederates in the battle of Atlanta captured two Union batteries and two guns of Company A, 1st Illinois Light Artillery. One of these batteries (De Gress') was recaptured when Cheatham's corps was repulsed. *Ibid.*, p 175.

11   Private Grunert reported that on the 22d, the foe made no effort to harass the Federals as they entrenched until dark. Their artillery then roared into action, but "by this time our breastworks afforded us good shelter." Grunert, *History of the 129th Illinois*, p. 87.

12   On July 20 as Thomas' Army of the Cumberland was crossing Peachtree Creek, it was attacked by the Confederates. The 129th Illinois, in accordance with Colonel Harrison's orders, crossed a low pine-covered ridge and a ravine, and ascended a steep cleared hill. When about halfway up the hill, the left wing was subjected to a galling fire from Rebel sharpshooters posted in the underbrush. Pressing on, the bluecoats reached the crest to discover a column of Confederates ascending the hill from the opposite direction. The right battalion of the 129th beat back the foe, routing them from behind a fence. When the Confederates recoiled, they left many dead and wounded on the slopes, along with two stands of colors. The 70th Indiana and 105th Illinois now came forward, scaled the hill, and took position on the left of the 129th Illinois. In the fight for the hill the 129th had 12 killed and 49 wounded. *Ibid.*, pp. 84-87; *O.R.*, Ser. I, Vol. XXXVIII, pt. II, pp. 344-46, 367-68.

Confederate assaults at other points along Thomas' front likewise failed, and they retired leaving the Federals in possession of the field. The battle of Peachtree Creek cost the foe about 6,000 casualties and the Union about 2,000. Cox, *Atlanta*, p. 158.

13   Regimental historian Grunert reported, "At noon our pickets were driven some distance by the enemy, being in too close proximity to him; but when our pickets advanced

again, the enemy retreated and our men resumed their old position." Grunert, *History of the 129th Illinois*, p. 88.

14  Probably sent with note written on July 25 or 26.

15  George W. Horton, a 25-year-old carpenter, was mustered into service on Sept. 8, 1862, as 1st lieutenant of Company F, 129th Illinois Infantry. He was promoted to captain of his company on June 11, 1863. On Jan. 11, 1865, he received a leave of absence, rejoining his unit in April, and was mustered out near Washington, D.C., June 8, 1865. Compiled Service Records of Union Soldiers, NA.

～∾⇒ 170 ⇐∾～

July 24th [1864]

Sunday morning.

All thanks to a kind Father, we are all safe & well. God has been with us. I saw Bro. John [Murphy] this morning, he is very well; Bro. Sammy was back with the wagons in the rear and is not very well.

The Enemy kept Shelling us until 8 o clock last night. They threw one shell into the fortifications on the left centre of my Company. It burst before it got through the Embankment & threw a vast amount of ground into the trenches covering Billy Hughes & Ed Geller and several others.[1] I expected to find some of them seriously hurt but no one was injured. We worked until a late hour last night, & I think we are shell proof unless some of the pieces come straight down. They have thrown quite a number of shells over us this morning, & a piece came down within a few feet of Major Hoskins a moment ago. We have recd. no injury thus far.[2]

I was told while up with Bro. John a little while ago that the carnage along the line of McPherson's Army was terrible. They buried 1,700 of the enemy killed; if that be true, their loss must be 8 to 10,000.[3] There will doubtless be a severe battle within a few days that will decide the fate of Atlanta. There was a large fire in the direction of the city last night, & it is supposed that some of our shells set fire to the city. We have several Batteries that can shell the city, but very few were opened.

It was almost cool enough last night for frost & is very pleasant this morning. How pleasant it would be to get away from all this tumult and enter the Sanctuary of the Lord this morning. I can imagine what a comfort it would be. Yet God is with us, kindly caring for and comforting us. Let our hearts praise him for all His mercies. We hope for a day of rest and quiet to-day. We have generally been moving or fighting and have seldom had the Sabbath as a day of worship. Our chaplain [Thomas Cotton] has not been visible since the day before the battle [of Peachtree Creek] of the 20th. He is somewhere in the rear, I presume, perhaps at the Hospital.

We have been favored with very pleasant weather except that some days were very warm. I presume you are not able to attend S. School and church this morning, may our Father comfort and bless you and give you Grace and Faith.[4] It is sweet to commune with Him, to comtemplate his Power and Glory with his Love for fallen creatures. With all our Sin and unworthiness, He neither leaves nor forsakes us but his mercies are extended every day and his invitations and promises are not withheld from us. Let us then trust in the Lord forever for in Him is everlasting strength.

I may make an effort to write to the Sunday School to-day if we remain quiet. I must write a letter to Sister Hannah this morning. We expect a mail to-day and an opportunity to send letters out. Bro. John will be here after a little while & may write a line.

Give my love to Mother [Murphy] and Maggie. Tell them to pray for us & especially for me that Grace may be given me to discharge my whole duty and find favor in the sight of God. Remember me kindly to all our friends. I know you will pray for me. Let our hearts constantly praise the Lord for all his goodness to us. Write often, &, when your health will not permit your writing, get Mother [Murphy] to write every day if it be only one line to tell me how you are getting along.

May our Father deal kindly with you in your coming trial and grant unto you the full realization of all your hopes and desires.

Good bye,

Your affectionate Husband

J. F. Culver

---

1   William E. Hughes, a 30-year-old miner, was mustered into service on Sept. 8, 1862, as a private in Company A, 129th Illinois Infantry. Serving with the regiment throughout the war, Hughes was mustered out on June 8, 1865, near Washington, D.C. Edward Geller, a 31-year-old farmer, was mustered into service on Sept. 8, 1862, as a private in Company A, 129th Illinois Volunteers. He was promoted corporal on April 7, 1865, and mustered out on June 8, 1865, near Washington, D.C. Compiled Service Records of Union Soldiers, NA. Allen was either Bartlett B. or Joseph, soldiers in Company A, 129th Illinois.

2   Historian Grunert recorded that the bombardment killed two blacks in the sector held by the regiment. Grunert, *History of the 129th Illinois,* p. 88.

3   Jacob D. Cox placed the Confederate dead in the battle of Atlanta on July 22 at 2,500. Cox, *Atlanta*, pp. 175-176.

4   Mary Culver was eight months  pregnant and would soon give birth to a second child.

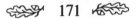 171

[July 26, 1864]

Dear Mary

Yours of the 4th & 17th just came to hand. Jim Rawlins has just left here, and he says Sammy was sent to the Hospital to-day. I am happy to know that you are so well.

In haste,

J. F. Culver

The above note probably was transmitted with J.F.C.'s "Names of Killed and Wounded in the 129th Ills. before Atlanta, July 20, 1864," a list of casualties arranged by company with a statistical summary.

```
Total
   Killed - 12
   Wounded
      Officers   3
      E. Men    49
   Total         52
```

[At the end of the list, J.F.C. penned this instruction:]

You can lend this to M. E. Collins if he wishes to publish it [in the Pontiac "Sentinel"], but I would like this Copy preserved.

J. F. Culver

## 172

Head Qurs., Co. "A" 129th Regt. Ills. Vols.
In the Field Near Atlanta, Georgia
July 28th 1864

My Dear Wife

Your letter of July 18th was recd. since I last wrote. I am very happy to learn that you enjoy such good health and also that my letters have added to your happiness. May our Father in Heaven, who has been so bountiful in blessings to us, continue to preserve us in life and health and give us Grace to discharge our duty in such a manner as may find favor in his sight.

Night before last we were moved into reserve, and we are now on the 2nd line resting. My health is still excellent, &, though I was quite ill for a few hours yesterday, I have every reason to be thankful for God's Goodness. The notice you saw in the papers about receiving pay on descriptive rolls must be a mistake as we have recd. no such notice. All sick and wounded are paid on descriptive rolls at the Hospitals in Nashville and places North of that, but that is all.

I am glad to learn that Lieut. Smith's health is improving so rapidly; I cannot imagine why he has never written to any of us. I saw Asa Alden yesterday; he is quite well and has escaped unharmed. He is an excellent soldier.

The account I wrote you in my last letter concerning the 20 Ills. is confirmed; only 16 of the men have escaped. The Lt. Col's. Adjt. & 1st Capt., Capt. Charles Paige is reported killed. Lieut. Donaldson of the 52nd Ohio was killed a few days ago and his company captured. I will try and get you a copy of Genl. Thomas' Order which gives the result of the fight for Atlanta. I saw Bro. John two days ago; he was well and says that Bro. Sammy is getting along as well as could be expected.

It was quite wet yesterday afternoon, and the weather is sultry and warm today and looks very much like rain. As we are expecting to draw clothing and I shall be busy, so I hastened to write to you this morning. The health of the Company is good. Green was quite sick for a day or two but is quite well again. The Campaign is still progressing favorably, and we trust in God that it may soon be successfully terminated. Let us continue to pray in Faith.

God is dealing very kindly with me, and my heart rejoices this morning in his presence. Who can tell the wonderful precious Love of Jesus? Though I have been most unworthy, yet am I not forsaken. May the richest of Heaven's blessings rest upon you. I have prayed that God would increase your Faith and fill you with His Love. Trust all to Him for He will never leave nor forsake you. You speak in your letter of the happiness you anticipate when, the war being successfully terminated, we may again enjoy the pleasures and privileges of Home. Let us hope that God in his good Providence may grant us that great blessing, but above all let us pray for Grace to be resigned to His will knowing that "He doeth all things well."

Allen Fellows just came to my tent and has just returned. He looks badly, and his health is not good. I wish he had remained in Chattanooga, for, should the Campaign be lengthened beyond Atlanta, his health is not sufficient for the task. He had a letter from home of date the 18th, the same date of my last. We expect a mail to-day.

There has been but little fighting on our front for the last few days. We may have a severe battle before we get possession of Atlanta, and we may get it without much effort. None but God knows, & we are willing to leave all to him. There appears to be no reason to doubt but that our Army will occupy it very soon, perhaps within a week.

Give my love to Mother & Maggie and remember me kindly to all our friends. May Our Father in Heaven be with you & hasten the day of reunion amid the Peace and prosperity of a happy people and a Country reunited and prosperous. Accept the constant love and affection of

Your Husband

J. F. Culver

P.S. I have tried to get the circular issued by Genl. Thomas, but fear I may not succeed until too late for the mail. The substance is as follows:

Our loss on the 20th was about 1,760 in killed, wounded, and missing, on the 21st, 22nd, & 23rd, about 2,150. Of the Enemy on the 20th, about 6,000; of the enemy on the 21st, 22nd, & 23rd, there was buried about 3,500 beside a large number the Enemy was permitted to bury. The Enemy's loss is estimated at from 15 to 20,000.

Should I get opportunity, I will still copy the circular and forward it.

## 173

Head Qurs. Co. "A" 129th Regt. Ills. Vols.
In the Field near Atlanta, Ga., August 3rd 1864

My Dear Wife

Chaplain Cotton starts for home to-day [1] & I hope to have an opportunity to send this by him. He recd. his resignation accepted yesterday. I have almost wished a few times that I was going with him but the campaign is not closed yet, and I must wait patiently. We moved from our position on the extreme right to the right of our Corps last night.

We are now within a mile of the city in the trenches built by the 14th Corps yesterday.[2] My health is very good. The Chaplain will have much to tell everybody when he gets home, & from him you will learn all the news. His health has been very poor for a long time. In my letter of day before yesterday I acknowledged the receipt of the handkerchiefs. The Chicago Tri Weekly is coming regularly; I shall try and continue the subscription if we get paid off in time.

Tell [Marcellus] Collins if he will continue the "Sentinel," I will send him the money as soon after pay-day as possible. I will enclose a note to him or send it separate by the Chaplain if he comes up.

Everything is progressing favorably here though slow, yet surely we are gaining ground. All the boys are well and in good spirits. The weather was quite cool yesterday but is very warm today.

Several letters were recd. yesterday of as late date as the 25th. I shall therefore confidently expect one by next mail. I would like very much to have written to the S. School, but did not have time on [the] Sabbath as I was on duty all day.

The right of our army is swinging around & will soon hold all the railroads to & from the city.[3] There is a hill between our trenches & the city that hides it from view. It is said to be visible from the Fort on our left.

I have not seen or heard of Bros. John or Sammy for a week or more; as we are several miles nearer each other, I may have an opportunity to hear from them soon. God has still been with and abundantly blessed us. We have had no [prayer] meeting for almost two weeks as we have been moving around most of the time. Sergt. Gaff wished to know yesterday what I would contribute yearly to make Pontiac a station again. I could not tell him as I feel very anxious to complete the payments on our house. I have never learned yet whether Thos. Hill paid the $100 in his hands on my notes. Though I cannot be as liberal as I wish, yet I will try and assist the Church & Sabbath School. We will not probably receive pay until the close of the Campaign. When that will be, no one, save God, knows. All the news recd. by the papers yesterday was good. The Army of the Potomac is again in motion, & we hope to hear a glorious account from them soon. I recd. a letter from Harry & Jennie [Cheston] yesterday. Jennie says she will write to you as soon as she gets home. They are visiting at his Father's. Marion (their baby, I suppose) was not well. The last news they had from Mother [Culver] all were very well at Home. Gaff has been posted about the state of affairs at home & pretended yesterday to have known it all the time. I think, however, he has been *fooled* & don't like to admit it.

I am very happy to know that your health continues so good & pray that God may continue to bless you & sustain you in your trial. Let us praise Him for the many manifestations of His Love and Mercy. Give my love to Mother and Maggie and remember me kindly to all our friends. May the richest of Heaven's blessings rest upon you.

Your affect. Husband

J. F. Culver

P.S. I am out of stamps.

1 Chaplain Cotton had resigned from the service and was returning to Pontiac, Illinois. Compiled Service Records of Union Soldiers, NA.

2 On July 24 the brigade had advanced its lines about 40 rods. Next morning men of the 129th Illinois were compelled to take cover behind their earthworks, as Confederate cannon hammered their positions. During the afternoon, enemy sharpshooters were active. On the 26th the bluecoats strengthened their works. Sharpshooters continued to bang away, killing one and wounding a number in Harrison's brigade. After dark the division was relieved by Geary's and placed in reserve.

The Confederates on the 28th again advanced out of the Atlanta defenses and assailed the Army of the Tennessee, which Sherman had shifted from his left to his right. Ward's division during the afternoon was ordered to reinforce the Army of the Tennessee. After the troops had marched about one and one-half miles to their right, Ward received orders to have them return to their camps, as the battle of Ezra Church had ended in the repulse of the Confederates.

During the day General Hooker, who was very popular with the men, at his request was relieved as commander of the XX Corps and started north. The senior division commander, Brig. Gen. Alpheus S. Williams, became interim corps commander.

On the 29th Ward's division again moved out, marching to the army's extreme right to support a forced reconnaissance down the Lick Skillet road, a mile west of the Alms House, by Davis' XIV Corps division. The line of march passed Ezra Church battlefield, and many Confederate dead and wounded were seen. The reconnaissance was made without any fighting, and the division camped for the night in a large field, about one mile in advance of the Army of the Tennessee. Next day, the 30th, Davis' division moved farther to the southwest and took position. Ward's formed to the right and rear of Davis' people. Earthworks were thrown up, but no Confederates were seen. Ward's troops held their ground on the 31st and August 1, as Davis' columns felt their way cautiously toward the Atlanta & West Point Railroad.

On the 2d Ward's division was relieved by the Army of the Ohio and marched northeast, rejoining the XX Corps near the Western & Atlantic Railroad. Next morning, the 3d, Harrison's brigade advanced and relieved a XIV Corps brigade. The brigade's left rested on the railroad, with the enemy works 800 yards to the front. *O.R.*, Ser. I, Vol. XXXVIII, pt. II, pp. 329, 349; Grunert, *History of the 129th Illinois*, pp. 88-92.

3   The Army of the Ohio, on the 3d, supported by the XIV Corps, forced its way across the north fork of Utoy Creek. Before the Federals could exploit this success and reach the Atlanta & West Point Railroad, General Hood's troops occupied and fortified a position covering East Point and the railroad. Cox, *Atlanta*, pp. 190-93.

 174

Head Qurs. Co. "A" 129th Regt. Ills. Vols. Infty.
In the Field Near Atlanta, Ga.
August 5th 1864

My Dear Wife

I recd. yours of the 27th yesterday and was very happy to learn that your health continues good. I sent a letter day before yesterday by the Chaplain [Cotton], but, as he intends going by the way of Middleport, it may be several days before he reaches Pontiac. He will give a full history of events.

My health continues good. We advanced our lines last night, and are now occupying trenches from 200 to 500 yards nearer the city than before.[1] There was hard fighting on the extreme right yesterday evening; the 14th & 23d Corps were ordered to take possession of the rail-road between East Point and Atlanta.[2] Rumor says that they succeeded.[3] Should it be true, the last rail-road communication of the Enemy with Dixie is in our possession. At East Point, the rail-road branches, one leading to Macon, the other to Montgomery. The rumor comes to us so well authenticated that I am constrained to believe it. The Rebs will now be compelled to fight or evacuate as they cannot supply their Army long in Atlanta.[4] May God give us Victory.

I wrote to Mother [Culver] this morning urging her to visit Pontiac, and asking her to fix the time so that I might try to meet her there. I also wrote to Harry & Jennie [Cheston] yesterday. I have not seen or heard from Bros. John or Sammy yet.

I recd. a letter from Miss Shellenberger requesting me to write an obituary notice of her brother. All the boys are enjoying good health, and though they have been working hard for the past two days & nights, they are in good spirits. Harry McDowell was sick for several days but is much better now. His health has not been good since his return [from Illinois], though he has managed to keep with the Regt. I should not be surprised if he resigned, and would not think it proper for him to attempt another campaign like the present unless his health should materially improve.

You can tell Miss Emma Thayer that I usually call him "Harry" & not "Billy" though I can readily change if she desires it. Remember me kindly to her and Miss Emma McGregor.

I heard that Abbie Remick expects to be married this fall when Milt. Lyons returns.[5] I am not sure that "Hardtack, &c." would be very acceptable at a festival, but I can assure all that it is very acceptable here.

I have not indulged in an ice cream since you left Gallatin, but I have no doubt I could do full justice to one. Perhaps I may give you sufficient evidence this fall.

I hope your anticipations of *coming events* may be realized.[6] May our Father in Heaven sustain you. I shall be content with the result if your life and health be preserved.

I recd. a letter from Lt. Smith two days ago; he says our property is in good condition. I will write a short letter to him to-day.

I have quite a "rustic seat" this morning, constructed by cutting a seat in the side of a trench & using the surface of the ground for a table. It is very comfortable and has all the advantages of a cushioned arm chair. The trench is about 3-1/2 feet under ground, & my seat is cushioned with green leaves. I shall spend a greater portion of the day in writing if I am not interrupted.

It has been my intention to write a detailed account of the battle of the 20th July [Peachtree Creek] to the S. School, but I have not had time. I enjoy the [Chicago] Tribune very much & shall try and continue the subscription. I will write to Lt. Smith requesting him to bring me a pair of boots, tin cup & plate, and the articles of clothing you are making. I shall be glad if you are able to get the shirts made as they are far preferable to those purchased in the stores.

We are very comfortably situated at present & hope to be settled down in Atlanta before another week. Give my love to Mother [Murphy] and Maggie. The kiss was very acceptable but lacks vitality. Tell Mother I am very much obliged for her kind expressions of Love. I hope she will promptly inform me of the state of your health, should you be unable for a time. Remember me kindly to all our friends. May our Father in Heaven bless and sustain you and continue his Mercies to us.

Your affect. Husband

J. F. Culver

---

1  Colonel Harrison reported that on the 4th, the brigade "built and occupied an advance line of works." During the day there had been heavy fire along the opposing picket lines. *O. R.*, Ser. I, Vol. XXXVIII, pt. II, p. 349; Grunert, *History of the 129th Illinois*, p. 92.

2  Efforts by Sherman's right (the Army of the Ohio and the XIV Corps) to secure a lodgment on the railroad connecting Atlanta with East Point were checkmated by the Confederates. In the fighting on August 4, the Federals had 26 killed and wounded, and no advantage gained. On the following day, Union operations were described as a "complete failure or worse." *O. R.*, Ser. I, Vol. XXXVIII, pt. V, pp. 364, 388.

3  There was no truth to this rumor.

4  J.F.C.'s estimate of the situation was correct. Following the battle of Jonesboro on August 31 and September 1, which placed the Federals astride the Macon & Western Railroad, the Rebels evacuated Atlanta.

5  D. Milton Lyons of Livingston County was born in Clinton County, Ohio, in 1841, the son of Mr. and Mrs. William B. Lyons. He moved to Pontiac with his parents in 1852, and entered Lombard University at Galesburg in 1858. Lyons enlisted in Company D, 20th Illinois Infantry. When discharged after expiration of this three-month term, he recruited Company F, 138th Illinois Infantry, which he commanded as captain until October 1864. Lyons married Abbie J. Remick on Oct. 25, 1865. *History of Livingston County*, p. 640.

6  This is a reference to the impending birth of the Culvers' second child.

 175

Head Qurs. Co. "A" 129th Regt. Ills. Vols.
In the Field near Atlanta, Ga.
August 6th 1864

My Dear Wife

Yours of July 28th came to hand this morning. I am very happy to learn that you still enjoy good health. I wrote to you by yesterday's mail and was not aware that a mail would go out until a moment ago, yet I hasten to write knowing that you may be anxious to hear and a letter unexpected always gives pleasure.

My health is very good and I have been blessed with all needful blessings for which all thanks and praise to our kind and loving Father.

The first train crossed the [Chattahoochie] river and run down near us yesterday evening.[1] The sound of the whistle was very cheering. As a result, fresh soft bread was issued to the Brigade this morning. A team was also sent back toward the river to procure green corn for issue to the troops.

All the Company are well. Nate Hill has been on picket to-day & Chris [Yetter] has been writing all day to someone. I recd. to-day one copy of the Chicago Tri-Weekly, 2 of the N.Y. Tribune, & 1 copy of the [Pontiac] Sentinel, besides a large package of the Christian Farmer so we have had a plentiful supply of reading matter.

The weather has been very pleasant. The Rebs made a charge yesterday all around our line but did not succeed in even starting our pickets. We have made every preparation to receive them that a Yankee can invent, & they are welcome to try our lines at any time now.[2]

The loss in our Brig. yesterday was two killed. One of them left his post and was wandering out in front of the line when a Reb. picket shot him, severely wounding him. A comrade, in endeavoring to help him, was instantly killed. The wounded man died last night. Both were of the 105th Ills.[3]

Major Hoskins is here in the Company & well. I saw to-day Capt. Reed, Jim Morrow, Harry McDowell and many others of your acquaintances, all well. The news in the papers are good. Give my love to all. May the blessings of our Father still attend you and His Grace richly abound in your heart.

Your affect. Husband

J. F. Culver

---

1 The Confederates, on abandoning their positions along the Chattahoochie in the second week of July, had destroyed the railroad bridge. Sherman's Pioneers rebuilt the bridge, and with locomotives now able to proceed south of the river, the task of supplying the "army group" had been simplified. The soldiers knew this, and received the first locomotive with "tremendous cheers." Grunert, *History of the 129th Illinois*, p. 92.

2 On the 6th the Confederates had repulsed a lunge by the Army of the Ohio toward the Atlanta & West Point Railroad. Along the fronts of the XVI, XVII, and XX Corps, Rebel skirmishers advanced and occupied the attention of Union pickets. This was to prevent General Sherman from withdrawing additional troops from his center and left, to bolster

his right in its fight to sever the Atlanta & West Point Railroad. *O. R.*, Ser. I, Vol. XXXVIII, pt. V, pp. 391-92, 404.

3  The killed were William Morrison and Seela Simpson of Company E, 105th Illinois. Compiled Service Records of Union Soldiers, NA.

 176

Head Quarters Co. "A" 129th Regt., Ills. Vols.
In the Field Near Atlanta, Georgia
August 18th 1864

My Dear Wife

It is just one week since I recd. a letter from you and just at this time it has seemed almost a month. Our communication has been interrupted, but we are informed that our mail came to-night and we will receive it in the morning. Hoping also that mail may go North to-morrow, I have been induced to write to-night.

We are enjoying most excellent health for which we have great reason to be thankful, and all the troops are in good spirits. We have had two weeks rest & feel like some new men, as we have for the past week been very comfortably situated. All we could desire might be a little more liberty, for, being continually on the front line and directly under fire from the Enemy's forts and sharpshooters, we are compelled to keep close under cover. The loss in our Regt. since Sunday has been very slight; I think not exceeding four or five wounded. In the Brigade several have been killed and wounded, but, taking into consideration our close proximity to the Enemy's fortifications, it seems miraculous that our loss has not been greater. Capt. Allen of the 105th Ills. had his right arm fractured last night by a musket ball. I do not recollect whether you were acquainted with him or not. Lt. Smith is getting along much better than he anticipated but would have been much better off at home for another month at least. He was on picket two days ago and was none the worse for it, he says. Lt. Burton was here yesterday; he says Bro. John is well and has been mustered as Lt. They have not heard from Bro. Sammy yet, but I presume he has written home ere this. Cris. is writing to Mrs. Hill to-night. All the Company are well.

Alf was up to see us last night; he is growing so large and fleshy that you would scarcely know him. He has just completed a very fine set of Maps of the Country from Chickamauga here for the War Department. He is rising rapidly and becoming quite famous. I hoped to get some more sketches for you, but he has been too busy for the past three weeks.

Genl. Sherman played off a rather serious joke upon the Johnies last night. Orders were given for the whole left wing of our Army to be ready to fall back to the river last night. Early in the day a Brigade was sent out to march over a hill in the rear of the 4th Corps, &, returning through a ravine, they kept moving over the hill in full view of the Enemy toward the left & returning until Johnie seemed convinced that we were evacuating. Shortly after dark, all the caissons of the Artillery and trains were sent out toward the river, and, to all appearances, the whole Army was in motion. The Enemy, who had been very happy and cheering all afternoon, commenced massing their forces in front of us intending doubtless to demolish the whole Yankee Army in their retreat, but about midnight the right of the 14th and all of the 23rd Corps moved out, took possession of the Macon Rail-Road, and fortified before *"Johnie"* found out how badly he was fooled and without the loss of a man to us.

At about 3 o'clock this morning, the skirmishers and forts on our front and left opened, but no reply was made until almost daylight when almost all the Artillery on our line opened & kept a steady fire till noon. The fort directly in our front is very much injured. Hood moved his Army again to our right and has been charging all afternoon endeavoring to regain the rail-road. We have heard the artillery & musketry, though 5 or 6 miles distant, and, judging from the sound, there must have been [a] terrific battle there. We hear indirectly to-night that our Army still holds its position and that the slaughter of the Enemy has been terrible.

Still other news reach[es] us of Genl. Kilpatrick who was not captured as supposed. Our Pontoon train left here last night to assist him to cross the river, and, more glorious still, the advance of Genl. Smith's Army is coming up. If all of this news be true, we are most favorably situated. We cannot expect the Enemy to fall back without one more desperate effort to break our lines, but unless surprised we feel fully able to hold them in check. We feel very sanguine of success, but God alone can foreknow the result.

Last night was most beautiful. The moon was shining brightly, and everything in nature seemed happy and evidenced the highest praise to Our Creator. I was very forcibly reminded of those days of quiet and unalloyed happiness *we* enjoyed "*3 years ago.*" There was very little firing in the skirmish line, and in imagination I could readily trace back through the past few years and fancy myself at "the Old House at Home" with Mary "by my side," and, when the illusion was dispelled, I tried by singing the songs we so often sang together to continue the "spell." "Beautiful Star," "Mother Dear, Oh, pray for me," &c. We lay at arms until a late hour as we heard the enemy moving and anticipated an attack. I have not often indulged in such "fancy dreams," for invariably the booming of the cannon or the roll of musketry would arouse me from my reveries and present the realities of the present.

I hope God is dealing most kindly with you. My hopes, which have been so strangely bright all through this Campaign, are still unchanged, that "God who doeth all things well" and who has been so bounteous in blessings to us is still caring for you. Let our hearts praise him. But I must close for to-night with a hope of hearing from you early in the morning.

Give my love to Mother and Maggie & Remember me kindly to all our friends. May Our Father in Heaven sustain you in all your trials and your fondest anticipation be realized. To Him we will commit ourselves, trusting that he will keep us by Grace Divine through life and bring us to "Sweet rest in Heaven" through Christ.

Your affectionate Husband

J. F. Culver

P.S. The tobacco you sent is the best I have had since I left home. Please accept my thanks.

 177

Head Qurs. Co. "A" 129th Regt. Ills. Vols. Infty.<br>In the Field, Chattahoochie River<br>August 30th 1864

My Dear Wife

The mail is late to-day & has not yet come in, while the time has arrived for the mail to go out. I am happy to say that my health continues excellent. The Bands have been playing all day and everything in nature seems happy.

I felt gloomy forbodings all day yesterday and this morning when thinking of the probable result of the Chicago Convention, but I trust in God that all may pass off quietly.[1]

Chris [Yetter] is on picket to-day and succeeded in trading for a few green peaches and beans of some citizens. I think we will soon open up a market for vegetables though they are not very plenty. All the Company are well.

I must close for Inspection & the mail. It seems like old times to be thus able to talk to you every day.[2] May our Father in Heaven bless you and grant you abundance of Grace. Give my love to all.

Your affect. Husband

J. F. Culver

**P.S. No news from *Sherman*[3]**

1 The date for the birth of their child was at hand, and J.F.C. was anxiously awaiting news of the baby's arrival. The National Democratic Convention had convened in Chicago to draft a platform and nominate candidates for the presidency and vice-presidency.

2 While the brigade had been on the march and in the riflepits, J.F.C. had been compelled to abandon his practice of writing almost daily to his wife. With the brigade posted north of the Chattahoochie, J.F.C. resumed his former habit.

3 General Sherman with five corps had advanced to the southwest. On the 28th the Army of the Tennessee reached Fairburn on the Atlanta & West Point Railroad. The next day was spent burning ties and twisting rails. On the 30th Sherman marched east, and nightfall found the Armies of the Cumberland and Tennessee camped a few miles west of Jonesboro, a station on the Macon & Western Railroad. Schofield's Army of the Ohio was posted near Red Oak Station on the Atlanta & West Point, where it could shield the movements of the supply trains. Cox, *Atlanta*, pp. 198-99.

 178

Head Qurs. Co. "A" 129th Regt. Ills. Vols.<br>Chattahoochie River, Georgia<br>August 31st 1864

My Dear Wife

A very light mail was recd. at noon to-day but none for me. We are being mustered for pay to-day, and rumor says we will receive 8 months pay in a few days. There is a paymaster here, and it is probable that he is making arrangements to pay.

We have as yet learned nothing from the Army though various rumors are afloat.[1] A reconnaisance was sent out yesterday from our Division in the direction of Atlanta but found no enemy within a mile and did not advance further.[2] If it is Sherman's intention to draw the enemy out of the city, it would be a bad policy to make any demonstration.

About 40 ladies who claimed they were only riding around the lines were seen yesterday riding about on mules. One or two more bold than the rest ventured so close [to] our lines that they were arrested as spies, which they undoubtedly are. One of the ladies captured is from Vicksburg and was known by reputation to Genl. Slocum.[3] She has left the latter place since the General, himself, but he was on a visit home for several days. She was very indignant that a Yankee should interfere with a ladie's ride, but, when informed that her name was upon the list of those who had taken the oath at Vicksburg & that she was found near our lines, she was much more civil.

Yetter had a severe chill at noon & has now a very high fever. I hope it is not serious. Nate [Hill] & all the boys are well. My health is excellent. May our Father in Heaven bless you. I look for the "good news" every day.[4]

Your affect. Husband

J. F. Culver

P.S. I have but two more stamps but will try and borrow.

---

1 On August 31 Union columns as they thrust toward Jonesboro and the Macon & Western Railroad encountered two Confederate corps. The battle that was to seal the fate of Atlanta commenced. Cox, *Atlanta,* pp. 199-200.

2 Sherman, not knowing what General Hood's reaction to his latest movements would be, had ordered the commander of the XX Corps to make a reconnaissance toward Atlanta on the 30th. This force found the Rebels strongly entrenched on Proctor's Creek and returned. *O.R.,* Ser. I, Vol. XXXVIII, pt. II, p. 330; pt. V, p. 203.

3 Maj. Gen. Henry L. Slocum had assumed command of the XX Corps, which had been led since General Hooker's departure on July 28 by Brig. Gen. Alpheus S. Williams, the senior division commander. Slocum had commanded the District of Vicksburg until August 14. *O.R.,* Ser. I, Vol. XXXVIII, pt. II, pp. 17, 21.

General Hood had been deceived by Sherman's movements. He deluded himself into believing that Maj. Gen. Joseph Wheeler's cavalry raid on the Western & Atlantic Railroad had wrecked the Union supply line causing Sherman to retreat across the

Chattahoochie. It was the 28th before Hood learned that he had blundered, and by then it was too late to keep the foe from securing a stranglehold on the Atlanta & West Point Railroad. Cox, *Atlanta*, pp. 197-98.

4   This is a reference to the birth of the anxiously awaited baby.

⛋ 179 ⛋

Head Quarters Co. "A" 129th Regt Ills. Vols. Inftry.<br>In the Field, Chattahoochie River, Georgia<br>August 31st 1864

My Dear Wife

I have given all my time for the past few days to writing up company business, and, as I shall be busy for some days to come, I scarcely take time to write to you, for, when not busy, my hand becomes tired and cramped so that my letters are made as brief as possible.

At noon to-day I lay down to rest but fell asleep & did not awaken until nearly mail time. It is 9 o clock, P.M. The evening is very pleasant. I have just laid aside the Muster and Pay rolls to talk awhile to you before retiring.

I was honored with a serenade to-night by the Brigade Band; they had been at Regtl. Hd. Qurs. playing and stopped on their way home. One piece they played was your favorite Quickstep, No. 1 in the 2nd book of the Cornet Band.[1] They did very well, as they have had very few opportunities to practice during the Campaign.

It is very quiet to-night and reminds me of those nights 3 years ago when we sat upon the door step or by the open window looking out into the future, to us then untried and unfathomable, now read and experienced. We have both learned and suffered much since then, but amid all our trials God has blessed us. How much of hope and anticipation have we realized? The future is mercifully sealed up and hid from our vision except such as is revealed by the light of Heaven. We live by Faith and rejoice in hope of the promises of God. I wish I could look in upon you to-night and know how you are situated, whether your heart is filled with joy for unbounded blessings received or whether your heart is sad and lonely. My emotions have been very conflicting for the past week. Sometimes anxiety and doubt, love and fear would predominate, but most of the time hope, bright hope, would drive all else away. God has been so constant in his care and blessings that I feel "all is well."

The stars shine dimly to-night, and the air is very cool but not too much so for comfort. There is but little comparison between the temperate climate here this season and the oppressive heat of the Prairies of Illinois. I know you would love this climate, especially if it is always as agreeable as this Summer has been. The cool nights will doubtless produce some ague and fever of different kinds, but I think the proportion will be much less than usual.

Yetter has been unwell for a few days, and to-day had a severe chill with a very high fever this afternoon. But to-night he is much better, and thinks that by a timely use of medicine he can ward off another attack. Lt. Smith came off Picket this evening. His health is not as good as it was before he was wounded, & I doubt somewhat the wisdom of his remaining in the service. He certainly could not stand a campaign. With every little effort, he suffers; and, on walking a mile or two, his bowels become very much enlarged. Nate [Hill] is well and hearty as ever.

We got some new potatoes to-day from the commissary & traded on the Picket line for some new beans.[2] I can assure you we relish them very much. Alf [Huetson] was up yesterday evening; he is looking very well and enjoys excellent health.

We have been speculating considerable for a few days past upon the result of the Chicago Convention. Day after to-morrow we will get the first day's proceedings. It is the general opinion that [Maj. Gen. George B.] McClellan will be nominated unless the convention should be divided, in which case candidates that have expressed more ultra views would likely be selected. I would not be much surprised if such a diversion were attempted to favor Vallandigham.[3] We are deeply interested, and, wherever the soldiers are permitted to vote, the policy of the administration will be sustained. We have all to hope for.

I succeeded in getting a little money this evening from a friend which I will enclose ($10.00). I know you must be very short of funds. Lt. Smith told me that his wife had recd. some money lately and that he had written to her to lend you some until pay day. I hope it will not be much longer deferred.

We have no news from Sherman. There was a rumor that a battle had been fought about 15 miles South East of Atlanta, but it could not be traced to any reliable source.[4] There is no communication with the army. Genl. Smith's forces must be with them ere this, but it is not known.[5]

The enemy is still visible along the front of our line across the River. A few days will probably reveal Sherman's policy. May God grant us a speedy victory.

Our mails have been very irregular for a few days past owing to some neglect of the Army Post-masters; the trains are very regular. There is a large body of troops gathering here for the various Corps at the front, which will help to swell the ranks considerable when the way is open.[6]

All the rest are fast asleep, and I must close or I will be unable to resume writing in the morning. My hand and arm get cramped very easily, as I have not been accustomed to write very long at a time lately. Last night they kept me awake until near midnight, which accounts for my long nap to-day. I hope to hear from you by to-morrow's mail.

I recd. the Chicago Tribune of the 26th this morning, & a letter should come through nearly as soon while my last letter was dated the 21st. I hope very soon to hear that your *trial* is over and your health good and that the desire of your heart has been granted.

May "our Father in Heaven" bestow upon you the richest of His blessings. You told me in one of your letters that after the first anticipated event "you would count the days and weeks until my visit home." I earnestly hope that our affairs may soon be so shaped by "Our Father's hand" that I may succeed in getting home.

I have not heard from Carlisle yet. I think they have forgotten me entirely. Give my love to Mother [Murphy] and Maggie. Tell Mother I look for her letter very soon; you know she is to write for you if you are not able. May Holy Angels guard thee this night and all your hours be replete with happiness.

Your affectionate Husband

J. F. Culver

---

1   J.F.C. had been a member of Pontiac's cornet band before being mustered into Company A, 129th Illinois.

2   Federals and Confederates were in the habit of trading necessities on the picket lines.

3   Clement Vallandigham, a leader of the Peace Democrats, had returned to Ohio in June 1864 and played a leading role in framing the Democratic platform, which helped doom his party to defeat in the November election.

4   The battle of Jonesboro had commenced on the 31st, and the Army of the Tennessee held its ground in face of a Confederate attack, permitting troops of Schofield's Army of the Ohio and Thomas' Army of the Cumberland to reach the vital Macon & Western Railroad at Rough and Ready, four miles north of Jonesboro. This led Hood to believe that Atlanta would be attacked, and he recalled one of the two corps battling the Army of the Tennessee west of Jonesboro. Cox, *Atlanta*, pp. 200-02.

5   This is probably a reference to the force commanded by Brig. Gen. John E. Smith, headquartered at Cartersville, and charged with guarding the Western & Atlantic Railroad from Dalton to Kennesaw. Smith was not en route to reinforce Sherman, so this may be classed as one of those rumors that have intrigued soldiers throughout history.

6   General Slocum had been ordered on the 29th to "collect together all stragglers" found in the area. Those that were armed were to be organized for defense of the line of the Chattahoochie and those without arms were to be put to work on the defenses. Convalescents would be handled in a similar manner. *O. R.*, Ser. I, Vol. XXXVIII, pt. V, p. 702.

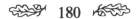 180

Thursday, Sept. 1st 1864

Dear Mary

The telegraph has just announced the nomination of Geo. B. McClellan by the Chicago Convention for President but lacks confirmation. We have no news from the Army yet. The mail came in about an hour ago but brought no letter for me. I still hope "All is well."

Chris [Yetter] is trying hard to have the ague again to-day & I think he will succeed. He accepts the issue very resignedly, and is hurrying Green [a black mess cook] up with dinner, so that he can eat a good mess of green beans and new potatoes before the "Shake" comes on.

We are all well. The weather is very beautiful. May our Father in Heaven bless You.

Your affect. Husband

J. F. Culver

## 181

Hd. Qurs. Co. "A", 129th Ills. Vols. Inftry.
Chattahoochie River, Ga.
Sept. 5th 1864

My Dear Wife

As we have orders to move to Atlanta to-morrow, I may not have an opportunity to write.[1] We have recd. no mail yet; I cannot understand it as the trains are running by here regularly.

I have just returned from the Picket line, where I was called to marry a couple, but they had no license & I refused as the laws of this state require a license. They seemed very anxious. The Lady was about 33 or 35 & had a daughter with her, about 12 years old. The man was 30 yrs. old. I was very sorry to disappoint them, but I sent them to Marietta where I think they can obtain a license.

We are all well. It has rained very heavy here this afternoon & we got slightly wet.

Sherman is returning to Atlanta with the Army.[2] We have not learned the full result, but 3,000 prisoners have arrived, & it is rumored that 7 or 8,000 more are on the road.[3] The enemy's loss is reported at 15 to 20,000. Our loss is slight, but we have not heard any numbers.[4]

I hope to hear from you very soon. May God bless you.

Your affect. Husband

J. F. Culver

---

1 Out-generaled by Sherman and defeated in the battle of Jonesboro, General Hood and his Army of Tennessee evacuated Atlanta on the night of September 1. Hood reassembled his army at Lovejoy Station on the Macon & Western Railroad, 25 miles southeast of Atlanta.

On the night of the 1st, soldiers of the XX Corps heard heavy explosions in the direction of Atlanta, and General Slocum ordered each of his division commanders to make a forced reconnaissance toward the city. A column from General Ward's division, on approaching the city, was met by Major James M. Calhoun, who formally surrendered Atlanta and informed Col. John Coburn that the Confederates had evacuated. The next day, September 3, the remainder of the XX Corps, except the units detailed to guard the Chattahoochie bridges, marched into and took possession of the city.

Harrison's brigade was detailed to remain on the Chattahoochie to protect the railroad bridge and the commissary and ordnance depots. *O. R.*, Ser. I, Vol. XXXVIII, pt. V, pp. 19, 330, 350, 392-93.

2 General Sherman on September 4 issued orders for his armies to take position in and around Atlanta, "until a new campaign is planned in concert with the other grand armies of the United States." Thomas' Army of the Cumberland was to occupy the city and protect the Western & Atlantic Railroad; the Army of the Tennessee would occupy East Point; the Army of the Ohio Decatur; and the cavalry Sandtown, Roswell, and "other points on the flanks and along our line of communications." *O.R.*, Ser. I, Vol. XXXVIII, pt. V, p. 801.

3 General Sherman reported that in the battle of Jonesboro, his "army group" captured two four-gun batteries, killed about 500 Confederates, and wounded another 2,500. Union losses during the period August 26-September 2 would not exceed 1,500. Confederates captured in this phase of the Atlanta Campaign totaled about 3,000. *Ibid.*, pp. 822, 830-31.

4 Confederate losses during this eight-day period were in excess of 6,000. On evacuating Atlanta, the Confederates destroyed seven locomotives, 81 cars loaded with ammunition, small arms, and stores, and abandoned 14 pieces of artillery and a large number of small arms. *Ibid.*, p. 778.

 182

Head Quarters, Co. "A" 129th Regiment Ills.
Vols. Infty.
Chattahoochie River, Georgia
September 7th 1864

My Dear Wife

Your letters of the 23rd & 25th August came to hand yesterday evening. To "Our Father" be all praise for his loving kindness and tender mercies. A week of intense anxiety was relieved by the news of your safety.[1] I would that I were more worthy of all the blessings bestowed upon me. As the mails are open again, I hope to hear from you often; but, as we are so far from the city, we get ours very irregularly.[2] Yesterday being the first we have recd. for 10 days.

Since the troops left here, it is very dull, and we get no news. The Campaign is over for the present, and I took advantage of the earliest opportunity, 3 days ago, to send up an application for a "Leave of

Absence."[3] There are so very many applications in that my chances seem very poor. I could do no better than try; even should I succeed, I will wait until after the troops are paid off.

Dr. [Darius] Johnson and Allen Fellows enjoy very good health. Allen has been pitching horse shoes in the Company all afternoon. He feels a little blue as he has not recd. a letter from his wife for a long time; his last was dated 16th or 18th of August. Dr. Johnson is in Atlanta.

The stamps you sent never arrived; I suppose there is a shirt also on the way. They will probably arrive soon.

I recd. a letter from Bro. Harry and Sister Jennie [Cheston] yesterday dated Aug. 20th. All were well, but they say nothing of Mother [Culver] and Hannah's anticipated visit to the West. The farms were to be offered for sale on the 23rd August.[4]

Sergt. Gaff has been selling me, I suppose, or else you are sadly mistaken. He told me a few days ago that by a letter he recd., dated the 21st Aug., he was informed of an acquisition to his family of a fine *Baby Boy*.

Your letter of P.M. August 25th made me feel very anxious, and I did not dare hope that any further news would reach me until next mail, but I was most happily disappointed in finding a Post Script, dated just 12 hours later, containing such glorious *"news."* You are certainly a "paragon" in your line.

May God restore you speedily to health and strength. I believe the desire of your heart has been granted unto you. I prayed that it might be so. Let our hearts be thankful for all the blessings we have received. I would be very happy, indeed, to give the carress you desire, & hope I may be blessed with the opportunity before long. I have written every day for the last two weeks, so that you must have quite a collection of mail when the communication opened.[5]

With the earnest hope that my application may be successful, and that I may very soon have the privilege of uniting my voice with yours in praise to "Our Father" for all his mercies, I remain as ever,

Your Affectionate Husband

J. F. Culver

---

1   Mary Culver had given birth to a son, Howard Dunmire, on Aug. 25, 1864.

2   The 2d and 3d Brigades, Third Division, XX Army Corps, were stationed in Atlanta, six miles southeast of the fortified camp occupied by Colonel Harrison's 1st Brigade.

3   Captain Culver on Sept. 5, 1864, had written to the assistant adjutant general, Army of the Cumberland:

> I have the honor to request a leave of absence for 30 days for the purpose of visiting my family in Pontiac, Livingston County, Ill.

My wife has been in delicate health all summer and is now quite ill. My child and my father have died since I entered service. I have not received a leave of absence since I enlisted Aug. 2, 1862. I have never been absent from my command either with or without leave, except on duty. 1st Lt. John W. Smith is serving with the company to which I am attached and my services can readily be spared for the period desired. Compiled Service Records of **Union** Soldiers, NA.

4  To settle the estate of Father Culver, it was necessary to sell the family farms in Cumberland County, Pennsylvania.

5  General Wheeler, with a formidable mounted force, in mid-August had been sent by General Hood to operate against the railroads over which Sherman supplied his armies. The Rebels had attacked Dalton, a station on the Western & Atlantic, but were repulsed. After breaking the subject railroad in several places and cutting the telegraph, Wheeler's horsemen swept into East Tennessee. When they returned from East Tennessee at the end of August, Wheeler and his cavalry raided the Nashville & Chattanooga Railroad. Track was twisted, bridges burned, and the telegraph cut between Nashville and Wartrace. While labor crews repaired the railroad and telegraph, Wheeler, pursued by strong Federal columns, retreated into north Alabama. Damage had been repaired by the 10th, when the first through train in 11 days left Nashville for Chattanooga. *O. R.*, Ser. I, Vol. XXXVIII, pt. V, pp. 789, 844; Cox, *Atlanta*, p. 196.

 183

Head Quarters Co. "A" 129th Ills. Vols.
Chattahoochie River, Ga.
September 8th 1864

My Dear Wife

We have no mail yet, and our opportunities for a regular mail are growing less unless some other method be adopted. We hope, however, if we remain here, our facilities will be much improved. The trains run regularly but do not stop here.

I hoped to see Bro. John before this, but the 4th Corps have not returned as was reported.[1] We know nothing of the movements of the Army and have no late news from the North. This place is exceeding quiet, &, if it had not been for the amount of writing and labor necessary to straighten up the books & papers, I fear I should have had the blues severely. I am almost done now, but I hope soon to have the assurance of a visit home.

I am going on Picket in a few moments, & hope to receive a letter from you before I return. Maggie's promised letter has not yet arrived. We are all very well. May our Father in Heaven bless you and our child & grant us life, health and all needful blessings. Give my love to all the family.

Your affect. Husband

J. F. Culver

---

1 The IV Corps was camped near Rough-and-Ready until the morning of September 8, when it started for Atlanta. The advance guard passed through Atlanta at 10:30 A.M. on the 9th, and the corps went into camp two miles east of the city, south of the Georgia Railroad. *O. R., Ser. I. Vol. XXXVIII, pt. V, pp. 827, 840.*

⟨⟩ **184** ⟨⟩

Head Qurs. Co. "A" 129th Ills.
Chattahoochie River, Ga.
Sept. 10th 1864

My Dear Wife

Though it seems very improbable that any letter will reach you for some time to come, as our communication is so seriously interrupted; yet, should this reach you, rest assured that we are all well and everything is prospering.

We have nothing to fear yet, for we have plenty of supplies for 3 months to come. We have had but the one mail since Aug. 26th. I heard this morning that the road was torn up near Wartrace, also at Gallatin and South Tunnel.[1] I think all will be well. I should prefer, however, if the letters on the road were safe in your hands or my own. I sent you a ten dollar Bill in one of them. I hope, however, none of them may fall into the enemy's hands. For fear that some of them may, & until the way is open & safe, I shall write but briefly.

May the richest of Heaven's blessings rest upon you and our child. Give my love to the family. With the hope of soon hearing from you, I remain,

Ever your affectionate Husband

J. F. Culver

---

1 General Wheeler had spent two days wreaking havoc on the Nashville & Chattanooga Railroad. In addition, the Confederates captured two trains, several stockades, and a number of small supply depots. There was no substance to the report that the Rebels had raided the Louisville & Nashville Railroad at Gallatin and South Tunnel. Wheeler, harassed by pursuing columns, had retreated into north Alabama, crossing the Tennessee River at Muscle Shoals on September 10. One of Wheeler's brigades, Brig. Gen. John S. Williams', had been unable to rendezvous with the main column and had recrossed the Nashville & Chattanooga Railroad on the 8th at Wartrace, but it was too hotly pursued to damage the track or telegraph. *O. R.,* Ser. I, Vol. XXXVIII, pt. V, pp. 841-42; pt. III, pp. 959-60.

 185

Hd. Qurs. Hospital, 3d Div. 20th A.C.
Atlanta, Ga.
Sept. 12th 1864

My Dear Wife

I came here on a visit to-day. I came down with Dr. Wood in an ambulance.[1] On our way, we met the mail going out, 8 sacks for our Brigade, so that I feel certain of some letters when I get back.

I am stopping for a few moments with Dr. [Darius] Johnson when I will return to camp. Josephus Ullery & Writtenhour are here.[2] Ullery is well & able for duty and Writenhour is getting better. I requested Seph. [Ullery] to go out & visit Bro. John [Murphy] to-morrow as I cannot get permission. I will write you at length to-night or to-morrow.

All the Co. are well except Sutcliff.[3] I heard just now that all the Leaves of Absence have been returned disapproved and that none will be granted. Mine is, of course, among the number — so ends my visit home. "God's will be done."

I hope to hear of your good health on my return to camp. May our Father in Heaven bless you & our child. Give my love to Mother and Maggie.

Good Bye.

Your affect. Husband

J. F. Culver

---

1   Orlando S. Wood, a 25-year-old physician, was mustered into service as 1st assistant surgeon of the 129th Illinois Infantry at Stevenson, Ala., on March 6, 1864. Dr. Wood was promoted to regimental surgeon on May 21, 1865, and mustered out with the regiment near Washington, D.C., June 8, 1865. Compiled Service Records of Union Soldiers, NA.

2   Josephus Ullery, a 23-year-old farmer, was mustered into service on Sept. 8, 1862, as a private in Company A, 129th Illinois Infantry. On Sept. 10, 1864, he was detached as a nurse in the Third Division, XX Corps hospital. Private Ullery was discharged with the regiment on June 8, 1865, near Washington, D.C. William Writenour, a 21-year-old farmer, was mustered into service on Sept. 8, 1862, as a private in Company A, 129th Illinois Infantry, and like Ullery had been detached for duty as a nurse in the division hospital. Private Writenour was mustered out with the regiment on June 8, 1865, near Washington, D.C. *Ibid.*

3   William Sutcliff, a 31-year-old farmer, was mustered into service on Sept. 8, 1862, as private in Company A, 129th Illinois Infantry. He received a 20-day furlough on Sept. 27 and it was extended until Nov. 5, 1864. Private Sutcliff was mustered out near Washington, D.C., on June 8, 1865. *Ibid.*

≪≫ 186 ≪≫

Head Quarters, Co. "A" 129th Regt. Ills. Vols. Infty.<br>Chattahoochie River, Ga.<br>September 13th 1864

My Dear Wife

On my return from Atlanta last evening, I found three letters awaiting me. I am most happy to hear that you enjoy such good health, and feel thankful to "Our Father" for the continued manifestation of "His" love and mercy so richly bestowed upon us. Your letters were dated respectively 27th, 29th, & 31st. I also recd. Chicago papers to the 3d inst. How greatly God has blessed us in all things.

I wrote a short note from the Hospital in Atlanta yesterday but had to send it without an envelope. Atlanta looked very desolate yesterday. Genl. Sherman ordered all the citizens to leave and gave them their choice to go North or South.[1] 1,000 teams started out to Rough & Ready loaded with families with a little furniture allowed to each. They seemed in good spirits generally, except some few women who had several children and seemed quite delicate in health. All the Ambulances of the Army were sent out also, some of them filled with fair looking ladies.

The city is not over half as large as Nashville,[2] but is very much scattered and in prosperous times was doubtedly a very pleasant place. I was only in the city a few hours. All that portion North of the square is very much injured with the shells, many houses are utterly ruined and quite a number burned to the ground. A majority of the principal business places are very seriously injured. There has been some fine gardens, but they are almost wholly destroyed. The citizens have dug large holes in their yards in which to protect themselves from shells. Nearly all the houses are vacated.

There are a few families which could not be moved at present. I saw one or two with very small infants & several whose condition would preclude the possibility of their being removed with safety; such, I presume, will be allowed to remain.

I am very much surprised that the Rebel Army should destroy all their commissary stores and abandon the wives and families of their soldiers to starvation. Had they left even a short supply, it had not been necessary to adopt such harsh measures as this seems to be. But it would be a matter of impossibility to take care of them here with our long base of supplies open to interruption all the time, and they did not wish to be sent North.[3]

I have not received Maggie's promised letter yet, but hope it may arrive by next mail. I am almost satisfied that I shall get no opportunity to visit home this season. We are preparing rapidly for the fall Campaign, and it will doubtless open by the 1st of next month.

I have had no letters from home except the one from Harry and Jennie [Cheston], which I mentioned ten days ago. I have not heard from Bro. John [Murphy] since about the 20th of last month. I sent Seph. Ullery out [to] the front yesterday evening and expect to hear from him in a few days.[4] I must close for the present but will try and add some this afternoon.

Till then, Good bye. I will write to-night. May our Father in Heaven keep & bless you and our child. We are all well.

Your affect. Husband

J. F. Culver

---

1  General Sherman, having "resolved to make Atlanta a pure military garrison or depot, with no civil population to influence military measures, issued orders deporting all citizen and family residents." In notifying General Hood of his decision on September 7, Sherman announced that those who preferred could go south and the rest north. For the latter the Union would "provide food and transportation to points of their election in Tennessee, Kentucky, or farther north." For the former, he would "provide transportation by cars as far as Rough and Ready, and also wagons; but that their removal may be made with as little discomfort as possible, it will be necessary for you to help the families from Rough and Ready to the cars at Lovejoy's." The refugees would be allowed to take with them their moveable property (clothing, trunks, reasonable furniture, bedding, &c.), and their servants, white and black, provided they did not coerce the blacks.

Sherman knew that this measure would "raise a howl against my barbarity and cruelty," and he answered that "war is war, and not popularity-seeking."

General Hood, in agreeing to Sherman's proposal for a "truce in the neighborhood of Rough and Ready" to facilitate the mass deportation, branded it as "an unprecedented measure," transcending "in studied and ingenious cruelty, all acts ever brought to my attention in the dark history of war."

On September 10 Sherman announced that pursuant to an agreement made with General Hood, "A truce is hereby declared to exist from daylight of Monday, September 12, until daylight of Thursday, September 22 . . . at the point on the Macon railroad known as Rough and Ready, and the country round about for a circle of two miles' radius, together with the roads leading to and from in the direction of Atlanta and Lovejoy's Station," for the purpose of affording the people of Atlanta a safe means of removal to points south.

Sherman's chief quartermaster at Atlanta was directed to afford the refugees "all the facilities he can spare to remove them comfortable and safely, with their effects, to Rough and Ready, using cars and wagons and ambulances for that purpose." *O. R.*, Ser. I, Vol. XXXVIII, pt. V, p. 822; *O. R.*, Ser. I, Vol. XXXIX, pt. II, p. 356; Sherman, *Memoirs*, II, pp. 111-12.

2  In 1861 the population of Atlanta was about 10,000 compared with Nashville's 37,000. By 1864 the number of people living in Atlanta had burgeoned to 20,000.

3  The destruction of the commissary stores did not trigger Sherman's decision to order the evacuation of Atlanta by the citizens, as J.F.C. supposed. In a letter to Maj. Gen. Henry W. Halleck on September 4, Sherman, in outlining an autumn campaign, announced his proposal "to remove all the inhabitants of Atlanta, sending those committed to our cause to the rear, and the Rebel families to the front." He would "allow no trade, manufacturers, nor any citizens there at all, so that we will have the entire use of railroad . . ., and also such corn and forage as may be reached by our troops." *O. R.*, Ser. I, Vol. XXXVIII, pt V, p. 794.

4  Company M, 1st Illinois Light Artillery, the unit to which John and Sam Murphy belonged, was camped two miles east of Atlanta, on the Decatur road. *Ibid.*, p. 840.

Head Quarters, Co. "A" 129th Regt. Ills. Vol. Infty.
Chattahoochie River, Georgia
September 13th 1864

My Dear Wife

Your letters of the 2nd & 4th came to hand this evening. I am very happy, indeed, to learn of your good health; God has very signally blessed us, and my heart is grateful. I shall endeavor to remember the 21st September, &, if in my power, will keep it sacred with you.[1] I did hope to spend it with you, but that seems more and more improbable every day.

You have doubtless learned before this that our loss in the capture of Atlanta was very light. We lost not a man in our Corps [the XX]. The death of John Morgan and the repulse of the Rebels in our rear are very gratifying.[2]

You have not yet acknowledged the receipt of the $10 I sent. I fear it was in some of the captured mails.

I am not aware that I feel any more dignified than usual, there is so very little of it in my nature. I will try and be very dignified when I get home. I have now no recollection of what transpired two years ago from Sept. 4th. Though I cannot fix dates, yet I have many, very many, recollections of the past. I have written of them to you.[3]

I am glad to hear from Bro. Thomas [Murphy].[4] I wrote to him a few weeks ago but have not heard from him yet. I would try and console him if I knew what was the matter.

I recd. the Tribune & North Western this evening of the 7th & have been reading to the boys until a late hour. I presume the draft has transpired.[5]

We are so far from the city that we get no letters except what come by mail. As the way is open again, I shall expect to hear from you very often until the Campaign opens again.[6]

I have not heard from Bro. John yet. You speak in your letter of writing to Hospital No. 19, Nashville. I presume therefore that Bro. Sammy is there and will write to him soon.[7] [Albert] Green is looking anxiously for his book. He was very much pleased to learn of the baby. Chris [Yetter] & Nate [Hill] are well & all the boys with the exception of Wm. Sutcliff. I sent forward an application for a furlough for him to-day; if that fails, I will try for his discharge.

The weather last night and to-day has been very cool. It is probable that there will be early frosts in the North.

I have not answered Harry & Jennie's [Cheston's] letter yet. Is it not singular that we have no letters from Mother or Hannah [Culver]?

Politics ran very high here until the Chicago platform was received;[8] the McClellan men have been very quiet ever since. We have considerable anxiety for results in the North this fall. The time is not long, but it will doubtless be hotly contested. I hoped to hear the result of the [Livingston] County Convention by to-day's mail but was disappointed.

The moon shines brightly to-night, & it is cool enough for an overcoat. If we could have a light frost to kill off the numerous insects that swarm around, it would be very acceptable.

Remember me very kindly to Mother and Maggie. I presume sickness in her family has prevented Sister Maggie [Utley] from writing. Mother [Murphy] was disappointed in writing, as she expected to act [as] correspondent during your disability.

I have not yet wholly abandoned the idea of getting home, though I do not anticipate too much. Let us still hope for the best. I feel assured that should I fail to make the anticipated visit, you have still a great comfort in our child. May God bless you both with health and bestow upon you the riches of his Grace.

I should have much liked to hear what Chaplain Cotton had to say. Were my letters to the Sunday School received? Remember me kindly to all our friends. Allen Fellows recd. letters from his wife yesterday. I have not seen him since the mail came in this evening. He is well. [Major] Hoskins is also well. Lt. Smith came off Picket this evening; he is improving in health slowly.

I may have opportunity to add a line to-morrow. Kiss baby for Papa. If Mrs. Smith's surmises be true, I may not have a right to the title. I shall take the credit, however, unless I am better informed. Hoping that the richest of Heaven's blessings may rest upon you, I remain, as ever,

Your affectionate Husband

J. F. Culver

Sept. 14th 64 — 1 P.M.

I opened my letter to say that we remain all well. We have orders to move to Atlanta to-morrow morning;[9] so, if they are not countermanded, we will be probably located in or near the city by this time to-morrow.

I intended to write to Bro. Tom but neglected it. I find I have to be very sparing of envelopes, as I have only a very few left & no way of obtaining more. As soon as I can get some money, I will get you to send me 100; by leaving the end open, the postage will not be much. I want the best. A very inferior article costs 50 cts per pack here, & just now they cannot be obtained.

The paymaster will arrive at Atlanta to-day or to-morrow, & we will probably be paid within ten days.[10] I have not heard from my Leave of Absence yet. The weather is very pleasant to-day. I presume we will get no mail until to-morrow. Remember me kindly to all. With much love, I remain, as ever,

Your affectionate Husband

J. F. Culver

---

1 Franklin Allen, the Culvers' first child, had been born on September 21, 1862. He died October 30, 1863.

2 Brig. Gen. John H. Morgan, the famous Confederate raider, had escaped from the Ohio State Penitentiary with a number of his officers. Making his way south, he was placed in command of the Department of Southwestern Virginia in April 1864. Morgan and his command camped in Greeneville, Tenn., on the night of September 3, while en route to attack Federal forces near Knoxville. Early the next morning he was surprised by a detachment of Union cavalry and was killed in the garden of the house where he had been sleeping. Warner, *Generals in Grey*, p. 221.

By September 10 trains were again operating over sections of the Nashville & Chattanooga Railroad wrecked by General Wheeler and his raiders. Wheeler, having been hounded out of Middle Tennessee, was camped near Florence, Ala., while General Williams' brigade, closely pursued by Federals, had fled eastward and had crossed the Clinch River, near Clinton, Tenn., *O. R.*, Ser. I, Vol. XXXIX, pt. II, pp. 356, 378, 381.

3 Mary Culver in her letters of September 2 and 4, missing from the Culver Collection, must have referred to something that had occurred on September 4, 1862.

4 Thomas Murphy, Mary Culver's oldest brother, was a Cleveland machinist and port engineer.

5 A draft to provide additional manpower for the Union armies began on Monday, September 12.

6 General Grant on September 10 notified General Sherman that "as soon as your men are sufficiently rested and preparations can be made, it is desirable that another campaign should be commenced. We want to keep the enemy constantly pressed to the end of the war." *O. R.*, Ser. I, Vol. XXXIX, pt. II, p. 355.

7 Pvt. Sam Murphy was hospitalized in Chattanooga on July 26, 1864, where he remained until rejoining his unit at Atlanta in September. Compiled Service Records of Union Soldiers, NA.

8 To please the war Democrats, Maj. Gen. George B. McClellan was nominated for the presidency by the Chicago convention, while the "peace faction" drafted the platform. After referring to "four years of failure to restore the Union by the experiment of war," the platform demanded the cessation of hostilities "to the end that at the earliest possible moment, peace may be restored on the basis of the Federal Union of the States." Randall, *Civil War and Reconstruction*, p. 619.

9 The 1st Brigade would rejoin the Third Division in Atlanta. The 2d and 3d Brigades had been in the city for almost two weeks. One regiment would remain at the Chattahoochie Railroad Bridge to protect the supply depots. *O. R.*, Ser. I, Vol. XXXIX, pt. II, p. 382.

10 General Sherman on September 11 learned that the paymasters had arrived in Nashville and would be joining his "army group" as soon as funds were available. He suggested that his troops be paid "in great part in checks on New York." *O. R.*, Ser. I, Vol. XXXIX, pt. II, pp, 358-59.

### ❦ 188 ❦

Head Qurs. Co. "A" 129th Regt. Ills. Vols.
Atlanta, Ga. Sept. 19th 1864[1]

My Dear Wife

Your letters mailed the 9th & 10th were recd. yesterday evening. I am very sorry to learn that your health is not good, but hope it is only a slight attack that will very soon be overcome.

I spent most of the day yesterday with Bro. John. Sammy was not at home, & I did not get to see him. Both are in good health.

It rained nearly all day yesterday, & this morning it is very wet and damp. We have not got our tent fixed up yet, as we did not wish to work on Sabbath. Chris [Yetter] is waiting for me to go with him for lumber,[2] so I will only write a line to inform you of my good health. To-morrow or next day at farthest I will write you a long letter. Give my love to all. Rumor says the pay master is here; if so, we will know it shortly.

May Our Father in Heaven bless you & Keep you both in health.

Your affect. Husband

J. F. Culver

1  The 1st Brigade took up the march from the Chattahoochee to Atlanta at 6 A.M. on the 16th, and, crossing the Peachtree Creek battlefield, reached the entrenchments they had occupied in front of the city at 8 o'clock. En route they "passed the graves of the fallen dear comrades, that were 'sleeping the sleep that knows no waking.' "

After a halt of several hours, the march was resumed, and the brigade passed through Atlanta, going into camp about one and one-half miles south of the city. After falling out, a number of men visited the abandoned Confederate works. "They were very strong and in their erection every modern invention in the art of war had been added."

On the 17th a suitable campground was selected by Colonel Case, and it was cleared of underbrush and debris. A number of abandoned frame dwellings nearby were razed by the soldiers, and the lumber and shingles used "in erecting tenements." Grunert, *History of the 129th Illinois,* pp. 102-04.

2  Colonels Case and Flynn on Sunday, the 18th, divided off the camp, assigning each company its area, within which "every four or five men were allotted a space of eight feet in width and twelve feet in length, to enjoy themselves in a glorious and noble style — in a straight line with the rest of the company." *Ibid.,* p. 104.

## 189

Head Quarters, Co. "A" 129th Regt. Ills. Vols.
Atlanta, Georgia  September 19th 1864

My Dear Wife

I have been very busy to-day fixing up Hd. Qurs. and this evening in preparing for Inspection to-morrow. We are now very pleasantly situated though we have not completed our work yet.

I saw both Bros. John and Sammy [Murphy] this morning; they are quite well. John is temporarily detailed in "Bridges Battery" and went on duty there this morning.[1]

You express some anxiety in yours of the 6th about my "Leave of Absence." You have learned before this that my application failed. I have had quite a fight with the "Blues" for a few days past, but I believe I have conquered. Let us not forget "Our Father" for all his mercies and blessings.

I hope you have not had a return of the chills. This season opens up sickly, I fear, in Pontiac. May Our Father in Heaven protect you and our babe. I had anticipated much pleasure in a visit home & must confess that I was very much disappointed, for I felt confident of success. God doeth all things well and doubtless he has some good purpose to accomplish thereby.

The tobacco, handkerchief, and book for Green have not yet arrived.[2] Green is looking very anxiously for his gift. Packages are generally delayed, & they will probably be along to-morrow or next day.

You say the Copperhead meeting has the appearance of being a success & wish to know if any one in Co. "A" will vote for "Mac" [McClellan], and what probability of the 129th getting home to vote. There is no probability of the 129th going home to vote; there will be too much on hand here at that time. Had McClellan accepted the nomination upon a strong war Platform, he would have had some friends and five or six of Co. "A" would have voted for him had opportunity offered. The Chicago Platform has no friends here that I know of, and McClellan's effort to kick aside the Platform and still accept the nomination by a strong copperhead convention has left him very few friends, indeed.[3] We prefer a continuation of the policy of the present administration & do not deem it advisable or necessary to make any serious changes. The Army is for Lincoln, though Illinois and Indiana troops cannot help elect him.[4]

I am surprised that a Copperhead meeting should be so largely attended in our county. I hope the friends of the Union are not idle.

The Chaplain [Brother Cotton] thought when he left us that he would rest a year but has accepted an appointment to Dwight. I should have liked much to have heard his speech in Pontiac. Did you hear it, or of it?

Tell Mother [Murphy] she does not long more for me to come home than I do to be there & kiss her for me. Sister Maggie [Utley] has never written. Give my love to her & kiss the children for me.

All the Company are well. We expected the pay-master here this week, but are told this evening that he will not be here until next week. Some of the men are becoming very impatient, & I fear some of their families are in want. There is something wrong as we should have been paid a month ago. Chris [Yetter] & Nate [Hill] are flourishing as usual; they are both striving very industriously to learn to play chess. What progress have you made? Green was almost as badly disappointed in my not going home as myself. He was intending to go along.

It is 20 minutes past 11 o clock; yet, late as it is, I must close my letter to-night or it will not get out in to-morrow's mail, as I shall be very busy in the morning.

Sherman is still shipping citizens South. I told you a short time ago that the cessation of hostilities was to continue until the 22nd of October; it is only until the 22nd of this month.[5]

Francis Van Doren gives rather an amusing incident that happened a few days ago.[6] He is driving team in the supply train and is at present engaged in moving citizens. On one of his Loads were two young ladies, one of which was very much grieved at being compelled to leave her home & was crying and lamenting her fate, when finally she consoled herself by saying "that she had a home from which Sherman could not drive her." Her companion, who must have considerable spice in her nature, warned her not to be too certain as Sherman might yet "flank her out of Heaven." It does seem hard to drive women and children from their homes when there are doubtless some who are innocent of any transgression of the laws, but it is a moral impossibility to subsist the citizens when we have so large an army & so extended a base of supplies.

I think it very probable that the Campaign will open about the 1st of October.[7] There is no news from Grant. All is quiet there.[8] We are still ignorant of the policy Genl. Sherman will adopt or the direction the Armies will advance. God, who has been so bountiful in blessings, is still with us, & we trust will guide us to certain Victory.

The Chicago papers report Genl. A. J. Smith [is] on his way here, but I think it must be a mistake.[9] We have heard nothing of him through military channels. We are looking anxiously for the result of the *draft*.[10] We would like to see the men coming along.

I recd. a letter from the editor of the Sentinel requesting me to write an article for the paper occasionally. If I get time before the campaign opens, I will, though I have but little inclination to engage in political discussions.

All the camp is quiet & the men sleep. The moon bright and clear shines sweetly upon us and a "Beautiful Star" is twinkling close by her. We dream of home and wonder whether in God's good Providence we are destined to enjoy its Sweets again. Who but "He alone" can tell, and yet we hope and anticipate trusting all to Him. Let us pray for Grace to be resigned to His will. May His richest blessings rest upon you and your babe.

I can imagine you both asleep now, & I would love dearly to see the reality of my dreams. Still "All is well," & if we only wait patiently for "God's good time" our enjoyment will be so much the sweeter. If not on earth, yet in Heaven we may meet. Remember me very kindly to all our friends and let us not forget that we are blessed far above thousands of those around us. May Holy Angels guard you.

Good night.

Your affectionate Husband

J. F. Culver

1   Bridges' Illinois battery, like Company M, 1st Illinois Light Artillery, was assigned to the IV Corps' Artillery Brigade.

2   Albert Green, a black freedman, had attached himself to J.F.C. while the regiment was at Nashville in the autumn of 1863.

3   General McClellan, embarrassed by the "peace plank," sought to repudiate it by placing the strongest emphasis on the Union in his letter accepting the nomination. He thus went before the country as a war leader. In the campaign which followed, Democratic speakers, taking their cue from McClellan, generally avoided mention of the "peace plank," while inveighing against Lincoln's policies and denouncing his so-called acts of usurpation. Randall, *Civil War and Reconstruction*, pp. 619-20.

4   No provision had been made by the legislatures of Illinois and Indiana to permit soldiers to vote by absentee ballot. To have their votes counted, soldiers from these states would have to return to their homes to cast their ballots.

5   On Sept. 10, 1864, General Sherman had issued Special Field Order No. 70, announcing that a truce is declared to exist from "daylight of Monday, September 12, until daylight of Thursday, September 22, . . . at a point on the Macon Railroad known as Rough and Ready, and the country round about for a circle of two miles' radius." *O. R.*, Ser. I, Vol. XXXIX, pt. II, p. 356.

6   Francis M. Vandoren, a 24-year-old farmer, was mustered into service on Sept. 8, 1862, as a private in Company A, 129th Illinois Infantry. On April 27, 1864, he was detailed as a teamster in the supply train of the Third Division, XX Corps. In the autumn of 1864 he rejoined the company and was wounded at Averysboro, N.C., March 16, 1865. Private Vandoren was mustered out with the unit on June 8, 1865 near Washington, D.C. Compiled Service Records of Union Soldiers, NA.

7   Sherman hoped to resume the campaign by October 1. When he did, he proposed to keep Hood's Army of Tennessee employed, and put his "army group" in condition "for a march on Augusta, Columbia, and Charleston, to be ready as soon as Wilmington is sealed as to commerce, and the city of Savannah is in our possession." Meanwhile, the Union armies with General Grant before Petersburg and those with Maj. Gen. E. R. S. Canby on the Gulf Coast would be reinforced "to the maximum." Grant's force would strike for Wilmington and Savannah, while Canby would "send a force to get Columbus, Ga., either by the way of the Alabama or the Apalachicola." *O. R.*, Ser. I, Vol. XXXIX, pt. II, pp. 358, 412.

8   Following the battles of the Weldon Railroad and Reams Station in late August, Grant's armies, having cut the Weldon Railroad south of Petersburg, paused to regroup. Grant's next attack was scheduled for the end of September, and would consist of thrusts at opposite ends of his long line. General Butler's Army of the James would attack north of the James, while units from General Meade's Army of the Potomac would thrust westward from the Weldon Railroad and attempt to reach the Boydton Plank road and the Southside Railroad.

9   Maj. Gen. A. J. Smith with his detachment of the Army of the Tennessee had spent most of the summer of 1864 in Western Tennessee and northern Mississippi, keeping General Forrest's cavalry corps occupied and away from Sherman's supply line. Smith, having accomplished his mission, had embarked his troops at Memphis, on the first leg of their trip to rejoin Sherman. Once again, as in June, Smith had to be diverted. This time it was into the trans-Mississippi to cope with Maj. Gen. Sterling Price's column which had crossed the Arkansas and was thrusting deep into Missouri.

10   President Lincoln on July 18 had issued a call for 500,000 volunteers. To fill this quota it was necessary to resort to the draft. Long, *Civil War Day by Day*, p. 541.

## 190

Head Quarters Co. "A" 129th Regt. Ills. Vols.
Atlanta, Georgia, September 21st 1864

My Dear Wife

I have not forgotten your request to keep this day as one of
thanksgiving to "Our Father" for the very many blessings He has
conferred upon us.[1] I thought yesterday that I would devote this day to
you and to memories of the past, but was detailed as Brig. Officer of the
Day, & in addition to that duty, I had to receive and issue clothing
which consumed the entire day. I have therefore devoted but very little
time to reflection.

My reading last night was in Psalms from the 111th including a part of
the 119th. The events of the past two years are so numerous and varied
that even a day seems scarcely sufficient to enumerate them. I regret
that I have spent them so poorly, yet God in his Infinite Mercy has
continually blessed me. My trials have been few and light. Part of the
time my heart has been filled with love, yet much of it has been spent
without profit.

To-morrow it will be two years since I left you in our home, delicate
in health and alone to bear your burdens and suffer your trials and
privations. God alone knew what was before us. Have we not gained
confidence in that hand that has protected us and that power which has
sustained us? We have not been without trials; God has visited us with
judgments. Our little boy, who had scarcely learned to lisp our names,
was called by a kind Father to His arms. To-night he appears as a
beacon light to guide us home, and surrounded with all the beauties of
Heaven he awaits our coming. Are not our ties stronger, our desires
more eager, our hopes brighter?

Nature smiles as ever, but the particles that form her beauty fade and
die and from the roots springs that beauty anew. So each successive
year adds its testimony to the power and goodness of our Creator. We
have also had witness of the love exercised toward us amid dangers
seen and unseen; we have been preserved in life, in health and to each
other.

God has also in his kindness given us another child to fill the vacuum
in our hearts. The ties of love which united our hearts have not been
loosened in all his dealings with us, but month after month we have

each become more necessary to each other's happiness. Let us look hopefully to the future. "Our Kind Father" will still care for us. The clouds, dark and lowering, which overhang our Country may dim our vision. We cannot divine futurity, yet trusting, hoping, loving, our "joy surely cometh in the morning." Above the clouds, the sun is shining brightly. I imagine at times its rays begin to break the vista and its rays will enliven the whole system of our body politic.

It would be a long story to tell you by what system of reasoning I have gathered my hope or to enumerate all the incidents that have made up my results. God who has thus far prospered and cared for us will develop all in His own good time. He is doubtless solving the great problem that has so long vexed the whole human family, "That the power lies not in *man* but in Himself." The establishment of this theory has cost us very dear, and the debt is not yet fully paid, but, true as the magnet draws the needle to the pole, will the hand of Omnipotence guide us safely through. "Let us praise Him for his marvelous kindness, for his wonderful works, and his boundless love toward the children of men."

I was disappointed in not hearing from you by to-day's mail. We recd. two days mail but only a paper for me. I have been thinking to-night of the many cares gathering around you, & I ought not to expect you to write so frequently. The tobacco, book, & handkerchief have not yet arrived. I presume they have been laid aside in some of the Post Offices & may be overlooked for weeks. It is not a very rare occurance.

Bro. Sammy and Jim Rawlins were here on a visit to-day & took dinner with us.[2] Sammy is looking very well. John is also well. John Lee came to the Regt. yesterday.[3] He is looking quite well & is able for duty.

There is a rumor here of a glorious victory in the Shenandoah Valley and of the death of Valandigham, both rumors lack confirmation.[4]

We were to have a review to-morrow, but it has rained so much to-day that it has been postponed. We are getting very comfortably situated here, though it is probable our stay will be of but short duration.

The city is almost deserted by citizens, almost all having been sent either north or south. We have an abundance of rations for present use, and the supply daily increasing. All the troops continue in good health. My own health continues excellent; I have been blessed very greatly. Oh, how I wish I was more worthy. Pray for me. I know you do.

I have no news from Carlisle yet. [Lt.] Smith is getting along very well, though he has not improved very rapidly in health. Nate [Hill] has been on duty since noon yesterday in the city. I do not know how long he will be detained there, but he is very pleasantly situated. He has charge of a guard at the Bakery. I will try & see him to-morrow.

It is still raining and the night is very dark. It is almost 11 o clock, & I must close. Give my love to Mother [Murphy] and Maggie, and kiss the children for me.

May "Our Father" bless you & your treasure with good health and happiness. The year is growing shorter rapidly. If I am not permitted to see you sooner, I hope through the kind interposition of Providence to be with you then. Let me find your love unchanged.

Good night,

Your affect. Husband

J. F. Culver

---

1   See J.F.C.'s letter of September 13, 1864. September 21 would have been Franklin "Frankie" Culver's second birthday.

2   James A. Rollins, a 25-year-old Pontiac Township farmer, was mustered into service on Aug. 12, 1862, as a private in Company M, 1st Illinois Light Artillery. He served with the battery throughout the war and was mustered out at Chicago, on July 24, 1865. Compiled Service Records of Union Soldiers, NA.

3   John Lee had been hospitalized since being wounded in the shoulder in battle at Peachtree Creek on July 20, 1864. *Ibid.*

4   Union forces commanded by Maj. Gen. Philip H. Sheridan, on September 19, 1864, had defeated General Jubal Early's army in the third battle of Winchester. General Grant, concerned by Early's successes which had compelled him to send two infantry corps and a third of his cavalry to guard the line of the Potomac, on August 6 had placed General Sheridan in command of a force with orders to destroy Early's command. Third Winchester was the first step in Sheridan's campaign.

There was no truth to the rumored death of Clement Vallandigham, leader of the "peace at any price" Democrats.

 191

Head Qurs. Co. "A" 129th Regt. Ills. Vols.<br>Atlanta, Georgia<br>September 22nd 1864

My Dear Wife

I was disappointed to-day in not receiving any letter from you to-day.

There must be something wrong with the mails as they do not come at all regular or else our friends at home are forgetting to write.

It is still very wet and has been raining most of the day. The news of Sheridan's victory in the Shenandoah Valley was confirmed this evening by telegraph from Sec. Stanton;[1] we gave three hearty cheers. We recd. no papers to-day.

I had a letter from [Erastus] Nelson by Lt. Edgington who returned from Nashville to-day. He will lose the use of his left arm and will be discharged in a few days.[2] Capt. Coppage of Co. "I" has been dismissed [from] the service for disobedience of orders.[3] Capt. Martin has resigned; his health is very bad.[4] Capt. Perry is still in the North somewheres. When we last heard of him, he was on his way to Lake Superior for his health; I presume he is resting upon the laurels he won in the rear.[5] Lt. Smith is well as usual; Chris [Yetter] and him are fast asleep. Nate [Hill] is on duty in the city. All are well. Capt. Walkley has been appointed A. A. In. Genl. of the Brigade.[6]

Our review which was to have been to-day has been postponed until Saturday on account of the weather. I was to see Frank Long to-day while in the city; he feels rather blue about his prospects.[7]

Chris had a letter from Tom Smith to-day; he is still at Quincy, Ills., and is rapidly improving.[8] Jim Chritten has the Jaundice but is not seriously ill. He is still at Kingston, Ga. [Pvt. W. H.] Bronson has returned to Chattanooga much improved in health; he has been home on furlough. Sutcliff's furlough has not yet returned; if it succeeds, it will be a good opportunity to send money home. I must close & go to bed. I wrote last night until nearly midnight, & I shall not wake at reveille if I dissipate too much. Give my love to all. May Our Father in Heaven bless you.

Your affectionate Husband

J. F. Culver

---

1 Secretary of War Stanton, on September 20, telegraphed General Sherman, "Yesterday, the 19th, Major-General Sheridan attacked the Rebel forces under Generals Breckenridge and Early near Bunker Hill, in the Shenandoah Valley, fought a hard battle all day and a brilliant victory was won by our forces. The Enemy were driven off twelve miles, 2,500 prisoners were captured, 9 stands of colors, 5 pieces of artillery were taken, and the rebel killed and wounded left in our hands." *O. R.*, Ser. I, Vol. XXXIX, pt. II, p. 423.

2 Pvt. Erastus J. Nelson of Company A was severely wounded by a gunshot wound in the chest at the battle at Peachtree Creek on July 20, 1864. He was hospitalized at Nashville, and given a medical discharge on Oct. 8, 1864. Compiled Service Records of Union Soldiers, NA.

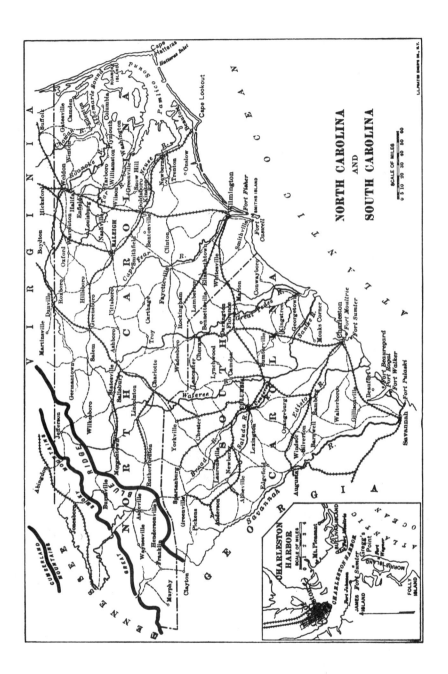

NORTH CAROLINA
AND
SOUTH CAROLINA

SCALE OF MILES
0 5 10 20 30 40 50 60

CHARLESTON HARBOR

SCALE OF MILES

3   Joseph W. Coppage, a 38-year-old farmer, was mustered into service on Sept. 8, 1862, as 3d lieutenant of Company I, 129th Illinois Infantry. He was promoted captain of the company on Dec. 3, 1862. Captain Coppage, on May 18, 1864, near Cassville, Ga., had refused an order to take charge of the regimental picket line, and when confronted by Colonel Case, who reiterated the order, Coppage shouted "I'll not [do] it, Sir, and you can show your favoritism as much as you please," and "I wish you would arrest me; I know my rights, Sir, and will just say what I please." Court-martialed, Coppage was dismissed from the service on Sept. 8, 1864. *Ibid.*

4   George W. Martin, a 35-year-old farmer, was mustered into service on Sept. 8, 1862, as captain of Company H, 129th Illinois Infantry. Captain Martin resigned his commission on Sept. 13, 1864, on receipt of a surgeon's certificate attesting to his disability because of chronic diarrhea. *Ibid.*

5   John B. Perry was mustered into service on Sept. 8, 1862, as captain of Company C, 129th Illinois Infantry. Captain Perry was hospitalized at Louisville on May 20, 1864, suffering with chronic diarrhea, and on July 11, 1864, he was given a leave from the hospital. He did not rejoin the unit, as he resigned from the service on Jan. 7, 1865, on receipt of a surgeon's certificate attesting to his disability. *Ibid.*

6   Samuel T. Walkley, a 44-year-old farmer, was mustered into service on Sept. 8, 1862, as captain of Company B, 129th Illinois Infantry. Captain Walkley was detached on Sept. 16, 1864, and assigned to duty as inspector general of the 1st Brigade, Third Division, XX Corps. He was mustered out near Washington, D.C., on June 8, 1865. *Ibid.*

7   Pvt. Frank Long was transferred from Company A, 129th Illinois, to Company H, 16th Illinois Infantry, on June 8, 1865. He was mustered out at Louisville, Ky., on July 8, 1865. *Ibid.*

8   Wounded at New Hope Church on May 27, 1864, Private Smith was hospitalized at Quincy, Ill., until receiving a medical discharge from the service on May 18, 1865. *Ibid.*

 192

Head Qurs. Co. "A" 129th Regt. Ills. Vols.
Atlanta, Georgia
September 25th 1864

My Dear Wife

An)ther day has passed, another week commenced, and God has been and still is with me. I long for some news from home. No mail to-day, and consequently no letters for me. The Enemy captured and destroyed the mail train supposed to contain several days mail.[1] I presume they have those intended for me. I still hope that you are well, but I cannot entirely remove the anxiety to know which continually haunts me.

The Sabbath Day has been unusually pleasant and happy. This morning I attended church in the city; this evening I preached at the Hd. Qurs. of Co. "G" from Hebrews, 2nd Chap. 2nd & 3rd verses. God was with me, & my soul is happy. We propose to commence a series of protracted meetings on Tuesday evening [the 27th] to continue so long as it may be profitable. Pray for us and ask all our friends to pray in Faith. We trust that God will pour out of his "Holy Spirit" upon us.

Lieut. Smith resigned some two weeks ago, and his papers returned home approved. He will start for home sometime next week. He was a good officer, & I am sorry to lose him.[2] I shall try to have [Chris] Yetter succeed him but may not succeed. Godfrey is entitled by rank,[3] but, having been promoted over Yetter without sufficient reason, I should much prefer Yetter, & I am satisfied the Company would also. Smith was loth to leave the company and service, but the condition of his wife's mind and health left him no choice. He has been in perfect misery ever since he returned [from leave].

I thank God with all my heart for giving me a wife, who, while she is strong and earnest in her attachment, is willing to sacrifice so much for her Country's good, who, instead of repining and mourning, can be cheerful and even comfort me. Believe me, I do not love you less than if you were less strong and self reliant; and, if I thought our Holy Father would not disapprove, I would pray to love you more. You have all my love, stronger than life and above all else, save God. I tried to imagine myself in the congregation at home, but there was so little resemblance. God is still the same in love and manifestations of mercy here.

All the Company are in good health. Nate Hill is still on duty in the city but was out to see us to-day. Alf Huetson was also here; he is well, & says there is a rumor afloat again that our Crops will be ordered to the Potomac.[4] I cannot think it true so soon after this last call. We have no news to-day owing to the loss of our mail last night. We recd. by telegraph yesterday news of another victory in the Shenandoah Valley,[5] also of rumors of Peace propositions from Jeff. Davis.[6] The latter is rather improbable. If God will speed our cause until the close of the coming campaigns here and elsewhere, we may hope to have them in such a condition that such propositions may come within the bounds of reason. Just now I believe they would ask much more than we could honorably grant.

Atlanta is almost rid of citizens. You have doubtless read in the papers the correspondence between Genls. Sherman and Hood.[7] To persons afar off the policy adopted may seem severe, but, under the circumstances, it was all that humanity could dictate. It was impossible to subsist them, & we have suffered so much from an inveterate foe in our rear that it has become a necessity to drive them before us.

The weather changed very suddenly last evening, and the night was very cold. We were scarcely comfortable with our overcoats this morning, but the day became very pleasant, though it is quite cool to-night.

Bill Myers of the 20th Ills. was here to-day.[8] Alva Garner is sick in Hospital at Marietta;[9] all the rest are well. [Lt.] Smith went to church in the city to-night with a squad of 12 of the Company. There is very encouraging revival in progress in several of the churches. May God increase the good work.

I saw a letter from Mrs. Paige to-day to Myers. She had heard of her husband's death only through the papers & was trying to cheat herself into the belief that it was not her husband. May God deal kindly and pour the oil of consolation into her heart. Poor woman. With all his faults, she loved him dearly, and the future will look very gloomy to her. He was an excellent and faithful soldier and a very efficient officer.[10]

Let us lift our hearts in praise and thanksgiving for his boundless mercies to us. Give my love to Mother [Murphy] & Maggie and kiss baby for me. I would like much to see him.

I fear Green's book & my stamps and tobacco have met the same fate of your last letters. May the richest of Heaven's blessings rest upon you, and the Grace, Love, and Peace of "The Father, Son, and Holy Spirit" abide with you. Write as often as you can make it convenient.

Your affectionate Husband

J. F. Culver

---

1 Confederate columns in the latter half of September again struck at Sherman's supply lines. General Forrest's corps advanced from its base in northeastern Mississippi, crossing the Tennessee River on the 20th, and headed north, wreaking havoc on the Tennessee & Alabama Railroad. Athens, Ala., was captured along with its garrison on the 25th. Next morning found Forrest's horse-soldiers striking toward Pulaski, Tenn., as Northern generals frantically deployed units to counter this thrust toward Nashville and the vital Nashville & Chattanooga Railroad.

Brig. Gen. William H. Jackson, whose cavalry division had remained with the Army of Tennessee when General Wheeler departed on his August raid, had forded the Chattahoochie in the fourth week of September at Phillips' Ferry. On the evening of the 24th, one of Jackson's columns captured a train near Marietta. *O. R.,* Ser. I, Vol. XXXIX, pt. II, pp. 646, 881; Cox, *Atlanta,* pp. 222-23.

2  Lieutenant Smith's resignation was to take effect on Sept. 23, 1864. Compiled Service Records of Union Soldiers, NA.

3  William A. Godfrey, a 35-year-old carpenter, was mustered into service on Sept. 8, 1862, as a corporal in Company A, 129th Illinois Infantry. Corporal Godfrey was promoted to 1st sergeant on Jan. 20, 1863. He was hospitalized at Savannah, Ga., in the late winter and spring of 1865, but rejoined the regiment in time to be mustered out with the unit on June 8, 1865, near Washington, D.C. *Ibid.*

4  There was no truth to the rumor that the XX Corps was to be transferred to the Army of the Potomac.

5  Secretary Stanton on the 23d had telegraphed Sherman that on the previous day Sheridan's army, following up its success at Winchester, had defeated General Early's army at Fisher's Hill. "Nothing saved Early's army from total destruction," he added, "but the cover of night." Leaving 2,000 prisoners in Federal hands, the Rebels retreated up "the Valley in the greatest confusion." *O. R.,* Ser. I, Vol. XXXIX, pt. II, p. 442.

6  In the summer of 1864 there had been several abortive efforts by well-meaning individuals to find a formula that would bring peace. Negotiations always broke down in the face of President Davis' "*sine qua non* of independence." Randall, *Civil War and Reconstruction,* pp. 614-18.

President Davis at this time was at Hood's headquarters, where plans were made and approved for the Army of Tennessee to take the offensive. Hood was authorized to advance and destroy Sherman's supply line, before the Federals could complete their build-up preparatory to a resumption of the campaign. Cox, *Atlanta,* p. 221.

7  See J.F.C.'s letter of September 13, 1864.

8  William H. Myers, a 21-year-old Pontiac carpenter, had been mustered into service on Aug. 9, 1861, as a private in Company D, 20th Illinois Infantry. Private Myers reenlisted as a veteran-volunteer at Big Black Bridge, Miss., in the winter of 1863-64. On May 28, 1864, he was detached to the Pioneer Corps, Third Division, XVII Corps, Army of the Tennessee, and in August was promoted sergeant. He was mustered out on July 16, 1865, at Louisville, Ky. Compiled Service Records of Union Soldiers, NA.

9  Alva Garner, a 23-year-old Pontiac farmer, was mustered into service on June 13, 1861, as a private in Company D, 20th Illinois Infantry. Private Garner was wounded in the arm at Shiloh on April 6, 1862, and in January 1863 was detailed as a nurse in a LaGrange, Tenn., hospital. In the autumn of 1863 Private Garner was hospitalized at Memphis. On Jan. 5, 1864, at Big Black Bridge, Miss., he reenlisted as a veteran-volunteer. Private Garner was promoted to sergeant on Oct. 3, 1864, and discharged with his regiment at Louisville, Ky., on July 16, 1865. *Ibid.*

10  Charles L. Paige, a 24-year-old Pontiac bookkeeper, was mustered into service on June 13, 1861, as a private in Company D, 20th Illinois Infantry. Private Paige was promoted regimental sergeant major on June 18, 1861. On Jan. 14, 1862, he was commissioned 1st lieutenant of Company D, and three months later captain. On April 20, 1863, he became acting lt. col. of the 9th Louisiana Colored Infantry, a position he held until rejoining his company in Sept. 1863. Captain Paige was killed in the battle at Atlanta, July 22, 1864. *Ibid.*

## 193

Head Quarters Co. "A" 129th Regt. Ills. Vols.
Atlanta, Georgia
September 30th 1864

My Dear Wife

As there is no mail, we suppose that our communications are interrupted somewhere, & probably no letters go north.[1] Bro. John [Murphy] was here last night & is well. Sammy [Murphy] has not gone to Chattanooga yet, but the "Battery" is expected to leave every day.[2] Lt. Burton is going home,[3] and, as Bro. John has recd. a portion of his pay, I got him to send you $20 by him. It will be expressed from Chicago.

We have not been paid as our money has not yet arrived, and, if the rail-road is injured as badly as reported, it may be a month before we receive it.[4]

We are all well. I wish you would please send me a box of cotton half hose by Sutcliff.[5] If [Lt.] Smith got through without interruption, you have all the news from us.[6] We are busy on reports; Yetter is learning. We are all well. With much love, I remain, as ever,

Your affect. Husband

J. F. Culver

---

1   To cope with Forrest's cavalry and protect the Western & Atlantic Railroad, Sherman had rushed General Newton's division to Chattanooga and Brig. Gen. John H. Corse's to Rome, Ga. The force guarding the Nashville & Chattanooga Railroad was also strengthened, while Gens. Lovell Rousseau and Robert S. Granger marched to intercept Forrest with 8,000 men. On the 26th Sherman learned from his scouts that Hood's Army of Tennessee had broken camp and had marched west from Lovejoy's Station, and was camped in and around Palmetto Station on the Atlanta & West Point Railroad. Upon receipt of news that Forrest's column was closing in on Pulaski, 70 miles south of Nashville, General Sherman ordered General Thomas with Morgan's XIV Corps to return to Tennessee. There he would push a column west through Stevenson to threaten Forrest's rear.

Forrest, after briefly occupying Pulaski on the 27th, had turned east toward the vital Nashville & Chattanooga Railroad. Fayetteville was occupied on the 28th, and small parties sent to cut the telegraph and railroad north and south of Tullahoma. Next day Forrest advanced toward the railroad, but at Mulberry, on learning that Thomas had massed a strong force at Tullahoma, he called a halt. Forrest now divided his corps: **Brig. Gen.** Abraham Buford with 1,500 men headed south toward Alabama, with instructions to wreck the Memphis & Charleston Railroad from Huntsville to Decatur, while Forrest with the main column turned west to raise additional havoc on the Tennessee & Alabama Railroad.

Damage to the railroad and telegraph, north and south of Tullahoma, caused by Forrest's raid on the night of the 28th was repaired in less than 12 hours.

General Thomas on the 30th from Chattanooga telegraphed Sherman that "this place" is "crowded with officers and soldiers on leave and furlough. No more should be allowed to leave until the [rail] road is reported clear to Nashville." Sherman was agreeable, and he notified his army commanders to stop all furloughs.

Although damage to the railroad and telegraph had been slight, all trains had been pre-empted to rush reinforcements north to cope with Forrest's raid. *O. R.,* Ser. I, Vol. XXXIX, pt. I, pp. 546-47; pt. II, pp. 459-532.

2   Although Company M was under orders to follow Newton's IV Corps division to Chattanooga, another month was to pass before the artillerists were able to board a northbound train. *Report of the Adjutant General of Illinois,* Vol. VIII, p. 667.

3   Thomas Burton of Chicago, a 20-year-old clerk, had been mustered into service on July 16, 1861, at Cairo, Ill., as a private in Company A, 1st Illinois Light Artillery. He was promoted to corporal on Dec. 1, 1861; was wounded at Shiloh on April 6, 1862; and promoted to sergeant on July 1, 1862. Sergeant Burton was discharged on Oct. 14, 1862, to accept a commission as 2d lieutenant in Company M, 1st Illinois Light Artillery. He was promoted to 1st lieutenant on March 31, 1864, and was mustered out at Chicago on July 24, 1865. Compiled Service Records of Union Soldiers, NA.

4   Damage inflicted by Forrest's raiders on the railroads over which Sherman supplied his "army group" was insignificant. But with Hood's army across the Chattahoochee and striking north, this situation was about to change.

5   Pvt. William Sutcliff, having received a 20-day furlough, had accompanied Lieutenant Smith. Regimental Papers, 129th Illinois, NA.

6   Lieutenant Smith, having received his discharge, had boarded a northbound train for Chattanooga on the 27th. Grunert, *History of the 129th Illinois,* p. 106.

 194

Head Quarters Co. "A" 129th Regt. Ills. Vols.
Chattahoochie River, Ga.[1]
October 9th 1864

My Dear Wife

It seems an age almost since I heard from you, and the prospects now are not very flattering as there is yet no communication with the north. I have commenced this letter in order to send by the first train that goes out. A longer time has elapsed since I last wrote, I think, than at any former time since I have been in the service. The interruption of our communication is much less serious than we anticipated as we have well authenticated reports that the railroad is free from farther molestation, and, as soon as it can be prepared, we shall again have the pleasure of hearing from home.

It looks just now very much like a premeditated affair of Genl. Sherman's.[2] For two weeks he was sending large numbers of troops to the rear, finally Genl. Thomas left also; but, instead of disposing the troops along the line of the road, all were massed at Allatoona pass awaiting the enemy. You will doubtless have full particulars of the Battle before this reaches you. We know but little yet save that Genl. Thomas defeated the Rebel Army with a loss of over 200 killed, many wounded, & several hundred prisoners.[3] We have heard nothing yet of Sherman's operations.[4] Kilpatrick with the Cavalry has captured and destroyed the enemy's Pontoon train and a large portion of their supplies.[5]

Our Corps, with a portion of each Corps of the Army, were left behind. We are very strongly fortified and would be able to withstand the Rebel army until the main Army returns. We entertained some fears about our supplies, as the Army took fifteen days' rations with them, but there was no need of alarm as there is amply sufficient for any emergency. Our ration of bread has been increased to 1-1/2 lbs. per day and all else in proportion except meat, and the boys have all they wish. The health continues excellent. Every man in my Company is fit for duty, & Dr. Wood told me yesterday that he had only one patient in the Regiment. Large numbers of those in the Hospitals have returned, & my Company is larger than at any time since the Campaign opened.

The weather since the first of this month has been very wet until two days ago. It is now very cold, &, if it were not for the continual high wind, there would be a killing frost. It is with difficulty that we keep comfortable with overcoat on over the fires. If it continues much longer, we will build chimneys.

I presume Smith and Sutcliff have reached home ere this, as they left the 27th Sept., though they were probably detained in Chattanooga several days.

I have no doubt but you feel great anxiety not being able to hear from the Army. Bro. John [Murphy] is with Sherman.[6] Sammy is in Chattanooga with his "Battery." I did not see John as he passed here as I was on duty, but several of the boys in the Company saw and talked with him.

I am sorry now that I did not keep a diary for you, but it rained so constantly, & we were continually moving from point to point strengthening the fortifications that I neglected it. Allen Fellows has a complete one, which he will send home by the first mail.

We moved from Atlanta to the river on the 1st two days before the Army commenced to move. Alf Huetson was out to see us yesterday; he is very well and is much pleased with his comfortable quarters in the city. I have not answered the letters I received from Carlisle yet, but will try and have them in readiness for the first mail.

As it was too cold for [church] service this morning, we will probably have preaching this afternoon if the weather is favorable. The sun is shining very brightly, but the wind is raw & cold. My hand becomes so numb that I cannot write with[out] going to the fire occasionally. The roads are improving rapidly; they must have been almost impassible in rear of the Army for the past week. Green was much disappointed in not receiving his promised book; it was doubtless captured on the trains that were destroyed yet may possibly come yet.

7 o'clock P.M.

I stopped writing for dinner, & it was so cold that I postponed writing thinking it would be more calm. At three o'clock, Lt. Scott invited me to go with him to the house of a citizen where he had been invited to preach. The time passed so pleasantly that I have just returned. The congregation was composed of several families, refugees from Atlanta and the surrounding country. The parlor is very nicely furnished, & I sat there trying to imagine myself at home. Oh, how I wished that this evening could have been spent at home.

I learned on my return to the Company that [Major] Hoskins intends to start home in the morning & that all letters must be sent up to-night, so I will haste to send this by him. I find it hard to forgive him for not giving me this opportunity since he was at home scarce six months ago. But it is doubtless all for the best.

The bridge is completed, & the first train passed over about an hour ago.[7] How earnestly we will look for mail now.

God grant that my loved ones are all well and happy. I have had the blues very badly several times during the past two weeks, but now I am living on hearing very soon from you. Kiss baby for me & tell him I would surely go to see him & Mama if it were possible. The picture [of the baby] will soon be coming, will it not? Give my love to Mother and Maggie. I would have written to the Sabbath School also if I had known Hoskins was going so soon. I did not think the way would be open for sometime yet, but I must close and gather up the mail. It is now past tatoo.

It seems so long since I had an opportunity to talk to you even by letter that I am loth to quit yet. Accept much love and a kiss, & may the richest of Heaven's blessings rest upon you.

Your affect. Husband

J. F. Culver

---

1   General Sherman on the 29th learned that two corps of Hood's Army of Tennessee had crossed to the north side of the Chattahoochie, about 25 miles southwest of Atlanta. To counter a Confederate thrust into Tennessee and an attack on his railroad supply lines, Sherman on October 1 notified his subordinates that he would reinforce General Thomas in Tennessee, and with the rest of his "army group" strike for Savannah and Charleston, believing that Hood would be compelled to follow. If, however, Hood turned his columns toward the Western & Atlantic Railroad, south of the Etowah, Sherman would fight him. Cox, *Atlanta*, pp. 223-24.

Consequently, on October 1, the 1st Brigade, Ward's division, was ordered to take position to protect the Chattahoochie Railroad Bridge. Breaking camp, the 129th Illinois passed through Atlanta and tramped up the Marietta road in a driving rain storm. It was dark by the time the regiment reached the river. After Colonel Case had detailed Company D to man a picket line, the rest of the regiment crossed the river and camped. During the night the rain-swollen river swept away the railroad and wagon bridges. A pontoon bridge was laid the next day, and Company D rejoined the regiment. Grunert, *History of the 129th Illinois*, pp. 107-08.

2   General Sherman, on October 3, satisfied that Hood was striking toward Marietta and the Western & Atlantic, put his "army group" in motion. Slocum's XX Corps would hold Atlanta and the Chattahoochie bridges and the other corps would march for Smyrna Camp Ground, south of Marietta. Hood, by this time, was near Lost Mountain with two of his corps, and the third (Lt. Gen. A. P. Stewart's) was driving for the railroad. On the 3d Stewart effected a lodgment on the Western & Atlantic, capturing Acworth and Big Shanty. After paroling the prisoners, damaging the railroad, and cutting the telegraph, Stewart sent one division (French's) to capture the post at Allatoona Pass and marched to rejoin Hood with the remainder of his corps.

Meanwhile, the Army of the Cumberland (less the XX Corps) had recrossed the Chattahoochie and by nightfall on the 4th was camped in and around Marietta. Howard's Army of the Tennessee was also north of the river at Smyrna Camp Ground, while the Army of the Ohio was preparing to cross at Pace's Ferry. Cox, *Atlanta*, pp. 225-26.

3   J.F.C. was mistaken as to details. General Thomas with two divisions had been rushed to Middle Tennessee to protect the Nashville & Chattanooga Railroad against Forrest's horse-soldiers. Their mission had been accomplished, and by October 6, Forrest had returned to his base, having seriously damaged the less important Tennessee & Alabama and Memphis & Charleston Railroads.

On the morning of October 5, Major Gen. Samuel G. French's division assailed the post at Allatoona Pass, defended by 2,000 men commanded by Brig. Gen. John D. Corse. There was a savage fight. When French learned that Sherman's infantry was at Kennesaw, 15 miles away, he broke off the attack and rejoined Hood's army at New Hope Church on the 6th. After the fight, Corse buried 230 dead Confederates and counted more than 400 prisoners. Union losses were 205 killed and wounded. *Ibid.*, pp. 227-31.

4   Sherman now massed his "army group" west of Marietta, while observing Hood's movements, and turned out large working parties to repair the railroad and rebuild the Chattahoochie Railroad Bridge. Having concluded that Hood's goal was to draw his "army group" out of the heart of Georgia, Sherman refused to be led away. General Corse was

sent to Rome with his division, from where he could cover the Western & Atlantic between Resaca and Cartersville. Sherman now repeated a proposal, previously made to General Grant, that he be allowed to abandon the Western & Atlantic, evacuate Atlanta, turn his back on Hood's army, and march for Savannah by way of Milledgeville and Millen. *Ibid.*, 233-34.

5  There was no truth to the report that Union cavalry under Brig. Gen. Judson Kilpatrick had "captured and destroyed the enemy's pontoon train and a large portion of their supplies."

6  John Murphy was still detailed to Bridge's battery and had accompanied that unit on its return to Middle Tennessee.

7  General Slocum on October 9 notified General Sherman that the railroad bridge, swept away on the night of the 1st, had been "repaired and the train has gone over." *O. R.,* Ser. I, Vol. XXXIX, pt. III, p. 163.

 195

Head Qurs. Co. "A" 129th Ills.
Chattahoochie River, Ga.
Octr. 13th 1864

My Dear Wife

The Post Master has just informed us that all letters sent in by sun down will catch the mail, &, as the sun is a few minutes high, I haste to inform you that through God's blessing, I am still enjoying excellent health. No word from home yet. Oh, how wearily the days pass round. "We are waiting, weary waiting" for good news from home.

We recd. by signal from Allatoona Mountains the confirmation of the rumor of the capture of Richmond.[1] God grant that it may be a permanent victory. Our Army is in motion, but we are still left.[2] We expect mail to-morrow, & then we will have news.

May God bless you and our babe. Give my Love to Mother & Sister Maggie. May Holy Angels guard thee. Kiss baby for me. Good Bye.

Your affect. Husband

J. F. Culver

1   The message reporting the capture of Richmond was false. On the 13th General Ben Butler had made a forced reconnaissance of Confederate defenses on the Darbytown road, 8 miles southeast of Richmond, and found them formidable and covered by an extensive abatis. Humphreys, *The Virginia Campaign of '64 and '65*, pp. 293-94; Grunert, *History of the 129th Illinois*, p. 111.

2   General Sherman on the 10th, learning that Hood's army was crossing the Coosa 12 miles west of Rome, ordered his columns to converge on Rome. General Thomas was to mass his forces at Stevenson, Ala., to oppose a possible crossing of the Tennessee by the Confederates. At Kingston on the 11th, Sherman temporarily lost track of Hood. The Confederates had pushed to the northeast, their line of march hidden by Johns Mountain, and on the 12th appeared before Resaca and called on the garrison to surrender. The Federals refused. Leaving one corps before Resaca, Hood marched Stewart's to Tilton and Dalton, capturing both towns and their garrisons. Sherman on the 13th put his "army group" in motion for Resaca, where he arrived the next day. Hood, having failed in his efforts to seriously damage the Western & Atlantic, retreated westward to Villanow. So far all he had accomplished was to draw Sherman 100 miles from Atlanta, but Slocum's XX Corps continued to occupy that place. Cox, *Atlanta*, pp. 235-37.

≈≈≈ 196 ≈≈≈

Head Quarters, Co. "A" 129th Regt. Ills. Vols.
Chattahoochie River, Ga., Octr. 18th 1864

My Dear Wife

There is no mail going or coming at present, but, as we are ordered out for forage in the morning with 5 days' rations, there may be an opportunity in my absence to send this to you.[1] I will leave it in the hands of some of those who remain to be forwarded. I did hope that some mail might arrive in the trains which passed this evening, but we leave so early that it will not reach here in time. So I am to wait 5 long days before I hear from you. If I only had the assurance that you are well. I cannot overcome the impression that you may be very ill, as my last letter was dated the 26th while several were received of as late date as the 30th.[2] I will trust all to "Our Father" who in his boundless Love has dealt so kindly with us. May He in the plentitude of his mercy preserve both you and our child in perfect health, and surround you with all necessary comforts to insure your happiness.

We have had no reliable news for several days though an abundance of rumors.³ I have kept myself very closely to my tent lately, having some unsettled business matters to occupy my time with and occasional reading. I preached last night in the Chapel tent of the 79th Ohio to a large & interesting Congregation from Deuteronomy 5-9. God was pleased to bless me.

Squads of Rebel Cavalry have been hovering around our lines for several days. To-day they captured 25 men & 150 mules with some private horses that were taken out to graze;⁴ once before, several men and mules. I think that is what gave rise to this Expedition which is for the double purpose of scouring the country & obtaining forage. Nate [Hill] is on picket and will be left behind. We will miss our comfortable tents and fires.

How very fortunate we have been thus far in being left to garrison this place. Our lot has fallen in the most pleasant places all through our term of service, and, though we have lost heavily during the Campaign of our best men, yet we outnumber a large majority of the Regiments in the service, and our Brigade is among the largest in the Army.

We have been gleaning from the papers recd. by Saturday evening's mail [the 15th], the particulars of the battles in the East and the aspect of political affairs in the North. Rumor is afloat here that the "Copperheads" have carried Indiana by considerable majority at the State Election on the 11th inst.⁵ We still hope it is an error. The soldiers of that State, like ourselves, are not allowed to vote.

The Pay-master paid off the 105th Ills. to-day but has run short of funds. As there has been no opportunity to transport funds with safety, we must abide by our misfortune without complaining. As [Lt.] Smith promised to see you supplied, & Lt. Burton has probably reached Chicago & ford. the money sent by him, I have given myself but little uneasiness on that score. I hope you will not hesitate to accept of any funds which may be offered that you need, for we have no assurance of being paid very soon.

Jim Mitchell was married on the 4th inst. to a Miss Clara Carter of New Albany, Ind. Dr. Reagan recd. their cards a few days ago. Col. Ben. Harrison is stumping the State of Indiana and has been nominated for a Brig. Genl.'s commission, Genl. Ward for Major Genl.⁶ Col. Smith, 102nd Ills. commands the Brigade at present, & Col. Dustin, the Division.⁷

I saw a letter from Sam Maxwell to Wm. B. Fyfe bewailing the fate of "Poor Culver," saying that his "Democratic friends pitied more than they derided him."⁸ I should take opportunity to answer it were it not that the time will be very limited after my return before the Election.

Jim Morrow is looking well. Allen Fellows has enjoyed very good health lately. I saw Connelly to-day;[9] he is well. Also Harry McDowell. Green is busy to-night preparing rations for our expedition.

I hear a train coming up from Atlanta which may possibly have mail for us, though it is doubtful, as there has scarcely been time to distribute it since the trains went down. But I must close for to-night. I will enclose three Photographs. I sent one in my last [letter] & think they will be very acceptable for your collection. I will get one of Genl. [O. O.] Howard as soon as opportunity offers.

Give my love to Mother and Maggie. Kiss baby for me & Remember me very kindly to all our Friends. Tell Remick that I will not probably be able to write such an answer to his letter as he desires, but, had the mails been going out, I would have been prompt in replying. I hope the letter written Mr. Decker arrived safely as it may answer, at least in part. May our Father in Heaven bless you with all needful blessings. Preserve us in life and health from danger and sin and fit our hearts for a close communion with him. If consistent with his will, our communion will be sweet when our duty to our Country is discharged. Let us pray and take consolation from His promises. Good Bye.

Your affectionate Husband

J. F. Culver

---

1  Attacks on the Western & Atlantic by Hood's army had by October 10 caused a great scarcity of forage in and around Atlanta to feed the horses and mules. It became necessary to forage upon the country. During the next several weeks, General Slocum sent four large foraging expeditions and a number of lesser ones into the neighboring counties. *O. R.,* Ser. I, Vol. XXXIX, pt. I, pp. 668, 680.

2  Soldiers of the 129th Illinois on October 14 had received the "first mail . . . for many days." Grunert, *History of the 129th Illinois,* p. 112.

3  Hood's army, with Sherman's columns closing in, had abandoned its efforts to destroy the Western & Atlantic Railroad and, covered by a strong rear guard, had turned southward after passing through Villanow. Sherman followed.

By the evening of the 17th, Sherman was satisfied that Hood had gone south by way of Summerville toward Gadsden, Ala., having given up his plans to cross the Tennessee River anywhere above Muscle Shoals. Next day found Sherman's "army group" continuing its pursuit through the mountains of northwest Georgia. On the 20th Hood's army was at Gadsden and Sherman's at Gaylesville. There Sherman halted for a week, watching Hood's movements, "proposing to follow him if he attempted to cross the Tennessee near Guntersville, but determined to carry out his plan of a march to the sea if Hood should go to Decatur or Florence." Cox, *Atlanta,* pp. 237-39.

4  A detachment from the 102d Illinois was ordered out on October 18 to recapture the livestock, and succeeded in recovering three horses and two mules. *O. R.,* Ser. I, Vol. XXXIX, pt. I, p. 684.

5  Rumors that Indiana had been carried by the "Copperheads" were wrong. Oliver P. Morton, the Republican wheelhorse, was reelected governor and the party made gains in the congressional contests. Long, *The Civil War Day by Day,* p. 582.

6  Captain Mitchell and Dr. Ragan had served with J.F.C. on Colonel Harrison's staff. General Ward was brevetted major general to rank from Feb. 24, 1865, and Colonel Harrison a brigadier general to rank from Jan. 23, 1865. Compiled Service Records of Union Soldiers, NA.

7  General Ward and Colonel Harrison having received leaves to return respectively to Kentucky and Indiana to campaign for the Lincoln-Johnson ticket, Col. Daniel Dustin of the 105th Illinois, as senior officer, had assumed command of the Third Division, XX Corps, and Col. Franklin C. Smith of the 102d Illinois, as senior regimental commander, had taken command of the 1st Brigade. *O. R.*, Ser. I, Vol. XXXIX, pt. I, p. 679.

8  William B. Fyfe, a 39-year-old lawyer, was mustered into service on Sept. 8, 1862, as a private in Company G, 129th Illinois Infantry. Private Fyfe served with the regiment throughout the war, and was mustered out near Washington, D.C., on June 8, 1865. Compiled Service Records of Union Soldiers, NA. Samuel Maxwell of Pontiac was elected treasurer of Livingston County in November 1860. An influential and popular politician, he moved to Missouri in 1866. *History of Livingston County*, p. 266.

9  Joseph B. Connelly, a 36-year-old farmer, had been mustered into service on Sept. 8, 1862, as a private in Company A, 129th Illinois Infantry. Private Connelly had been detailed as an orderly with the First Division, XI Corps, on Jan. 14, 1864. When the XX Corps was constituted, Private Connelly was re-assigned as orderly with the 1st Brigade, Third Division, XX Corps. Compiled Service Records of Union Soldiers, NA.

 197

Carlisle, Penna.[1]
Febr. 9th 1864 [5]
10 A.M.

My Dear Wife

I arrived here about an hour ago & am at Harry's; found all well & Sister Hannah here. I will go out to Mother's after dinner.[2] All the friends so far as heard from are well, & all I have seen wonder why you are not with me.

The snow is very deep, about 18 or 20 inches, & the sleighing, of course, excellent. The meetings are still in progress in the lower charge with glorious results. I shall doubtless be busy while here.

I have seen but few acquaintances yet. I shall certainly expect to hear from you at New York if not here. I shall leave for N.Y. on Monday morning [the 15th] if not sooner.

Jennie says that Harry & her wrote to us over two weeks ago. I presume you recd. the letters before this. She is very anxious to hear from you. All send much love. I will write again soon. Kiss Howard for me. May the richest of Heaven's blessings rest upon you. Enclosed is a photograph for Mrs. & Dr. Capron.[3] Please deliver it.

Good Bye,

Your affect. Husband

J. F. Culver

---

1 J.F.C., his leave due to expire in four weeks, was en route to rejoin his unit. When last heard from, the 129th Illinois, along with other units General Sherman had led on the "march to the sea," was encamped near Savannah, Ga. J.F.C. planned to proceed to New York City by railroad and there board a ship for Savannah and a rendezvous with his regiment.

Harry Cheston was married to J.F.C.'s sister, Jennie C. Hannah M. Culver was J.F.C.'s youngest sister.

2 Mrs. Martha Dunmire Culver, J.F.C.'s widowed mother, was currently living in the family home in Carlisle's east ward.

3 Dr. and Mrs. Elisha Capron of Pontiac were close friends of the family. While J.F.C. had been on leave, Dr. Capron had treated him for piles, which had plagued him since June 1864. Pension File, J.F.C., NA, Application No. 960, 772, Certificate No. 766492.

 198

Carlisle, Penna.
Febr. 10th 1864 [5]

My Dear Wife

I came to Mother's yesterday afternoon & stayed until evening. Charlie was down at the Pagues', but she was expecting him home so I went back to Harry's & with Jennie to church.[1] There was a *concert* in town, and the church was quite full and the meeting quite interesting.

There were about 15 or 18 forward for prayers and the interest seems to be general.

I remained all night at Harry's & came out to Mother's this morning. Gustie & Charlie were up this afternoon. All are well.

I saw Mrs. Caldwell this morning, and she inquired very kindly about you.[2] To-morrow morning I shall go to Millers[3] on business & to Pagues in the afternoon & come back to Mother's Sunday morn [the 14th].

Bro. Harry [Cheston] is to preach to-night. I wish you could be here to hear him. Mother & I will go in.

Hannah is with Jennie but will be home to-morrow. Bro. Charlie has left College. His guardian says he will have no more money until Spring, but it is only an excuse, I think, as he has been urging him to stop for several months. Charlie has an idea of going to a Commercial College in the spring & intends to go to Illinois with Mother & Hannah if I get back in the fall. I want you to tell me candidly, are you anxious or willing to have them live with us? I never thought much about it, as I did not think they would come, but they seem so confident now that I wish to know your desires. Do not hesitate to tell me.

[The] Pagues have [their] sale on the 6th March.[4] If I could remain a few days longer, I would like to see the place he has purchased, but I must hasten to the Regt.

The sleigh bells are ringing in every direction, & the sleighing is excellent. I have been feasting on Mother's large *apples*. I wish I could send you one. I shall look anxiously for a letter to-morrow. Remember me in love to all. Kiss Howard for Papa. Marvin can walk quite well & say a number of words. The snow is so deep that I will not go to Frankie's grave though I would like very much to have seen it. Write often. I want to receive letters soon after I reach the Regt.

May God bless & make you happy. Good Bye.

Your Affect. Husband

J. F. Culver

---

1 Eighteen-year-old Charlie Culver was J.F.C.'s youngest brother, while his sister, Rebecca, was married to S. Augustus Pague and lived on the family farm in Middlesex Township.

2 For biographical data on Mrs. Caldwell, see J.F.C.'s letter of September 14, 1863.

3 John Miller, a prosperous Middlesex Township farmer, was married to J.F.C.'s half sister, Lucetta. In 1860 the Millers were living with their six children, four boys and two girls. Eighth Census, Cumberland County, State of Pennsylvania, NA.

4 To settle the estate of J.F.C.'s father, it was necessary to sell the family farm on which the Pagues were living.

## 199

Harrisburg, Pa., Febr. 13th 1865.

My Dear Wife

I left home on the afternoon train and have to wait until 3 o'clock to-morrow morning for the N.Y. train. The Dr. says Mother has Erysipelas, but he thinks it will not be severe. Bro. Charlie & Sister Jennie both promised to write to you.

I called to see Mrs. Annie Van Horn Daires this evening & found the family well.[1] Mr. Daires was not at home but is well. Annie played a few new pieces on the Piano for me. I left at 8 o'clock, & on my way back to the hotel came by a church where they were holding a revival meeting. I went in & remained until half past ten. They are having a good meeting, & I enjoyed it very much. There were fine ladies at the altar. It was a Winebrenenan Bethel, a denomination not much known in the West.[2] I presume you would scarcely have enjoyed it as it was a very noisy meeting. But the Spirit of God was manifestly present.

I am in a study whether to go to bed to-night or not. It is nearly 11 o'clock & the train leaves at 3. I am not sleepy. I have been thinking much of Home. I wish I could spend the hours intervening with you. "When shall we meet again?"

I did not enjoy my visit [to Carlisle] as much as I anticipated. The only sleighride I had was from John Miller's to Pagues' & from there to Carlisle.[3] The roads were so drifted that we could not drive off a walk. The sleigh bells are jingling merrily around the city to-night.

Sherman is still moving North.[4] I cannot imagine where I will find the Regt. I look for a letter on my arrival in New York to-morrow morning. Kiss Howard for me. Give my love to all. May Our Father in Heaven bless you both. Do not fail in writing. With much love, I remain, as ever,

Your affect. Husband

J. F. Culver

---

1 Annie Van Horn Daires by 1867 was a widow and dressmaker and was living on Harrisburg's Canal Street, near Walnut. *The Harrisburg City Directory 1867-68,* compiled by William J. Divine (Harrisburg, 1867), p. 53.

2 The Winebrenenan Bethel Church met on Fourth Street at the corner of Strawberry Alley. *Ibid.*, p. 193.

3 The Miller farm was in Middlesex Township, on the Sterretts Gap Road, six miles north of Carlisle.

4 General Sherman had advanced into South Carolina. Ward's Third Division of General Slocum's wing had crossed the Savannah River into South Carolina, at the beginning of the New Year, at Screven's Ferry, and had marched to Hardeeville, while General Howard massed his wing in and around Pocotaligo. On January 29 the 129th Illinois marched from Bethel Church to Robertsville, where it rendezvoused with the remainder of the XX Corps. Four days later, on February 2, the Third Division broke camp and started north. Near Lawtonville, the 1st Brigade was engaged by Rebel cavalry. The Confederates were bested, and the Federals continued to advance, having lost ten men in the skirmish. The XX Corps, along with Sherman's other columns, pressed steadily ahead, crossing the Big and Little Salkehatchie, and on the 7th reached the South Carolina Railroad. The next 72 hours were spent wreaking havoc on the railroad between Graham's and Williston. Meanwhile, Howard's wing had reached the railroad at Midway.

On February 11 the XX Corps left the railroad and started north toward Columbia. Destruction of the bridge across the South Fork of the Edisto caused a short delay. Fording the river on the 12th, the XX Corps forged ahead, and nightfall on the 14th found the troops camped at Tucker's, 18 miles southwest of Columbia. Howard's wing meanwhile had reached Orangeburg, as it converged on Columbia from the south. Grunert, *History of the 129th Illinois*, pp. 163-196; Cox, *March to the Sea*, pp. 168-70.

 200

Sweeny Hotel, New York
Febr. 14th 1865

My Dear Wife

I arrived here at 4 P.M. & recd. your letter of the 8th. The one sent to Carlisle I did not get. The mails must be much delayed by the deep snow. I am sorry to hear of your own and Howard's ill health, but hope you have both recovered ere this.

I went to the Q. M. Dept. and secured transportation on the "Constitution" which is to leave at noon to-morrow if not prevented by the ice on the Bay.[1] I shall probably go aboard at any rate, and this is probably the last letter I shall write before I reach Savannah, so that it will probably be two or three weeks before you hear from me again.

I hope Maggie Chappell has done well, yet I was not at all favorably impressed with the reputation I heard of him.[2] I wish them much happiness.

There is but little snow here though the streets are quite slushy.

If I thought you would do much of your writing from the "preacher's," I should certainly "donate a new pew," however, I was too glad to hear from you to find fault with the penmanship. You may direct your letters hereafter to the Regt., though I have no idea when I shall reach it.

I wrote to you from Carlisle yesterday morning concerning the disposition of the money coming from Father's estate in April.[3] If it does not reach you, let me know.

I feel uneasy about Howard's arm; I did not expect him to get so sick.[4] I learned in Carlisle by letters received from Bloomington, Ills., that the Small-pox had become epidemic there, so much so, that the schools are suspended. I hope it will not reach Pontiac.

Your letter does not mention the progress of the [revival] meetings, yet I hope they are still improving in interest.

Rumor says Sherman has possession of Branchville.[5] I hope it is true, as it will compel the evacuation of Charleston.[6] In that event, I may land there instead of Savannah. I anticipate a few days sea-sickness; I hope not severe. My health is good.

You do not mention in your letter the money I sent you from Chicago, either for yourself or for Goodwin & Smith. I presume, however, it reached you; there was $25.00 for you & $10.00 for the others. The first (yours) was enclosed in a letter with the S.S. books, the other I sent by mail.

I thought I should write to the S. School or church from this place but do not feel like it to-night. There are very many things I should like to talk with you about to-night if I were with you, as it seems such a long time before I can reasonably expect to hear from you again. Keep in *Good* heart, let us trust in God to control all things for our good. I know you will be very lonely, but make use of every means in your power to keep cheerful. Be assured that whatever contributes to your happiness will meet my approbation.

We can hope for the future trusting in God. I feel that He will bless and keep you both. Kiss Howard for me & Sister Maggie [Utley] & the children. I ought to have written to Bros. John and Sammy again but have neglected it. Remember me to them when you write. Jennie & Hannah complain that you do not write to them often enough.

Remember me kindly to all our friends, especially those who have recently espoused *Christ*. I shall remember them at a Throne of Grace. I have committed both Howard and you to the care of "Our Father in Heaven," and I feel content though it is hard to be so far from you. May He abundantly bless you with health, happiness, and a sufficiency of Grace. With much love and a lasting remembrance of your pure and holy affection, I must say Good Bye.

Your affectionate Husband

J. F. Culver

---

1  *Constitution* was a 944-ton screw-propelled steamboat, built at Mystic, Connecticut, in 1863. She was wrecked off Cape Lookout, North Carolina, on December 12, 1865, with the loss of 40 lives. The Quartermaster Department had the responsibility of providing transportation for soldiers traveling on orders and en route to rejoin their units. *Merchant Steam Vessels of the United States, 1807-1868, "The Lytle List"* (Mystic, 1952), pp. 40, 264.

2  Maggie Chappell was born in Indiana in 1836, and in 1860 she was living in Pontiac at the home of Joshua and Harriet Whitman. She had apparently married or was engaged to marry someone of whom J.F.C. disapproved. Eighth Census, Livingston County, State of Illinois, NA.

3  The subject letter is missing from the Culver Collection.

4  Before leaving Pontiac, J.F.C. had had Howard vaccinated for smallpox.

5  Sherman's line of march passed west of Branchville. On February 7 soldiers of General Howard's wing reached the South Carolina Railroad at Midway, eleven miles west of Branchville. From there, they advanced on and captured Orangeburg.

6  With Sherman's columns astride the South Carolina Railroad, the defenders of Charleston found themselves in an increasingly precarious position. If Sherman turned his army toward the coast, they would be encircled by an overwhelming force and destroyed.

 201

Home Insurance Company
Office No. 135 Broadway.
New York, Feby. 15th 1865

My Dear Wife

I went to the Dock this morning to see what time the boat would leave. We may possibly not get away to-day on account of the ice. I met Capt. Horton, Co. "F", on the boat & went with him up to the Lovejoy Hotel to see Capt. Coolidge, Brigade Quarter Master, and Capt.

Endsley, 70th Ind.[1] I will have plenty of good company & feel much happier this morning than yesterday. I was a little blue yesterday when I thought of making the trip with strangers, perhaps sea-sick most of the way. God has been very kind and good to me, & I feel very happy in His love.

Capt. Horton & myself went down Wall Street to the Ferry this morning to see the sights. The gold market had not opened yet, so we will go again about noon. On our way back, we called in here at the Home Ins. Co.[2] They greeted me very kindly and offer[ed] to do anything in their power to make my stay in New York pleasant. I am writing in a very neatly furnished little office for private uses. Am all alone. There is an arm chair just to my right, & I have been trying to imagine Howard and you in it, while I talk with you. "Oh, how I wish you were here."

There will be a vessel in from Fortress Monroe [Va.] at 12 o'clock with the latest news. You will receive them by the Chicago papers to-morrow.

I am extremely fortunate in meeting Capt. Horton, as I will have barely sufficient funds to pay my living to Savannah. I have tried to be very economical but everything is so enormously high. I wished to send you some nice book from here, but you must "take the will for the deed" this time.

I see by the telegraph news this morning that it is snowing in Chicago, and probably in Pontiac also. The snow in Western New York is reported 4 feet deep. All the roads running West are blocked up, so that I cannot expect another letter before I leave.

Capt. Horton left the Regt. on the 10th January at Savannah & has been home on leave of Absence. He gave me quite a history of the Campaign through Georgia. The boys were all well. The news of the capture of Branchville and evacuation of Charleston are repeated this morning. It will either be confirmed or denied by the news on the noon Steamer.

The boat that we go down on ("Constitution") is not a very fine one but looks strong and good. Horton says all were sea-sick coming up, so you can imagine what my condition will be two days hence. We will be Six days going to Savannah unless we have better luck than common. The sea is very rough. The weather this morning was very clear and pleasant, but it is quite cloudy now & looks as if we might have rain.

Horton went around to the Lovejoy Hotel to see what time the other Officers intended to go on the Boat. I expect him back every moment when we will return to the Sweeny Hotel for my baggage.

If I have opportunity, I will write on the boat on the way down. It will be all new to me as I was never on the water. I would like very much to hear from Howard and you this morning. I presume you are at Maggie's, & I hope well and happy. If it be true that we have presentiments of good or evil of those we love, you are indeed happy. I had very sweet communion with Our Father last night before retiring and feel this morning as if I can freely trust in all things. May he bless you always with health and happiness. The clock is striking 12, so I must again say Good Bye. Kiss Howard for Papa and accept a sweet one for yourself. May Our Father bless you.

Your affectionate Husband

J. F. Culver

---

1   George W. Horton, a 25-year-old carpenter, was mustered into service on Sept. 8, 1862, as lieutenant in Company F, 129th Illinois Infantry. He was commissioned captain of his company on June 11, 1863. When the regiment left Nashville in February 1864, Captain Horton remained behind in the hospital but rejoined the company in time for the Atlanta Campaign. On January 11, 1865, he received a leave at Hardeeville and rejoined the regiment on April 4. Captain Horton was mustered out near Washington on June 8, 1865. Benjamin F. Coolidge was mustered into service on Aug. 23, 1862, at Camp Piqua, Ohio, as lieutenant and quartermaster of the 99th Ohio Infantry. In November 1862 he was assigned to General Ward's staff as brigade quartermaster. Lieutenant Coolidge in January 1865 had been ordered to proceed to Nashville on official business. On rejoining the XX Corps at Goldsboro, he was given a temporary assignment as division quartermaster. Henry M. Endsley of Shelby County was mustered into service on Aug. 1, 1862, at Indianapolis, Indiana, as captain of Company F, 70th Indiana Infantry. Captain Endsley, having received a leave, left his unit on Oct. 20, 1864, and rejoined it in late March 1865. Compiled Service Records of Union Soldiers, NA.

2   Before entering service, J.F.C. had been the Livingston County agent for the Home Insurance Company of 135 Broadway, New York City, New York.

 202

Charleston, S.C.<br>March 7th 1865

My Dear Wife

Almost two weeks have elapsed and we are still in Charleston, with no better prospect of getting to our commands than when I last wrote.[1] I am looking for some word from you by next mail. How long we may remain here, I am unable to determine.

My health has been excellent for which I have every reason to be thankful. We have been spending our time reading such books as we could get from the houses in the neighborhood and making a tour through the city each day seeking information of Sherman's whereabouts.[2] We recd. a small mail from New York on Saturday [the 4th] consisting of papers chiefly, the latest being of date the 23rd February. There is nothing new, and the place is as dull as you can possibly imagine.

I was at church on Sabbath morning and afternoon. The Sacrament of the Lord's Supper was administered after the morning Service, & Col. Merrill & myself were partakers.[3] I felt very much blessed. The congregations were not large, yet they seemed kindly disposed toward us.

The weather for the past few days has been very pleasant, and the gardens are being cultivated. There are peas, beans, onions &c. up in our garden, yet we do not anticipate remaining long enough to receive the benefit of them.

Schools have been opened for the negroes, and the streets are thronged with them about school hours. They seem to enjoy it very much.

We have been making good use of our piano and have a concert every day. Some new music would be very acceptable, however; we have repeated all we can remember so often that we are getting tired of them. I have just finished reading the 2nd volumn of "Queechy" & must hunt up something new to-morrow.[4] The only excitement we have is an occasional fire. We had quite a large one last Sunday evening down town, three unoccupied buildings were burned.

The streets of Charleston are becoming quite lively. Stores are being opened up in those portions that have been vacated for the past two years on account of our shells.[5] They are also patching up their houses where the shells in many places have entered. The city is garrisoned almost entirely by negro troops.[6] I have heard of no disturbance thus far. I have not been on the streets at night, and do not know whether the city is lighted up or not. The part we occupy is very quiet and two blocks from the business portion of the city. The citizens are flocking to the Provost Marshall's Office to take the oath [of allegiance]. They cannot open a store or get a letter out of the office without showing their papers having taken the oath. It seems rather hard but it will undoubtedly do good.

We are still getting along very comfortably here, though we cannot wholly escape the "Blues." We might be in a much worse condition, however. My Leave of Absence will expire in 13 days more, & then I will be in the same boat with the rest. I feel sorry that I did not spend another month in Pontiac regardless of *Public Opinion;*[7] but I doubt not all will yet be well.

Dr. Bennett had a conversation with a Rebel Surgeon to-day who told him that he thought there would be no fighting.[8] Yet it looks very probable that there will be a battle somewhere before the war ends. Many here are of the opinion that they [the Confederates] will evacuate Petersburg & Richmond & retreat in the direction of Lynchburg.[9] I hope no more fighting will be necessary, yet cannot realize so happy a termination of the war.

Burk is upstairs playing "Home Sweet Home," & I can almost imagine myself there at times.[10] I dare not think too much of it for fear of the Blues. I have neither seen or heard anything worthy of note.

This is my fifth letter from Charleston. How happy I would be to hear from you & Howard to-night. Remember me in love to all the friends. I must try & write to the boys soon. I fear I am very, very lazy; don't you think so? I have written but two letters, except to you, since I am here — one to Mother and one to the [Pontiac] "Sentinel," but I will try & do better.

May Our Father bless and make you happy. Col. Merrill & Dr. Bennett insist on my reading my letter, so that they may gather items for a letter home. They offer three cents in money & a sentence each to fill out the sheet, but I could not accept such a proposition. There is sufficient evidence of nothing to write about. Write often. Direct to the Regt. Good night.

Your affect. Husband

J. F. Culver

---

1 The occupation and destruction of Columbia by Sherman's army on February 19 compelled the Confederates to evacuate Charleston. Employing the Northeastern Railroad, General Hardee moved his troops to Cheraw, where great quantities of stores, both public and private, had been previously sent. Cotton, which was stored in the city in large quantities, was burned in the warehouses, and the fire, spreading, caused much damage. A powder magazine caught fire and exploded, killing about 200 civilians. Union forces led by Rear Admiral John A. Dahlgren and Maj. Gen. John G. Foster that had been blockading the harbor and bombarding the city and its defenses from James Island occupied Charleston on February 18, the morning after it was evacuated. Cox, *March to the Sea,* pp. 178-79.

Since arriving in Charleston in the fourth week of February, J.F.C. had written four letters to his wife, but these are missing from the Culver Collection. This is unfortunate, because in these letters he would have described the voyage down from New York, the receipt of news of the fall of Charleston, and identified where he was quartered.

2 Sherman's columns had resumed their advance through South Carolina on February 19. Evacuating Columbia, the army marched north. Slocum's wing, traveling by way of

Winnsboro, crossed the Catawba River near Liberty Mills on Washington's birthday, camped in and around Chesterfield on March 3, and advanced into North Carolina the next day, the 129th Illinois going into camp in a forest of young pines. General Howard's right wing had occupied Cheraw the previous day, after a slight skirmish. On the 7th the XX Corps crossed the Great PeeDee at Cheraw, and, after making a 17-mile march, halted for the night near Laurinburg, a station on the Wilmington, Charlotte & Rutherfordton Railroad. Grunert, *History of the 129th Illinois*, pp. 197-207.

3  Samuel Merrill was mustered into service on Aug. 1, 1862, at Indianapolis, Ind., as captain in Company K, 70th Indiana Infantry. He was promoted to major on April 11, 1863, and to lieutenant colonel eleven months later. Colonel Merrill on Jan. 8, 1865, having received a 30-day leave, left his regiment at Hardeeville, S.C., and rejoined his command in late March. Compiled Service Records of Union Soldiers, NA.

4  A popular novel, *Queechy*, by Susan Warner was first published by G. P. Putnam of New York City in 1852.

5  On August 22, 1863, the Federals had opened fire on Charleston with a 150-pounder Parrott (The Swamp Angel), emplaced in the Marsh battery, near Morris Island. Although the Swamp Angel burst on the 24th round, it was replaced by other heavy-rifled guns. Additional batteries were erected on Morris Island, armed, and the bombardment of downtown Charleston continued. Warren Ripley, *Artillery and Ammunition of the Civil War* (New York, 1970), pp. 118-22.

6  On February 28, 1865, the Charleston area was garrisoned by the following black units: 54th and 55th Massachusetts Infantry Regiments; and the 21st, 33d, and 35th U.S. Colored Troops. White units posted in the area were: the 54th and 56th New York Infantry; 52d Pennsylvania Infantry; Battery B, 3d New York Light Artillery; and the 1st Battalion, 3d Rhode Island Heavy Artillery. *O.R.*, Ser. I, Vol. XLVII, pt. II, p. 626.

7  Apparently, a number of the neighbors had complained about J.F.C.'s long absence from his unit.

8  It has been impossible to further identify Dr. Bennett.

9  Those holding this opinion were correct. On April 2-3, following the battle of Five Forks, General Lee's Army of Northern Virginia evacuated Petersburg and Richmond and, with the Armies of the Potomac and James in close pursuit, started for North Carolina and a hoped for junction with the Confederate armies led by General Joseph E. Johnston.

10  It has been impossible to further identify Burk, other than that he was a member of the brigade band.

## 203

Charleston, S.C.
Monday morning, March 13th 1865

My Dear Wife

I went to the Post Office this morning with bright hopes of hearing from you but was doomed to disappointment. I can only wait patiently hoping that I may be more successful next mail if I should be in the city so long.

We have had no opportunity to get farther north as yet, & we are seriously debating the policy of returning to Hilton Head to try our chances there.[1] This place is growing so dull to us that we must do something desperate soon. If the army was lying idle, it would not be so unbearable; but with our commands in motion, while we can contribute nothing, is more than we can patiently endure.[2]

My health is very good and the weather in this vicinity is beautiful, such as we enjoy in the north in late May & early June.

I had the pleasure of attending two Sabbath Schools yesterday. In the morning at 10 o'clock at Bethel Church (white).[3] The attendance was not very large but those present seemed much interested. I spoke about ten minutes. At 11-1/2 o'clock I went to Zion's Church S.S. (white & black);[4] there were about 130 or 140 children present. I talked to them 10 or 15 minutes; they seemed very much interested. In the afternoon Rev. James Beecher, Bro. of Henry Ward Beecher of N.Y. & Colonel of the 35th U.S.C.T. preached in Zion's Church.[5] There were about 12 or 1500 present. It is a Methodist church & has 1200 members. After the Sermon, the Sacrament of the Lord's Supper was administered. I preached in the evening at 7-1/2 from Romans, 3rd Chap, 23rd verse; there were some 800 or 1,000 present. The building is a very large one and seats 1500 easily. It was a happy day; God was with us.

The Steamer "Arago" arrived at Hilton Head on Friday,[6] & we recd. northern news this morning to the 5th inst. There is no important war news, except a probability that Sherman may open communication with the coast at or near Wilmington, N.C.[7]

Everything is quiet in and around Charleston, and remaining indoors you would not realize the existence of war. We are to be honored with the company of a *Lady* in our house. She stepped into our parlor just now, & we became so excited that we came near upsetting all the chairs in the room. Her name [is], I think, Mrs. Moss, & [she] is from New York. Her husband is principal of some of the public schools, &, as they could find no place so convenient as this, we gave one of our front rooms up stairs.

I learned from Mrs. Beecher in a conversation on Saturday evening that she plays the Piano, so we hope to have some good music. Dr. Bennett removed over the river last week, & I have not exercised much on the Piano since he left.

The weather is very beautiful to-day, & our garden, which is in full view of my Desk, would astonish you. We have Peas, Beans, onions, watermelons & radishes all up & looking finely. The birds sing very sweetly among the trees in the garden, & everything out-doors looks happy. We have not been able to get a Northern paper yet, but may succeed throughout the day.

How much pleasanter it would have been if I had remained at *home* until now. I think the prospects are brightening for the termination of the war. Then "Home Sweet Home." Remember me kindly to all our friends, Kiss Howard for me. It would be a great comfort to know just now that you are both well. May Our Father bless you. I feel so Blue to-day that I cannot write.

Good Bye,

Your affect. Husband

J. F. Culver

---

1   This statement suggests that J.F.C. had disembarked from *Constitution* at Hilton Head, S.C., and had boarded another ship which brought him to Charleston.

2   In the period March 7-13, the 129th Illinois, along with other units of the XX Corps, had continued its advance into North Carolina. The Lumber River was crossed on the 10th, and the next day the troops, after a 25-mile march, reached Fayetteville, on the Cape Fear River. Grunert, *History of the 129th Illinois,* pp. 207-11.

3   Bethel Church was on Pitt Street at the southwest corner of Calhoun. *Sholes' Directory of the City of Charleston, 1883* (Charleston, 1883), pp. 37-8.

4   Zion Presbyterian Church was on the south side of Calhoun, east of Meeting Street, *Ibid.,* p. 39.

5   James C. Beecher of Hartford, Conn., was mustered into service on April 28, 1863, at Boston, as lieutenant colonel of the 35th U.S. Colored Troops, and was promoted to colonel on June 9, 1863. Colonel Beecher was wounded at Honey Hill, S.C., on Nov. 30, 1864. In March 1865 his regiment was stationed at Mt. Pleasant, S.C.; and in April in Charleston, at the Citadel. Compiled Service Records of Union Soldiers, NA.

6 *Arago* was a 2,240-ton propeller-driven steamer, built 10 years before in New York City. *Merchant Steam Vessels of the United States, 1807-1868,* p. 11.

7 On March 12 a steamboat ascended the Cape Fear River from Wilmington, N.C., and for the first time since the last day of January, Sherman's army was again in communication with Union forces operating along the coast. Grunert, *History of the 129th Illinois,* p. 211.

 204

Charleston, S.C.
March 14, 1865

My Dear Wife

We have just returned from a visit to "Fort Sumpter." The water was not very rough, but it rained quite hard part of the time, & as a consequence we got wet through. We went out in a small rowboat, about as large again as old Charlie Jones's in which you may recollect taking a ride one beautiful *moonlight night* several years ago.[1]

"Fort Sumpter" is to-day probably the strongest of its kind in the world, & it looks like an impossibility to have captured it by direct assault.[2] We were shown through it by a man who was in it with Major Anderson when he surrendered it, and was also among the first to enter it after its evacuation by the Rebels.[3] It is not quite as large as I expected to find it, yet much more complicated. I gathered a few shells as relics which I will try and preserve. There is only a sergt. & 8 men in the "Fort". Those portions [of Fort Sumter] facing our Batteries on the Island [Morris] are all battered down, & over the ruins are various kinds of abattis, over which it would have been impossible for troops to force their way against even a feeble resistance. We came by "Castle Pinckney" on our way in;[4] it is very well finished but has never been used. Around two sides of Sumpter there are tons of iron (solid shot & shell) which it would seem might occupy years in throwing there.

I will enclose in this some papers that I should have left at home. The two receipts put in the drawer with my other recpts, & the license in an envelope marked "Licenses." I think it probable we will try & get to Hilton Head to-morrow, & from there to Wilmington.

We received the New York Herald & Tribune yesterday but there is but little news. We have no news here, and it is as dull as you can possibly imagine. I can scarcely expect to hear from you if we leave here before the next mail arrives, but I shall hope that you are all well and happy.

May God bless you. It is wet & gloomy this afternoon. Remember me in love to all our Friends. Kiss Howard for me.

Good Bye.

Your affect. Husband

J. F. Culver

---

1  Charles Jones was a prosperous Livingston County farmer.

2  Fort Sumter had been attacked by Union ironclads on April 7, 1863. Repulsed with the loss of one vessel, the Federals retired. They returned that summer, and, having secured possession of Morris Island, opened fire on the morning of August 17 on Fort Sumter with all their batteries. A number of ironclads at periodic intervals joined in the bombardment. The masonry walls were pounded into ruins at a number of points, but the Confederate defenders burrowed into the rubble. On the night of Sept. 8, 1863, the Rebels repulsed a landing party. The bombardment was resumed, but failed to dislodge the defenders who remained in possession of Fort Sumter until the night of February 17, 1865, when Charleston was evacuated. D. Ammen, *The Atlantic Coast* (New York, 1883), pp. 91-110, 130-156.

3  Maj. Robert Anderson on April 13, 1861, had surrendered Fort Sumter to Confederate authorities after a 34-hour bombardment. This event was the point of no return on the road to the Civil War. On April 14, 1865, Anderson, now a brigadier general, returned to Fort Sumter to raise the same United States flag that he had lowered four years before. Warner, *Generals in Blue*, pp. 7-8.

4  Castle Pinckney was a masonry fort guarding the entrance to Cooper River. Situated as it was in the inner harbor, it had not been subjected to bombardment as had Forts Sumter, Moultrie, and Johnson, and the defenses of Sullivan's and James Islands.

 205

At anchor off Morehead City, N.C.
Sunday night, March 19th 1865

My Dear Wife

We arrived here at dark & cast anchor, as our vessel draws too much water to cross the bar except at high water & in daylight. We will not get in until noon to-morrow. We hope to get direct to the Army.[1]

The New York papers of 16th, which we recd. off the "Atlantic" off Fort Fisher this morning, state that Sherman is at Goldsborough & the rail-road runs within 15 miles, & Schofield is represented at Kingston.[2] We may be disappointed, however.

Our trip from Charleston has been very pleasant. The sea has been smooth as glass. I expected a rough trip at this season of the year but was happily disappointed.

We met the "Fulton" on her way to "Hilton Head" with the mail.[3] I have not heard from you since I left, except yours of the 8th Febr. recd. in New York. You can imagine my anxiety to receive some intelligence of you. I will hope that you are well & happy. May God bless you.

It is six weeks tonight since I left you. Aside from the sights and changes, it has been about the dullest time I most ever passed. To-day has been but little like Sunday though the day has been very beautiful. We have not been out of sight of land to-day, but the coast from Wilmington up is very barren. We were not sufficiently near Fort Fisher to see its arrangement;[4] it looks very formidable at a distance.

The name of this vessel is "New York" & belongs to the Vanderbilt Line.[5] There are 1200 troops on board — 52nd Penna, 54th New York, 159th New York, & some detachments.[6] Col. Merrill & Capt. Endslee, 70th Ind., and Burk of the Brig. Band compose our party. We left Dr. Bennett at Charleston.

I will write to-morrow if we stop long enough. I have written to-night so that should an opportunity offer we will go forward, and I might not have a chance to write before reaching the command. I am sorry that I have no good news to communicate. Let us hope, however, that God will be pleased very soon to bring this war to a close. Remember me in love to all our friends. I should have written more, but I lacked the energy or disposition, or something else, I don't know what.

I have had the blues ever since I left home. Write very often. Kiss Howard for me, Pray for me.

Good Bye.

Your affect. Husband.

J. F. Culver

---

1 Sherman's army had started from Fayetteville for Goldsboro on March 15, the First and Third Divisions of the XX Corps taking the road for Averysboro. The next day near Averysboro, the 129th Illinois, along with other units of Slocum's wing, engaged a

Confederate force led by General Hardee. After a severe fight lasting until dark, the Confederates retreated. The Federals occupied Averysboro on the 17th. Grunert, *History of the 129th Illinois,* pp. 212-17.

2 The New York papers of the 16th were premature in reporting Sherman at Goldsboro. On the 16th Slocum's left wing was fighting the battle of Averysboro, and Howard's right wing was near Owensville. General Schofield, following the defeat of General Hood's Army of Tennessee at Nashville in mid-December, had been transferred to the Atlantic seaboard with his XXIII Corps. After capturing Wilmington, N.C., Schofield directed his attention to opening a route for supply of Sherman's army by way of Morehead City and New Bern.

By the last day of February, General Cox's XXIII Corps divisions had been shifted from Wilmington to New Bern. Thrusting inland, the Federals on March 14 occupied Kinston. It was 65 miles from Kinston to Averysboro. Cox, *March to the Sea,* pp. 147-62.

3 *Fulton* was a 2,307-ton propeller-driven steamer, built in 1856, and calling New York her home port. *Merchant Steam Vessels of the United States, 1807-1868,* p. 69.

4 Fort Fisher, one of the Confederate strongholds guarding the approaches to the Cape Fear River and Wilmington, had been captured by a Union amphibious force on January 15, 1864. Until the fall of Fort Fisher, the mouth of the Cape Fear had been a focal point for blockade runners.

5 *New York* was a new propeller-driven steamer of 2,217 tons. *Merchant Steam Vessels of the United States, 1807-1868,* p. 138.

6 The 52d Pennsylvania and 100 men of the 54th New York had been embarked at Charleston on March 17, while the 159th New York had boarded the ship at Savannah. These units were under orders to proceed to the mouth of the Cape Fear River, where they would report to the commanding officer, U.S. Forces. *O. R.,* Ser. I, Vol. XLVII, pt. II, p. 897.

 206

New Bern, N.C.
Mch. 22nd 1865

My Dear Wife

We arrived here safe & well yesterday evening, and leave at 8 A.M. for Kinston.[1] The information is quite reliable, though not positive, that Schofield has formed a junction with Sherman, and that we can go through directly.[2] We will have to march from Kinston to Goldsboro — 25 miles, but that is a very small item if we can only get through.

New Bern is a very pleasant place of about 5000 inhabitants. The weather to-day is pleasant but rained last night. I stepped up to a Q.

M.'s Desk, while Burk was getting breakfast, and have only time to write a line. May God bless you with health and happiness. Kiss Howard for me.

Your affect. Husband

J. F. Culver

---

1  The trip of 33 miles from Morehead City to New Bern was made by rail.

2  On March 19, as Sherman's columns marched east toward Goldsboro and a rendezvous with Schofield, General Johnston attacked Slocum's **wing.** near Bentonville. The Confederates gained ground at the expense of the XIV Corps. Reinforced by the XX Corps, the Federals stiffened and held. Next day Sherman arrived on the field with Howard's wing, and orders were sent by courier for Schofield to march at once from Kinston upon Goldsboro. On the 20th Sherman's troops felt their way forward, and during the night Johnston's army abandoned its position. The next day, the 22d, Sherman put his columns in motion for Goldsboro, which had been occupied by Schofield's troops the preceding day. Sherman entered Goldsboro on the 23d, at the head of Howard's wing. Cox, *March to the Sea*, pp. 186-96.

 207

Kinston, N.C.
March 24th 1865

My Dear Wife

We arrived here two days' ago but had no opportunity to get to the command.[1] Our train arrived this morning & will start back to-night; we will go with it. I have seen several men of the Regt. to-day, but none of my company. The loss of the Regt. in the last battle [Averysboro] is two killed and 14 wounded. James M. Pemberton of Co. "A", & one man (Bullman) Co. "H", *Killed*; & F. M. Van Doren, Co. "A", Sergt. Mason, Co. "E", Corp. Onstott, Co. "H" are among the wounded.[2] I could not learn the names of all. There were three in Co. "K". Francis Van Doren is but slightly wounded. David Jones, Co. "A", died in South Carolina of Chronic Diarrhea.[3] Henry Snyder, Co. "A", has been quite sick but is much better.[4] One man said he heard that Sam Hill was captured but had been exchanged & was again with the Company.[5] Major Hoskins is here & will go with us. All the Co. not mentioned are reported well.

All say that the Regt. never fought better. Col. Case commanded the Brigade & did well. He is reported slightly wounded but was able to run around when the train left.[6] The Rebels were badly whipped & in full retreat.[7] Sherman will stop only a few days for supplies. I feel in better spirits than at any time since I left home. There is a large mail (100 sacks), & I will hear from *you* soon.

It is very windy and dusty. My health is excellent. The boys represent the trip from Savannah as very severe, yet they lived well. The country has been very Swampy. The train brought several hundred families of refugees, & they sit in groups all around the field. It looks terrible. Both young & old without any one to protect or provide for them, surrounded with soldiers & doubtless often insulted by reckless men.

Remember me in love to all. Tell [John] Smith the result of the battle as soon as you can so that he can inform Pemberton's family. He was a brave & noble soldier. May God bless & protect you & make you happy. I will write as soon after my arrival at the command as possible.

Good Bye.

Your affect. Husband

J. F. Culver

---

1 Captain Culver had traveled the 32 miles from New Bern to Kinston by rail. Goldsboro, where Sherman had rendezvoused with Schofield, was 24 miles west of Kinston.

At 2 A.M. on the 24th the 129th Illinois had been turned out by an alarm, and five hours later the regiment broke camp at Waynesboro, on the final leg of its 55-day march from Hardeeville. At noon, the regiment entered Goldsboro, their route passing Sherman's headquarters. Sherman stood bareheaded as the troops marched by with bands playing. The regiment, along with other units of the Third Division, camped two miles north of Goldsboro. Grunert, *History of the 129th Illinois*, p. 223.

2 According to the regimental returns, two men were killed and 17 wounded at Averysboro on March 16. Two of the wounded subsequently died. The three wounded in Company K were: Corp. Andrew Salgman, and Pvts. Joseph Caley and Philip Wilderwood. *O. R.*, Ser. I, Vol. XLVII, pt. I, p. 799; Regimental Papers, 129th Illinois, NA, RG 94.

James M. Pemberton, a 23-year-old farmer, was mustered into service on Sept. 8, 1862, as a private in Company A, 129th Illinois Infantry. He was killed in action at Averysboro, March 16, 1865, Edwin P. Bulmer, a 32-year-old shoemaker, was mustered into service on Sept. 8, 1862, as a private in Company H, 129th Illinois Infantry. Private Bulmer was mortally wounded in the chest at Averysboro and died the next day in a field hospital. Francis M. Vandoren, a 24-year-old farmer, was mustered into service on Sept. 8, 1862, as a private in Company A, 129th Illinois Infantry. From April 27, 1864, until autumn, he was detailed as a teamster in the supply train, Third Division, XX Corps. Wounded at Averysboro, Private Vandoren was mustered out with the regiment on June 8, 1865, near Washington, D.C. Otis S. Mason, a 30-year-old blacksmith, was mustered into service on Sept. 8, 1862, as a sergeant in Company E, 129th Illinois Infantry. Sergeant Mason was wounded at Averysboro, and was hospitalized at Quincy, Ill., where he was medically discharged on March 25, 1865. John H. Onstot, a 35-year-old clerk, was mustered into service on Sept. 8, 1862, as a corporal in Company H, 129th Illinois Infantry. Onstot was promoted to sergeant on May 16, 1864, and was wounded at Averysboro. He was given a medical discharge while hospitalized at Madison, Indiana, on May 25, 1865. Compiled Service Records of Union Troops, NA.

3  David Jones, a 37-year-old miner, was mustered into service on Sept. 8, 1862, as a private in Company A, 129th Illinois Infantry. Private Jones died on March 3, 1865, at Chesterfield, S.C., of a "congestive chill." *Ibid.*

4  Henry E. Synder, a 20-year-old farmer, was mustered into service on Sept. 8, 1862, as a private in Company A, 129th Illinois Infantry. He was mustered out near Washington, D.C. on June 8, 1865. *Ibid.*

5  Nathan W. Hill, a 24-year-old farmer, was mustered into service on Sept. 8, 1862, as a private in Company A, 129th Illinois Infantry. He was promoted to corporal on Dec. 30, 1862, and to sergeant on May 9, 1863. Sergeant Hill was discharged on June 8, 1865, near Washington, D.C. *Ibid.*

6  General Ward reported that at Averysboro, he "directed Colonel Case to move with the First Brigade well around to the left and feel for the rebel flank, at the same time directing Colonel Dustin and General Cogswell to press the enemy in their front. I cannot speak too highly of the manner in which Colonel Case executed this movement." The 1st Brigade led by Colonel Case closed on the Confederate flank, just as Dustin's men swept over their earthworks. The Southerners took to their heels, leaving three cannon and 100 prisoners, not counting 68 wounded, in the Federal's hands. *O. R.,* Ser. I, Vol. XLVII, pt. I, p. 784.

7  Following the battle of Bentonville and the occupation of Goldsboro by Schofield's army, General Johnston retired northward to the Smithfield area. Here astride the North Carolina Railroad, he would be in a position to cover Raleigh, if, as expected, it proved to be Sherman's next goal on his march through North Carolina. *O. R.,* Ser. I, Vol. XLVII, pt. II, pp. 1453-54.

 208

Head Qurs. Co. "A", 129th Ills.
Goldsboro, N.C., Mch. 26th 1865
Sunday Eve

My Dear Wife

I rode from Kinston to this place yesterday on horseback, 37 miles, & arrive[d] just before dark. I recd. 12 letters brought through from Atlanta & 10 more by to-days mail, the last from you bearing date Feb. 20th. I am very happy indeed to learn that you are well & Howard also.

I am at home again; I found all the boys present in good health &

most of them glad to see me. I wrote to you just before I left Kinston of the result of the battle on the 19th inst.[1] J. M. Pemberton killed. Mark Stevens[2] & F. M. Van Doren slightly wounded. Henry Polk was captured on the 15th inst. while out foraging. The boys have fears that he was killed, but I hope he will turn up soon all right.[3] Green [the freedman] was the happiest boy I seen. Christ [Yetter] has been getting along finely. Nate [Hill] is flourishing. All of them are fat & hearty. David Jones died on the march from Savannah up; Mark Stevens is in the Hospital but Van Doren is with the Company.

7-1/2 P.M.: I quit writing to go to Supper, & after Supper the Chaplain came after me to preach. I preached from Romans, 6 Chap, 23rd verse. It was so cold that there was not a great many out though all the fires in the neighborhood were surrounded.

I saw Bro. [James H.] Gaff & [John S.] Lee this evening, both are well. Allen Fellows was also here to-day & is well.

We have just recd. orders to prepare immediately for another campaign.[4] 50 men of our 1st Div. were captured to-day while out Foraging.[5] The Band of the 3rd Brig. is playing a beautiful air. It is very cool to-night, & I should not be surprised if there is a frost.

I will not undertake to answer your letters to-night. I have read all of them once over but have been busy making estimates of clothing, camp, & Garrison equipage for the Company, & there are very many reports to make & things to look after at the close of so long a campaign, so you must excuse me if I am not so punctual for a few days. I thought of very many things I wished to write about this afternoon, but my tent is constantly full, & I am interrupted so often.

Mat Harber is here from the Hospital.[6] He says Mark Stephens is getting along very well. Col. Case commands the Brigade. We ate part of the fruit cake for supper this evening, & I gave its history. Our Regt. lays about two miles North West of Goldsboro. I have not been to the Town yet.

I would have been pleased to have seen Howard playing in the water. Kiss him for me. I have letters from Carlisle of the 14th Feb. Mother was better at that time. I will close for this time. The mail leaves at 5 A.M. to-morrow.

Remember me in love to all our friends. Let us thank God for his mercies & take courage. Do not give way to despondency; God will care for us. I hope you will be happy. Accept the love of your

affect. Husband

J. F. Culver

---

1 The battle to which Captain Culver referred is Averysboro, fought on March 16, not Bentonville which raged on the 19th and 20th.

2 Mark Stephens, a 24-year-old farmer, was mustered into service on Sept. 8, 1862, as a private in Company A, 129th Illinois Infantry. Wounded at New Hope Church on May 27, 1864, Private Stephens was hospitalized at New Albany, Ind. He rejoined the company in the autumn of 1864 and was wounded at Averysboro, March 16, 1865. Rejoining the unit, Private Stephens was mustered out near Washington, June 8, 1865. Compiled Service Records of Union Soldiers, NA.

3 Henry M. Polk, a 21-year-old farmer, was mustered into service on Sept. 8, 1862, as a private in Company A, 129th Illinois Infantry. Private Polk was captured foraging at Blackwater, N.C., on March 15, 1865, and was paroled at Aikins Landing, Virginia, March 26. He was furloughed at Benton Barracks, Mo., on April 7, 1865. *Ibid.*

4 On the 25th General Williams alerted the division commanders of the XX Corps to "at once have estimates and requisitions prepared and forwarded for a full supply of all articles needed to thoroughly equip their commands. The Corps must be put in condition for another campaign. A full supply of all needed articles can be obtained and full requisitions should be made." *O. R.*, Ser. I, Vol. XLVII, pt. III, p. 2.

5 A failure to file "after action reports" by the officers involved limits details of this affair.

6 James Mat Harber, a 21-year-old farmer, was mustered into service on Sept. 8, 1862, as a drummer in Company A, 129th Illinois Infantry. Drummer Harber was detailed on Sept. 13, 1864, as a nurse in the Third Division Hospital, and was mustered out with the regiment on June 8, 1865, near Washington, D.C. Compiled Service Records of Union Soldiers, NA.

 209

Head Quarters Co. "A" 129th Ills.
Goldsboro, N.C., March 28th 1865

My Dear Wife

The mail leaves at 4 P.M., & I must spare a few minutes from my papers to write to you. I recd. 4 letters from you yesterday, one from Hannah [Culver] and one from Cousin Electa Wallace, Mansfield, Ohio, with Photograph enclosed.[1] I dare not take the time to answer your letters in full; they were very interesting, indeed. The latest bears date Febr. 29th. I hope you are enjoying yourself. I should have enjoyed the Communion Season very much. I earnestly hope all the converts may prove faithful.

You were not more surprised at Nannie Barrett's joining our Church than I was when she told me her intention. She spoke to me just before I left the church the last evening; I advised her to study the discipline & then do as she thought best. I hope Charlie Murphy may not suffer from the dog's having bitten him, yet I have very little faith in a mad stone.[2]

I am sorry to say that I kept no diary, but I will try & write up one the first leisure time I have. I cannot imagine wherein your "married life has been a failure" except in the realization of that enjoyment you anticipated.[3] The pleasures of a home & its comforts we have known but a few weeks during our married life. It is hardly fair to conclude that all is a failure. I trust God will spare us for the enjoyment of many years of peace and prosperity when we may forget past sorrows in present enjoyments. Your married life has been experienced by very few in this country, so much of sorrow and so little of comfort.

I am glad to hear that the church has secured a new cabinet organ. I agreed to give $10 if necessary.

The boys are all well as usual. We are drawing new clothing, & the men will soon be comfortably clad. Quite a number have been barefoot, some for a couple of weeks, & must have suffered greatly.[4] The wounded are getting along finely. We have learned nothing of Henry Polk yet; I will write to his father to-day.

Mother's health is much improved. Hannah says she wrote to you. Green is flourishing & would like to see you & the baby.

I cannot tell what our prospects may be for getting home in June; it is doubtful. Tell J. W. Smith that I could not get to Savannah, Ga.; therefore I did not attend to his business. There are a great many things that I wish to write about & will in a few days if we are not hurried off. I hope Howard is entirely well. Kiss him for me. Remember me kindly to all our friends. Accept much love & may God bless & keep you.

Your affect. Husband

J. F. Culver

---

1  Electa Wallace of Mansfield, Ohio, was a relative of the Dunmires'.

2 Charlie Murphy was the 8-year-old son of William and Adaline Murphy, whose farm adjoined Mrs. Culver's father's property in Pontiac Township. Eighth Census, Livingston County, State of Illinois, NA.

3 Mary Culver in one of her letters had complained that her "married life has been a failure," which elicited these reassurances from her devoted husband.

4 The regimental historian wrote, "New clothes arrived this evening and were distributed, and it seems as though General Sherman did not intend to remain long, as the rumor of an advance was current." Grunert, *History of the 129th Illinois,* p. 224.

General Sherman on April 1 reported that the "suffering of the troops for want of shoes" could not be blamed on a want of foresight on the part of his chief quartermaster, but could be attributed to "mud banks, storms at sea, difficulties of navigation, &c." *O. R.,* Ser. I, Vol.XLVII, pt. III, p. 29.

 210

Head Qurs. Co. "A" 129th Ills. Vols.
Goldsboro, N.C., March 29th 1865

My Dear Wife

By to-day-s mail I recd. letters from Bro. Sammy [Murphy], Chattanooga, Tenn. of Mch. 2, & from Springfield, Ills. of the 2nd also, but none from you. Yesterday I recd. yours of the 29th Feb., being the latest. We have news from Pontiac of the 8th & 10th inst. I hope, however, you are not ill. Your letters may have been delayed.

It is quite cloudy & threatens rain. Yetter went on a visit this morning to the 17th Corps & has not yet returned. John Lee just came into my tent; he is quite well. His last letter is dated the 1st March & came by Major Hoskins.

I read a number of your letters over just before dinner. I find some of them as old as October & one from Maggie [Utley] of Oct. 14/64.[1] I thought of all the changes that have taken place since they were written; and, though the ways of Providence are past finding out, yet God has been very good to us. I think of Dear Mother very often.[2] I felt very happy last night after I lay down, & I thought she was near me though I could not see her.

We have not yet heard when the Army is expected to be put in motion. Genl. Sherman has gone to Washington & will doubtless return with his plans for the coming Campaign completed.[3] Unless the Rebel Army should retreat from our front, we anticipate a campaign similar to last summer, only doubly severe. I think it probable they will contest every inch of the ground stubbornly.

I recd. a letter from Saul to-day of Jan. 31st. He says if the war does not terminate with this Campaign, he will be in the Army. A few weeks may make a vast change in the aspect of affairs in this Country.

Jim Morrow was up at my tent last evening, he is in good health. Harry McDowell was here until a late hour last night, he is very well.

I heard yesterday of Thad. Keyser's marriage. Rumor says Abbie Remick has returned, & she & Milt [Lyon] are to be married very shortly.[4] Is it true? Has Ed. Cook returned yet?

Remember me to all our friends. Kiss Howard for me. Love to Maggie & children. Hoping Our Father will bless you, I remain, with love,

Your affect. Husband

J. F. Culver

---

1   The October letters were written before J.F.C. received the orders detaching him from the regiment and sending him to Chicago as a witness in the Beatty trial.

2   Mrs. Nancy Murphy, J.F.C.'s mother-in-law, had died under the wheels of a railroad train on November 10, 1864. Mary Culver, from that day forward, was unable to mention her mother's name. Culver, "Robert Murphy and Some of His Descendants," p. 40.

3   General Sherman on March 26, leaving General Schofield in command of the armies, boarded a train at Goldsboro for the trip to New Bern. There he embarked on the steamer *Russia* and landed at Old Point Comfort, Virginia, from where, on the afternoon of the 27th, he telegraphed General Grant and Secretary of War Stanton. Next day found General Sherman at Grant's City Point headquarters. There they discussed with President Lincoln plans for defeating the armies of Generals Lee and Johnston and ending the war. When he returned to New Bern by boat on the 30th, Sherman was accompanied by his brother John, United States senator from Ohio. *O. R.*, Ser. I, Vol. XLVII, pt. III, pp. 32-3, 42-3, 59-60.

4   Abbie J. Remick on October 25, 1865, married D. Milton Lyon, son of William M. Lyon.

## 211

Head Qurs. Co. "A", 129th Ills. Vol. Inftry.
Goldsboro, N.C., Mch. 30th 1865

My Dear Wife

I was the happy recipient of three letters from you to-day, of date of
6th, 7th & 9th inst., all of which confirm what your former letters say
that your health is good. I am very thankful for the good news. I hope
Howard will become more manageable, possibly his teeth trouble him as
you intimate.

I did think it possible Bro. John [Murphy] had some serious intentions
of addressing Jennie Gutherie, but his letter sets that matter at rest.[1] I
shall expect you to keep the correspondence of Mrs. Maurice if you find
it profitable. I have now more on hand than I can do justice to. I am
happy to hear that Mrs. Collins has so far recovered that she can go out.
I hope you will not rely too much on my getting home in June, as I think
it doubtful.

I am sorry that you were compelled to testify in that horse suit. I
would much rather pay for her myself. As it is probable Bro. Utley lost
the suit, do you try & find out quietly what he values the mare at, and I
will pay for her as soon as I can.[2] I am surprised at Mathis' conduct and
will write to W. B. Lyon about it. Do not settle it again. I have an acct.
at Lyon's of things I brought for the boys & forgot to set down the
amount.[3] If you have an opportunity, I wish you would please get it for
me, & I will send the amt. when we are paid. We expect pay in a few
days.

Send for the bolt of muslin if you have sufficient funds to spare. I
wrote in one of my letters a request for you to keep an account of the
time you stay at Utleys with the time I spent there. Possibly that letter
may not have reached you.[4]

The band of the 2d Brigade has been playing for an hour some very
sweet airs. They were playing "Home Sweet Home" when I sat down
to write; they have just ceased. We have a great deal of good music as
there are six bands within a few hundred yards of us. We are quite well
fortified here, but I have not heard of any enemy in our immediate front
for several days.[5] There was a rumor in camp to-day that Grant has

taken Richmond at a loss of 25,000 men, but it lacks confirmation.[6] The Rail Road is opened up with Wilmington, & trains arrive and depart regularly to & from both Wilmington & Morehead City.[7]

We recd letters to-day from Pontiac as late as the 20th March which is only 10 days. The men begin to count the days now for the 8th Sept. to come round.[8] They talk a great deal about home & the prospects there.

Christ. [Yetter] went on duty (picket) in my place this morning to give me an opportunity to complete the muster rolls. It rained so much this forenoon, however, that I did not get through. Nate [Hill] is out visiting & has not come in yet.

You asked me in one of your letters what I used to cure the Inflamatory Rheumatism. I used nothing but cold water in the shape of baths three or four times a day at first — decreasing in number gradually. It is a never failing cure. I had the water poured from a water pot in a stream of 1/2 inch in size upon the affected parts, gradually increasing the height to 10 or 15 feet. It will certainly scatter the swelling & drive away the pain. I hope Bro. Harrington will try it & keep it up all summer.[9] Harry McDowell spent an hour here early in the evening. He is very anxious for the expiration of his term of service so that he may enjoy the pleasures of home with a wife; he is devoted as ever. Jim Morrow & I had quite a chat last night; he had a great many questions to ask about his lady friends in Pontiac. Nate is just coming home, he has spent the evening with Charlie Peck.[10] Charlie is acting Commissary of the Regt. John Wilson has not yet returned.[11] Weiser (the bugler) has just heard of the death of his wife.[12] She has been sick for several months; but, as he had no opportunity to hear from her, he did not learn that she was sick until the mail reached him here. She leaves 3 small children.

Saml. McGooden is not with the Army. He went home from Atlanta to have an operation performed on his eyes, & they have not heard from him since. I saw [William] McCartney yesterday, he is well & has stood the march very well.

There is a band about a quarter of a mile off, & the music comes this way carried by the breeze. It sounds so very sweet that it reminds me of those times at home when we could hear the band in the court yard. "When shall we meet again?" I like the song very much but hardly think it conducive to happiness to dwell on it too often. God, who has thus far shown us only love and mercy, will perform all his promises in His own good time. I stood out in front of my tent awhile to-night watching the stars & listening to the music & found myself at home directly. So for fear of the blues, I hastened into my tent & commenced writing.

There is quite a circle of the boys around the fire talking of their marches through Georgia & South Carolina. I can only be a listener &

have but a faint idea of all their exploits as they take occasion to tell me many times each day.

I had a long letter from Saul yesterday.[13] He says if this campaign does not end the war, he is coming into the service and California will put forth her strength.

The "Sentinel" has not reached the Company since I left. I spoke to Decker about it when I was home, & he promised to see to it.[14] If you have an opportunity, please remind him of it. Send me the No. containing my Charleston letter. I have not had time to write to him or the paper since my arrival here. It is 20 minutes of ten, & I must close if I would write any other letters to-night. I hope Our Father will still preserve you in good health & make you happy. Remember me kindly to all. Kiss Howard for me. Tell our Friends to write. Accept much love, Good Night.

Your affect. Husband

J. F. Culver

P.S. I have had such a call for stamps that I must ask for a few.

J.F.C.

---

1   On February 28 John Murphy, who was stationed in Nashville, had written his sister, "Of course I'll take your advice kindly, and not only that but I prize it very highly. But I have no notion of making overtures for the hand of Jennie Gutherie, and I think she does not understand it otherwise. I do not think I have been the cause even indirectly of a rupture between her and Kelly. Mollie, don't you know that I can never marry a woman that can't sing?" John Murphy to Mary Culver, February 28, 1865, Culver Collection.

2   A suit had been brought against Leander Utley by certain parties for a mare in which J.F.C. had an interest.

3   W. B. Lyon owned and operated Wm. H. Lyon & Son, a prosperous Pontiac dry goods store. *History of Livingston County, Illinois*, p. 640.

4   The letter referred to is missing from the Culver Collection. Apparently, Mary Culver and Howard were staying with the Utleys, as had J.F.C. during his Pontiac leave.

5   Upon going into camp, soldiers of the 129th Illinois, like those of other XX Corps units, began erecting cabins. On the 28th orders were issued by General Williams for his division commanders to "pay particular attention to the establishment of their picket-lines, having them so placed and with such connections right and left as will enable them to entirely prevent any person from passing them." *O. R.*, Ser. I, Vol. XLVII, pt. III, p. 47; Grunert, *History of the 129th Illinois*, pp. 224-25.

6   There was no truth to this rumor. But on March 29 General Grant sent two corps and Maj. Gen. Philip H. Sheridan's cavalry sweeping westward across Hatcher Run in an effort to reach the Southside Railroad and force General Lee's Army of Northern Virginia to evacuate Petersburg.

7   J.F.C. was mistaken about the resumption of through rail traffic between Goldsboro and Wilmington. It was April 4 before the bridge across the Northeast Branch of the Cape

Fear was rebuilt, and the 5th before through trains again made the run between these two cities. *O. R.,* Ser. I, Vol. XLVII, pt. III, pp. 65, 91, 96.

8   As a three-year-regiment, soldiers of the 129th, unless they chose to reenlist as veteran volunteers, would be mustered out on September 8, 1865.

9   Robert Harrington, running on the Union ticket, had been elected county clerk of Livingston County in the autumn of 1861, and was reelected four years later. After leaving office in 1869, he moved to Mississippi and from there to Beatrice, Nebraska. *History of Livingston County, Illinois,* p. 266.

10   It has been impossible to further identify Charles Peck, unless he was Darius R. Peck, a 32-year-old engineer, who had been mustered into service on September 8, 1862, as a private in Company A, 129th Illinois. Compiled Service Records of Union Soldiers, NA.

11   John T. Wilson, a 24-year-old farmer, was mustered into service on Sept. 8, 1862, as a private in Company H, 129th Illinois Infantry. He was detailed as quartermaster clerk on Oct. 1, 1862, and on Nov. 1, 1863, he was promoted to commissary sergeant. Wounded on Aug. 19, 1864, before Atlanta, Sergeant Wilson was hospitalized and did not rejoin the regiment, being discharged at Camp Butler, Ill., Jan. 24, 1864. *Ibid.*

12   Joseph C. Weiser, a 31-year-old jeweller, was mustered into service on Sept. 8, 1862, as a private in Company H, 129th Illinois Infantry, and was mustered out near Washington, D.C., on June 8, 1865. *Ibid.*

13   S. S. Saul moved to Pontiac from Pennsylvania in 1854 and taught school for several years. In 1857 he was elected county clerk, a position he held until 1861. Saul had been instrumental in prevailing on J.F.C. to settle in Livingston County. They had been partners before J.F.C. was mustered into service in September 1862. *History of Livingston County, Illnois,* p. 324.

14   Henry S. Decker and James Stout were owners of the *Sentinel,* having acquired it from M. E. Collins in 1863. Decker, the editor, had moved to Livingston County from Chicago, while Stout was an "abolitionist of the most ultra character, at a time when it was anything but popular to promulgate the doctrine." *Ibid.,* p. 318.

꤮ 212 ꤮

Head Qurs. Co. "A", 129th Ills. Vol. Inftry.
Goldsboro, N.C., April 1st 1865

My Dear Wife

The Leader of the Brig. Band is discharged & starts home to-day & thinking a letter would reach you more directly through him, I hasten to write. I wrote to Lt. [John] McKnight to send you $12 that he owes me & which I had directed him to pay to [Christ] Yetter at Atlanta. I will inclose $10 — if you have no use for it, you can pay it on my acct. with Wm. B. Lyon & take his receipt for it.

I wrote to you a few days ago to get a bill of my purchases & send it to me. I think I wrote the same to Lyon when I wrote about Mother's transactions. If we receive pay, I will ford. sufficient to pay Lyon & Smith both. I recd. a letter yesterday from Fanny Miller of the 19th inst.

We are all in good health, & the weather is beautiful. I have not had time to write up that diary for you yet. We have no late news. All the company are well. I expect letters from you by to-day's mail. Letters come through from home, some in 10 to 12 days.

Rumor says we will leave here on the 12th, but no one knows as Genl. Sherman has not returned yet.[1] No enemy have been seen on our front for a couple of days. Alva Garner of the 20th Ills. has just come & brings a New York Herald of the 27 Mch.[2] The news are very good.

I have been talking until my time for writing has almost expired. Sailor[3] leaves at noon from Brig. Hd. Qurs., & it is after 11. I must send this over, or it will be too late. Remember me to all our friends.

With much love, I remain, ever

Your affect. Husband

J. F. Culver

---

1 J.F.C. is mistaken on one point. General Sherman returned to his Goldsboro headquarters from City Point on the night of March 30. On April 1 Sherman alerted several of his subordinates to be ready to resume the offensive on the 10th. *O. R.*, Ser. I, Vol. XLVII, pt. III, pp. 80-1.

2 Alva Garner of Pontiac was mustered into service at Joliet, Ill., as a private in Company D, 20th Illinois, on June 13, 1861. Private Garner was wounded in the arm at Shiloh on April 6, 1862, and on returning to duty was detailed as a nurse in the hospital at La Grange, Tenn. He reenlisted as a veteran volunteer at Big Black Bridge, Miss., on Jan. 5, 1864, and was promoted to sergeant on Oct. 3, 1864. Compiled Service Records of Union Soldiers, NA.

3 W. F. Sailor was drum major of the brigade band.

 213

Goldsboro, N C.
April 2nd 1865

My Dear Wife

I recd. by to-day's mail yours of the 16th inst. & was very happy to learn that you are well. Letters were recd. two days ago from Pontiac of as late date as the 21st, one from Mrs. Fellows, but she made no mention of you & I presume had not seen you.[1] The condition of the roads and your few opportunities are sufficient reasons for your letters not reaching me sooner and perhaps are the reasons why mine are so long on the way.

The day has been very pleasant, & the night is beautiful. I preached in the 79th Ohio last night & to-night in our own. We had a good meeting. We will hold meetings every evening throughout this week. Four arose for prayers to-night. Pray for us. As I never recd. any account of the meetings after I left, there must be some letters that did not reach me.

I will try and write to Maggie [Utley] before we leave here but dare not promise positively. Tell her I will do the best I can. I thought I should write several letters to-day, but I was very tired & thought it best to rest in order to be ready for the morrow.

I was glad to hear that Howard is growing so rapidly as it is a sure indication of good health, yet I know he must be a great burden to you. I wish I could assist you to take care of him this summer, but, if God spares me, I will try & assist you more than when I was last at home. I feel very sorry when I think how little I done to make you happy while I was at home. You have not told me whether you expected to be *able* to *visit* Penna. next fall or not.

Alva Garner and Josephus Ullery took supper with us this evening. Both are well. I was at the hospital to see Mark Stephens yesterday; he is getting along very well & expects to go home on furlough shortly.

The Chaplain preached the funeral sermon of those who have fallen since the Regt. left Atlanta.[2] All the detachments of Sherman's Army from Chattanooga and along the coast are expected here in a few days. The Army will be made as effective as possible, and be prepared for the strongest opposition the Rebs. can muster.[3] We have had all kinds of rumors to-day, the wildest being that Peace was declared & the Army ordered north.[4] Our latest news is the New York Herald of the 27th containing a short account of Grant's last battle.[5] The prospects look flattering but not enough to dispel our anticipations of a severe campaign.

I have not yet written to the Sabbath School. I may try to to-night if I am not too late in closing this. Alf Huetson was here to-day. He inquired very particularly about you & wished to be kindly remembered. I will inclose a little shell that was picked up in "Fort Fisher" by an Officer of the 23rd Corps.

Among the numerous grape vines this evening, was one that our Corps was going to Washington to relieve Hancock's Veteran Corps.[6] Sherman has returned, & we are ordered to be ready to move by the 10th inst. which will be one week from to-morrow.[7]

Our camp is very nicely fixed up with pine trees lining both sides of all the streets. The boys have built comfortable houses and was there any prospect of remaining here long enough to justify it, we could make this camp very beautiful.[8] We have good water in abundance which is a great blessing.

Some of the members of our Regt. captured on this last raid have been exchanged and are on furlough home. We hope to hear from Henry Polk soon.[9] I have not yet written to his parents hoping to see or hear from him each day.

I hear trains whistling for the last hour. The rail-road is complete from Wilmington to this place giving us two avenues of communication with the coast.[10]

I see by the New York papers of the 27th inst. that both Wilmington and Charleston are soon to be made "Ports of Entry" which is certain evidence of the determination of the government to garrison and hold them. They will be garrisoned, doubtless, with colored troops while all the others will be sent to the front.[11] There is one Division of Colored Troops here, but I have not learned where they are stationed.[12] The Regt. of which Jos. Z. Culver is adgt. is in the Division;[13] I would like to see him.

I sent ten dollars in a letter I sent by Wm. F. Sailor to be mailed at Chicago, Ills. Chris [Yetter] asked me just now whether you had forgiven him for the letter he wrote to you over a year ago; he says you have never written to him since. I had forgotten all about it but have an indistinct recollection of the affair.

We have just recd. orders to be ready to go on a forage expedition at 6-1/2 A.M. to-morrow. The whole Regt. is ordered out, &, as we will probably have a hard day's march, I cannot write any more letters and must close this one soon. I hope there will be some letters awaiting me on my return. How cheering it will be.

I am glad you are contented, & I hope God will make you happy. I spent your birthday [March 17] in Charleston. Had I thought of it, I would certainly have written, but I have been very thoughtless lately. I know not why.

Remember me kindly to all our friends. Give my love to Maggie & family. What is Bro. John's address? How I wonder how you are enjoying yourself to-night & where you are. I can imagine both Howard & you in bed sound asleep. May Our Father kindly watch over you & preserve you. Kiss Howard for me. I will write soon after my return. I do not know how long we will be absent but probably not over one day. Accept a kiss. With much love, I remain,

Your affect. Husband

"Frank"

---

1  Mrs. Fellows was the wife of J. Allen Fellows, the regimental hospital steward.

2  Abel H. Scott had succeeded Thomas Cotton as chaplain of the 129th Illinois. Scott, a 37-year-old minister, had been mustered into service on Sept. 8, 1862, as a sergeant in Company F, 129th Illinois Infantry. He was promoted to sergeant major on March 7, 1863, and was commissioned 2d lieutenant of Company F on June 11, 1863. Lieutenant Scott was wounded at Resaca on May 15, 1864, and did not rejoin the regiment until July 13. He resigned his commission in December to accept appointment as regimental chaplain. Compiled Service Records of Union Soldiers, NA.

3  General Sherman in the last week of March had reorganized his army into the Army of the Tennessee commanded by General Howard and the Army of Georgia led by General Slocum. The XX Corps, to which the 129th Illinois belonged, was a part of the Army of Georgia. Also reporting to Sherman was General Schofield's Army of the Ohio.

When Sherman's "army group" resumed its advance, the railroads leading from Kinston and Wilmington to Goldsboro would be abandoned. O. R., Ser. I, Vol. XLVII, pt. III, pp. 75, 80-1.

4  There was no truth to the peace rumor.

5  Units of General Lee's Army of Northern Virginia on March 25 had assailed Union positions east of Petersburg held by the IX Corps, Army of the Potomac. Fort Stedman was stormed by the Rebels, but they were unable to exploit this success. Counterattacking Federals soon recovered Fort Stedman, and the Confederates, having suffered heavy losses, were driven back into their Petersburg defenses. Humphreys, The Virginia Campaign of '65, pp. 316-20.

6  Maj. Gen. Winfield S. Hancock, plagued by his Gettysburg wound, in the autumn of 1864 had been called to Washington to recruit a "Veteran Reserve Corps." His efforts met with slight success, and on February 27, 1865, he was placed in command of the Department of West Virginia. Consequently, there was no truth to this rumor. Warner, Generals in Blue, p. 204.

7  The report that Sherman's "army group" was to be ready to resume the advance on April 10 was correct. O. R., Ser. I, Vol. XLVII, pt. III, p. 65.

8  A soldier of the regiment had written on March 23, "We have been fixing up some log shanties to stay in, four of us in a shantie." The regimental historian recorded on the 28th a good many of the cabins, which were started on the 25th, "were done while others are approaching completion." Through the South with a Union Soldier, p. 167; Grunert, History of the 129th Illinois, pp. 224-25.

9  Henry Polk had been paroled at Aikens Landing, Va., on March 26, 1865, and ordered to Benton Barracks, Mo. Compiled Service Records of Union Soldiers, NA.

10  It was April 5 before the first through train reached Goldsboro from Wilmington.

11  J.F.C. was only partially correct in his assumption that Charleston and Wilmington would be garrisoned by black units. The 1st Separate Brigade charged with occupation of Charleston on April 30, 1865, included four black commands among its 16 units. No black commands were currently attached to Brig. Gen. Joseph R. Hawley's District of Wilmington, *O. R.*, Ser. I, Vol. XLVII, pt. III, p. 362.

12  One of the three divisions constituting the X Corps, Army of the Ohio, consisted of U.S. Colored Troops. The X Corps was camped in and around Faison's Depot, 20 miles south of Goldsboro, on the Wilmington & Weldon Railroad. *Ibid.*, p. 50.

13  Joseph Z. Culver was mustered into service on Feb. 29, 1864, at Baltimore, Md., as 2d lieutenant of Company K, 39th U.S. Colored Troops. He was promoted to 1st lieutenant on Sept. 13, 1864, and assigned to duty as regimental adjutant. Adjutant Culver was wounded on Feb. 12, 1865, but soon rejoined his command. Compiled Service Records of Union Soldiers, NA.

 214

Head Qurs. Co. "A" 129th Ills. Vols.
Goldsboro, N.C.
April 4th 1865

My Dear Wife

We have had no mail for two days. The last news I have from you is of the 16th ult. I hope to be more successful, however, by to-morrow's mail.

Our Forage Expedition of which I spoke in my last letter was of short duration. We were not over two miles from camp & returned at noon.[1] The weather continues to be very pleasant, and our preparations have been going on rapidly. It is a current rumor that we will start on Monday next [10th], & we are using every effort to be ready. We had Brigade Inspection to-day & will have Division & corps reviews during the week.

All the sick and wounded that could bear removal have been sent to Newbern & the coast. The detachments of this army are coming up from Nashville, Tenn., Charleston, & Blairs Landing, S.C. & will soon all be here.[2] The troops are nearly all supplied with clothing, and a very few days will suffice to complete their equipment. The news by the New

York papers of the 29th ult. are good, and I hope by God's help we will soon see the end of the war.

We are having a glorious meeting in the Brigade. The Regts. have joined in a Union meeting, & we have a very pleasant place for worship. There were 13 forward to-night. This was our first effort united. I preached to-night from 95th Psalm, part of 7th & 8th verses. God was pleased to bless me, and we hope for glorious results during our short stay here. Pray for us.

The health of the Company and Regt. is good. Bronson's discharge has gone forward, & I think he will be able to start for home in a few days.[3] He is in very poor health, & I fear will not survive long. We have heard nothing of Henry Polk yet; we expect daily to hear of his return home. Several of the boys that were captured about the same time he was have reached their homes & have been heard from.

Capt. Horton arrived here to-day from Blairs Landing. Genl. Ben Harrison will be up in a few days & will doubtless command the Brigade in the coming campaign.[4] Jim Chritten, Winnie Kelley, Mat. DeLong & Wm. Sutcliff are on their way & will be here this week.[5]

It is quite late to-night, but I could not lie down without talking awhile with you. There is a string band serenading Lt. Col. Merrill of the 70th Ind. & the music sounds very sweet. The moon shines beautifully every night. Everything seems so calm and beautiful to-night that it seems almost impossible that such a thing as war can exist. How forcibly it reminds me of a night long ago when we sat at Mother's door one night singing "With Maggie by our side." Do you remember it? I wonder if Maggie [Utley] does. It was before you went to Cleveland to school. Those & many others that followed were happy days, yet I trust there are many more equally happy in store for us. God is kind and merciful, let us trust him still.

Nate [Hill] has gone to bed & is asleep. Christ [Yetter] is writing yet. I am sure he writes 4 letters to my one. I was not aware before that he had so large a correspondence. Mrs. Hill wrote to him a few days ago that she knew I was responsible for Jennie Gutherie's refusing Kelley; I hope she is mistaken. I only spoke once to her about it & that was after her father & mother assured me that they would not be married. I am very sorry that I even spoke of it.

I must close for to-night. May God bless you. Kiss Howard for me. Remember me kindly to all our friends. As communication will be kept open with the rear, I hope to hear from you often. Good night.

Your affect. Husband,

J. F. Culver

The 129th moved out early, marching in a westerly direction. After proceeding about two miles, they found a good supply of corn and fodder. While the soldiers were loading their wagons, one of the pickets was surprised and shot to death. Grunert, *History of the 129th Illinois,* pp. 225-26.

2 The returning soldiers, along with many recruits, were disembarking at Wilmington, where they were organized into casual companies and issued rations by General Hawley. They then marched to Goldsboro. *O. R.,* Ser. I, Vol. XLVII, pt. III, pp. 87-8, 91.

3 William H. Bronson, a 25-year-old jeweller, was mustered into service on Sept. 8, 1862, as a private in Company A, 129th Illinois Infantry. Private Bronson was hospitalized much of the time from Dec. 1863 until receiving his medical discharge on April 10, 1865. Compiled Service Records of Union Soldiers, NA.

4 Benjamin Harrison had been brevetted brigadier general to rank from Jan. 23, 1865.

5 Winfield S. Kelly, a 20-year-old farmer, was mustered into service on Sept. 8, 1862, as a private in Company A, 129th Illinois Infantry. The autumn of 1864 found Kelly hospitalized in Nashville, Tenn. Rejoining the regiment in the spring of 1865, Private Kelly was mustered out near Washington, D.C. Martin DeLong, a 21-year-old farmer, was mustered into service on Sept. 8, 1862, as a private in Company A, 129th Illinois Infantry. Wounded at Resaca on May 15, 1864, Private DeLong was hospitalized at Jeffersonville, Ind., and on rejoining the unit in the spring of 1865 was hospitalized in the division hospital. He was mustered out with the regiment on June 8, 1865, near Washington, D.C. *Ibid.*

 215

Head Quarters Co. "A" 129th Ills.
Goldsboro, N.C.
April 5th 1865

My Dear Wife

Yours of the 23rd ult. reached me to-day. I am very happy to learn of your good health and that the condition of the roads gives you an opportunity to get around. I shall look for letters more regularly now. I know it is much more pleasant for you to get out among your friends, & I hope you will be happy.

I was not aware that Dr. Johnson was at all seriously ill.[1] I hope most earnestly that he will heed the voice of God and yield submissive to His will. He might do much good in Pontiac. He shall have my prayers for God's blessing. I am happy to hear that Bro. Crist received so handsome a donation. It must be very gratifying to himself & family to be so substantially remembered. I thought I had answered Sister Kate's letter. I must try and write to her before we leave here.

You need feel no alarm about the insurance on our property. You recollect you have both policy & receipt. The last policy is a new one which accounts for the notice. Had the old one been only renewed, the notice would not have been sent.

I would like to receive a box from home as you desire, but I am in need of nothing, & it is not probable it would ever reach me.

We had a good meeting to-night, & God was pleased to bless several souls. The meetings in the 2nd & 3rd Brigades have not closed yet though it is nearly ten o'clock; I hear they are resulting gloriously. May God continue the good work.

Capt. Wm. Strawn of the 104th Ills. was here to see me to-night.[2] He lives near the line between Newton & LaSalle County. You doubtless remember him.

The news from the North to-day are very flattering.[3] We have Division Review to-morrow at 8-1/2 A.M. which indicates an early departure. It is generally thought, however, we will not leave until Monday, yet it may be before or after. Our Army was reorganized: the 15th and 17th Corps forming the Army of [the] Tennessee, the 10th and 23rd Corps the Army of [the] Ohio, & the 14th and 20th Corps the Army of Georgia. We belong to the latter & will be the left wing, &, as a matter of course, farthest from the coast.[4] It is very probable that we will have very few mail facilities, but I hope you will write every day, & I will do so every opportunity.

Bro. Jim Gaff was here to-day; he is quite well. Capt. Reed has been ailing for a few days but is around again. The health of the Regt. is good. Bronson's discharge papers have not been received yet, but I look for them every day. I think the idea of paying the Army before we leave has eked out. I see no signs of a Paymaster at present. We are almost fully equipped & lack only a few pairs of shoes. There is an immense quantity of "Grape Vine" afloat to-night, & there has been cheering all along the lines of the army for 4 hours past. Nothing reliable has been received, however, that I can learn. The Army is in jubilant spirits, & I should not be surprised to hear of marching orders any day.

Chris & Nate have been fast asleep for an hour. I wish I could look in upon you to-night. May God bless you & our babe & preserve you both in good health. May His richest blessings of health & happiness be yours and the enjoyment of many years in such home joys & comforts you have so patiently awaited and which you so richly deserve. Kiss

Howard for Papa & love to all friends. With love and affection, I remain,

Your Husband

Joseph F. Culver

1 Dr. Darius Johnson, having resigned as regimental surgeon, had returned to Pontiac to resume his practice. Compiled Service Records of Union Soldiers, NA.

2 William Strawn was mustered into service on Aug. 14, 1862, at Ottawa, Ill., as lieutenant of Comapny F, 104th Illinois Infantry. He was promoted to captain on July 26, 1863. *Ibid.*

3 The Union advance toward the Southside Railroad gave promise of success. Sheridan's cavalry and foot-soldiers of the V Corps had occupied Dinwiddie Courthouse and had secured a lodgment on the White Oak road. To cope with this increasingly grave threat to his supply line, General Lee was compelled to pull troops out of the Petersburg defenses and rush them to the point of danger. On April 1 at Five Fork, Sheridan's cavalry, bolstered by the V Corps, routed the Confederates led by Maj. Gen. George E. Pickett. Early next morning, Grant followed up this victory by launching an all-out assault on the Petersburg defenses, while Sheridan's columns blocked the Southside Railroad. Humphreys, *The Virginia Campaign of '65*, pp. 322-62.

4 Special Order No. 44 reorganizing the army was issued on April 1. The Army of the Tennessee would constitute the right and the Army of the Ohio the center. With General Slocum leading the Army of Georgia, Maj. Gen. Joseph A. Mower commanded the XX Corps. *O.R.*, Ser. I, Vol. XLVIII, pt. III, p. 75.

≈≈≈ 216 ≈≈≈

Head Quarters Co. "A" 129th Regt. Ills. Vols.
Goldsboro, N.C. April 7th 1865

My Dear Wife

We have had great rejoicing yesterday and to-day over the success of Grant's Army, the capture of Petersburg and Richmond with 23,000 prisoners, guns, &c.[1] There is also a rumor afloat that Genl. Lee has been captured by Sheridan,[2] yet every one is so wild with joy that we are afraid to believe it lest it be only the production of some fertile

*425*

imagination. We hope, however, that God is about to bring the war to a close. To His name be all the Glory.

I have never witnessed such manifestations of joy as we have witnessed within the past two days. The cannon were booming thunder until a very late hour last night. I quit writing to attend the meeting. When I commenced, it was raining, but the cloud passed & for 1-1/2 hours it was quite pleasant. We had a good meeting. There were eight at the altar and two converted. The attendance is very large, and, if the weather permits, we anticipate more glorious results during the few days we may remain here. We have made arrangements for Sacramental Service on Sabbath.

The trains are being loaded, and we expect to move on Monday. The successes of Grant's Army will doubtless change our programme materially. Orders were received this evening to move light for a rapid march, &, if we have to get to the rear of Lee's Army, it will be a severe chase.[3] This Army has had so much experience in marching that I fear my five months' idleness will be a decided disadvantage.

All the company are well. Asa Alden of Co. "G" was removed to the hospital quite ill.[4] I sent a letter yesterday by McDonald of the 53rd Illinois whose time is out, & he was going direct to Pontiac.[5]

I was disappointed in not receiving a letter from you to-day, but Bro. Gaff had a letter of the 26th March in which his wife said she had seen you at church that day and you were well. Allen Fellows has been a little under the weather for a few days but will be all right in a few days. The health of the Regt. is good.

There has been a continuous shouting all along the lines of the Army to-night, & several Batteries have fired salutes. We recd. New York papers of the 3d & Newbern dispatches of the 6th to-day. We have details of the battles before Richmond on the 31st, 1st, & 2nd. All that we have heard since is what is termed grape vine. We were reviewed yesterday by Maj. Genl. Mower, our new corps commander. He is a fine looking Officer & has the reputation of being a good fighter.[6]

It has ceased raining again, & we hope the few [remain]ing days we stay here may be bright and pleasant. I have not been able to banish from my mind for the last two days the probabilities of a speedy termination of the war and the prospect of soon getting home. God grant that it may be so, yet it is not safe to be too sanguine. It is almost too much to hope for so suddenly, & disappointment would be terrible.

The mails will either confirm or deny these rumors to-morrow. We find it impossible to get a paper for a day or two after it gets here, the demand is so great. Again the cannon are booming all around the lines, & the cheering commencing in Goldsboro goes round from camp to camp until the sound dies away in the distance. It has heretofore been a certain indication of battle when so many rumors became rife in camp. It was so before every severe battle of last summer's campaign.

We hear the bands striking up in the direction of Goldsboro, &, if any news is passing, ours will be out when they reach here. I wonder if the Army will become quiet at all to-night. It is near ten o'clock. I am afraid that whiskey may have a hand in, yet none has been issued that I know of. Green was very happy to-day over the news, but said he was trembling for fear they might not prove true. [We] have heard of no enemy in our immediate front for several days, & refugees coming into our lines report Raleigh evacuated and all the Rebs gone to Lee.[7]

Stoneman with our cavalry & one Division of the 4th Corps is reported at Boon, N.C. which is about the same distance from Danville that we are, but the country very mountainous.[8]

I will not close my letter until I learn if there is anything new. The bands of the 14th A.C. on our immediate left are out playing, & the boys are getting up to learn if possible what the excitement is. The cannon still keep firing.

God has been very kind to us this far, though there has been so much wickedness He has not cast us off. I hope to hear from you by to-morrow's mail. I think my letter from Kinston [dated March 24] informing you that I was near the Army must have reached you in time for your answer to reach me here, & I expected a letter every day when you knew I was with the Regiment. I wrote a letter to the "Sentinel" night before last, also one to Mother. I have been expecting news from Carlisle all week but have heard nothing yet.

How I would like to be with you to-night that we might rejoice to-gether over the glorious news. Kiss Howard for me. May Our Father continue his blessings toward us. Remember me kindly to all our friends. The Army is becoming quiet, & we have learned nothing yet. I will leave my letter open until morning & add any news we may receive. I can imagine yourself & Howard sleeping sweetly & with thoughts of home and joy I must say Good night.

Your affect. Husband

J. F. Culver

Apr. 8th

The cheering last night was over Sherman's official report of the fall of Richmond.[9]

J.F.C.

427

1   On the evening of the 6th, General Sherman had received a message from General Grant sent on the 3rd. It reported that the movements commenced on March 29 had "terminated in the fall of both Richmond and Petersburg this morning. The mass of Lee's army was whipped badly south of Petersburg, and to save the remnant he was forced to evacuate Richmond. We have about 12,000 prisoners, and stragglers are being picked up in large numbers. From all causes I do not estimate his loss at less than 25,000." The Confederates, he continued, were in full retreat, "and there is every indication that they will endeavor to secure Burkeville and Danville." Grant was pursuing with Sheridan's cavalry and five infantry corps. *O. R.*, Ser. I, Vol. XLVII, pt. III, pp. 89-90.

2   There was no substance to this rumor.

3   General Sherman on April 7 notified his army commanders that "the capture of Richmond and retreat of Lee's army to the west . . . necessitates a change in our plans. We will hold fast to Goldsborough and its [rail] lines and move rapidly on Raleigh." General Slocum's Army of Georgia was to be ready to move "on Monday straight on Smithfield and Raleigh by the most direct road." *Ibid.*, pp. 121-22.

4   Asa N. Alden, a 30-year-old carpenter, was mustered into service on Sept. 8, 1862, as a private in Company G, 129th Illinois Infantry. Hospitalized in the division hospital on April 6, 1865, Private Allen was mustered out one month later at David's Island, New York Harbor. Compiled Service Records of Union Soldiers, NA.

5   Dennis McDonald, a 16-year-old Pontiac laborer, was mustered into service on Feb. 24, 1862, as a private in Company G, 53d Illinois Infantry. Private McDonald was captured near Canton, Miss., Feb. 24, 1864. He was confined in Southern prison pens until exchanged at Charleston, S.C., on Dec. 11, 1864. Rejoining his unit, Private McDonald was transferred to Company B and was mustered out near Washington, D.C., May 27, 1865. *Ibid.*

6   General Mower, formerly a division commander in the Army of the Tennessee, had been named to lead the XX Corps on April 2. He had been hand-picked by General Sherman for this position. *O. R.*, Ser. I, Vol. XLVII, pt. III, p. 111.

7   As it had been for the past two weeks, General Johnston's army was camped in and around Smithfield. Consequently, the stories told by refugees that Raleigh had been evacuated and that Johnston's columns were en route to join General Lee were false.

8   Maj. Gen. George Stoneman with 4,000 cavalry had ridden out of Jonesboro in East Tennessee on March 20 to raid across the Appalachians into western North Carolina. By the 29th Stoneman's horse-soldiers had crossed into North Carolina and had occupied Boone. The next day they advanced to Wilkesboro. Long, *Civil War Day by Day*, pp. 655, 658-59.

9   On the 8th General Sherman notified his subordinates that he had "Official intelligence from General Grant of the defeat of Lee's army and occupation of Petersburg and Richmond." Grant's columns were pursuing fragments of Lee's army, "represented at 20,000, toward Danville." *O. R.*, Ser. I, Vol. XLVII, pt. III, p. 132.

## 217

Head Quarters Co. "A" 129th Ills. Vols.
Goldsboro, N.C.
April 9th 1865

My Dear Wife

We have just recd. notice that the last mail leaves at 3 o'clock, and it is now 1/2 past one. The whole Army will move on Raleigh in the morning;[1] it is about 50 miles. Whether we will have much hard fighting or not, God only knows. There cannot be many more battles.

I was very sadly disappointed in not getting any letters to-day; & now the last mail has come in, I shall not probably hear from you for several weeks. Yet I trust you are well. I thought my letter from Kinston [of March 24] would surely reach you in time for your answer to reach me before we left here. I believe I should have been fully satisfied but must content myself without. The last I recd. was of date the 23rd March & the one before the last the 16th, but I heard from you through Bro. Gaff of the 28th March.

We have been very busy to-day, & I was thinking I would write you a long letter to-night, but that prospect was blighted by the notice recd. a few minutes ago that no more mails would leave after 3 o'clock. We just recd. a letter from Henry Polk; he was at Annapolis, Md., on the 28th March & was to leave for St. Louis next day. His safety causes great rejoicing; he will doubtless get home.

Jim Chritten, Wm. Sutcliff, Winnie Kelley, & Sherman McQuown came up to-day. Mat DeLong will be here to-morrow.

We had a most excellent meeting this morning, & the Sacrament of the Lord's Supper was administered. It was a blessed time. God grant that we may soon enjoy such a privilege at home with our loved ones. Wm. Bronson's discharge papers came this morning, & he starts for home to-morrow. I do not think we will get to see him again. WE HAVE (I commenced a sentence but was interrupted & forgot what it was). Alf Huetson has just come in & brings glorious news. Genl. Grant has telegraphed us to move on Johnson[sic] & end this matter as soon as possible.[2] Henry Snyder was sent to the rear yesterday sick;[3] he is not very bad but was unable to march. All the troops are in good spirits &

are tired of camp. We are well prepared for the campaign. The weather is beautiful.

I took my chair to the fire after breakfast this morning & reread & burned all your letters, 13 in all. It seemed sacriligious, but I could not run any risk of their falling into strangers' hands. I wished very much to preserve them. I kept only the last one & hoped to place another in my pocket this afternoon & burn it, but I will carry this one to read occasionally.

We have just learned that John Harper has been exchanged so he will probably be at home soon.[4] I find it almost impossible to write as there [are] so many questions to answer & things to attend to. Everyone is busy packing up. I will not get time or opportunity to write to the Sunday School or Church; I intended to do so this afternoon. You must remember me to them & tell them that I have been so very busy, but I have prayed for them every day since I left. I think Bro. Crist might have answered my letter but presume he had not time.

Give my kind regards to all my friends. I intended to write to Abbie & Lida Remick but have the same excuse to all. Want of time. My "Sentinel" has not come yet through. I saw one to-day of the 16th containing my Charleston letter full of mistakes. Before this reaches you, we will be beyond Raleigh, or at least fight[ing] for it.

We are to draw some clothing in a few minutes, & I must cut my letter short. There are so many things I wished to write about, but in the hurry I shall not be able. If it be Our Father's will, I will make up for it when the campaign is ended. Be of good cheer, &, during the long weeks in which you may not hear from me, trust more in God. He will care for us. I feel that I can trust him wholly. If I should fall, we will certainly meet in a better and happier world, & you must teach Howard to remember me. Kiss him Good bye for me.

I feel very happy to-day knowing that God is ours and that his love is exercised toward us. I feel very thankful to our friends in Pontiac who are trying to make you happy by their kind attentions. Remember me particularly to Mrs. Johnson, Emily, Mrs. McGregor & family, Mrs. Smith, Lou, & all others who by their kindness comfort you in my absence. And now, dearest, I must say Good bye for a short time. Kiss Howard occasionally for me. I commit both you & him to the kind care of Our Father in Heaven. Write often. Should communication be kept open, I might possibly hear from you, & at all events, I will get them when the campaign closes. By orders just recd. our letters must be directed as follows.

May the richest of Heavens blessings rest upon you. With a kiss and much love, I remain through life,

Your affect. Husband

J. F. Culver

Co. "A" 129th Ills.

1st Brig., 3d Div., 20th A.C.

Army of Georgia

Fortress Monroe

---

1   General Mower on the 8th had notified his division commanders that at daylight on the 10th they would start for Smithfield, taking the river road. The First Division would have the lead. Each division would be accompanied by its ambulance and tool wagons, and ten ammunition wagons. The remainder of the train, with the exception of four artillery ammunition wagons, would follow the XIV Corps trains. *O. R.,* Ser. I, Vol. XLVII, pt. III, pp. 132, 145.

2   The dispatch referred to is probably General Grant's Burkeville telegram of April 6 which read, "We have Lee's army pressed hard, his men scattering and going to their homes by the thousands. He is endeavoring to reach Danville, where Davis and his cabinet have gone. I shall press the pursuit to the end. Rush Johnston at the same time and let us finish up this job all at once." *Ibid.,* p. 109.

3   For data on Henry Snyder see J.F.C.'s letter of March 24, 1865.

4   John A. Harper, a 21-year-old carpenter, was mustered into service on Sept. 8, 1862, as a corporal in Company G, 129th Illinois Infantry. Corporal Harper served with the regiment throughout the war. Compiled Service Records of Union Soldiers, NA.

218

Head Qurs. Co. "A" 129th Ills.
Raleigh, N. C. April 14th/65

My Dear Wife

I have just learned that there is a possibility of sending out letters, & I haste to write hoping it may reach you. We arrived at this place yesterday evening & have not yet started out & will not probably until to-morrow as it is already late in the afternoon. We left Goldsboro at sunrise on Monday morning [the 10th] moving in the direction of Smithfield, our corps being on the extreme left. We had several light skirmishes which retarded our progress; &, the country being very swampy, we moved only about 8 or 9 miles & went into camp. It rained considerable during the afternoon & evening.[1]

We broke camp Tuesday morning [the 11th] about day-light & moved very rapidly. There was only one light skirmish during this day. The weather was very warm & many fell by the way. Two of our Brigade died & several took sick. We reached Smithfield about 4 P.M., having marched about 20 miles. When we halted for dinner, I had but six men of my Company with me, all the rest had fallen out. At Smithfield we recd. the news (official) of the surrender of Lee's Army.[2]

At an early hour on Wednesday [the 12th], we started for Raleigh,[3] our Brig. acting as train guard until near noon. There was skirmishing in our front but done by Kilpatrick's Cavalry. In the evening the cavalry captured over 60 wagons loaded with ammunition.[4] It was the rear of the Rebel Army retiring from Smithfield. We marched about 16 or 18 miles & went into camp near Swift Creek at about 4 P.M.

Yesterday morning we started at daybreak for this place anticipating a hard day's battle.[5] After moving about 5 miles, we heard the cannon booming in our front, & we supposed the time was near at hand but we kept moving on & on until we came in sight of this place but found no enemy. It seems that the 14th Corps having had some ten miles the shortest route, were two or three hours in advance of us & kept up a skirmish with the Rebel rear guard.[6] We are therefore in possession of Raleigh without a battle.

We have lost track of Johnson's [sic] Army which accounts probably for our stay here to-day.[7] Gov. Vance surrendered the city on the approach of our army.[8] There are a vast number of Rebel sick & wounded here with their Surgeons, nurses, &c. I was through the City this morning. It is quite a small place, though in its prosperity has been beautiful. The Rebs blew up the depots.

Citizens say that Johnson's Army passed through in great haste the evening before we came & that Johnson declared he would not fight another battle. They have no Official news of the surrender of Lee's Army, Grant having destroyed their communication. Some of our boys saw a rebel soldier who was present when Lee surrendered but escaped afterward & reached his home. He was hid while Johnson's Army passed through but made his appearance this morning. He said that all of Lee's Army supposed Johnson had surrendered to Sherman. Unless Stonemann's or Sheridan's cavalry stop him, we will have a severe foot race yet.

The prospects look glorious. Let us praise God for all his blessings. We had good meetings after going into camp at Smithfield & Swift Creek & a most excellent one here last night. There were three forward for prayers, & God was with us.

We recd. to-day New York papers of the 7th with full acounts of the battles. This is doubtless a day of great rejoicing in the north as it has been set apart especially for that purpose.[9]

I have felt like getting home soon. I do not think we will have any more severe battles. So far as we have learned, Johnson's Army is very much demoralized & have no intention of fighting longer if they can help it. May God grant us a bloodless victory. I am unable to see what they can gain by holding out longer. The train is expected from Goldsboro to-morrow, but, as all our mail was ordered to Fortress Monroe, I cannot expect a letter.[10] We are all well. The weather is very pleasant though a little warm. We have a beautiful camp in a pine grove near the city.

Give my love to all. Kiss Howard for Papa. May Our Father in Heaven keep & bless you. With much love, I remain

Your affectionate Husband

J. F. Culver

---

1 The XX Corps camped on the night of the 10th at Atkinson's, one mile west of Moccasin Creek. During the day, Slocum's advance had skirmished with troopers of the 1st South Carolina Cavalry, losing two killed and five wounded.

Orders for the next day's march called for General Geary's Second Dvision to take the advance, followed by the Third and First Divisions. *O.R.*, Ser. I, Vol. XLVII, pt. III, pp. 155-157.

2 General Sherman, in acknowledging receipt of Grant's telegrams reporting surrender of Lee's army, replied on the 12th, "I hardly know how to express my feelings, but you can imagine them. The terms you have given Lee are magnanimous and liberal. Should Johnston follow Lee's example, I shall, of course, grant the same. He is retreating before me on Raleigh, but I shall be there to-morrow." *Ibid.*, p. 177.

3 Mower's orders for the day's march called for the XX Corps to cross Neuse River, and march on the Leechburg road to the intersection of the Elevation and Raleigh roads, where it would turn north to Swift Creek. General Ward's Third Division had the lead, with the 1st Brigade guarding the trains. *Ibid.*, pp. 170-71.

4 Brig. Gen. Judson Kilpatrick's cavalry, as it spearheaded the Union advance from Swift Creek toward Raleigh, skirmished frequently with Confederate horse-soldiers of Lt. Gen. Wade Hampton's command covering the retreat of Johnston's army. *Ibid.*, p. 186.

5 Swift Creek was 14 miles from Raleigh. On the 13th the XX Corps marched in the following order : First, Second, and Third Divisions. *Ibid.*, p. 185.

6 Sherman's cavalry entered Raleigh on the morning of the 13th, the city being surrendered by the mayor to General Kilpatrick. Johnston's army, covered by Hampton's and Wheeler's cavalry, had evacuated the city on the 12th, retreating toward Hillsboro. Kilpatrick's horse-soldiers, not wanting to give the Rebels a chance to regroup, pressed on

ten miles to Morrisville, and in doing so, smashed a number of roadblocks manned by Wheeler's troopers. *Ibid.*, pp. 197-98.

7 On the 14th Generals Sherman and Johnston had agreed to a temporary suspension of hostilities, with the object of finding a formula for ending the war. Sherman accordingly promised to limit the advance of his main columns to Morrisville and his cavalry to Chapel Hill, while expecting Johnston to maintain his present position. Johnston's army was camped in and around Hillsboro. *Ibid.*, pp. 206-07.

8 J.F.C. was mistaken. The mayor (not Governor Zebulon B. Vance) surrendered the city to the Federals. *Ibid.*, p. 197.

9 The War Department on April 9 had ordered "a salute of 200 guns to be fired at the headquarters of every army and department, and at every post and arsenal in the United States, and at the Military Academy at West Point, on the day of the receipt of the order, in commemoration of the surrender of General R. E. Lee and the Army of Northern Virginia to Lieutenant-General Grant and the army under his command." *Ibid.*, pp. 351-52.

Meanwhile, President Lincoln was getting ready to call for a day of national thanksgiving.

10 Working parties had been turned to repairing railroad bridges and trestles burned by the retreating Confederates. By the 17th the only bridge not rebuilt spanned the Neuse, and trains were running north from Goldsboro and south from Raleigh to the Neuse, where transfers were effected. *Ibid.*, p. 238.

 219

Head Qurs. Co. "A" 129th Ills.
Raleigh, N. C., April 18th 1865

My Dear Wife

Since I last wrote to you from this place we have been laying quietly in camp awaiting the result of the interview between Genls. Sherman & Johnson.[1] They met yesterday at Hillsboro, & Genl. Sherman left this morning for the same place. It is generally believed that Johnson has surrendered his army but the arrangements have not been completed yet.

This is a sad day in the army. The news reached us officially this morning of the assassination and death of President Lincoln.[2] We heard it rumored yesterday but did not credit it. I never saw so much sadness manifested. The whole army is silent as the grave. Groups are gathered here & there discussing the sad event. I have heard only one sentiment expressed, & it seems to be universal throughout the army. Woe to the South if this Army is compelled to pass through it again. Woe to the Rebel Army that compels us to fight longer, & Woe to the copperheads of the North. You cannot imagine what deep hatred exists against the latter class.

The army expects to be mustered out next month. We all anticipate spending the 4th of July at *"Home."* There is no possible escape of Johnson's army, & the news of Forrest & Rhoddy's capture have reached us.[3] As Johnson has command of all the rebel armies in the South, we expect their Surrender to Sherman before these negotiations close.[4]

Yesterday the news would have been received with wild acclamations of joy, to-day there would be no outburst at all. We have a meeting of the Brigade at 6 o'clock this evening to pay due respect to the dead. May God be merciful to us in our great affliction.

The weather is beautiful. Our meetings continue, & God is doing a great work for us. There were 10 forward Sunday night & 9 last night & numerous conversions. Over 160 have joined the church. The attendance is very large. I preached last night from Mark 16 Chap. & 16th V., & God was pleased to bless me.

All are in good health. I saw Allen Fellows this morning, Bros. Gaff & Lee yesterday. All well. I cannot find my ink & Yetter is on Picket, so you must excuse the pencil this time. My heart is too sad to write much to-day. We have recd. no mail yet. I will write soon again if we do not move. We will not remain here long as it is too far from our base of supplies. We will either go North or South. Write often. Give my love to all. Kiss Howard for me. May God bless you with His richest blessings. I remain, Very affectionately,

Your husband

J. F. Culver

---

1　General Sherman, on the evening of the 17th, notified General Grant that he had just returned from a meeting with General Johnston at the Bennett House, 27 miles from Raleigh. There had been a "full and frank interchange of opinions," with Johnston endeavoring to make terms for surrender of all Confederate forces still in the field. But to do so, he would have to discuss the subject further with Secretary of War John C. Breckinridge. Sherman was agreeable, and promised to meet again with Johnston at noon on the 18th at the same place.

As he informed Grant, "we lose nothing in time, as by agreement both armies stand still and the roads are drying up, so that if I am forced to pursue we will be able to make better speed." The one thing that both Sherman and Johnston feared was that the Confederate armies would "dissolve and fill the whole land with robbers and assassins." *O.R.,* Ser. I, Vol. XLVII, pt. III, p. 237.

2  Sherman's headquarters on the evening of the 17th issued a special field order, announcing, "with pain and sorrow," the assassination of President Lincoln by one "who uttered the State motto of Virginia." To calm passions, Sherman informed his soldiers "that the great mass of the Confederate Army would scorn to sanction such acts, but he believes it the legitimate consequence of rebellion against rightful authority." *Ibid.*, pp. 238-39.

3  A powerful column led by Maj. Gen. James H. Wilson had advanced deep into Alabama. At Selma on April 2, Wilson's horse-soldiers had routed Lt. Gen. Nathan B. Forrest's once formidable corps. Forrest and Brig. Gen. Philip D. Roddey had narrowly escaped capture by swimming the rain-swollen Alabama River under cover of darkness. Warner, *Generals in Gray*, p. 262.

4  J.F.C. was mistaken. General Johnston commanded the Department of South Carolina, Georgia, and Florida. But by involving Secretary of War Breckinridge in the negotiations he hoped to effect the surrender and parole of the remaining Confederate armies, as well as his own.

 220

Head Qurs. Co. "A" 129th Ills. Vols.
Raleigh, N. C., April 20th 1865

My Dear Wife

Your letter of the 9th inst. I found on my table to-night on my return from Church, and, as I have not written for two days past & will probably be very busy to-morrow, I will write to-night. I feel very thankful to our Father that you are both [Mrs. Culver and Howard] in reasonable health & trust you may be very soon perfectly well. Good health is one of the greatest blessings our Father bestows upon us. My health has been most excellent with the exception of a few days shortly after we came into this place.

The prospects for Peace are very flattering & possibly by this time has been consummated. Genl. Sherman notified this army yesterday that all had been accomplished, & he was awaiting the approval of the Government at Washington.[1] If Lincoln is still alive, we have no doubts; but, as a doubt was cast around the first rumor & we have no certain information, yet we are much in the dark not knowing what a new Govt. may demand. The probability of the President's death has cast a greater gloom over the Army than the severest defeat of this war, &, while we fear the rumor may be too true, yet we pray God it may prove untrue.[2]

We held a mass meeting of the Brig. yesterday to receive Genl. Sherman's order, &, though every heart rejoiced at the prospect of so soon returning home, yet the occasion more resembled the commemoration of departed ones than the anticipations foreshadowed by the order. Cols. Case, Dustin, Doan, & Genl. Harrison addressed the meeting. Three cheers were given for Genl. Sherman & the Union restored, then every one retired to his Quarters.[3] You receive all the news long before we do, as we are very far from our base of communication, &, before this reaches you, you will know all the results of present negotiations.

We have Johnson's army securely hedged in, but it is not impossible that he might turn one of our flanks and get away should the present efforts fail to bring Peace.[4] We have gone into camp here & are very pleasantly situated. I am busy with my Ordnance returns & other reports, preparing for our muster out of the service.

I am very much surprised at Mrs. Remick's representations. I agreed if absolutely necessary to give $10—on the instrument but never thought or spoke of doing more. Do not agitate the matter by raising the question. I am very much grieved over misconduct of that kind. I have overlooked a great deal for I felt deeply indebted to the family for their kindness in my extremity, &, while I have often earnestly desired that the most friendly relations might ever exist between my family & theirs, yet I have no wish paramount to your happiness. I hope I never have, & by God's grace, I never will lay any restrictions upon your judgment in your choice or rejection of friends and associations. Your opportunities for judging social character far exceed mine. I do not think I ever have informed you my real opinions of the worth or demerits of their society, yet I hope you will not think me unkind or thoughtless. I have thought in my own case that our obligations might be of such a nature as to overbalance everything of self but would never yield at the sacrifice of happiness or even feelings of love of those I love as life itself & better than all else save God. Believe me then, I confide wholly to your own judgment the selection of your friends & associates believing that I can fully enjoy with you all social blessings & believing also in my heart that you would readily yield as much and infinitely more to any request I might make.

I shall rejoice with you to find Howard well & able to creep when I return. I wrote from Goldsboro concerning Asa Alden & presume you have recd. the letter ere this. He is in the Hospital there & is doing very well. We had a letter from Henry Polk to-night from Dwight. I suppose all know he is safe ere this. The boys are all well.

Allen Fellows was in my tent a few minutes ago inquiring the news. As you did not mention Lou's name, we presumed she was well. He has not heard from her since we left Goldsboro though I have recd. two letters. Bro. John Lee was here to see me this evening; he & Bro. Gaff are well.

We had a good meeting to-night, five at the alter [*sic*]. God is still with us. Pray for us.

Remember me very kindly to Mrs. Johnson & family. I feel that I owe them much for their kindness to you & their efforts to make you happy. I shall not forget their kindness should I be permitted to return home. Remember me kindly to all our friends. I have had so many things upon my mind all day that I cannot write with that ease I could wish.

By Genl. Harrison's return, Col. Case comes back to the Rgt. Cris [Yetter] & Nate [Hill] are well. Cris seems to be bored somewhat over Lib Keif's fortune and his. Nate says he intends to get married & settle immediately. I suggested to the boys that there was one portion of the military drill they should study more closely now: that is the "guard against *Infantry.*"

From present prospects, we all expect to start for home in a few weeks. "Home, Sweet Home." These war worn veterans are well prepared for its enjoyments. I trust in God we may lose none of our numbers before that happy time arrives.

I must bid you "Good Night." The wind is troubling my candle & will soon leave me in darkness. May Our Father in Heaven bestow upon you the riches of His grace & our hearts' most ardent desires be speedily granted.

Your affect. Husband
J. F. Culver

---

1  On the 18th General Sherman had returned to the Bennett House, where he met with General Johnston and Secretary of War Breckinridge. There he prepared a paper outlining terms for surrender of all Confederate forces still in the field. The terms were very liberal and in general provided for "the war to cease; a general amnesty, so far as the Executive of the United States can command, on condition of the disbandment of the Confederate armies, the distribution of the arms, and the resumption of peaceful pursuits by the officers and men hitherto composing said armies." It also provided for recognition by President Andrew Johnson of the "several State governments, on their officers and Legislatures taking the oaths prescribed by the Constitution of the United States, and where conflicting State governments have resulted from the war, the legitimacy of all shall be submitted to the Supreme Court."

This agreement, as it touched on both military and civil affairs, would have to be submitted to Presidents Johnson and Davis for their approval. John G. Barrett, *Sherman's March through the Carolinas* (Chapel Hill, 1956), pp. 239-40.

General Sherman on the 19th had issued Special Field Order No. 58, announcing ,"a suspension of hostilities and an agreement with General Johnston and other high officials, which when formally ratified, will make peace from the Potomac to the Rio Grande." *O.R.*, Ser. I, Vol. XLVII, pt. III, p. 250.

2  Although it had been announced officially, J.F.C. and many others were unable to make themselves believe that Abraham Lincoln was dead and Andrew Johnson had succeeded to the presidency.

3  Bvt. Brig. Gen. Harrison again commanded the 1st Brigade, Third Division; Col. Daniel Dustin, the 2d Brigade; Col. Henry Case, the 129th Illinois; and Lt. Col. Azariah W. Doan, the 79th Ohio Infantry. General Harrison told the brigade that he hoped the Confederate leaders would not accept Sherman's "terms of surrender, that we might get a chance to tame the enemy, who had given a terrible blow to the army by this foul murder, and that we might subdue the enemy, and drive the last remains of rebel spirit out of them." Grunert, *History of the 129th Illinois,* pp. 236-37.

4  In accordance with the agreement with General Johnston, a line passing through Tyrrell's Mount, Chapel Hill, University, Durham Station, and West Point on the Neuse River would separate the armies. *O.R.,* Ser. I, Vol. XLVII, pt. III, p. 250.

 221

Head Quarters Co. "A" 129th Ills. Vols.
Raleigh N.C., April 23rd 1865

My Dear Wife

I commenced to write about an hour before the mail left to-day, but Harry McDowell came in with the New York Herald containing an account of the Assassination & death of President Lincoln, and I laid the letter aside to read the particulars. It is now too late for to-day's mail. The mail has not come in yet. I anticipate a good long letter from you; I have recd. none since yours of the 9th.

This has been a beautiful day and very pleasant. The first sound that greeted my ear on awaking this morning was the sweet warbling of a bird. I heard several sing very sweetly this morning. During the few years of the war, the birds have been very scarce in the neighborhood of the Army, at least, & to hear them again is a great treat.

Bro. John Lee has been sitting here for the last 30 minutes talking. He is in good health & recd. a letter from home yesterday of the 12th inst. I laid aside my letter to converse with him. I am not certain that I shall accomplish much in the way of writing until after church to-night as there are so many around. Alva Garner & James Maxwell are here,[1] & there is a constant crowd around, talking of going home; but then the wind is so high that if it continues it will be impossible to keep a candle burning to-night.

It seems as if the war was over.[2] Everything bears the impress of the Holy Sabbath. We had an excellent meeting this morning. Genl. Class at 9-1/2 & preaching at 10-1/2. Our Brig. Church numbers 195 members, ten joined to-day. The ordnance [*sic*] of baptism was administered this afternoon; I was not out. Our night meetings continue to be very interesting; there were five at the Alter [*sic*] last night & some conversions every day during the week.

The news of the death of the President is now established beyond doubt, and the developments implicate the "'Knights of the Golden Circle.'"[3] I am not surprised. Everyone here when the rumor first reached us exclaimed that it was the work of the Copperheads. We have spent three years in honorable warfare; this event foreshadows what we must anticipate at our "Homes." It will be much more difficult to meet successfuly, & many innocent will doubtless suffer with the guilty. But the issue must be met, & the Army is preparing for it. Genl. Sherman's order indicates the line of policy to be pursued.[4] The order proclaiming Peace has been delayed beyond our anticipations, owing no doubt to the change of the Government and the additional time required to define the policies to be adopted.[5]

I was interrupted by the return of Alva Garner & James McCabe.[6] They remained for supper, & I had no opportunity to write before Church as I was notified that I must preach if the Chaplain of the 70th Ind. did not come, & as it was late & quite cool, I thought I would postpone writing until morning, but I have just been notified to be ready to start on a Forage Expedition at 6-1/2 A.M. I must close my letter to-night late as it is (10-1/2).

Your letter of March 12th directed to Charleston, S.C. has reached me this evening. All the questions I believe have been previously answered save one, & that is that it is Clymer who wishes to join our Conference. He is to be married in June or July. I recd. a note from Lou Fellows through Allen this evening, dated the 9th inst., the same date of your last letter recd. She was expecting you to pay her a visit.

I have no late news from Carlisle. I hope to find mail here for me on my return. We go with two days' rations. Bart, Allen, & Burton got up last night from Charleston.[7] All our friends here are in good health. I must close for to-night. Remember me in love to all our friends. Kiss Howard for *"Papa"*. Write very often. I hope soon to be "Home" if it be God's will. May His richest blessings rest upon you. Good Bye.

Your affect. Husband

J. F. Culver

---

1   It has been impossible to further identify James Maxwell.

2   At 10 A.M. on the 22d, Generals Sherman and Slocum had reviewed the XX Corps. Two hours before, the troops, leaving their knapsacks in camp, had formed in the streets west of Fayetteville Street. The Third Division, preceded by the Second Division, had marched past the reviewing stand at the Market House on Fayetteville Street. As the troops tramped by, in light marching order, the bands played familiar airs. *O.R.*, Ser. I, Vol. XLVII, pt. III, pp. 268-69; Grunert, *History of the 129th Illinois*, pp. 238-39.

3   The theory that the assassination of President Lincoln and attempts on the lives of Vice-President Johnson and Secretary of State William H. Seward was part of a conspiracy involving Confederate leaders and Knights of the Golden Circle had been fostered by Secretary of War Stanton.

4   On April 17 General Sherman, in announcing the President's assassination, had informed his soldiers, "We have met every phase which the war has assumed, and must now be prepared for it in its last and worst shape, that of assassins and guerrillas; but woe unto the people who seek to expend their wild passions in such a manner, for there is but one dread." *O.R.*, Ser. I, Vol. XLVII, pt. III, p. 239.

5   Secretary of War Stanton, on April 21, notified General Grant that President Johnson had disapproved the memorandum of agreement between Generals Sherman and Johnston. Grant would relay this news to General Sherman and direct him "to resume hostilities at the earliest moment." *Ibid.*, p. 263.

6   James J. McCabe of Pontiac, an 18-year-old, was mustered into service at Joliet, Ill., as a private in Company D, 20th Illinois Infantry, on June 13, 1861. He was promoted corporal on April 25, 1863, and was wounded at Raymond, Miss., May 12, 1863, and captured and paroled 12 days later. He reenlisted at Big Black Bridge, Miss., as a veteran volunteer on Jan. 5, 1864. Corporal McCabe was wounded a second time at Kennesaw Mountain on June 27, 1864, and was promoted to sergeant on Oct. 31, 1864. Compiled Service Records of Union Soldiers, NA.

7   Robert Burton, a 30-year-old farmer, was mustered into service on Sept. 8, 1862, as a private in Company A, 129th Illinois Infantry. Hospitalized at Bowling Green, Ky., on Dec. 30, 1862, Private Burton was medically discharged on Nov. 1, 1863, and reenlisted as a private in Company A in Chicago on Oct. 12, 1864. Compiled Service Records of Union Soldiers, NA.

222

Hd. Qurs., Co. "A", 129th Ills.
In the fields near Holly Springs, N.C.
April 26th 1865

My Dear Wife

I closed up my last letter on Sunday night [the 23d] to go foraging. We left camp at 6 o'clock & moved in the direction of Cape Fear River. The country is much finer than any we have passed through lately. When we were 23 miles from the city, we recd. orders to return to camp immediately as our corps was to march early next morning.[1] It was then 4 o'clock. We fed the train & started back, arriving in camp about 2 o'clock yesterday morning after 46 miles travel. We had 4 officers & 200 men of the Regt.

Early yesterday morning we broke camp & marched to this place. It is 13 miles from Raleigh & near Holly Springs. I have not seen the Springs yet. We will remain in camp to-day, but how much longer, I do not know.[2]

The rumors are so numerous & so vague that we have no idea of the condition of affairs. Genl. Grant is in Raleigh. We hear one hour that Johnson has surrendered which is discredited the next. Our movement in such haste rather implies an effort to intercept him if he attempts to turn our flank. We are marching light prepared for fight & are on half rations for 30 days. The boys are out foraging to-day to make up the deficiency.[3] There has been a rumor afloat for the last two days that Genl. Sherman is relieved for halting at Raleigh & capitulating with Johnson instead of pressing forward. It will be a sad hour for this Army if it prove true.[4]

We met a great many of Lee's army on their way home while we were out foraging Monday. I begin to think we have accomplished much more than we ever anticipated in this war, i.e., the subjugation of the South. Their spirit is certainly broken.

We are all in good health. This is a splendid country much resembling Northern Georgia. Large fine oak timber. It is a relief from the pine forests that have lined our march all the way through from Atlanta.

I recd. your letters of the 14th & 15th on my return Tuesday morning. I am happy to hear that your health is improving. Your letter of the 15th is the first intelligence I have recd. of Leander's [Utley] success in his suit. Is he satisfied with the amount or does he value the mare at more; if so, find out the amount & I will pay it.

Father's estate was settled April 1st, & the money should reach you by the 15th or 20th, yet it might be delayed a couple of weeks longer. Bro. John Miller will doubtless inform you when he pays over the money.[5] If we stay here a few days & get fixed up a little, I will write again. Remember me kindly to our friends. Kiss Howard for me. May Our Father in Heaven bless you. Good Bye.

Your affect. Husband

J. F. Culver

---

1   General Grant, who hand carried the message from the government that the agreement Sherman had negotiated with Johnston and Breckinridge was unacceptable, had reached

Raleigh on the morning of the 24th. Word was immediately sent by Sherman to Johnston, notifying him that "the truce or suspension of hostilities agreed to between us will in forty-eight hours cease after this is received at your lines."

Sherman at the same time notified his army commanders of the situation and alerted them to have their troops ready to resume the offensive at noon on the 26th. The movement against the foe would be governed by "the plan laid down in Special Field Order, No. 55, of date of April 14, 1865." To facilitate operations, the army commanders on the 25th would marshal their corps ready to cross the truce line at the time indicated. *O.R.*, Ser. I, Vol. XLVII, pt. III, pp. 208-09, 293, 295.

2  The XX Corps, with the First Division in the lead, had marched at 7 A.M. to Jones' Cross-Roads. This was on the road to Avens' Ferry, where it was to cross the Cape Fear River at noon on the 26th. *Ibid.*, pp. 297-98.

3  On the evening of the 25th, Sherman had received a message from General Johnston, announcing receipt of Sherman's dispatch of the 24th, reading "I am instructed to limit my operations to your [Johnston's] immediate command and not to attempt civil negotiations, I, therefore, demand the surrender of your army on the same terms as were given General Lee at Appomattox."

It and a dispatch received the next morning indicated that Johnston was agreeable to an agreement for surrender on the terms drawn up by Sherman on the 18th for "disbanding this army, and a further armistice and conference to arrange these terms."

Sherman accordingly agreed to return to the Bennett House at noon on the 26th for another meeting with Johnston. This resulted in orders for the army commanders to suspend their advance across the truce line and for the troops to remain in camp until receipt of further orders. *Ibid.*, pp. 294, 303-306.

4  Although General Grant did not do so, he was under orders to supersede Sherman in command. Grant did not have the heart to tell his friend this, nor of the instructions from the War Department directing the troops in the South not to obey Sherman's orders. Barrett, *Sherman's March through the Carolinas*, pp. 267-68.

5  For additional information about John Miller, see J.F.C.'s letter of February 10, 1865.

 223

Head Qurs. Co. "A", 129th Ills. Vols.
Raleigh, N. C., April 28th 1865

My Dear Wife

We marched from Holly Springs to this place to-day and are making preparations for our coming Campaign. We will leave here on Sunday or Monday morning next, "Homeward bound." The last mail leaves at 11 o'clock to-morrow, the last opportunity to send letters from this place & the last we will have until we reach Richmond, Va.

Our present destination is supposed to be Alexandria (near Washington) though we may turn up somewhere else. We have 15 days' supplies & have orders to average 15 miles per day which will take us fully to Richmond by the route designated for us.[1]

We had a mail both yesterday and to-day, but I recd. no letters from you. I recd. one to-day from Maggie Guthrie of the 10th inst.[2] Your last was the 15th. The war is over, & I doubt not fills the hearts of the people with joy.[3] I cannot express my own feelings. If God spares our lives, we hope to be in a few weeks quietly at our homes. We are very restless, & the days seem long that keep us from our loved ones.

I have been suffering for the last few hours from severe headache, but it will all be gone I hope by morning. I cannot say how soon you may look for us. We will doubtless be delayed at Alexandria a couple of weeks & possibly longer. I must try and get home to attend court the first Monday in June, & we may all possibly be there by that time.

The Campaign before us is a severe one. We sent to the rear to-day all that were not in good marching trim, of my Company, Haley, DeLong, Noyes, & Cook.[4] They may reach home several weeks before us. All the rest of the Company are in good health. I cannot write much to-night but will try & add a few lines in the morning. Perhaps my head will feel better. Good night. May Holy Angels guard you & Our Father in Heaven keep & bless you.

Saturday morning, Apr. 29th

I arose this morning in the enjoyment of excellent health. We recd. the order of march this morning & will be in Richmond by the 12th or 14th of May.[5] We will have no mail facilities until we reach there. We will leave here either to-morrow or Monday. Joy fills every heart, yet there has been no demonstrations. A few more days hard marching, & we will be at Home. I must close as I am busy on the muster rolls & must complete them by noon. Let us thank God for all His mercies. Remember me to all. Kiss Howard for *Papa*.

Your affect. Husband

J. F. Culver

---

1 General Sherman, on the 27th, notified his generals that the Army of the Ohio would remain in the Department of North Carolina, while the Armies of the Tennessee and Georgia would march to Richmond. The Army of the Tennessee would travel via Louisburg, Warrenton, Lawrenceville, and Petersburg, while General Slocum would route

his Army of Georgia through Oxford, Boydton, and Nottaway Court-House; roads to the west of those followed by Howard's army. The Armies of Georgia and the Tennessee would, before leaving Raleigh, turn in the contents of their ordnance trains, and use the wagons for extra forage and rations. The columns would "be conducted slowly and in the best order, and will aim to be at Richmond ready to resume the march by the middle of May."

On the 28th the commander of the XX Corps, General Mower, notified the troops that hostilities had ceased, and they would be marched at once via Richmond to Washington "to be mustered out of service and return to their homes." While en route there would be no foraging upon the country and private property would be respected. *O.R.*, Ser. I, Vol. XLVII, pt. III, pp. 323-25, 341.

2  Maggie Gutherie was the 17-year-old daughter of George and Sarah Gutherie. Her father was a prosperous Pontiac Township farmer. Eighth Census, Livingston County, State of Illinois, NA.

3  In their afternoon meeting at Bennett's on April 26, General Johnston had agreed to surrender all the troops under his command on these terms: (a) all acts of war on their part to cease; (b) all arms and public property to be deposited at Greensboro, and delivered to a United States ordnance officer; (c) all officers and men to give their "individual obligation in writing not to take up arms against the Government of the United States until released from this obligation;" (d) the officers to retain their side-arms, "private horses and baggage;" and (e) this done, all officers and enlisted men "to be permitted to return to their homes, not to be disturbed by the United States authorities so long as they observe their obligation and the laws in force where they may reside." *O.R.*, Ser. I, Vol. XLVII, pt. III, pp. 313, 321.

4  John E. Haley, a 23-year-old farmer, was mustered into service on Sept. 8, 1862, as a private in Company A, 129th Illinois Infantry. Private Haley was mustered out with the regiment near Washington, on June 8, 1865. Joseph G. Noyes, a 28-year-old farmer, was mustered into service on Sept. 8, 1862, as a private in Company A, 129th Illinois Infantry. He was assigned to a Nashville convalescent camp from Jan. 30, 1864, until June, and in April 1865 was confined to the Third Division hospital, XX Corps. Private Noyes was mustered out on June 8, 1865, near Washington, D. C. Charles Cook, a 42-year-old farmer, was mustered into service on Sept. 8, 1862, as a private in Company A, 129th Illinois Infantry. Private Cook was captured by Rebel partisans on April 26, 1863, at Richland, Tenn. Exchanged, he rejoined the company at Gallatin, Tenn., on June 17, 1863. He was hospitalized in Atlanta at the beginning of the "March to the Sea." Rejoining the regiment in the spring of 1865, Cook was mustered out on June 8, 1865, near Washington, D. C. Compiled Service Records of Union Soldiers, NA.

5  The troops were cautioned that upon leaving Raleigh, "the march will be continued from day-to-day until our destination is reached or until orders are given from these or higher headquarters to halt." The XX Corps divisions would "habitually march and encamp from three to five miles apart." The commander of the lead division would post guards to look after the security of all buildings and private property along the route. These guards would be relieved by the succeeding divisions as they passed. *O.R.*, Ser. I, Vol. XLVII, pt. III, pp. 341-42.

## 224

Hd. Qurs. Co. "A" 129th Reg. Ills. Vol. Infty.
Raleigh, N.C., April 29th 1865

My Dear Wife

We expect to start on our march to Washington in the morning at 5 o'clock, & though the last mail went out for the Corps, yet I will try & mail this in the 23d Corps which is to remain here for the present.[1] It is raining to-night & bids fair to be a wet day to-morrow. I was in hope that we would rest until Monday morning [May 1], but, though we do not see it, doubtless the necessity exists for our immediate departure.

We are in good health & all ready for this our last campaign. The cannon have been booming at intervals of 30 minutes throughout the day, & all Officers of the Army assume the badge of mourning for 6 months. We have not yet learned the particulars of the negotiations. Many vague rumors are afloat, but we must wait until we get through to the north for more definite information.

Chris [Yetter] has not been well for a couple of days, but I think it is only a slight cold. Nate [Hill] has had headache for two days. Allen Fellows in playing with Billy Perry this evening received a severe cut in his hand from a knife Perry was whetting.[2] His hand is doing quite well to-night, & I think will be well in a few days. I saw Bro. John Lee this evening at Church. We had a good meeting.

We were inspected & mustered to-day; only once more, & we hope to be done. Every day & every hour of the day, you may hear the boys talking of "Home Sweet Home." I have been so busily engaged with papers that I could not enter into their enjoyment as much as I would like.

By the time this reaches you, we will be doubtless at Richmond, Va., or beyond it. I hope to receive several letters from you there. I would like very much if our house could be vacated so that we might go immediately to housekeeping on my return, yet I can give no definite idea of the time we will reach home. If convenient for Mr. Mathis, ask him to leave by the 1st of June.

It is getting quite windy, & the light will not last much longer, so I will close. Remember me kindly to all our friends. Tell Maggie Gutherie that

I did not get time to answer her letter here. Kiss Howard for me. May the richest of Heaven's blessings rest upon you & preserve us for future enjoyment in this life. With much love, I remain, Ever,

Your affect. Husband

J. F. Culver

---

1 General Grant, on the 29th, wired Washington that four corps would march from Raleigh to Alexandria, passing near Richmond. General Mower, during the day, informed his XX Corps that they would "commence the march to-morrow." The First Division would take the lead, followed by the Second and Third. Mower hoped the march would be so regulated that the corps would be across the Neuse when it halted for the night. *O. R.,* Ser. I, Vol. XLVII, pt. III, pp. 345, 348.

2 William W. Perry, a 20-year-old drayman, was mustered into service on Sept. 8, 1862, as a private in Company A, 129th Illinois Infantry. Private Perry was detailed as regimental ambulance driver on Dec. 2, 1862, and did not rejoin the company until May 5, 1864. On Aug. 28, 1864, he was detailed for duty in the regimental medical department, where he remained until mustered out on June 8, 1865, near Washington, D.C. Compiled Service Records of Union Soldiers, NA.

 225

Head Qurs., Co. "A", 129th Ills.
Near Richmond, Va., May 11th 1865

My Dear Wife

We start at 11 A.M. for Alexandria. We recd. no mail here & will not until we get through. We were saved the trying ordeal of a Review yesterday by the timely arrival of our good friend Genl. Sherman. The men are much rejoiced as the route advertised by Genl. Halleck would have been most tedious.[1]

I was in Richmond yesterday. Saw Libby Prison & Castle Thunder & rode through the greater portion of the city.[2] I have not time to give you a lengthy description this morning. The half of the business portion of the city is in ruins by fire. It has been quite a pretty place. I rode out to the camp of the 39th Ills. and took dinner with Lace, the Leader of the

Band.[3] All the boys were over here, & I did not see them until on my return home. I met Charlie McGregor, Addie Wilson, & Jones.[4] They are all well; Charlie looks *very* well. I had not opportunity to talk with them, but we will see them to-day as we pass through the city.

We were cheered a few moments ago by the news that a mail had arrived, but it proved to be a very small one—only two letters for my Company & none for me. We must be content to wait until we reach Alexandria.

I have a negro [freedman] for Bro. Utley on trial. If he proves to be worth anything, I will try & take him through; if not, I will drop him at Alexandria.

All the boys are in good health. We will be about 7 or 8 days on the way. The papers speak of a Grand Review of all the Armies at Alexandria, the 20th inst. I must close & pack up. We hope to be at home early in June.

May Our Father in Heaven bless us with life & health. Kiss Howard for *Papa*. Remember me kindly to all. I shall look anxiously for late news at Alexandria as it will only require 4 or 5 days for mail to reach us there from home.

Good Bye, God bless you,

Your affect. Husband

J. F. Culver

---

1 On May 8 orders were issued by Maj. Gen. Henry W. Halleck, commanding the Military Division of the James, that the Army of Georgia would pass through Richmond on the 10th. It was to cross the James on the upper pontoon bridge at the foot of 17th Street, and pass through the city by way of 17th, Cary, 21st, Main, 13th, Capitol, Grace, and Adams Streets, to Brook Avenue. The XIV Corps was to have the lead, and the troops would be reviewed by General Halleck from a stand at the courthouse near Capitol Square.

General Sherman, who had left his "army group" at Raleigh on April 28, rejoined it near Manchester on the 9th. His first order on arrival was to cancel the review. *O. R.*, Ser. I, Vol. XLVII, pt. III, pp. 437-39, 446.

2 Libby Prison and Castle Thunder were notorious prisons, where the Confederates held Union prisoners of war.

3 The 39th Illinois was assigned to the 1st Brigade, First Division, XXIV Corps, Army of the James. Philip M. Lace of Pontiac on Oct. 11, 1861, was mustered in at Chicago as leader of the regimental band, 39th Illinois Infantry. He was mustered out on June 4, 1862, at Washington, D.C. Lace was reenlisted in the regiment on Jan. 12, 1864, at Joliet, Ill., as a private in Company H, in May he was detached as leader of the regimental band, and on Sept. 23 he was promoted to fife major. Compiled Service Records of Union Soldiers, NA.

4 Charles A. McGregor, a 22-year-old clerk, was mustered into service at Chicago on Feb. 22, 1864, as a private in Company C, 39th Illinois Infantry, and on March 22 was detailed to the regimental band. James A. Wilson, an 18-year-old clerk, was mustered into service at Chicago on March 15, 1864, as a private in Company C, 39th Illinois Infantry.

Private Wilson was detailed to the regimental band seven days later. Henry T. Jones of Cook County was mustered into service at Chicago on Oct. 11, 1861, as a fifer in Company C, 39th Illinois Infantry. On Nov. 1, 1861 he was appointed principal musician, and on June 13, 1862 he was discharged at Washington, D.C. Twenty months later, on February 29, 1864, Jones reenlisted in the regiment as a private in Company C and was detailed to the regimental band. *Ibid.*

 226

Burke's Station, Va.
May 19th 1865

My Dear Wife

As I was trudging along yesterday evening longing for camp, I was most agreeably surprised to meet Bro. Wes. [Culver] coming after me with a horse & permission for me to leave the column.[1] I mounted & we came to this place, where I found Sister Hannah, Mary, Willie & the baby.[2] All very glad to see me. We have but 7 miles more to camp.

The column left at 5 o'clock this morning, & I presume are at the place by this time. I will start in a few minutes. I hope to hear from you this evening or to-morrow. We are all very weary but will be recruited up in a few days.

I wish you could be here at the Review next week.[3] I will write as soon as we get into camp. Bro. Wes & family are all well, so are all at Mother's. It rained very hard last night & is cold this morning. I must close for the present with love to all. May God bless you.

Your affect. Husband

J. F. Culver

---

1 Wesley Culver was one of J.F.C.'s younger brothers, and he was currently stationed near Fairfax Station. Wesley had been mustered into service on Nov. 22, 1862, as assistant surgeon of the 56th Pennsylvania. On Feb. 26, 1863, he was medically discharged, because of a "dropsical leg" occasioned by an 18-foot fall from a tree at the family home which fractured several small ankle bones. By Oct. 27, 1864, his injury having healed, Wesley reentered service as assistant surgeon of the 202d Pennsylvania Infantry. March 1865

found him on detached duty, near Burke's Station, with Companies D and I of his regiment. Compiled Service Records of Union Soldiers, NA.

2 Wesley was felled by "consumption" in March, and his wife Mary had come down from Carlisle to help nurse him, bringing with her their two sons, five-year-old Willie and Charlie who had been born in December 1864.

3 It had been announced on May 18 by Army headquarters that there would be "a review with marching salute, of the Army of the Potomac, the Army of the Tennessee, the Army of Georgia, and General Sheridan's cavalry" on Tuesday and Wednesday, the 23d and 24th. On the 23d would be reviewed the Army of the Potomac and Sheridan's cavalry and on the following day, General Sherman's two armies. *O. R.*, Ser. I, Vol. XLVII, pt. III, p. 526.

 227

Hd. Qurs. Co. "A" 129th Ills. Vols.
Near Alexandria, Va., May 21st 1865

My Dear Wife

Yours of May 2d came to hand this afternoon. I am happy to hear that your health & Howard's is as good as it is & hope God may bless you with good health. I intended to write you a long letter to-day, but it rained hard until noon & threatens to rain again. For three days it has been raining almost constantly, & it has become very muddy & unpleasant.[1] To-morrow we will move a few miles nearer Washington & get ready for our Review on Wednesday.

Sister Hannah & Bro. Wes & family were to be here to-day, but the rain has prevented them. Sister Hannah expects to return home soon after the Review. Bro. Charlie [Culver] is expected here to-morrow.

We have a miserable camp here with no facilities for fixing up. We are all impatient for the time to arrive when we shall start homeward. We have learned nothing since our arrival here. I will try & go to Washington on Tuesday [the 23d] & get what blanks & papers I need to settle up my accounts. I think it very probable we will be mustered out at Springfield or Pontiac though it may possibly be done here.

Our Review on Wednesday will be very tedious & wearisome, but we hope 'twil be the last. We recd. notice that all troops whose time expires by Octr. 1st next will be sent off as soon after the Review as possible, though we may be delayed for want of sufficient transportation. I have but little idea of the route we will take, but think it probable we will go on the Baltimore & Ohio rail road.

This has been a dull Sabbath: The rain has kept us confined in our little tents all day; I hope it will clear up soon so we can get around. I have not been in Alexandria yet; we are about 4 or 5 miles distant. I saw the dome of the Capitol at Washington from the summit of a neighboring hill day before yesterday evening.

I saw Allen Fellows to-day, he is quite well, also Crist [Yetter], Nate [Hill], & all the boys. The mail is making up, & I must close. As I cannot tell when we will leave here, I hope to hear from you often. The letter recd. today is the only one recd. since we left Raleigh. Letters should not be more than 5 days coming through. I wrote to you from Richmond & also from Burke's Station where Bro. Wes is on duty. Remember me kindly to all our friends. Kiss Howard for me. Hoping to see you safe & well, I remain,

Your affect. Husband

J. F. Culver

P.S. Your letter recd. to-day contained 6 postage stamps. Please accept my thanks. I have now a large supply on hand.

J. F. C.

---

1 The regimental historian reported that on the 21st, "the rain continued to pour down in torrents. . . . We had the greatest trouble in preparing our meals, got wet to the skin, and had to remain in the tents until more favorable weather commenced." Grunert, *History of the 129th Illinois*, pp. 257-59.

 228

Hd. Qurs., Co. "A" 129th Ills. Vols.<br />Near Alexandria, Va., May 23d 1865

My Dear Wife

We are very busy preparing for the Review to-morrow, but I haste to write a few lines.[1] I have recd. only three letters from you since our

Hd. Qrs. Co. "A" 129th Ill. Vol
New Alexandria Va. May 23" 1865

My Dear Wife

We are very busy preparing for the Review to-morrow but I haste to write a few lines. I have recd only three letters from you since our arrival here but presume you thought we were cut off from communications & therefore did not write. Sister Hannah did not get here on Sunday. It has been raining ever since our arrival untill to-day. It is very warm & we fear to-morrow will be a hard day We leave here at an early hour as we have 8 or 10 miles to march before we reach Washington. Our days march can be little less than 20 miles & march of the way in line which at best is very severe. If it is warm as to-day many a poor fellow will fall by the way. We are all in good health All nescessary arraingments are being made for our muster out. yet we will hardly be able to leave here for a couple of weeks yet. I will write when we reach camp after the Review I hope to hear from you more frequently. We are all well Remember me in love to all

Your affect Husband
J. F. Culver

arrival here, but presume you thought we were cut off from communications & therefore did not write.

Sister Hannah did not get here on Sunday [the 21st]. It has been raining ever since our arrival until to-day. It is *very* warm, & we fear to-morrow will be a hard day. We leave here at an early hour as we have 8 or 10 miles to march before we reach Washington. Our day's march can be little less than 20 miles, & much of the way in line which at best is very Severe.[2] If it is warm as today, many a poor fellow will fall by the way.

We are all in good health. All necessary arrangements are being made for our muster out, yet we will hardly be able to leave here for a couple of weeks yet. I will write when we reach camp after the Review. I hope to hear from you more frequently. We are all well. Remember me in love to all.

Your affect. Husband

J. F. Culver

---

1   Those that did not draw new clothes repaired and cleaned their old uniforms. Small arms and accoutrements were cleaned and polished, "and preparations made . . . to appear in a proper condition" for the review. Grunert, *History of the 129th Illinois*, p. 258.

2   Orders issued by General Sherman on the 20th called for soldiers of the Armies of the Tennessee and Georgia to be ready to march at daybreak. The men would fall out without knapsacks, with canteens and one day's rations in haversacks. Understrength regiments would march in close columns of divisions, and the others in close columns of companies; the artillery in battery front, with close intervals. Regimental and headquarters pack mules would be led in close order in rear of the brigade ambulances.

With the Army of the Tennessee in the lead, the columns were to cross Long Bridge and take position on Maryland Avenue at the foot of Capitol Hill and east of the canal. At 9 o'clock a signal gun would be fired, and the head of the column would move out, the units marching by close columns of companies, right in front, guide left. Passing around the Capitol to Pennsylvania Avenue, the column would proceed down the avenue, and past the reviewing stand in front of the White House. All colors would be unfurled from the Capitol to a point beyond the President's reviewing stand.

After passing in review, the units would proceed to their new camps, those of the Army of Georgia to be located northeast of Washington and those of the Army of the Tennessee northwest of the city. *O. R.,* Ser. I., Vol. XLVII, pt. III, pp. 526, 539-40.

## 229

Head Qurs. Co. "A" 129th Regt. Ills. Vols.
Washington, D.C., May 27th 1865

My Dear Wife

I learned through J. A. Fellows this evening by a letter from his wife of the 22d inst. that you are well. I have been sadly disappointed in receiving no letters this week, & it is now Saturday night. I have felt uneasy thinking you must be sick. I hope, however, to hear from you by to-morrow's mail.

It has been raining hard for three days, & we have been wet most of the time. Our Review came off very well on Wednesday [the 24th]. You will get the full particulars through the papers. Bro. Charlie came down Tuesday & found his way to camp in the evening. Bro. Wes. with Mary & Hannah were on a stand in front of the President's Mansion, &, after the Column had passed the Reviewing Officer, I fell out and went back to them. I saw two Brigades of our Division & two Divisions of the 14th Corps pass.[1]

It was the first Review I ever seen & was quite interesting. After the Review was over, I brought Hannah & Charlie out to camp with me. I got a place for Hannah with Major Richardson & wife, the former commands "Fort Lincoln."[2] She has a very pleasant place. Charlie stays with me in camp. Our camp is 4-1/2 miles from Washington on the Baltimore Pike & 1-1/2 miles from Bladensburg. The situation is a very pleasant one.

We are hard at work preparing for muster out & hope to finish all our papers next week. We have not learned yet what time we may expect to go home, but 'twill not be long.

I was in Washington yesterday in company with Hannah, Charlie, Maj. Richardson & wife, & Mrs. Cartwright. The latter is wife of Lt. Cartwright, Bro. of Mrs. Richardson, & have been married but a week.[3] It rained very hard all day, & we were kept close to the houses & the ambulance. We visited the Capitol & Patent Office. Considering the weather, we had a very pleasant trip.

Hannah & Charlie will go home on Monday morning [the 29th]. I could not drive from my mind the idea as we passed down the Avenue on Wednesday [24th] that you might be present. I thought there would certainly be a delegation from our part of the State thus affording you an opportunity to come. I know you would have enjoyed it. It occurs to me just now, however, that you could not leave Sister Maggie [Utley] which may also account for the long intervals in your letters.[4]

Another week has passed away, & another Sabbath approaches. I hope soon, very soon, to spend them with you in God's service. I will probably write to-morrow if I am not called on for too many reports. Always when we get into camp as now there is a few months back work to make up, & the calls for papers are almost incessant. I made up the Muster & Pay Rolls to-day. We will receive part pay before we start home.

I will close for to-night; it is almost 11 o'clock. Charlie & I spent the evening with Hannah at the Major's. All the boys are well & are making good use of the time looking around Washington. Remember me in love to all the family. Kiss Howard for Papa. May God bless you & keep you safe from harm until my return.

Your affect. Husband

J. F. Culver

Sunday morning, May 28th 1865

My Dear Wife

I will add a postscript this morning as the mail has not gone out yet. Charlie has gone up to the house to bring Hannah to camp. We are now very nicely fixed up. Cris [Yetter] has been very busy preparing for the reception of ladies this morning. A large bouquet of Laurel decorates the table, & the cedar boughs surrounding the tent & the arbor in front combine to make it very comfortable & pleasant.

It is a beautiful morning. The birds are singing sweetly & the sun shining brightly for the first time in four days. The band of the 2d Brig. is playing some very fine airs. How I wish I could be with you to-day. The band is now playing "Ever of thee I'm fondly dreaming." I hope before many Sabbaths pass around, we may be all at *home*. It is time for Inspection. I may add a line or two again before I seal my letter up. Good Bye.

Your affect. Husband

J. F. Culver

1   The XX Corps moved out with the First Division in the van and General Ward's Third Division bringing up the rear. In Ward's division, General Harrison's 1st Brigade had the lead. The unarmed men were left to guard and move the knapsacks, camp, and garrison equipage to the new camps east of the Potomac.

Marching by way of Columbia Pike, the corps passed Fairfax Seminary and Fort Richardson and crossed Long Bridge at 7 o'clock. *O. R.*, Ser. I, Vol. XLVII, pt. III, pp. 563-64.

2   Fort Lincoln was near the district line, a few hundred yards east of the Bladensburg Pike. James M. Richardson, a 36-year-old Brookline merchant, entered service on Nov. 20, 1863, as captain of Company H, 3d Massachusetts Heavy Artillery. He was promoted major on Nov. 30, 1864. In the spring and early summer of 1865, Major Richardson served as acting inspector general, Hardin's division, XXII Corps, with his duty station at Fort Lincoln. Compiled Service Records of Union Soldiers, NA.

3   Edward G. W. Cartwright, a 19-year-old Nantucket clerk, was mustered into service on Dec. 3, 1863, as a 2d lieutenant in Company H, 3d Massachusetts Heavy Artillery. He was promoted to 1st lieutenant on Dec. 15, 1864, while stationed at Fort Lincoln. *Ibid.*

4   Maggie Utley gave birth to a child, her third, in May 1865. Culver, "Robert Murphy and Some of His Descendants," p. 129.

 230

Head Qurs., Co. "A" 129th Ills. Vols.
Washington, D.C., May 28th 1865

My Dear Wife

We received a mail this morning but no word from you; possibly I may be more successful next mail. I shall go to the city with sister Hannah & Bro. Charlie at 5 o'clock in the morning. Bro. Wes & wife did not come up to-day as they promised; I presume the mud prevented them. The weather has been beautiful to-day.

I just recd. yours of April 2nd. It has been lying doubtless at "Fortress Monroe." I shall be very busy now until all my papers are made up. My Desk arrived this evening. Write often; do not delay on account of my going home. I cannot tell when that will be, but probably by the 10th June. I hope to receive a dozen letters before that time. I will write frequently.

I must go up to the house & see Hannah. I will add a few lines on my return if I can get at the table.

I have just returned. 9-1/2 o'clock. It is raining hard & promises fair for a wet day to-morrow. Frank Long's trial comes off to-morrow, & Yetter, Hill & myself are summoned.[1]

We are all well. Alf Huetson was up here to-day. The days seem long as our return approaches. Remember me kindly to all. May the Richest of Heaven's blessings rest upon you. Good night.

Your affectionate Husband

J. F. Culver

---

1 Frank Long was court-martialed for desertion and sentenced to forfeit 88 days' pay. To do so, he would be retained in service in such regiment as Colonel Case might designate for the subject period. Compiled Service Records of Union Soldiers, NA.

 231

United States Sanitary Commission. [letter head]
Hd. Qurs., Co. "A", 129th Ills.
Washington, D.C., May 29th 1865

My Dear Wife

Another day has passed without any word from you. I begin to fear that you are sick. The last I have recd. was of the 11th inst. while everybody is receiving letters two & three days from home. I have thought that possibly you may be expecting me home on the 1st of June. I shall not go until the Regt. does if I can help it, as I wish to get all my accounts settled as soon as possible, & it will save me a great deal of trouble.

Sister Hannah & Bro. Charlie went home to-day, & I presume are at home with Mother at this hour. They enjoyed their visit very much.

The weather to-day has been beautiful. I do not remember when I enjoyed a morning as I did this one. We [J.F.C. and his brother and sister] started to the city at 5 o'clock. The birds sang so sweetly, and all nature wore a beautiful aspect.

We are all in excellent health. The days seem long to the boys waiting for their discharges, but I am kept so busy that the time passes rapidly. The moon shines brightly to-night. I wish I could look in upon you this evening & know how you are getting along. I think I surely will hear from you by to-morrow's mail.

We cannot tell when we will start for home, yet we know 'twil not be long. May Our Father in Heaven bless you. Kiss Howard for me. Remember me kindly to all our friends. With much love, I remain,

Your affect. Husband

J. F. Culver

232

U.S. Sanitary Commission [letter head]<br>Washington, D.C., June 2nd 1865

My Dear Wife

Yours of the 29th ult. recd. last night. I am very happy to hear that you are well. This was the 1st recd. since yours of the 11th ult. I have written 3 to 4 times a week ever since we arrived at Alexandria; before that we had very few mail facilities.

I am happy to hear that Maggie is doing so well. Present my congratulations.[1]

I am busy day & night but will be partially done by Saturday.[2] I will then write. I do not know when we will start home, probably not for a couple of weeks yet.

I recd. a letter from Charlie [Culver] yesterday. Judge Watts told him that he wrote to you inquiring when & where he should send the money but recd. no answer.[3] I presume he has lost your address. I will write to him next week if we are not nearly ready to start. I expect to call at

Carlisle a few hours on my way home. I drew one hundred dollars from Watts by Charlie yesterday; it will be here to-day.

Mollie is lying very sick at the National Hotel, Washington. Bro. Wes' Regt. has been sent north & is in camp near Philad. Penna. Wes will go as soon as Mollie can be removed. I have not had time to go & see them, but recd. a letter from Wes. I must close for the present.

May God bless you.

Your affect. Husband

J. F. Culver

---

1   Mary Culver had undoubtedly written her husband that Maggie Utley had given birth to a baby girl.

2   Orders were received on the 21st for company commanders to have all their returns, muster rolls, and accounts up-to-date and in order by June 1. General Sherman, on the previous day, had notified the adjutant general that much progress has been made "in the muster out and rolls of discharges." General Slocum had given assurances that he could complete "the rolls and discharges" for his Army of Georgia within ten days.

Distractions were numerous and work lagged. All trains departing Washington were crowded with discharged soldiers on their way home. The cheering of these men, as the trains rumbled northward, was heard in the camps clustered around Fort Lincoln, about one-fourth mile east of the right-of-way of the Baltimore & Ohio.

General Sherman on the 30th had issued his farewell order to his troops, thanking them for their love of the Union, for their fidelity to him, for enduring so bravely the privations and hardships, and for their bravery in numerous battles. Grunert, *History of the 129th Illinois*, pp. 265-66; *O.R.*, Ser. I, Vol. XLVII, pt. III, p. 598.

3   Judge Frederick Watts of Carlisle, as administrator of the estate of Joseph Culver, was charged with disbursing the assets to the heirs.

 233

Hd. Qurs., Co. "A", 129th Ills. Vols.
Washington, D.C., June 5th 1865

My Dear Wife

We are still very busy preparing for our muster-out & are expecting our turn to come every day. The 102d Ills. was mustered out yesterday evening & start home very soon.[1] I hoped to hear from you by yesterday's mail but was doomed to disappointment. I hardly expect to hear again unless you have written yesterday, which, if mailed to-day, will reach me Wednesday [the 7th].

We are all well. Alf [Huetson] returned to the Company yesterday evening & will help me with my papers. I hope to have all completed by to-morrow.

I am going to the city this morning to get the money out of the express office that Charlie sent me. I sent down for it twice but did not succeed in getting it. We hope to get home sometime next week if nothing happens. Hoping to find you well & happy with God's blessing resting upon you, I remain, as ever,

Your affect. Husband

J. F. Culver

---

1 The 102d Illinois, like the 129th Illinois, belonged to the 1st Brigade, Third Division, XX Corps. That evening General Ward had his brigade commanders assemble their men to listen to his farewell address. Ward had had too much to drink, and "words as well as sense were wanting or but half understood." He was interrupted several times by cheers and jeers from his soldiers. General Harrison and Colonel Doan of the 79th Ohio also made speeches, dwelling on the privations, hardships, and battles they had shared. They were interrupted frequently by applause. Grunert, *History of the 129th Illinois*, p. 267.

# INDEX

Arabic numerals indicate the **numbers of the letters** in which persons, places, organizations and other subjects are discussed. Roman numerals indicate page numbers in the introduction.

Harrington, Robert B., 69, 69n, 211, 211n

Harrison, Col. Benjamin (later U.S. President), xii, 103, 103n, 104, 104n, 105, 107n, 109, 110, 110n, 111, 112, 129, 135, 136, 139n, 196, 196n, 214, 220, 229n, 233n

Harrison, Mrs. Benjamin, 103, 103n, 104, 115, 161n, 174n

Home Insurance Co., 201, 201n

Hooker, Gen. Joseph, 98, 107n, 132, 132n, 133, 135

Hoxie, David, 83, 83n

Hoxie, John, 83, 83n

Horses, 140, 143, 145, 149, 211; sale to army, 25, 25n; tack, 103, 140n

Horton, Capt. George W., 169, 169n, 201, 201n, 214

Hoskins, Capt. John A., 28, 28n, 30, 30n, 47, 52, 58, 74, 111, 114, 125, 126, 128n, 133, 145, 161n, 194

Huetson, Alf, 65n, 79, 83, 86, 108, 110, 124, 125, 128, 130, 150, 155, 176

Illinois legislature, 155, 189, 189n

Illinois Regiment, 129th, vii-viii, x, 79n, 80, 80n, 81, 86, 86n, 196; families of soldiers in, vii; questions of excessive or unnecessary hardship, 18, 18n, 29, 29n, 30, 100, 196, 209, 209n; commended, 74n, 86, 86n

Indiana legislature, 189, 189n

Inspections, x, 29, 78, 86, 86n, 124, 125, 135, 136, 154, 214, 224-229 *passim*

Johns, Dr. Henry C., 47n, 85, 113, 113n

Johnson, Dr. Darius, 34n, 66, 67, 215, 215n

Johnston, Gen. Joseph E., 218, 218n, 222, 222n

Jones, David, 112, 112n, 208

Keene, Laura, 96, 96n

Kenyon, Earl H., 41, 41n, 42, 43

Landscaping (of camps), 132, 132n, 135, 213; construction of arches, 135

Leaves of absence, 56, 63, 64, 68, 68n, 72, 72n, 73, 77; 80, 87, 114, 152, 156, 182n, 185, 194, 201. *See also* Culver, Joseph Franklin: seeks leave; Visits: by soldiers on leave

Lincoln, Abraham, 189; reaction to his assassination, 219, 219n, 220, 221, 221n, 224

Long, Frank, 148, 148n, 156, 191, 230, 230n

Lookout Mountain, 125, 126, 139

Louisville, Ky., 4, 6; expected attack on, 3, 3n, 4, 4n

McClellan, Gen. George B., 179, 189, 189n

McDowell, Lt. William H., 115n, 125, 136, 136n, 138, 151, 151n, 154, 161, 174, 211

McKnight, Lt. John P., 55n, 94

McLemore's Cove, Ga., maneuvers at, 83, 83n, 86n

Maples, Edwin R., 8, 8n, 21n, 24, 24n, 36, 39, 43, 56, 74, 74n, 78

Maps, 58, 165

Mitchellville, Tenn., 29

Moran, Thomas, 162, 162n

Morgan, Gen. John Hunt, 39-43 *passim*, 51, 51n, 57-61 *passim*, 66, 66n, 69, 69n, 187, 187n

Mower, Gen. Joseph A., 216, 216n

Mules, 119

Murphy, Mary. *See* Culver, Mary Murphy

Murphy, Nancy, 210, 210n

Murphy, William John, 2, 7, 25, 25n, 79, 79n, 90n, 111, 124, 124n, 138, 138n, 139, 189, 194, 194n, 211, 211n

Music, instrumental, xii, 76, 79, 117, 126, 155, 161, 177, 179, 198. *See also* Culver, Joseph Franklin: and band equipment

Muster-out, 227-33 *passim*

Nashville, Tenn., 77, 77n

Negroes. *See* Blacks

Nelson, Erastus, 66, 66n, 81, 81n, 82, 83, 191, 191n

Nelson, Gen. William "Bull," 7, 7n

New Year's Eve, 42

Newspapers, 78, 79, 86, 87, 104, 124, 149, 149n, 153, 156, 158, 161, 169, 187, 201, 216; unavailable, 16, 18, 24, 26, 41, 44; reasons for unavailability, 20, 44, 91; inaccuracy of, 154; of Nashville, 42, 86, 86n, 124, 154; of Louisville, 144; of Chattanooga, 153; *Pontiac News*, 31, 36; *Philadelphia Ledger*, 86, 104, 125; *Pontiac Sentinel*, 94, 99, 104, 160, 169, 173, 175, 202, 211, 217; *Chicago Tribune*, 124, 160, 164, 173, 174, 175, 179, 187; *Chicago Times*, 129; *New York Ledger*, 129, 130; *New York Herald*, 153, 204, 212, 213; *New York Tribune*, 154, 160, 175, 204; *Christian Farmer*, 175

Oaths of allegiance, 202
129th Illinois Regiment. *See* Illinois Regiment, 129th

Paige, Capt. Charles L., 66, 172, 192, 192n
Pay, 100, 103; system for dispensing, 2, 16, 18, 20, 22, 47, 78, 140, 142, 155, 164, 172, 178, 212, 229; delays in, 16, 18, 20, 23, 86, 163, 189, 193, 196; hardships caused by delays in, 16, 23, 27, 34, 39, 47, 47n, 87, 101, 125, 133, 153, 164, 169, 189, 196; pay days, 42, 77, 87, 108, 166, 178, 229
Perry, Capt. John B., 19n, 133n, 147, 191, 191n
Photographs, 19, 19n, 25, 25n, 83, 83n, 87, 91, 92, 93, 99, 107, 111, 141, 142, 196
Pillage. *See* Destruction of Confederate property, cities
Plattenburg, Phil, 66, 128, 128n, 140, 145, 146, 146n
Pollard, E. A., 58, 58n
Pontiac, Ill., 72, 96, 169, 202. *See also* Sickness: in Pontiac, Ill.
Postal system, 14, 17, 20, 21, 29, 52, 62, 81, 105, 109, 116, 117, 118, 122, 134, 149, 149n, 157, 160, 165, 185, 187, 189, 196, 202, 217, 231; delays, xiii, 26, 36, 37, 39, 41, 41n, 43, 43n, 45, 60, 65, 66, 69, 109,

138, 142, 143, 144, 149, 184, 190, 191, 193, 194, 200; stamps, xiii, 5, 14, 36, 36n, 47, 47n, 133, 173, 227; informal arrangements, xiii, 24, 24n, 30, 36, 43, 44, 46, 51, 71, 161; lost mail, 13, 31, 37, 58, 58n, 66, 83, 93, 187, 192, 215
Postlethwaite, Mary, 83, 83n, 96, 96n
Prisoners of war: held by Union, 7, 16, 16n, 56, 56n, 58, 58n, 59, 59n, 69, 69n, 83, 166, 166n, 181; held by Confederacy. 208, 208n, 213, 214
Privacy, lack of, 1
Provisions. *See* Food; Supply lines; Sutlers

Quartermasters' work, 19, 20, 200, 200n, 209, 209n

Racism (in Carlisle, Pa.), 99, 99n
Ragan, Dr. Amos W., 132, 132n, 196, 196n
Railroad schedules, 70, 199
Railroads. *See* Supply lines
Raleigh, N.C., 218
Recruitment, 66, 95, 95n, 110, 110n
Refugees, 9, 56, 186, 186n, 189, 207, 216
Religious services and meetings, 11, 40, 78, 80, 83, 86n, 92, 109, 109n, 125, 126, 128, 129, 133, 139, 161-169 *passim*, 173, 192, 198, 199, 199n, 202, 203, 203n, 213-221 *passim. See also* Culver, Joseph Franklin: his Sunday school class
Republican Party, 21n, 93n, 96n, 99n, 139n, 155, 155n, 179, 189
Reviews. *See* Inspections
Richmond, Va., 225
Rosecrans, Gen. William S., 63, 63n, 99
Rousseau, Gen. Lovell H., 21, 21n, 111, 111n
Rumors, xiii, 56, 66, 87, 213, 215, 216, 220, 222; concerning the war in the west, 16, 16n, 17, 17n, 39, 43, 43n, 44, 44n, 56, 56n, 57, 57n, 76, 76n, 83, 91, 91n, 122, 122n, 132, 132n, 137, 167, 174, 174n, 176, 179; concerning the war in the east, 57, 57n, 155, 155n, 160, 190, 195, 211, 213, 216; concerning the

Carolinas campaign, 200, 200n, 201; concerning the 129th Illinois Regiment, 22, 22n, 71, 74, 74n, 128, 128n; concerning events in Pontiac, Ill., 25, 25n, 47; cumulative effect of unfounded, viii, 39, 154, 155, 179, 216, 222

Rush, Marion, 25, 25n, 26

Russell, William L., 33n, 34, 34n, 54, 54n, 58, 65, 67, 71, 74, 74n, 78

Sanitary Commission, 169

Saul, Samuel S., ix, 31, 31n, 210, 211

Scouting expeditions, 51, 52, 55, 55n, 57, 61, 69

Shellenbarger, Joseph, 68n, 128-132 *passim*, 136

Shelter, 5, 23, 27, 28, 37, 40, 43, 69, 70, 70n, 84, 85, 100, 103, 104, 124, 124n, 127, 127n, 132, 134, 153, 159, 213, 213n, 227; heating, 21, 27, 33, 39, 43, 92, 107, 113, 126, 127, 127n, 130

Sherman, Gen. William T., 176, 186, 186n, 189, 189n, 194, 194n, 210, 210n, 212, 212n, 220, 220n, 221, 221n, 225

Ships, 66, 66n, 200, 200n, 203n, 205, 205n

Sickness: among soldiers, 17, 20, 20n, 22, 25, 25n, 30, 30n, 41, 41n, 42, 46, 46n, 47, 66, 72, 78, 80, 83, 139, 147, 156; in Pontiac, Ill., 34, 34n, 39, 47, 136; in Bloomington, Ill., 200

Singing, xii, 1, 6, 42, 76, 78, 86, 91, 109, 109n, 128, 129

Sleeping arrangements, 18, 21, 28, 33, 79, 99, 113, 179

Smith, Col. G. P., 14n, 29n, 30, 30n, 37n, 47n, 172

Smith, Lt. John W., 11n, 23, 25, 28, 80, 145, 150, 154, 156, 158, 166, 174, 179, 192; concern for his wife, 11, 11n, 29, 31, 72, 72n, 86, 130, 192; sick, 41, 44, 48; friendship with J.F.C. broken, 98, 125, 125n; wounded, 11n, 148, 148n, 149, 150, 160, 164, 164n, 176, 179, 187

Smith, Mrs. John W., 11, 11n, 29, 34n, 51, 51n, 54, 63-78 *passim*, 83, 91, 94, 98, 125, 187

Southern population. *See* Civilian population in areas occupied by Union armies; Blacks

Speechmaking, 1, 220, 233n

Spies, Confederate, 7, 7n, 79n, 178

Sports and games, 182, 189

Stewarts Creek, Tenn., fort at, 117, 117n

Stones River: battle of, 43, 43n, 45n; fortifications at, 79, 79n

Suffrage, 155, 189, 189n, 196

Supply lines, 14, 29, 29n, 79, 79n, 93, 100, 100n, 117, 118, 128, 153, 155, 155n, 156, 175, 194, 211, 213; disrupted, 39, 41, 41n, 42, 42n, 57, 57n, 61, 61n, 79, 94, 119, 124, 124n, 127, 156n, 159, 184, 184n, 192, 193, 193n, 194, 194n

Surrender of Confederate forces, 218-224 *passim*

Sutlers, 7, 7n, 33, 33n, 74, 74n, 78, 99

Telegraph, 41, 41n, 46, 58, 58n, 60, 79, 103, 180, 217

Thanksgiving, 28

Theatre, 96, 96n

Theft, 23, 62, 87, 165; defenses against, 9, 19, 36n

Thomas, Gen. George H., 136, 136n

Timepieces, 19, 54, 92

Trading with the enemy, 33, 33n, 179, 179n

Tullahoma, battle of, 56, 56n, 79

Union Leagues, 139, 139n

Utley, Leander, 6n, 25, 25n, 51, 51n, 52n, 87, 88, 211, 222

Vaccination, 66

Vallandigham, Clement L., 93, 93n, 179, 179n, 190

Vandoren, Luther, 14n, 51, 51n, 83

Vicksburg campaign, 56, 56n, 58, 58n

Visits: by civilians to soldiers in camp, vii-viii, 23n, 29, 30, 33, 33n, 34, 38, 41, 51, 70, 70n, 78, 78n, 81, 101, 114 (*See also* Culver, Mary Murphy, contemplates visits to J.F.C.; Culver, Mary Murphy, visits J.F.C.); by soldiers on leave, viii, 65, 66, 67 (*See also* Culver, Joseph Franklin: round trip north; Leaves of absence)